A History of Infamy

VIOLENCE IN LATIN AMERICAN HISTORY

Edited by Pablo Piccato, Federico Finchelstein, and Paul Gillingham

1. *Uruguay, 1968: Student Activism from Global Counterculture to Molotov Cocktails,* by Vania Markarian

2. *While the City Sleeps: A History of Pistoleros, Policemen, and the Crime Beat in Buenos Aires before Perón,* by Lila Caimari

3. *Forgotten Peace: Reform, Violence, and the Making of Contemporary Colombia,* by Robert A. Karl

4. *A History of Infamy: Crime, Truth, and Justice in Mexico,* by Pablo Piccato

A History of Infamy

CRIME, TRUTH, AND JUSTICE
IN MEXICO

Pablo Piccato

UNIVERSITY OF CALIFORNIA PRESS

University of California Press, one of the most distinguished university presses in the United States, enriches lives around the world by advancing scholarship in the humanities, social sciences, and natural sciences. Its activities are supported by the UC Press Foundation and by philanthropic contributions from individuals and institutions. For more information, visit www.ucpress.edu.

University of California Press
Oakland, California

Library of Congress Cataloging-in-Publication Data

Names: Piccato, Pablo, author.
Title: A history of infamy : crime, truth, and justice in Mexico / Pablo Piccato.
Description: Oakland, California : University of California Press, [2017] | Includes bibliographical references and index.
Identifiers: LCCN 2016042800 (print) | LCCN 2016043730 (ebook) | ISBN 9780520292611 (cloth : alk. paper) | ISBN 9780520292628 (pbk. : alk. paper) | ISBN 9780520966079 (ebook)
Subjects: LCSH: Crime—Mexico—History—20th century. | Crime—Press coverage—Mexico—History—20th century. | Crime writing—History and criticism. | Justice, Administration of—Mexico—History—20th century.
Classification: LCC HV6813.5 .P53 2017 (print) | LCC HV6813.5 (ebook) | DDC 364.97209/045--dc23
LC record available at https://lccn.loc.gov/2016042800

Manufactured in the United States of America

26 25 24 23 22 21 20 19 18 17
10 9 8 7 6 5 4 3 2 1

para Xóchitl, Catalina y Aída

Soñé con detectives helados, detectives latinoamericanos
que intentaban mantener los ojos abiertos
en medio del sueño.
Soñé con crímenes horribles
Y con tipos cuidadosos
que procuraban no pisar los charcos de sangre
y al mismo tiempo abarcar con una sola mirada
el escenario del crimen.
Soñé con detectives perdidos
en el espejo convexo de los Arnolfini:
nuestra época, nuestras perspectivas,
nuestros modelos del Espanto.

ROBERTO BOLAÑO,
La Universidad Desconocida

CONTENTS

Acknowledgments ix

Introduction: A National History of Infamy 1

PART ONE: SPACES

1 · From Transparency to Darkness: Justice and
Publicity in the Mirror of Criminal Juries 17

2 · A Look at the Crime Scene: The *Nota Roja* and
the Public Pursuit of Truth 63

PART TWO: ACTORS

3 · Lost Detectives: Policemen, Torture, *Ley Fuga* 107

4 · Horrible Crimes: Murderers as Authors 126

5 · Careful Guys: *Pistoleros* and the Business of Politics 161

PART THREE: FICTIONS

6 · Our Times, Our Perspectives: The Emergence
of Mexican Crime Fiction 193

7 · Our Models of Dread: Crime as Revenge,
Justice, and Art 231

Conclusion: Trying to Keep Our Eyes Open 261

Appendix: Quantitative Evidence about Crime in
Mexico in the Last Century 271

Abbreviations for Archival Sources 279

Notes 281

Index 367

ACKNOWLEDGMENTS

If I had not witnessed the exemplary rigor, hard work, and long hours that my daughters Catalina and Aída put into their high school and college study, I would probably have taken many more years to write this book. As it is, their love for knowledge made me realize that it was worth joining them in more than a few sleepless nights to produce something that one day might be of interest to other students. All of this, of course, was possible because Xóchitl Medina, my wife, a teachers' teacher, taught us how to work hard and do things well. My conversations with the three of them about the stories in this book helped me improve it and see its relevance. Whether written close to or far away from them, every line that follows is owed to them.

I probably started this book, without knowing it, the first day of class at the Facultad de Filosofía y Letras of the Universidad Nacional Autónoma de México, in 1983. While I waited for a teacher to show up, I read André Gide's tale of the mysterious case of a woman who had been locked in a dark room for twenty-five years; my sister had given me the book for my birthday. Thirty-two years later later I came across a quote from the same book in Sara Maza's *Violette Nozière:* "The more we know of the circumstances, the deeper the mystery becomes, taking leave of the facts to settle in the personalities."*
The coincidence speaks much about the reasons why I studied and wrote history in the intervening years, but also about the debts I have incurred in the meanwhile. The thirst to read broadly, but always returning to Jorge Luis Borges, I owe to my family, including my sister Cecilia, my brother Antonio,

* Sarah C. Maza, *Violette Nozière: A Story of Murder in 1930s Paris* (Berkeley: University of California Press, 2011), p. 197; André Gide, *La secuestrada de Poitiers,* trans. Michèle Pousa (Barcelona: Tusquets, 1969).

my mother Ana, and my late father Miguel Angel. I read Maza's book because Kate Marshall, the University of California Press editor, sent it to me, as part of the guidance and impulse she gave to this project. I am also thankful for the work of Luis Herrán, Bradley Depew, Francisco Reinking, and Sue Carter. My collaboration with the coeditors of the series on the history of violence in Latina America to which this book belongs, Paul Gillingham and Federico Finchelstein, has also been an invaluable factor. Paul has been a source of energy and knowledge. His understanding of twentieth-century Mexico helped me sharpen my argument and place it in the right context. Federico was also central in the drive to finish this project, but also for my effort to conceptualize violence and politics. I am much obliged for their reading of the manuscript, which brought out ideas that had not been well formulated initially. My debt to the readers for the University of California Press is very deep: Mary Kay Vaughan, Elaine Carey, and Robert Buffington improved this book in decisive ways. Rob has read my last three books, so my gratitude to him is especially deep. Adela Pineda, Thomas Rath, and Benjamin T. Smith were extremely generous in reading, commenting on, and enhancing the manuscript. Ben's generous erudition has enriched this book, which I can only hope will establish a dialogue with his forthcoming work on crime and the press.

Acknowledging the help of many people in the production of this book is not a chore but a way to remember many good conversations and collaborations. First among them are those with my colleagues and friends Caterina Pizzigoni, Nara Milanich, and Amy Chazkel, who gave insightful first readings to these chapters. Decisive encouragement, questions, and suggestions came from Claudia Agostoni, Marianne Braig, Lila Caimari, Gabriela Cano, Hélène Combes, Angélica Durán Martínez, Tanya Filer, Gustavo Fondevila, Cathy Fourez, Serge Gruzinski, Ruth Halvey, Paul Hathazy, Aída Hernández, Marc Hertzman, Eric A. Johnson, Ryan Jones, Dominique Kalifa, Alan Knight, Regnar Kristensen, Alejandra Leal, Eugenia Lean, Annick Lempérière, Everard Meade, Daniela Michel, Mariana Mora, Saydi Núñez Zetina, Nadège Ragaru, Margareth Rago, Ricardo Salvatore, Gema Santamaría, Luana Saturnino Tvardovskas, Elisa Speckman Guerra, Pieter Spierenburg, Mauricio Tenorio, Geneviève Verdo, Edward Wright-Rios, Rihan Yeh, René Zenteno, and my compadres Theo Hernández and Carla Bergés. Students at Columbia deserve a separate mention for their sustained interest and their keen commentaries on long chapter drafts: Sarah Beckhart, Andre Deckrow, Marianne González le Saux, Sara Hidalgo, Paul Katz,

Daniel Kressel, Daniel Morales, Rachel Newman, Allison Powers, and Alfonso Salgado. Rachel's collaboration was essential in the latter stages of the process, improving the manuscript and obtaining the images. I also had the invaluable assistance of Laura Rojas, who discovered María del Pilar Moreno for me, Xóchitl Murguía, Julia del Palacio, Natalia Ramírez, Kimberly Traube, and María Zamorano. I thank Susan Flaherty and Rodrigo Moya for their help in obtaining the image on the cover, Carlos Peláez Fuentes and Luis Francisco Macías, from *La Prensa,* and Marina Vázquez Ramos from the Fototeca, Hemeroteca y Biblioteca Mario Vázquez Raña.

I received financial and institutional support from Columbia University through the Institute of Latin American Studies, the Department of History, the Institute for Social Research and Policy, and the Alliance Program, which made possible a stay at the Université de Paris 1, Panthéon Sorbonne. I also had the support of the Center for U.S.-Mexican Studies at the University of California, San Diego, for a useful stay in La Jolla; the Desigualdades Project at the Freie Universität Berlin, for a productive time in Berlin; the Universidade Estadual de Campinas, for another fruitful month in Sao Paulo; the American Council of Learned Societies; and the Shorin-Ores family, for some quiet time in Lakeville, Connecticut.

Introduction

Like any other history book, this one tries to understand the present. For Mexico, the present means violence and impunity of such scale that the name of the country has become virtually synonymous with infamy. Violence and impunity seem to be rooted in the dehumanization of victims, which both the government and a large sector of the public accept as inevitable. Murder is not usually investigated but rather is simply explained on the basis of disputes among victims or criminals whose rights are routinely violated. This book argues that this neglect is the product of a historical process. The political regime that emerged from the 1910 revolution was a model of stability for Latin America during the twentieth century, yet not a successful example of transition to democracy and the rule of law. Looking at national history through the lens of crime and justice, this book examines the emergence, by the middle decades of the century, of a broadly shared tolerance in Mexican civil society for extrajudicial punishment and the victimization of the innocent. This tolerance developed despite the parallel emergence of critical perspectives sharply condemning the inability of the state to seek and acknowledge the truth.

The nexus of crime, the truth, and justice is a premise of modern society: we all believe that there should be a relationship between the three. Once a crime is committed, the police must establish what happened and who is responsible, and the judiciary must follow up with an appropriate punishment. In Mexico, that premise is as old as the nation. Yet during the middle decades of the twentieth century, Mexicans came to define reality by the absence of that connection: the truth about specific crimes was often impossible to know, and as a result, justice could be achieved only occasionally, more often than not outside state institutions. From the twenties to the fifties, we also see the development of language and themes that allowed citizens to talk about the problem and keep it in a central place in public life. This book is not just about symbols or ideas, however. Even perceptions—a word commonly used today by contemporary politicians to suggest that they know more about reality than the public does—are the product of practices enacted by social actors and the state. This book traces the ways in which the crime-truth-justice nexus broke down and looks at civil society's attempts to restore it. Preceded by a dictatorship and a civil war, the period of national history considered in this book saw the development of a coherent set of knowledges and practices around crime and justice. These basic notions survived beyond the end of this period, when new forms of organized crime and state complicity with violence overwhelmed civil society's ability to cope with them.

The history of crime in postrevolutionary Mexico is intertwined with the country's political history. Beginning in 1876, the Porfirian regime managed to project an image of peace over a reality of social and political violence. The government cited crime, particularly petty theft, and alcoholism, as reasons to deploy punishment as a form of social engineering. During the revolution, the legal definition of crime was almost meaningless, as collective acts of robbery, murder, and rape went unpunished, and authorities were powerless to guarantee life or property. Immediately after the civil war, the confluence of widespread access to guns, class conflict, and the government's laxity in relation to crime broadened the gray zone for transgression.[1] A government based on a broad alliance between labor and peasant organizations, progressive intellectuals, and national capitalists consolidated in the 1920s. Starting in 1929, a unified official party system minimized electoral competition and disciplined the political class across the country, although this system hardly eliminated patronage. About the same time, new codes and other legal reforms portended a modern penal system. Yet behind the façade of corporatist stability, public life was fractious and decentralized, as diverse social actors were finding new ways to negotiate relations with the state and across class divides. While old criminal practices subsisted, modern forms of criminality emerged and became more prominent in public life.

A distinct era in the history of crime began in the late twenties, with massive urban growth in the forties. Recent studies confirm the connection between modernization and new forms of criminality, viewing crime as a symptom of new forms of urban individualism associated with capitalism, the emergence of national mass media, and U.S. cultural influence. The archetypal urban gangster—earlier associated with the U.S. side of the border—became the dominant trope of the new Mexican underworld. Those violent men of humble origin displayed their success through the highly visible consumption of expensive clothing, cars, and weapons. In this new era of the pursuit of prosperity, legality became an inconsequential, marginal component of what was seen simply as business. The moral lessons of gangsters' stories were founded purely on the basis of personal success or failure. The criminological paradigm dominant in the late nineteenth century, which viewed the criminal as a primitive individual who was separate from the civilized world, could not account for this new expression of criminality, in which the gangsters defined success. The sharp line dividing criminal from lawful had become dulled.[2]

Quantitative evidence, described in the appendix, supports the idea of a distinct period between the twenties and fifties. Overall crime rates decrease nationally from the end of the revolution, around 1920, until the eighties, when property crimes begin to increase, while violent crimes continue a downward trend only reversed by the so-called war on drugs of the first decade of the twenty-first century. By the late sixties, the number of indictments for drug trafficking had increased, indicating the state's newfound interest in these offenses. The effects of these new policies in terms of corruption and violence ushered in a new phase in the national history of crime, an unfinished era that is beyond the scope of this book. At the same time as drugs became its obsession, the federal government also revealed its propensity to use violence against political dissidents. Since the sixties, rural guerrilla, labor movements, and student protesters denounced and often responded in kind to the underlying violence of Mexican politics. Repression was most dramatically exemplified by the October 2, 1968, massacre of students in Tlatelolco, Mexico City, an emblematic episode of the dirty war against social movements in which presidents gave intelligence and armed services great leeway to use violence. The members of these branches of the state also used their enhanced power to exploit the increasingly profitable business of extortion and drug trafficking. Politics combined with social and cultural changes to transform criminal practices themselves, now typified by drug trafficking and consumption, juvenile delinquency, and some notorious examples of cops turned robbers.[3]

Crime was always present in Mexico, but it was not until after the revolution that it became the most prominent fact of urban life and the object of systematic investigation. Each crime left material evidence, most notably a corpse and a thick trail of testimonies, feelings, opinions, and other traces. Detection was the basic operation to reveal what had happened; in Mexico, it involved methods and skills mastered by professionals, called detectives, but regular citizens also appropriated these techniques. Professionals and civilians operated on the assumption that there was one truthful answer to the riddle posed by crime. Yet this was also the time when the link between the reality behind crime and the truthful public knowledge of its causes and penal responsibility became a problem.[4] Institutional and political constraints limited the capacity and prestige of Mexican detectives, and they did not care much about collecting physical evidence, relying instead on their ability to deceive, threaten, and torture suspects. This opened up the task of detection to other actors. A diversity of readers and writers presented their opinions about the famous cases that seemed shrouded in mystery. This civic engagement had no parallel in other fields of public life, especially as political mobilization, electoral politics, and open debate about the regime in the public sphere were increasingly controlled by the official party and its ruling elite.

This engagement is all the more remarkable because everyone knew that the truth about a crime did not determine the punishment administered by penal institutions. Judicial processes were slow and difficult to understand. For victims and their kin, delays diminished a sense of vindication—when trials did not actually inflict more humiliation and pain. Impunity was high: in cases of murder, between 1926 and 1952, and throughout the country, only 38 percent of the indicted were found guilty, and a large percentage of investigations did not even yield an accusation.[5] Presidential archives during these years contain thousands of letters from relatives of murder victims denouncing the impunity of killers and demanding the president's intervention. In the case of minor crimes like theft or extortion, newspapers published abundant examples of impunity and corruption among judges and police officers. Incarceration was not necessarily related to criminal culpability. Prisoners lacked information about their status. They did know that the guilty often walked free, and the innocent often remained behind bars.

Truth, in other words, has a history and a set of local particularities. In Mexico, the middle decades of the twentieth century saw the emergence of new questions that could be answered truthfully. In the past, all that was needed was to establish the facts of the crime, usually in the form of a narrative where criminals, victims, and authorities were clearly distinguished. The revolution was a time of lawlessness, when crime and politics mixed, making it more complicated to establish the truth about a crime, particularly in cases of murder. The flawed methods used by Mexican authorities turned citizens' focus to the suspect's own words as the most reliable version of what had really happened. As Manuel Múzquiz Blanco put it in a 1931 story published in *Detective,* "If the judicial truth, the trial records, the imagination of reporters, the viciousness of prosecutors, and the witnesses' accounts gave the affair the appearance of a puppet show, the simple truth, presented by the main character in the drama, Dolores Bojórquez ... is even darker, colder, more brutal."[6] Now, for example, it was legitimate to explore the subjectivity of the criminal with the aid of journalism, science, and even fiction. While the police and judiciary lacked the social authority to provide a credible account of events, criminals' thoughts, feelings, and impulses were seen as a legitimate basis for public discussion. In determining the truth about crime, once-authoritative scientific methods now competed with the moving sincerity of personal accounts, particularly murderers' confessions. Criminologists had to adapt their approach to their favorite object of study, "the criminal." Although positivist ideas about born criminals as primitive human beings continued to be cited, they now shared the scene with those of psychiatrists, physicians, and psychoanalysts, who explored criminals on the assumption that they had complex personalities, and that their words could hide but also reveal the truth.

Confessions were not above criticism, of course. Relatives of murder victims could participate as the civil part in trials, or through the press, to defend the reputation of victims. Newspaper and crime fiction readers were aware of the ineptitude, corruption, and impunity of law enforcement. They learned that confessions could be obtained through coercion. Still, most people believed that the truth lay somewhere in the crime pages. The Mexican history of detection, therefore, defies the premise that the state was a known quantity in the judicial process, and that once proof was established, a guilty sentence was assured. In Mexico, multiple actors, including journalists, lawyers, jurors, witnesses, suspects, and victims, argued about what constituted the truth. The state played a part in the process but did not control it. Even writers had a difficult time restoring a sense of order through fiction. Detection, in sum, was a complex process, but not so much that people lost hope of ever reaching the truth. Their debates might not always lead to a judicial sentence, but they achieved some degree of validation in the court of public opinion.[7]

Crime was a central theme in the public sphere. It was narrated, explained, pictured, and debated by people from all walks of life. Analyzing these discussions allows us to show how crime produced representations of reality that, in turn, shaped it.[8] Detectives, suspects, victims, witnesses, judges, journalists, and readers came together to discuss stories of crime. The evidence they summoned was variegated and confusing, unencumbered by legal criteria or even moral norms. Crime provided objective facts, independent from state-sanctioned scientific or legal knowledge. Narratives of famous cases, images of murderers and dead bodies, were as real as any fact about social life could be. Jury trials, crime news, and crime fiction gave citizens a platform for disseminating their own explanations and becoming authors of stories and narratives—some suspects were even allowed to give speeches and interviews. In these accounts, murder was an act full of meaning, something to be explained and interpreted with the use of reason and sentiment, and even judged from an aesthetic perspective.

These narratives and debates created what I term "criminal literacy"— basic knowledge about the world of crime and penal law. Criminal literacy included eclectic information about institutions, famous cases, everyday practices, and dangerous places that helped people navigate the complex practical problems of modern urban life. The uncertainty surrounding justice and the police only made that knowledge more necessary. The basic fact of criminal literacy in Mexico was that the truth was never definitive, but always debatable. Reality, in other words, was not the raw information one gathered by walking the streets of the city or peeking at crime scenes: it was the organization of that information into predictable patterns that made crime the object of a productive dialogue and promised the restoration of safety after a transgression.[9]

Mexico's reputation, both within and outside the country, has long been tainted by violence and impunity. In the eyes of outsiders, the country was practically in the hands of highway robbers during the unstable years that followed independence. During the Porfiriato, prisons and city streets seemed to be infested with drunks and marijuana-fueled, knife-wielding degenerates. The 1910 revolution came with an explosion of violence and disorder on such a massive scale that images of Mexican executions and corpses were printed on postcards. By the mid-twentieth century, Mexico was a calmer place, a tolerant haven for psychoactive, erotic, or otherwise illicit entertainment for travelers. William Burroughs praised Mexico City in 1949 for "the general atmosphere of freedom" that violence and illegality offered. (It certainly helped him to escape punishment for the accidental shooting of his own wife.)[10]

This book understands infamy, to use Jorge Luis Borges's words, as a "surface of images."[11] Yet behind the apocryphal or distorted stories that form his 1935 *Historia universal de la infamia,* there is a subtle argument about the need to revisit the connections between fiction and reality, and reputations and facts. Borges writes about despicable characters throughout world history whose common achievement is infamy itself. Tom Castro, for example, is the impostor who, after leaving prison, holds news conferences in which he either defends himself or confesses his guilt—according to the preferences of the audience. Such criminals are to be praised, suggests Borges, because they provide "the dark and necessary occasion for an immortal undertaking"— the telling of their story. The *compadritos* from Buenos Aires kill their adversaries and "devote their old age to recounting that clean duel."[12]

Mexico's infamy has been a domestic product for universal consumption. According to Carlos Monsiváis, crime news, the most popular journalistic genre of the twentieth century in Mexico, reproduced violence on a massive scale, highlighting the most barbaric aspects of the country's culture and reinforcing images of Mexicans as a people inclined to commit violence for trivial reasons. Since the late nineteenth century, the enduring prints of *calaveras* by José Guadalupe Posada have provided an iconography for the idea. Reporter Pepe Nava put it plain words in a 1936 column in *Excélsior:* "For the Mexican, death is a silly thing without importance. Here it is the same to kill as to be killed." Such images were also embraced by intellectuals looking for a definition of national identity, *lo mexicano,* during the middle decades of the century. Authors like Octavio Paz and Samuel Ramos saw violence and death as both the distinction and the burden of the nation. Crime stories portrayed an aspect of Mexican popular culture that, in their view, the nation had to transcend in order to become truly modern, like the United States.[13]

Infamy refers to both reputation and morality. The double meaning of the word is central to this book's project: to understand the intersection of practices and perceptions that, in the eyes of the public, defined actions as criminal and punishment as just. Thus, this is a *history,* because its premise is that notions such as truth, justice, and even reality change over time; they are the product of debates where multiple social actors participate. This is a specifically a *national* history because, in contrast with Borges's project, it focuses on the infamy of crime *in* Mexico, and in so doing, it tries to explain the infamy *of* Mexico, the reputation of the entire country. But from this historical perspective, the book criticizes the naturalization of crime implicit in that reputation. Unlike most national histories, therefore, it cannot offer a portrayal of "the Mexicans" or take the structure of a unified narrative. This book is instead a series of stories that include a diverse cast of actors and refer to both fiction and reality, just as in the book by Borges. This is not a book of fiction, of course, but a study of fiction's role in creating an experience of reality as part of criminal literacy, that cautionary experience that people assemble to navigate everyday life. Although experience and stories are always local, the national scale is necessary in order to address the broader linkages between social practices, institutions, the press, and literature. Most of the evidence in the following chapters, therefore, comes from Mexico City because it was the place of famous criminal cases, the newspapers that covered them, and the legislators and policymakers who tried to deal with their consequences. Murder stories set in the capital played a central role in structuring criminal literacy across the country, without eliminating regional differences.

Historians have used famous cases as narrative references to delve into the microhistory of moments and places. There is nothing like a good criminal case to exemplify a historical circumstance, presenting the context and reproducing a diversity of voices while maintaining a suspenseful plot that is to be solved not necessarily through detection but by uncovering the broader historical meaning of the anecdote. The following chapters, however, stay away from that narrative structure. They do not use cases as metaphorical vehicles to make a point of more general significance. Instead, the book shows how each case, with its unique characteristics, shaped criminal literacy. Cases, therefore, are not examples but the very object of the knowledge that I am trying to reconstruct. In other words, I will not be the detective but will merely watch how others played the detective with the materials that life provided them.[14]

The following pages explore several arenas in which the public debated about the difficult connections among crime, truth, and justice. The chapters are organized into three parts that follow a loose chronological order. The first part of the book, "Spaces," is concerned with the venues in which crime and justice were discussed. Jury trials, in chapter 1, provided the site for a multiplicity of actors to debate felonies and criminals. Trials in which regular citizens, rather than a judge, decided on the facts of the case were a novelty in the country's legal history. In Mexico City, jury trials gave a prominent role to suspects and also created a setting in which other voices proposed alternative interpretations of events and motivations. Prosecutors and defenders gave long speeches, attacking or praising the character of victims, witnesses, and suspects. Participating in any of those capacities, suspects were exposed to the gaze of the public in ways that were unflattering yet also allowed some of them to challenge gender and class roles. Jurors themselves were involved, while judges tended to let everyone speak their minds and were not always able to prevent disorder. People attended jury trials in large numbers; they loudly voiced their opinions, often disrupting the proceedings. When juries were abolished in 1929, penal processes became increasingly opaque, playing out in small court offices and thick written files. It was then that the police news, or *nota roja,* the topic of chapter 2, took over as the realm where crime and justice were openly discussed. The transition from jury trials to the nota roja as the focal point of crime in the public sphere reflected the increasing alienation of Mexican citizens from the judicial system. Crime-centered newspapers and magazines contrasted their openness and dynamism with the obscurity of the courts. Newspaper readers believed that they had to search for the truth, and sometimes also for punishment, beyond state institutions. Just as the press was seen as a reliable source of facts, it was also an emotional vehicle to express support for punitive violence. Thus, newspapers were at the center of public debate about crime and fostered widespread support of extrajudicial violence against suspects. Columnists argued that since the death penalty could not be applied, and prison sentences were not long enough, infamous criminals should be punished with direct violence, including torture, lynching, or death at the hands of their guards—the so-called *ley fuga.*

The second part, "Actors," focuses on the central characters of those discussions. Detectives and policemen, tackled in chapter 3, were supposed to establish the truth behind crimes and allow judges to impart justice. Yet they did not always succeed, or they succeeded using methods that undermined the public's belief in their accounts, such as torture, extortion, and extrajudicial executions. Illegal violence was meted out by representatives of the government. The use of ley fuga occurred in a few exemplary cases as the culmination of a public debate, thereby enforcing "the sentence of public opinion." Death was a fitting end for a parallel trial in the public sphere that, as everyone knew, was not as prone to corruption as those taking place within the judicial system. Thus, extrajudicial violence was a way to break the law in order to achieve justice. But it came at the cost of the dehumanization of its victims and only deepened the gap between truth and justice. Despite the glaring contradictions between these practices and liberal notions of justice, public opinion granted torture and ley fuga a veneer of coherence and legitimacy unavailable in official channels. Chapter 4 looks at murderers, and at murder as a communicative act—an action that always has public repercussions, usually visible in the press. Murderers, particularly when they had the attention of the media, used their crimes to convey a message, an explanation for their behavior, or just a story. Their narratives often challenged the legal truth: given the ineffectiveness of official procedures to clarify the facts, firsthand testimonies became essential even if they came from despicable characters, and confessions became the dominant evidence of the truth about a crime. Chapter 5 considers a very real stereotype, the *pistolero*, or gunman, an expression of the violence and impunity that most Mexicans associated with crime and politics during these decades. Pistoleros populated the gray zone between crime and justice and thrived on the support of their powerful employers, often politicians, particularly after the 1940s.

The third part of the book, "Fictions," argues that literary narratives were integral to people's understanding of the dilemmas of truth and justice, and that these narratives were a central vehicle for the formation of criminal literacy. Chapter 6 looks a the origins of the genre of crime fiction in Mexico and the emergence of readers and writers, and chapter 7 focuses on four authors and their efforts to reconcile art, crime, and justice. Science and legal thinking were only part of the broadly shared knowledge about criminals, police stations, courts, prisons, and the customs of the underworld. This knowledge was never presented in an encyclopedic format but was condensed in literary narratives that deployed imagination in the plot but realism in the details. Crime fiction was produced and consumed by all kinds of people who deemed it useful in everyday life. After all, any modern, resourceful, and literate inhabitant of the city had to possess some knowledge about these themes. As we will see in chapter 6, detective and murder stories were a popular literary genre that included both translations and original works by Mexican authors. In early Mexican narratives, as in American hard-boiled, the intuition of fictional detectives was seen as more reliable than the lies of evasive suspects—and certainly more persuasive than the stupid or, at best, dissembling methods of the police. Hard-boiled Mexican detective authors elaborated on the central role of crime news to reach the truth and on the aesthetic appreciation of homicide that newspapers only hinted at. In Rodolfo Usigli's masterful 1944 novel *Ensayo de un crimen,* examined in chapter 7, Roberto de la Cruz, the main character, decides to commit a beautiful murder. He tries a couple of times and is frustrated when newspapers misinterpret his artistic work or attribute it to someone else. He wants to use murder to achieve a higher artistic truth but needs newspapers to publicize and validate it. As if to contrast reality with de la Cruz's delusion, the novel itself often invoked criminal literacy, alluding to cases and practices familiar to knowledgeable readers. Other contemporaries tried variations on these situations. Chapter 7 shows how, as it matured, the genre began to neglect detection in its plots in favor of the perspective of criminals who deployed cruel forms of direct justice. These stories may have channeled the frustration of readers disappointed by the official justice system; in any case, they maintained the notion that punishment had a direct connection with the truth. In doing so, they expressed illiberal impulses inherent in the naturalization of violence and impunity. Following this insight, the epilogue tries to connect some of these themes with the present.

Other countries offer examples of the ways in which crime stories and stereotypes generated debates of great political consequence. There is plenty of evidence about the role of crime as the focus of civil society's critical engagements with the state. In the words of Josefina Ludmer, crime is a "critical instrument." The criminal, Karl Marx noted, is a producer of norms, knowledges and relationships.[15] In the case of Mexico, as we will see, crime was a central theme for the emergence of critical publics—audiences which not only consumed information but also defined themselves by actively expressing their opinions. Mexico's weak police and judicial system meant that civil society played a significant role in crime prevention, especially compared to countries where those institutions had greater strength and legitimacy. In Mexico, the smallest cases became politicized: Concepción Dueñas, a regular citizen, informed President Adolfo Ruiz Cortines in 1954 that the killer of her daughter was at large because the "authorities do not pay attention to me and investigate as they should." She wanted justice, while investigators were satisfied with the idea that it had been a suicide.[16] That kind of unmet demand for justice is a running theme in this book, always in tension with the "immortal undertaking" of remembering the criminal stories that came to define a national Mexican identity. Like Dueñas, the majority of the Mexicans cited in the following pages did not particularly relish living in a violent place, and they strenuously objected to impunity. Finding out the truth, and connecting truth to punishment, brought crime to the center of the public sphere.[17]

This was not a history of unanimity, however. Disregard for due process and general acceptance of violence were the paradoxical products of the civic engagement made necessary by the weakness of state justice. Nota roja and crime fiction produced narratives that were all the more convincing because they involved multiple voices challenging the state, not because they aped its rhetoric. The opinions expressed in those debates appealed to violence without undermining their rational authority. Not in spite of but because of its cacophonous combination of feelings, deduction, intuition, and random evidence, this version of justice in the public sphere could be brutal, but it at least claimed to have a strong link with the truth. It empowered some individuals to take justice into their own hands and in doing so legitimized collective prejudices.

Infamy touched both women and men. From the suspects and victims in jury trials to the writers and characters in crime fiction, gender inequality in terms of access to safety and justice defines the history contained in this book. These differences could be symbolic and material. Women were more often victims than perpetrators of violence, and victims of both sexes were expected to be passive and vulnerable regarding their dignity and bodies. At the same time, men had a near monopoly over the legitimate, if not legal, use of violence. They also excluded women from the key legal roles held by policemen, lawyers, juries, and judges. Crime challenged social norms, however, opening spaces for women to defy expectations, though often at the cost of their honor. Thus, crime reporting was a masculine job, but women also consumed and produced stories: readers included women, and famous cases often focused on women as victims or criminals. Criminal literacy helped the public make sense of a time of great changes in gender roles in Mexico, when urbanization, education, and democracy were making women more prominent at work and in public spaces, allowing them to gradually acquire political rights (the vote was only fully granted to them in the early 1950s). Yet the processes surveyed in this book cannot be summarized as a progressive transformation in terms of gender equality. If anything, stories about violence and punishment confirmed that women had a subordinated place in social life, however tantalizing the stories through which they challenged expectations.

Something similar can be said about class differences, which underwent decisive change during the middle decades of the twentieth century, paralleling changes in gender norms. The conflicts created by crime and efforts to restore order through investigations and the administration of justice brought people of different social classes into often uncomfortable proximity. Access to money and connections filtered most middle- and upper-class suspects out of the nightmare of prisons and police stations, but not all of them.

Fewer still escaped the prying eye of police reporters and photographers. Crime stories offered readers a fascinating window into upper-class private spaces and the prestigious places where modernity seemed to reign, like fancy night clubs, restaurants, and even government offices. Illegality and violence forced intimacy on people who in normal circumstances would have remained safely isolated in their own social spaces by a deeply rooted notion of honor. Educated men monopolized the administration of justice, yet the pursuit of the truth opened up debates in the public sphere where participants could not be easily separated on the basis of their social standing.

This book encompasses two simultaneous trends. First, violence and impunity were normalized on the assumption that there would always be victims and suspects, and that their rights would always be limited. Gender and class divides expressed through crime were, in other words, the basis of authoritarian attitudes that tolerated inequality and the selective application of the law against a disenfranchised group of society. Second, public debates about crime and justice, although unresolved, expressed a common wish to find out what happened and to restore some balance to the lives disrupted by violence. This wish often entered into tension with assumptions about a fit between the roles created by crime and social difference. Restoring balance did not necessarily mean restoring hierarchies. The opposite of infamy, in sum, was not honor but the truth.

PART ONE

———

Spaces

ONE

From Transparency to Darkness

JUSTICE AND PUBLICITY IN THE MIRROR
OF CRIMINAL JURIES

BETWEEN 1869 AND 1929, MEXICO'S capital housed the institution that best embodied the possibilities and limits of the pursuit of truth in crime: the jury system in penal courts. A group of randomly selected male city residents had the power to decide over the facts in felony cases. Attorneys and judges maintained a prominent role in the process, and the voices of witnesses and suspects were also heard during public audiences, but the decision about justice was ultimately in the hands of a few good men who, lacking any direct interest in the conflict at hand, voted with their conscience to represent public opinion. Despite constant criticisms from legal experts, the popular juries, as they were often called, worked with sufficient transparency and independence to achieve considerable authority. By the 1920s, the institution had reached the peak of its influence, but it was abolished in 1929 by a presidential decree that replaced the Federal District's penal code. Criminal processes then followed an inquisitorial system, identical to the one already established in other jurisdictions, which kept most of the work of prosecutors and judges out of the public eye. The reasons for the abolition of the jury system, as we will see, were as much political as juridical. Starting in 1929, in any case, the penal process became completely opaque to common citizens.

During the 1920s, jury trials were prominent in the public sphere as the venue where diverse actors presented narratives and explanations of crime to broad audiences. Famous cases mobilized the rising power of newspapers and the radio. Those cases were particularly fascinating to the public because they exposed the subjectivity of those actors to the public's probing scrutiny while simultaneously channeling criticism of the postrevolutionary regime.[1]

Jury trials were the framework for influential debates about femininity, and they in turn contributed to the transformation of the role of women in public life—although, as we will see, not necessarily in a way that empowered them. Jury trials were a key site for constructing criminal literacy, and they catalyzed the emergence of publics that would tackle the problem of violence and impunity in subsequent decades. Studies of criminal juries in other countries stress their role as a space in the public sphere to explore many topics other than justice: emotions, gender roles, privacy, race. Jury trials did look like theater, and it is indeed tempting to see them as a stage where a variety of interesting plots and roles were performed as melodrama. Changing expectations about women in relation to violence and domesticity played out in this theater. In Mexico, however, jury trials were also the main stage for the pursuit of truth and justice. Multiple actors, from lawyers and suspects to audiences and journalists, participated in contentious debates, while jurors considered competing narratives.[2] State agents had only limited control over the process. The result was the emergence of an enduring skepticism toward the law. Looking at how jury trials operated beyond the structure of melodrama shows that women and political adversaries of the government could also use them to challenge their subordination.

After a brief history of the jury trial and its political context, this chapter will describe its operation through the testimonies of its defenders and adversaries. It would seem that nothing about jury trials was serene or balanced: the debates among lawyers about a particular case could be as acrimonious as the disputes on the way the institution worked. The basic question that divided those opinions was whether jurors were easily manipulated by base emotional appeals or hidden interests, or whether they were the custodians of a truly democratic institution. The second part of the chapter will deal with a famous case that marked the zenith of the jury trial's influence in the public sphere, when in 1924 a girl was acquitted after murdering a politician. The third part will consider the fall of the institution, after the trial of the assassin of the president-elect in 1928, and a verdict that was reached in the context of political pressure, religious conflict, and the media's obsessive interest. These two cases exemplify another lasting legacy of jury trials: the open vindication, by members of civil society, of informal justice and extrajudicial punishment as the best ways to deal with the limitations of the state.

Established after half a century of civil war and foreign invasion following independence, jury trials promised an enlightened way to address the conflicts that still riddled the nation at every level of public and private life. Justice Minister Ignacio Mariscal and other liberals who proposed the institution identified it with democracy and progress and offered a prestigious genealogy: the jury was an invention of ancient Rome and Greece, perfected by the English people, codified by the French Revolution, and embraced by the United States.[3] The Mexican 1856 Constitutional Congress, summoned by a liberal coalition, had debated the idea of including criminal juries in the new constitution, failing to approve it by only two votes. After the civil war with conservatives (1857–1861) and the French invasion in support of a monarchy (1861–1867), the same group of liberals returned to the idea. This time they established jury trials in the Federal District through a law that Mariscal proposed, Congress passed almost unanimously and President Benito Juárez signed in April 1869. As a space where the common citizens could, at least in theory, intervene directly in the process of justice, "the popular jury," as it was often called, seemed to be a lively expression of popular sovereignty.[4] There was a Mexican antecedent that Mariscal was reluctant to acknowledge. Journalists had been tried before juries from the 1820s until 1882, with some interruptions brought by political instability. In 1869, however, Mariscal was trying to avoid the impression that criminal juries would have the same flaws as press juries, which many saw as chaotic and biased in favor of suspects.[5]

Proponents of the jury believed that it could teach the public to tackle complex ethical and political situations while redeeming a justice system that lacked authority. Benjamin Constant, a strong influence on early Mexican liberals, argued that the jury was a mainstay of governance because it channeled private citizens' concern about the law.[6] The jury was valuable because it allowed ordinary citizens to not only enforce but also transcend the law, using their common sense to perform a basic function of public opinion in its classic role of judging reputations. Even though they were asked to decide only on the facts of a case, jurors took their common sense further, embracing the emotions of the trial and adopting a negative view of the law when they thought it was flawed. Jurors in criminal cases placed their conscience above the letter of the law and judges' instructions. For old liberal Guillermo Prieto, too much guidance from authorities altered the essence of the jury and turned it into merely another branch of the judiciary.[7] If education could lead to injustice, ignorance was a virtue.

And ignorance was not difficult to attain. By 1869, penal legislation was still a hodgepodge of colonial codes, national laws, and traditional norms. Upheaval and civil war had made magistrates vulnerable to corruption, political pressures, or, among lower-court judges, inexperience. Liberals argued that only the direct participation of citizens could remedy such "judicial putrefaction."[8] The jury's democratic nature helped it to gain the broad support it won early on as a testimony to the struggles that the country had just survived. Writing from *El Monitor Republicano,* "Juvenal" argued that the people had to claim the power to judge: "Let's not delegate to the hands of power," he admonished, "the very rights that we have been able to take from it only with great effort." Mariscal contended that the jury was a new right of the Mexican people: as a representation of the people, the jury would prevent the politicization of justice and other abuses of power.[9]

More than a right, the jury was an expression of popular sovereignty, a direct representation of the popular will through the conscience of individual citizens. Prestigious liberal ideologue Ignacio Ramírez explained that "the sovereign people" were the quintessential judge, just as they had been in the public square of antiquity and were at the time in the United States.[10] According to the 1869 law, jury verdicts could not be appealed if nine jurors out of eleven were in favor of conviction. A simple majority was enough for a verdict even if it led to a death penalty. In the following years, critics saw this broad authority as an idealistic aberration. Subsequent reforms gave judges authority to hear an appeal against the jury's decision in case of procedural error, but maintained the exception when the vote was close to unanimous. The premise was that only individual citizens could be honest, free from the influence of money and power that so easily corrupted public officials. Each juror decided within the subjective realm of his beliefs, where he was accountable to no one, except perhaps God.[11] Thus, for example, even if a juror was asked to vote on the facts of the case, he was free to rule instead on the basis of his appraisal of the morality of the suspect's action. Unlike the judge, by "applying the moral law that each man carries in his conscience," the juror was above the letter of the law and the intentions of the legislator.[12]

The letter of the law, however, was equivocal about jurors' obligations. The questions posed to them by the judge were restricted to matters of fact ("Is J. Jesús Soto guilty of having taken the life of Marcos Tejeda by inflicting the wound described in the medical certificate?" Or, "Was the death of N caused by peritonitis caused by the wound?").[13] Yet when jurors began to deliberate, they were sworn "to fulfill the obligations of the jury without hate nor fear and to decide, according to your conscience and your intimate belief, the charges and the means of defense, conducting yourself with all impartiality and firmness."[14] Beyond that subjective demand, the law did not impose any rule as to how jurors should reach their decisions. After all, the jury's authority resided in the individual conscience of each juror: it was not his intelligence or knowledge that mattered but his sincere belief about the moral value of the suspect's actions.[15]

From its inception, the jury trial elicited resistance from sectors of the legal profession. At first, lawyers could see the benefit of a system that enhanced the impartiality of judges. Before juries were tasked with deciding on matters of fact, judges had to carry the double role of prosecutor and adjudicator, gathering evidence and then dictating the sentence. The popular jury, and the special prosecutorial office created to supplement it, would leave the judge to coordinate the process and decide on matters of law, thus preserving his impartiality. But as the legal profession grew in size and expertise, some began to voice criticism of such "democratic improvement" on the administration of justice.[16] Thus, the 1869 law was followed by rulings and legislation that reflected growing skepticism. The Federal District's highest court proposed to eliminate criminal juries as early as 1880. Instead, the 1881 Code of Penal Procedures for the Federal District narrowed the jury's purview to crimes with a penalty of more than two years of jail. A new code of procedures from 1894 further limited the crimes that juries could decide and expanded the role of judges. More crimes, like bigamy, were excluded in 1902, and in 1907 juries were restricted to crimes with penalties of more than six years of prison; juries were also excluded from hearing cases involving dueling, adultery, and attacks on public officials. During those years, other states that had also had criminal juries abolished them.[17] Just before the revolution, jurists augured that the days of the popular jury were numbered. However, Primer Jefe Venustiano Carranza included the popular jury in his project for a new constitution in late 1916, and this time constituent deputies approved it.[18] Regulations for the Federal District remained in effect until 1929, when a new penal code was approved. The possibility of using juries instead of judges remained in the constitution until 2008, but only for a few crimes, like treason and libel.

Critics of the jury system voiced pessimism about the average citizen and his ability to express the popular will. For Santiago Sierra, the illusion of "our democratic experience" had consecrated an institution that was a poor and ephemeral reflection of justice.[19] Forty years later, another Porfirista, Francisco Bulnes, argued that the jury's authority had to be constrained because "we do not deserve justice, because whoever cannot make it does not deserve it."[20] Bulnes described the jury in Mexico as bad parody of august models: "The twenty six just men of the prudish England ... became in Mexico twelve coarse men who congratulated rapists for the good bodies they have enjoyed, mocked husbands who suffered scandalous adulteries, admired the exquisite horror of those who murdered their concubines or public women, exalted in the heroism of the troublemakers, the astuteness of treacherous murderers, the trickery of thieves."[21] The most coherent indictment against the jury, however, came from prominent lawyer Demetrio Sodi, a judge and jurist who acquired considerable influence and wealth during the Porfirian period. Sodi published *El jurado en México* in 1909, calling for the end of the jury trial, which he believed was imminent: most states had already eliminated it and established "procedures that are in accordance with the scientific advances of penal law."[22] The book echoed the positivist critique against liberalism but stressed the perspective of a legal profession that had already acquired greater prestige by the time. Sodi argued that the jury was not a democratic institution (how could it be, if the lists were arbitrarily produced by government officials?), and he dismissed the idea that juries were necessary because of the flaws of the judicial establishment. Even if most judges were poorly educated, the defects of the jury were such that its abolition was still a better option. Based on his long trial experience, Sodi combined the usual quotations from legal authorities with outrageous anecdotes from actual Mexican jury trials. He listed the many ways in which justice could be undermined. One of the main dangers were lawyers' tricks and rhetoric "because juries decide by impression and not by intimate belief."[23]

Reports of frequent irregularities in the court buttressed calls to abolish jury trials. Courtroom spectators tried to influence the jurors with their vociferous responses to speeches and testimonies. Bribes and threats were discovered in some cases. Jurors often hurried, not taking the time to seriously consider the evidence. Lawyers used sophistry or encroached on the court's roles. The strongest indictment of jury trials came from a few particularly scandalous cases in which juries acquitted suspects of crimes like homicide. Although newspapers reported most of these instances as routine, a few examples seemed particularly outrageous, prompting early calls for abolishing the institution or temporarily suspending constitutional guarantees.

There were plays inspired by such injustices, and extensive coverage of particularly grievous acquittals resulting from jury votes that contradicted the evidence. Even faced with a suspect's multiple confessions, as in the case of accused murderer Felipe Guerrero in 1895, juries did not always deliver a guilty verdict. For critics, the conclusion was plain: the kind of people who served in juries were selfish and therefore sympathized with the criminal, or they were so crass and base that they failed to see the abnormality of crime.[24]

These arguments neglected the fact that in many cases acquittals were supported by strong evidence, and guilty verdicts in others led to the death penalty.[25] A count made in 1929 by judges who presided over jury trials found that of 260 trials, 70 percent resulted in a guilty sentences, 5 percent were "absurd verdicts, mainly because of defects in the way the accusation was formulated" (where prosecutors requested harsh punishment for minor offenses), and the rest were acquittals for "crimes of passion."[26] The numbers, even if partial, contrasted favorably with the data collected in 1880, when juries in a small sample of cases acquitted more than 70 percent of the accused.[27] The improvement, newspapers argued, was the result of their coverage, which had made the operation of the trial more transparent. Even the jury selection could become a public event, with newspapers printing the names and portraits of those chosen.[28]

The social profile of jurors was the main reason for professional lawyers' opposition to jury trials. According to the 1869 law, juries were composed of eleven members. There were no income requirements, but jurors could "not be an employee, public official, physician, nor hold a profession that would prevent them from having free time without losing wages."[29] They simply had to be, legislators explained, men of "good habits and good common sense."[30] Thus, the exclusions were based on social status and not ideology. The illiterate were excluded, as well as artisans, and later those below a certain income level. Lucio Duarte, who owned a pulquería, successfully petitioned to be excused from jury obligation "for lack of the knowledge that must be held by the person who fulfills such commission."[31] Foreigners with three years of residency, and former supporters of the Second Empire, otherwise deemed traitors, could be included—they tended to be educated, upper-class men, after all. In 1880, moderate liberal Santiago Sierra called for a smaller "but well-chosen [jury] of citizens who satisfy the qualities that constitute honorability."[32] A 1891 reform to the law reduced the number of jurors to nine and established that they had to earn one hundred pesos a year or have a profession.[33]

Before each trial, the names of the jurors were randomly drawn from a list compiled by municipal authorities of "well-known persons" in each neighborhood.[34] In practice, the social profile of jurors was determined by the process of selecting the names to be on the list. Many citizens asked to be excluded, claiming illness, ignorance, deafness, old age, or other reasons. Those with friends in government could easily be removed from the list. The result was arbitrary, incomplete, and out-of-date lists, which often included people who did not exist. According to one judge, this caused "great problems that, little by little, destroy[ed] and degrade[d] the institution of the jury."[35] Juries, critics claimed, included people with little education, merchants, shady Spanish immigrants motivated by interest, and even drunkards. Demetrio Sodi denounced the existence of "professional jurors," also known as "coyotes," or "milperos" (corn farmers), who were familiar with legal procedures. They were "vagrants" who arranged to be selected for juries in order to receive the small stipend that came with the job. Their trick was to guess the judge's desired outcome in order to be "selected" again.[36] Twenty years later, newspapers continued to pillory jurors for hire who did not represent "the clean and spontaneous naivety of the humble citizen" but rather the cunning of slightly educated urban characters seeking profit in the interstices of a flawed system. Turning jury service into a job, they perverted the institution's goals and made possible a "threatening sewer where corruption boils."[37] Corruption could work for all sides. The jurors for a 1929 murder case came together from Ixtapalapa; they were, according to El Universal, "Indians" sent by a cacique. During a break in the court sessions, they had lunch with an employee of the defense who told them how to vote.[38]

A look at the rest of the participants in trials suggests that there were indeed other actors who could undermine the expression of popular sovereignty through the jury. Judges controlled the process of trials before the final public audience. They were in charge of the initial investigatory phase of the process, which consisted of gathering all the evidence in a written file. Public hearings before the jury began with the court's secretary reading the prosecution's indictment and the defense's case in a monotone that put jurors and audience to sleep. Then suspects answered questions, and additional evidence was presented to jury. During this phase of the trial, according to the law, the judge "can do whatever he deems necessary for the clarification of the facts: the law leaves to his honor and conscience the use of means that might strengthen the manifestation of the truth."[39] The judge was the most aggressive and powerful actor in the proceedings, grilling and scolding the suspects if their statements contradicted any part of the existing evidence, or if they claimed not to remember the events. According to Carlos Roumagnac, a keen observer of the world of crime and prisons, judges acted on the assumption that the suspect was guilty, leaving aside "the calmness and the impartiality . . . that must be the main features of a true judge."[40] Judges lost some of their power in the next phase of the trial, when the prosecutor and defense lawyer summarized the case using all their rhetorical weapons. This was the moment when everyone paid attention, and oratory acquired a central role because skillful defense lawyers could turn the jurors and the audience against the prosecution.[41]

Attorneys deployed the tools of rhetoric and personal emotion, undermining the structure of the process established by the law. The code instructed prosecutors to limit their conclusions to "a clear and methodical exposition of the charges lodged against the accused," without citing authors or laws, and it allowed the defense attorney to speak "with all freedom except to attack the law, morality or authorities, or insult any person."[42] In practice, there was considerable leeway. Although the judge could stop the speeches if they transgressed these boundaries, attorneys used a variety of resources in order to influence jurors. Some began with jokes. Prosecutors cited criminologists to stress the obvious criminal features of the suspect. Both sides deployed "flashy rhetorical figures and dramatic effect" in which literary inspiration took precedence over facts.[43] But it was the defense that could most effectively use art to elicit emotions and to encourage jurors' empathy for suspects. The same effect was harder to achieve with victims: revenge was easier to imagine than suffering.

Their ability to mobilize sentiment over the law made a few defense lawyers quite popular. They were talented orators regarded as artists whose work had political significance. The best known among them was Querido Moheno. A lawyer and congressman during the Porfiriato, Moheno advocated for a parliamentary regime and strong restrictions on voting rights in order secure a peaceful transition out of the benevolent dictatorship of the aging Díaz. This meant, in his writings, a greater role for public opinion, which he defined as the voice of the most educated sectors of society. During the civil war that started with the coup against President Francisco I. Madero in 1913, Moheno joined General Victoriano Huerta's cabinet, and he had to leave the country when the revolution prevailed. He returned in 1920, ostensibly renouncing politics, to work as a journalist and defense attorney in Mexico City. During that decade, his speeches, some of them several hours long, were praised as works of art, while his newspaper columns lambasted the postrevolutionary regime. He was so popular that audiences applauded him before he started to speak, and listeners celebrated the conclusion of his speech with "shouts, applause, cries, wriggling hands, all combined in honor of the great tribune"; they even carried him on their shoulders, despite his considerable weight.[44] His successes in court were often interpreted as political victories. Government deputies referred to him as "the cynic Querido Moheno who, not satisfied with having tarnished himself with the crime of *huertismo,* now wants to be tarnished by his complicity with all the crimes committed by prostituted women in Mexico City."[45] Moheno used all the resources of oratory to persuade jurors to vote for acquittal, combining the basic dictates of classical rhetoric with a cunning manipulation of the audience's emotions.

Moheno embraced political sociologist Gustave Le Bon's ideas about the crowd. In doing so, he made the jury trial the keystone of a broader political theory about the role of sentiment and violence in public life. Le Bon, admired by Porfirians and revolutionaries alike, argued that crowds could be studied and manipulated as living organisms. He described them as impulsive, simplistic, authoritarian, and conservative. Juries were just a particular variety of crowd, and as such, they were influenced more by imagination than reasoning or evidence. Le Bon offered a few rules to influence juries: exploit their tendency to be lenient with crimes that usually do not affect them, modify the speech according to jurors' reactions, and address those who seem to be the leaders within the group.[46] *El Universal* translated this to the Mexican context: "A jury is a crowd, and a crowd does not operate by reasons but by feelings. Nobody can persuade a crowd, but it seems very easy to move it. And to move it is to defeat it . . . even at the cost of justice."[47] From this perspective, emotions could be a legitimate foundation for verdicts; jurors were assumed to simply channel the judgment of public opinion. This obviously contradicted the model of the rational, logical truth that was supposed to characterize judicial investigations. But it worked as part of Moheno's rhetorical strategies. He often refused to base his defense on factual details, arguing that the fate of his clients "will not be decided with those details but with great facts and generalizations."[48]

For Le Bon, "to know the art of impressing the imagination of the crowds is to know the art of ruling them."[49] The political implications of these ideas were particularly relevant in 1920s Mexico. In Moheno's hands, they made oratory a weapon against the postrevolutionary regime's abuse of power. In his speeches before juries and in his newspaper columns, he defended the use of violence as heroic resistance against tyranny. As a lawyer in the 1920s, Moheno argued that the jury was the highest representation of public opinion—much as he had argued about Congress before 1913. He and other famous defense lawyers insisted that the jury was the only institution that could provide a measure of justice in a corrupted judicial system—"the only true guarantee that the citizen enjoys among us." The jury superseded written law because it was "the summary of social conscience." [50] "Official justice" was nothing more, after all, than a temporary delegation to the government of people's right to seek justice. Jurors' "intimate conviction" translated into public action a deep skepticism of the state, which Moheno cultivated in speeches that framed defendants' actions as resistance against the regime's corruption. Defending Alicia Jurado, who had killed her husband, he argued that the revolution had created moral confusion and impunity, and that as a consequence justice had lost its authority; if the murderers of Madero and Zapata had not been punished, and the men who had stolen Moheno's own furniture during the revolution now used it without fear of punishment, how could the jury condemn a defenseless woman? [51] The revolution had been "this horrible nightmare, these ten years of butchery between brothers in which a million Mexicans died." [52]

Moheno's vindication of public opinion was based on a racialized view of society. He claimed that a truly independent jury had to be drawn from a list that represented the "intellectual level" of Mexican society: neither intellectuals nor ignorant "huarachudos" (sandal-wearing people), [53] and he argued that "the only possible form of democracy is the rule of the people by the best of the people." [54] The judiciary's decadence was a result of the *mestizaje* (interracial mixing) that was "strangling the republic." [55] Moheno, who had lived in Cuba and the United States during his exile, alluded to the "African savagery" of blacks in Cuba who, he claimed, killed and ate white children. In his writings, he praised the U.S. South, where "the Lynch law authorizes certain kinds of popular executions" as a protection for white women's honor and a direct representation of popular sovereignty—the same reasoning used by liberal Ignacio Ramírez six decades earlier, when jury trials were first proposed. [56] Other Mexican authors shared Moheno's racially tinged view of social hierarchies, and his conservative rejection of the revolution. [57] The success of Moheno's speeches probably pushed the government to eliminate the institution in 1929. [58] While these ideas did not lead to fascist ideologies similar to those developing at the time in other countries, in Mexico they left a less overt but more resilient legacy of generalized skepticism toward the judiciary and the police, as well as tolerance of extrajudicial punishment.

Only after hearing these speeches and the judge's instructions did the jury become the key actor in the proceedings. The judge presented jurors with the questions upon which they had to vote. The questionnaire followed a logical order in which a negative response to one question would preempt discussion of the next one. Mitigating and aggravating circumstances, therefore, were considered only after the jury had voted on the suspect's guilt. The judge had to avoid technical terms and make the questions as simple as possible, but often the jury's answers were illogical—offering aggravating circumstances after declaring that there had been no crime, for example. Along with the questions, the jury received a handbook with relevant articles from procedural codes. The judge also gave them instructions intended to preserve the integrity of the decision process. For example, jurors were told to disregard the fate that the suspect would expect according to their verdict. Nobody took these orders too seriously, and the jury did keep punishment in mind when voting on the facts of the case. Beyond this, there were no rules for the jury's deliberation. The judge could only enter their chambers to clarify a point of law, but he could pressure the jury to reach a prompt verdict, ordering jurors not to leave court until they voted or refusing to bring food to them, even though sessions were scheduled in the afternoon and evening. These tactics, some critics argued, led to obviously erroneous votes caused by exhaustion.[59]

The role of the jury was not limited to its deliberation and vote after the hearing. The jury provided a unifying perspective throughout the trial, actively engaging with the other participants and maintaining, despite the arguments of critics of the system, a fair competition in the pursuit of the truth. The best panorama of the diversity of voices heard at jury trials during the 1920s comes from the 1961 memoirs of Federico Sodi, *El jurado resuelve*. Unlike his half-brother Demetrio, who in 1909 wrote *El jurado en México*, Federico celebrated the institution and its polyphonic chaos, and he did not pay much attention to juridical questions. The great speeches by famous lawyers, according to Sodi, "never determined the fate of an accused. A case was won or lost through the evidence placed in front of the jurors." Rather than being the object of emotional manipulation, "the jury's instinct allowed it to distinguish truth from lies with mathematical precision . . . through a wonderful intuitive phenomenon," so that its opinion was already formed before the lawyers' closing remarks. Thus, for example, Sodi was able to get an acquittal for homicide suspect Bernice Rush despite the prejudice against her U.S. nationality and her past as a prostitute. Over several days, jurors began to understand her, despite her poor Spanish, thanks to "those small, fleeting elements . . . that can only be perceived and transmitted between human souls."[60]

Evidence came to jurors from different perspectives. Four parties interrogated suspects and witnesses in order: the judge, who usually tried to support the results of the prior investigation; the prosecutor, who contributed to the case hoping for a guilty verdict; the defense attorneys (often a team, including court-appointed and pro-bono lawyers), who were trying to both cast doubt on the accusation and create an alternative story; and the attorneys representing the civil party. The latter were hired by the victims or the family of a murder victim to seek monetary compensation and defend the reputation of the deceased. They sat at a table on a platform next to the judge, prosecutors, and defense attorneys; they participated in the interrogations, and they also gave a concluding speech. Their role could be important: in María del Pilar Moreno's case, the representative of the victim's family was more vociferous in demanding punishment than the prosecutors.[61] Representatives of the civil party could also add to the emotional color of the trial. In a case in which a man who had killed his cheating wife and her lover moved the audience with his tears, the lover's relatives countered the effect with a lawyer who was, in Sodi's opinion, ridiculous but effective: "Some said that he charged a schedule with three categories of fees: defense with teary voice, defense with cries, and defense with continual sobbing cries."[62] All lawyers could work, at different points in their careers, in any of the four capacities mentioned above. Thus, even after the worst battles, they sought to have a drink together with their adversaries, often in a bar across the street from court.[63]

Jurors also heard other voices during the presentation of evidence. Prosecutors and defense attorneys, in Sodi's view, could be overpowering during speeches but lose control during interrogations. The best ones, like Moheno, gathered information about the witnesses before the trial, surprising them by revealing information about their lives, and laying the groundwork for the summation, a melodramatic narrative with starkly delineated characters. The truthfulness of testimonies was exposed also during the *careo,* a face-to-face confrontation between the suspect and witnesses or victims. The judge enjoined both parties to reconcile their testimonies, and let them speak freely, without the intervention of the attorneys. The result yielded little new evidence but produced fascinating dialogues spiced with insults and gossipy accusations, as in one case involving two wives of a murder victim who challenged each other's morality, or another between two men involved in a duel who were reluctant to admit that the cause of the dispute was someone else's wife. Suspects could otherwise intervene in the discussions, and even under the prosecutor's interrogation they conveyed their own explanations and criticisms of the evidence. Jurors could also ask questions through the judge or, as in the case against Rush, comment on the accuracy of the translation of her deposition.[64] Witnesses were also active in the process beyond their testimonies. They included all kinds of fascinating people, from a mentally ill man brought from the asylum to a famous detective; they could sleep while waiting for their turn or remain actively engaged as part of the audience.[65]

The most dissonant among these voices, of course, was that of the suspect. Some of them had such a commanding presence that they became celebrities of sorts. Women acquitted thanks to Federico Sodi's work ended up, as he feared, victims of their own sudden fame, but others acquired enduring reputations.[66] Audiences came to court to see those fascinating characters up close. A Spanish man accused of murder, for example, attracted everyone's curiosity because his appearance did not fit any of the stereotypes of the criminal offered by science. In the famous Desierto de los Leones case, the image of a woman in black, covered by a veil, sitting next to the skull of the man she helped kill and bury, surpassed any movie in terms of its impressive staging.[67] Suspects manipulated the jury, according to Sodi: "They tried to ingratiate themselves with the court, making the judges laugh, or moving them with sentimental stories and faked afflictions"; female suspects rented children "to cause pity, with a feigned maternity, among the simple and naïve jurors." Some also hid the purported anatomical evidence of their criminal propensities, such as large ears, long arms, dark skin, or sparse beard—all of which, as a good positivist, Sodi considered objective evidence of criminal tendencies.[68]

The staging was much appreciated by the crowds attending jury trials. The court distributed a limited number of free tickets, which in famous cases were sold outside the courthouse. The spectators' physical presence in the courtroom was palpable; as the temperature in the courtroom rose, the smells of sweat, food, cigarette smoke, and flashbulbs could be suffocating. People hissed, booed, cried, clapped, and in some cases, chanted "Acquittal! Acquittal!" as if they were attending a sporting event.[69] In at least one case, examined below, they physically attacked the suspects. Those who could not enter the courtroom had to be kept out by soldiers, but these would-be spectators could still express their opinion from the street. Lawyers and journalists liked to compare these crowds to the audiences found in theaters, cheap cinemas, street markets, or cabarets. In 1907, writer Federico Gamboa

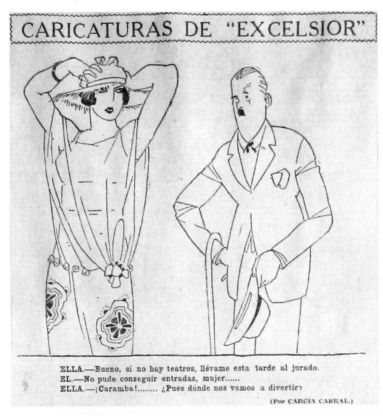

CARICATURAS DE "EXCELSIOR"

ELLA.—Bueno, si no hay teatros, llévame esta tarde al jurado.
EL.—No pude conseguir entradas, mujer......
ELLA.—¡Caramba!........ ¿Pues dónde nos vamos a divertir?

(Por CARCIA CABRAL.)

FIGURE 1. Jury tickets. *Excélsior,* 29 April 1928, p. 6.
  "She: Well, if there are no plays, take me to the jury.
  "He: I could not get tickets, woman . . .
  "She: Damn! Where are we going to have fun, then?"

attended jury trials in the morning to hear promising orators and then enjoyed lunch at the country club. He was fascinated by the diversity of the audiences. People from all walks of life could get tickets and make their presence felt: from upper-class women, highly placed bureaucrats, foreign diplomats, and other "decent people," to the "gangsters" and assorted rabble from the neighborhoods around Belem prison where the Mexico City courtrooms were housed.[70] For the sensual and bored woman shown in figure 1, the jury was a necessary distraction if theater was not available; she was annoyed because her husband could not get tickets for her.

By the 1920s, jury trials had their own specialized reporters, who generated innovative photographic and narrative coverage. Chronicles featured the dramatic intensity of the setting, the personality of the actors, and the sequence

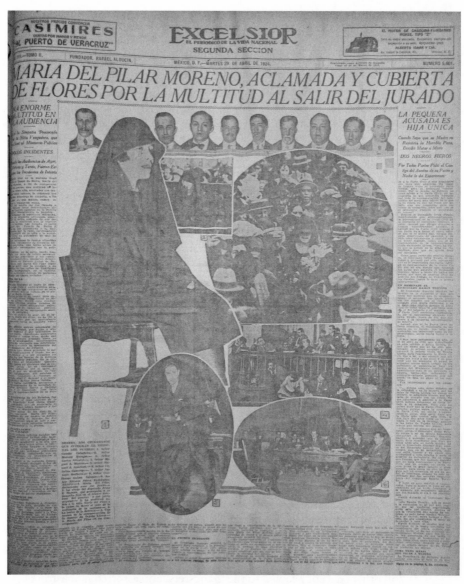

FIGURE 2. María del Pilar Moreno's acquittal. *Excelsior,* 29 April 1924, sec. 2, p. 1.

of events, from the crime scene to the final speeches in the courtroom.[71] Figure 2 captures the most striking elements of María del Pilar Moreno's case: her slight yet dignified figure, the support of her mother, the crowds in the street, the jurors' faces, a reconstruction of the moment of the shooting, and the desks of judge, attorneys, and journalists in the courtroom.[72]

Though jury trials were a spectacle, they were not frivolous. Women, as we will see in the next section, probed the limits of the female exercise of violence in defense of dignity. Jury trials were living laboratories of justice and schools to build criminal literacy. Chroniclers of a famous case in 1906 noticed members of the audience, including law students, commenting on points of jurisprudence. Gamboa kept coming back to trials in order to gather material for his fiction, even as he decried the jury as a "democratic stupidity."[73] Criminologists observed a variety of criminal types and situations in a setting that, like the prison, was inherently connected to the "world of crime." Roumagnac recommended that those studying the science of policing should attend jury sessions; among the "public in attendance it is rare not to find members of the underworld and particularly recidivists."[74] Roumagnac himself interviewed prison inmates who told him that they attended trials not only to pass the time but also to learn lawbreaking techniques and ploys to avoid investigators. The radio, a medium that emerged during the mid-twenties, only expanded the reach of these lessons. The political ramifications of jury trials, as we will see in the next section, were also multiplied by audiences and the media.[75]

MARÍA DEL PILAR MORENO

The case of María del Pilar Moreno is useful in order to understand how the practices and arguments related to the criminal jury came to produce enduring narratives. Her story became a powerful focus of public interest throughout the country because it incorporated several plotlines, both political and private. As a current affair, a theme of *actualidad,* the details of the case circulated across the country by word of mouth and through the mass media over the course of several months. Newspaper readers, judges, lawyers, suspects, students, women, and even writers ("all social classes," according to *El Heraldo*) knew about the details of the case and spoke about it with emotion and knowledge. The coming together of such a diverse public was the consequence of a complex story that was rich in meaning. The opinions inspired by the murder and the trial reflected changing understandings of age, gender, privacy, and justice.[76]

On July 10, 1922, when she was fourteen years old, María del Pilar killed Senator Francisco Tejeda Llorca outside his house at 48 Tonalá Street, Mexico City. Two months earlier, Tejeda Llorca had killed her father, Deputy

Jesús Moreno, but he had escaped prosecution because he was a member of Congress. María del Pilar's action provoked demonstrations of popular support immediately following her crime, and there were celebrations after her acquittal in April 1924. She owed the result in large part to Querido Moheno's defense, but her case was also helped by her own explanation of her motivations, disseminated through the press, a volume of her childhood memoirs, and the trial itself. The "tragedy," as contemporaries labeled the case, would not have been so powerful had it not taken place in the middle of a political upheaval that endangered Álvaro Obregón's government from several sides. In that setting, the story of María del Pilar exposed the masculine ferocity of politics, the widening gap between judicial institutions and true justice, and the uncertainty about the role that women had to play in a new era of increasing political participation. The trial garnered more public support for the use of private violence to remedy the flaws of the law and the impunity associated with politics.

The characters of the story presented that dilemma in the stark lines of melodrama. On May 24, 1922, Tejeda Llorca bumped into Jesús Moreno at the doors of the Secretaría de Gobernación. The two were trying to meet with Minister Plutarco Elías Calles. A scuffle ensued and Tejeda Llorca, encouraged by his friends, who were holding the victim, shot Moreno at close range. Tejeda Llorca surrendered and gave a statement at the police station. As a federal deputy, however, he could not be charged unless Congress stripped him of his *fuero*, or parliamentary immunity. In the following weeks, María del Pilar and her mother, Ana Díaz, met with several high-ranking politicians, including Calles, asking for the arrest of Tejeda Llorca. Nothing could be done, they were told, because of Tejeda Llorca's immunity. Tejeda Llorca exemplified the privileges enjoyed by a political class of violent men who seemed to be above the law. Congressmen were the object of particular scorn, as Congress itself was losing influence in relation to the presidency and as a representation of public opinion.[77] The press attributed Moreno's death to "political passion" and electoral struggles in the state of Veracruz. Although both men belonged to the Partido Nacional Cooperatista, they were trying to undermine each other's run for Congress—Moreno for deputy again, and Tejeda Llorca for senator. Both claimed to have popular support, but they knew it was Calles, Obregón's likely successor, whose blessing would decide their future. The following year, while the trial hearings were under way, a military rebellion supporting Calles's rival for the presidency within Obregón's cabinet, Adolfo de la Huerta, created a serious threat to the government, magnifying the political implications of the case. Friends of Jesús Moreno were now among the Delahuertistas, and during the trial María del Pilar's lawyers paid homage to some of the rebels executed by the government.[78]

The fourteen-year-old girl at the center of the case seemed to be above politics, though, as she attracted the sympathy of everyone interested in the case. After her father's death, María del Pilar reacted with dramatic gestures: when she saw his corpse at the hospital she tried to climb over a railing to kill herself; then, she embraced his body and promised to seek revenge. At the funeral, under heavy rain and in front of politicians and relatives, she erupted in "moving cries" and exclaimed, "Justice, sir! My father has been villainously murdered!"[79] After her crime, she confessed that she was finally at peace. She received flowers at the police station, the Correctional School, and during the trial, and after her acquittal she left the courtroom "walking on flowers" into a crowd outside the Belem courthouse that stopped traffic for almost half an hour.[80] People from around the country wrote to her or approached her in person to embrace her or to kiss her hands. María del Pilar inspired these feelings because, after her crime, she constructed a narrative of her life that pitched her vulnerable femininity against the violent disruption of domesticity brought by politics. According to her memoir, *La tragedia de mi vida* (written with the help of journalists and published in 1922, after the homicide), she was not afraid to intervene in defense of her father: she once threw herself in front of officers coming to arrest him, and on another occasion she followed her mother on a long trek into the countryside in order to nurse her sick father.[81]

María del Pilar's killing of Tejeda Llorca was just another demonstration of her filial love. When she decided to shoot him, she dressed herself in white and ordered her chauffeur to take her to her favorite church, the Sagrada Familia, at the Colonia Roma. Her aunt Otilia accompanied them. In Tonalá Street, two blocks away from the church, María del Pilar stepped out of the car and approached Tejeda Llorca, who was standing on the sidewalk with other men. She grabbed him by his lapel and told him, "Kill me, like you killed my father." He grabbed her arm and tried to force her to her knees, but she was able to draw her gun and shoot him four times. There were more gunshots, it seems, and Manuel Zapata, a friend of Tejeda Llorca who had also been involved in Jesús Moreno's death, disarmed María del Pilar and beat her. Her mother arrived shortly afterward in another car and took her to the offices of *El Heraldo,* the newspaper that Jesús Moreno was running at the time of his death. The newspaper's new director accompanied them to the police station, where María del Pilar confessed, was arrested, and spent the night in the company of her mother.

In her statements, María del Pilar gave differing accounts, first saying that she had done it for revenge, then adding details that diminished her penal responsibility. At first she said that the crime was premeditated and that she was satisfied with having avenged her father; she did it also "to defend my life, . . . my father's honor, and . . . my orphanhood." But when questioned about the facts of the crime, she stated that she was not looking for her victim on Tonalá Street, that she had used her gun because she believed that Tejeda Llorca was going to draw his, and that she did not intend to kill him but was forced to pull the trigger by the victim's painful pressure on her arm. Witnesses, however, suggested that it had all been planned; some had seen, days before the crime, a "mysterious car" parked on their street with a man and two women inside; others stated that they saw a "strong man" shooting twice at Tejeda Llorca as he stumbled, already wounded, toward his house. The autopsy later revealed that Tejeda Llorca's body contained a .38 caliber bullet, along with the .32 caliber bullets from María del Pilar's gun. The ensuing investigation, however, did not lead to another arrest, and the contradictions between her statements, those by witnesses, and the physical evidence were never resolved.[82]

The proceedings following María del Pilar's indictment focused less on the facts than on the antagonism between multiple actors. Tejeda Llorca's relatives sued María del Pilar for 30,000 pesos, and thus became directly involved in the trial. More than money, their goal was to clear the victim's name before public opinion. María del Pilar framed the process as a confrontation against powerful adversaries. When she was offered freedom on bail, she refused it against the advice of her lawyer, explaining that she felt safer at the Correctional School. This implied that her enemies might use violence against her, but it was also a way to declare her trust in justice: rather than obtaining freedom without a clear resolution, she preferred to wait in prison and let the jury decide her fate. The case, however, dragged on for almost two years, a delay that was in itself a form of punishment. María del Pilar stayed eight months at the school, leaving only twice a week to place flowers at her father's grave, until it became clear that prosecutors and judge were delaying the conclusion of the trial, at which point she moved back in with her mother.[83]

The delay allowed María del Pilar to put forth a narrative of her own life that expanded on the contradictions between the violence of politics and the happy domesticity of a prosperous and protective household. She had studied with private tutors, at the prestigious Colegio Francés, and at the Escuela Normal para Profesoras. His father encouraged her to learn piano, singing, and embroidery, and he hoped she would become a journalist. He instructed his wife to spare María del Pilar any domestic chores that might hurt her hands, and he expected her to dress well but without ostentation. The respectability of the family was embodied in the house where they lived in 1922. Her father had built it, naming it "María del Pilar," and he put the deed to the house in his daughter's name. She had told him she liked the Colonia Portales, a sparsely populated area south of downtown. Journalists and Moheno himself in his concluding speech at the trial described the house to evoke the bliss of the modern, self-sufficient life of American-style architecture and automobiles characteristic of Mexico City's new *colonias*.[84]

Politics, the source of the prosperity that had made this happiness possible, also threatened it. María del Pilar and her mother often asked Jesús to abandon his run for Congress and focus on journalism. His political work had brought him time in prison, persecution, exile, illness, and duels. In the 1920s, the job of congressman still implied considerable risks, with gunfights and even homicides taking place on the very floor of the Chamber of Deputies. Political intrigue was probably the reason that several masked men stalked the Colonia Portales house at night and tried to climb onto María del Pilar's terrace. However, María del Pilar's defense of a vulnerable household departed from the femininity found in most respectable families: she fired a small rifle she had received as a gift to call attention to the intruders. Since the rifle was too flimsy, her father gave her another one which proved too heavy, and he later gave her a small handgun that she kept in her night desk and eventually used to kill Tejeda Llorca. During the trial, Moheno tried to downplay María del Pilar's unfeminine familiarity with firearms because it could evoke foreign *criminelles passionnelles,* and influence juries against her. Despite Moheno's strategy, her male admirers could not help but notice her courageous use of such a masculine symbol of her father's legacy. She trusted such identification would help her, knowing that jurors "had a father and have children" and would have to acquit her.[85]

María del Pilar's clearest departure from normative age and gender roles, however, was her awareness of the impact of her actions and words on public opinion. After she killed Tejeda Llorca, she described to journalists the emotions that had moved her to commit the crime. She wrote a memoir and continued to give interviews to newspapers up to the final days of the trial, always stressing her vulnerable but dignified femininity. For example, she assured *Excélsior* that she was calm despite her "feminine and nervous temperament."[86] Her performance during the jury hearings was fine-tuned to affect the audience. She cried several times during the interrogations and speeches, but when it was time for her to testify she delivered a clear and moving version of her story. In addition to narrating the basic events, she derided Calles's rejection of her pleas for justice. In contrast to the usual image of mournful and silent women in criminal trials (which she and her mother nevertheless provided for photographers), she was outspoken, almost commanding: she asked the judge not to expel the boisterous public from the courtroom, she invited the audience to show respect to her prosecutors, and she thanked the victim's relatives for dropping their request to have her father's murder discussed as part of the trial. The latter intervention prompted "a storm of applause from a deeply moved audience."[87] María del Pilar was thus able to invest her deed with a clear moral meaning. She would not write again, as she promised in her book, but her gestures and words before the jury audience, her memoirs, and her pictures in the press created a paradigm of filial love and dignity. Her triumph was celebrated as one of femininity, but her active defense of domesticity and her claim for revenge seemed to confound gendered contemporary notions of the use of violence.

Moheno's summation before the jury provided an effective rhetorical form for this tension between gender norms and the use of violence in the name of justice. He began in a minor key: mercy, he argued deceptively, was the goal of a good defense speech, so he professed humility. But he then introduced himself as a man who had successfully defended other women accused of homicide. In those cases, he had also faced the hostility from the government which characterized him as "a representative of the reaction" whose triumphs were "a threat to the nation." He reminded jurors and the audience that he was working pro bono, having previously rejected a retainer from the relatives of Tejeda Llorca.[88] Moheno's presence dominated the stage and contrasted with María del Pilar's image; sweaty and corpulent, at one point he requested a break, explaining that he was very tired.

In the main part of the speech, he framed the jury's decision in terms of the crime's moral implications rather than the facts. He painted an idealized scene of the Morenos' domestic bliss at the Portales house, contrasting it with "the sordid two-room apartment in a horrible tenement" where the accused and her mother had to move after the father's death. María del Pilar now had to do domestic work.[89] Such misfortune was the product, Moheno explained to a teary audience, of "our lowly, bloody, and suicidal politics."[90] The strategy was calculated to steer jurors' reasoning toward causes that were both larger than the crime at hand and equally emotionally charged. The real crime, Moheno stated, had been the electoral fraud that gave Tejeda Llorca a seat in the Senate, maintaining his impunity, after he had committed murder. Lifting a page from Le Bon's ideas about the crowd, Moheno encouraged the intervention of the courtroom audience and of public opinion more generally; he cited his own books, newspaper columns, and interviews. He also sought to move jurors to action, as classic rhetoric dictated, through the warmth and passion of emotions. His tools in this and other speeches were few but effective: repetition of "great ideas" and metaphors, constant references to religion, mythology, national history, and literature, attacks against the prosecution's witnesses, depictions of the defendant's suffering, and pathetic calls for forgiveness. The climax, however, was a vindication of violent revenge that showed little mercy for the victim. Moheno appealed for jurors to take justice into their own hands, as María del Pilar had done, and to acquit her, voting with their conscience but disregarding the letter of the law. He was applauded for several minutes, and even the judge congratulated him on the beauty of the speech. After the verdict, he was carried out of the courtroom on the shoulders of the audience.[91]

The resolution of María del Pilar's trial was an emblematic example of how jury trials had become a venue where gender roles could be openly discussed and transformed to a certain extent. Her case and others during the 1920s created a prominent space for the public to hear stories that brought together women and violence. These were fascinating narratives, complex enough to allow for different interpretations, all sharing a strong female protagonist. Through the words and images produced in the courtroom, these women explained how they used violence to defend their honor and physical integrity. The acquittals that several of them obtained, as in the case of María del Pilar, demonstrated that juries were willing to vote in favor of defendants even when such a vote contradicted a strict interpretation of the law.

It would be a mistake, however, to conclude that these cases were part of a process of female empowerment through socially legitimate uses of violence. The system that gave these female murderesses a public voice and impunity was, after all, entirely controlled by men. As a result, the emotions that lawyers mobilized in jurors were not associated with gender equality, although these feelings could lead jurors to interpret suspects' actions as a plea of weak women for masculine help. Moheno's defense of María del

Pilar invoked patriarchal gender roles and depicted her story as a tragedy in which the duties of daughter and wife had been challenged by external factors (namely, Mexican politics), and had to be restored to their proper balance by a countervailing force, the jury system. Thus, when jurors and public opinion defied the written law to enact their moral interpretation of violence, they were protecting the same masculine order that excluded women from any prominent role in the penal system. The cases of female defendants in front of the jury could be fascinating, but they were not a chapter in an unequivocal trend toward gender equality.

Women were central in the public created by juries. *Excélsior* noted that the audience in María del Pilar's trial and the crowd outside Belem little resembled the usual group of jury spectators: this time, women outnumbered men in the courtroom, which held a large number of middle-class people and many "beautiful and elegant women."[92] These "señoras and señoritas from the best of society" brought María del Pilar flowers, listened to her every word, cried with her, visited and hugged her at the Correctional School, and even offered their homes as surrogate prisons.[93] *El Heraldo* justified its extensive coverage of the case arguing that "we are interested in the Mexican woman, whether she is a mother, daughter, wife or sister."[94] This presence of women in jury trials was also a feature of other famous cases. Writing about the audience for the trial of Luis Romero Carrasco, in 1929, José Pérez Moreno described for *El Universal* an anxious audience whose "curiosity had reached paroxysm." Elderly ladies trained their binoculars at the lawyers, an elegant man struggled for a good seat, and "many women" provided the color, their garments creating "red or lilac blots" in the room. Pérez Moreno compared the scene in the courtroom with that of a "theatrical stage."[95] Even cases in which men were accused of killing their wives provided an opportunity to express normatively feminine sentiments: army officer Alfonso Francisco Nagore shot his beautiful wife and her lascivious boss and photographer in 1928. During the trial, and against the advice of his attorney, Nagore cried openly and at length, as did many women in the audience.[96] Female spectators may have been attracted to these trials by something more than seedy stories, artistic oratory, or melodrama. In the courtroom, they also laid claim to criminal literacy and participated in debates about women's place and rights in postrevolutionary society.

Critics were concerned about the capacity of jury trials to undermine gender hierarchies: in addition to Moheno's cases, they viewed other famous trials involving women during the 1920s as a symptom of the institution's decadence. Something about the presence of women in courts seemed to be changing in ominous ways, starting with the presentation of female suspects before juries. The recent past offered a contrasting example of order. In several famous cases during the Porfiriato, lawyers characterized some murderesses as lowly "rags of societies" who deserved mercy because of their ignorance even though they also represented the worst moral attributes of their sex. Such was the case of María Villa, a prostitute found guilty of killing another woman out of jealousy; her own attorney called her a "terrible panther who does not have cranial resources." These perceptions of female offenders, informed by positivist criminology, were giving way to new attitudes.[97] By the 1920s, women who killed appeared more complicated and interesting even if juries still found them guilty. Newspapers printed female suspects' portraits, and people at their trials wanted to see them in person. Defense attorneys asked judges to have the soldiers guarding them step aside to avoid blocking the audience's view. With her use of violence, María del Pilar provided an example for others to follow. *El Universal* suggested as much when a thirteen-year-old girl in Torreón shot a soldier who was accosting her mother. Now men felt endangered by popular reactions instigated by women: friends of Tejeda Llorca received anonymous threats and refused to attend the jury trial in fear for their own safety. The personal stories of other suspects, not just the fact that they were women, became relevant in order to understand their need to use violence against men. Such was the case of María Teresa de Landa, the first "Miss Mexico," who in 1929 killed her bigamist husband, General Moisés Vidal, and who was acquitted thanks to her defense by Federico Sodi. Another similar case was that of sixteen-year-old María Teresa Morfín, who killed her husband when he announced that he was leaving her, and was acquitted in 1927. To critics, her case perfectly illustrated the negative consequences of jurors' lenience: after her release, Morfín became a cabaret dancer and was later murdered in Ciudad Juárez.[98]

María del Pilar's experience demonstrated that women, even very young women like her, could now be praised when they engaged in violence. María del Pilar, Moheno argued, had committed a crime of passion. Her behavior compared with that of "strong men deserving reverence."[99] It was commonly accepted that the usually male perpetrators of crimes of passion were not authentic criminals—not at least in terms of the somatic classifications and hereditary causality of positivist criminology—because they committed crimes inspired by heightened emotions, raising honor above the law. Moheno appealed to male jurors' "intimate" identification with the female suspect. He asked them to imagine the cadaver of their own father and invited them to empathize with the "tempestuous disorder of [her] feelings of tenderness, hopelessness, and indignant rage." In such circumstances, taking justice into one's hands deserved anyone's praise.[100] Women also had the right to kill when they were exploited or dishonored. Responses to María del Pilar's predicament from male members of the public echoed these feelings: Federico Díaz González, for example, declared his "respect and veneration" for her as she had no choice but to "take justice in her own hands" and to fulfill the "duty of a loving daughter."[101] Other men emphasized the importance of her age and filial duty, and her bravery in placing her love as a "model daughter" above the law. Some offered their help to complete the manly deed: Adolfo Issasi was willing to provide 40,000 pesos to cover the girl's bail, and others offered their own bodies to take her place at the Escuela Correccional or at the Islas Marías penal colony if need be. For these men, María del Pilar had acquired masculine traits that were all the more admirable because of her sex: a "strong personality" and a "virile attitude." After all, a group of "obreros honrados" (honorable workers) from Matamoros argued, with some irony, she had accomplished what neither men nor revolutionary institutions could do: she had punished a politician.[102]

This enthusiasm for women performing masculine actions coexisted with views that stressed more conventional roles. María del Pilar was the embodiment of femininity: other women had killed men who lived with them, but she came from "the heights of her virginal bed" as "a strong and avenging virgin" in a slight body.[103] Tejeda Llorca offered a suitable contrast: he was muscular, wealthy, and untouchable, and he threatened the purity of the defendant. Even her defense lawyers played the part of the chivalrous protector of powerless women. Moheno's reputation, after all, was based on a perfect record defending female murderers.[104] The moral lesson of the melodrama was as strong as its characters were emblematic of gender roles.

It should not be surprising, therefore, to see negative responses to women's criminal agency in the same venues and sometimes from the same actors who praised María del Pilar's actions. In multiple cases in which men murdered women out of jealousy, attorneys justified homicide as a natural reaction against the freedom that women were gaining. In a 1925 speech in defense of a fellow deputy who had killed another congressman who had accused him of being of "dubious sex," *agrarista* deputy Antonio Díaz Soto y Gama argued that murder was an obligation in such situations. "Had [Deputy Macip] not done that, women would become more terrible to men, like the prostitutes that Moheno defends."[105] Díaz Soto y Gama warned about the challenges to sexual hierarchies such cases seemed to encourage: "The Mexican woman is becoming a criminal woman, wild . . . Now our women are almost not women at all; it is frightening."[106] Tejeda Llorca's murder by a weak, young woman gave a graphic example of gender disorder. The press transcriptions of his autopsy graphically presented the politician's body exposed and vulnerable: one of the bullets, according to the doctors, had exited through his penis. Violence against women could therefore be excused as a way to restore balance. While María del Pilar's trial unfolded, several other cases of men who killed in defense of their honor ended in acquittals or the early dismissal of charges. This was the result of the Federal District attorney general's instruction for prosecutors to facilitate the release of men accused of murder in such circumstances. In a later trial, Moheno, never one to worry about contradictions, asked the jury to acquit a man who had killed out of jealousy.[107]

The end of the jury system in Mexico City can be interpreted, in this context, as an effort to maintain the masculine monopoly over justice. The last three notable cases brought to the jury before its abolition in 1929 involved women who had killed men. Courtrooms henceforth became spaces even more dominated by men, where women were losing even a modicum of protection. Preserving a limited role for women in national life was clearly the general goal when the 1916–1917 Constitutional Congress debated voting rights: assemblies and crowds were not rational, representatives argued, but governed by "sentimentalism" and the influence of "idealists[,] dreamers," and the clergy. Deputies decided then not to pass a proposal to extend voting rights to women.[108] By contrast, during the 1920s, the government saw state intervention in the domestic realm as a key tool for social and economic reconstruction. This meant a greater concern about childhood and a renewed emphasis on women's domestic responsibilities. The suffragist movement failed to capitalize on women's mobilization during the 1920s and 1930s and could not achieve a constitutional reform despite attempts by the sympathetic government of Lázaro Cárdenas (1934–1940).[109] But this might not be the right way to assess the legacy of this particular story. María del Pilar Moreno personified a courageous brand of femininity, yet she was also an example of domesticity disrupted by politics. After her moment of fame, she seems to have completely departed from public life. Her trial mobilized emotions as a legitimate element of public life, cultivated new audiences that included women, and recast the links between truth and justice in a way that, however briefly, challenged state power.

An example of this challenge to state power can be found in the most important case ever tried before a jury in Mexico. On July 17, 1928, president-elect Álvaro Obregón was murdered by José de León Toral at a restaurant in the southern Mexico City suburb of San Ángel. The assassination came at a moment of great tension within the political elite marked by threats of military rebellion, a religious war raging in some western states, and confrontations between obregonistas and political groups more closely identified with President Plutarco Elías Calles. Such was the complexity of the situation that those who watched Toral shoot Obregón stopped short of killing the assassin in order to find out who had sent him. A group of politicians confronted Calles in the following hours and told him that public opinion was blaming Luis N. Morones, leader of the Labor Party, loyal to the president, and open enemy of Obregón; they told him, according to the memoirs of Emilio Portes Gil, that the people did not trust the current police chief and demanded that well-known obregonista General Antonio Ríos Zertuche be put in charge of the department and the investigation.[110] Calles was quick to recognize that the caudillo leadership inherited from the revolution, and epitomized by Obregón, had to be replaced with a more stable system. In the following months, Calles negotiated an end to the civil war with the church hierarchy, put to rest any notion of his own reelection, assured that Portes Gil was named interim president, and founded a unified party. He also maneuvered politically to maintain a preeminent influence for the next six years.

Calles had no choice but to agree with the demands of the men who confronted him after the assassination: he saw that his position was weak and did not know himself what had transpired. Although he could not sacrifice Morones right away because doing so would make him look weak, as he explained to Portes Gil, Calles made sure that the truth of the case was brought to light. He interrogated Toral himself soon after the murder but extracted nothing from him; the murderer refused to talk, other than to say that he was doing God's work. Although the investigation itself did not depart from the usual practices of the Mexican police, the political and juridical consequences of the trial itself were unexpected. The agents working under Ríos Zertuche included the famous detective Valente Quintana (further discussed in chapter 3), who was recalled from private practice to join the efforts, and other men who were close to the victim, including the vengeful Colonel Ricardo Topete, who had seen Toral acting suspiciously at the restaurant but failed to prevent the shooting of his boss. They tortured Toral and threatened his family for several days before he decided to talk, revealing his true name, and take Quintana and Topete to meet Concepción Acevedo de la Llata, "madre Conchita," a nun who would also be accused of the murder. An explanation emerged in a matter of days: Toral was a religious fanatic who had decided to kill Obregón in order to stop the state's persecution of Catholics. People who had influenced and aided him were also arrested, but the findings did not lead to a clear intellectual author other than Acevedo. She was an independent-minded nun who hosted Toral and other figures of the urban Catholic resistance in an illegal convent where she lived with other nuns after they had to vacate their original dwelling because of a government decree.

The prosecution against Toral was intended to be part of Calles's efforts to advance institutionalization. Discovering the true motivations behind the crime through a regular judicial process was supposed to restore a sense of normalcy to otherwise extraordinary circumstances. As a consequence, Toral was not executed immediately after his crime, as the police had done with other Catholic would-be assassins of Obregón the year before. On November 1927, days after a bomb was thrown at the caudillo's car on his way to a bull-fight, four men were shot by a firing squad, without a trial, at police head-quarters. Even though the evidence against some of them was weak, Calles ordered a swift execution as a lesson against the Cristeros—as the Catholic fighters were called. The event was carefully photographed but, rather than instilling fear, the images became part of the popular devotion to one of the victims, Jesuit Miguel Agustín Pro.[111] His funeral was attended by tens of thousands, and in the eyes of the public his sacrifice became an example of the regime's abuses.

One year later, the political context and the growing strength of the Catholic resistance forced Calles to try a new approach. A judge granted Toral an *amparo* (order of protection) after his arrest to prevent an execution, and he was properly indicted, interrogated by a judge, and tried, along with Acevedo, before a popular jury just like other common criminals. Treating the crime as a common homicide was central to the government's strategy. The goal was to project an image of peace and progress to Mexican public opinion and the world. The hearings took place at the San Ángel municipal building, not far from the site of the murder, in the local city council's meeting room. Nine local residents of humble background were chosen to be jurors. Toral and Acevedo were represented by good lawyers, the main one being Demetrio Sodi, the Porfirian critic of the jury, already an elder figure in the field. Since Toral confessed and chose not to claim insanity, Sodi focused on avoiding his execution by invoking article 22 of the constitution, which prohibited the death penalty for political crimes. The prosecution ignored the constitutional protection by closely following the penal code's definition of aggravated murder. Federal District *procurador de justicia* Juan Correa Nieto, acting as the prosecutor, did not foresee any problem since the crime was almost universally condemned. The judicial setting was only a way for society to channel the nation's "just outrage." Even the Catholic Church hierarchy distanced itself from Toral and Acevedo, keen to manage its conflict with the government and control a religious rebellion that was escaping the church's own authority.[112]

However, as in other jury trials of the period, things found a way to get out of the government's control. Even though Toral's culpability was beyond question, the trial hypnotized the nation and echoed the trials of other famous criminals. With its political and religious undertones, it invited too much attention, and according to *Excélsior,* it was comparable only to Maximilian's trial in 1867, another case in which a liberal regime executed a conservative enemy. As with Pro's execution, an event that was intended to serve as propaganda would ultimately further tarnish the government. Media coverage was extensive. The proceedings at the San Ángel courtroom were broadcast by the Secretaría de Educación Pública radio network across the country.[113] A movie camera captured footage of the suspects. There was a special table set up for the numerous reporters and photographers from the national and international press. *Excélsior* vowed to offer "the greatest, as well as the truest and most impartial information that has ever been published in any organ of the national press," and the paper deployed photographers, famous caricaturist Ernesto García Cabral, writer Rafael Heliodoro Valle, and several reporters. The newspaper also paid for stenographers to write down every word uttered during the trial. Querido Moheno wrote comments and observations, and M. de Espinosa Tagle offered a column entitled "What a Woman Thinks about the Jury."[114]

During the first few days of the trial, which started on November 2, 1928, *Excélsior* devoted several pages to it, at least two of them with large photographic compositions depicting the "main persons" in the drama, the crowds outside and inside the courtroom, the gun used in the crime, and the drawing of Obregón that Toral had used as an excuse to approach his victim. Readers were immersed in every detail of the proceedings. Short interviews with the main actors provided a sense of proximity to the events that complemented the use of photographic and hand-drawn portraits. After the jurors' names were drawn by lot, a reporter found their addresses in San Ángel, interviewed them, and took their pictures. Several of them were textile workers, a couple owned pulquerías, and all responded to the reporter's questions about the jury as an institution and their expectations for the case. J. Cruz Licea, an employee at a nearby mill, declared that he would offer no opinion until he was shown the evidence and could "decide according to my conscience" without any external influence.[115] Reporters carefully recorded the gestures and reactions of judge, jurors, lawyers, witnesses, and suspects, and feature columnists wrote their "psychological observations." García Cabral showed his drawings to Toral, who was also an artist, and the suspect nodded his approval. Acevedo had photographers take a picture of her with Toral and prosecutor Correa Nieto outside the courtroom. Foreign journalists praised the "color" and "intimacy" of the setting. *Excélsior* received congratulations for its coverage during the first days of the trial, including the crowd's applause outside the courtroom. Its printings sold out during those days, even though sellers raised its price to one peso.[116]

The people who gathered outside the courtroom, according to a reporter, wanted to see the trial "in a setting of Greek tragedy." Yet they were not different from "those crowds that attend impressive spectacles: people of peaceful faces, good bourgeois like those you see in festivities and parks, and above all young women, flapper style, who laugh and comment with an indifference that borders on perversity." [117] Women were prominent in the courtroom, too. Besides Acevedo, there were Toral's mother, his wife, who was about to give birth to their third child, and Sodi's daughter, among many others. According to Espinosa Tagle, women used to be excluded from jury audiences, but "today, when modernism has changed habits, we can see the enthusiasm among women to attend these debates. . . . Toral's case has demonstrated this great interest." [118] As with María del Pilar's trial, the visibility of women in the court of justice raised concerns from some male observers. *Excélsior* detailed the feminine behavior in such crowds: "Juries are theater shows paid for by the state. Its audience swings according to its feelings, according to the impulses of its affections." [119] The events in the last days of the trial would come to reverse the initial lighthearted tone.

As often happened in high-profile jury trials, the suspects became the protagonists. José de León Toral (figure 3) was, by all accounts, a shy young man, a devout Catholic, a good father and husband, art student, and soccer player. He did not fit very well at the center of a cause célèbre. When he arrived for

FIGURE 3. José de León Toral, Concepción Acevedo de la Llata, and guards outside San Angel courtroom. Colección Casasola, Fototeca Nacional, Instituto Nacional de Antropología e Historia.

the beginning of the trial in San Ángel, he was surrounded by a crowd and greeted them with a relaxed demeanor—he even took off his hat for the pictures. In one image, he smiled at the camera while eating a humble meal inside his cell. In another, he seemed to have a pleasant conversation with madre Conchita. Yet he would most likely be executed in a few weeks. Rafael Cardona explained: "The personality of José de León Toral has aroused great curiosity since the events of last July 17. Lawyers, physicians, psychology aficionados, and writers, all those capable, in sum, to penetrate the mystery of criminality . . . have proposed hypotheses and suggested ideas about Toral's character, his criminal motives, his background, his mental constitution." Cardona believed that Toral did not lie during his testimony, although he did reveal a susceptibility to female influence: he was, by his own admission, driven to act by some words from Acevedo (who had casually said that only the death of Obregón and Calles would solve the situation of Catholics), and by the biblical story of Judith, who seduced and decapitated the Assyrian Holofernes in defense of her city. Although "effeminate" or similar terms were not among the insults directed at him during the trial, Toral's persona little resembled the dominant masculinity of revolutionary politics. His clean-cut, lean, and youthful appearance might have helped him approach Obregón at La Bombilla, where he passed as an artist without raising suspicion.[120]

From the outset, Toral deflected the antagonistic interrogations of judge and prosecutors, and he presented his story with great deliberation, looking at the jurors, occasionally consulting his notes, citing the newspapers, showing his drawings, and making sure the microphone captured his voice. The English section of *Excélsior* noted that thanks to his "remarkable composure, demonstrating intelligence, and an intense religious fervor, the youthful murderer practically conducted his own case."[121] Although his initial plan was to be killed right after murdering Obregón, he explained, he now embraced the platform provided by the trial. He told *Excélsior* that he did not know how jury trials worked but trusted there would be justice if the arguments made by his defense and Acevedo's were heard. He accepted Sodi's strategy to spare him the death penalty; doing otherwise, he explained, would mean committing suicide. Putting up a defense also meant extending the opportunity to speak directly to the country through the media, which he did carefully. Before the start of the trial he gave interviews, and during the the San Ángel hearings, he asked the judge's permission to read the newspapers so that he could respond to them and avoid repetitions in his statements.[122]

Toral did not present an openly political argument—even though that would have supported Sodi's case—but offered what he thought was a deeper message. He confessed, detailing the preparation of his crime and its execution. He stressed that he had acted alone, and that Acevedo had only inadvertently influenced his decision, but she was not otherwise involved in the crime. Toral explained that he was concerned about religious freedom and admired the example of his friend and soccer teammate Miguel Agustín Pro. Toral did not hate Obregón but had to kill him at the service of a higher cause. For that cause, too, he expected to suffer like a martyr and, as such, to become a witness for the truth. This resonated in the media. Toral was, for *Excélsior,* "a walking dead man" who "looks at the world as do ghosts: without any moral condescension." [123] Citing his legal and religious obligation to speak truthfully and thoroughly about the circumstances of the case, Toral interrupted the prosecutor's questioning at one point and began a detailed account of the way he was tortured at the police station. Though shocking in its detail and surprising to everyone, the revelation was not challenged by the judge or prosecutors, nor was it invoked by the defense to disregard his previous statements.[124] Rather than using his torture as an argument against the government, Toral presented it as evidence of his sacrifice and faithful adherence to the factual truth.

Renato González Mello has argued that Toral's drawings also reveal his central concern, as an artist and juridical subject, for the truth. While in jail, he drew on a piece of paper the different positions in which he had been tortured (hanging from his thumbs, from his armpits, from ankles and wrists), wrote on it "my martyrdom," and with the judge's permission, showed the drawings to the jurors. Although he was ready for martyrdom from the moment he conceived the crime, Toral wanted also to achieve it within the rules of secular justice: "I want this to be clearly understood, that what I am saying is the truth, in case one day I am justified." When Toral met with Calles, the day of the murder, he told him that "what I did was so that Christ would reign over Mexico." Asked by Calles to explain what kind of kingdom that was, Toral told him that "it is a reign over the souls, but far-reaching, absolute." [125] He was probably alluding to John 18:36–37, where Jesus states that "my kingdom is not of this world" and that "for this I have come into the world, to testify to the truth. Everyone who is of the truth hears My voice." [126] The trial provided Toral with the best opportunity to embrace the martyr's role of witness of Christ's suffering. He explained that after his arrest, "I only asked for one grace during the days of the jury trial: that He spoke through my mouth. I did not want to defend myself but to justify myself and to invite love for Him in preparation for his impending arrival." [127] Toral's truth, which he conveyed with apparent sincerity to jurors, was subjective. The naturalism of his drawings of torture and other images with religious themes produced in jail used his youthful, masculine body to convey the solitary pain and humility that emulated Christ's sacrifice. In the three months of imprisonment between the sentence and his execution, Toral wrote religious thoughts on small cards and presented them to those who visited him: "To know Jesus is to love him," read a typical one.[128] The truth, in Toral's testimony, was the word of God.

Concepción Acevedo de la Llata (1891–1978) also claimed to speak the truth, but she offered a sharp contrast with Toral, as a defiant woman at the center of an unruly entourage of Catholic activists. She was a Capuchin nun who ran a convent in Tlalpan until the government closed it in 1927. Despite official orders from the church hierarchy, she continued to live with the other sisters in houses where, free from the strict rules of the convent, she was visited by men and women who wanted to read the Bible, hear mass, or socialize. She met Miguel Agustín Pro there, and after his execution she began to take food to other Catholics in prison. Her popularity in Catholic circles often resulted in conflicts with her superiors, who had criticized her emphasis on harsh physical penitence at the convent. During the trial, Correa Nieto revealed that she used an iron brand to mark her arms with the initials of Christ and had encouraged other nuns to do the same. Members of the Catholic resistance then used the brand as a way to mark their commitment to the cause.[129] Acevedo did not seek to be at the center of the trial, but neither did she avoid its consequences. When Toral brought the police to her door, he asked her if she was ready to die with him, and she said she was. The political circumstances that had caused the convent to be closed were now thrusting her into a new kind of mystical suffering. Acevedo was imprisoned, tried, and sent to the Islas Marías penal colony. In her memoirs, she described her suffering at length: hunger, humiliation, illness, and even a broken bone as a result of the attacks by Obregonistas in the courtroom. Her notoriety itself was a form of punishment, for she had vowed to dedicate her life to God in silence and humility. She became the object of lurid speculation: while prosecutors tried to characterize her as a powerful figure who pushed Toral to commit the crime, others on the government's side castigated her on moral grounds: "She was very perverse and good looking, very sensual . . . and had great orgies with champagne."[130] Hostile crowds in the courtroom called her "whore."[131] She rejected false accusations against her because she wanted to "go to martyrdom through truth and justice." The truth she pursued centered on the government's persecution of Catholics. In her statements during the trial and after, she defined her sacrifice as a religious and political obligation. She had to be cautious, however, not to demonstrate vanity. She was a woman, after all, whose religious role called for patience and piety.[132]

Like Toral, however, Acevedo was not shy to embrace her central role. Following her arrest, she denied her participation in the preparations for Obregón's assassination yet also stubbornly refused to condemn the crime.[133]

She gave interviews to the press before the trial, posed for the cameras, and was heartened by the crowd that received her outside the San Ángel courtroom. While Toral's words fascinated the public because they came from a man who was certain to die soon, Acevedo's comments intrigued audiences in ways that resembled those of other cases of women accused of homicide who challenged gender roles in jury trials. During the hearings, she spoke with considerable freedom, adopting a defiant tone toward lawyers, addressing the audience directly, and criticizing those who booed her but applauded the prosecutor. Later, at the penal colony, where she became friends with the warden, General Francisco J. Múgica, and after she married another man accused of conspiring to kill Obregón, Acevedo wrote her memoirs, in which she defended both her political commitment and her reputation in the eyes of public opinion and the church.[134]

During the trial, Toral and Acevedo shifted the focus of the trial onto a terrain that tended to undermine the state's accusation. Correa Nieto and the other prosecutors berated the suspects, portraying Toral as a single-minded, fanatic avenger of Pro, and Acevedo as a conniving woman who manipulated him and other would-be assassins in the pursuit of darker goals. These characterizations were meant to counter the justification that both advanced, and to prove that theirs was not a political crime inspired by religion but a vulgar homicide motivated by lowly passions. Yet both suspects consistently offered an alternative that was politically plausible and apparently sincere. At the heart of Acevedo's narrative during the trial was a defense of the political value of her kind of religious resistance. When asked by the prosecutor whether she was aware that her influence, through a casual comment heard by Toral, might have caused the crime, she retorted that "it was the national influence": in other words, it was a broad social reaction to state religious persecution that had caused it. She argued that she only spelled out what many people in Mexico believed—though, she added sarcastically, not all of them would be prosecuted.[135] Her words at the trial and her later writings intimated that higher church and even political figures were behind the assassination. But her defense lawyer proposed that she was not the "intellectual author" of the crime or any other conspiracies, as the government claimed, and that she rejected the Cristeros' military approach. Several witnesses were brought to testify against her, but they did not provide any incriminating evidence. While Toral's culpability was beyond doubt, her attorney asked the jurors to acquit her.[136] Acevedo's willingness to abandon the role of a quiet and passive religious woman undermined her claim of complete innocence, yet under the government's custody and in national broadcast, she advanced the thesis that the assassination of Obregón was justifiable.

Toral's words lent themselves to further elucidation. In his columns, Moheno wrote about Toral as "the regicide," one of those criminals who, offering their lives in exchange, murder the monarch or head of state in pursuit of a higher good such as religious freedom. Regicide, added Moheno, had a long history but was new in Mexico. Other presidents had been assassinated (most recently Madero and Venustiano Carranza), but, according to Moheno, the label fit this case because of the crime's deeper meaning. Without openly embracing the Cristero cause, Moheno explained the regicide (he did not use the word *tiranicidio* but *regicidio,* to avoid implying Obregón was a tyrant) by noting that the country suffered under a "state of intense hopelessness that demands a new faith." [137] Toral, therefore, killed Obregón for political reasons, yet "he feels chosen by God for that mission." Toral was a mystic, according to Moheno, who expiated the sins of others with his suffering. His crime was political in the same way Lombroso classified as political the resistance of Christian martyrs in Rome. Understanding Toral's deed required a definition of politics that encompassed, as in Le Bon's views of the crowd, the role of emotions. Religion, wrote Moheno, shapes politics when "the religious feeling of the masses plays the role of instigator." [138] Yet the conflation of sentiment, religion, and politics personified by Toral was anathema to the liberal tradition embraced by the postrevolutionary regime. Moheno exemplified the consequence of this chasm with the exchanges between the suspect and prosecutor Correa Nieto: "That interrogation resembled a dialogue between two people who spoke different languages." Unable to understand the suspect's logic, Correa Nieto gave speeches rather than asking questions. This, in turn, gave Toral room to present his religious mission, recounting his torture in every painful detail, with the monotonous voice of "an indifferent witness" who believed himself a martyr beyond suffering. [139]

Another interpretation of Toral is found in his attorney's interrogation and summaries. Demetrio Sodi wanted to avoid the death penalty for his client, arguing that he had committed a political crime. Sodi was therefore forced to straddle the required adherence to the penal code and an expansive definition of what constituted a political crime; in other words, he was trapped between upholding the law and advancing a critical notion of justice. As a result, his defendant's account contradicted his own strategy. Sodi was further undermined by a hostile courtroom environment aroused by the political implications of his argument. He challenged the evidence against his client when he pointed out that there was no proper autopsy and that Obregón's body presented many bullet holes of different calibers. This would have meant that there were other shooters shielded from prosecution. The assertion, however sound, proved to be a strategic mistake, as the prosecution accused Sodi of telling a national audience that there had been a cover-up in which Calles was involved. This indignant reaction forced Sodi to quickly abandon the idea. Toral insisted that he had acted alone and tried to exculpate Acevedo, but Sodi had to prove that she had influenced Toral and other Catholic adversaries of the regime. Furthering the thesis of the political crime, Sodi argued that the case was of great historical significance and that even the prosecutors admitted the crime was directed "against the government."[140] In terms of motivations, added Sodi, Toral's crime was equivalent to those for which other men and women sympathetic to the Catholic Church had been recently accused, yet he reminded the court that his client's action did not constitute an endorsement of the Cristero war.[141] Sodi echoed Moheno's argument that Toral had not killed Obregón out of hate but because of a martyr's sense of duty. Citing other cases of regicide in history, Sodi argued that the penal law would have wrongly classified all of them as common crimes. But this was another losing strategy. In his final speech, Sodi made multiple references to the Bible and persecutions against early Christians and other martyrs of intolerance, yet he had to agree with the prosecutor that the murder of Obregón could not be justified by Catholic doctrine, which had condemned tyrannicide since the Council of Trent.[142] His key argument, however, encapsulated a dilemma familiar in jury trials: while the letter of the law defined the crime in its external aspects, if jurors understood the crime's deep reasons, their votes against the indictment were justified.

By spelling out the contradiction between the penal law and the political significance of the crime, Sodi was invoking jurors' honor. When the judge admonished him for discussing the penalty Toral could receive, Sodi responded with frankness: "This is another fiction of the law, a lie in the law. We live amidst complete lies."[143] In his 1909 critique of the jury system, Sodi had argued against the democratic fiction that nine common men could objectively decide on complex questions that were better understood by legal experts. Nineteen years later, as a litigant for the downtrodden in a highly visible case, he expressed a new appreciation for the integrity of the system. When leaflets and voices coming from the back of the room claimed that jurors had received money from Sodi, he reacted with indignation, saying that he himself was not being paid for his work, much less provided with funds to buy jurors' votes. The accusation also prompted some jurors to break the silence they had maintained during the trial. According to *Excélsior*, "Juror Ausencio B. Lira gets excited and complains, full of indignation, saying that all his life has been one of pure honesty."[144] During his closing speech, Sodi embraced the postrevolutionary racial rhetoric of *mestizaje* by reminding the audience of the "beautiful outrage portrayed in the bronze faces, that are our national pride, of the jurors!" He emphasized the "honesty" of the "humble people" who integrated the jury.[145]

Demetrio Sodi's praise of jurors' "honesty" projected onto the institution his own family's pride in their role against a regime that they saw as increasingly tyrannical. Despite their differences in the past (when Demetrio had collaborated with Moheno against Federico), both Sodi brothers now had a favorable view of the perspicacity of jurors. What Federico would later remember as a space of free speech and camaraderie among lawyers was overwhelmed by the government's hostility in 1928. Demetrio had been "cruelly insulted" and prevented from speaking several times during the sessions.[146] In a book published eight years after the trial, Demetrio's daughter, María Elena Sodi de Pallares, highlighted the irony of that moment: after losing his prominent political position and his money with the revolution, Demetrio began to work in courts again. His defense of Toral was undertaken as a moral obligation although it could also help business. María Elena's book, however, suggests a deeper ideological commitment. Demetrio Sodi thought that Toral "was the deserving representative of the youth of our time, the youth who heroically died moved by mystical feelings." He had planned to present further evidence of the government's attacks against Catholics and freedom of speech, but he was not allowed to do so.[147] *Los Cristeros y José de León Toral* also contains an explanation of the religious conflict from a Catholic perspective, as well as sympathetic biographies of Acevedo and Toral, the latter based in part on his mother's memoirs, reproductions of his drawings, and testimonies of Toral's involvement in the civic life of Catholics during the late 1920s.[148] For María Elena and her father, the jury, however flawed, seemed to be the last space to openly express an oppositional Catholic point of view in the Mexican public sphere.

The Sodis' bitter memories of the case derive from the violent way in which Demetrio's case was thwarted by external interventions in the judicial process. Even though Calles had intended Toral's trial to signal the triumph of the government's even-handed administration of justice, the proceedings descended into a chaotic fiasco that only fueled the religious opposition and laid bare the ineptitude of law enforcement. During a break in the trial, jurors sent a message to Acevedo, telling her that she was going to be convicted and asking for her forgiveness. She obliged, and in her memoirs asked the reader: "Is this a free people? Sure, we have to believe in that freedom, the judges asking for forgiveness from the suspect, how ironic!" [149] Even an Obregonista insider like Deputy Antonio Díaz Soto y Gama expressed skepticism toward what he saw as a government's farse: as good revolutionaries, "today we are not interested in this case of 'courtroom justice,' nor do we believe in it"; it was all a "maneuver to distract public attention" away from the true culprit—Morones, Soto y Gama's rival.[150]

The government could only blame itself for the fiasco, and it resorted to a heavy hand to change course. With the radio broadcast, authorities had allowed the alleged authors of the murder of the president-elect to speak to the nation about religious persecution. The judge and prosecutors had done a poor job: their interrogations, particularly those of Correa Nieto, were overly aggressive, too general in their questions, and more concerned with communicating a political message against Cristeros than with properly presenting evidence. On November 4, the third day of the proceedings, things began to change. The judge cut the session short, and the defense complained that the interruption was due to instructions from political authorities. The radio broadcast was interrupted, and photographers were prevented from entering the room for the session of November 5. On that day, Correa Nieto excused himself from the trial, alleging that he had been threatened. He appointed assistant prosecutors who took over the case, including Procurador General Ezequiel Padilla. The new team focused on proving Acevedo's involvement in other conspiracies and limiting opportunities for the defense and the accused to speak.[151]

That same November 5, in the chambers of Congress, federal deputies discussed the need to make a forceful intervention in the Toral trial. Representatives affirmed Congress's responsibility to voice support for the revolution in order to counter the onslaught of messages from "reactionaries" on the radio. In the "deifying of crime," argued congressmen, "the criminal becomes the martyr." [152] They agreed to act forcefully to protect "the masses of the country." More specifically, this meant that if Toral was not found guilty, as the notoriously violent San Luis Potosí cacique Gonzalo N. Santos claimed, "I will empty my gun on him and the jurors." The trial, other deputies argued, was a national embarrassment: "In other countries, even those that seem more civilized, like the United States, León Toral would have been lynched, but here he is being handled with white gloves."[153] That very afternoon, a group of several dozen federal deputies led by Santos burst into the San Ángel courtroom. Waving guns and sticks, they insulted Sodi, who had to climb on a chair to fight back. The deputies also attacked the suspects, kicking and breaking madre Conchita's leg, and pulling Toral's hair. They also threatened jurors. In subsequent days, the deputies maintained control of the courtroom, disrupting the defense and creating a tense situation. Some of the members of the jury asked the judge to be excused, arguing that they feared for their lives. The judge denied their requests and guaranteed their safety, but several brought their own handguns to the courtroom. A heavily armed group of soldiers took positions in the courtroom while mounted troops fought demonstrators outside. Although things seemed to calm down on November 6 and 7, the diverse crowd of the first days was gone, and the only woman in the room by that time was Acevedo. On November 8, the final day of the trial, the radio broadcast was restarted, but the large audience, which included public officials and congressmen, made enough noise to cut Sodi's last speech short. When the jury returned with a guilty verdict (only one vote was cast for Acevedo's innocence), there were cheers among the progovernment crowd outside the courtroom.[154] The trial had become a showcase for the violence of Mexican politics.

The actions of Santos and the other deputies demonstrated a concerted albeit belated effort to limit the public impact of the trial. Until their intervention, defense attorneys had relied on the media to prevent distortions to their message: "Fortunately yesterday the entire country heard our words, all the press talks about what we said, and they can attest to the fact that we did not attack anyone," stated Ortega on November 4.[155] By the following day, however, there were no more opportunities for Toral and Acevedo to be heard on the radio. National newspapers did not report on most of the violence taking place inside the courtroom, probably after receiving instructions from the government. In the November 5 debates at the Chamber of Deputies, *Excélsior* was mentioned as a specific target: "The enemies of the revolution: the press and money," declared deputy Manuel Mijares; "the reactionary press," claimed Alejandro Cerisola. Deputies agreed to begin an economic boycott against *Excélsior*, suspending government advertising, canceling subscriptions, and engaging in other forms of direct action.[156] The newspaper drastically reduced its coverage of the trial, replacing the transcripts of the

proceedings with a synthesis. After November 7, *Excélsior* gave more prominence to U.S. election results. It stopped printing Moheno's articles on the
trial as well as those of the other writers and artists. The editors tersely noted
in an editorial that their journalistic duty had been "interpreted in a twisted
way" by the government, leading to threats against them.[157] The newspaper
was soon punished in a more permanent way: its circulation was blocked, and
Consuelo Thomalen, the widow of founder Rafael Alducín, was forced to sell
it to a group of businessmen with close connections to the government.[158]

Toral and Acevedo's appeals were denied, and Toral was executed on
February 9, 1929. In front of the firing squad, he began to shout, "Viva Cristo
Rey," as his friend Agustín Pro had done just before his death two years earlier. The bullets interrupted Toral's voice. His burial instigated demonstrations and riots, and as Cristero resistance raged on, assassination attempts
continued, the next one against President Portes Gil on the very day of the
execution. Instead of serving as an example of good administration of justice,
the trial left a lasting legacy as an example of the abuse of power, a stain on
the legitimacy of the justice system.[159] Toral was remembered in popular bal-
lads, *corridos,* although he did not acquire the posthumous cult of Miguel
Agustín Pro. Decades later, plays by Jorge Ibargüengoitia and Vicente Leñero
used the records of the trial to reflect on the authoritarianism established in
those days, in the form of a regime for which words had no meaning in the
face of power. Written in 1962, *El atentado* by Ibargüengoitia makes the 1928
trial the climax of a historical comedy that pokes fun at the postrevolutionary regime's discourse of justice. All actors assume that there was a conspiracy
involving the Abbess and Pepe to kill president-elect Borges, and they see the
trial as merely a theatrical setting for a preordained sentence.[160] Leñero's play,
El juicio, consists of fragments from the 1928 trial's transcripts. Through the
voices of suspects, lawyers, and witnesses, the story is presented in all its ominous ambivalence. Toral, Acevedo, and other men and women accused of
plotting against Obregón and Calles claim that violence is a right they can
exercise in defense of their religion; government investigators use torture as
a normal element of the investigation; prosecutors make their case in terms
of realpolitik. The threatening voices that burst into the courtroom on
November 5 remain, in Leñero's play, anonymous and in the dark: their
power, just like the truth about the crime, is unassailable. The play was first
staged in 1971, and its audience could easily have connected the darkness
surrounding the story with the violent authoritarianism of the PRI regime
of their own time.[161] Both plays reflect another historical lesson from the San

Ángel courtroom in November 1928: either as a tragedy or a farce, the jury trial of Toral and Acevedo was an inconclusive, sordid affair that little resembled justice.

CONCLUSIONS

Educated Mexicans always viewed the criminal jury negatively. Their mistrust articulated Porfirian notions about ordinary Mexicans' unfitness for democracy and lack of integrity. Federico Gamboa threw up his hands: "What great errors are, in my opinion, the famous jury and the no less famous universal suffrage!" [162] Even Querido Moheno, who owed whatever good reputation he had to jury trials, declared after the revolution that juries were in the hands of inferior people only interested in money. If the jury was taken as an "index of collective feelings regarding morality," reasoned *El Universal,* then "we have to mourn a tremendous decline in the ethical level of Mexican society." [163] These views were based largely on the melodrama and rhetoric that seemed to dominate the most famous cases. Suspects inevitably became the main characters, but other actors—victims, witnesses, lawyers, judges, and journalists—also embraced their roles as characters with a stark moral valence; jurors and audiences comprised a sort of chorus which judged the story unfolding in front of them on its aesthetic and moral value. The exchanges between all these actors were emotionally intense, and the stage was charged with echoes of other stories. Melodrama, in other words, provided a set of roles and a narrative structure embraced by actors and public alike. Even critics shared an aesthetic criterion: the jury represented "theatrics of the lowest kind" in which the problem was not the dramatic structure so much as the poor quality of the performances and script.[164]

Yet the histrionics of a few conservative lawyers and the violent femininity of famous suspects were only the most visible part of the process. The motley cast of characters, and the vagaries of jurors who used their votes to acquit, undermined the control of the legal profession over justice. Unexpected voices could challenge the government in the public sphere. The diversity of players involved in jury trials was the defining trait of the institution's influence in public life, and the main source of its enemies' exasperation. Perhaps the most prominent among those players, and the reason for male commentators' anxiety, were a few women whose crimes catapulted them into the center of public life. They had used violence to defend their honor, their family, or their religion, and did not shy away from telling their story once they sat as the accused. The prominent place they briefly occupied thanks to these trials challenged patriarchal notions about women's silence and proper domesticity. Yet their effort to escape conviction led them to embrace the less threatening aspects of modern femininity. Social uses of the law, in other words, could challenge conventions or buttress conservatism. From today's perspective, reading these trials as mere melodrama, a spectacle with a limited cast of contrasting characters, does not help our understanding of the breadth of those social uses of the law.

Over six decades, the trajectory of the jury in Mexico City reflected a deep transformation in notions of justice. The institution came into existence shortly after an era of civil strife, and jury proponents hoped that it would foster transparency in the judicial process. While this basic belief persisted in the following years, in reality the effect of criminal juries was rather diffuse, blurry in the details and often morally ambiguous. In the 1920s, after another civil war, the institution made its greatest impact on the public sphere, but in the eyes of lawyers and politicians, the jury also appeared to erode respect for the law and to politicize justice. As this chapter has shown, it could not have been otherwise: the criminal jury put into practice a popular notion of justice grounded in republican skepticism toward the state. At the most basic level, the jury was a bastion against the abuses of the government because it gave public opinion a tangible role in governance. A premise of Mexican criminal literacy was that, in the circuitous path leading from the truth to justice, it was legitimate to take some shortcuts even if they violated the law. The flaws of jury trials were only the most visible aspect of general decay in the justice system: suspects, witnesses, and lawyers came in many moral shades, nuances which melodrama could not fully express. By the 1920s, mistrust of the entire justice system was widespread. Luis Cabrera, a key intellectual of Carrancismo, decided during those years to return to legal practice because he needed work. Yet he hesitated because of the corruption he observed in the courts, a low "moral level" which, he recognized, had to be blamed on lawyers themselves.[165] Venal jurors, the "milperos" described by the Sodis, were only a symptom of that corruption. By the end of the decade, longstanding skepticism toward the judiciary was turning into disappointment. The Toral and Acevedo trial was just the last straw.

The criminal jury was abolished through a 1929 presidential decree that replaced the 1871 Federal District's penal code with a new one with a strong positivist imprint. The committee that drafted the new code explained that the jury would be replaced by "a technical committee formed by psychiatrists, psychologists, and other scientific professionals who will sentence according to the new modalities of penal law." [166] Science, not common sense, was better able to understand crime. This had been the opinion of Porfirian critics of the jury, including Demetrio Sodi, but it could only be put into practice at a specific political juncture. The Toral case had revealed the potential damage that a high-profile case could do to the government's efforts to control a fractious body politic. The Federal District's city council had been eliminated in late 1928, reinforcing presidential control over the capital's governance. Judges now had complete dominance over the investigation and sentencing; hearings were no longer public events. The opacity long associated with routine penal procedures now set in over the most visible part of the system; melodrama gave way to other narrative forms. [167]

The abolition of jury trials marked the end of an era. After 1929, actors continued to take shortcuts in the pursuit of justice: prisoners and victims turned to presidential intervention, policemen to the ley fuga, and almost everyone accepted the fact that press reports were more reliable sources of truth than were sentences. The involvement of public opinion in matters of crime and justice no longer took place in the institutional framework of the jury system but in the virtual space of crime news, to be examined in the next chapter. Yet this was not a sustainable structure to maintain the pressure of civil society on the justice system or the police. A paradoxical effect of this transformation of skepticism into disappointment was the acceptance of extrajudicial violence in place of legal punishment. Moheno articulated the theory, and others followed in practice: the sentiments of the Mexican crowd, juries or their audiences, could be channeled as violence and intolerance in the name of justice. This explains his admiring invocations of lynching in the United States. This theory was not often voiced in the following years but remained latent in the apologies for ley fuga found in the press and literature after the demise of the jury system.

The memory of the criminal jury continued to influence ideas and representations of crime and justice in other ways. As soon as it was abolished, newspapers and books began to commemorate it with some nostalgia. There were rumors and discussions about reestablishing it. But the negative resonances of its melodramatic excesses prevailed over any argument in its favor. For criminologist Francisco Valencia Rangel, its return would only have encouraged the morbid interest in the crime news which invaded newsstands just as the jury was going away. The jury survived as a trope of popular culture.

It inspired comedies, including plays about famous cases like that of María del Pilar Moreno, and satirical movie scenes, where the stage created by jury trials continued to be useful to talk critically about justice.[168] As we will see in the next chapter, crime news embraced this legacy, particularly the vision of justice as the product of multiple actors' participation in a system that was flawed but at least offered the people a chance to speak up.

TWO

A Look at the Crime Scene

THE *NOTA ROJA* AND THE PUBLIC
PURSUIT OF TRUTH

With their images of crimes and criminals, their strident headlines and bloody images, crime news magazines and newspapers were an important part of the landscape in Mexico City from the 1920s onward. They were displayed and sold in prominent places to attract readers ready to steal a few minutes away from the bustle of everyday life. The nota roja was the journalistic genre with most readers in the country, its style the most recognizable. Headlines used wordplay, conveyed moral outrage, and synthesized crimes in brutally direct terms, characterizing victims and criminals in sardonic and memorable ways: "The plumber who killed a cobbler in an absurd fight," or "Murdered his buddy because he demanded a hat."[1] Street sellers (*voceadores*) cried out the front-page headlines, and nota roja papers reached every corner of the city a few hours after events—moving information faster than any other media. The suspect in the 1934 murder of three women at a Tacubaya barbershop was arrested at 5:30 P.M., and "by 7 pm," boasted *La Prensa*, "we had flooded with copies . . . the entire capital and its farthest suburbs."[2]

Beginning in the late 1920s, journalistic innovations in crime news nurtured a broad and engaged public. The accounts of famous cases that attracted tens of thousands of readers were initially a printed extension of the criminal jury trial's high-stakes drama, but they survived as a narrative form for decades after 1929. Reporters, editors, and photographers developed an effective language to tell stories to an avid and critical audience. Criminals, particularly murderers, also reached the public via interviews and confessions. Journalists and criminals, after all, were more credible than judges or detectives in revealing the details of a crime. With time, the authorities, who resented the scrutiny of the nota roja but were unable to curtail it, began to appropriate its communicative resources, now using them to propagate their own perspective. By the 1960s, the nota roja had mostly settled into a moralistic support for the police, with an emphasis on images over narrative and a flattened view of suspects. In the process, it lost much of the critical and engaged tone that marked its early, golden age.

As the focus of news coverage, crime reporting served as the context for spreading critical views of the state. If we examine the production of nota roja, its content, and its interpretations of crime during the middle decades of the twentieth century, we recover a central chapter in the development of Mexico's public sphere. The nota roja was a highly political form of journalism, although its politics are difficult to classify along ideological lines. Thanks to the commercial success that supported their autonomy, these publications could present objective evidence of the ineptitude and corruption of officials and encourage readers' involvement in public affairs. Crimes provoked unanimous condemnation but also created fascinating characters; they also reinforced the public's endorsement of extrajudicial violence. Yet the nota rota was not just about morality: crime news conveyed a shared sense of reality, one that was morally compelling and relevant to everyday life: it was the daily encyclopedia of criminal literacy.

The approach I propose challenges prevailing interpretations that see the nota roja as a minor journalistic genre defined by its unpleasant and vulgar contents. Histories of journalism in Mexico neglect it, with most focusing on the struggles between the philistines in the trade and the heroic defenders of free, critical, and cultivated speech, particularly after President Luis Echeverría's attack on the independence of *Excélsior* in 1976.[3] From this perspective, although the nota roja is understood to have increased the number of newspaper readers, it could not be a vehicle for consolidating democracy. This contempt resonates with academic views of Mexican mass media in general as devoid of intellectual merit and co-opted by a powerful state. During the middle years of the twentieth century, the government did offer economic support and political access in exchange for the loyalty of large newspapers, while editors cultivated a close relationship with presidents and ministers and abstained from criticizing the regime's venality. Nota roja reporters were close to the police, so they became the lowliest example of journalism's ethical poverty. This is the effect of a foreshortened historical perspective: by the 1960s, the association of press and state had indeed incorporated the nota roja, which had lost much of its earlier critical independence.[4]

Commentators saw the undeniable popularity of the nota roja as a social pathology rather than as part of the country's intellectual history. Carlos

Monsiváis pointed to the deep roots of Mexican readers's "intense ghoulish fascination with crimes."[5] During the second half of the nineteenth century, a diversity of cheap publications, loose leaves, and penny press periodicals conveyed bloody stories to a broad, semi-literate public. The engravings of José Guadalupe Posada have become iconic and are often cited as an early version of the nota roja. These publications were artisanal in their craftsmanship and limited printings. Although they contained a mix of bloody crimes and fantastic events similar to those in twentieth-century tabloids, recent scholarship has proposed an interpretation of nineteenth-century popular press as a satirical genre that broadened the reading public and conveyed political messages through an astute use of demotic language and images.[6] Despite this lineage, prevalent views still characterize the nota roja as a medium akin to pornography that from its inception appealed to a morbid sentimentalism, peddling escapist stories that lacked structure or any meaningful relationship to reality. For editors like Félix Palavicini, founder of *El Universal,* there was nothing wrong with laughing at the pain of others. He said, according to Eduardo Téllez Vargas, that the police section was "the society pages of our people." When humble people read them, Palavicini joked, they found reasons to celebrate: "It turns out that my goddaughter was abducted so we are going to have a wedding," or "they killed my *compadre* and we missed the funeral."[7] Studies of the nota roja have focused on its graphic content, further cementing the similarity to pornography, with the increasingly frequent pictures of scantily clad women illustrating the pages of some publications. For Monsiváis, the genre satisfies an "unconscious ... addiction" for blood and mayhem, while its headlines offer a "symbolic nod to morals." Paradoxically, he and others also used the nota roja as an archive of real examples of the misery, violence, and disregard for life that, in their view, kept Mexico in a state of backwardness.[8]

Recent reappraisals of police news in Mexico recognize its culturally productive role, if not its journalistic virtue. Scholars and artists now acknowledge the nota roja's connections with art and literature and its transformative influence on newspaper journalism in general. In Mexico, as Ricardo Pérez Montfort has pointed out, journalists beginning in the 1930s "valued in a positive way that urban and marginal world" of cities, and accordingly expanded the themes of their chronicles and reportages.[9] Turning the tables on modernity, these commentators suggest that gore and vulgarity express an aesthetic of "the ordinary" and celebrate the pathological traits of urban culture that nationalism and elites had tried to sanitize.[10] A famous, probably apocryphal example of nota roja poetics was the chorus of a Botellita de Jerez song, "Violola, matola, con una pistola" (He raped her, he killed her, with a gun).[11] Literary approaches to *fait divers* and other forms of crime news mock the inane, casual tone of headlines ("He wanted to have fun and they destroyed his face with bottles"), but also recognize it as an inspiration for literary authors. Novelist José Revueltas began his career as a journalist with *El Popular* writing nota roja pages. Another author, Max Aub, found inspiration in the synthetic language of *La Prensa* headlines for his *Crímenes ejemplares.* "I killed him because they gave me twenty pesos to do it," reads one of its epigrams.[12] More recently, artists like SEMEFO and Teresa Margolles have deployed the shock value of nota roja aesthetics in performances and installations, although they tend to reproduce the same dismissive views of popular consumption of nota roja described above.[13]

In contrast to such views, the following pages will shun any normative assessment. I do not define nota roja by the lowbrow quality of its contents or by its penchant for making private lives the object of public scrutiny, as in American tabloids.[14] What gave coherence to the genre in Mexico was the way in which stories were displayed and narrated, and the nota roja's form of interacting with readers. The nota roja was the modern journalistic expression of the old interest in crime that inspired Posada and other popular chroniclers. By the mid-twentieth century, the genre connected that interest with the objective reality of an unreliable judiciary and police system. Through images and text, the nota roja became the foundation of criminal literacy. Unlike the penny press, its production was no longer artisanal but the center of a profitable business. It did not sell fear or pornography, or at least not only that: to an audience of critical readers, it presented the reality of violence and impunity that defined urban life.

THE BUSINESS OF CRIME PAGES

In order to understand it as a business, we must situate crime news within the history of Mexican journalism. The model for commercially successful dailies catering to a broad readership (unlike the educated audience of old liberal, opinion-centered newspapers) was *El Imparcial,* created in 1896. It was a newspaper with modern machinery, inexpensive for readers, sensible for advertisers, informative, and visually attractive. It also served the political purposes of the government and in exchange received a steady subsidy. On

the eve of the revolution, political competition led to an ideological diversi-
fication of newspapers, although most of them tried to follow the model of
El Imparcial. The large newspapers that emerged during the later stages of the
civil war, notably *El Universal* (1916) and *Excélsior* (1917), combined a political agenda with the goal of profit. Their publishers were closely connected to
the political elite and stood to gain considerable money and political capital.
The market allowed for growth: newspapers served the propaganda needs of
a consolidating state but also responded to the tastes of a growing readership.[15] Thus, after an initial period of instability in ownership and vulnerabil-
ity to attacks from political actors (such as those suffered by *Excélsior* in
1928), the 1930s were characterized by financial consolidation and a cozier
relationship with the federal government. Although scholars today suspect
that political protection and official subsidies were the key to success for
national newspapers, further research is needed to determine the extent to
which these papers relied on their own revenue from sales and advertisement.
We do know that relentless competition for readers was a priority in news-
rooms. Daily circulation numbers and advertisement receipts did not lie, and
they spurred continuing technological and journalistic innovation.[16]

The number of newspapers printed and sold is notoriously difficult to
establish. Even the Secretaría de Gobernación, usually in charge of relations
with the media, gathered widely different numbers for major newspapers:
120,000 a day for *Excélsior* in a 1961 estimate; 20,000 in another from 1966.[17]
Editors tended to exaggerate the numbers, and the powerful Unión de
Voceadores, which monopolized street distribution, also manipulated sales.
Scattered information suggests strong sales of nota roja newspapers and
magazines along with the afternoon edition of mainstream newspapers. In
1966, *La Prensa,* which devoted its first and last pages and the majority of its
content to crime news, sold between 35,000 and 70,000 a day, approximately
the same circulation as in the 1940s. In 1923, *El Universal Gráfico* sold 20,000
copies in the afternoon, while the morning editions of *El Universal* and
Excélsior sold 60,000.[18] The low cost of each copy was a key factor: when the
administrators of *La Prensa* raised the price per copy in 1939, trying to compensate for lost profit due to increased production costs, daily sales dropped
from 70,000 to 50,000.[19] A magazine with a police theme, *Detectives,* published since 1931, claimed to sell 42,720 copies.[20] In the 1960s, *Alarma!,* the
most popular magazine of the genre, was said to sell half a million copies
during a famous case of multiple homicide in a brothel in Guanajuato.[21] The
numbers above might not seem especially high for a city with a population of

3,137,600 inhabitants and a literacy rate of over 80 percent in 1950. Yet given the large number of publications and their rapid circulation throughout the city, we should not underestimate the impact of the copies in circulation. One fact was well known, as revolutionary writer and editor Martín Luis Guzmán pointed out: "Crimes are the key to circulation."[22]

Government pressure on newspapers relied on money rather than overt censorship. Thus, after the trial of José de León Toral, despite calls to use direct violence against *Excélsior,* the government established control by forcing publisher Consuelo Thomalen to sell the newspaper.[23] In 1935, the dispute between President Cárdenas and *jefe máximo* Calles played out in newspapers and on the radio. Instead of silencing critics, Cárdenas granted interviews and deployed union support in the streets to dominate coverage. Aware of the new weight of the media, he laid the groundwork for a more stable relationship between the federal government and newspaper editors with the creation of the Departamento Autónomo de Prensa y Publicidad (DAPP), charged with streamlining communication of official information to the media. Cárdenas also replaced the powerful supplier of newsprint Papelera San Rafael with Productora e Importadora de Papel, S.A. (PIPSA), a state-owned entity that monopolized paper imports from Canada and assigned quotas to each publication.[24] PIPSA became a way for the government to lean on newspapers by selectively granting loans or reducing the supply of paper. Simultaneously, the purchase of advertising space by the federal government became an important (although not exclusive) source of revenue for the industry. The Unión de Voceadores was another government tool to limit the circulation of dissenting content; it could simply stop the sale of any publication deemed to have inappropriate content. After World War II and the embrace of Cold War anticommunism reduced the space for ideological dissent, the relationship between federal officials and publishers became more harmonious, often facilitated by gifts and assorted benefits to the latter.[25]

State-centered histories of the press tend to stress only one kind of reader: a politically literate man able to decipher the cryptic editorials, signed columns, and interviews in the first section of the newspaper. This type of history suggests that the need to communicate with such a reader was the only reason the government would care about the press. Yet focusing on this ideal reader does not explain the business side of that history. Editors knew that the key to increase sales and advertising was to put out a newspaper "for all tastes and financial means."[26] This meant embracing multiple styles and topics. Separately folded sections invited different kinds of readers to simultaneously read the paper. These sections dealt with national and international politics, society gossip, culture, sports, and economic activity. Announcements of raffles, contests (cutest newborn baby, best Christmas ornament, best speaker, most beautiful woman), and new celebrations (Mother's Day, invented by *Excélsior*'s Alducín) increased the number of subscribers and street sales. Brand advertisements and classified ads addressed a consumer culture that featured commercial brands but also incorporated private individuals into the daily exchanges of the market. This diversity of readers and varied content allowed for new forms of critical engagement to grow under the radar of conventional politics. Audience opinion became central to the news and commentary on bullfighting and sports, for example.[27] But it was crime news that provided the more expansive terrain to critically address the performance of the state. Despite Palavicini's prejudices about nota roja readers, good police section editors knew that their numerous readers were not exclusively male or working class.[28]

The first crime news publications in the nota roja mold appeared in the 1920s. *El Universal*'s afternoon edition, *El Universal Gráfico*, was the first one in 1922. A similar afternoon edition, *Últimas Noticias*, by *Excélsior*, appeared in 1936. These were shorter versions of the morning editions with a greater percentage of crime and sports news, smaller ads, and fewer political articles. Companies saw these editions as a low-cost way to increase sales while fully using the capacity of their expensive imported machines. But they were also an opportunity to experiment with a populist tone, to print more graphics, and to offer coverage on lowbrow themes that did not suit the more respectable morning papers. A typical *El Gráfico* edition began with the accidental death of a general on the cover, followed by articles on the organization of the Inspección General de Policía, on money counterfeiters, and a satirical piece on a dispute between two women. Afternoon editions also featured opinion pieces and articles that challenged the government: for example, one endorsed the *falangista* side of the Spanish civil war even as the morning edition maintained the official stance of support for the Republicans.[29]

The genre's most successful publication, and the first newspaper to center on crime news, was *La Prensa,* founded in 1928 shortly after the Obregón assassination. Like other newspapers of the time, following an early period of consolidation it achieved stability by the 1940s. *La Prensa* innovated in its reporting and use of photography; it printed in rotogravure, which allowed for large numbers of copies and extensive use of graphics. Most of its pages, including the front and back covers, were devoted to crime news, while international news was kept to a minimum, although there was flexibility according to the stories of the day.[30] *La Prensa* often claimed to have the highest circulation in the country and a diverse readership.

Under its first director, José E. Campos, *La Prensa* began as a public corporation, raising funds from businesses by issuing promissory notes redeemable for advertising space. Confidence was not lacking: in 1929, the paper changed its motto to "The newspaper that conquered Mexico in a month." Sales were strong from the outset, and the newspaper was soon able to reduce its price from ten to five cents.[31] Success was largely thanks to editor Miguel Ordorica, who gave *La Prensa* a distinctive style, aggressive in its reporting and its criticism of the government. Ordorica had strong conservative affiliations: he had worked for *El Imparcial* and was an unrepentant supporter of Victoriano Huerta, the general who overthrew and had Madero killed, and after leaving *La Prensa* in 1935 he moved on to *Últimas Noticias,* a more strident platform for his views. After being displaced from *Últimas Noticias* when his opinions became too problematic during World War II, he eventually acquired a prominent role in the Cadena García Valseca, a national network of newspapers, first as founder of *El Sol de Guadalajara* and then in 1948 as director of the organization. In all his endeavors, Ordorica espoused right-wing views which brought trouble for *La Prensa* during the Cárdenas presidency, but were no longer politically costly for him under Manuel Ávila Camacho (1940–1946) and Miguel Alemán (1946–1952).[32]

Ordorica had to leave *La Prensa* in 1935 after the newspaper's criticisms of Cárdenas's labor and foreign policies, as well as the death of founder Pablo Langarica, brought about a crisis in the company. Papelera San Rafael tried to collect on debt incurred by the newspaper, and the government refused to extend further credit. Unions and peasant organizations denounced editors' reactionary tendencies and encouraged internal labor disputes.[33] Temporarily run by the paper company, *La Prensa* was plagued by grievances from fired workers; publication was interrupted for five months, at which point President Cárdenas endorsed the creation of a worker-controlled cooperative to take over the bankrupt company's property and authorized a new line of credit. The arrangement, however, excluded some of the journalists who had worked at *La Prensa* from the beginning, including Ordorica.[34] The cooperative still faced demands from creditors as well as litigation from former employees. Some of these employees even tried to publish another newspaper with the same name.[35] Eventually, the management of the cooperative increased its control over the unruly general assemblies, although not over its fractious politics: the newspaper sided with Cárdenas when he broke with Calles but also managed to express support for Mussolini, Franco, and Nazi Germany before the entrance of Mexico into World War II. A 1936 column, for example, defended Hitler's racial policies by arguing for the need to preserve "Western civilization" against "the Jewish people." [36]

Despite ideological disagreements, Cárdenas recognized that the newspaper reached popular audiences. During a trip to Yucatán in 1937, Cárdenas told George W. Glass, the manager and president of the cooperative, "I am interested in what *La Prensa* says, and not in the other newspapers." [37] Vicente Lombardo Toledano, a stalwart supporter of the regime in the 1930s and a prominent antifascist, noted with concern that *La Prensa* reached "the home of the worker and the peasant" while other newspapers could not. [38] The editors capitalized on this. In 1938, manager Luis Novaro offered Cárdenas *La Prensa*'s services as a means to defend the government's achievements. Its "enormous circulation among all popular classes," argued Novaro, guaranteed that propaganda in *La Prensa* would yield greater returns than propaganda disseminated through official channels, perhaps alluding to the official daily *El Nacional,* founded in 1929, which was of good quality but had a limited circulation. [39]

However, *La Prensa* did not need Cárdenas to expand its circulation and increase advertisement sales. It added new sections and a photography department directed by Miguel V. Casasola. By 1942, Novaro explained the newspaper's success and its unique place within the industry: "We are the main newspaper in Mexico because in reality, we are the truly popular newspaper, and thus we can sustain ourselves without great problems." [40] Although circulation oscillated due to competition and other factors, the newspaper was able to cope with the occasional bad times without excessive reliance on government support. In the same year that, for example, sales reached critically low levels (32,000 copies), publishers raised its circulation to twice that number by establishing a lottery. But the bases were strong. In 1938, the newspaper received 64,842 pesos from direct sales and 44,041 from advertisements. In 1943, total revenue reached 2,246,859, with only 25 percent from advertisement sales. Of those sales, about 17 percent came from government agencies, including ministries and state governments. [41] Around half of the copies were sold in Mexico City and the rest in other Mexican cities, thanks to more than a thousand sales representatives based as far away as Texas and Guatemala. Despite Novaro's departure in 1950, the newspaper remained profitable. Acquired by a Spanish conglomerate and then by Mario Vázquez

Raña's Organización Editorial Mexicana (OEM) in the 1990s, *La Prensa* continued to have the highest circulation after the sports-focused paper *Esto.*[42]

The cooperative guaranteed stability for workers and healthy finances, but the editorial process was tightly controlled by a few managers and editors who also handled relations with the political class, as was the case with other privately owned newspapers. Thus, while *La Prensa* supported Manuel Ávila Camacho during his 1940 campaign, tensions arose when the new president's brother, Maximino, learned that the editors had refused to publish favorable coverage for his work as governor of Puebla and that one of them had privately called him a "clown." The managing editor himself had to offer explanations to the irascible politician in order to avoid further damage.[43] When revolutionary general and historian Vito Alessio Robles angrily asked why his latest reply to former minister and sugar magnate Aarón Sáenz was not going to be published, manager George W. Glass was frank: "We cannot accept your articles because licenciado Sáenz has paid us for a series of ads and could take it away."[44] During the presidency of Miguel Alemán, *La Prensa* adopted a sycophantic attitude toward the president, published a section entitled "The Catholic World," and berated union protests against the government.

Yet ideological or personal disputes at the highest levels of government cannot explain the diversity of agendas that found an outlet in *La Prensa*. While the editorial page could be conservative and pro-government, smaller news articles conveyed a populist outrage that could only be interpreted as critical of the government. Strong sales driven by crime stories insulated the newsroom from management interference and allowed for sharp reporting on the corruption and brutality of the police and local authorities. The paper published readers' letters and daily columns that persistently complained about urban governance and security.[45]

The cooperative structure gave particular autonomy to workers in their daily production of the "pages of blood news." Reporters and photographers gathered the material on the streets and in police stations, returned to the newspaper office, wrote the copy, and developed the photographs with just enough time for editors to revise the text and write headlines before closing the edition. Management tried to separate news gathering from writing in 1942, telling reporters to phone in the information for staff writers to compose the articles. But custom prevailed, and reporters continued to write their own pieces, maintaining a tone of immediacy that readers appreciated. This decentralized approach meant that even the shortest article reflected the activist tone that had defined *La Prensa*'s reporting from the beginning. For example, when a woman was stabbed in 1929, the reporter concluded with skepticism about the possibilities for a clear resolution from the authorities: "This underworld drama seems to be wrapped in the thick veil of mystery, and all the investigations into it have failed." [46] *La Prensa* criticized the police relentlessly while pointing to its own decisive interventions in famous cases, as well as in smaller grievances against the government brought by readers. The newspaper's aggressive style defined its dominance during the golden years of the nota roja, from the 1930s to the 1960s. [47]

La Prensa was the most prominent and successful newspaper, but there were other nota roja publications in circulation that reflected the heterogeneity of the genre. Many magazines, printed mostly in Mexico City after the 1930s, reached a large number of readers. In contrast with newspapers, their articles were complete narratives that included the resolution of each case and background information on the actors. *Alarma!*, published in different versions since the 1950s, sold hundreds of thousands of copies. [48] It was the model for the kind of direct, dramatic style that many associate with the genre. A typical story ran the headline "Santa, move over! I am going to kill your godmother!" Shoemaker Manuel Tapia Pérez shot his wife, got drunk, and, as he was entering prison, shouted, "I regret it because I adored her!" [49] Magazines integrated images in a sequence that paralleled the written narrative. Photographs ranged from crime scene carnage to female nudes (or "artistic nudes") or some combination of the two. Covers would feature voluptuous women suffering or instigating crime, next to smoking guns and men of action, even if the images bore no connection with any story inside. Magazine contents were not necessarily driven by the news value of a story. Along with local crime, they included articles about famous cases abroad or graphic stories about violence during the revolution, exploiting the abundant photographic archive of corpses and executions captured during the Cristero war and the various military rebellions of the 1920s. [50] They cast a suspicious gaze on common crime and national history alike. From that perspective, the recent past was not so different from the present, for in both moments politics was founded on violence.

Nota roja magazines had more ideological diversity than large newspapers. From the 1950s, magazines like *Alarma!* and *Por Qué?* combined gore, female nudes, and acerbic critiques of the government. In the pages of these magazines, police officers were little more than thieves in uniform. Complaints against the "gangsters with a shield" would be printed because, as the editors of *Alarma* promised, "This magazine does not mince words." [51] As with newspapers, however, denouncing some state officials did not prevent magazines from extoling others. *Alarma!*, for example, reported on the inept investigation of a series of crimes against homosexuals (without reproducing the homophobic language dominant in the press), in the same issue in which it published extensive propaganda for the official presidential candidate, Luis Echeverría (1970–1976).[52] *Por Qué?* was a starker example of opposition through nota roja in the late sixties and early seventies. This short-lived magazine followed all the visual and journalistic conventions of the genre but combined them with increasingly open attacks against the authoritarian tendencies of President Gustavo Díaz Ordaz (1964–1970). Despite an initial understanding, the Unión de Voceadores boycotted the magazine, and its editor and reporters were the objects of attacks from the government. Yet sales remained strong, no doubt because of the images of naked women, corpses, and, unlike other publications in the genre, soldiers shooting at demonstrators.[53] Indeed, *Por Qué?* was probably the only popular journal to publish pictures of the victims of the October 2, 1968, massacre at Tlatelolco.

A group of crime magazines, some of them dating back to the 1930s, like *Detective, Detectives, Guerra al Crimen, Policía Internacional, Gaceta de Policía,* and *Argos,* adopted the perspective of law enforcement, stressing technical and historical knowledge about crime and offering practical advice to detectives.[54] For journalists closer to this tradition, like Eduardo Téllez Vargas, by the 1960s the rest of the nota roja had degenerated because of the proliferation of "tasteless and obscene pamphlets . . . [with] pages full of stupid narratives in which a perverted criminal always wins." The distinction, according to Arellano Martínez, reflected the difference between the French and American styles of crime news: while the former praised criminals with biographical narratives, the latter made a tight "synthesis of the events of the criminal class" based on the files of police investigation.[55]

Yet even police-centered magazines catered to the less respectable interests of their readers, with contradictory results. For example, a single 1959 issue of *Detectives* praised Federal District major Ernesto P. Uruchurtu for closing seedy nightclubs while publishing ads for cabarets like "Arena," "Las Cavernas," "Bombay," "La Perla," and others.[56] *Revista de Policía* printed so-called artistic nudes on the cover while its interior pages criticized actress María Félix and French movies for their depiction of nudity and sexual acts.[57] There was no contradiction, however, if the reader was an experienced man who could deal with vice and pornography without losing his moral compass.

Less concerned about reaching a diversity of readers than were newspapers, nota roja magazines assumed a knowledgeable complicity with an ideal reader who enjoyed life yet was ready to face the dangers of the city. Ads for cabarets, sports, and a few political stories combined with the promise to uphold "strict ethical and professional norms," in the words of *Argos* editors. They contended that the knowledge they imparted had practical purposes: it was necessary to know crime in order to avoid it, placing "society in constant alert against the criminal activities of those who operate outside the law."[58] Criminal literacy, in these magazines, was a male privilege in which realism transcended prurient morality.

In addition to magazines, the nota roja style could also be found in the police sections of newspapers across the country. Most days, local news had little room and probably no taste for crime news. Stories had to be shorter for lack of space but also because the supply of mayhem was more limited. Investigations were a luxury that speculation tried to replace: an anonymous body was found in Culiacán, and *El Sol* guessed from its hands that the victim was a tomato picker. Yet crime news could have political effects and consolidate new publications. In towns like Apizaco, Tlaxcala, local politics reached such levels of antagonism and publicity that partisan newspapers used the graphic resources of crime news to attack their adversaries.[59] Other media better reflected the impact of the nota roja on everyday life. The radio program *Cuidado con el hampa* (Beware of the Underworld) aired more than 115 episodes in the 1950s, serving as a dictionary of criminal customs. Each episode described the modus operandi of a specific kind of criminal in terms intended to help the audience avoid the danger. Movies used the nota roja's alacrity and its ability to dramatically condense information. Pedro Infante, in the role of Pepe el Toro, holds a copy of *La Prensa,* reading, "I did not kill her!" in a scene from *Nosotros los pobres* (1947), one of the most popular Mexican movies of the era. As we will see in chapters 6 and 7, authors like Juan Bustillo Oro and Antonio Helú wrote scripts and stories inspired by newspapers. Directors also took inspiration from the nota roja in films with noir themes and allusions to famous cases: movies set in the urban underworld produced in Mexico increased from three in 1946 to fifty in 1950.[60]

Government attempts to both censor and exploit the nota roja confirm the influence of this genre. Officials used informal mechanisms to impose prior censorship on movies and plays, but nothing of the sort could be used against the press. Cárdenas's minister of gobernación, Silvano Barba González, declared in 1936 that stories about crime undermined the goals of moral development outlined in the president's six-year plan. Others officials advocated sweeping measures to stop the flood of sex, gore, and degradation.[61] Barba González proposed changes in penal legislation to prevent the publication of the nota roja altogether. He defined the genre as "the scandalous publication of crimes and misdemeanors with all kinds of details about their circumstances and procedures, as well as the apology . . . of the personality of the criminal . . . in a way that would make him seem, before those who are vulnerable to influence or who have antisocial tendencies, as a subject worthy of imitation." [62] The idea was discussed in committees at the Chamber of Deputies two years later, but it was not put to a vote because congressmen determined that it contradicted article 7 of the constitution, guaranteeing free speech.[63] In 1942, a new proposal in Congress, which also failed, tried to ban the publication of "falsified" news.[64] Concerned about the fact that women and children read comic strips and were exposed to the pornography that often accompanied it, President Alemán prohibited the printing and circulation of "obscene objects" in any media in 1951. This led to the closing of some publications and charges against their editors, including the magazine *Nota Roja,* which was deemed particularly offensive for the large size of its images. It probably had a large audience since it used *La Prensa's* distribution network. New criminal charges were filed against other titles under President Ruiz Cortines in 1954.[65] Stressing the negative side of criminal literacy, the argument behind these attempts was that the nota roja worked as a handbook for would-be criminals, as dangerous for its influence on "morbid" brains as was time in prison.[66] *El Nacional* eliminated its crime news section in 1968 on the orders of Díaz Ordaz.[67]

The commercial success of these publications made such blanket measures unlikely to work on private publications, and these attempts exposed the government to further criticism. *La Prensa* countered "sentimental Quakerism" with the argument that good press coverage did not always exalt criminals but often led to their capture.[68] Readers from Querétaro, Matamoros, and other cities wrote to *Alarma* in 1951 asking for more copies to be sent to their cities, encouraging the magazine: "Don't pay attention to the propaganda of supposedly moralistic people . . . because many of us, the youth in the provinces, do not have means to entertain ourselves like those in the capital." [69]

More discreet attempts to rein in journalists focused on specific cases and publications that linked local news, crime, and politics.[70] Thus, judges and prison authorities limited the coverage of some politically charged cases by holding suspects incommunicado. Editors protested these measures but also negotiated. *La Prensa* agreed to be less thorough in certain cases and to avoid showing blood in its color images.[71] But the contents of reporting was of greater concern. Articles about small miscarriages of justice and acts of corruption could be as worrying as broader political criticism of the regime. This is particularly clear in the scrutiny of *La Prensa* by intelligence agencies. Clippings from the newspaper were common in files on opposition movements gathered by the Secretaría de Gobernación. The Dirección Federal de Seguridad, an agency created by Alemán in 1947 and modeled after the FBI, kept tabs on editors' ideological tendencies, noting when they published a manifesto by the Partido Acción Nacional (then a Catholic, centrist party) denouncing electoral fraud or when they refused to publish statements by the Communist Party and railroad workers.[72] But DFS agents also monitored seemingly nonpolitical issues, such as the activities of two reporters who pressured crime victims into denouncing slow police investigations. The reporters used the argument (probably correct) that giving a statement to the press would help victims obtain justice. Agents also followed the activities of a correspondent in Ixtapan de la Sal who, after he lost his regular bribe from the State of Mexico Judicial Police, used "any conflict" as a pretext to paint police authorities in a bad light.[73] This unfocused spying suggests the absence of a single government strategy to control *La Prensa*. During the sixties, Mario Santaella, the newspaper's administrator, received 50,000 pesos a month from the Secretaría de Gobernación. At the same time as DFS agents followed prominent columnist Manuel Buendía and incited conflicts within the *La Prensa* cooperative, in the pages of the paper itself Secretary of Gobernación Luis Echeverría anonymously published a column spreading theories about conspiracies by foreign governments and ambitious politicians behind student movements.[74]

PRODUCERS OF REALITY

A focus on censorship and co-optation is of limited value for understanding the history of the nota roja. The government could do little against the effective ways in which the nota roja constructed its narratives. The nota roja was the product of a collective craft that gave coherence to the genre across time, institutions, and political eras. Reporters were fundamental to building a story. They entered the crime scene on the heels of the police or even before them. On the day of Leon Trotsky's assassination in 1940, Eduardo Téllez Vargas of *Novedades* arrived at the house in Coyoacán minutes ahead of the police because he had informants in the emergency medical services. He was able to pick up the murder weapon used by Ramón Mercader and have it photographed; he was even tempted, as he acknowledged in his memoirs, to smuggle out the manuscript of a book about Stalin that the victim had been writing. Others succumbed to this kind of temptation and took evidence with them. Reporters, after all, were there to act as the eyes of readers: they presented any slightly relevant piece of information, witnessed the initial questioning, and interviewed suspects immediately after the crime.[75] As we will see in chapter 6, journalists were the heroes of detective novels more often than police detectives were. When circulation was down, a good reporter could find a story or make one up to improve sales. For a few of them, recognition could pave the way for a long, successful career. David García Salinas, for example, drew from his experience and connections at *La Prensa* to write books, produce radio programs, and edit official publications. Téllez Vargas made a name for himself because of the quality of his work for *Novedades*. But crime reporters never earned as much money as some reporters in the political section, like Carlos Denegri from *Excélsior*.[76]

Photographers became more important in latter decades. Early on, the Casasola family and the Mayo brothers built their studios by selling graphic material to newspapers, but soon publications began hiring photographers as full-time employees. The 1939 internal bylaws of *La Prensa* required photographers to pick up their assignments by 10 A.M., return with their material by 6 P.M., and call the offices every hour to receive new jobs throughout the day. By the 1960s, according to *La Prensa* veteran Carlos Peláez Fuentes, photographers were driving coverage. They let reporters know about the "graphic information" they had captured so an article could be written, or gathered information themselves when the reporter could not be reached in time. Photographers, or *fotoreporteros* as they began to be called, were often the only representatives of nota roja newspapers at the crime scene. Upon their return to the newsroom, they conveyed the information to a desk writer, who composed the text that would accompany the image.[77] Most of the photographs they brought were composed in haste, framed frontally, and illuminated with a direct flash. They left little room for background or other details and did not seem to have any aesthetic value, at least in comparison with the often flowery prose of reporters and columnists. Thus, few photographers acquired a reputation beyond the newspapers: Enrique Díaz and Nacho

López produced "graphic stories," or *fotoreportajes,* narratives made of a series of images with themes related to the world of crime and justice, for general interest magazines.[78] Enrique Metinides, who began working for *La Prensa* at a young age, made a name in art circles only after retiring from the newspaper in 1979. His pictures of people surprised by death or catastrophe, now exhibited outside the context of the newspaper, invite a voyeuristic gaze, both among 1960s readers and 2010s gallery patrons; but if we place them back within the context of nota roja journalism, we can see their editorial significance. As Jessie Lerner has suggested, with López and Metinides the realism and spontaneity of crime photography became a journalistic indictment of the police and justice system, particularly in comparison with the stock images provided by the Casasolas.[79]

For the anonymous majority of nota roja journalists, conditions were not particularly good. Authorship was rarely accredited in a byline, and the pay was low. According to *La Prensa*'s internal accounts, reporters and photographers earned 300 pesos a month in November 1938, 60 pesos less than the newspaper's cashier but the same as the bookkeeper. They were closely supervised, like other employees: every morning, the assignment editor reviewed the day's newspapers and counted how many important stories had been "won" or "lost" to rivals.[80] Most journalists had little education and earned their position through apprenticeship within the newspaper. Although their material conditions probably improved over the course of the century (the first union was created in 1922, and there were several strikes across the industry), salaries remained meager. Many reporters had to make do with additional rewards from their sources (in the form of cash payments, called *embute,* or no-show jobs) and commissions on the sales of advertisement. Unsurprisingly, reporters in general had a reputation as "rude, careless, undisciplined, skeptical," and were often associated with vice and illegality; nota roja reporters in particular had a bad reputation because of their close association with the police.[81]

Reporters had no choice but to maintain these relationships. A few police detectives had previously worked as journalists; some journalists, in turn, would pass as police officers in order to get a scoop, as Téllez Vargas did to get into the hospital where Trotsky lay dying. In most cases, the relationship was straightforward. Contacts at the police and the Cruz Roja emergency services allowed a reporter or photographer to be the first one to reach a scene, look at evidence, interview suspects, borrow particularly interesting objects, or arrange objects for a photograph that would produce a more eloquent picture—as happened with the bottles, glasses, ashtrays, and gun found in the house of John Healy, where William Burroughs accidentally killed his wife in 1951. It was common for reporters to spend hours at police stations waiting for the next story. According to one reporter's testimony, in the early 1930s the chief of the Federal District's Secret Service presented difficult cases to the journalists playing dominos at headquarters. He would ask them for a "sentence" on the suspect, and his agents would follow their advice.[82] Protection from friends in the police would always come in handy. Nota roja reporters seem to have been particularly fond of enjoying nightlife in cabarets and other places associated with drugs and prostitution—the heart of "the world of the *hampa*."[83] Some carried police badges and guns given to them by their contacts in the police. Manuel Buendía, who began his career in *La Prensa* and became editor-in-chief of the newspaper from 1960 to 1963, owned both a badge and a gun thanks to his friends at the DFS. He used the privileged information they gave him in his *Excélsior* column, "Red Privada." However, when he turned his attention to drug trafficking in 1984, the gun was of no use and he was killed by members of the DFS.[84]

In most cases, the relationship between reporters and the police was not as extreme. Police officers of all ranks had strong incentives to maintain a close connection with journalists since their jobs hung in the balance; their careers could be impacted by both good press or a sudden exposé, or *periodicazo*. The Mexico City chief inspector and his direct subordinates served at the pleasure of the president, who until 1997 also appointed the mayor of the Federal District. Police chiefs were usually members of the military and did not last very long in the position. Thus, to have police "triumphs" publicized in the press could be very valuable. Articles written by their press offices could be published in newspapers with no indication that they were actually paid ads, although their origins were betrayed in the text; one such article praised the heroic performance of agents in front of dangerous crowds from Mexico City neighborhoods where "people love to see the police become the victim of any predicament."[85] Police chiefs would let their favorite reporters know when they were about to stage a "blow against crime," but they could also ask the press to remain quiet about events that might damage police credibility in the eyes of the public. The police used the press to condemn suspects by staging images in which the suspect held the weapon, stood next to the booty, or reenacted the crime.[86]

As self-appointed representatives of the public, journalists could help win an indictment from judges who would otherwise be reluctant to do the police's bidding. Just as they denounced abusive policemen, the nota roja voiced criticism of the weaknesses and corruption of the justice system. There was a difference that gave an advantage to the police in front of reporters, however: their activity provided the raw material for nota roja narratives, with shocking images and exclusives, whereas the judicial process was of less interest because it was slow, took place in offices without much drama or an audience (after 1929), and developed under the control of lawyers and judges whose work was never transparent. A guilty verdict did not guarantee closure, given the uncertainties of the penitentiary system. The section entitled "Cortes Penales" in *La Prensa* provided a few lines of follow-up to cases that were easily remembered by readers ("undesirable pornographers" or the "murderous physician").[87] Beyond that, little was reported on the fate of suspects after their indictment, the point when punishment really began, since suspects often waited months for a sentence in nasty prisons where they had to mingle with the guilty. Sentences were also irrelevant for those who had money or powerful sponsors. It was as if the true proceedings against the suspect had taken place on the pages of the newspaper while the case was under investigation, and the official trial was redundant.

Reporters, in other words, were not completely subordinated to the state. Guillermo Mellado remembered his times as a reporter in the 1920s (before becoming a policeman) as marked by relentless competition: "We reporters knew more than many detectives who carried identification and big guns but who, when required, completely ignored the basics of a good investigation." He felt compelled to intervene when police ineptitude resulted in a wrongful arrest.[88] Even in the postwar decades, when publishers generally adopted an uncritical tone toward the government, nota roja publications still reported on the abuses, ineptitude, and criminal complicity of police forces throughout the country.[89] This was facilitated by the fact that multiple police agencies were often involved in big cases, with agents competing at the crime scene and carrying out parallel investigations. Reporters sought information from different agencies that were trying to upstage one another, and editors published competing explanations. Multiple articles on an important case could be written by different authors drawing on different sources. As Téllez Vargas acknowledged, it was always useful for a reporter to present information that might contradict the official hypothesis; besides satisfying readers, it helped him earn the trust of suspects and other informants.[90] By offering alternative explanations and presenting suspects' points of view in the form of interviews, rather than in the main feature, journalists avoided the appearance of justifying the crime.[91]

The complex relationship between reporters, agents, and criminals made sense to savvy readers. Téllez Vargas and his colleagues knew that people from all walks of life read the nota roja not because they wanted to escape reality but because it helped them navigate the perils of everyday life in the city. Those readers framed their interpretations in the context of their experience of the police and judicial systems. Stories were useful when they dealt with dangerous places, people, and situations, and with agents of the state who victimized citizens instead of protecting them.[92] The nota roja's crude or sarcastic tone was not a sign of callous disregard for life among these readers but rather served as a way to highlight the disjuncture between justice and the truth about a crime.

For its readers, crime news provided the definitive record of crime, a necessary part of everyday life. They attributed to the thoroughness of its coverage an almost official quality: what happened was registered there, and vice versa. Among the thousands of letters addressed to Mexican presidents requesting their intervention in cases of homicide, usually penned by relatives of the victims, many contained newspaper clippings which documented both the crimes and the impunity of the alleged killers with an accuracy and openness that were absent from judicial or police investigations. For example, in November 1955 the widow of Demetrio Varela, from Milpa Alta, D.F., sent President Adolfo Ruiz Cortines a letter with a clipping from *La Prensa*. She demanded the arrest of Gregorio Silva, who remained free because of his political connections. Even the police relied on the press for their investigations.[93] The dangers of urban life (robberies, suicides, shootouts, accidents, drinking binges, cadavers found, children lost) were meticulously compiled in the nota roja and rendered memorable through the power of images or the wit of headlines. The same day on which *La Prensa* devoted several pages to the kidnapping of Charles Lindbergh's son, a small article entitled "A mother-in-law killed her daughter-in-law with a quarrel" explained that the cause of Maura Romero's death might have been an "attack of bile" while she and her mother-in-law argued. Before an autopsy could determine the cause of death, the elderly María de Jesús Ramírez Romero was put in Belem prison, accused of murder.[94] Readers probably did not consume too many of these stories in a single sitting, but read one or a few each day. Over time, the effect was nevertheless powerful: each piece was a detailed observation of urban life which, like a David Hockney Polaroid collage, could be assembled together to form a large and untidy, yet sharply focused, picture.

Nota roja, we can argue, created reality, if we understand reality as a commonly shared reference among the participants in a conversation, a way to organize the complexity of life that makes agreement possible. People might have doubted the promises of politicians, gossiped about artists, or debated the competitive drive of sportsmen, but everyone agreed that a triple murder had been committed at a barber barbershop at 80 Avenida Patriotismo on the night of April 23, 1934: it was confirmed by pictures, witness accounts, and a crowd of Tacubaya neighbors outside the place. Accepted as a faithful depiction of life, the pages of nota roja created a common terrain on which citizens could interact critically with the state and among each other.[95] The relatively few opinion pieces in those pages included arguments in favor of the death penalty, premised on the need for a direct connection between actions and consequences. Other references to policy were concrete and pragmatic. Even public opinion was an objective fact. In its early days, *La Prensa* published brief surveys on the thoughts of "common citizens" on themes of current interest.[96] The everyday life of common citizens, its routine and material conditions, was more tangible there than in other kinds of news. Images of car and railroad accidents whose mangled victims were "humble people" served as a stark warning that this could happen to anyone. Lesser mishaps (a young man crushed by the cart he was pushing, a fatal bicycle fall) were useful reminders of mundane dangers. Everything was connected by the inaction of the state: the daily reports of potholes or garbage in the street appeared next to the missing persons announcements placed by relatives.[97]

The most valuable service provided by the nota roja was its daily reporting on the faces, whereabouts, and methods of criminals. Below an image of one Manuel Infante, *Alarma!* suggested: "If by chance you find him in the street, and he invites you to play billiards, run away from him because is trying to scam you ... or call the police."[98] Magazines and crime radio shows stressed the social utility of criminal literacy. The motto for radio program *Cuidado con el hampa* was "To warn society against crime is to serve it." Each show described the modus operandi of a different kind of robber or con man in precise detail.[99] To consume that information was not an exercise in paranoia but a basic way to get ready for life in the city. "A maniacal strangler is on the loose and killing! Danger for everyone!" might sound like an expression of panic, but the article behind it contained specific warnings about fleabag hotels and the nightlife characters associated with the strangler.[100] Images of criminals shocked, just like pictures of accidents, but they also conveyed useful information about the dangers of everyday life; they produced a methodical kind of fear, perhaps, but not paranoia. Indeed, after seeing the portraits of criminals at large, readers would write to authorities to help in their capture.[101]

Letters to the editors were part of this construction of reality. They included complaints about routine annoyances of everyday life and the unresponsiveness or dishonesty of authorities. Many more may not have been published: *La Prensa*'s op-ed page asked readers to refrain from sending anonymous mail or letters denouncing personal or political enemies. Columns like "Vox Populi" in *La Prensa* registered citizens' demands and authorities' lack of response. For the column's anonymous author, the proper administration of justice in Mexico was no more than "a dream." [102] Articles and opinion pieces elaborated on the corruption or ineptitude of government officials, from judges to street cops who abused their positions or acted in collusion with criminals, to the impunity of men and women accused of crimes. They described police agents who were thieves, murderers, kidnappers, or extortionists, or who beat citizens, fabricated charges, or made money illicitly. Articles could be quite specific about abuses and extortion by judges and inspectors, printing their names for greater shame. In 1959, for instance, *Detectives* exposed an "*influyentazo*" (politically connected person), a relative of a former president, who avoided punishment after killing a sanitary inspector. [103] Not all critical references to authorities were dismissive; when described in a benevolent tone, the shortcomings of the police could justify readers' involvement: "The police need help," argued *La Prensa* when offering a reward for locating Santiago Rodríguez Silva, the Tacubaya murderer. [104]

Nota roja's realism defined itself in opposition to the banality of established newspapers. *La Prensa*'s motto was "To say what others keep quiet." It boasted of its extensive readership and its ability to represent "the entirety of public opinion in Mexico." [105] *Detective* justified its articles on "hair-raising crimes" on the basis that all civilized countries needed police news, and Mexican newspapers refused to provide it in order to avoid being called "yellow and scandalous." [106] The motto of *Alarma!* was "Only the truth." It often reminded its readers of the "journalistic deterioration" in the country while emphasizing that "we have always been guided by the goal of clean, useful, healthy journalism." [107] Many readers shared these assessments: those of *Nota Roja* praised the newspaper as "a magazine that has defended the people of Mexico." [108] This ability to counter official silence was more noticeable when crimes made it possible for nota roja reporters to penetrate into the private lives of politicians and celebrities, uncovering the vices and delinquency behind power. [109]

Savvy readers, unlike contemporary critics, were able to distinguish the nota roja's pursuit of the truth from other kinds of stories. In the 1960s, some magazines began to publish fantastic stories. Headlines like "In Chiapas the strangest monster of all times was born. The prophets Nostradamus and the Madre Matiana predicted it," or "I am an extraterrestrial agent. A case that will leave you astonished," appealed to readers' black humor, humor that was itself a form of critical commentary.[110] While a number of these stories were translations from American tabloids, others attributed collective hallucinations to Mexican popular religiosity. The *Alarma!* report on a girl who cured sick people in Agua Dulce, Veracruz, included a disclaimer: "This magazine is produced by a complete journalistic organization with the strictest principles of professional ethics."[111] Translated from nota roja hyperbolic language, the statement meant: while in our pages incredible stories appear next to realistic crime news, the smart reader knows that the fantasy of the former does not weaken the truth of the latter.

NARRATIVES OF NOTA ROJA

Reality, however, was not a collection of isolated events. It appeared in the public sphere as truthful stories structured by a conventional set of rules. These rules included the priority of detailed observation of the events by nonstate agents, and the certainty that justice could not be expected from judicial institutions. The use of these rules was best illustrated in a limited number of famous cases. On any given day, there was always one crime story that could attract many readers, usually a murder that distinguished itself from the ordinary stories because it did not have a clear culprit, was particularly bloody, or involved criminals, victims, and witnesses who were themselves interesting characters. The case of "the passion tragedy of the Restaurant Broadway" is an example from 1932 in which "a cheated husband, of German origin, killed his rival when he found him with his deceitful wife." Although the guilt of Guillermo Gosserez was not in question, the reasons for his violent behavior were of interest. The coverage included a back-page portrait of the relaxed and well-dressed Gosserez, information concerning the last time husband and wife had had sexual relations, and discussion of her past romantic liaisons.[112] Cases like this could last days or weeks in the pages of newspapers, making the names and likenesses of the main characters familiar to readers.

It was essential to get these stories quickly and correctly. In the 1934 case of the Tacubaya barbershop, *La Prensa* bragged of the accuracy of its reporting when compared to the error-laden accounts of its competitors. It was not only a matter of providing the best images and most comprehensive reports, but also of having the correct hypothesis and making the most direct contribution to the investigation. The newspaper immediately accused Rodríguez Silva, reproduced his likeness, and a few days later, thanks to the work of its correspondent in León, Guanajuato, led the police to his capture. With this, trumpeted the editors, "*La Prensa* achieves one of its greatest and most celebrated journalistic triumphs." [113] A timely and original approach to the story translated into better sales. After the discovery of the Goyo Cárdenas murders in 1942, *La Prensa* general editor Fernando Mora summoned the experienced reporter Miguel Gil and told him to take charge of the case and to find a "completely different" interpretation from that advanced by the police. Gil brought artist Jesús Nieto to draw scenes from the story, including the hands, feet, and eyes of the suspect. The circulation of the newspaper doubled to seventy thousand. [114]

"The passion tragedy of the Restaurant Broadway" included several characters connected by complex relationships. Probing the violence in those relationships exposed the realm of domesticity to the scrutiny of public opinion. Like most other famous cases, it featured both challenges to and the violent enforcement of gender roles. Gosserez's wife, Mercedes Santibáñez, admitted that she felt "passionate love" for the victim, Hernán Lizárraga, before her wedding to Gosserez, and that she had seen him again lately. She admitted also that she was planning to divorce Gosserez, even though on the day of the crime they had reconciled and had sexual intercourse. [115] Crimes of passion, which in many cases involved the victimization of women and leniency toward males, were more than news: they confirmed prevalent patterns of violence in social interactions, and they made for fascinating reading because they came in a narrative form and had a subjective dimension. What actors had thought, felt, and done in the past was more relevant in these cases than for other kinds of violence. Science and the law acknowledged the importance of this subjective dimension by classifying passion as a temporary disease that was not limited to men. Passion, however, was a deceiving label for characterizing complex plots. Against the romantic notion of love that underlay these "tragedies," the violence here was merely the climax of relationships in which sex, the physical act of love, conflicted with sentiment, interest, and masculine control. [116]

Despite their complexity, these stories were truthful because they were based on testimonies and records of a past that seemed to contradict the present. The attacker usually confessed, providing subjective details that were often lacking in other crimes. The investigation, therefore, did not center on the identity of the culprit but on the reasons for the violence, for these reasons could determine the sentence if, for example, honor was at stake. Female witnesses provided a different perspective from that of the male attackers, and they turned some of these cases into debates about relationships. In the "crime of passion" committed by sixty-five-year-old poultry merchant Patricio Cárdenas de la Cruz against his wife, twenty-five-year-old Teresa Suárez, the killer justified his actions by arguing that she had mocked his honor. He also bragged that he had enough money to leave prison if he were ever incarcerated. *La Prensa,* however, registered the interest of Santa María la Ribera residents in the case. A picture on the back cover, shot from a high angle, showed the crowd gathered around Teresa's body (she had died on her knees with her head down), next to an image of the .32 caliber gun used by Cárdenas de la Cruz (figure 4). Teresa's sister, Virginia, was also photographed, gesturing as she gave her version of the story: Teresa had suffered abandonment, deprivation, infidelity, and mistreatment at the hands of the man who eventually killed her. Virginia disparaged Cárdenas and told the reporter that he once had almost killed Teresa but had suffered no consequences.[117] "Passion" worked as a label that assembled personal histories and everyday details, even if they lacked glamour. The brother of another woman killed by her lover "told the story of the relationship" between victim and murderer: he exploited her into prostitution, yet in a letter he reproached her: "In the eyes of your family I am a pimp and you know that is not true."[118] The *Alarma!* title cited earlier ("I killed Edilberta because I loved her") made the story sound like a crime of passion, but the narrative was in fact one full of sordid detail: incest, poverty, a corpse found by a dog. For the magazine, there was no romance here but a lesson about the dangers for "innocent girls" exposed to interactions with men "hungry for sex."[119]

Crimes of passion were instructive because reasonable interpretations of the crime assumed that male domination was a natural equilibrium disrupted by violence. *El Universal Gráfico* gathered comments from passersby about a street scene in which a jealous woman had stabbed a man:

A gentleman walking by commented on the customs of the race:
—Strong passions . . . The woman who kills when people think she is bad, although she is good. That man, fallen in a pool of blood, is the man of our race, generous, gentle, who before wounding a woman prefers that she, blinded by fury, sacrifice him.

LA PRENSA
Diario Ilustrado de la Mañana 50 ¢

MATO A TIROS A SU ESPOSA UN COMERCIANTE

Tragedia por Celos en Santa María de la Ribera

FIGURE 4. Murder of Teresa Suárez. *La Prensa*, 5 Mar. 1957, p. 40.

Another spectator said, mistakenly:

—The great tragedies of our people are here: the good, simple, humble, lovable woman who becomes a wild beast when she is mistreated. The hard working, honest, good father and excellent husband who falls in the face of tragedy rather than raising a hand against the mother of his children.

The preliminary findings, however, complicated stereotypical views: the victim "was a professional thief and as a certificate of good behavior he had no less than eighteen scars on his body." [120] Crimes of passion mobilized romantic notions of the tragic links between violence and love but also uncovered details that muddled the lesson. Serious coverage was necessary, therefore, to make these stories meaningful. Otherwise, as veteran journalist Gonzalo Jordán warned with a probably apocryphal tale, they could inspire misguided responses: when a young, blonde, wealthy woman was found dead in her room, the mystery inspired a flood of interpretations: the left blamed capitalism, the right suspected "some intelligent communist, that is, a born murderer," experts and astrologers opined, reporters became famous, comparisons with foreign cases abounded, and hairstyles, dresses, movies, and music appeared, inspired by the case. It turned out, however, that the woman had died of a heart attack. [121]

Although stories about passion crimes were especially popular, all crimes could boost newspaper sales. When they chose to focus on one, nota roja publications deployed all their resources to capture any piece of evidence that was fit to print. One edition was usually not enough. As the days went by, headlines and texts assumed an increasing level of knowledge on the part of readers. There was indeed an implicit order in this exhaustive coverage. Stories usually began with a detailed description of the crime scene, including photos, drawings, and even diagrams. Images, sounds, and smells placed the reader at the scene (figure 5). [122] Narratives gained traction as characters became more defined. The main one, in cases of murder, was the criminal. His or her name kept the interest of readers in focus over several days and encouraged the ignorant to catch up. In the case of Alberto Gallegos, a notorious 1932 murderer, *La Prensa* used prominent headlines over several days to tell the story: "Gallegos lost!" "Gallegos confessed!" "Gallegos is a cynic"; and "Exemplary punishment for Gallegos." [123]

Characters took shape through interviews, a key format for the press coverage of famous cases. The murderer's point of view had a ring of authenticity because, as often happened, it provided the only direct testimony related to the crime. Aware of this, some suspects granted interviews strategically: they

FIGURE 5. Crime of Tacubaya. *La Prensa*, 24 Apr. 1934, p. 1.

could reward journalists with an exclusive or stop talking when coverage seemed to be going against them, as did multiple murderer Goyo Cárdenas. Others, like María del Pilar Moreno, turned their confessions into accusations against their victims.[124] For most readers, voluntary confessions, published as first-person accounts in the form of interviews or transcriptions of letters or statements, were more persuasive than any other kind of evidence. As a format, the interview became popular during the second half of the century, to the extent that politicians would pay large sums to answer softball questions to be published on the front page of important newspapers. Lowly nota roja reporters, by contrast, had to earn the trust of prisoners, who had nothing to gain other than the risk of revealing self-incriminating details. Authorized by judges or wardens, reporters sat down with suspects in their cells. The results included information about their personality, life, and customs, as well as explanations of the crime. Writers avoided sounding apologetic by shifting to the suspect's first person to recount the events. Yet these interviews often implied a criticism of confessions coerced by the police to deceive "those who have the noble duty to inform the public." [125]

Open-ended interviews and photographs built a nuanced understanding of the suspect and his or her actions. In its early characterization of Rodríguez Silva, *La Prensa* compared him with other "examples of the Lombrosian." But as more information came along, editors recognized that he "is no longer the morbid, marijuana-smoking, hypersexual being we first thought, but presents himself with new attributes: astute, of many resources, with a magnetic power that seals the lips of the men and women he lives with." [126] He talked to reporters over the phone after his arrest and then spoke to them again while eating in a cell in the company of his mother. Other interviews conveyed a sense of intimacy that bordered on admiration. In one with Gallegos, entitled "En confianza" (In confidence), the reporter described a cultivated and attractive persona: "We found him freshly shaved and whistling a funeral march set to rumba while reading a morning paper with visible satisfaction." [127] He denied having killed an elegant socialite, although did not deny having befriended her.

Nota roja interviews were central to criminal literacy, reflecting contemporary ways of understanding crime. Journalistic tête-à-têtes certainly contrasted with the rigid interrogations of criminals favored by Porfirian criminologists like Carlos Roumagnac. Their questionnaires looked for criminogenic factors: family degeneration, sexual deviations, alcoholism. The premise was that "the criminal" was a barbarous subspecies of the human race, an impression that seemed to be confirmed by the closely cropped rows of identification portraits that illustrated police magazines in Porfirian Mexico. These images of disheveled, angry, or disoriented suspects proved that criminals looked different from peaceful people but not from each other. In postrevolutionary Mexico, however, the theory was of little use: criminals could be anyone in the crowd or the neighborhood, people who might be well dressed or not. Mid-twentieth-century media depictions of criminals paid attention to skillful, elegant individuals. *Cuidado con el hampa* described the cunning modus operandi of different criminal specialists, from fraudulent funeral parlor agents to *guitarreros* who operated a machine that printed bank notes. A gang of Argentines who swindled large amounts of money from wealthy Mexican men became an example of the smooth operations of the "international underworld."[128] Criminal behaviors were changing in an increasingly cosmopolitan society. In nota roja narratives, this meant a deeper construction of the criminal: someone with a past and sometimes even a conscience.

Nobody seems to have been troubled by the fact that while criminals talked, victims remained silent. Coverage seldom tried to compensate for this absent perspective. On the contrary, stories and photographs showed little regard for their dignity: images identified bodies and presented them at the crime scene as just another piece of evidence. Crime opened the doors of privacy to the prying eyes of public opinion. In Rodríguez Silva's case the bodies of the victims were prominently displayed on the front page, and reporters gave details about the women's sexual transgressions and the possible homosexual relation between the murderer and the brother of two of the victims, living as they did in such crowded quarters. The details suggested that victims got what they deserved due to their lack of prudence and morality.[129] News coverage, as well as judicial investigations, often meant the sometimes posthumous humiliation of being publicly accused of immorality, as happened to Teresa Suárez (figure 4), whose husband and killer accused her of cheating on him.

Criminals anchored the narratives of famous cases, but they were only one piece in a puzzle that included many facts. At first sight, nota roja accounts seemed to have no organization after they introduced the crime scene. Information was published as it came to light, on the assumption that readers would assemble the pieces of the puzzle. Texts did not follow a prescriptive structure, such as the "inverted pyramid" of U.S. newspapers, nor was there an obvious sequence of cause and effect, or even a unified chronological flow. Although some reporters played the role of snoops, nota roja narratives never followed the structure of detective stories, with their careful measuring of information and inference, ever moving toward an irrefutable denouement. Instead, they resembled the early "construction of murder as mystery" that Karen Halttunen described for the late eighteenth- and early nineteenth-century United States: stories that were "usually fragmented, chronologically jumbled, and incomplete," where contradictory perspectives coexisted, and plots were not always easy to follow. The absence of a master intelligence to organize the information, which in crime fiction was provided by the detective, required nota roja readers to play the same kind of active role that juries had played in criminal trials.[130] Counting on the complicity of those readers, Mexican journalists produced stories that were not random or opaque but rather suggested that the truth was out there.

As soon as the crime was discovered and the public eye began to scrutinize the crime scene, the narrative began to flow in two temporal directions.[131] On the one hand, moving toward the past, readers learned about the protagonists, their lives, and the conflicts that might have pushed them to crime. Victims, suspects, and other characters gradually acquired depth as reporters interviewed them and investigated their past. Thus, for example, the transformation of Rodríguez Silva from a brutal murderer to a more complex character who had deep relationships with his victims; and of David Heredia, the street cop who was the son and brother of two of Rodríguez Silva's victims, and who cried and promised vengeance at the funeral. Days later, readers learned that according to detective Valente Quintana, Heredia had had intimate physical contact with the suspect at the barbershop. In this investigation of the past, crimes of passion were the archetype. Nota roja reporters might have been following the dictum of nineteenth-century New York editor Lincoln Steffens, who in order to cover the case of a woman murdered by her axe-wielding husband instructed a reporter, "If you can find out just what happened between that wedding and this murder, you will have a novel for yourself and a short story for me. Go on now, take your time and get this tragedy as a tragedy."[132] Mexican newspapers constantly used the word "tragedy" to describe even the most sordid crimes. Fate seemed indeed to be inscribed onto the past of the characters. It is a mistake, however, to confuse tragedy as a dramatic form dealing with serious events and inspiring cathartic feelings with the pathos emanating from the crime scene. Nota roja narratives could not follow a strict dramatic style because they were subordinated to the continuing influx of information from too many voices, each with a different moral weight, all participating in the construction of that past.[133] The whole experience could be called a tragedy only retrospectively. Yet it was never clear when the end of a case had arrived. There was only a painstaking gathering of facts about the characters' past that lasted as long as did the readers' attention.

On the other hand, the narrative moved forward with the present, providing all the information that the police revealed or industrious reporters procured. Large and small facts constituted the raw material for the inner detective in every reader. Reporters were more visible in this strand of the chronicle. Their entrance into the crime scene signaled their commitment to follow the case to its resolution and to link their gaze with that of readers. When the reporter reached the site of Rodríguez Silva's crime, he surveyed the "pigsty" where the bodies of Juana Castañeda, María Estela Heredia, and Teresa Pulido were found (figure 5). These initial descriptions were often written in the first person and included the name of reporters, photographers, and graphic artists. With emphatic precision, they conveyed the sensory impact of the crime: in the barbershop, "on the floor of a miserable room . . . turned into a huge pool of blood," there were "cots . . . rags" and murder weapons forming the "horrific scene."[134]

The reporter's individual perspective soon fragmented into multiple points of view. Brief testimonies, rumors, vague tips, revealing photos, and other items appeared in a proliferation of articles, captions, text boxes, and headlines. Long articles began on the front page and continued in different sections, forcing readers to move back and forth through the pages of the newspaper. Texts recapitulated the names and places visited in previous days but also introduced contradictory pieces of information. In the Tacubaya case, separate pieces said that drops of blood suggested the murderer was wounded; that there had been no rape of the victims; that multiple tips were emerging as to the whereabouts of Rodríguez Silva, and that "all available accounts on the motive of the crime are mere suppositions."[135] This fragmentary but persistent building of the case both replicated and critiqued the police investigation, which often consisted of little more than cobbling together of evidence without any concern for motives or an overarching hypothesis. The ideal nota roja reader could make sense of it all because he or she resembled a character imagined by literary fiction: the armchair detective who did not have to leave his room to solve the mystery because he or she was omniscient through the newspapers.[136]

Images, especially photographs, reinforced the impression that newspapes provided comprehensive knowledge. Studies of the nota roja have focused so exclusively on the role of photographs that the photographs seem to have no connection to textual reporting. It is easy to see why: photos of corpses covered in and surrounded by blood were increasingly frequent beginning in the 1920s. When color began to be used on *La Prensa*'s cover in 1972, and blood no longer looked black, photographers were told to find new angles in order to avoid the vast expanses of red. Photographs of female bodies at the crime scene or in the morgue, iconic images that had fascinated Porfirian writers, were legitimized in the name of forensic interest, allowing for the publication of nudity that would otherwise be censored. However, with time "artistic nudes" without any forensic rationale became more frequent.[137] The charge of pornography was often leveled against newspapers and magazines, but if we look at the connections between images and text, we can see that the even the most shocking images were part of a narrative.[138]

Photographers did not work in isolation. The images they produced were assembled in compositions, sometimes filling entire pages, presenting a rich array of data that enhanced the coverage contributed by reporters: portraits of those involved, the crime scene, the crowds, the police station, and court depositions. In some magazines, reenacted stories arranged in frames formed *fotonovelas* similar to comic books. Illustrations identified the elements of the case and synthesized the action with images from the reconstruction of the events at the crime scene. By the 1960s, the work of photographers had become more autonomous while the written component of crime coverage had lost weight. The camera itself grew in importance even as it actually decreased in size. According to photographer Enrique Metinides, the crowds of spectators standing close to a horrific crime scene were attracted by the camera as much as the tragedy; Metinides called them "voyeurs" (*mirones*).[139] In 1970, *Alarma!* writers ascribed a certain agency to the camera: given "the orgy of vice and prostitution" prevalent in Ciudad Netzahualcóyotl, they claimed, "the camera refused to capture such ignominy." [140]

In the best study on the subject, Jessie Lerner proposes that this style of photography dealt with modernization and its impact on people's lives. This, I would add, applies not only to the object of those images but also to the way in which they encouraged active reading and political engagement. There was no better way to contradict the government's statements than to show, as *Alarma!* did, the cabarets, prostitution, and drug trafficking that were not supposed to exist.[141] Just like pornography in other societies, after all, racy nota roja images expanded audiences, expressed political dissent, and challenged the authority of normative sexual, age, and gender roles. However, the images in the pages of newspapers and magazines were not self-explanatory; their meaning was the product of a collaboration among coworkers and a dialogue with readers. Recognizing this collaborative process is also key to understanding these images' interactions with other genres and media. For example, the links between political, artistic, and nota roja photography examined by Lerner are evident in the work of artist Manuel Álvarez Bravo. Crime scene and corpse pictures, in turn, owed much to the technical conventions of forensic photography, and in some cases they even aided police investigations. As Metinides himself admitted, both noir movies and the work of New York freelance photographer Arthur Fellig (aka Weegee) were his inspirations—just as movies and novels took inspiration from forensic images.[142] More than testimonies of modern life, nota roja images were the lynchpin of a new perspective on reality.

The visual vocabulary of these images was integral to the criminal literacy nurtured by the nota roja. Unlike the rows of mug shots favored by Porfirian publications, suspects' portraits enhanced the psychological depth of interviews.[143] They conveyed the fashion sense and environment of their subjects, providing names and addresses, capturing them individually or in groups, opening the frame as much as possible given the space available on the page. Details defined characters in terms of class, reflecting Gallegos's elegant demeanor (figure 6). The faces of some suspects, like Rodríguez Silva, were reproduced frequently and sometimes in large drawings or photographs, creating a sense of intimacy that gave ammunition to official accusations that crime news idealized criminals. On the cover of *La Prensa*, he opened to the viewer's eyes his bandaged hand as proof of the truth that he had been attacked by his victims (figure 7).

The image and the confession of the murderer were both fascinating and threatening. Thanks in part to photography, nota roja narratives had an emotional force that no other journalistic genre could achieve, and this force could express itself in multifaceted ways. The feeling usually evoked was vengeful rage toward the criminal, with little sympathy toward victims. The appeal was clear from the headlines, which vilified suspects and demanded swift justice. "The jackal's paw" was the headline above the photograph of Santiago Rodríguez Silva (figure 7). A few days earlier, in relation to the same case, an editorial exclaimed: "Revenge! is the unanimous and justified outcry . . . *La Prensa* is shaken by the same feeling of social outrage and, being the representative of the people, offers its cooperation in the capture."[144] The emotional language was not purely manipulative but rather formed part of

FIGURE 6. Gallegos (center) and accomplices. *La Prensa*, 3 Mar. 1932, p. 1.

FIGURE 7. Santiago Rodríguez Silva. *La Prensa,* 1 May 1934, p. 1.

an interaction between newspapers and readers intended to stir the latter's feelings and encourage their participation in resolving cases. *La Prensa* defined the "fascinating and brutal crime" at the barbershop by "the cruelty, the viciousness, the ferocity" of the violence.[145] It presented pictures of angry crowds and sorrowful images at the funeral, attended by an "enormous multitude, mostly of the humble class." Editors appealed for the capture of the "heinous criminal," echoing Tacubaya neighbors who "demand the head of the murderer; that he be hanged from a tree; that he receive the ley fuga." [146]

This case, however, was not only "brutal" but also intellectually "absorbing," deserving readers' participation beyond expressing their feelings. They might contribute by denouncing the runaway suspect or responding to the questions that peppered articles: Was there an accomplice? What was Rodríguez Silva's motive? Was it attempted rape? *La Prensa* offered a reward to readers who helped in his capture and fifty pesos to the person who could explain the true motive behind the crime in a hundred words. Prizes and questions within articles served "the goal . . . of stimulating the instincts of observation, deduction, and investigation of its readers." [147] The line between reader and reporter seemed porous at times: *La Prensa*'s representative in León wrote about how he began to look for Rodríguez Silva in his city after reading the newspaper's coverage of his crime and family antecedents. Involvement in the story created engaged readers. A witness told the police that he sat on a park bench with two men to read the newspapers and comment on the murder of Jacinta Aznar; one of them bet one hundred pesos that the main suspect, Alberto Gallegos, was the only killer.[148]

By arousing emotions and readers' "instincts of observation," the nota roja inspired citizens' engagement with broader social issues. In relation to the Tacubaya barbershop murders, the newspaper published one of its "Encuestas Relámpago" (flash polls) to passersby, asking, "Is the regeneration of criminals possible?" Another poll sought opinions about the reestablishment of the death penalty, which the newspaper favored.[149] When the nota roja gathered opinions, however, it was not only with the goal of amplifying the editors' ideological positions or provoking emotions among readers. More generally, these polls sought to involve audiences in the pursuit of truth through the use of critical reason.[150] Skepticism of judicial institutions made citizens' use of common sense essential for public opinion to demand justice. A man from Xochimilco wrote to President Ávila Camacho denouncing a prosecutor who had failed to accuse his brother's killer. The letter writer explained that he was going to deliver his findings to the press, too, "so this agent at least has the very mild sanction that, like the tree, he will be known by his fruits." [151] *Detectives* encouraged readers to bring their grievances against the justice system to the newsroom, promising a thorough investigation: "If you are the victim of injustice, *Detectives* will defend you. We have private policemen, lawyers, physicians, etc." [152] The goal was to achieve a truthful result that could withstand scrutiny in the press and eventually lead to a just outcome. However, as the examples cited above suggest, civic engagement also included calls for the extralegal use of violence against criminals.

The narratives of famous cases often reached their climax with the capture of the criminal. The pursuit of the suspect and the truth formed a single goal in the case of the Tacubaya barbershop: "Follow the fascinating search for the killer in *La Prensa,* and [find out] whether justice manages, in the end, to uncover the motives of this sordid tragedy." [153] People volunteered wild tips on the suspect's whereabouts to the police, but the newspaper scored a triumph when its correspondent led the way to Rodríguez Silva's capture in León. Although prosecution and explanation were different processes, journalists hoped to resolve them simultaneously with a confession and an indictment. The denouement, at least for the most satisfying stories, did not have to wait for a sentence: it came with a confession heard just before the prison doors slammed shut.

The crime of the Tacubaya barbershop turned out to be more complicated than that. Rodríguez Silva maintained, implausibly, that he had killed in self-defense. Although his hands were wounded, the ferocity with which he had stabbed and slashed the women, added to the fact that he had previously bragged of having killed a man, raised doubts about his exculpatory account. The police believed he had tried to rape one of his victims. In order to advance the investigation, Rodríguez Silva was taken to the barbershop to reconstruct the events in front of detectives and prosecutors. The procedure took place at midnight, with officials and suspect arriving through the back door to 80 Patriotismo in order to avoid the crowds of neighbors that still wanted to lynch Rodríguez Silva. (The possibility of a violent end was indeed in the air. When he returned from León, his custodians had to take him off the train before reaching the station, where an irate crowd was waiting for him. Newspapers and public petitions demanded his prompt execution.) During the reconstruction, according to the police, Rodríguez Silva suddenly tried to attack his custodians with one of the razors still at the crime scene, and he was shot to death. The autopsy found twenty bullet holes in his body. No reader would be able to claim the fifty-peso prize offered by *La Prensa* for the correct hypothesis about his motives. Other than that, nobody lamented his end, except perhaps his mother, although she admitted that she had expected her son to come to such an end.[154]

CONCLUSIONS

Starting gradually in the 1960s, the nota roja changed, a shift that might at first seem like decadence. Reporters entered into subordinate relationships with the state institutions they were supposed to scrutinize, while editors imposed an uncritical tone of support for the government. The presentation of suspects to the cameras became a ritual that supplanted the detailed report on the investigation. Images replaced text on newspaper front pages and magazine covers. The "blood pages" lost space within mainstream newspapers and on corner newsstands, ceding ground to increasingly popular sports publications like *Esto* and *Ovaciones*. Critics and insiders recognized the loss of journalistic and literary quality in comparison to the golden age of the 1920s to the 1940s. Radio and television proved more successful at attracting the interest of growing audiences.[155]

This panorama is deceptive, however. If *Alarma!* and *La Prensa* had lost prestige, they still continued to sell in large numbers. The new lowbrow marginality allowed for a freer use of stylistic features that no longer had to be contained to fend off censorship: irony in the use of adjectives and superlatives in headlines, dark humor that reinforced the complicity with knowledgeable male readers, extremely gory images, and more explicit "artistic nudes." The influence of the nota roja on other media persisted. Radio programs with police themes amplified the emotional color of headlines and provided useful information. *La policía siempre vigila,* first aired in 1959, defined itself as a "radio program taken from the archives of the Secret Service." *Cuidado con el hampa,* mentioned above, used a similar format. *El que la hace la paga* dramatized true cases solved by the police.[156] Like radio, television was limited in the content it could broadcast because the airwaves concession system made companies dependent on the government's good graces. A couple of shows in the 1990s echoed nota roja, but they were canceled by presidential orders. The legacy also survived within print journalism. Beginning in the 1980s, print dailies like *unomásuno* and *La Jornada* adopted a more critical stance toward the government. In these publications, petty corruption and police abuse gave way to denunciations that adopted the language of human rights, although a few nota roja chroniclers and photographers continued to produce old-style, quality journalism.[157] Today, *La Prensa,* many local newspapers, and the internet retain the visual languages, engagement with public opinion, and disregard for victims' rights that the nota roja established during its golden age.

This history is similar to that of other countries. Studies of U.S. tabloids, French fait divers, and other forms of crime news show that drawing a too-sharp distinction between these genres and "serious" journalism can lead to a condescending neglect of an important arena of the public sphere. The nota roja also generated narrative innovation, well-defined actors, compelling plots, and a sharp sensibility for the weird, funny, tragic, and unfair in everyday life. Its narratives also had political meanings that a superficial examination can easily miss.[158] What is unique about Mexico's nota roja, I argue, is the role that crime news played in the public sphere. The nota roja became prominent after the late 1920s because after the abolition of criminal jury trials, the judiciary and the police rapidly lost authority when it came to producing a full and definitive account of the causes of and culpability of a crime. The nota roja created a public that could agree on a basic fact of Mexican life: impunity. From that basis, the genre offered a persuasive depiction of reality that incorporated multiple voices. It engaged readers as citizens whose opinions and experience could help solve a case—and pressure authorities to investigate more doggedly. Truth, in sum, was the product of a deliberative and informal process registered by the press as it collected interviews, confessions, letters, and other morsels of evidence. There was no ultimate arbiter for this process. Yet for writers and readers of the nota roja, for relatives of murder victims, and sometimes even for the authorities, truth could only be found in this terrain.

Translating the truth into justice was another problem. Victims or their kin denounced the impunity of criminals in the penal system, and they saw delays and uncertainty spoil any vindication a sentence might eventually provide. Against this backdrop, it is not surprising to see that for criminally literate Mexican citizens, justice was only tangentially associated with the law, and crime was seldom related to punishment.[159] Newspapers came to partially restore these linkages by metaphorically issuing the sentence of public opinion, and through narrative, producing a kind of truth that was more persuasive than that coming out of the judicial system. There were consequences to this sentence of public opinion, however, which were not metaphorical at all. In their coverage of some famous cases, nota roja publications implied that the extrajudicial punishment of suspects or convicts by the police was a more satisfactory alternative than the imprisonment dictated by judges.[160]

Thus, a distinctive aspect of Mexican crime news was the recognition that violence was part of everyday life and governance. From extrajudicial punishment to the mistreatment of prisoners and victims, there was a dark side of reality that readers needed to incorporate into their experience of urban life and citizenship. Male domination was another fact of Mexican reality that the nota roja did not question. Crime news was, increasingly, a domain of public life that excluded women and denied any value to crime victims. In parallel to the growing use of photography, a masculine gaze on female bodies and corpses became dominant, though it had long been part of criminological views of Mexican society. Despite these biases, the criminal literacy built on the nota roja codified the perceptions of corruption, ineptitude, and violence that characterized the postrevolutionary political order from civil society's perspective. But rather than signifying a fatalistic acceptance of things, readers' desire to access objective information was essentially pragmatic: knowledge was useful to chart a daily path in the city so that one could avoid becoming a victim.

The nota roja's view of justice did not serve any narrow political purpose supporting or opposing the dominant party: its critique was political in a broader sense, for it portrayed the national infamy and channeled citizen participation. Its history might not make for an edifying chapter in the narrative of Mexican democratization, but we cannot define the genre as simply propaganda for dehumanizing violence. Lynching, as demanded by the crowd outside the Tacubaya barbershop, and extrajudicial executions, like that finally committed against Rodríguez Silva, remained rare. Behind their threat was a more prevalent social demand for truth and justice expressed by publications like *La Prensa*. The state did not usually meet this demand. Nota roja readers, as citizens, nevertheless continued to see justice as a right associated with the truth, a constantly renewed claim rather than a privilege of modern life.[161]

PART TWO

Actors

___

THREE

Lost Detectives

POLICEMEN, TORTURE, *LEY FUGA*

Detectives and policemen stood on the opposite side of the pursuit of the truth that juries and the nota roja undertook on behalf of the public. This part of the book will shift the focus to actors and practices that undermined justice. The spaces of publicity examined in the previous chapters fostered open discussions about crime and punishment, yet the implicit premise was that impunity prevailed in everyday life. That facet of Mexican reality was central to criminal literacy, yet was not easy to document and debate. Rather than examining famous cases, this chapter deals with the experts who had the modest task of finding the truth but who usually failed to achieve it. More often than not, the work of detectives and policemen dealt with crimes that did not need to be made known to the public. As a result, we have scant information about their procedures. Policemen and detectives were closely connected to each other, as most private detectives had been policemen at one time or another. They shared the basic ability to navigate the underworld and the willingness to produce and keep secrets, whether they worked for the government or private customers. Their lack of social prestige is not surprising given their avoidance of publicity and their tendency to use violence.

This chapter looks first at detectives, including both private sleuths and well-known police investigators; then, it examines the common police agents who, in conducting investigations, preferred results over fame. The contrast in their methods seems obvious: intelligence and astuteness versus brutality and violence. Yet policemen and private detectives were more similar than different. In postrevolutionary Mexico, the promise offered by sophisticated models of detection collided with the primitive reality of routine investigative practices, which depended on confessions obtained through physical abuse or death threats. Both detectives and policemen relied on torture, the possibility of ley fuga, and deception, offering a flawed foundation for official justice and feeding widespread skepticism of the official truth.

ANOMALOUS DETECTIVES

The history of private detectives in the countries where the profession emerged in the nineteenth century, namely France and the United States, does not offer a very useful framework for understanding the Mexican case. In those countries, private policing and investigation were the result of massive changes in economic life. The proliferation of transactions between individuals who did not know each other (when honor and reputation were not enough to guarantee trust, in other words) made snooping useful. In industrial centers, detective agencies offered a means of labor control with a precision and at a scale that local police forces could not reliably provide to companies. Solving crimes was not the main concern for private detectives in either the United States or France: their business was to dig out information and to release it according to their employers' needs. Detectives offered their services for hire through advertisements, paradoxically leaving a small documentary footprint of their existence and their interest in publicity. They were often associated with blackmail and did not enjoy much prestige until the turn of the twentieth century, when they became the protagonists of an entire literary genre.[1] Some of these traits were integral to the identity of the profession in Mexico, even if its development responded to different conditions.

At least through the Porfiriato and until the end of the civil war, economic reasons to hire detectives in Mexico did not exist. Paternalistic labor control and a close scrutiny of public opinion over individual reputations made them unnecessary. The services of the Pinkerton Agency were hired to harass Mexican anarcho-syndicalists in U.S. exile but were not required south of the border, where a few policemen close to the government were in charge of repression and spying.[2] Conditions changed in the 1920s: a new political elite invaded the national and state capitals, and profitable business spilled beyond the control of the oligarchy that had maintained a tight grip on the best opportunities until the fall of Díaz. As we saw in the previous chapter, the daily press rose to such prominence and autonomy that the ability to ensure secrecy acquired new value. Meanwhile, police agencies' capacity to solve serious crimes vanished, overwhelmed as they were by the new power of the revolutionary army and the proliferation of large and small forms of corruption. It is during this decade that some "very skillful detectives," like Valente Quintana and others, rose through the ranks of the Mexico City police to gain public recognition and in some cases started their own business or worked for other state agencies.[3]

In those early decades, there was a new enthusiasm for detective work and for the possibilities of civilians participating in solving crimes. Before the business could be regulated, it seemed to be an open field which anyone with method and initiative could enter. There were journalists who tried their hand, like Guillermo Mellado, a newspaper reporter, author, police officer, and private detective who claimed that journalists often knew better than police agents. His chronicles of famous cases, published under the pen name of Nick Carter, celebrated the wisdom acquired through experience and audacity—a higher form of criminal literacy but one that was not restricted to experts.[4] Detection aficionados, mostly self-taught civilians, offered their services to authorities in difficult cases. Juan González Alejo, from Veracruz, explained to the Federal District police chief that he wanted to help solve a case "so I can have more practice in my studies for Private Detective" and also to serve society.[5]

Such optimism was based on the idea that anyone could learn the trade. As González Alejo said, all that was needed was practice, which could certainly be facilitated by "an identification that will authorize me to undertake all kinds of investigations." Police badges, after all, were liberally dispensed by state agencies. At the same time, knowledge about the techniques of detection was available from multiple sources. Textbooks in English (on fingerprints, ballistics, forensic medicine) were found in detectives' offices. Correspondence courses granted certificates, some rewarding successful students with Sherlock Holmes hats and magnifying glasses. *Argos,* a trade magazine published in the 1930s and 1940s, included articles on technical matters such as the collection of fingerprints.[6] Detective schools, as in other countries, advertised their courses in newspapers. Besides a diverse range of expertise, textbooks characterized detectives as men who could deploy physical energy, realism, and cool thinking. Alongside these options for private education, there were schools formed by police departments and trade organizations. Gradually professionalized, experts coming from these schools could also receive scholarships to study abroad.[7]

High theft rates, weak police institutions, new commercial demand for background checks, and the trade's openness encouraged the emergence of private detective agencies beginning in the 1920s. Some of these agencies advertised in the newspapers and magazines. An agency established by Valente Quintana offered "secret investigations, thefts, vigilance, location, credit, collections, etc.," done by "expert detectives."[8] Agencies also provided technical expertise in graphology, ballistics, and surveillance according to the latest U.S. models.[9] As individuals and companies saturated the business, many complaints against these agencies reached federal and Mexico City authorities. One citizen characterized an agency as "an extortion factory."[10] From a legal perspective, detective companies potentially violated article 21 of the 1917 Constitution, which established that only the Ministerio Público (public prosecutor's office) could be in charge of crime investigations. In practice, private investigation of crimes meant additional protection for those who could afford it. Applicants for official authorization claimed to provide valuable services to commercial firms.[11] In the early 1930s, authorities were trying to rein in the business by restricting licenses. Cristóbal Trápaga, a lawyer hired by the Secretaría de Gobernación to review a petition by Agencia Polmex, concluded that it was not realistic to eliminate all these establishments since they already existed with the blessing of the government; they provided useful surveillance of "damaging and dubious social types," argued Trápaga, at a time when the economic situation was increasing the frequency of theft, and the police were proving increasingly unable to investigate crimes successfully.[12]

This ambivalence was reflected, and probably enhanced, by the law. The Secretaría de Gobernación had to admit that there was no official regulation for private detective agencies in 1934.[13] It was only in 1948 that President Alemán decreed the Reglamento para los Investigadores, Detectives y Policías Privados. It required all private police and detective agencies to request authorization from the Procuraduría General de Justicia and to register the cases they took and the identity of all their agents; they could issue identification cards to their employees, who could not be current agents of official police institutions. Signaling the existence of a widespread problem, the Reglamento banned the use of IDs that bore the national seal or had the shape of the metallic "shield" used by the police. The Reglamento nevertheless allowed for collaboration between detective agencies and the judicial police. If private detectives investigated a crime or a missing person, they had to notify the judicial police and act "as their auxiliary," with the only limitation that they could not take affidavits. State agencies could have their own departments of investigation to look into the probity of their personnel and to investigate crimes that affected them directly. In other words, the

Reglamento opened a broad and poorly defined realm of involvement for private and semi-official detection, only supervised by the same judicial police whose shortcomings required companies and private individuals to pay for the investigations in the first place. Increasing this slippage, police and army officers were often hired by these companies, which provided better salaries and a smooth continuity between the public and private sectors. The porous borders between the two realms were recognized and partially formalized through the creation of a specialized police force at the service of banks and industrial companies. This evidence suggests that the proliferation of police agencies that Diane Davis has attributed to internal political competition was also the result of the police and public prosecutor's limited ability to investigate crimes.[14]

The careers of successful private detectives exemplify the overlap between public and private service. Those who had a name recognizable enough to attract customers often emerged from the ranks of the police, usually moving up the ladder, solving some famous cases that put them in the newspapers, and then commercially capitalizing on their reputation. They did not sell their technical skills so much as their ability to venture into the underworld and use whatever trick worked, relying upon an odd mix of experience, social capital, and arcane knowledge about crime. *Argos,* the trade publication, portrayed the eclecticism of this high form of criminal literacy when it advised prospective detectives to learn slang, fingerprinting techniques, and the tricks and stories used by con men. Such immersive acquisition of knowledge was the best path to deal with crime.[15] Silvestre Fernández, one of the editors of the magazine, was also owner of a detective agency in the 1940s. He moved to Mexico City from Jalisco as a young man. His father worked for the Servicio Secreto of the capital police. Silvestre began with a desk job, became a street cop, and later an agent of the Policía Judicial and the Servicio Secreto. He helped solve the case of the Tacubaya barbershop and many others until "it was difficult not to give him a promotion." He then turned to a more lucrative job as the head of security for the Monte de Piedad (the institution with the official monopoly over pawning), and he later worked for several aviation companies.[16] In early 1946, when he was the manager of the Policía Privada Continental, Fernández solved the "crime that . . . caused the deepest impression in Mexico in the last hundred years." In October 1945, brothers Angel and Miguel Villar Lledías were killed in their opulent home in downtown Mexico City, and many valuables were stolen. The Policía Judicial descended on the crime scene, only for its agents to steal what money was left. When the victims' sister, frail, seventy-year-old María, complained about the police thievery, she was accused of the murders despite evidence that the culprit had overpowered the two victims and then murdered them in a violent fashion. Fernández became interested in the case out of curiosity and because of his friendship with the suspect's lawyer. María's innocence was evident to him from the beginning, as was the "mountain of failures and mistakes by the official police." Thanks to information volunteered anonymously, a 50,000-peso reward offered by María, and his friendship with the governor of the state of Hidalgo, Fernández was able to find the true criminals (a construction worker and a ex-convict who had fled to the state of Hidalgo) and recover part of the bounty.[17]

The most famous Mexican detective was Valente Quintana. He was born in the border city of Matamoros, Tamaulipas, in 1889, and as a young adult moved to Brownsville, Texas, where he studied at the Detectives School of America, and worked for the police. In 1917, he joined the Mexico City police, beginning as a cop in uniform but eventually reaching the highest rank. His role in solving a large train robbery in 1921, the famous Tren de Laredo case, made his reputation. Yet his relationship with the government had its ups and downs. Several of the criminals he captured, according to his memoirs, escaped prison or were acquitted in suspicious circumstances. He used to joke that the only case he could never solve was that of "the gang of the politicians." In 1926, he left the police force to establish his Bufete Nacional de Investigaciones, but he was brought back to work on important cases, including the 1927 and 1928 attempts against Obregón discussed in chapter 2. In 1929, President Emilio Portes Gil made him chief of the Mexico City police, the only civilian to occupy the position for many decades.[18] In that capacity, he participated in the repression of Vasconcelista demonstrations and uncovered a plot to assassinate President Ortiz Rubio in 1930.[19] However, he was accused of taking bribes from a gang of swindlers and had to resign. Until his death in the late 1960s, he worked as a private detective in Mexico City as well as promoting boxers. The exploits of this "Mexican Sherlock Holmes" were praised by the foreign press, he became the subject of comic book series, of a couple of movies in the 1950s, and was the inspiration for a character in Rodolfo Usigli's 1944 murder novel *Ensayo de un crimen*, discussed in chapter 7.[20]

Quintana's successes were based on a very pragmatic combination of showmanship, knowledge of the underworld, and discreet use of force. He often disguised himself, changing his clothes and voice to appear as a lowly mule driver, a drunkard, an upper-class tourist, or a hunter. He had been an actor before coming to the capital, after all. The goal of his disguises was to gain the confidence of possible witnesses and suspects and to get them to talk about the crime. The device worked best during his incursions into the city's underworld, where he would overhear conversations between ruffians. His memoir, written with the help of a journalist, contains descriptions of dangerous places that readers were advised to shun, and where criminals had their natural habitat, like the barrio Atlampa, "the Sodom of Modern Mexico." For one investigation, he dressed as a tramp in order to join a group of men smoking marijuana under a bridge. In several cases in the book, Quintana does not explain how he managed to identify the suspects: he simply knew a lot of people in the world of crime.[21] In a visit to Texas, when he was chief of the capital police, he told newspapers that he kept "a complete history, past and present, of every resident of Mexico City. Not a single individual escapes. If a man cannot show proof that he is engaged in a legitimate trade of some kind he is either deported, jailed, or required to engage immediately in some legitimate pursuit." As a result, he bragged, felons have been "entirely eradicated" from the city.[22] This vast archive might have been a fantasy of social hygiene: there is no other evidence that it existed or even that it helped him solve specific cases.

In practice, Quintana applied rather conventional means. He used deception both in the field with disguises and during in the interrogation of suspects. Quintana would tell them that their accomplices had already incriminated them, extracting confessions that in the case of the 1927 attempt against Obregón led to the arrest and execution of four men, including Agustín Pro.[23] Quintana also used violence. In his memoir, he had no qualms about describing how he detained suspects at gunpoint, promising immediate death if they did not surrender, and how he obtained statements with similar threats. Although he never tortured prisoners, according to his account, he had a reputation for doing so and certainly coordinated with others who used torture. In the case of Obregón's assassination, Toral acknowledged the participation of Acevedo only after other agents had tortured him. Quintana told Toral that he could end his suffering and protect his family from similar treatment if he cooperated.[24]

All the detectives mentioned here were at odds with the Mexican justice system. Fernández's most famous case, the Villar Lledías double murder, was an indictment of the dishonesty of the Policía Judicial. Quintana saw some of his victories thwarted by porous prisons and accusations of corruption. Other detectives criticized the inability of prisons to rehabilitate criminals and claimed that the police could solve only a small fraction of homicide cases.[25] The two were admired for their skills and knowledge about the world of crime but did not claim to embody the inexorable arm of justice. For Quintana, punishment was merely an afterthought, even when it took the form of the ley fuga against rape suspects he had captured in Veracruz.[26] Detectives generally enjoyed little prestige: reporters claimed to best them at every turn, and as we will see in chapter 6, even fiction writers made fun of them. The main reason for this was not corruption so much as the fact that the methods of Mexican detectives could hardly be understood as a scientific path to the truth behind a crime. Immersion in the underworld, threats, deception, and violence were the antithesis of the public use of reason in matters of crime. Rather than offering a technically advanced model for this endeavor that would strengthen the role of public opinion in the pursuit of the truth, detectives remained too close to the police and their methods.

OBSCURE POLICEMEN

When detection was in the hands of actual policemen, it took place mostly through agencies that were no more transparent than private investigators. The 1917 Constitution gave the judiciary the authority to investigate crimes and mandated the creation of the Policía Judicial. This left the Mexico City and other police departments in charge only of preventive policing. For decades, the police department nevertheless maintained an office, ominously called the Servicio Secreto, charged with investigating high-profile crimes, usually homicides and large robberies. The office was not strictly constitutional, perhaps, but it was necessary according to its apologists. Conceived as an elite group of agents, which in the early days included Valente Quintana, the Servicio Secreto had an ambiguous reputation as an effective although poorly regulated office. It received political directives regarding the crimes that would have priority. Its agents gained favorable nota roja coverage in some cases, but with time, the agency came to be synonymous with spying and political repression rather than detection. Agents usually ascended through the ranks of the department, as had Quintana, and like him, they could easily be fired or depart for better jobs. Their methods, documented in the Federal District Historical Archive, did not give much weight to scientific procedures, instead mostly relying on testimonies and confessions obtained through diverse and sometimes brutal methods.[27]

Concerned about the appearance of empiricism, police authorities sponsored several schools for agents. Although the technical foundations of the field of detection were prestigious enough, the actual schools associated with the Federal District's police department failed to dispel the perception of improvisation and violence that characterized the institution in the public's view. Foreign teachers were brought for some subjects, but the notion prevailed among cadres that experience and an intuitive knowledge of human nature were irreplaceable, and that training was only a waiting period in the process of recruitment. Superiors placed less importance on academic education than on personal ability when assigning cases to agents. Thus, for example, the investigation of sexual offenses was often trusted to female agents, who were thought to have a special expertise on rape because of their sex. Despite their role in solving such cases as the Goyo Cárdenas multiple homicides, none of these women ascended the ranks.[28]

For the majority of police officers, male and female, the rewards were nil in terms of social recognition and precarious in terms of reumuneration. Their uniforms were dirty and old. Their salaries were low and subject to discounts in the form of fees to the Partido Nacional Revolucionario, and they saw wages withheld for other, often unexplained, reasons. Their pension funds could disappear, and they could lose the bond they had to post when they started working.[29] They were always exposed to danger, but investigations of the murder of police agents did not always result in arrests.[30] Promotions and hires were often influenced by recommendations from powerful people rather than merit. In the mind of some agents, this situation might have justified engaging in practices that came to define the vices of the profession. Policemen stole from victims and suspects and demanded money in exchange for the arrest or release of suspects.[31] Although turnover was high, it remained difficult to make a career in the force for those who persevered. The chief of the Mexico City police was usually a member of the military. The job of police agent in Mexico City "has been considered a perk for some military chiefs and for civilians who are relatives or friends of high-level officials."[32] In 1946, policemen and detectives created the Instituto Mexicano de Policía, a trade organization intended to establish modern police methods, foster professionalization, improve wages, and achieve full insurance coverage for police agents.[33] It does not seem to have lasted long.

Among the few agents who made a career of policing, experience and direct knowledge of the practices, spaces, and languages of criminals was the key qualification but not a guarantee of success. For example, Jesús Ríos

Guzarnotegui began in 1914 at the lowest level, joined the Servicio Secreto, and became an officer. He then moved to the Ministerio Público and later back to the Servicio Secreto.[34] Veterans had no time for science; they knew there were certain inexplicable patterns in the world of crime that only experience revealed: if a body was found in a prone position, one agent claimed, the murderer was going to be arrested, just as inevitably as criminals returned to the crime scene after some time.[35] Known to specialize in "the most lurid and mysterious murders," agent José Acosta Juárez acquired some celebrity when he participated in the capture of Goyo Cárdenas in 1942. This did not have a great impact on his career: in 1948, after twenty-eight years on the force, from his initial position as a street cop, or gendarme, he still worked as a detective.[36]

Technical knowledge was no match for resourcefulness when there was pressure to obtain quick results. If an agent had to use political influence in order to capture a suspect, or if he had to pretend to be a lawyer in order to obtain information leading to the killers of a fellow officer, so be it. There was no point in keeping data organized during the investigation. Through the 1930s, before forensic experts began to exert some influence, the Mexico City police department had very limited technical capabilities. Evidence was collected haphazardly at the crime scene, with such carelessness in some cases that much of it was lost. It did not help that journalists and other busybodies crowded the crime scene, often taking objects with them like mementos or photographs to be published in the newspapers.[37] In fact, crime scenes could become stages for the competition between journalists, local residents, and policemen from different agencies. The Servicio Secreto often competed with the Ministerio Público and the city's Policía Judicial. If the last two prevailed, their rivals claimed, then judges would give light sentences to the accused. Rather than sharing information, agencies hid it from each other, and there were frequent moments of tension. With time, the number of government investigative agencies increased, all of them striving for the public reward that followed a break in a case or the capture of a suspect. Collaboration was exceptional and only happened when ordered from above. Many crimes, including some homicides, were simply not investigated because they did not attract press interest, had no political value, or no victims or relatives intervened. Some were abandoned without investigation after being labeled suicides.[38]

Once an investigation began, the most direct path to a resolution was to single out and capture a suspect and then create a situation that would induce a confession. Detention in the police cells or the municipal jail was not a pleasant experience, and ideally this would be enough to push the suspect to give up. After the indictment, prosecutors often conducted a reconstruction of the events at the crime scene, in the presence of the judge, jury, and sometimes the press. The ostensible goal of the procedure was to reenact the events according to existing testimonies in order to reconcile any apparent contradiction or gap in witnesses' and suspects' accounts. Yet there were two implicit purposes that were more important. One was to prompt the suspect to describe the crime in his or her own words one more time, with the expectation of eliciting a contradiction that would force him or her to acknowledge previous lies.[39] The second was to create a dramatic moment, an almost theatrical re-creation of the crime that would, in the eyes of the public, confirm the criminal nature of the indicted and hopefully sharpen his or her feeling of guilt. In a 1951 reconstruction of the events outside Mexico City, a sibling of the victim played the role of the deceased—both brothers were shepherds—and tension escalated to the point that the brother began to strike the suspects, who then confessed. The neighbors who were watching the procedure demanded that the suspects be hanged on the spot.[40] In most cases, the drama was covered by reporters and photographers. The prosecutors served as stage directors. In the case of the Tacubaya barbershop, discussed in the previous chapter, their role went much further when they killed suspect Rodríguez Silva as he was allegedly trying to attack them during the reconstruction at the crime scene.

Torture was a more reliable tool of police investigations. The practice of inflicting physical or emotional suffering on prisoners became commonly associated with police work beginning in the 1920s. Victims of torture, their relatives, and even newspapers denounced it, sometimes with euphemisms such as "energetic interrogation," while police authorities strenuously denied it or vowed to punish those agents who used it. Although it could occur at any stage of the investigation, torture was frequently used before the indictment.[41] In contrast with the reconstruction of events, it had to take place behind closed doors. Before torture began to be denounced by human rights organizations in the 1980s, it was barely documented. Its use during the middle decades of the twentieth century can be pieced together from a few direct testimonies, glimpses from diverse perspectives, and multiple silences that need to be interpreted in the context of social perceptions of the police. But it certainly happened and was an open secret of police stations. Informants recommended that detectives use it in order to obtain confirmation of their hypotheses; Servicio Secreto agents were often accused of using torture simply to obtain money from the prisoner.[42]

Several techniques were available. Prisoners could be hanged in particularly painful positions: from their thumbs, feet, armpits, knees, or wrists, to then be beaten and burned; their heads could be submerged in water buckets or tubs (the infamous *pocito,* little well, in the basement of police stations); they could be forced to squat with their arms wide and be hit in the stomach if they moved; or carbonated water, sometimes mixed with chili powder, could be sprayed up their nostrils. They could be deprived of food or prevented from sleeping by having their cells flooded, as happened to Toral and other suspects in his case. Rape could be used against women. Prisoners could be told that their relatives were being tortured and made to hear voices of agony to prove it. Other forms of psychological torture such as simulated executions were also used.[43] Later testimonies also describe the use of electric shocks, but I have not found evidence of their use before the 1970s.

Unlike its use as part of counterinsurgency and state terrorism in Latin America later in the century, torture in postrevolutionary Mexican police stations was not conceived as a form of psychological warfare or as a performance of the ideological dehumanization of enemies.[44] For Mexican policemen, there were two main purposes. The first was to obtain a quick confession. Once the prisoner had admitted his or her guilt, all other kinds of investigation were unnecessary, and the investigator's job was done. *Detectives,* usually not a critic of the police, lamented that torture persisted as "the police force continues to fabricate criminals in a rush because of its desire to claim success in its investigations."[45] The legal value of these confessions was only slightly undermined when suspects recanted on the advice of their lawyers and claimed their innocence. Yet judges could easily disregard statements in which suspects recanted. This response seems to have been common enough for the police to call it a habit among prisoners and to print a generic form in which they denied the allegation, leaving only a blank space to enter the name of the alleged victim. They used the form to counter the allegation by the wife of Alejandro Ponce de León about the "savage physical and moral torture" inflicted on her husband, a suspect in a 1954 homicide. However, an internal document in this same case recognized the effectiveness of "severe interrogations."[46] The second reason to use torture was to obtain information about accomplices or the whereabouts of the bounty. Even when the victim of torture was not a suspect, police agents were confident in the value of the information thus obtained.[47]

Torture, in sum, was at the heart of police investigation, hidden from sight but widely known to occur. Even when torture was only a possibility, it defined the dangers faced by citizens when dealing with the police. Thus, agents used the mere threat of arrest as a tool to extract information from witnesses. Gabriel Alarcón requested an amparo from a judge against a warrant arguing "that my life is in danger if I go to the court to tell the truth that I know." [48] Other suspects admitted they preferred to remain at large, even if they were innocent, rather than suffering the torments they expected at the police station. The threat was also used against suspects who contradicted the official version of events. [49] The fact that the police and judiciary insisted that torture could produce the truth about a crime was the key contradiction between their perspective and civil society's perceptions of justice.

LEY FUGA

This threat was all the more effective when it was accompanied by the possibility of death at the hands of the police. According to Martín Luis Guzmán, in 1931, "criminals acquired the habit of killing themselves in the cellar of the police headquarters, and all of them, strangely enough, committed suicide with a .45 caliber automatic handgun." [50] In 1936, *La Prensa* presented such cases as routine: "Two suicides at the police headquarters. Only one of them managed to kill himself immediately. The killer of an alcohol inspector hung himself in his cell. A con man named José Fuentes Núñez tried to slit his throat with a razor blade and is dying." [51] Other cases of dubious suicides took place at the penitentiary.

That tone of irony was absent when the prisoners officially died in the hands of the police. The case of Rodríguez Silva, killed during the reconstruction of the crime at the Tacubaya barbershop, was reported as anything but an accident (figure 8). [52] His death was an extension of the police investigation and explained as a consequence of his reluctance to fully confess. He had been interrogated for days after his capture, and he had continued to argue that he had killed the women in self-defense, showing the wounds on his hands as proof. In a bulletin to the press issued after his death, the police explained that Rodríguez Silva, "like everyone who lies, fell into numerous contradictions," compelling investigators to set up the reconstruction of events at the barbershop. The result was not a confession, but Rodríguez Silva's death provided a successful end to the investigation. In the words of

¡LO GALLECUEARON!

INFORMACION EN PAGINA TRES

LA PRENSA
Diario Ilustrado de la Mañana

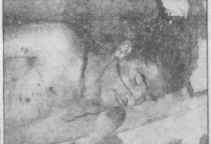

| AÑO VI | NUM. 2082 | MEXICO, D. F., JUEVES 3 DE MAYO DE 1934. | FUNDADOR: PABLO LANGARICA |

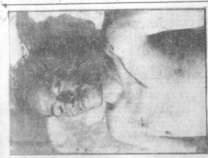

HE AQUI AL CHA-CAL.—Santiago Rodríguez Silva, el asesino de las calles del Patriotismo, arriba, a la izquierda, completamente desnudo en la camilla en que fue transportado de Tacubaya hasta el Juárez. A la derecha, el cadáver mostrando los orificios que hicieron las balas disparadas por empleados policiacos al darle muerte la madrugada de ayer.

EN EL HOSPITAL JUAREZ.—Grupo de estudiantes de Medicina en los momentos en que observaban el cadáver de Santiago Rodríguez Silva en el anfiteatro del Hospital Juárez adonde fue conducido para que se practicara la autopsia de ley, después de llevar el cadáver desde las calles del Patriotismo hasta esa institución de Beneficencia y estudio.

PARECE QUE FUE ENCONTRADO EL "CUATRO VIENTOS"

INFORMACION EN PAGINA DOS

FIGURE 8. Death of Rodríguez Silva. *La Prensa*, 3 May 1934, p. 1.

the police chief, General José Juan Méndez, the death of the suspect meant that "the horrible crime on Patriotismo street has found an epilogue."[53] The implication was that the suspect's death was not only the immediate result of his attempt to attack agents with a razor blade but also proof of the accusation against him: he had killed the women with the same weapon he tried to use against the police, after all. Rather than denouncing a possible abuse, *La Prensa* editors depicted the shooting as a logical response to Tacubaya residents who demanded "the head of the murderer; that he be hanged from a tree; that he receive the ley fuga."[54]

The ley fuga, in which prisoners were killed by soldiers or policemen alleging that they were trying to escape, was an extension of the practices described above which took place outside police stations but had a similar value in terms of the investigation. Public by definition, the ley fuga was also a form of extrajudicial punishment that often won support from the press. Alberto Gallegos, sentenced for killing Chinta Aznar, was an emblematic victim of the practice. At one point during the trip to the Islas Marías, he stood up to grab the typewriter he had placed above his seat, and Captain Armando Vázquez Cavazos shot him in the neck. His body was dumped by the train tracks, and Vázquez Cavazos explained that Gallegos had tried to escape and had to be killed.[55] A textbook example of the ley fuga, this was not a rarity "because," according to a reporter, "guards usually eliminated the most dangerous criminals even though they were sentenced to spend several years in prison."[56] Gallegos had been shaken by the realization of his possible fate when he had learned that Luis Romero Carrasco (who had killed his uncles, their maid, and their parrot in 1929) had been shot while en route to the Islas Marías. *La Prensa* celebrated the guard's bullets for "freeing society, once and for all, of a constant danger."[57] Gallegos's story generated a verb: "galleguear," a euphemism for the ley fuga applied to other cases during the 1930s, including *La Prensa*'s coverage of Rodríguez Silva's end.

The ley fuga became a broadly cited reference in public culture, appearing in contexts ranging from political conflict to law enforcement. Everard Meade has documented increasing press interest in ley fuga cases in the 1930s after the abolition of the death penalty, including cases of lynchings that ended as ley fuga.[58] Editorials in favor of the reinstatement of the death penalty included language that demanded that it be applied swiftly; one called for "identification and death. No more" as the only way to stop crime waves.[59] Thus, the ley fuga was not merely a demonstration of the weakness of the state: by ironically referring to the legality of executions (it was not a law, after all), and giving a central role to state agents, it was justifiable as a complement to state action, increasing the severity of punishment and instilling fear in would-be criminals.

Dating back to the civil wars of the nineteenth century and the Porfiriato, the ley fuga maintained considerable public support after the revolution. Even though it was carried out by state agents, it was associated with lynching (a practice in which officials were not involved) as a response to a state that could not be trusted with the protection of honor and property. Querido Moheno, as quoted in an earlier chapter, defended extrajudicial violence as a social reaction to a state that would not guarantee honor and justice.[60] For nota roja readers and editors, there was no clear hierarchy distinguishing legal and informal justice, so they were not shy about expressing support for the extralegal use of violence. In a 1932 editorial entitled "Crime and Impunity," *La Prensa* formulated the argument in terms that would remain valid in the following decades: legal penalties were too benign, prisoners escaped, and the "ineptitude and impotence of the police" encouraged the activity of criminals.[61] When the murderers of Senator Mauro Angulo (a case discussed in chapter 5) suffered the ley fuga in 1948 on a Veracruz road, the press claimed that in the absence of the death penalty, the outcome was as good as could be expected.[62] *Últimas Noticias* claimed that the ley fuga could be understood as a "defensive reaction of society" which involved "the collective subconscious."[63]

Despite the support it found in the press, the ley fuga faced the same kind of resistance from potential victims as did torture. After Marciano Armenta and his two alleged accomplices in the Angulo case were arrested, authorities received letters and telegrams from their lawyers and relatives protesting their irregular detention and torture. Armenta's lawyer accused the Federal District's police chief of ignoring an amparo.[64] The sister of one of the suspects, Elvira Armenta Barradas, presented another writ of habeas corpus and warned that "such extended and unjustified detention makes me think that the goal is to kill my aforementioned brother with the use of the famous Ley Fuga."[65] The suspects were indeed killed on a Veracruz highway, as will be discussed further in chapter 5. The response of authorities in this case was slightly more substantive than the preprinted denial they often used when accused of practicing torture. According to Pedro J. Castro, chief of the Federal District's Servicio Secreto, he had to shoot them.[66] Castro declared, in response to criticism from Federal District prosecutor Carlos Franco Sodi, that he was not "a killer" and that the death of the suspects under his direct custody was "very embarrassing" for him, as he was a member of the army with a clean record. He explained that he did not apply the ley fuga because doing so would tarnish his honor as a military man. Yet his reputation was at stake: if he had allowed Armenta to escape, he acknowledged, suspicion would have fallen on him because of the suspects' wealth; he had no choice but to kill them. He also recognized the logic of the ley fuga as punishment: facing the dilemma between failing in his assignment to guard the suspects and "avoiding, by any means necessary, that the crime remained unpunished," he chose the latter.[67]

In the following decades, the practice continued to be recognized as a possible outcome in every case. A civilian from Nayarit offered his help to the Mexico City police chief to capture the suspected murderer of two police officers, suggesting that he could do more than merely conducting an arrest: "Mr. Inspector, I want to know if you only want the person mentioned alive, I am asking instructions from you in case it is not possible to catch him alive, so you can decide." [68] Even though the ley fuga could not be publicly acknowledged, it remained part of police methods. Along with torture, it helped investigators extract confessions. In some cases, the use of the ley fuga reflected the involvement of civil society: Gallegos and Rodríguez Silva were killed after newspapers had interviewed them and depicted both as undeniably guilty. In their cases, and many others, the death of the criminal was a fitting end for a trial that had already taken place in the court of public opinion. The ley fuga was a form of punishment, even if in that role it undermined the fundamental separation of police, judiciary, and penal functions in Mexican law.[69] In less visible cases, however, the ley fuga illustrated the idiosyncrasies of Mexican investigations. Policemen often argued that their efforts to find criminals were sabotaged by the judiciary. Unlike torture, the use of the ley fuga could lead to tensions between police officers and judicial authorities, as happened in Armenta's case.[70]

CONCLUSIONS

Torture and ley fuga were the most visible among other practices whose lack of transparency defined Mexican detective work. Just like private detectives, policemen were responsible for finding the criminal, but they lacked the authority to explain and punish the crime. While the press aired hypotheses about crimes and suspects, and judges dispensed punishment, policemen and detectives were often forced to keep the methods and results of their work a secret. Despite the merits some police and detectives may have had, the criminally literate public assumed that detection in Mexico had an uncertain link to the truth.

Some policemen explained this frustrating perception of inferiority as a product of the undue influence of politics on their work. Among the hundreds of pages that Servicio Secreto agents kept from their investigation of the 1936 murder of Deputy Manlio Fabio Altamirano (to be discussed in chapter 5), someone inserted an undated newspaper clipping entitled "Politics versus Police" that expressed the dilemma between obedience and the truth that police investigators faced in high-profile cases. The clipping is worth quoting at length, while we imagine the approval its words invited among readers at police stations:

> The main difficulty that the police has to face when it is trying to solve so-called political crimes ... is the veto power of friendships over detection.
> The police easily discovers the mechanism of a crime, defines responsibilities and identifies the culprits, but it is not uncommon for it to be forced to keep the result of its work quiet, even if it looks inept, because that is demanded by political influences. . . .
> Thus when a crime is committed in which professional politicians seem to be involved the public tends to doubt that the police will get to the bottom of the affair. Some cases partly justify that skepticism. Haven't we seen the material perpetrators of certain crimes overcome by a sudden desire to kill themselves before they could say what they knew? There have been cases like these, and the best part is that when they commit suicide, public rage is satisfied and the investigation is closed.[71]

Policemen in the middle decades of the twentieth century faced an epistemological trap: the greater a crime's public impact, the stronger the urgency to obtain the truth about it through any means available, even if those means further undermined civilians' trust in their profession. Agents had "to fabricate criminals." While low-level police officers lacked social recognition, elite branches of the police force like the Servicio Secreto remained associated with violence and abuse of power. The problem, of course, was of their own creation. But it was also insurmountable: everybody knew that impunity, rather than justice, was the most likely outcome even for the smallest cases. The hope that detectives' technical knowledge and intuition would bring out the truth disappeared in the hands of policemen.

Many of the features of the Mexican police described in this chapter resonate strongly with recent scholarship and experience. Studies of contemporary police institutions and their members take corruption as a basic, almost self-evident starting point. Bribery moves up from the lowest levels of the ranks to the upper brass, encouraging predatory behaviors that seek to extract resources from poorly regulated or illegal sectors of the economy, including robbery, prostitution, and drug trafficking. The discretionary application of the penal law and administrative regulations and the lawlessness of police behavior are compounded by the rivalry between different agencies, creating an environment of violence and distrust both within these institutions and in their interactions with citizens. Several of the methods described in the previous pages have survived, if not expanded: the murky association with informants, the use of torture, the reliance on confession, and the politicization of investigations.[72] Although documenting the continuity of these practices from the 1920s to the present would require another book, it is safe to say that the relationship between the police and the truth has remained problematic. Today, any hope that police investigators might uncover the culprits of a crime is based on the assumption of an intimate relationship between cops and criminals, rather than on detectives' technical acumen or intuition. While in the 1920s it was possible to imagine Valente Quintana infiltrating the underworld to solve a case, today it is easier to imagine that police findings are the result of transactions between criminals and their official sponsors. The illusion of detection has been permanently lost, but its demise had been in the making for almost a century.

FOUR

Horrible Crimes

MURDERERS AS AUTHORS

The infamy of killing was a form of truth that promised immortality. Even authorities had to recognize it. When the police department set out to create a museum at the Escuela de Policía in 1932, the school's director gathered "photographs and other valuable objects" linked to a list of "murderers" whose last names sounded familiar to everyone: Gallegos, Romero Carrasco, Toral, Teresa de Landa, Vilchis, madre Conchita. These names were at the heart of criminal literacy. They condensed useful lessons: Juan Guerrero Lemus, for example, asked the police to send his son Esteban, who had acquired the habit of stealing, to the Islas Marías "before he becomes another Romero Carrasco." [1] They also provided ignominious examples: lesser criminals admitted to drawing inspiration from the famous ones, such as an imitator of Goyo Cárdenas who buried his victims. Cárdenas was so famous that his nickname, el Goyo, was all that needed to be mentioned. There were jokes, plays, pornographic movies, and according to newspapers, a wave of crimes dubbed "goyomanía." [2] Other cases resonated for many years, even when their protagonists were less famous. Such was the case of Petra the tamale vendor from the Lagunilla neighborhood, who in the early twentieth century was rumored to stuff her product with human flesh. She was emulated by another woman in the 1970s who used the remains of her abusive husband. [3] Petra's legacy did not carry her name but exemplified the creative and disturbing possibilities of crime.

Although famous criminals were nothing new, the stories of individual infamy to be examined in this chapter signaled a new way to understand crime and, by extension, urban life and individualism. I did not select those stories because they best represented the many others that were ignored by the press. As discussed in chapters 1 and 2, certain institutions and media decided who would acquire criminal fame. Those characters were then further mythologized by literary fiction, as will be shown in chapters 6 and 7. They have also helped historians understand modernization in original and productive ways.[4] Rather than studying their cases to understand broader social problems, however, this chapter will show how they transformed the meanings of murder. They were not just examples, I argue, but key references for speaking about crime and violence in postrevolutionary Mexico.

Until the 1920s, murderers were considered through the lenses of romantic passion or positivist science. Romantic conceptions of crimes of passion took the form of tragic stories in which the murderer was a good man, usually not from the lower classes, driven to kill his loved one by the inevitable obligation of honor.[5] Although crimes of passion continued to feature in the press during the twentieth century, they were now limited as forms of individual expression. Passion was becoming simply a psychological force that overwhelmed the intelligence of the killer. Thus, the 1932 "passion tragedy of the Restaurant Broadway" provided some salacious details about a couple's life, but coverage presented little of interest on the personality of Guillermo Gosserez, who killed his wife's lover at the restaurant upon discovering her infidelity. What once could have been a compelling moral tale was now simply a defense of male prerogative. Society, argued lawyers like Moheno, had to forgive these crimes rather than delve into their psychological origins since anyone would commit them in defense of honor.[6] Like Gosserez, postrevolutionary criminals of passion seemed to lack any interesting features. Fernando García Castillo, for example, killed his ex-wife in 1941 simply "because I had to do it." The reporter who interviewed him in the prosecutor's office presented him as barely able to speak. "I am an imbecile," García Castillo recognized. Instead, for the reporter, the story was an example of a worrying social trend: "the decomposition of the Mexican household" owing to the "many Mexican mothers who allow modernism to take over their customs."[7] Though the label of passion continued to be applied to stories of domestic violence, these now seemed to lack any redeeming moral value. Instead, these crimes were merely symptoms of the ills of the times. As with a 1970 murder-suicide, little was left to reconstruct the tragedy other than grizzly images of bodies. "The grave keeps the secret of love!" concluded *Alarma!*.[8]

The decline of crimes of passion coincided with that of "the criminal" as a well-defined human type. The idea of a criminal type was at the center of positivist criminology's authoritative diagnostic of the deleterious effects of Mexico's late nineteenth-century modernization. The biological theses of criminal anthropology acquired hegemonic influence during the second part of the Porfiriato, when members of a small but influential group of positivists around Díaz wrote about crime, endorsed the construction of a modern penitentiary, and cited the findings of the Italian school of criminologists, particularly Cesare Lombroso, as self-evident truths applicable to Mexican society. The theory behind the science involved a racially charged division between "the criminal" and other kinds of human beings.[9] Among the most famous murderers of the Porfirian period were Francisco Guerrero, known as "El Chalequero," who killed a number of prostitutes in the desolate outskirts in the city in the late 1880s, and Jesús Negrete, "El Tigre de Santa Julia," an urban bandit who gunned down several men in the course of robberies, escapes, and acts of revenge. Both were poor and uneducated men whose indigenous appearance seemed to reflect the threat of old Mexican habits of violence. Criminologists described them as typical examples of the "Lombrosian" criminal, with primitive cranial features and other telltale signs of deviant propensities.[10] After the revolution, this expert knowledge began to lose its ideological value, even though Lombroso and others continued to be read and cited by lawyers and journalists. The 1929 Federal District penal code, inspired by a positivist notion of punishment as a defense of the social organism, gave scientists a role in determining the length of sentences according to the criminal potential of the convict. But the code was soon replaced by a new one in 1931 which recovered classical ideas about crime as a voluntary act and punishment in proportion to the crime's gravity.[11]

The characters at the center of infamous cases in the twentieth century were difficult to interpret within the frameworks of passion or science because their actions had a subjective dimension which demanded new ways of understanding violence. Murder stories now provided opportunities to look into killers' mental lives and undermine their radical otherness in the process. Put differently, famous criminals provided new ways to think about oneself, to link the subjective realm and social life in a changing world.[12] But this did not make them less disturbing—on the contrary, the murderers examined in this chapter were harder to explain and the narratives they provided, although detailed, often failed to make any moral sense. As we will see, they seemed to kill for pleasure, their choice of victims seemed arbitrary, only intended to satisfy their appetites or to acquire fame, and each represented a unique case that could not be reduced by generalizations.

The best way to cope with the new complexity of murder was to tell it as a story. Journalists, scientists, writers, and readers apprehended the new criminals through narratives, complete with a plot and a cast of characters in which the personality of the criminal was both the centerpiece and its most memorable feature. As a result, the confession, an account of the crime that came from the suspect rather than investigators, became the best representation of the truth of the events, if not always the motivations, of a crime. In public or legal form, voluntary or given under duress, confessions had articulated individual responsibility in judicial and religious venues since colonial times, marking the intersection of individuals' conscience and social norms. Recognizing guilt could win leniency from criminal juries. During the era of the nota roja, confessions were no longer expected to elicit mercy; if anything, they were the product of reporters' perseverance in bringing to light the truth of a suspect's conscience. In detective stories, the resolution coincided with the confessions of suspects pushed to admit their guilt by the skillful detectives' tricks.[13] In judicial and police practice, agents commonly extracted confessions by means of torture or threat. After all, as noted in chapter 3, confessions simplified their work and were readily accepted by judges.

These confessional narratives are part of a long literary tradition in which murder was discussed as art form and murderers compared to artists. Thomas de Quincey provided the most commonly cited formulation of this idea in *On Murder,* an 1827 ironic take on romantic notions of beauty and authorship. The impact of de Quincey's idea on Mexican writers will be explored in chapter 7, but I found no reference to him in actual murder cases. The Marquis de Sade, by contrast, was frequently mentioned in discussions of the association of violence and pleasure. The word "sadist" was applied to criminals by the early decades of the twentieth century, usually referring to the use of violence in the context of sexual attacks. By the 1940s, "sadism" was often applied by experts and laymen to criminals like Goyo Cárdenas. The term was not simply an adjective but also referred to the troubling link between murder and erotism that Sade explored in his books. These were not translated to Spanish until the 1960s, but the notion of sadism became widely known among experts through Richard von Krafft-Ebing's 1886 *Psychopathia Sexualis* and later Sigmund Freud's work.[14]

Sade's ideas served as a theory of crime in Mexican interpretations of infamous Mexican murderers. For Sade's characters, murder heightened sexual pleasure, making libertinage "always ... preferable to the monotonous and lackluster charms of virtue." Thus, the pain and destruction inflicted on victims (usually women and minors) could only be called a crime in reference to mistaken human laws: they were in fact a service to Nature, for which death and desire, in its highest expression, always went together.[15] Roumagnac and Alfonso Quiroz Cuarón alluded to Sade in their studies of Mexican criminals. While he was in France writing *El laberinto de la soledad*, Octavio Paz wrote "El prisionero," a poem that paid tribute to Sade's revelations about the integral connection between death and pleasure. Paz pointed to the broad appropriation of Sade's "truth" by "the wise man, the writer" but also by "the maniac." Perhaps referring to figures like Goyo Cárdenas and other "maniacs," Paz added that Sade's name was "a tattoo of infamy on certain foreheads."[16]

Paz listed criminals next to writers because murderers became authors in the era of the nota roja. Since the nineteenth century, there had been infamous characters who inspired widely circulated stories, particularly highway bandits and thieves like Chucho el Roto. Positivist obsession with the biological causes of crime gave some common criminals the opportunity to get their own stories in writing, as did the murderer and prostitute María Villa.[17] María del Pilar Moreno's saga, examined in chapter 1, hailed a new era in which the words of murderers were widely published and closely scrutinized. The term "autor del crimen" was commonly used, reflecting a double meaning of the Spanish word *autor* (creator and culprit) not present in English.

The "author of the crime" provided readers with an individual perspective that reporters or detectives could not offer consistently: the former because they usually did not have a byline, and the latter because, as we saw in chapter 3, they had a complicated relationship with the truth. By contrast, murderers left material traces of their crimes and, through confessions, produced the most direct account of their actions.[18] Authorship encompassed the performance of violent acts that were invested with meaning as well as oral or written accounts of those acts. The modern definition of literary authorship is problematic: it can be an arbitrary way to classify and explain actions and words. The emergence of the modern notion of the author was in itself an act of transgression, subject to juridical constraints. Michel Foucault explored this in his study of the nineteenth-century account produced by a barely literate French patricide, Pierre Rivière, for whom "the murder and the narrative of the murder were consubstantial."[19]

Postrevolutionary journalists and experts looked for firsthand accounts from the underworld. The *Revista de Policía* published a selection of the diary of a woman found dead in a hotel room. The document, "a poignant drama," described her arrival in the capital, her work as a *fichera* dancing for money and as a prostitute, and her addiction to morphine, which brought her to the lowest levels of the underworld, next to other "degenerates like me."[20] In the nineteenth century, fascinating texts were produced in prison by suspects awaiting a sentence. The Porfirian dictatorship sent political journalists to Belem prison so often that they had their own area, with better appointments than those available to common criminals, where they were able to continue work for their newspapers. Under the right conditions, prison offered the ideal setting for a writer: solitude, silence, and time. Famous criminals enjoyed similar privileges when wardens treated them like "aristocrats of crime."[21]

The perception of criminals as authors was reinforced by the visual resources of the nota roja. Diagrams of the crime scene contained fingerprints and footprints that worked as a signature. Photographic and hand-drawn portraits suggested psychological insights. Alberto Gallegos appeared as both an author and a criminal on the front page of *La Prensa,* where a cropped image of his portrait, with carefully combed hair, was superimposed on the facsimile of his typewritten confession; he sold photographic portraits for a living and was therefore better able to control his image in the press.[22] Toral was pleased by the drawings made of him by an *Excélsior* artist during his trial. The composition on the front page of *La Prensa* certified Rodríguez Silva's authorship of the Tacubaya crime: his face looking into the camera, an extended hand showing the wounds he received when he killed the women, and a brief note in his handwriting ("I am ready to confess my crime"), verified with his fingerprints and a seal from the León police department (figure 7).[23]

The basic question in public discussions of these criminals was no longer whether old pathologies and family history caused the crime but whether the crime was exceptional or in keeping with the suspect's past. It was inevitable to ask this question when considering the trajectory of chemistry student Goyo Cárdenas, the morally dubious past of Ema Martínez, or the wrestling career of Pancho Valentino. These suspects, and the scientists who examined them, shared the assumption that the criminal act was the most authentic expression of individuality. Murder gave a few people an opportunity that most others lacked: to have their image, words, and past presented in public to explain their actions.

ALBERTO GALLEGOS

People had knocked on Jacinta Aznar's door at 17 Insurgentes Avenue for weeks with no response. A strange smell came from the house, but nothing was done until her friends called the police. On February 23, 1932, firefighters broke into the house, followed by detectives and journalists. The intolerable stench, they discovered, came from Aznar's body, which lay on the living room floor. She laid supine, with arms and legs outstretched, her face disfigured by trauma. Based on the size of the larvae in the body, and the dates of the newspapers under the door, police technicians wearing gas masks dated her death to around a month earlier. Thus began a case that would become paradigmatic for narratives of detection and justice in the following decades, auguring "a new and staggering form of criminality" and the emergence of the murderer as a public figure.[24]

The ingredients of a mystery in the style of Agatha Christie seemed to be all there—except perhaps for the putrefying body. The victim belonged to the Yucatecan upper class. She had studied and traveled around the world, claimed to have been close to the king of Spain, and frequented the most elegant places in Mexico City, always noticeable because of her beauty and distinction. She had a darker side, too: she lived alone, her lawyer and other employees could barely tolerate her irascible character, and her family kept her at arm's length.[25] The rental income that made her fancy lifestyle possible was beginning to diminish. Young male friends escorted her to restaurants and jewelry stories, but nobody knew of any stable relationship. For a while, the police looked for an elegant gentleman who sported a silver-handle cane and a tailored suit, whom witnesses had seen leaving her house; some believed he was from Argentina, others from Cuba, but he was never found.

The case inspired the involvement of the public. It was passionately discussed "in cafes, in cantinas, in the tramway and everywhere, even in homes."[26] *La Prensa* in Mexico City, and *La Prensa* in San Antonio, Texas, among other newspapers, followed the investigation very closely. The magazine *Detective* presented its coverage as a parallel investigation to that of the police, a new "special police service."[27] Through the press, authorities encouraged witnesses to come forward, and some did: people wrote to the police to offer "a lead," "or maybe a hypothesis that is not so harebrained," suggesting names to look into and scenarios to explain the crime.[28] There was no shortage of expressions of outrage and shock, and pressure on investigators mounted as days went by. "Society is attentive to the punishment of these vile assassins," warned an anonymous letter to the police chief.[29] Detectives and judges were disoriented by the motley cast of characters that emerged: the victim's driver; the main suspect, Alberto Gallegos, a portrait salesman; his father, a humble former Zapatista, and his boss, a bespectacled man who retouched photographs; the missing Argentine dandy.[30]

Gallegos could not have been more different from the cerebral Christie murderer. He was a tall man with large hands and the kind of protruding lower jaw that, according to positivist criminologists, suggested innate criminal tendencies. He had been in prison in the United States and Mexico, and experts deemed that he had a "highly erotic temperament."[31] When he saw his name in print (his signature had been found on a partially burned piece of paper at the crime scene), Gallegos came forward and presented a story so far-fetched that the police arrested him on the spot. He declared that he sold framed and retouched photographic portraits and that Aznar was a client. On January 22, he called at her house and an elegant man, whom he had seen before arguing with her over the signing of some papers, came to open the door. As he walked to his car, he told Gallegos: "Go upstairs and do not say anything about what you will see there unless you want the same thing to happen to you." Gallegos climbed the stairs and found Aznar on the floor, bleeding from her head, mumbling for help. He went for some water and saw her die. Scared by the threat of the stranger, he hurried out of the house and left, intending to keep his silence—until he saw his name in the newspaper. After the arrest, he maintained his innocence despite long interrogations. The police chief himself tried to elicit contradictions in his account, but only got him to admit that, even though he claimed to be a brave man, he was scared and ran away after Aznar's death. Although Gallegos declared that he had not suffered any form of torture, the Texas newspaper reported that he was kept awake for four days, agents taking turns asking him questions, until he broke down in tears. Yet he maintained his implausible account, and "the fog that continues to encircle judges, police officers and journalists." Questioned about some inconsistencies,[32] he responded with literary flair: "The illogical has always been the seed of the truth."[33] Even the police chief told him during an interrogation that he had "a talent for making things up."[34]

Gallegos only confessed on March 18, when two men, Eugenio Montiel and Juan Sánchez, declared that they saw him beat Aznar with a tube before ransacking the house and sharing the spoils with them. Other witnesses declared that Gallegos had been speaking about a plan to rob a wealthy woman he knew. From his cell, Gallegos typed a confession confirming these accounts in general terms. A few days later, however, he changed his mind again. He asked to cross-examine the two witnesses who claimed to have seen him commit the crime. The judge allowed it, and Gallegos was able to bring out contradictions in their accounts. He shouted that he was innocent, as were the two alleged accomplices that had testified against him. When confronted with the pages of his confession, Gallegos took it from the judge's hands and used a lighter to bring out a message he had written with invisible ink: "Everything written here is false, I have done it to prove that I am innocent."[35] He explained that the police had pressured him to sign it. Montiel and Sánchez also changed their statements, claiming that interrogators had threatened them with prison or death if they did not blame Gallegos. These sensational revelations had no effect on the trial or public opinion: newspapers had already characterized Gallegos as a cynical but intelligent liar, spectators at the court hearings called him a fake, and the judge declared him guilty. He was sentenced to twenty-two years in prison, and his alleged accomplices received shorter sentences. Upon review by a higher court, his sentence was reduced to twenty years, and Montiel and Sánchez were absolved.[36]

Shortly after his arrest, Gallegos began giving interviews to the press from his cell. These were intimate yet wide-ranging conversations in which he spoke about the case but also his literary and musical tastes. Gallegos admitted enjoying the newspapers, particularly "the letters from my [female] admirers, and the police stories, which fascinate me." In another "moving interview," he cried when his father visited him.[37] He also cried when the police chief told him that his reputation was at stake, and he raised his voice in anger when somebody in the crowd called him "the murderer": "Scoundrel! How do you dare calling me a murderer!" In his statements to the police and the press, he insisted that "I am not afraid of justice because one day the truth will be known."[38] Gallegos was aware of public perceptions of his person. He was careful about his presentation to the camera, and during police interrogations he expressed his feelings yet kept his stylish demeanor, always well dressed and with a relaxed pose (figure 6). For Miguel Gil, a reporter for *La Prensa,* Gallegos was smarter than most journalists; he commented that Gil's was "a pretty newspaper" and pleaded: "Let's see if you can help me."[39]

Gil's reporting probably did help Gallegos. *La Prensa* reproduced Gallegos' written confession on its cover, combined with his portrait, and transcribed it inside (figure 9). He had written it over two nights of pacing inside his cell, crying in his bed, and typing under the light of a candle. The text was a skillful piece of self-presentation. Addressed to the assistant director of the Belem prison, César Cervantes, it thanked him for words of kindness that "have reached the bottom of my heart," because "you saw in me not a despicable criminal of habit for whom any attempt at regeneration was

FIGURE 9. Gallegos's confession. *La Prensa*, 21 Mar. 1932, p. 1.

almost impossible, but a poor unfortunate pushed by fate to commit a crime in a moment of insanity." He had decided to confess "everything" because "the voice of my conscience has not died inside me," and he could not bear to see two innocent men imprisoned for his crime. He knew that the confession would shame his parents but also expected their forgiveness. On January 21, he had breakfast with "my beloved Anita" and left her with a kiss, promising to come back for dinner. "The morning was full of sun and joy and I walked these streets, happy, relaxed and confident, carrying my suitcase and smoking a cigarette." Aznar approached him in the post office while he was selling portraits. She was "a respectable lady of some 45 or 50 years, well dressed, almost elegant." She told him to come to her house to work on a couple of portraits. When he arrived, she was not home, so he left the message the police found later. She came later that afternoon and handed him a portrait of King Alfonso XIII to colorize. When she took him to her bedroom, to show him other portraits, he saw a set of earrings with stones. "In those moments, . . . the damned idea of theft possessed me, and I felt something horrible." She noticed his intentions, they struggled, and he beat her to death. After the crime, he was overwhelmed by remorse: "With my hands covered in blood and having turned into a lunatic, I stood up, I felt that my legs were failing me, and when I walked my steps were like those of a drunkard, I thought I was going crazy, I sat on a chair because I could not walk and I started crying like a madman." He then erased his fingerprints, washed his hands, and took a few things. Of Cervantes, Gallegos only asked him to "judge me as you want, I did it in a moment of insanity, of fear, I will never be able to explain to myself how I committed that crime." He finished begging for forgiveness, and promising to confess everything to the judge.[40]

Gallegos recanted this confession days later. Perhaps he expected his newly acquired celebrity to afford him some protection from the dangers of imprisonment, but it was to no avail. After the sentencing, when he was told to prepare for the trip to the Islas Marías, fear kept him speechless for several seconds. He had already been struck when he heard that Romero Carrasco had suffered the ley fuga on the way to the islands and reportedly attempted suicide.[41] Preparing to leave for the penal colony, Gallegos told journalists that he was not going to attempt an escape from the train. But his fate was sealed. Some newspapers even predicted the place and time of his death days in advance. It was a brutal end for a short-lived celebrity, and a warning for criminal suspects who were willing to use their newfound fame to avoid punishment.

Ten years later, another man who left decomposing female bodies in his wake became the object of everyone's attention. Like Gallegos, Gregorio "Goyo" Cárdenas, a bespectacled chemistry student at the National University, was a talkative prisoner who relished celebrity and was eager to share his feelings. Their two stories were otherwise very different. Contemporary scholarship about Goyo Cárdenas argues that in his case, science was decisive in saving him from meeting an end like that suffered by Gallegos. Multiple studies commissioned by judges made Cárdenas the object of intersecting disciplines vying for scientific authority. *Novedades* joked that readers were more interested in whether Cárdenas would take a shower in jail than in "the situation in Stalingrad."[42] His celebrity was a product of his willingness to talk to the media and his shrewd manipulation of the different knowledges that were supposed to explain him and treat his deviance. Goyo, as he was known by all criminally literate Mexicans, was not so different from other famous murderers, but he was better than most at playing the hand he was dealt.

The story began on September 1942 with lawyer Manuel Arias Córdova frantically looking for his daughter, Graciela Arias Ávalos. As was the practice in similar cases, female police agents assigned to the case looked first for her boyfriend, who happened to be Goyo. Agent Ana María Dorantes found that Cárdenas, on the advice of his mother, had checked himself into Dr. Gregorio Oneto Barenque's private mental sanatorium.[43] The police sent two other female agents disguised as nurses, and soon got Oneto Barenque to admit that Cárdenas had confessed to killing Arias Ávalos and three other women.[44] While this was going on, Goyo's neighbors in Tacuba told the police that somebody had to break into his house at 20 Mar del Norte: they had noticed big green flies and a smell of putrefaction, and from a nearby roof, someone had spotted a human foot sticking out of the recently disturbed soil in the backyard. By the time policemen, investigators, journalists, and Arias Córdova reached the house, a bare, rather dirty, but ample structure where Cárdenas went to study and conduct experiments, a crowd of neighbors was waiting outside. Workers extracted four shallowly buried bodies. In addition to Arias Ávalos, there were three other victims, all prostitutes. Cárdenas confessed that he had picked them up on separate nights, taking them to the house to have sex. Afterward, he had strangled them with a rough cord he used to hold test tubes. His account would evolve in the following weeks, but it was the shocking images of the crime scene, including newspaper photographs of the disinterred bodies, that came to define the story. While posterity remembered this as simply the case of Goyo Cárdenas and focused on his psychological state, labels applied to the story early on suggest that at first this case was not seen as very different from other episodes of moral aberration: "the Tacuba strangler," "the Totonac Blue Beard," "the monster," "troglodytic student," "the ferocious jackal."[45]

Strong reactions from the public resembled those voiced about Gallegos. Housewives wrote to the president and newspapers, congressmen gave speeches demanding the reinstatement of the death penalty, and even female prisoners asked for swift justice, similar to that met by Gallegos. People insulted and threw stones at Cárdenas as he was taken to the hospital or to prison. There was something new about him, though. He was a student, drove his own car, read, and enjoyed modern life, yet also performed brutal acts that evoked primitive criminal behavior. An anonymous letter to the police argued that Cárdenas represented an extreme version of the same threat that all students posed to downtown residents going about their daily life: "the indications of indescribable cruelty, of savagery, of true barbarism, of stupidity, of rudeness, of cruelty . . . that university students boast . . . [as] individuals thirsty of pleasure, orgies, concupiscence."[46]

Cárdenas did not fit the mold of the Lombrosian born criminal. He came from Veracruz, where his family owned rural properties. In the capital, he was one of the founding members of the Oil Workers Union in 1936, worked as a typist in several state agencies, and studied chemical engineering at the National University with a scholarship from the state oil company, although by 1942 he was only in the second year of the program and had not graduated. His car and house indicated some prosperity and independence, although he still lived with his mother. When he was arrested, the family had enough resources to hire prestigious lawyers and seek the advice of Oneto Barenque and other experts. Unlike Gallegos, Cárdenas had not been motivated by robbery: his murders seemed to be an extension of his sexual impulses, and there was no evidence that he had any accomplices.[47]

Diverse interpretations soon emerged, sharing the unanimous condemnation of the crimes but differing on the causes and meaning of Cárdenas's behavior. Experts and lay people joined in a true "interpretive feast," to use Carlos Monsiváis's apt words, based on the criminal's own accounts of his deeds and character.[48] Exiled Spanish sexologist and herpetologist Martín de Lucenay did not know Cárdenas but sent La Prensa a manuscript where he

FIGURE 10. Gregorio Cárdenas typing. *La Prensa,* 10
Sept. 1942, p. 40.

offered a critical interpretation that was, he argued, as good as any other: "We
do not need to reach the heights of Freudian theories to speculate, without
exacting scientific rigor, about the really extraordinary case of the great sadist
Gregorio Cárdenas Hernández, whose crime has prompted morbid publicity." [49] As in Sade's books, according to Lucenay, Goyo killed as part of his
need for sexual satisfaction; love, passion, or any kind of sympathy for victims
was foreign to his behavior.

Cárdenas managed to profit from that "morbid propaganda" by retaining
some control over accounts of his life and crimes. He had multiple opportunities to put forward his own explanation, as journalists attended his depositions and were authorized to visit him during his first days in jail. [50] He had a
facility for writing, and one psychiatrist called him "an intellecualized criminal." [51] At the police station, he typed his first confession, which he titled
"Statement by the suspect chemical engineer Gregorio Cárdenas Hernández"
(figure 10). His accounts pointed to deep psychological impulses. Just after

having sex with the prostitutes, he wrote, something overcame him. He described his behavior almost as an out-of-body experience: "My brain was not right." Switching to the third person, he continued: "Cárdenas was not there . . . he had turned into a beast," full of hate toward women. The split was even starker in the fourth crime, the murder of his girlfriend, Arias Ávalos: "Life smiled upon both of us, always in love, always satisfied," but they had had an argument in his car because he was jealous and even though "I loved her dearly," "again the beast took over me . . . I was insane, I killed that which I adored so much." [52] After each crime, Cárdenas wrote, he was overcome by remorse, buried his victims, prayed for them, and went to church to seek God's forgiveness.

Professing to be puzzled by his own actions, Cárdenas later offered various accounts. He alternatively blamed jealousy, mental disease, and the pursuit of science. In interviews with journalists, psychiatrists, and criminologists, he claimed that he had conducted experiments on the first victims, trying to see if adrenaline extracted from the glands of one would revive another. He said he had sex with them before or after killing them. Judges ordered multiple studies of his personality in order to ascertain whether he was criminally responsible or should be committed to a mental institution instead. [53] He was questioned at length, injected with truth serum, and subjected to electroencephalograms and electroshocks. Voluntarily or not, he provided ample information about his life, his relationships with the victims, and just about any topic he was asked about. He liked movies "of scientific character or with a philosophical plot, because I have never liked romantic movies"; he said "[I] preferred to read poems in general and the literary works of Sor Juana Inés de la Cruz, Fray Luis de León, Fray Servando Teresa de Mier, philosophical works, among which I have preferred the doctrines of Kant and Auguste Comte, and the Catholic Bible." [54] Anything, he seemed to assume, could be relevant to help explain such a disturbing anomaly in his behavior.

Cárdenas, perhaps advised by lawyers and doctors, complicated all explanations but fundamentally tried to seem mentally insane in order to avoid prison. When he was arrested at Oneto Barenque's clinic, he performed as a rather clownish "crazy," claiming to be invisible and scribbling formulas on an imaginary blackboard. His attorney requested a psychiatric examination, and Goyo's behavior persuaded the judge to suspend the proceedings of the criminal case and have him interned at the state mental institution, La Castañeda. [55] For five years, Goyo thrived there, taking on the administration of a store, developing a relationship with a female employee, and going out with her to hotels and the movies, all while keeping experts believing that he could not be declared legally responsible for his crimes. The director of La Castañeda, Dr. Leopoldo Salazar Viniegra, explained that during his internment, Goyo "educated himself for simulation" in order to deceive experts, reading what had been written about him, and "invoking public fame; the opinions of people who were lay in psychiatry but had the opportunity to meet him. . . . He attended psychiatry classes and took shorthand notes." Concerned that such freedoms would cause further scandal, Salazar Viniegra added that he could not provide the vigilance necessary to ensure prevention of future escapes. After another doctor proposed that Goyo should receive a lobotomy, Cárdenas fled, only to be immediately captured in Oaxaca. In all, his escapades made a mockery of the justice system. A sister of Graciela Arias Ávalos wrote to President Alemán in 1948, demanding justice. She suggested that she could have obtained revenge using her own money but hoped that there would be real punishment for Goyo: "I put the murderer in the hands of Justice," yet now he enjoyed all kinds of freedoms at La Castañeda, going to the movies and cabarets.[56]

After Cárdenas was captured in Oaxaca, the judge ordered new tests to evaluate his mental state. Salazar Viniegra declared that there was no longer anything wrong with Goyo's mind, so he could be tried as a normal criminal. Another study proposed that he should continue his internment in La Castañeda until cured. A third evaluation, by Alfonso Quiroz Cuarón, concluded that Cárdenas exhibited physiological and mental anomalies and a "perverse disposition." His simulations of mental imbalance were a reflection of "the excitement of his personality" but were also intended to avoid punishment. Quiroz Cuarón proposed that Cárdenas not be tried as a sane person: he was still potentially dangerous to society and had to be permanently isolated in prison.[57]

Cárdenas was thus sent to the Lecumberri penitentiary, punished without a sentence for his devious manipulation of science. He shifted strategies there, now emphasizing his legal rights. He and his sisters wrote to President Alemán complaining that, according to the constitution and the penal code, he could not be imprisoned at the penitentiary if he was mentally ill; and if he was not, he had to be sentenced in order to set a term for his incarceration. With the same diligence he had applied to psychiatry in La Castañeda, he studied the law. Even though he now endured harsher conditions, he conducted himself as a rational person. He wrote three books, played music, gave legal advice to other inmates, knit bags, got married, and had five children. Yet judges and defense lawyer were reluctant to touch his case, and successive presidents ignored his pleas for a pardon, even when his wife and children engaged in a hunger strike in front of the presidential palace. He was only able to leave in 1976, after his lawyer argued that he should be found guilty of his crimes and released, as he had already served more time than the maximum penalty for his offense. By that time, his relation with prison authorities had improved. In probably the strangest scene in the history of Mexican penology, he was invited by the minister of gobernación to a session of the Chamber of Deputies and applauded as an example of a regenerated criminal.[58]

Contemporary scholars have interpreted the Goyo Cárdenas case as a moment in which psychiatrists, doctors, and criminologists imposed their authority over the judiciary. When Cárdenas was first declared mentally unfit to stand trial, as Everard Meade points out, he avoided both the harsh treatment usually faced by suspects reluctant to confess and the dangers of an incarceration that might very well have ended in the ley fuga. Bringing the focus back to Goyo's own story, rather than to the cultural or juridical implications of his case, suggests a different conclusion. He chose the terms in which his deeds and his psyche were going to be discussed by both laymen and experts: he first pretended to be insane, but by the end of his incarceration he adopted a strictly legal perspective on his rights. Early on, he used the interest of the nota roja to protect himself, and throughout his years of confinement, he accepted his celebrity with resignation as people continued to visit him in prison, seeing him as a kind of freak. From that relatively autonomous position, Cárdenas antagonized both judges and doctors. He argued, for example, that the Quiroz Cuarón's report, which sent him back to Lecumberri, was just the penal system's underhanded way to punish him, not a scientific effort to find the truth about his health.[59]

There seemed to be an undercurrent of antagonism between the murderer and the experts. In his report, Quiroz Cuarón included photographs of Cárdenas dressed as a geisha as evidence "that his sexual evolution was not correct, it was not differentiated and he had a homosexual tendency."[60] Cárdenas, in turn, claimed that Quiroz Cuarón was himself a homosexual who made unwanted advances on prisoners. In general, Cárdenas expressed a very low opinion of the science of mental disease. Of his interactions with famous Spanish doctor Gonzalo Rodríguez Lafora, he wrote: "Of course I was never sincere with him and gave him false answers; I had no reason to be frank. I had read some psychiatry and knew his goal; Dr. Lafora, like any physician . . . wanted to have unseemly facts to apply norms, psychological as well as psychiatric, that nobody believes in . . . because this branch of medicine still leaves much to be desired." Rodríguez Lafora did not like it when Cárdenas asked him how many patients he had cured. He had been invited by the defense to offer his expert advice but was later sued by Goyo's family for publishing embarrassing information about them.[61]

Despite Cárdenas's infamy and the "interpretive feast" around him, the truth about his crime was never officially confirmed: he was not found guilty of his crimes, and his motivations were never clarified. He did not mention the murders in the books he wrote from prison. His victims were not prominent in scientific or popular discussions of his case, as if their status as prostitutes or girlfriends made them natural prey for a deviant mind. His enduring celebrity meant the persistence of a vague threat: young women were potential victims if they dared walking the streets of the city at night. The press dubbed other episodes of violence against women "goyomanía," detectives interrogated suspects about their knowledge of Goyo's case, and pornographic movies, jokes, and theater shows played out on the legend.[62] This was the tacit counterpart to the detailed psychological knowledge Gregorio Cárdenas bequeathed Mexican criminal literacy.

Of the cadre of experts involved in the Cárdenas case, Dr. Alfonso Quiroz Cuarón (1910–1978) was the most celebrated and is an apt exemplar of the new, scientific, approach to crime that was called for by the times. As a young man, Quiroz Cuarón migrated from northern Mexico to the capital and began working for the government as a secretary in a penal court. He then became a forensic technician, studied medicine, and had a successful career as an expert on crime working in state and academic institutions. Two events in his youth left a strong personal impression on him and marked his professional calling; they also exemplified the dangers of modern crime and the limits of official justice in postrevolutionary Mexico. The first was the death of his father, who was killed by a fellow railroad employee during a robbery when Alfonso was fifteen years old. The murderer was later killed in an incident orchestrated by the prison director, a friend who wanted to avenge Quiroz Cuarón's father. The second event was the 1928 assassination of president-elect Álvaro Obregón, whose autopsy Quiroz Cuarón was able to attend as a medical student. The procedure was so poorly conducted that it created serious doubts about the accusation against Toral and raised the possibility of a cover-up (as discussed in chapter 1).[63]

Shaped by direct experience and scientific aspiration, rather than academic structures, Quiroz Cuarón devoted his career to elevating the intellectual level of forensic science by exploring the minds of criminals in depth. His name was associated with detective work against international criminals. One example of his accomplishments in this field was the identification of Leon Trotsky's assassin, Ramón Mercader, who for years would only give his name as Jacques Mornard. Quiroz Cuarón claimed to have found the true identity of the suspect in Spanish police archives.[64] Another, probably more productive aspect of his law enforcement interests were his books and work on organized crime, which emphasized the cross-border dimensions and sophistication of modern criminals, including in this category some guerrilla organizations. Dismantling gangs devoted to forgery required expert local knowledge and international collaborations made possible by relationships which Quiroz Cuarón developed during his frequent travels. In the course of his work, he organized an office of detective services for the Banco de México. Although this corporative brand of detective work was intended to help banks prevent losses, it also reflected an expanding concern about the activities of organized crime. In Mexico, these gangs often found their victims among the wealthy, both locals and tourists. They were involved in fraud, kidnapping, drug trafficking, and prostitution. Unlike the typical criminal, they included elegant, smart, cosmopolitan men and attractive women, and they used their own international criminal slang.[65] Detectives had to learn their language and modus operandi, wrote *Argos,* but above all, they had to collaborate with police agencies in other countries. Just as they encouraged this outward-looking modernization, however, these slippery criminals also threatened detectives' integrity: for example, a group which included Peruvians, Spaniards, and Mexicans defrauded the Banco de México of large sums in the early 1930s; those arrested managed to escape, and there was a rumor that they had shared their gains with Valente Quintana.[66]

A well-known expert when the discipline of criminology was still not fully professionalized, Quiroz Cuarón became the government's go-to man in matters of crime: he worked as advisor to penal institutions, performed psychological evaluations, wrote books, and taught on multiple topics. For Spanish jurist Mariano Ruiz Funes, Quiroz Cuarón embodied the variegated sources of the discipline: he "knows criminology, that is, anthropology or biology, criminal psychology and sociology," accumulating the kind of expertise that would in normal circumstances have required the collaboration of several experts.[67] He combined work in prisons and laboratories with a variety of methodological inspirations. He used Lombroso, whose biological reasoning had been temporarily rejected by the discipline but, Quiroz

Cuarón argued, was now vindicated by medicine; he also drew from the findings of anatomy, pathology, and psychiatry; he applied psychoanalysis liberally through citations of Freud and references to the "collective subconscious."[68]

Quiroz Cuarón applied his robust but eclectic knowledge to themes as diverse as prostitution, sexuality, psychiatry, political violence, statistics, and bank robbery. But his reputation as a scholar mostly derived from his texts on the crimes and personalities of murderers like Gregorio Cárdenas, Higinio Sobera de la Flor, and Mercader. These extensive reports were intended to help judges decide on the criminal responsibility of the suspects and their treatment; their reports included large amounts of information on a variety of aspects of the criminals' bodies and minds, from urine samples to cranial configurations, speech patterns, and dreams. Rehabilitation, however, was not the goal. Recommendations included life custody for a mentally disturbed man who still posed a threat (Cárdenas), a lobotomy for a violent offender (Sobera de la Flor), and the longest possible sentence for a sane man who murdered with deliberation (Mercader).[69] Although the basic question was simple (whether the suspect was "*loco*" according to article 68 of the penal code), Quiroz Cuarón managed to produce meandering studies in a prose laden with jargon and quotations from authorities. The technical and obscure quality of Quiroz Cuarón's explanations may have been intended to satisfy the judges who requested the studies, but the publication of the reports undoubtedly catered to readers' fascination with the murderers that occupied the nota roja. His 1952 book *Un estrangulador de mujeres* included photographs of Goyo Cárdenas naked (his identity feebly protected with the use of initials and a black box over his eyes) and of the corpses of his victims.[70] Proceeding through accumulation rather than following a guiding principle, Quiroz Cuarón had little concern about the compatibility of the theories behind each authority he cited. He used psychoanalysis extensively while also explaining very specific aspects of the suspects' behavior through anatomical abnormalities, inherited predispositions, or other pathologies. Quiroz Cuarón also judged their actions in moral terms, citing passion, revenge, and other feelings. Among the social bases of criminals' behavior he included the "ethnic element of revenge."[71] His method, in sum, only expanded and updated the eclectic accumulation of explanations that had characterized Porfirian criminologists.

Criminology after the revolution did not achieve the coherence and influence that its practitioners had hoped for since the Porfiriato. This was not

Quiroz Cuarón's fault, of course: the borders of his discipline were not clearly set, and the sprawling research approaches that he and his colleagues embraced were not easily taught. Despite his academic standing, Quiroz Cuarón never saw the creation of a professional school of criminology at the National University, where he studied and taught until the end of his life. The problem was the centrality of criminals in the public sphere, which overshadowed the status of transgression as a scientific object. Quiroz Cuarón's recommendations after his studies of specific cases were to individualize punishment or treatment and to reform penal legislation in order to give greater power to medical experts. Yet his report on Cárdenas reflects the fundamental failure of criminological knowledge to impose itself on the penal process and more pointedly on interpretations of crime. Asked by the judge to deliver an opinion on the criminal responsibility of the suspect, after two contradictory reports, Quiroz Cuarón summarized all previous studies of Cárdenas and produced a table detailing the methods, theories, and conclusions of each one. He then added his own tests and recommendations. Yet neither Quiroz Cuarón nor the other experts who examined and proffered opinions about Cárdenas ever conceived the debate in terms of the superiority of one framework over the others: they applied criminal anthropology, pathology, psychiatry, and psychoanalysis like so many layers of paint over a canvas.

The wide-ranging use of diverse authorities and methods concealed a contradiction at the heart of Quiroz Cuarón's intellectual project. He vowed to expand the authority and capability of science applied to crime, yet he made the individuality of the criminal the key to that knowledge. Quiroz Cuarón shared a premise with many lay and expert contemporaries, namely that the history and mental state of the criminal were the ultimate, irreducible explanation of each crime. In a study of the cranium of the Tigre de Santa Julia, Quiroz Cuarón explained that "the criminal act is the most intimate and individual of each criminal. It is the deepest product of his entire personality; in that act intersect hereditary tendencies and the forces of learning. . . . temperamental tendencies and character. In the moment of crime the present forces of his life but also all his past act upon the subject. Therefore, criminal behavior is only technically understandable through the comprehensive study of the personality of the criminal." [72] Thus, his brand of criminology was a continuation of public fascination expressed by the popular press, not its polar opposite. Since his studies dealt with cases in which the authorship and basic facts of murder (the who and the how) were not in question, Quiroz

Cuarón could only use science to solve the problem of the why. Discussing Mercader, he conceded that it was difficult to understand how an otherwise normal person would kill an old man in such violent way, and he concluded that "to interpret this enigma the best techniques were required; to discover the truth not in the books, but inside the criminal, who in the last analysis is the only owner of his secret."[73]

Mercader's case, however, proved that it was not always possible to reach inside the criminal's mind. The man who in 1940 murdered Leon Trotsky in his Coyoacán house gave his name as Jacques Mornard. Authorities realized that he was obviously an educated, healthy, intelligent man, not a *loco*, yet they could not extract any evidence from him about a Stalinist conspiracy similar to others associated with previous attempts against Trotsky. Mornard stated that he hated his victim because of his interference in his relationship with a woman, and because he thought he had betrayed the working classes. Mercader was the first suspect in Mexico to undergo an electroencephalogram, which revealed only that he understood Russian. Quiroz Cuarón and psychiatrist José Gómez Robleda interviewed him for hundreds of hours, examining his dreams, drawings, anatomy, and brain functions. Dismissing the communist conspiracy, they came to the conclusion that Mornard had killed Trotsky because he saw him as a representation of his father and was suddenly overcome by his Oedipal impulses.[74] Yet nothing was known about the murderer's family, as the name he provided could not be verified. In 1950, taking a set of fingerprints to Spanish archives, Quiroz Cuarón was able to identify Mornard as Ramón Mercader. Further information about Mercader confirmed the decisive role that his mother, Caridad del Río, had in the crime—not as a result of an Oedipus complex but rather because she had recruited her son to participate in a complex operation ordered and financed by the Soviet government.[75]

Mercader was the opposite of the famous Mexican criminals of his era: he refused to give interviews to the press, worked modestly in the penitentiary as a teacher, and kept quiet on the reasons for his crime through the twenty years of his incarceration. On Quiroz Cuarón's advice, Mercader was denied early parole. He managed to survive Lecumberri, despite a guard's offer to Trotsky's widow, Natalia Sedova, to kill him for money.[76] After his release in 1961, Mercader was treated as a hero upon his arrival in Moscow, where he received a medal, a dacha, and a pension. Even then, instead of publicity and fame Mercader chose silence and isolation, biding his time until he was able to fulfill his desire to return to Paris and then Cuba, where his mother was born, and where he died three years after her, in 1978.[77] As with the other famous murders examined here, however, his crime gave him a place in history and explained his life.

The murder of Catholic priest Juan Fullana Taberner on the night of January 8, 1957, seemed to be one of those outrageous crimes that could easily unify public opinion. Crowds outside the church, at the funeral, and near the police station demanded that the culprits be lynched or suffer the ley fuga. Newspapers saw the case as a symptom of the "endemic putrefaction . . . that Mexico is suffering in these days," in "a time of multiple subversions to spiritual values." Fascinated by the case, people from across the country offered to collaborate with the authorities to find the criminals.[78] Yet the story had such a motley cast of characters that it was impossible to reduce it to a conspiracy or a sadistic act of pleasure. It was as if the famous murderers who preceded this case had created expectations for complex and sophisticated criminals that could not always be fulfilled. As in many other contemporary examples of homicide, the culprits were not particularly articulate, and their actions did not have much meaning beyond the satisfaction of their predatory needs.

The victim, by contrast, was an educated man, Spanish by origin, who had just officiated mass in the church of Fatima, at 107 Chiapas St., in the mostly upper-class Colonia Roma. Fullana Taberner's body was found tied and gagged in the kitchen of the house adjacent to the church, with death caused by trauma and asphyxiation. The house and temple had been ransacked and an image of the virgin destroyed. Liturgical objects and money had been stolen. The press called it a "sacrilegious theft" and reported that about fifty agents had been assigned to the case.[79] Police set out to question people who might have had a motive to kill Fullana Taberner, but it turned out there were several since the victim had an irascible disposition. Servicio Secreto detectives wasted little time on the niceties of forensics: the criminals had been careful enough to leave no fingerprints but otherwise proved to be quite disorganized, suggesting that they were "professional but coarse."[80] Thus, agents went straight to their contacts in pawnshops and hung out under cover in places where criminals were known to socialize, in the neighborhoods of Tepito, Jamaica, and Tacubaya. Soon enough, they arrested a suspect who confessed after "broad and detailed interrogations" and led them to other participants.

The testimonies of those involved were contradictory in some details but overall revealed a sloppy bunch of amateurs. It was a poorly conceived plan from the start. Ricardo Barbosa, an aspiring bullfighter and nephew of the other priest in the parish, father José Moll, told his old friend, out-of-work wrestler José Valentín Vázquez, "Pancho Valentino," that Moll had millions of dollars hidden in the house. Valentino went to the barrio Tepito to recruit a couple of men to help him do the job. In a place of ill repute, El Paraíso, Rubén Castañeda Ramos, "El Boxer," arranged a meeting for Valentino with Pedro Linares Hernández, "El Chundo," an inveterate marihuana smoker, and Pedro Vallejo Becerra, "El México," a decadent pimp and an old dancing partner of Valentino's at the Salón México.[81]

Barbosa drove the three men to the church. Armed with a gun that did not work, a metal rod, and a baseball bat, they rang the bell. Nobody answered except for a barking dog, so they went back to the car. They drove around for hours, frustrated, and thought about robbing a driver for money, but could not find a suitable victim. They found out later that the bell of the parish house did not work, so they tried again a few days later. They lost some time looking for a place to leave Valentino's six-year-old son, Panchito. After trying to entrust him to one of his father's old girlfriends, the men left the boy alone in a room at the Hotel Terminal, near the bus station.

Once they arrived at the house on Chiapas Street, they poisoned the dog (Duque was his name, and he survived) and then knocked hard on the door, overpowering the priest who opened it. He was not Moll (although they would not realize it until they read it in the newspapers days later) and did not know where the money was. Fullana Taberner was a former boxer so he put up a fight. He was beaten and tortured. Valentino applied a wrestling armlock to strangle him, and the priest died in the kitchen. After going through the parish house and the church for more than an hour, they left with about 4,000 pesos, some jewels, two chalices, two silver pitchers, a silver tray, a radio, an electric shaver, and a portable typewriter. As they got away in Barbosa's car, where he had stayed in order to avoid being recognized, they split the money and divided the rest of the loot in the hotel room where Panchito had waited. El Chundo got the radio, which he wanted to give to his mother, and Valentino kept the typewriter. They went to the state of Hidalgo to see a cousin of Valentino's who could melt the objects they had stolen, but he said that they were not made of silver. Valentino, Panchito, and

El México took a bus heading toward the U.S. border. El Chundo was later arrested carrying around a bloodied cassock in Tepito; Barbosa was detained soon thereafter.[82]

The group, in sum, did not offer a flattering portrait of the underworld. The cover of the Servicio Secreto file on the case showed that all of them went by several names (El México used six), and with good reason. El México had killed a police officer in 1937, spent a year and a half in prison, had a total of twenty-four entries in the prison book, and currently made a living as a "coyote," an intermediary, around pawnshops. He had lived in the United States, liked to read books and newspapers, wrote well, and had a deep scar on his face.[83] Barbosa was a bullfighter wannabe who got Moll to pay for his international trips. He went around with another man "who said he was his pistolero" but was simply his sword-bearer in bullfights (*mozo de estoques*). El Chundo just hung around El Paraíso, in Tepito, and he was none too bright. He was soon found by undercover agents after clumsily trying to get rid of some objects obviously linked to the crime.

Pancho Valentino was the most notorious of the lot. He was the center of public attention from the moment he was identified as a suspect. Described by the police as "tall, strong," he was born in Celaya in 1918. His father worked for the Secretaría de Educación Pública, and his two sisters were also decent folk, but Pancho turned out to be a restless man. In 1942, through the bracero program, he went to California to work in the fields and later tried to find a job in Hollywood. He joined the U.S. armed forces and served as a mechanic in a B29 squadron. Although he had told his mother that he had fought in the Philippines, was a great marksman, and had earned a medal, he confessed to the police that he was never in the front lines. After being discharged, he used the scholarship he earned with his service to study dance and tried his luck at the movies. He also painted and failed miserably as a bullfighter. Eventually, he became a wrestler in Mexico, enjoying a degree of success that took him to arenas in the United States and Europe. The newspapers published his professional picture, which showed him dressed with a sarape and sombrero over the wrestling outfit, smiling and playing the guitar (figure 11). He also had problems with the law: four years before the crime, he had slashed the face of his French wife, Andrea Van Lisum, in the Broadway restaurant, and as a consequence he had lost his license to fight. He was also accused of rape by another woman. He had married seven times and had four children, including Panchito. He also had fifteen prior entries in prison—for the attack on his wife, drug trafficking, and pimping. Because he had spent

"No Maten a mi Hijo", Implora la Madre de
Pancho Valentino; Portugués Contra Barbosa

FIGURE 11. Pancho Valentino. *La Prensa,* 21 Jan. 1957, p. 1.

so much time in the United States and had U.S. citizenship, the press called him "el pocho." [84] He was indeed an example of the ambiguities of national identity at a time of increasing interactions with the United States.

The police chased Valentino for two weeks, sending agents and requests for help to San Luis Potosí, Jalisco, Tamaulipas, and other states where they thought the fugitive might be hiding or passing through on his way back to the United States. He took his son and the typewriter but had to get rid of both along the way because they slowed him down. He left Panchito in a Tamaulipas village with a note addressing "to whom it may concern" to "please deliver this child to his granny who lives at Gacetilla 18, colonia Aztcapotzalco." [85] Secret Service agents found Valentino in the state of Querétaro. When they approached him in a field, he ran away but stopped after the agents shot into the air. He confessed on the spot.

Valentino mobilized his celebrity to save his skin. Even before his capture, his mother begged through the newspapers: "Do not kill my son." She promised that if she knew where he was hiding she would go there "on my knees [and] even if I fell I would stand up again and would reach him to implore that he turned himself in." She heard that he was going to suffer the ley fuga but only wanted him to be tried, and she hoped her grandson would be delivered to her custody. [86] When Valentino arrived in Mexico City, reporters and the Servicio Secreto Chief were waiting for him, expecting him to make a statement. What he offered was more of a press conference. At one point, he asked Colonel Manuel Mendoza, the Servicio Secreto chief, whether he should answer one of the journalists' questions. The colonel encouraged him to do it "so the public knows the truth and responsibilities can be allocated." Valentino was clearly ready to talk. He explained his crime as a result of his poverty and other people's wealth: "I am a product of Mexico, of the Mexican environment, and I do not want to escape from it." He quoted poet Salvador Díaz Mirón's dictum ("Nobody has the right to the superfluous while somebody lacks the strictly necessary") as "my best philosophy," and he justified his sacrilegious behavior on philosophical grounds: "This is a cruel God who is constantly punishing us." Yet he also acknowledged that he had been "'influenced' by modernism and gangsters."[87] Eventually sentenced to thirty-three years in prison, he tried to escape from the Lecumberri penitentiary but suffered a serious beating. Some say that he had to beg on his knees for the warden not to use the ley fuga on him. He was instead sent to the Islas Marías, where he repented of his crime and led a peaceful life, dying of a heart attack a month before his release.[88]

THE MULTIPLICATION OF KILLERS

The cases discussed thus far were exceptional; they counted among the handful every week that captured the interest of the readers. Publicity was not evenly accessible. Many homicides did not prompt more than a brief mention in the newspapers, leaving few traces of victims and suspects. A few murderers who did attract the press chose to keep quiet rather than exploiting celebrity. Among these was Luis Romero Carrasco, who in 1929 killed a wealthy pulque trader, his lover, two maids, and the house's parrot. He was incriminated by his fingerprints on a bloodied knife, and the trial was straightforward. He was reluctant to speak, even though the press followed every step of the process and a crowd attended the jury trial. In fact, he slept through the defense's speech, refused to testify, and when a reporter asked him if he intended to say anything, he answered: "What for? If you will only go ahead and act like intriguing gossip mongers ... Why should I talk, I better keep quiet." Romero Carrasco confessed only to a criminologist, saying that he had done it for revenge, not money. After his sentence he was killed by ley fuga on the train to the Islas Marías.[89]

If a murderer was already famous, punishment was easier to avoid. Emilio "El Indio" Fernández, a prestigious movie director, could get unruly after a few drinks. In 1938, he killed a technician while filming *Herencia macabra* because he had challenged his authority on the set. He had to flee to Cuba for a while but was able to return shortly afterward. In 1959, he invited some journalists to talk about his success at the Cannes Film Festival. After consuming several drinks and smoking marihuana, he took offense about a question, went upstairs for a gun, shot and wounded the *Excélsior* reporter, and told everyone to leave. He was found guilty of a murder in 1976 but only spent a few months in a Coahuila prison. While his movies helped create an image of Mexico as a country of violence and beauty, and he otherwise liked to talk about his exploits, when it came to actual murder accusations he followed good legal advice and avoided punishment.[90] In a famous 1960 scandal, Guillermo Lepe killed singer and actor Agustín de Anda, the fiancé of his daughter, actress Ana Berta Lepe, because he had besmirched her honor. Lepe was sentenced to ten years in prison but only served five.[91] These stories contained an implicit lesson for the criminally literate: with money and a good lawyer, building a public narrative was not necessary.

The choice between publicity and silence was different for women. Experts and the press reserved their expectation of psychological depth for male criminals, and after 1929 there were no cases like that of María del Pilar Moreno, in which their motivations were discussed in a jury trial. Thus, female murderers were less likely to be treated like authors, even when judges and journalists allowed their stories to emerge in full. Ricarda López Rosales killed her two daughters in 1942. She was pregnant, had lost another child years before, and could not sustain herself and her daughters with her work as a maid and a seamstress. When her female neighbors discovered the bodies of her eight- and ten-year-old daughters, they wanted to lynch her, and the police had to protect her. In jail, other female inmates threatened her. But a reporter from *Novedades* interviewed her, and the judge encouraged her to talk at length, which she did "intelligently" according to the newspaper. Her account was clear, but her delivery lacked emotion: the fathers of her children had completely abandoned Ricarda. She had begun planning the murder months beforehand, buying five tubes of Veronal, a barbiturate, which she had the girls drink and which she intended to take herself later. She declared that her life had been difficult since her own mother died when Ricarda was six: "Since I was very little life has been repugnant for me, because it is so ugly and only gives bitterness." As a mother herself, Ricarda felt it was her right to take the lives of her children and felt no remorse because she had fulfilled her responsibility: "Since I could not give them what they had the right to have,

I preferred to put a stop to their suffering." The judge ordered psychiatrists to examine her, reasoning that the syphilis from which she suffered or her parents' alcoholism might diminish her penal responsibility.[92] The case, like others, quickly disappeared from public memory. Forty years later, by contrast, a similar story found more receptive audiences, when Elvira Luz Cruz killed her four children in a situation of extreme poverty. Her plight inspired support from feminist organizations and two movies.[93]

When female murderers tried to explain themselves, they faced steep barriers. There was little sympathy for those who were suspected of killing their husbands out of greed. A word coined to refer to several of these women was *autoviudas,* alluding to the fact that they caused their own widowhood but also, at least in one famous case, because a woman killed her husband inside a car. In 1959, Magdalena Hernández shot her wealthy husband, Andrés Echenique Sagarramundi, in a case that unleashed a wave of nota roja populist vitriol. Newspapers relished the unraveling of her far-fetched claim that the gun went off by accident—a typical stratagem of lawyers. Portraits of Hernández were not flattering (figure 12), and *La Prensa* published details of the couple's extravagant lifestyle, their disputes about money, and the luxurious car in which Echenique Sagarramundi died. Her lawyer, Felipe Gómez Mont, earned particular scorn as an "old fox" who had defended other autoviudas yet ironically was president of the Liga de la Decencia, a moral vigilance organization, and member of the Catholic Partido Acción Nacional.[94] For *La Prensa* columnist Manuel Buendía, Gómez Mont was nothing more than a "pharisee" who would use any trick, including a late visit to prison with a priest, in order to defend his client.[95] According to *Detectives* most autoviudas could not escape justice, but one in Acapulco succeeded by paying the judge. When murderesses seemed to have legitimate reasons to use violence, they were less interesting as individuals than as a symptom of the "influence of ideological trends that every day give more support to materialism."[96] In cases of lower-class women who cited abuse from men as a justification for murder, the moral coordinates were even simpler. As Dolores Ramírez from Guadalajara explained after killing her husband, Esteban Pérez García: "How can I regret it if. . . . I finally freed myself from him?"[97] The press did not look for psychological nuance: these women, it seemed, simply responded to situations that they could not fully articulate.[98]

A caricature by Don Yo in *La Prensa* (figure 13) compared Magdalena Hernández with another woman who killed a man, Ema Martínez. The two women were indistinguishable in their appearance, according to the drawing;

FIGURE 12. Magdalena Hernández. *La Prensa*, 19 Mar. 1959, p. 20.

FIGURE 13. Magdalena Hernández and Ema Martínez. *La Prensa,* 19 Mar. 1959, p. 9. Caption: "Such is life.... One should not criticize, my dear friend, because it is proper that the leader and lawyer of the League of Decency, Felipe Gómez Mont, should defend decent married ladies who have kept a horribly decent conjugal life and who have killed their husbands with all decency. This lawyer cannot defend Ema, the one [who killed] the senator. She was not married, she does not have millions . . . therefore she is not decent."

the difference was that the first had millions to pay for her defense, so she was "decent," unlike Martínez, who could not afford the services of Gómez Mont and had to rely on a public defender.[99] Martínez had shot and killed Senator Rafael Altamirano a few months earlier. She did it at his office, in front of multiple witnesses, and was arrested on the spot. The scene was still chaotic when journalists reached her: the victim's family arrived unaware of his death; a press photographer slipped in the senator's blood; Martínez had an "attack of hysteria" in the next office.[100] With tears in her eyes but without remorse, she claimed, "He sank me . . . he finished my life and left me in the streets!" The scandal she opened up not only revealed Altamirano's profligate behavior but also, and with scintillating detail, corruption within the federal bureaucracy. She told reporters that she had been a victim of the sexual debauchery reigning in the Federal Pensions Office (Dirección de Pensiones), where she had been Altamirano's secretary four years ago and had been coerced into having a relationship with him. For a year and a half they were lovers, he paid for her apartment, and they often went out at night. When they broke up, because she was tired of him forcing her to drink too much, they had a fight, and she slapped him. According to Martínez, Altamirano had her fired, then had her arrested and beaten by agents of the Dirección Federal de Seguridad. She was taken to Dr. Oneto Barenque's psychiatric clinic (the one where Goyo Cárdenas went to feign insanity) and was declared mentally ill without so much as an examination. She spent several months in La Castañeda. When she was released, she was not allowed to collect her savings from the pensions office. An underling of Altamirano, licenciado Rafael Aréchiga, brought Ema to his own apartment, drugged her, took pictures of her in "inconvenient positions," and circulated them among her coworkers. She sued Aréchiga and Altamirano for defamation, but the case was dismissed. Fearing for her safety, she left for Chiapas and then to Guatemala, but she continued to receive threats and to be the object of gossip. She returned to Mexico City in 1959 and finally was able to collect the money she was owed thanks to the intervention of a labor court. She used it to buy the .25-caliber gun she fired at Altamirano's back.[101]

Ema Martínez's crime was intended, in her words, to clear her name. After her arrest she refused to argue that she was mentally ill or had acted in self-defense: she simply laid out her accusations. Her claims fueled comments in the press about the corruption reigning among bureaucrats; Altamirano now seemed an example of the politician who moved from obscure jobs to elected office because of personal connections and who used his position for profit and sexual advantage. Members of Congress and newspapers began to receive letters confirming that "true orgies or bacchanals" took place in Altamirano's offices, where female employees were photographed naked and in "in positions that offended the most elementary rules of morality."[102] Martínez was clearly aware of the political implications of her accusations. In a telegram to President López Mateos two months before the homicide, she conveyed her personal predicament with a reference to her enemies' improper influence over the previous government: "Save me, Mr. President. The savage persecution continues to deprive me of work, honor, dignity. They continue to torment me, all because of the schemes brought by the Pensions Director to [former president] Ruiz Cortines."[103] In an interview from prison, she promised that in the next proceedings of the case, "public opinion will learn about many things not known until now."[104] The implication was so subversive that the judge in charge of the case stopped Martínez's interviews with reporters, did not allow publication of her long deposition, and made further hearings private, to the displeasure of editors. He decided that she was to be interned until a psychological evaluation established that she was fit to stand for trial.[105] The case soon disappeared from the news.

Press coverage of Ema's case oscillated between the scorn directed at autoviudas and a sympathetic regard for the immorality that made her a victim. Conservative *Novedades,* for example, did not mention her alleged relationship with Altamirano, and described her as "a woman of 43, curly hair, slightly dark skin, not physically attractive who . . . did not show the slightest emotion for what had happened." [106] *El Universal,* also close to the government, ran the story without much sympathy toward Martínez, yet allowed reporters to transcribe and confirm her statements while its opinion columnists suggested that other bureaucrats were involved in the scandal. Even *Amanecer,* from Altamirano's home state of Querétaro, began the coverage calling her "a crazy Guatemalan," but eventually published a lengthy interview with her and accepted her argument by characterizing the assassination as a "crime of passion" [107] and thus an excusable product of violent emotions.[108] From the start, *La Prensa* condemned Martínez and suggested that she was indeed mentally unstable, but it also gave her ample space and ultimately embraced her narrative. Editorials and caricatures denounced the corruption and immorality that she had revealed. Ema Martínez knew that a gesture like hers authorized newspapers to pass over the boundaries of privacy and criticize politicians. Her crime allowed her to briefly put her story before public opinion.

CONCLUSIONS

Each one of these men and women used different ways to tell his or her story of murder. In 1932, Alberto Gallegos profited from his brief celebrity to present nota roja readers with a complex persona, torn between the joy of life and the fear of the police, forced to confess but nevertheless willing to tell a different story to whomever cared to listen. In 1942, Goyo Cárdenas exploited new ideas about the mind among scientists and laymen, using his education and eloquence to describe the mysterious psychological forces that possessed him and pushed him to kill. This strategy, and his study of the law, allowed him to survive. Pancho Valentino was not much of an intellectual, but he hoped to be in show business, so when the cameras and reporters turned to him, he presented himself as a man with an interesting life: a migrant who had made the most of his journey in the United States, a wrestler, a seducer, and a victim of poverty forced to steal. The three were prominent references in Mexican criminal literacy, but they were not the only famous murderers. Over the decades when they committed their crimes, even as murder rates were decreasing, the public's concern about violent death remained high, and may have even increased, as an effect of the expanding diversity of slightly less famous murderers who presented their stories in the nota roja. From thieves who killed for practical reasons, to murderesses whose story was a hard sell, to quiet serial killers, criminals multiplied and began to lose the prestige of authorship as time passed.

During their heyday as authors (of both crimes and narratives), though, they acquired a public voice that was more compelling than that of detectives or policemen when it came to knowing the truth. This was the reason their infamy acquired national proportions and their names were preserved through the years. There was an aesthetic side to killers' endurance in collective memory. The association linking murder, narrative, and pleasure was a good explanation for violence, as experts had argued by using the concept of sadism to account for men like Goyo Cárdenas, and as intellectuals like Octavio Paz unwittingly confirmed with their reflections on Sade. "His greatest originality," wrote Paz about Sade, "lies in having thought about erotism as a total, cosmic reality, that is, *as the reality*." Sade's narratives built a utopia in which there was no crime because the fulfillment of pleasure through cruelty was both ancient and natural. From this perspective, the laws of the state were but brittle, man-made attempts to stem legitimate natural urges; violence against the weak was not immoral because it allowed the libertine to obtain pleasure.[109] Of course, this aesthetic reflection on murder could not be openly embraced in a judicial setting, but it did point to a fundamental aspect of murderers' centrality in the public sphere: theirs was a form of pleasure in which violence was meaningful only when committed by men. Women were not called sadistic, and as we just saw, faced steeper obstacles when trying to convey the purpose of their actions.

One can take the analogy between murderers and literary authors only so far. As we will see in chapter 7, some fiction writers played with this connection in stories told from the criminal's perspective. But if we try to understand the logic of homicide suspects in their own terms, we must remember that aesthetics were always subordinated to more pressing needs. This chapter has dealt with individuals who were accused of murder, and it has not attempted to account for the causes of their transgression: what they did up to the alleged crime is interesting only as a causal part of the explanations they offered. Once they were arrested, all the accused discussed here faced imminent dangers: they could suffer violence from the police, enraged neighbors, and fellow inmates. Thus, they had to tread carefully: being too smart and evasive, as Gallegos tried to be, could result in extralegal punishment; total silence, as maintained by Mercader, only worked if one wanted to sacrifice one's freedom to a higher cause. In between, a feasible goal was to use words and images in order to steer the judicial process toward a more benign outcome. Even when prison was inevitable, the continuing ability to bring the attention of authorities and outside observers to one's plight could mean the difference between life and death. As in other penal systems, Mexican suspects realized immediately after the crime that all their acts and words would henceforth be part of the public realm.[110] As the previous three chapters have shown, the police investigation and subsequent judicial process were important, but a decisive section of that realm lay beyond penal institutions. Suspects needed to understand that the audiences at jury trials, or the readers of newspapers and magazines, could be as influential as lawyers and reporters. They all could be swayed by the voice of public opinion.

In a world that defined itself as modern because of its rapid cultural change, urban anonymity, and extensive presence of the media, murderers as authors exemplified a notion of individualism that could not be erased by the generalizations of science. They made the subjective realm, in which they chose to use violence perhaps in the pursuit of pleasure, an inevitable aspect of any understanding of the truth about crime. Explanations of their behavior were therefore always tentative and any assessment of the effectiveness of justice mostly speculative. In sum, they fascinated readers because they exemplified a modern subjectivity that was adversarial toward the state and accepting of violence.

FIVE

Careful Guys

PISTOLEROS AND THE BUSINESS OF POLITICS

You knew a pistolero when you saw one. Dr. Joaquín Maas Patiño was driving in Mexico City one day in 1948 when another car suddenly cut into his lane. He decided not to quarrel with its driver because the man was "tall, lean, with black trimmed mustache, dressed with blue denim pants, Texan hat, white shirt, so he gave me the impression of being a pistolero [literally, gunman] or some politician's bodyguard."[1] Maas Patiño thus avoided entering a world of pain associated with characters whose mere appearance spelled trouble. The men who came to beat a journalist some five years later, also in Mexico City, were according to a witness "two typical pistoleros: Texan hats, raincoats . . . the bulk of guns in their waists."[2] They were less elegant but equally recognizable outside the capital: a "famous pistolero" in Tlapacoya, Puebla, according to police notes from 1936, was "about twenty eight years old, slightly dark complexion, short stature, strong build, dresses with a dark suit, beige hat, a trench coat, has a golden tooth. He might be with a woman who is his lover and is called Aurora, and is tall, dark skinned, slender."[3]

The woman who accompanied the "famous" Tlapacoya pistolero was part of his description because, for their contemporaries, pistoleros were exhibitionists.[4] They were easy to find in the spaces of nightlife, creating all sorts of disorders in cantinas, cabarets, and other places of dissipation where they flaunted their immunity. Miguel Chavero, for example, did just that in Apizaco, Tlaxcala, when he insulted everyone in a brothel and then bragged that the police chief protected him.[5] Pistoleros combined those connections with illegal businesses. Some pistoleros worked as bouncers, while others controlled their own clandestine establishments, like "El Cementerio de Elefantes," a joint in Tacuba owned by an "influyentazo" (influential man), a relative of a former president. They could also act as "raqueteros," extorting

FIGURE 14. Rodrigo Moya, *El pistolero,* portrait of Roberto "El Güero" Batillas.

money or favors from legitimate cabaret owners.[6] The point, in any case, was to be well known in places of ill repute. Roberto "El Güero" Batillas founded his reputation when he appeared one day in the famous cabaret Waikiki, asked who was the toughest guy in the joint, and proceeded to offend his girlfriend and beat him up. This was the start of a career as bodyguard and enforcer for movie stars, drug traffickers, and politicians.[7] Batillas modeled for a Rodrigo Moya portrait in the sixties, his glory days gone yet still keeping the style that made him fearsome (figure 14).[8]

The main element of the pistolero's public persona was his gun, usually big and barely hidden from sight.[9] Most people in politics carried a gun, but in the ironic words of *Excélsior,* the prototypical pistolero used his weapon as an "accurate expression of his legal truth."[10] This meant that they could carry and use their guns without fear of reprisals, legal or otherwise. Another accessory that signaled the pistolero's immunity was the *charola,* the official identification or badge of a police, military, or intelligence agency that any self-respecting pistolero carried with him. One such identification issued by the Senate allowed Marciano Armenta (on whom more later) to force the builders of the Prado Hotel to give his crew favorable contracts.[11]

Visually recognizable, mid-twentieth-century pistoleros were nevertheless not defined by the penal law, as much as they liked to break it. Unlike famous murderers, no scholarship focused on them, and the nota roja barely paid any attention to them. Pistoleros, after all, used violence like professionals and lacked the psychological depth, if not the sadism, of criminal celebrities like Gallegos or Goyo Cárdenas. But the key difference with common criminals was that pistoleros were rarely punished because of their important function in politics. Loyalty to their bosses (public officials, caciques, landowners, etc.) guaranteed pistoleros protection from the law. Thus, it was risky to denounce them, and it was also useless. In contrast with the engagement of Mexican citizens with justice and the truth described in chapters 1 and 2, the silence around pistoleros defined a darker subfield of criminal literacy, antithetical to civic participation and open debate. Knowing about crime in Mexico meant knowing about pistoleros but also maintaining a cautious silence, like Dr. Maas Patiño did.

In Mexican politics and businesses, pistoleros were the dirty secret that everyone knew about. Thus, they must be understood beyond the usual parameters of the study of the public sphere. From the state's perspective, they did not exist, and they were certainly not a voice of civil society, yet they played an essential role in the development of an authoritarian regime. Their odd combination of visibility and invisibility poses a challenge to the historian. The abundant visual representations of the pistolero, like that of Batillas, both influenced and drew from popular culture. Yet it would be a mistake to understand the trade as a mere stereotype or a cultural construct. The violence behind those images was real, just like the gun Batillas reaches for in the picture. While the usual record of politics ignores pistoleros, they did show up in police records. In this chapter, I will draw from those scattered appearances to describe them in terms of their public and private functions. I will go into more detail on three exceptionally publicized cases of murder committed by pistoleros because they illustrate the complex relationship between violence, politics, and business that defines pistoleros as a historical phenomenon. Those stories are not representative precisely because of their publicity, but to their contemporaries, they nevertheless constituted a prominent, if particularly embarrassing, example of national infamy.

Before delving into the stories, practices, and political uses of pistoleros, I will look at the "surface of images," to use Borges's words, that constituted their fame. Sharply dressed gunmen populated the cinematic ambiance of cabarets, a key setting for depictions of urban life and its dangers in Mexican movies.[12] The pimp and robber of Emilio Fernández's 1949 masterpiece *Salón México*, played by Rodolfo Acosta, dressed and behaved the part with flair but in the end received his comeuppance. Slightly more celebratory was the 1947 film *Gángsters contra charros* by Spanish-born director Juan Orol. The naturally skilled fighter Johnny Carmenta, played by Orol, has been abandoned by his wife, played by Cuban dancer Rosa Carmina. Tired of a boring but honest life as a mechanic, Johnny decides to follow the path of crime and become a pistolero—defined as a man ready to steal anything because "he is courageous and strong," in the words of Carmenta's Italian trainer.[13] The movie pits city pistoleros against rural *charros* (cowboys) with predictably bad consequences for all. Other depictions were less flattering: for example, a caricature by Carreño in *La Prensa* showed a smiling, robust, and elegant man wearing a white tie over a black shirt, the gun visible in his belt, strolling along holding the hand of a fancily dressed female skeleton (figure 15).[14] José Martínez de la Vega inserted a character in his detective stories that seemed pulled out of police descriptions: "Matías, the pistolero . . . a coarse guy, with a trimmed mustache over a thick lip. Dark, square built, with a light gabardine trench coat."[15]

Pistoleros were the emblematic inhabitants of an underworld defined by dangerous populations and spaces. That *mundo del hampa* included professional criminals, loose women, drug traffickers, pimps, and a motley crew of ancillary characters. As in other countries, the spatial and social definition of crime became a more persuasive explanation of deviance than biological generalizations. It had the advantage of precision, a world easily mapped by newspapers: on Palma Street there was a "mafia" of thieves; Candelaria de los Patos was a "dramatic center of delinquency"; Romita neighborhood was a "nest of murderers and junkies"; and the brothels on Cuéllar and Monterrey Streets were the meeting place of "upper-class criminals, drug traffickers, top-notch rateros, and even the odd public official who turns a blind eye."[16] At the center of this world were "the cabaret, the dance hall, the centers of prostitution and vice."[17] Establishments like Salón México, Salón Colonia, Club Smyrna, and La Playa were the classiest among them, known as the gathering places for "the authentic aristocracy of the underworld."[18] However, the stories of most denizens of that world were a "daily novel of real life" tragically illustrated by the exploited women who succumbed to vice, prostitution, and

CARICATURAS DE CARREÑO

Del brazo...

—Confiamos en la voluble condición femenina de la muerte...

FIGURE 15. Pistolero and Death. *La Prensa,* 18 Aug. 1954, p. 8. Caption: "By the arm. We trust the fickle and feminine nature of death."

crime.[19] The police just kept a constant watch on the nightlife, controlling the occasional fights and scandals and tapping into a steady stream of kickbacks. This was not a self-contained world, however. The hampa threatened all citizens, as the radio program *Cuidado con el hampa* reminded XEW listeners. Criminal gangs, often including foreigners, acted skillfully and easily crossed back and forth from the underworld to the respectable economy.[20]

Pistoleros were associated with the more attractive aspects of modern life, like American sports. Batillas had been a boxer active in the U.S. border region before his splashy appearance at the Waikiki. Famous detective Valente Quintana had a side career as a promoter of Mexican fighters on the border and in the United States. Fiction and movies demonstrated the suggestive connections between sport and crime. In *Gángsters contra charros,* Johnny takes lessons on the techniques of hand-to-hand combat as part of his criminal training. A short story by Francisco Talán focused on a Mexican boxer who proved his mettle in New York despite local gangsters' attempts to force him to take a dive during a fight.[21]

Blending fiction and reality, "truculent North American movies," many believed, taught Mexican criminals how to carry out their attacks. For example, the press alleged that the movies inspired the stony performance that distinguished the killers of Deputy Manlio Fabio Altamirano in 1936, to be discussed below.[22] Borrowed from English, the terms *"raquetero"* and *"gángster"* expressed the association between the trade of pistolerismo and its U.S. models, yet the Spanish words gave the concept a specifically Mexican brand of exuberant impunity. For a columnist in *La Prensa,* the difference was that "autochtonous" gangsters were not exclusively interested in commercial profit like their North American counterparts. Mexican pistoleros could kill for sport, love, or politics, as their craft "is based, mainly, on the disdain for life, which is one of the characteristics of our people and the ardent Mexican character."[23] Conversely, for some U.S. expatriates, the spaces and practices associated with pistolerismo in Mexico exuded freedom. Writing to Jack Kerouac in 1949 from Mexico City, poet William S. Burroughs explained why he liked the country, besides the availability of drugs: "Anyone who feels like it carries a gun. I read of several occasions where a drunken cop, shooting at the habitués in bars, were themselves shot by armed civilians who don't take no shit from nobody."[24]

This apparent carelessness, which as we will see cost Burroughs's wife so much, pointed to the real impunity behind the pistolero images. The pistolero was not just a stereotype that expressed cultural anxieties caused by rapid modernization.[25] It was an inevitable part of everyday life. Stories about the abuses of power committed against civilians, both in the city and in the countryside, referred to the pistolero as a symptom of the "rotten environment" that had characterized broad areas of the country since the 1920s.[26] Regardless of whether the pistolero was acting on behalf of a political boss or just out of "the stupid habit that some people have of reaching for their gun for any reason," their crimes were never punished.[27] Police investigators received anonymous letters with names and antecedents of murderers, men of "very bad background" linked to politics and responsible for "countless crimes." The letters often came from relatives of victims who lamented their powerlessness against those men and their sponsors.[28] When the police did nothing, as was often the case, letters went to higher authorities. In 1958, licenciado Javier Torres Pérez wrote to President Ruiz Cortines that air force pilot Sergio García Núñez had killed several people in addition to engaging in kidnapping and gun trafficking. Two of his murders were committed "in a treacherous and cowardly manner" in a cantina. Yet he avoided prison, "claiming that he had been attacked." Torres Pérez reasoned that García Núñez's reputation was part of his threat: "The captain goes around in uniform, obviously armed, is almost two meters tall, Herculean build and since he lives in the neighborhood his deeds are well known." He now walked the same streets where the relatives of his victims lived, in Colonia Moctezuma, bragging that the judge released him for 50,000 pesos and that the newspapers were silent about his case on orders from the president himself. Torres Pérez warned about the consequences of these cases: "The people get tired, Mr. President, of so many García Núñezes."[29] One anonymous letter called police chief Pedro J. Castro a pistolero and murderer: "You might laugh," stated the letter, "but that is how public opinion is formed . . . the voice of the people, the voice of God."[30] Pistolero threats against and murders of journalists suggest that such accusations had unmistakable political implications.[31]

POLITICS AND PISTOLERISMO

The word "pistolero" was increasingly common from the late 1930s on, but politicians were reluctant to use it because it also signaled the weaknesses of the postrevolutionary state. The "Diario de los Debates de la Cámara de Diputados" (the best searchable corpus for public discourse) registers the first use of the term in legislative debates in the early 1940s.[32] Deputies could not use the word lightly because they themselves carried guns, and their debates sometimes devolved into gun battles.[33] Politicians were also the victims of pistoleros. On the way to a Mexico City police station after the brazen killing of fellow Veracruzano and *agrarista* leader Eduardo Guichard, Armando Armenta Barradas offered the policeman fifty pesos, then threatened him, reasoning in reference to yet another murder, that "if I shot a deputy, why not a street cop?"[34] Guichard's case revealed a new reality of "murders committed with premeditation, treachery, advantage, by individuals with local notoriety, accomplices and friends of the leaders or officials, or at least their pistole-ros."[35] The abuses of revolutionary commanders during the civil war lingered in urban memory as a concrete reminder of the violent origins of the regime. Although by midcentury it was not possible to link every instance of crimi-nal abuse of power to the revolutionary legacy, its imprint was clear in the methods of pistoleros. Impunity linked them to the past even as popular culture associated them with modernity.[36]

Despite President Cárdenas's intolerance toward such disorder and several campaigns to have civilians surrender their guns, the fact was that pistoleros were integral to the regime. For *La Prensa* columnist Mateo Podan, just as politicians carried guns and needed the services of pistoleros, so pistoleros were becoming politicians.[37] The relationship was symbiotic: "Pistolerismo is, for high level politicians as much as for provincial midgets, like water for the life of a plant. And the politician is, for the pistolero, everything that an organic being is for the existence of a parasite. They need and complement each other."[38] The memoirs of regional cacique Gonzalo N. Santos cynically document his own use of violence as well as his reliance on his loyal, machine-gun-wielding "gargaleotes." He had no compunction about listing his own crimes ("a lousy death more or less is not going to make me lose my sleep") but was careful to credit his employees, too.[39] The skills of pistoleros were particu-larly useful in electoral struggles, but agrarian and labor disputes also spilled into violence in which the "sempiternal bigwigs of revolting small-town poli-tics" got the upper hand.[40] From the perspective of educated critics, pistoleros embodied the legacy of barbarous rural practices in the modern city.

With the brutality of the pistolero's executions, *La Prensa* could not help but wonder whether "the pistolero believes himself strong enough, or public power is so weak, that he can establish the law of the jungle in the capital of the country?" Their practices were, in other words, "a direct challenge to police authorities, whose effectiveness is in doubt," and even called into ques-tion the good name of presidents.[41] Lázaro Cárdenas tried to place himself above petty political violence but could not avoid allying with unsavory caciques. His successor, Manuel Ávila Camacho, maintained appearances, despite the scandals committed by his brother Maximino. A military general, governor of Puebla, and minister in his brother's cabinet, Maximino had "a small private army of murderers" and engaged in all kinds of shenanigans.[42] Miguel Alemán, who came to office in 1946, brought a new style to high poli-tics, relying on younger civilian administrators like himself. Further down the chain of command, however, this simply meant that politicians were now reluctant to get their hands dirty and came to rely on the violence experts. Against the imaginary omnipotence of the man at the apex of the pyramid, therefore, murder was the inevitable consequence of petty conflicts that could not be arbitrated. The nota roja documented this dimension of politics because homicide spilled out of the secretive world of power into that of crime. It seemed natural that violent people would gravitate toward public life. For an informant of anthropologist Oscar Lewis in Mexico City: "There's nothing dirtier than politics. It's pretty rotten and there's been a lot of bloodshed too. How many people die so a man can get into power!"[43]

Recent scholarship has begun to recognize and explore the integral role of interpersonal violence in twentieth-century Mexican politics. Paul Friedrich places the origin of the pistolero in the "fighter" of revolutionary and agrarian strife of the early decades of the century. The political violence established after that was the work of "the more enterprising fighters," a product of personal enmities rather than ideology.[44] Recent studies, however, propose that strong men in the countryside used "direct violence" according to certain rules that guaranteed a degree of consensus. Pistolerismo was an effect of caciquismo—a locally rooted system of allocation of public resources based on loyalty, clientelism, and a good dose of illegality. The role of caciques was fundamental as intermediaries between a rural society still accustomed to violence and more institutional structures of domination at the national level. Violence is not itself the object of these analyses, which instead stress the functional roles of actors within the system. A closer look at the "individualization of violence" embodied in the cacique-pistolero symbiosis, however, inevitably pushes political history closer to the history of crime.[45] From that perspective, violence does not require a retrospective structuralist explanation but a good eye for its logic and history. In the words of Paul Gillingham, pistoleros were "violent entrepreneurs who struggled for power across most of Mexico after the armed revolution."[46] The blurring of boundaries between public and private interests incarnated by these entrepreneurs and their routine use of illegality also undermined the divide between modern and traditional actors.[47]

Paradoxically, that combination of roles justified pistolero exploits as a form of crime control: if those "shady businesses" were profitable for actors connected to power, they would become less attractive for more numerous, low-level criminals. Considering the costs and benefits of illegality, a more limited police intervention against pistoleros allowed for a more effective organization, if not eradication, of criminal activities.[48] In 1943, *El Momento* of Oaxaca reported on the "First Pistolero Congress" convened in that city. No association seems to have been founded then, but the joke was in the unholy combination of professionalization, law breaking, and politics suggested by the story. For a criminally literate reader, it implied that the only way to control the underworld was to leave it in the hands of those denizens who had the best political connections. The cost was uncertainty: how could one really know if a given crime had political connotations?[49]

THE ETHOS OF THE TRADE

The cardinal rule for a pistolero was to make sure that the question about whether a crime had political connotations would have no clear answer. The symbiosis between politicians and pistoleros took the form of a personal relationship that exchanged protection for loyalty. It was articulated as a code of behavior above the law. For Gonzalo N. Santos, his cousin Braulio embodied the virtues of this code: "He was very smart, extremely cruel with his enemies, loyal to his friends, to his group, his party, and especially to me." [50] The pistolero's job was an extension of the duties of the *guarura,* or *guardaespaldas* (bodyguard), who offered physical protection to his employer but was also his strong arm. The slippage between these two roles was the problem that the Secretaría de Gobernación wanted to tackle in 1942 when it proposed reforms to the penal code against "pistolerismo," "paid killers," and "armed citizens," or "bodyguards." [51] The most egregious example of this trajectory was Arturo Durazo Moreno, who began as a guarura, rose to policeman and pistolero in the 1940s, and was appointed Federal District police chief by his old friend President José López Portillo (1976–1982).[52] Durazo was so blatantly venal that he ended up in jail after López Portillo left power, deprived of the kind of protection that had defined his career.

The good pistolero was quietly loyal, while his boss was discreet in his generosity. When Donato Fernández was killed, his boss Manuel Parra and his remaining men buried him with "all the honors" in a lonely forest.[53] Santos learned from an early age that it was not wise to flaunt illegal gains, but to distribute them among friends.[54] Gestures like Parra's toward Fernández remained private so as not to attract attention. José Canchola broke the rules when he bragged to a friend in a pulquería of Colonia Vallejo: "The lousy police suck my dick." Canchola's crimes included the murder of military and police officers in different cities, and this eventually led to his death at the hands of the army in Guanajuato in 1946.[55] In other words, there were limits to impunity, and those who boasted too loudly, like Canchola, could soon overstep those limits. His mistake was not that he broke the law but that he did it in such a way that would force authorities to do something about it. Pistoleros demonstrated that finding the culprit for a crime in Mexico was a political decision.

As with most observations on pistolerismo, there is scarce evidence to confirm this. The "paid pistoleros" who committed a murder and flaunted the protection of authorities in several towns in Puebla prompted a victim's relative to ask President López Mateos to intervene in the hope he could do something about that impunity.[56] But in most cases protection was taken for granted, to the point that *Alarma* could predict that Arturo Herrera Pérez would not be arrested or accused of the murder of his wife because he was on the payroll of the leader of the Chamber of Deputies. According to *Detectives,* the relative of a former president who killed an inspector in a bar would avoid capture because he was an "influyentazo." [57]

The pistolero's sponsors provided safety from prosecution through a variety of means. One was to help him skip town after a crime, preferably to a jurisdiction where local authorities would be benevolent. The killers of Marcelino Jara were arrested in the Federal District, where the crime was committed, but "because of political influences," the investigation was interrupted, and they were transferred to Tlalnepantla, State of Mexico, and promptly released.[58] Another way to avoid arrest was to display a government identification card. The victim of the influyentazo who died in a bar, Miguel Ángel García González, was himself the nephew of a high official; at the time of his death, he carried a gun with ten rounds, 1,200 pesos in cash, and identifications issued by the Oficina de Reglamentos, the Tribunal Superior de Justicia del Estado de México, the government of the Federal District (crediting him as a judge in an Iztapalapa court), and the Secretaría de Gobernación.[59] He also carried a document that identified him as a lawyer. These affiliations were not always entirely fictitious: work in the police was a profitable side job for some pistoleros, and police agencies often hired pistoleros as temporary aides in their investigations, a role known in recent decades as the *madrina*.[60] The army was not immune to this slippage of roles: officers got involved in illegal businesses, including extortion and drug trafficking, forcing the Secretaría de la Defensa Nacional to rotate military commanders as often as possible.[61] The police chiefs of the Federal District had been members of the military since the thirties, and their subordinates were often involved in illicit practices.[62]

It was also useful for pistoleros to know some law. Although most of them did not have a law degree, some lawyers became masters in the art of breaking the law and avoiding punishment. Common language coined the term *abogángster* (gangster plus *abogado*) to name those who combined the credentials of lawyers and the attributes of pistoleros. The most famous among them was Bernabé Jurado (c. 1908–1980). He was tall, hedonistic, good looking, and diabolically smart. He knew all the tricks needed to avoid prison. His prowess was so widely known that William S. Burroughs used his services to avoid prison after killing his wife, Joanne Vollmer, in Mexico City in 1951. Burroughs made bail, with Jurado's assistance, after changing his confession: he first accepted killing her while playing William Tell, as he tried to shoot a glass on top of her head, but then he claimed instead that the gun had fallen and discharged itself. Jurado paid the ballistics expert to alter his report and manipulated other witnesses. Once he was released, Burroughs left Mexico never to return, but not before buying an ounce of heroin from Jurado. Jurado's services also helped well-known drug traffickers and "criminals of the worst ilk." He patronized cabarets of all categories, and his parties were attended by "people from the artistic and journalistic world as well as criminals and politicians," from movie director Emilio "El Indio" Fernández to assassin Hugo Izquierdo Ebrard. Jurado's flamboyant lifestyle won the admiration of judges and others employees of the judiciary who easily fell for his stratagems. Even though the police could not prove his involvement in any crime, he was dubbed "the Mexican Al Capone," and he inspired a play at the Teatro Iris— "Un jurado a Bernabé" (A jury for Bernabé) with actors Palillo and Borolas. He killed a man after a traffic dispute, left the country after being indicted, obtained an amparo from the Mexican Supreme Court, and returned without having to face jail. Eventually, life caught up with him. He continued to involve himself in thefts, accidents, drinking binges, and in the end, he killed himself after shooting his wife—his seventeenth, by some accounts.[63]

These different ways to avoid punishment amounted to an advantage that pistoleros exploited when they engaged in their own business after having earned an employer's trust.[64] The famous Fidel Corvera Ríos began his career as a bodyguard for politicians; "While he protected them from attacks he was free to commit crimes, certain that his patrons would defend him in case he had a problem with justice." He went on to have a criminal career of bank robbing and drug-trafficking punctuated by episodes of extreme violence.[65] Success in illegal businesses eventually afforded independence. When a group of politicians in Tampico tried to bribe him, while he was still only a customs agent, Santos showed them a closet full of money and told them: "I am a bandit and bandits do not sell ourselves; honest people like you sell themselves." He called them hypocrites and announced with pride: "This money is the product of my wrongdoings, of my struggles, but nobody bought me with this money . . . I earned it with the right of the winner."[66]

THE BUSINESS OF THE PISTOLERO

In addition to the pistolero's work for his political boss, he also typically engaged in his own criminal activities, particularly those in which violence played an important role like car theft, bank robbery, kidnapping, extortion, and other "shady businesses."[67] The common denominator of these activities was the pistolero's partnership with authorities. Pistoleros were criminals with impunity, recognized experts in the use of violence who deployed their talent at the service of men and women with power, as well as in their own illegal activities where their connections gave them the upper hand. For example, a 1937 murder case prompted an obituary of sorts for a pistolero in *Detectives:* Miguel M. Miravete, stabbed to death by an unknown assailant, had been a customs agent, had tried to buy a seat in Congress, was involved in drug trafficking and extortion, and although he was married, had multiple lovers.[68] The 1948 murder of Mauro Angulo, discussed later in this chapter, inspired a report entitled "Political Gangsterism in Government" from the U.S. embassy, which outlined the intricate web of "shady businesses" centered around police corruption: the main suspects, all close to President Alemán, used the services of pistoleros in connection with narcotics smuggling, pimping, and extortion.[69] A profitable area of business, particularly after the fifties, was urban land speculation. Arturo Herrera, the wife murderer mentioned above, owed his protection from a congressman to their collaboration in "businesses with real estate lots."[70]

For all these lines of business to prosper, however, pistoleros needed to be capable of killing. Murder had to be a credible threat in order to facilitate other operations, particularly extortion. It could also have a good payoff. "Paid pistoleros" who pulled the trigger or thrusted the knife were only the "material elements" used by "intellectual" authors to achieve their goals, as one witness in the Angulo case put it.[71] Luis Saldívar Martínez was persuaded to try to kill the senator, he explained, because "I would earn more than I earn in the field as the peasant I am."[72] Some commissions could be well remunerated. Rafael Barradas Osorio admitted to having been offered 20,000 pesos for the murder of Angulo, receiving a 500-peso advance and a gun from Marciano Armenta.[73] In 1954, Alejandro Ponce de León (on whom more below) received 25,000 of 75,000 pesos promised to him for arranging the murder of Alfonso Mascarúa, and Ponce de León in turn paid 5,000 plus 100 pesos of expenses to Antonio Trujeque, who completed the job.[74] Murder was a service available to a broad range of clients. Some could hire a murderer to deal with family disputes, like doña Trini Castañeda, a merchant from the town of General Anaya, Federal District, who in 1937 had Eduardo Franzoni killed to avenge her brother's murder. For that purpose, according to *Detectives,* she hired a man dressed like a charro, "as a pistolero, to kill Eduardo, paying him 4,000 thousand pesos, because she is a wealthy woman." She advanced a thousand and paid the rest upon completion of the job.[75] Thirty-six years later, according to *Alarma!,* a woman was going to pay 20,000 to have her husband, an unfaithful musician, murdered, although she was only able to pay 1,200 pesos as the "down payment."[76]

Murder could be a productive activity for rookies, but other pursuits provided more stable income and required an established reputation. In the early 1930s, drugs were only just becoming a significant part of the nightlife world populated by pistoleros and their ilk. But with a growing regime of prohibitions and a new diversity of products, the role of criminal entrepreneurs began to expand. The following passage from *Detective* is worth reading in extenso:

> Until recently the hampa, the tough guys, the dissolute ones at the barracks and prisons, the women who exchange their caresses for blows and stabs, they only knew about the domestic marihuana, the magic herb that drives people crazy, breaks the will and releases the human beast thirsty of pain and blood.... Today ... the hooked in the underground have moved from the plebeian marihuana to the aristocracy of cocaine and morphine, and there are coalmen who dream of the paradise of opiates, and the muleteer or pulquería busboy who hide a small syringe in the dirty red bandanna, just like any perverse upper class lady.[77]

The cast of characters expanded with the new drugs, as did the possibilities of commercialization. Pistoleros offered their services to big operators in the trade. El Güero Batillas worked for a while as the bodyguard of Graciela Olmos, "La Bandida," one of the main distributors of drugs in the capital. Others engaged in the trade themselves. Corvera Ríos did it during his stay in prison. Outside urban centers, the cultivation of marihuana and opium poppies prompted "an openly gangster-like behavior" among law enforcement authorities.[78]

Closely linked with the business of drugs was control of prostitution. Although prostitution had been regulated since the nineteenth century, it was in the 1930s that abolitionism and eugenics inspired the press to denounce the tragic stories of women who had been forced into prostitution by the shackles of drug addiction and the threat of violence. Efforts to rescue women from exploitation only increased the profitability of police protection. The pimp, called the *cinturita*, or *padrote*, acted as protector, lover, and punisher of female prostitutes. Pistoleros became features of the *zonas de tolerancia,* where they collected the bribes sex workers had to pay to the police.[79] Cabarets and brothels' semi-legality made them particularly vulnerable to violent entrepreneurs linked to police authorities.

Robbery committed by pistoleros was less common because it tended to be more spectacular, although it could provide a good reward if done properly and with the collaboration of authorities. There were hierarchies, of course. Small-time "hampones" based in cabarets used fists and wrestling moves to rob individuals. In rural settings, murder and cattle rustling were associated with pistoleros In the big city, bank robberies, which often necessitated the murder of guards or bystanders, attracted intense public attention toward men like Corvera and Jurado.[80]

THREE MURDERS

This sketch of pistoleros' image and of the rules of their trade implies an artificial coherence. What most people knew about them came in the form of stories. Criminal literacy, after all, was not just a collection of principles or a theory, but a sprawling knowledge about places and people. A close look at three cases briefly mentioned above provides a deeper understanding of the way in which experience informed action. The following section will also show how pistoleros were an integral yet disruptive part of public life. They were not, as we will see, untouchable or isolated figures, but operated in relation to their bosses, their victims, and their colleagues. There was a logic to those relationships that illustrates how public power was deployed in transactions involving money and violence.

The three cases that follow occurred between 1936 and 1954, a key period in the development of pistolerismo. Featuring the murders of public men ordered by other public men, they are by no means typical. The prominence of the victims prompted thorough police investigations and press coverage, leaving a good documentary record, at least by the standards of pistolero history. Although the crimes were committed in Mexico City, the three cases found their explanations and main actors outside the capital. We know more about them precisely because they involved the Federal District's Secret Service and prompted the interest of Mexico City nota roja journalists and readers. Unlike most other cases discussed in this book, the identities of the material and intellectual authors of the crimes were not known from the beginning. As a consequence, the investigations involved conventional detection as much as political speculation. All that was known from the outset was that they were the handiwork of pistoleros.

The afternoon of June 25, 1936, Manlio Fabio Altamirano was having an ice cream with his wife at a table close to the front door of Café Tacuba when a short, dark man with a mustache in the style of Hitler entered the restaurant and shot him in the hands, chest, and head. Altamirano did not have time to draw his own gun.[81] A witness outside the restaurant declared that after the shots were fired, he saw a man with a gun in his hand emerge and climb into a car that was already pulling away. Expertly driven, the vehicle soon disappeared from sight, but not before somebody wrote down the license plate number; the car later turned out to have been stolen. The alarmed customers of Café Tacuba included painters Diego Rivera and Frida Khalo.[82]

Altamirano, a congressman from Veracruz, was no stranger to the use of guns. In 1924, for example, he had been involved in a shootout in the Chamber of Deputies that resulted in the death of another congressman.[83] In 1936, he was likely to become the official candidate for the governorship of the state. He had already received letters from supporters warning about the murder plans of hacienda owner Manuel Parra, who employed "armed workers and full time pistoleros" and favored another candidate for the governorship.[84] People had heard suspicious conversations in buses and hotels in the previous days. However, many were surprised by the murder itself: it did not look like the typical attack by a "Veracruzano rancher" in which the shooting would usually follow a verbal confrontation, or the victim would be killed in a field with a rifle shot from a distance ("*venadear*" was the verb used for this method). In this case, according to press columnists, "the pistolero who killed Altamirano looked more like a city gangster."[85]

The political plot behind the crime quickly emerged. At the crime scene, with Altamirano still in her arms, the widow shouted, "The men of Quiroga killed him," referring to the former minister of war and the navy general Pablo Quiroga and his associate, Manuel Parra. She explained that the killer was smartly dressed like a "dandy" in order to deceive, because that was not the way people dressed in Veracruz.[86] That was the same accusation made by several leftist Veracruzano politicians who visited the newsroom of *Excélsior* the following day. They also accused interim governor Guillermo Rebolledo and his preferred candidate for the governorship, Joaquín Muñoz. The leader of the Partido Nacional Revolucionario, former president Emilio Portes Gil, arrived at Café Tacuba minutes after the crime and confirmed to reporters that the crime was politically motivated, although he gave no names. A few days later, he met with President Cárdenas and they decided to postpone the gubernatorial elections in Veracruz.[87]

Anonymous letters to the police and speeches at the funeral advanced the idea that Altamirano had been killed by reactionary political enemies. Vicente Lombardo Toledano warned that the working classes in Mexico needed to be ready to deal with the kind of political violence found in contemporary Germany and Italy. As the coffin was placed in the ground, the assembled mourners sang "The Internationale." For Senator Ernesto Soto Reyes, it was imperative to go beyond the material author of the murder (a "troglodyte . . . lombrosian"). He declared, "It is a crime of the Mexican bourgeoisie, of imperialism, against the working class." The intellectual authors of the crime had to be punished because doing otherwise "would give birth to a nefarious school of crime, which besides encouraging all sorts of evils and undermining the morality of the public, would devote itself to killing those committed to holding public office." [88] Newspapers of different ideological positions echoed this interpretation, which linked the debasement of politics and social morality through the emergence of "the procedure of elimination by pistolero." [89] Yet characterizing the murder of Altamirano as political ("if politicians commit it or order it") meant only that it would be harder to reach justice, as the police could easily find the culprit but nevertheless be "forced to keep silent about the results of their work." [90]

Pressure on federal authorities led to partial results. Military officers in Veracruz arrested Gildardo Lobillo, who had been part of the plot to kill Altamirano but did not participate directly. Lobillo named one of the material authors, Rafael Cornejo Armenta, and the immediate instigator, Manuel Parra, who was promptly arrested. Jorge Bernal, another participant, was captured while trying to flee to Guatemala.[91] But not much else was achieved. Cornejo Armenta was not captured, although it was well known that he lived around Plan de las Hayas, Veracruz, and Parra was released months later thanks to an amparo, rearrested, and let free for good in August of 1937. In July 1939, another suspect, a member of the same clan, Armando Armenta Barradas, was detained after killing a man at a café on Uruguay Street and, as mentioned above, bragged about his role in the murder Altamirano.[92] The victim's widow and other witnesses recognized him as the shooter. Nevertheless, he was not accused of Altamirano's murder, and he was still free on bail in 1941. In 1949, Altamirano's brother wrote to President Alemán to thank him for sending a representative to the commemoration of the death of Manlio Fabio, and to remind him that Rafael Cornejo Armenta was still free in Plan de las Hayas, and that of those involved in the murder, only Armando Armenta Barradas had died as a consequence of his participation in the murder of Senator Mauro Angulo—a case which we will discuss later.[93]

Veracruzano politics had been particularly violent since the 1920s, mainly because of agrarian disputes which by some accounts had led to thousands of deaths. An epicenter of violence was the region around Plan de las Hayas and Misantla, where suspects in the Altamirano case hid and enjoyed local support. According to an anonymous Servicio Secreto source, investigators could trust only a few people in the region. When information came it was from family members of victims, like Feliciano López, from Misantla, whose mother was killed by the Armentas, or from Zenón López, from Juchique de Ferrer, who stated that he "is no longer scared" of the clan because they had already killed his brother.[94] Witnesses reported that Parra's group had long engaged in organized violence targeting *agraristas,* peasants, and local politicians, whom they killed without worry of receiving punishment. In the late twenties, Parra ("the greatest pistolero of them all," in Gillingham's apt words) had been sent troops from Quiroga, then secretary of the army, in order to defend his Almolonga hacienda from attempts to distribute its lands among peasants. In association with other owners, Parra organized a group of *guardias blancas,* a private police force that had been commonly found in haciendas since the Porfiriato. The Armentas were part of that network, which spread fear and death under the name of the Mano Negra.[95] Editorials and parliamentary speeches described the Mano Negra as a criminal organization at the service of hacendados, yet Parra's leadership combined local paternalism with regional and national connections, making the outfit more than a mere gang of vigilantes.[96] The name of the organization was a reference to early iterations of the *mafia,* or *cosa nostra.* Like the Italian Mano Nera, Parra's organization was secretive and tried to instill fear among its enemies.

The Veracruz Mano Negra was a regional organization based on kinship ties with no ideological program, and it shared much of its business logic with contemporary pistolerismo.

Pressed by investigators, participants in the plot against Altamirano began to talk, revealing the inner workings of the organization. According to Heriberto Ramírez López and Juan Armenta Ceballos, in May of the previous year, Parra had invited them and other men to enjoy dinner and cognac at his hacienda. He told them that Altamirano "would not reach power" because "he was a bandit." Then he announced that he had summoned them to see "who had the balls to kill deputy Manlio Fabio Altamirano." As in other *cacicazgos,* some degree of discussion was a requirement for any important decision.[97] At the Almolonga dinner, all agreed that Rafael Cornejo Armenta should take care of it with the help of Gildardo Lobillo. Parra promised both men 500 pesos and warned them: "Boys, you know that if I learn that you are talking about this you will not last 24 hours." Although a judge later decided, against usual practice, that the testimony from Ramírez López and Armenta Ceballos was not valid evidence because it had been extracted with torture, the statement by Lobillo to the Mexico City Servicio Secreto agents confirms the basic facts. Lobillo had come to work for Parra as baker in Almolonga, but his boss knew about his experience during the revolution and as a policeman in Coatepec, Veracruz, where he fought bandits, killed a few men, and helped pacify the place. Lobillo claimed to have spoken to Parra five times, most of them about the proper preparation of the bread, and only in the last conversation did they discuss the murder of Altamirano. Parra gave him a handgun and 50 pesos for expenses, and warned him about keeping his mouth shut. Parra promised him 5,000 pesos if he completed the task—not the 500 mentioned by the other witnesses. Lobillo went to Mexico City and waited for Altamirano outside his office, but he had to return to Veracruz before he could carry out the murder. Rafael Cornejo Armenta stayed to complete the assignment.[98]

The contrast with Toral's assassination of Obregón eight years earlier could not be more striking. Despite the initial confessions, and abundant evidence of Mano Negra involvement, the investigation resulted in no punishment. Veracruzano pistolerismo had invaded the capital.[99] The official party candidate after Altamirano's death was Miguel Alemán. He became governor of Veracruz until 1939, then minister of gobernación, and president from 1946 to 1952. According to journalist Roberto Blanco Moheno, Alemán consulted frequently with Parra while he was governor. Parra preserved his power after the 1936 incident, and the Mano Negra became a "state within the state" until Parra's death of natural causes in 1943. The organization killed thousands. Working with brutal simplicity, it had "iron-clad discipline with clearly established hierarchies." Blanco Moheno wrote an exposé for *Excélsior* that the newspaper did not publish, fearing retribution.[100] The network was not immune to internal strife, and it would be weakened by the rivalry between Rafael Cornejo Armenta and Crispín Aguilar, the putative successor of Parra as regional strongman until his own demise in 1950.[101] Altamirano's murder was part of a broader change that probably escaped the imagination of those present at the Almolonga dinner: the ascent of Alemán, the consolidation of caciquismo's violent rule, but also the growing agreement among politicians in Mexico City, embraced by Alemán himself, that such straightforward use of murder for political gain had to be contained.

Reining in political murder was not achieved by strengthening the role of institutions and citizens' participation, as the next case shows, but through violent means that, paradoxically, maintained pistoleros' silent presence in the shadows of public life. The murder of Tlaxcala senator Mauro Angulo occurred the morning of February 17, 1948, when he was leaving the Aragón bath house, as he did every morning. A man walked up to him and shot him four times in the head, then shot and wounded a witness, climbed into a waiting Jeep with another man at the wheel, and disappeared in the Mexico City traffic. The efficiency of the murder and the immediate public reaction indicated that it had been the work of professionals. President Alemán soon received anonymous letters denouncing the violence prevalent in Tlaxcala and the impunity enjoyed by thugs at the service of Governor Rafael Ávila Bretón. Angulo's funeral was the occasion for renewed speeches and editorials against pistolerismo. According to an Apizaco, Tlaxcala, newspaper, failure to act would cause "pistolerismo, racketeering, the swindlers of public ballots and all the anti-social pests [to seize] power, holding honest people in a reign of terror for many years."[102] Citizens demanded that the president himself oversee a proper investigation since state authorities could not be expected to solve the crime. Alemán ordered "all the police agencies" to collaborate in the investigation, including the newly created Dirección Federal de Seguridad. The Federal District's Servicio Secreto took the leading role in the investigation because the crime had taken place within its jurisdiction.[103]

As the analysis of evidence and interrogations proceeded in the following days, the political motivations behind the crime became clear. Angulo, who was not a leftist like Altamirano, had agreed with the other senator from

Tlaxcala, Gerzayn Ugarte, and with governor, Ávila Bretón, to moderate the competition for the next gubernatorial election. Assassination was already part of the campaign: in November of the previous year former deputy Aurelio León, also involved in Ávila Bretón's succession, had been murdered in Apizaco with the same gun used to kill Angulo.[104] To preempt accusations, Governor Ávila Bretón hurried to Mexico City to meet with Alemán, and he later participated in the interrogation of suspects. Many names were mentioned at first, including a duo of radio singers. Soon, however, members of the same Veracruzano clan linked to Altamirano's death emerged as suspects. The first to be arrested were Marciano Armenta Castillo, Armando Armenta Barradas, and José López Hernández. The Jeep used to escape belonged to Armenta Castillo. Another suspect, Rafael Barradas Osorio, told Servicio Secreto agents that he had recently met "Armando Barradas" and Hugo Izquierdo Ebrard at the construction site of the Hotel del Prado in Mexico City. As Barradas Osorio read to him the murderer's description from a newspaper, Izquierdo Ebrard acknowledged that he had to "finish off the affair" and kill Angulo and that he expected to be arrested.[105] Marciano bragged that he would never be brought to justice because he could count on the loyalty of his men. He told agents that "my boys do what I order because I have disciplined people and we all work in coordination." When a detective told him that there was indeed a confession, Armenta Castillo refused to believe it, as the alleged informer "is too much of a man and also knows our code, because in our family whoever speaks or confesses and endangers our lives, will die."[106]

Politics explained the assassination but also got in the way of punishment. Servicio Secreto agents, with the collaboration of Tlaxcala state prosecutors, called a meeting with Armenta Castillo, Ugarte, Ávila Bretón, the owner of a brothel in Apizaco, and other local Tlaxcalteca authorities. The discussion seemed less an interrogation than a closed-door council. According to the agents' report, Marciano Armenta Castillo candidly stated that "it is not to my advantage to confess because it will hurt me politically." He did tell Ugarte and others that he had asked Armenta Barradas and brothers Hugo and Arturo Izquierdo Ebrard to kill Angulo because he wanted to be governor, and because during the Almazán campaign Angulo had killed his brother Teodoro Armenta "by crucifixion."[107]

Armenta Castillo's words were lent credence by the violent reputation of his subordinates. The anti-agrarista activities of the thirties, in which the Armentas had participated as members of the Mano Negra, had expanded into robbery, extortion, and other businesses outside their region by the late forties.[108] Just days before the murder of Angulo, the Dirección Federal de Seguridad had begun to investigate Marciano Armenta Castillo for his behavior in the construction of the Hotel del Prado. As a contractor, he was overcharging for work poorly done, employing men who had criminal records, and using official badges and guns to threaten and beat engineers who complained.[109] Statements and reports on the Angulo investigation were leaked to the press. Headlines dubbed Armenta Castillo and his men "sinister and somber superpistoleros." [110]

In a way that he probably did not expect, Armenta Castillo was correct in predicting the ultimate failure of the investigation. The reason why Veracruzano "superpistoleros" were involved in a Tlaxcalteca political conflict was never clarified because the ley fuga brought the case to a premature conclusion. As mentioned in chapter 3, Armenta Castillo, Armando Armenta Barradas, and José López Hernández were killed on a Veracruz highway by Servicio Secreto agents who were taking them to locate the Izquierdo Ebrard brothers.[111] The trip took place even though the first three had not yet been officially charged, and their lawyers, fearing the ley fuga, had presented amparos to keep them in Mexico City. The caravan with the suspects and the agents stopped in a lonely area near Magueyitos, Veracruz, so that the three men could attend to their bodily needs. Instead, according to Servicio Secreto chief Pedro J. Castro, they ran in different directions, and they were shot just before they disappeared into the fog that surrounded the highway.

Although this was hardly the proper conclusion from a judicial point of view, from the public's perspective, it closed the case in a legitimate way, demonstrating authorities' strong hand against "professional pistolerismo." [112] Veracruz governor and future president Adolfo Ruiz Cortines told a Servicio Secreto agent sent to Xalapa to ask for Ruiz Cortines's opinion that "he hoped this would end the era of terror that these men had established in the state." He added that he had "not received any complaints" and "that opinion accepts what happened." [113] It was a textbook example of the use of ley fuga. Once the detective work was over, and Armenta Castillo refused to confess, the agents in charge of the investigation case moved it toward a resolution focused on the concerns about public perception articulated by Ruiz Cortines. In the press, the Magueyitos episode meant that justice, if not the law, had been served.[114] *La Prensa* put the image of the pistoleros' bodies on its front page, reproduced "the executioners' version," and described the scene as the epilogue of "a long career of crimes and professional pistolerismo, when everything had finished and senator Angulo's blood, among the blood of others, had been avenged."[115] All parties seemed to accept this version. In a letter to Alemán, Gloria Flores, a relative of Armenta Castillo, agreed with the idea that the death of the three men was an execution, meant to make someone pay for the deaths of León and Angulo. She only challenged the fairness of making three men pay for the deaths of only two.[116]

The murder of Senator Angulo and its resolution suggest a forking path of the history of pistolerismo. On the one hand, the creation of the Dirección Federal de Seguridad by Alemán expressed the willingness of the federal government to centralize and institutionalize some of the functions that pistoleros had thus far served on an informal basis. From the time of Alemán's election in 1946, the regime was particularly concerned about improving the country's image. In Veracruz, as Gillingham notes, the caciques who dominated through the Mano Negra had become enmeshed in suicidal infighting by the late forties. Crispín Aguilar was imprisoned between 1947 and 1950 and was killed soon after his release. Rafael Cornejo Armenta, Aguilar's adversary and the material author of Altamirano's death, suffered a similar fate. Violence began to decrease as the state reined in the activities of pistoleros, or at least some of them.[117] Other pistoleros, though, survived modernization by taking a different path, forsaking politics and focusing only on illegal business. The brothers Izquierdo Ebrard, eventually captured by a military officer in Veracruz, were sentenced to nineteen years of prison for Angulo's murder, but they remained powerful enough in prison to influence events and people outside.[118] Hugo Izquierdo Ebrard was free by 1958, and he was arrested again as a member of the gang of violent robbers lead by Fidel Corvera Ríos.[119] If there was a lesson, it was that assassination in Mexico City was no longer a cost-free way to solve local disputes.

As the next case suggests, however, we should remain skeptical of the narrative proposing a dichotomy between institutionalization and crime. Alemán's ascent to the presidency could be interpreted simply as elevating pistolerismo to a higher level, not ushering in its obsolescence. After all, he owed an important step in his career to the murder of Altamirano and the support of the most traditional caciquista leadership, including Manuel Parra. When he joined Manuel Ávila Camacho's cabinet as minister of gobernación, he brought his own pistoleros from Veracruz. Some of those who had protected him as a governor became part of the Dirección Federal de Seguridad, which he initially put in charge of his personal security as president.[120]

Alemán modeled the DFS after the U.S. Federal Bureau of Investigation. The apparent contradiction of having bodyguards staff a modern investigation agency is less puzzling when we consider the multiplication of police agencies during the postrevolutionary period. There were institutions for preventive and investigative policing at the municipal, state, and federal levels, plus police agencies attached to specific aspects of governance (highways, banks, military, drugs, and migration). Rather than being a coherent expression of state sovereignty, the plurality of agencies expressed, as noted in chapter 3, their limited ability to investigate, while at the same time maintaining political equilibrium among their respective bosses.[121] After the revolution, according to *Detectives,* the Federal District police department was filled with men who had no credentials, and in some cases could not even read, who were hired because they had sponsors, like senators or mayors from other cities, or were able to buy the position.[122]

When Alemán ordered that "all the police agencies" collaborate in the investigation of Angulo's death, he was implicitly recognizing the problems caused by that diversity. Forensic method, for example, was less important than overpowering the competition. Multiple agencies usually descended on the crime scene, as in the case of Angulo; some agencies could detain suspects for periods longer than what was authorized by the law before releasing them to the judicial authorities (the only ones authorized to bring charges) or dispatching them with the ley fuga. According to *La Prensa,* "Each police body has created its own clues." [123] The DFS, like the Servicio Secreto, worked in a juridical "limbo" that allowed it to investigate other agencies and use force with little oversight, but with implicit presidential support.[124] While this lack of regulation facilitated the work of agents-pistoleros, it also undermined public trust in the result of their investigations. Agents from different institutions could be found among suspects and witnesses, as we shall see in the following case.[125]

The assassination of labor organizer Alonso Mascarúa shows that the violence of pistoleros continued to be a viable business connected to a range of economic and political activities, in and around police agencies. In this case, the victim was not a high-level politician but an activist in the union of movie theater employees. On the night of August 10, 1954, Mascarúa was returning to his house in Colonia Asturias when a man shot him from a car and another stabbed him to death. Minutes before, he had been at a restaurant near his house. Upon leaving, he told the owner that he wanted to be back home early because there were robbers around the neighborhood. He added, however, that he was not afraid of them, and he showed the owner the gun tucked under his belt. Mascarúa was also carrying fifteen hundred copies of a flyer he was planning to distribute the following day. The flyers disappeared, but the police and newspapers learned that they accused Mascarúa's rival at the union, Pedro Téllez Vargas, of misappropriating union funds. The killers disappeared without leaving more than a vague description from a couple of witnesses.[126]

Mascarúa's family and supporters immediately accused Téllez Vargas. Newspapers echoed this suspicion in the days following the crime. Yet Téllez Vargas adamantly denied having ordered the crime, and he even attended Mascarúa's funeral.[127] It was easy to see the imprint of violent labor politics. Since the early postrevolutionary years, most notably in the 1948 "charrazo" against railroad workers, the government deployed violence as one of its tactics against independent unions. Téllez Vargas had his own "grupo de choque" of armed men to intimidate rivals. Editorials claimed that the murder only demonstrated that "union gangsterism is reviving in its greatest opprobrium."[128] Labor leaders often enjoyed a degree of protection against prosecution for common crimes. Some labor sectors, like sugar mill workers, were particularly violent, but unions associated with modern industries like cinema also saw their share of beatings and bullets.[129]

The police investigation targeted "hundreds" of suspects. Some of those mentioned as possible intellectual authors besides Téllez Vargas included communists, the powerful union leader Fidel Velázquez, Deputy Alberto Hernández Campos, and a group of distributors and theater owners controlled by William Jenkins. The potential ramifications of the case were so complicated that police officers told *La Prensa:* "'This is an issue that burns the hands.' ... it will very difficult for this treacherous crime to be properly solved, and ... the involvement of powerful interests is ... an obstacle to taking the investigation in the right direction."[130] Téllez Vargas and the union offered a reward of 10,000 pesos for information leading to the capture of the murderers.[131] A month went by without any results, and then José Antonio Arredondo, aka El Jarocho, was arrested by Servicio Secreto agents in relation to another crime. He was a pistolero who had worked as confidential agent for the police, had been previously accused of two murders, and had participated in the repression of the Rubén Jaramillo movement by the judicial police of the state of Morelos.[132] Arredondo declared that four months earlier Alejandro Ponce de León had asked him to kill Mascarúa for 20,000 pesos on behalf of a third man, but that he had rejected the offer, arguing that "if when I was in bad shape I did not do it, much less [would I do it] now that I do not have the need."[133] Arredondo looked like a witness produced by the police in order to push forward an investigation that seemed to be stagnating. He came to judicial proceedings well dressed and in the company of Secret Service agents, one of whom was seen giving him a gun before he climbed into a car with other police officers.[134] Arredondo claimed that he testified out of his "affection" for the Secret Service, but he also received the reward offered by the union.[135]

Arredondo's statements, whether truthful or fabricated, led to the arrest of Ponce de León in Puebla. According to Ponce de León's wife, "Four guys in leather jackets with Texan hats" kidnapped him, kept him for several days, and subjected him to "savage" torture.[136] The men were Federal District Servicio Secreto, and it took several days before the government of Puebla allowed them to transport Ponce de León to the capital, where he finally testified in court. Ponce de León was probably protected in Puebla: he owned a gas station that was a gift from his father, a wealthy businessman, he had worked as confidential agent for the state of Puebla police, had killed a man, and sometimes had worked as an extra in the movies. The press characterized him as professional pistolero. His own nephew, Joaquín Vigueras Ponce de León, told journalists that "my uncle never left his 38 . . . he always carries it in the right pocket of his pants, and he is very dangerous," adding that "he is one of the bloodiest murderers . . . He can kill any person with a smile on his lips, and can sell his own mother."[137]

Ponce de León had asked Vigueras to find somebody "to come with him, as a pistolero, because he had to beat somebody up." Vigueras told him he "already knew a person, who was a boxer and could do what he was asked to." This person was Antonio Trujeque, who "has a reputation of troublemaker and in street brawls he slammed his adversaries' heads against the floor, and he has previously committed a murder." Trujeque was arrested and confessed to his participation in the murder of Mascarúa. He also confessed that he had killed a boy of fourteen at a party by stabbing his jugular and that he had used the same procedure with Mascarúa, with the complicity of two other men and Ponce de León, who had promised to pay him 10,000 pesos.[138] The Puebla police later found a 150-peso receipt for expenses signed by Trujeque to Ponce de León. The deal may have also included promises in case Trujeque was arrested: he later got into a fight with Ponce de León at the Mexico City penitentiary, arguing that Ponce de León had promised to pay for his food while he was in prison and to provide him with good lawyers.[139]

Ponce de León was only an intermediary. From the moment of his arrest, in early September, *La Prensa* speculated that his testimony might lead to the true author of the crime, and that the delay in presenting him to judicial authorities was a scheme by "extremely powerful influences that have moved to prevent public opinion from learning what Alejandro Ponce de León is really saying."[140] Eventually, he declared that the crime had been commissioned by his former boss, powerful businessman Gabriel Alarcón, who had first asked him to kill another union leader, Salvador Carrillo, an ally of Téllez Vargas.[141] Alarcón promised to pay Ponce de León 100,000 pesos upon completion of the job.[142] The idea was to ruin Téllez Vargas's reputation and thus pave the way for Alarcón's company, Cadena de Oro, to buy more theaters in addition to the four hundred it already owned. Alarcón was a partner of Jenkins and both were known to use any means necessary to consolidate their monopoly of movie screens.

As the case advanced, and despite the confessions of the material authors, the impotence of Mexican justice became the object of derision. Ponce de León recanted his confession and said he had been tortured. The press mentioned other crimes in which Jenkins and Alarcón were suspects, but only the latter was charged with Mascarúa's death. When a judge issued the arrest warrant, police surrounded Alarcón's house in Puebla, but refrained from capturing him. He finally presented himself to the police with the protection of another judge's amparo so that he would not be detained. Alarcón's lawyers used various maneuvers to keep him out of jail. He was sentenced to twenty years, but the sentence was later annuled.[143] In the end, his business career was not fundamentally altered by the case. He went on to found a newspaper, *El Heraldo de México,* and he died with his wealth intact in 1986. Jenkins and Alarcón were, after all, close to all the Mexican presidents after 1940, and they wielded great influence. They had been partners of Maximino Ávila Camacho and his brother Rafael, governor of Puebla in 1954, both of whom were brothers of the former president.[144] Once again, politics and business had come together seamlessly thanks to the handiwork of pistoleros.

CONCLUSIONS

The cases discussed in this chapter resemble many others in their intertwining of violence, crime, justice, and politics. Investigations and sentences did not provide closure because there was always an ultimate explanation that could not be supported juridically: that someone in power had ordered the crime. It would be a mistake, however, to simply blame "power." If the historian tries to take the place of the judge, cause and effect are as evasive as legal responsibility.[145] In this regard, pistoleros' violent methods can be more illuminating than their putative goals. In each of the three cases, men came to kill without so much as a word or a provocation, and then walked away without concern: they did not need to hide their faces. They simply climbed into a car and disappeared into the city, relying on anonymity, the inability of investigations to reach them, and the porosity of prisons. After they finished their job, they returned to the places where they were well known and protected. It is only thanks to the unorthodox methods of the Federal District's Servicio Secreto and the persistence of the newspapers that they did not escape us entirely.

Pistoleros were known by the criminally literate as experts on violence who relied simultaneously on visibility and secrecy. The murderers in the three cases examined here were professional pistoleros; they had the technical capacity and the will to use violence, and they were part of networks in which those attributes were rewarded. Testimonies of the Armentas' use of violence in the region of Veracruz they dominated are abundant. Like the Izquierdo Ebrards, they were prone to boasting about their exploits, and they became involved in different kinds of illegality. Trujeque's brutality in fights and a previous murder served as a recommendation of his services for Ponce de León, as was also true of Lobillo when Parra sought him out. Some, like El Güero Batillas, deliberately constructed their public personas, offering a variation of the criminal-as-author role that the nota roja and criminology had established.[146] More performers than authors, pistoleros understood the power of their image. They used it to further their goals by instilling fear but also by preserving and expanding their cultural capital. Violence was a well-advertised signal that could reach potential partners in illegality.[147] But all of them also knew to be careful, leaving no traces or confusion behind them. In other words, pistoleros moved between ominous secrecy and obnoxious visibility. The cause for this was their double role as political and economic actors. They had to serve their bosses by using violence against adversaries in a way that could not be traced back to its intellectual authors. At the same time, pistoleros benefited from impunity by engaging in a diversity of illegal business, murder being one of them.

Many feared that pistolerismo could degrade public life into a violent state of nature, bringing to the cities the kind of brutality urban residents associated with rural life. Successive governments, particularly after the Alemán presidency, sought to rationalize pistolero violence, yet they were not able to eliminate the profession. If anything, as we saw, institutional change only brought "good" pistoleros to bear against those who were too disruptive. What the state never seriously attempted was to control them through the law. Impunity was less the product of a totalitarian conspiracy than the result of a system in which multiple players conducted a variety of illegal activities under different sorts of official sponsorship. The judicial system's failure to rein in pistoleros revealed the growing difficulty of drawing a line between politics and illicit business, and the recognition of pistoleros' competence in crossing back and forth over that line. Pistoleros lent their expertise in the use of violence and their social connections to the daily operations of politics and business. Whether moved by loyalty, money, or most commonly both, pistoleros participated in a range of activities that were advantageous for both their bosses and themselves. They were emblematic of that mixing of public and private roles through combining a clientelistic sense of obligation with shameless individualism.

At different levels, this complex relationship between politics and business defined the entire postrevolutionary regime. Authoritarianism is often used as the category that best defines this regime in institutional terms, from the presidency down to the ballot. Single-party rule, coercion combined with consent, and corporative structures severely constrained representation and democracy. However, observed from the ground level, the label of "authoritarian" suggests a bottom-up coherence. In Mexico, the history of pistoleros shows how authoritarianism was embedded in everyday life. The system was based on a decentralized use of violence, involving multiple actors with various degrees of official authority—a form of "soft authoritarianism." [148] Violence cemented the stability of the groups in power at all levels of government. With their apparently arbitrary power and their tacit logic, pistoleros were the fulcrum of the political system. While political history has focused on their role in repressing agrarian, labor, and electoral opposition, the evidence in this chapter suggests that pistolero violence was a pillar of authoritarianism that constantly demonstrated the absence of justice, and profited from that absence. [149]

This manifestation of authoritarian rule was harder to denounce than others because the only way to prove that justice had failed required universal agreement regarding the truth about crime. As previous chapters have shown, that truth was obscured by the shortcomings of detectives, and by judges' and public opinion's excessive reliance on confessions. The result was a widely held belief in the existence of conspiracies behind every serious crime. The impunity of some of the pistoleros discussed in this chapter seemed only to prove these theories. Impunity thus became the keystone of a system in which the state lacked the monopoly of the legitimate use of violence, yet maintained the appearance of an unlimited ability to use it.

As a consequence, citizens saw the political and criminal functions of pistolero violence as almost natural. This impression was based on several assumptions. The central one was that public life and business were fundamentally masculine realms. Pistoleros excluded the "weak" in ways that required no explanation. Another assumption was that they practiced a quintessentially Mexican trade. The stereotype of the sharply dressed, badge-holding, gun-toting tough guy permeated popular culture, and educated commentators explained it as a Mexican phenomenon. For example, Eduardo Luquín's 1950 novel, *Aguila de oro: Espejo del pistolero,* suggested that pistolerismo was the combined product of the revolution and "the coldness with which murder is committed in Mexico, the disdain for human life," an atavistic expression of "the voice of Huiztilopochtli." [150] Burroughs admired Mexicans "who don't take no shit from nobody," and the fact that "all officials are corruptible" in the country.[151] Even recent historical scholarship is tempted by explanations of pistoleros that refer to a general "habitus" of Mexican culture or a "Mexican psyche." [152]

That national reputation was based on the belief that crime and impunity were inevitable parts of life in Mexico. Yet such naturalization contradicted the evidence, also presented in this chapter, that many citizens resisted the arrogance of pistoleros. The next chapters examine one kind of reaction against infamy. Denouncing impunity in the absence of the truth required a collective effort of imagination, which was expressed by crime fiction. Fiction created a realm where intelligence defeated brutality, dispelling the dark presence of pistoleros and offering some control for Mexicans over the "surface of images" that was their infamy.

PART THREE

Fictions

SIX

Our Times, Our Perspectives

THE EMERGENCE OF MEXICAN CRIME FICTION

Crime fiction was the most popular literary genre in Mexico in the mid–twentieth century. During its golden years, between the forties and sixties, the genre satisfied different tastes, encompassing a great variety of titles, translations of foreign authors, and a number of local writers. It had educated readers who appreciated bookish references to justify the ephemeral joy of a seedy story; it also had less pretentious readers who carefully assembled a novel out of the comic pages of the newspaper on the corner newsstands. Magazines encouraged budding or occasional writers to submit their manuscripts. Editors selected national and translated stories for publication, providing readers with references and basic facts about the genre.

Mexican crime fiction was also required reading for understanding the broken nexus between crime, truth, and justice. Novels and short stories published between the forties and sixties established a realm of the imagination where the violence and impunity associated with policemen, murderers, and pistoleros could not undermine the pursuit of the truth and some form of justice. Fiction was not a way to escape uncertainty but to embrace it with irony. Crime novels and magazines were printed on the same cheap paper as the nota roja, and they were found in the same places: offices, markets, barbershops. Reading them was not a leisurely pastime but a moment of pleasure stolen from the urgencies of everyday life. Actors from different classes and countries interacted in those pages, playing the roles of victims, detectives, policemen, politicians, and criminals; they were moved by greed, revenge, naïveté, or other emotions that in their diversity were a reaction to popular vices and government weaknesses. Critical views of justice found their best expression in narratives that took the form of fiction but consistently referred to reality. Just like court testimonies, police reports, or newspaper articles, crime fiction documented the tangled paths that led to the truth. Its writers and readers had a morally ambivalent relationship with violence, the police, and the judicial system.

Reading crime fiction was a reliable way to enhance criminal literacy: it helped readers to understand the city and its puzzling combination of modern life (consumer culture, cosmopolitanism, free speech) and a restrictive political system. The genre, in turn, shaped discussions about that new world: by looking at justice and violence through the eyes of criminals or detectives who were outsiders, Mexican readers developed a skeptical attitude toward the state.[1] This does not mean that realism defined Mexican crime narrative: its plot was more important than the setting or the psychological depth of the characters. Nor was nationalism a characteristic feature of the genre, since crime stories were not concerned with the Mexican essence that prestigious intellectuals of the time looked for, mostly in the countryside. Instead, stories took place in urban settings involving a motley cast of locals and foreigners. National identity had little relevance for fictional Mexican detectives; they preferred to tackle murder as a concrete problem rather than as a sign of a collective psychological trait. Otherwise, what was the point of finding a culprit?[2] There was no political program in this search other than a sardonic awareness of the infamy of a country that wanted to be progressive but could not do so. The urban setting was not a cause of crime; it just offered segmented spaces, anonymity, and a fast pace for social transactions—in other words, an opportunity to challenge the oppressive hierarchies that nationalist intellectuals believed to be an essential feature of Mexican society. Until the sixties, Mexican crime writers did not see corruption as a weapon of an authoritarian state but simply as a fact of life that had to be dealt with.[3]

Rather than looking inward for Mexican essences, crime fiction was in constant dialogue with foreign interlocutors. Its detectives emulated the methods of their counterparts in the United States, England, and France, and stories often included foreign criminals. As Mexico acquired new ties with the outside world, from the Spanish Civil War through the Cold War, there was no choice but to take sides with or against "imported" ideologies like fascism and communism. Consumer culture and Americanization, brought in part by returning Mexican migrants, transformed habits and shaped cultural products.[4] The pages of crime magazines and the shelves of bookstores reflected this new openness: Mexican authors offered their stories next to foreign counterparts, and Mexican readers did not seem to favor authors based on nationality.[5] The earliest Mexican detective novel I found compares its hero, Pancho Reyes, "the Mexican detective," to the likes of Holmes and Nick Carter.[6] The parallelism would become a trope of the genre. It is inaccurate, however, to think that this conversation with foreign authors and references made Mexican crime fiction artificially cosmopolitan: instead, it was a way to approach Mexican reality through one of the most salient aspects of contemporary life. World War II and the connections built by consumption and migration provided a fertile setting and demonstrated the urgency of engaging with the rest of the world.[7]

However, the essential link with reality and the common denominator of the genre was murder. As a danger of everyday life, murder bridged fiction, social life, and politics. For W. H. Auden, "Murder is unique in that it abolishes the party it injures, so that society has to take the place of the victim and on his behalf demand restitution or grant forgiveness; it is the one crime in which society has a direct interest."[8] Since its origins with Edgar Allan Poe, detective fiction has tried to give rational meaning to an act that was difficult to explain from an enlightened perspective, if not outright monstrous, a sign of a failure of society, according to Raymond Chandler. Through the nota roja, homicide in Mexico demonstrated its ability to bring together large audiences. Common homicide was a political topic because it exhibited the moral limits of government, not only in its inability to reveal the truth but also in its complicity with violence and illegality. The multiplicity of voices and media mobilized by murder occupied the space that authority vacated in the public sphere.[9] Fiction went further than any other media in exploring the physical and moral variations of murder.

Mexican writers put murder at the center of complex storylines. In order to enjoy murder, readers needed to have some knowledge about the rules that structured mystery plots. Although some authors in Mexico were quite strict about how stories should be written, readers did not see theory as a requirement for enjoying a good account, and in practice, there were many plot variations. In the classical form, a smart criminal challenges an even smarter detective who is at the center of the cast of characters. This unity of perspective was important to establish the narrative's connection to social life and politics. A recurring protagonist made it possible to repeat themes and structure, and it allowed publishers to attain a production speed that guaranteed an ample supply of cheap titles for a growing numbers of readers. Thus, for example, some early Mexican stories parodied Sherlock Holmes: instead of possessing a methodical intelligence, Mexican detectives were multi-talented, clever schemers whose genius also contrasted with the clumsiness of the police.[10]

Common narrative elements included suspense (the author knows more than the reader and administers the information to achieve tension), legibility (stories are written in a clear way), simple characters (often little more than stereotypes), and intellectual rigor (reason always wins). Fair play was a basic assumption, a pact that guaranteed the reader would have all the necessary information to solve the case using common sense. In the classic model, two narratives merged, one of the investigation centered on gathering facts to find out who was the criminal, and one of the crime itself, centered on the events. The first one reveals the second, but the plot cannot work if it excludes either one. As in the nota roja, the reader follows the investigation from the perspective of the detective or journalist, reconstructing the events preceding the crime, the crime itself, and the subsequent pursuit of the criminal. Beginning with Edgar Allan Poe's foundational tales, the identification of detective and reader was suggested by the key role of newspapers in solving crimes.[11]

With regard to the setting, as in Agatha Christie's stories, private, upper-class spaces were common, and the act of murder was physically simple, representing an intellectual challenge more than a true moral violation. Hard-boiled authors like Raymond Chandler dismissed these conventions and instead stressed the author's honesty through his own voice, keeping the detective at the center of the plot "because he seeks the truth."[12] This was not easy for Mexican writers because "honesty" and "detective" were two words that did not easily go together to describe Mexican reality. By contrast, it was not such a dishonest thing for authors to adopt the murderer's perspective or blur the distinction between detective and criminal. The fact that the detective was a man of honor did not mean that he did not have an ambivalent relationship with the law. Chandler's words applied to Mexico very well: a good crime author "writes of a world in which gangsters can rule nations and almost rule cities."[13] In Mexican crime stories, collaborations between the detective and the police were close but never friendly, sometimes antagonistic, and always colored by mutual scorn. U.S. hard-boiled and Mexican stories shared another implicit rule: justice could arrive indirectly, frequently with the offender's death, for causes unrelated to his or her transgression. "Hell with loose ends," as a Chandler detective put it, as long as the detective and the reader knew that the result was fair.[14] Hard-boiled novels had a greater diversity of relationships between characters, and the investigation focused on the reconstruction of the selfish reasoning of diverse actors in a context where violence and corruption prevailed. In the "messy and morally ambiguous" novels of Dashiell Hammett and others, escaping reality through mental exercise was no longer the goal, a happy ending was not guaranteed, and the detective was a hero in spite of himself.[15]

The genre evolved and expanded over the course of the twentieth century, but what most Mexican crime fiction shared during its golden years was a focus on a moral plot, parallel to that of detection. The detection plot could be quite intricate, sometimes technical, but its basic question was simple: Who did it? In the moral plot, uncovering characters' motivations was as important as following the procedures used to discover the culprit. The questions were more complicated (Why did he do it? Who is really to blame?). The goal was to arrive at the truth through the intelligence and daring of detectives who relied on the critical observation of the behavior and testimony of characters, and only marginally depended on evidence. The resolution could include public punishment or individual redemption. Although the detection and the moral plots were inextricably linked, Mexican stories of this era used the former the same way the detective of Dashiell Hammett's *Red Harvest* used dynamite: to uncover power relations and the web of loyalty, betrayal, and deceit behind the real crimes. The truth resided in an ethical and political dimension that was at the heart of the connection between fiction and reality. In the case of Hammett, the bitter conclusion was that, against expectations under the rule of law, solving the investigation did not mean solving the moral problem. All that writers could do, he argued, was to maintain "the integrity of their disenchantment," their ability to see with clear eyes the mechanisms that moved each character.[16] In depression-era United States, this meant understanding the rationality that a capitalist economy had imposed over the imagined moral simplicity of established social customs. The disenchantment in mid-century Mexico centered on the fact that the state failed to provide a framework for justice. Both in Mexico and the United States, the game played by writers and readers was seldom satisfactory in the sense of offering the neat restoration of order sought by classic detectives. All the moral plot could do to reestablish balance after the crime was to signal the possibilities of justice outside the law.[17]

The genre was accessible to readers and authors because it was particularly able to absorb different languages and incorporate a diversity of voices. As a result, it could present social relations in ways that were less weighed down by literary pretensions than in other genres of national literature. The role of authors was not as dominant as in those other genres: some hid their names, others plagiarized; very few wanted to be remembered as crime writers. Pseudonyms were so common that when José Dibildox submitted a manuscript to the magazine *Aventura y Misterio,* editors assumed the name was not real.[18] Unburdened by prestige, these writers inhabited a literary field that was open to many kinds of readers and writers.[19] Different models inspired local stories (detective, mystery, noir). Plots, authors, and audiences frequently crossed over to other media, like the nota roja and the movies.[20] Even the name of the genre was disputed. *Literatura policial* was the term used by most contemporaries, but the police were rarely the center of the story, and the privileged perspective was often that of criminals. Murder was the common denominator, but the genre was never called the murder novel. Even the term "literature" can be deceiving. It could be said that these stories, their readers, authors, and publishers came together in a "field," a structured and relatively autonomous social space. But it was also a "genre" in the coherence of its narrative devices.[21] Thus, the term "crime fiction" is appropriate enough to distinguish it from the other ways to talk about crime as considered in this book.

Despite its role in discussions about crime and justice in the public sphere, history and literary criticism have not taken midcentury Mexican crime fiction very seriously. Scholars have defined it by its authors, noting their dilettantism and parasitic relationship with foreign models. Not surprisingly, most prominent Mexican writers avoided the genre, and the few who tried it found their experiments ignored for decades, their attempts receding into oblivion together with those of lesser-known authors. Only a fraction of the national production of detective and mystery stories from the initial and most productive period, between the forties and sixties, has been reprinted, and for the most part, contemporary libraries have failed to preserve original books and magazines. State-supported publishers and intellectuals were more interested in narratives with rural settings and revolutionary themes that addressed national identity; these offered better chances for literary recognition. With few exceptions, studies of Mexican crime fiction also judge its authors, particularly those writing before the 1970s, as having lesser aesthetic and social value. According to this perspective, Mexican crime fiction did not faithfully reproduce "Mexican reality" and was plagued by artificial situations and characters, constituting an eclectic and derivative version of foreign recipes.[22]

Part of this contempt is based on national infamy: since there is no justice in Mexico, critics argue, one cannot take seriously a genre whose central theme is the search for truth and the restoration of the moral order altered by transgression. No reader could believe in the existence of a Mexican Sherlock Holmes because there was no Mexican Scotland Yard or Old Bailey. Yet authors were aware of the paradoxes of detection and justice in Mexico. María Elvira Bermúdez, discussed in the next chapter, explained that "the Mexican distinguishes himself by his unashamed skepticism toward the power of abstract justice and by a bitter disdain toward the actions of the representatives of concrete justice. For the Mexican, revenge is synonymous with justice . . . he does not care about the quest for justice."[23] For other early writers and editors, "justice was so unreliable and corruptible that it almost made no sense to adapt the police detection procedures of Anglo-Saxon stories. Here, they claimed, everything is simpler and more brutal. . . . In an environment ruled by the venality of justice, it makes little difference the capacity to establish complex logical sequences, the marvelous reading of the criminal's mind."[24] By defining Mexican crime fiction's shortcomings in terms of its tenuous connections with Mexican reality, scholars have ignored these authors' efforts to critically engage with the dilemmas of crime and punishment.

This chapter examines that effort through three manifestations of early Mexican crime fiction. In the next section I will examine two writers, Antonio Helú and José Martínez de la Vega, who played a key role in building the popularity of the genre beginning in the 1940s. They wrote stories that made fun of police ineptitude and celebrated the ingenuity of detectives who skirted the law. The product of a generation disappointed by postrevolutionary politics, their stories tried to make sense of the violence and corruption of public life. In the second section, I will look at mystery magazines and their construction of savvy new readers and writers. Editors like Helú wanted to engage international authors and bring them to Mexican audiences, educating local readers on the rules of logic and intuition behind a good plot. In the third section, I will discuss some of the social attitudes implicit in those plots through a series of short novels published by *La Prensa* about the adventures of fictional reporter and detective Chucho Cárdenas. These stories stressed the role of public opinion and drew a map of Mexican society in which women were often reduced to objects of desire, and humble but upwardly mobile men proved their worth to foreigners and those who still lived in cultural backwardness. Together, these three cases help us understand the basis for the genre's popularity. The following chapter will delve into a few other authors who more systematically explored Mexican conditions in the pursuit of justice and the truth.

At first, Mexican crime fiction opted for satire instead of technical accuracy and realism. The works of Antonio Helú and José Martínez de la Vega parodied the classics and mocked the justice system, setting up the baseline of skepticism that would define the national narrative. The first writer to embrace the genre was Helú (1900–1972). Of Lebanese immigrant parents, he was forced to leave the country after his participation in José Vasconcelos's 1929 presidential campaign. Vasconcelos was the founder of the Secretaría de Educación Pública under Álvaro Obregón. After the caudillo's death, he mounted a strong challenge to the candidate supported by Plutarco Elías Calles. Vasconcelos's followers included many students like Helú, whose hopes for a democratic and enlightened end to the rule of revolutionary caudillos were frustrated by the violence and electoral fraud of 1929. In exile in Los Angeles, Helú learned about movies and worked as a journalist. Upon his return in the thirties, he wrote for different media, but crime fiction remained his passion. In 1946 he founded the Club de la Calle Morgue along with Rafael Bernal, Enrique F. Gual, and other aspiring writers. The reference to Poe was clear in the group's name, but there was also inspiration from the Mystery Writers of America and the English Detection Club. The latter, once presided over by G. K. Chesterton, required members to swear an oath in which they promised "never to conceal a vital clue from the reader." [25] The goal of the Mexican Club, as Helú wrote to Frederic Dannay, editor of *Ellery Queen's Mystery Magazine,* was simple: "Few are those in our country who write detective fiction. We want many more writers of this 'genre,' and many more readers." [26] Helú was instrumental in achieving both goals by founding the magazine *Selecciones Policiacas y de Misterio* in 1946, which he edited with some interruptions until the fifties. He also established the publishing house Editorial Albatros, which sold detective and mystery novels as well as books on diverse popular topics. [27]

Helú was able to eke a living out of his passion. In 1944, he thanked Dannay for the seventy-five dollars he received in payment for a story and explained why he had to engage in other professional activities: "You can not make your living, here in Mexico, by writing short stories, not even detective short stories. I wrote six. . . . and I got about $50.00 (Mexican money) for each one. I was 25 then and I was ambitious, so I left short stories and began writing plays which met with some success. Then, the Mexican era of the movie picture started, and here I am now writing and directing for the movies."[28] Between 1936 and 1960, Helú worked on eighteen movie scripts and directed seven films, including one based on a story he wrote ("La obligación de asesinar," 1937). His texts were also published in magazines, newspapers, and edited books.

Helú simultaneously played with the conventions of the genre and used the detection plot to criticize contradictions in the Mexican cult of honor.[29] His 1925 story "Pepe Vargas al teléfono" is a dialogue in the format of a radio script and centers on the sleazy morality of journalists. The character is a up-and-coming reporter who engages in fights, writes on many themes, benefits from diverse official perks in exchange for libelous articles, and receives romantic favors from actresses.[30] In the 1928 story "El fistol de la corbata," Máximo Roldán solves a case by simply reading the newspaper at home. He scans the police section with great attention to detail and a dose of street smarts. He learns about the antecedents of the case because "lately I have been interested in browsing old newspapers and reading about the most famous cases." The rest of the story explains what Roldán knows before even arriving at the crime scene. He knows that the murderer is a woman because the two pieces of evidence left in the scene—the title's tie clip and a garter—are masculine objects intended to deceive the police. Her name is Isabel, and she was the victim of mistreatment at the hands of the deceased, her stepfather. Years earlier, he killed Isabel's mother and escaped punishment because she had a lover, and authorities at the time decided that homicides committed in "legitimate defense of honor" would not be prosecuted. Isabel confirms Roldán's deductions by showing him her diary, where she wrote how she conceived of the murder of the man she hated so much. Instead of denouncing her to the authorities, Roldán steals jewels belonging to the victim, gives Isabel some money, and allows her to escape.[31]

This cynicism toward the law is also evident in *El crimen de insurgentes,* a play Helú cowrote with Adolfo Fernández Bustamante, another member of the Club de la Calle Morgue. The play was staged at the Teatro Arbeu in 1935. The story takes place during a criminal jury trial, a common setting for Mexican stories even after its abolition in 1929. The detective, Carlos Miranda, begins as a mere spectator but soon demands that lawyers place him on the witness stand so he can address the jury. Using the same information everybody else has, Miranda solves the mystery and exonerates the suspect, who happens to be his girlfriend, Matilde. The trial brings together characters from different social classes: while the educated Miranda surprises everyone with his intelligence, witnesses, policemen, and lawyers are comically stupid. As in other Helú stories, an admiring audience validates the detective's findings without needing a representative of the state to confirm them. Jurors vote and the acquittal is celebrated in the courtroom. The true murderer turns out to be the family's domestic worker, who earns the sympathy of the audience because she killed the victim in defense of Matilde. When the judge commands her to show "more respect for justice!" she responds in the lower-class inflection that defines her voice: "Who is justice?"[32] Helú makes fun of justice's lack of prestige as an allegory, but he also displays the judge's real inability to control juries and audiences, who jeer at authority, hug the suspect, humiliate policemen, and cheer the murderer. As in "El fistol," the detective corrects the official investigation, the victim is a despicable paternal figure, and the murderer does not deserve punishment.

The ethical ambiguities of Helú's detectives reflect these views of justice. In a letter to Dannay, Helú proudly corrected Ellery Queen's statement that Arséne Lupin was the only character in the detective genre in which thief and detective were combined: Roldán (whose letters can be rearranged to spell "ladrón," thief) has both roles in a story that Helú offers to send Dannay, probably "El fistol," later published in the New York edition of Ellery Queen's.[33] Roldán becomes a thief and a murderer in "Debut profesional" when he uncovers fraud at his workplace and is forced to kill the embezzler, who was about to kill him—even though Roldán proposes that they split the money. He escapes with 20,000 pesos, reasoning that he was going to be accused anyway. Calling the police would only mean going to jail, when just yesterday he imagined himself "among the most honorable men on earth." He might go to Russia, then, since "the world is upside down!"[34] In "La obligación de asesinar," a fast-paced comedy of errors, Carlos Miranda is burglarizing a house when a murder takes place. The story follows his efforts to escape prosecution. Other crimes, however, take place while he does this. Miranda solves them through action rather than deduction: he tricks the murderer into trying to kill him, but the police, an otherwise useless bunch of dimwits, save him just in time. The plot is punctuated by comic scenes involving upper-class characters and an announcement addressed to the reader inviting her to solve the case.[35]

The complicity between Helú and his readers evokes an implicit view of Mexican justice and crime which absolves the detectives from any moral fault. The victims of Roldán's thefts are already dead, absolving him of guilt from the perspective of the reader. As with Miranda, circumstances force him to be a detective. They meet and become friends in "Cuentas claras," a story in which they steal money from a group of thieves.[36] In "Las tres bolas de billar," they also join forces to solve murders in a pool hall. They let the murderer escape because they think he was only trying to prevent a robbery, yet they also take the money that was going to be stolen since the runaway murderer is going to be blamed anyway.[37] Miranda and Roldán use their street smarts and intelligence to manipulate other characters and avoid the inept representatives of justice, in the process committing thefts and murders that are not morally wrong.

The irrelevance of formal justice acquires a darker tone in "Un día antes de morir," a story in which the narrator is a murderer awaiting execution. The death penalty was rarely used in Mexico, but as with the jury trial, it provided a dramatic scenario to frame a struggle against the mistakes of the state. The unnamed narrator had carefully planned to kill his friend in revenge for old offenses. When he arrives to execute his plan, he realizes that somebody has already killed his intended victim, and that the killer has tried to incriminate him by using his left hand to stab with a knife. The narrator soon comes to the conclusion that the real killer is a man named Obregón, the lover of the victim's wife, who in the past had also been the lover of the narrator. Thus, he finds and must kill Obregón to avoid being killed himself. In contrast with the murder he had planned, this time the narrator leaves his fingerprints and other evidence to incriminate himself. He is arrested, accused of the two murders, and sentenced to death. He writes now only to clarify that he is only responsible for one, although "it makes no difference whether I had killed one or the other, or both," or that he had done it in self-defense.[38]

The first stories by José Martínez de la Vega (1907–1954) supported the notion that early crime fiction in Mexico was a lighter version of the foreign original. He was a journalist at *Excélsior,* where he became director of the afternoon edition, *Últimas Noticias.* Two of his brothers were notable vasconcelistas, and his own production as a journalist reflected a conservative stance in line with *Excélsior.* His books and stories, published in the mid-forties, offer a humorous take on the detective form and illustrate the impossibility of real detective work in Mexico. Yet his peers recognized in him a keen observer of social mores. For Bermúdez, his stories are an example of that "Mexican neglect for anything that would involve precision, detail, routine."[39] Martínez de la Vega spelled out the national infamy: Mexican police were a joke, like the postrevolutionary regime in general; the Mexican people were laughable in their lack of intelligence, their immorality, and their propensity for violence. He used the detection plot to reiterate a simple moral truth: justice cannot be expected from institutions or civil society, so we might as well laugh at violence.

Parody assumes readers' prior knowledge of the classics.[40] Péter Pérez, the detective in Martínez de la Vega's stories, was himself a caricature of the stereotypical detective: poor, badly dressed, he dwells in a room of the working-class Colonia Peralvillo, and eats tacos in the street without much concern about hygiene ("Maybe the barbecue was dog, but with the guacamole you cannot even notice").[41] He needs to borrow or steal money from others in order to get to the crime scene. He used to be called Pedro, but he "internationalized his name." At the beginning of a case he sports a fake beard and a Sherlock Holmes hat and pipe. Yet people recognize him, the pipe makes him sick, and his deductions often turn out to be wrong.[42] The parody includes idiosyncratic forms of investigation "that many envious observers consider idiotic."[43] To find out, for example, whether a man had been poisoned, he has a puppy lick the hand of the corpse, with dire results for the puppy. Exaggerating the armchair detective trope, Péter locks himself in his house to think, explaining that "I am a mental detective" and that "I use my brain and nothing else."[44] He adds a Mexican twist to the pure logic of the classics: when solving a locked-room mystery, similar to those faced by "the brightest novelist detectives of the world," Péter's solution is embarrassingly obvious and is based on the fact that the room has no roof.[45] The smooth resolutions contrast with the violence of the crimes themselves: a corpse abandoned in a barrel; a man who enters a taquería and kills all the customers; a merchant lynched for promising low prices ("from before the times of Cárdenas"); a judge who is strangled, quartered, and sent in the mail. The cruelest death might be that of exotic dancer Mensolele (a reference to the U.S-born artist Tongolele): a student ties her to a chair and for six hours reads the Divine Comedy to her.[46]

Verisimilitude or literary accomplishment were of less concern to Martínez de la Vega than reaching a large readership. Péter Perez's stories were short and did not bother to build suspense. Suspects' confessions took care of the details, whether prompted by Péter's surprising intelligence or the police's threats of torture.[47] Drawings by famous caricaturists Armando Guerrero Edwards and Rafael Freyre resonated with the comics and editorial sections of newspapers. Other media broadened the audience. Some stories were in the format of radio scripts with directions for sound effects and musical intermissions. His adventures were broadcast on the radio. In the movies, popular comic Antonio Espino, known as "Clavillazo," played the title role in *El genial detective Péter Pérez* (Agustín Delgado, director, 1952).[48] The nota roja, a central component of *Últimas Noticias,* was simultaneously a popular vehicle for the stories, a tool of detection for the detective, and an object of derision for the author. Péter reads newspapers avidly and collects the comics; in a dialogue with another character, he parodies the language of the social section ("Cuquita Bertóldez got married; an elegant wedding, right?; Fulana wore turkey blue and mango from Veracruz; Zutana prickly pear with ornaments in goat milk tones . . . Ah, the elite!") and the police pages ("Horrible affair, miss; dreadful, tremendous, cruel, mysterious, fantastic, horrifying . . . gloomy, chilling, fatal, mortal").[49]

The relationship between Péter and the police is typical. The detective's official counterpart is Sergeant Vélez, who sometimes buys him food or a bus ticket, and even gives him a medal (for the wrong reason, it turns out). Most of the time, however, their relationship is competitive, as each tries to steal "glory" from the other. Martínez de la Vega also interjects his negative views of the police through editorial asides, denouncing agents who classify murders as suicides in order to avoid the work of investigation, as in "El misterio del gendarme desdentado," in which a police agent bites a street food vendor to death because she refused to pay the daily bribe (called *mordida,* bite, in the parlance of the times).[50] Police foibles were a vehicle for Martínez de la Vega's antigovernment views, which extended to other agents of the state. Political references appeared in brief jokes: the victim is "deader than effective suffrage,"[51] or through characters who portray the idiocy and criminality of public life, including union and agrarian leaders, or the murderer in "El crimen del estudio," a "professional pistolero, small-time political wannabe, and mental retard to boot."[52] However, the sarcasm goes beyond the state: lower-class characters are just as slow-witted and vulgar as police officers, and female characters are little more than the object of Péter's lewd insinuations.[53]

Parody was Martínez de la Vega's way to share with criminally literate readers a conservative view of society in which the lower classes deserved authoritarian rule, but the postrevolutionary state only offered corruption and ineptitude. Péter Pérez worked as a narrative caricature that pointed readers' attention toward the only angle that could make sense of that mess: crime. The detective does not read the political section of the newspapers because it reminds him of the ruling party's fraudulent electoral victories; homicides related to politics are not interesting because as everybody knows, "Electoral murders are never punished."[54] By contrast, the crime section is more engaging because murder turns "private life into public things."[55]

The moral and intellectual limitations of Helú's and Martínez de la Vega's detectives played a double role in these foundational stories of Mexican crime fiction: they established a sarcastic complicity with Mexican readers at the same time that they appropriated the classics of the genre. Both authors stated a reality few disputed: justice and the truth could not come from the police and the judiciary; it could only come from the picaresque wit of urban dwellers. This was an ironic version of nationalism that worked very well among readers. Their stories circulated through diverse media, cementing the popularity of crime fiction.

MAGAZINES CREATE READERS AND AUTHORS

The author is a thorny category of analysis for the historical reading of fiction texts. As Helú and Martínez de la Vega demonstrate, their political and journalistic experience provides some keys to understanding their stories. But there were many authors of crime fiction in mid-twentieth-century Mexico, and not much is known about the majority of them. This section tries another angle: understanding the conditions for the production of stories. In Mexico, as in other countries, most stories circulated in slim, pocket-sized magazines published every other week or in the daily section of newspapers, occupying an intermediate place between comics and books. This format contributed to the neglect of posterity: magazines have not been collected systematically, and many of those cited in the following pages come from used bookstores.[56] By contrast, single-author books were more prestigious. It was a different experience, for example, to read Bermúdez's "Muerte a la zaga" in volume 70 of *Selecciones Policiacas y de Misterio* in 1950, compared to reading it in *Los mejores cuentos policiales mexicanos,* edited without superfluous modesty by Bermúdez herself in 1955, or in a nicely designed volume devoted to her work by the reputable Editorial Premià in 1985. The latter book consecrated Bermúdez as a pioneer of "Mexican literature" in the context of the genre's revival during the eighties. The 1955 anthology paired Bermúdez with established and prestigious Mexican authors like Helú, Bernal, Martínez de la Vega, Antonio Castro Leal, and Rubén Salazar Mallén. The 1950 magazine sandwiched her story between pieces by Cornell Woolrich and Georges Simenon.[57]

Translated stories by the classic early authors of crime fiction were published in Mexico in different periodicals beginning in the late twenties, but only in the mid-forties do we see publications devoted to the genre.[58] These magazines followed U.S. commercial models. *Selecciones Policiacas y de Misterio* was first published in 1946 as a subsidiary of *Ellery Queen's Mystery Magazine,* created in New York in 1941. *Selecciones* had the mission of translating stories originally published in English and adapting them to a Latin American audience.[59] In the introduction to the first issue of *Aventura y Misterio* in 1956, editors framed their publication as a continuation of *Ellery Queen's.* This was not a renunciation of literary status but the opposite. *Aventura y Misterio* only published originals in Spanish with the purpose of consolidating the popularity and "artistic dignity" that "adventure, police, mystery or 'suspense'" stories had in countries like the United States and England.[60] The choice of *Ellery Queen's* as a model (in favor of dozens of other U.S. detective magazines published since the 1920s) signaled the high hopes of Mexican publishers. "Ellery Queen" was a pseudonym used by Frederic Dannay and Manfred B. Lee, names that were actually the anglicized pen names of Daniel Nathan and Emanuel Lepofsky, respectively. The two men founded the magazine, and Dannay edited it until his death in 1982. The Ellery Queen franchise was a commercial success thanks to its comic books, radio, television, and movie productions. The magazine, however, defined itself as a high-quality alternative to pulp outlets like *Black Mask.*[61]

Helú's first contact with "Mr. Ellery Queen" was in December 1943, when he sent Dannay a book, and, contradicting a claim made in the New York magazine, affirmed that Péter Pérez actually preceded Arsène Lupin as the first thief-detective. The correspondence with Dannay continued at least until 1955. They exchanged more books, and Helú submitted the stories "El fistol de la corbata" and "Debut profesional," both eventually published by Dannay as "The Stickpin" and "Professional Debut." They also discussed business. In January 1944, Helú told Dannay that *Ellery Queen's* had about seventy-five buyers in Mexico City's American Book Store. Helú, of course, was one of them, and he also owned one of the thousand copies of Dannay's *The Detective Short Story: A Bibliography,* demonstrating that he was "an enthusiastic 'fan.'"[62] The letters show that for both editors the monetary value of stories was as important as their literary status. Helú informed Dannay that *Leoplán,* an Argentine magazine, had printed *Ellery Queen's* stories in what "must certainly be piracy."[63] It is not clear if Helú and Dannay ever met, but the relationship helped Juan Bustillo Oro secure the rights to adapt Cornell Woolrich's "Collared" into a movie entitled *El cuello de la camisa,* discussed in chapter 7. Helú had to pay only "a ridiculous amount" and was able to obtain Woolrich's literary approval for the adaptation.[64]

In contrast to *Ellery Queen's, Selecciones* had precarious existence. In 1947, Helú resigned from the magazine, but he had to face the debts incurred with his American partners. In a 1948 letter to Dannay, he confessed to being "ashamed": the Mexican magazine owed over $600. One Mr. Morales (perhaps Pio Morales Suteras, manager of the first issues and again in the 1950s), who had signed the contract with *Ellery Queen's* along with Helú, sold the magazine to another publisher and left for Havana, where he "lost all his money gambling." Helú promised to pay back the money in installments in 1948 and then again in 1949. He offered as payment the rights to "The Stickpin" and any new story of his that would be published in *Ellery Queen's,* including a planned series of stories on a barber who shaves the police chief and solves cases while doing so. The fact was that the Mexican magazine did not have steady earnings. It published no ads, except a few for the American Book Store (probably in exchange for books), and initially sold for one peso. As costs and debt increased, the price went from 1.60 to 2.00 pesos in 1950. Publishers explained that the price of paper and ink had increased by 30 percent and that the translation rights for each story had increased from $4.85 to $8.25.[65] Yet the magazine survived until 1957 and published hundreds of stories, a feat compared with others that followed. *Aventura y Misterio* appeared under the imprint of Editorial Novaro, a large publishing house that produced a variety of popular books and magazines. Although it printed twenty thousand copies, it did not last beyond its fourteenth issue in December 1957. *Novelas y Cuentos Mercury,* also short-lived, followed *Aventura y Misterio* in the fall of 1957, also under Novaro but now by arrangement with Mercury Publications, publishers of *Ellery Queen's.*[66]

Sales were not helped by the fame of famous Mexican writers. Most stories were signed by names that then as now "mean little or nothing to us."[67] The magazines saw this lack of prestige as a challenge: in 1957, the editors of *Aventura y Misterio* wrote that their goal was to encourage national authors to reach the levels of U.S. and European counterparts. They admitted that "in Spanish the genre is new and until recently there was a general skepticism about it among intellectual circles."[68] Even in the Spanish-speaking world, Mexico was behind. Among the volumes Helú sent Dannay was *Seis problemas para don Isidro Parodi,* by Honorio Bustos Domeq (a pseudonym for Jorge Luis Borges and Adolfo Bioy Casares), deemed by Helú in 1944 to be the only "book of detective short stories written in Spanish."[69] *Selecciones* counted twenty-one authors writing in Spanish by issue 69 and promised to increase the number. *Aventura y Misterio* published only originals in Spanish, including authors from countries like Argentina and Cuba.[70] Besides the savings of paying less for permissions, the strategy was intended to attract more national readers and future contributors.

Mexican authors in crime fiction magazines came from different places and backgrounds. None had the literary fame of Borges, very few were women, and in general represented an array of professions. They included movie directors (Bustillo Oro), criminologists (Luis Garrido), university presidents (Garrido and Eugenio Trueba), literary scholars (Sergio Fernández), sports journalists (José Manuel Enríquez, Vicente Fe Alvarez), actors (Ulalume), art critics (Gual), and several writers whose main body of work was in other genres (Rafael Solana). The majority of them seem to have been only fleetingly involved with the trade. A typical case was Roberto Cruzpiñón. The first story he published in *Selecciones* arrived in the mail. Editors did not know him then, and only years later would introduce him as a pharmacist from the isthmus of Tehuantepec, a lover of books and jazz, sometimes a poet, and an employee of a large laboratory. He published six stories in *Selecciones*.[71] E. Varona was a teacher and textbook author who explained her ironic pseudonym (*varón* means male): "I am the 'crazy' one in the family and I do not want to risk my neck giving you my real name. Police novels fascinate me as reading material, and one day I might be able to write them, but I do not want to live them ... at least not as a victim."[72] Hiding one's identity did not necessarily mean relinquishing status. The editors of *Aventura y Misterio* explained that Diego Cañedo (probably a pseudonym), the author of "El misterio de las gafas verdes," was "probably a professional, businessman, or politician who devoted himself to literature on occasion but who could very well be considered an authentic author."[73] Pseudonyms and anonymity were common. Helú's name was rarely mentioned in *Selecciones* despite his central role in the project. Authorial fame was less important than pleasure, and money was not the priority for anyone with realistic expectations. While authors like Bermúdez and Helú had a respectable output over several decades, for most Mexican writers a couple of published stories marked the high point of their careers.

Editors encouraged the emergence of authors by raising their awareness of the possibilities offered by the genre and, when able, providing symbolic or material rewards. When selecting stories, editors chose original manuscripts from among hundreds of submissions, or they picked stories for translation from "our library [containing] one of the most extensive anthologies of police stories from all over the world, unknown in Spanish."[74] The priority was to look for those manuscripts which met certain standards: they needed to have "basic cleanness of the language ... clarity, emotion, expressive force, dramatic tension, intrigue."[75] Editors also had to obtain permissions, translate, copyedit, and to the extent possible, make sure that the pieces were originals. *Aventura y Misterio* added a new dimension to the job by turning editors into judges: following the example of *Ellery Queen's,* they offered prizes of 1,000, 500, and 100 pesos to the best three manuscripts published in each issue of the biweekly. Prizes expressed a very pragmatic notion of literature. As Helú complained and Morales Suteras proved, although the profits reaching editors were not large, there were other social and material benefits. Thanks to *Selecciones,* Helú nurtured his friendships with Bermúdez, Bernal, Martínez de la Vega, and Bustillo Oro, with whom he had a particularly productive relationship: Helú wrote movie scripts, which by his own admission paid much more than the stories, and he directed a few films.[76]

Translations of the best examples of the genre were part of these magazines' effort to increase the number of Mexican authors. Editors wrote short introductions to the stories to further their didactic effort, identifying existing narrative models and styles. *Selecciones* pointed to the influence of authors who created a national version of the genre (like Chandler and Hammett) or skillfully combined two variations, "the intellectual and the action" styles (Rex Stout).[77] Although complete adherence to any model was difficult to achieve, the best stories tried it as a matter of pride. Introducing a text "of perfect police structure" by criminologist Garrido, the editors of *Aventura y Misterio* celebrated that the story "demonstrates how a genre frequently mistreated can appear with dignity, without losing its traditional values of interest, action, intrigue, and surprise."[78] Local writers proved willing to embrace this influence, and the line between plagiarism and variation on a theme was never clear, explaining Helú's need to tell Dannay that Arsène Lupin was not the first detective-thief, as noted above. In fact, Máximo Roldán was frequently compared to Lupin, and the editors of *Ellery Queen's* noted the similarities in the "basic conception" between "El fistol de la corbata" and "The Red Silk Scarf," by Leblanc.[79] Although Helú was beyond reproach, the similarities were not always licit. Editors had to remind prospective authors "that any similarity with short stories, novels ... by other writers will be their exclusive responsibility," even when their purpose was not "plagiarism" of works published "in the countries where police literature has developed so much."[80] Striking a balance between originality and adherence to the genre required editorial interventions. The introduction to "Un corazón amante," by José Manuel Enríquez, described one such intervention: "One good day a tall, lean, dark young man, with an aquiline nose (not as aquiline as ours, of course), presented himself in front of our desk, humble but at the same time nervous." He brought a few pages that he wanted to show to the editors. They responded, "with all the pain in our hearts," as was their duty: "after suggesting that he made some modifications, that he be more careful with style, and that . . . well, that he think of something more original. . . . he disappeared. We are sure that we were as upset as him." Enríquez returned some time later with a new manuscript that was now being published.[81]

The tension between adhering to the rules of the genre and maintaining originality was expressed in the choice of settings and characters. Mysteries could be staged in the sixteenth century at the Vatican, in India, or in Burma.[82] Several took place in the United States in prisons, desert towns, or Hollywood.[83] "Sin novedad en Berlín" (1954), by Raymundo Quiroz Mendoza, is set in postwar Germany, and the main character is a U.S. journalist who realizes, in the middle of a dense plot of murder and conspiracy, that Hitler has survived the war and only recently died in obscurity, having passed as mental patient.[84] Other stories featured foreign criminals in Mexico, like Juan de Mora's "Estar de suerte," in which a traumatized U.S. war veteran roams Mexican cities looking for young female victims. Like a tourist seeking exotic places, the killer in the story expects to find easy prey but is instead murdered by two thieves. De Mora vindicated the Mexican capital as a modern setting: "Mexico is a beautiful country, no doubt. A bit surprising for those who have never thought about Latin America and suddenly find themselves in a city full of sky scrapers, noisy, with magnificent hotels and a great number of cars."[85] But editors could also challenge abuses in this regard. "It is a shame that Henry García Cisneros," wrote the editors of *Aventura y Misterio,* "just like others among our young authors, persists in setting the action in a land that is not his."[86] They also scolded Habacuc Pérez Castillo because "he tried to adopt the perspective of a writer used to the customs and environment of the United States, maybe because he is a devout reader of police literature in that country. . . . Now . . . we would like him to write about Mexico and, why not? about his patria chica, Guerrero."[87]

When stories relied on local color, as with Martínez de la Vega, they played with the contrasts between national characters and international examples. In a story by Arturo Perucho, Lieutenant López, with "indigenous parsimony," solves the murder of a opera singer and explains to a foreign character: "Here we lack many things . . . devices like those that the

Americans have to find the liars . . . and the money they have. But we have a machine that does not work badly at all: this," says López, pointing at his head.[88] Rural settings lent themselves to proper mystery and detection. The editors of *Aventura y Misterio* introduced Luis Gutiérrez y González's story "Junto al zapote, licenciado" as an example of the "regionalist literature" exemplified by Juan Rulfo's work, with accurate dialect and "pathetic situations [where] solitude and death are the central themes." The story has no mystery or detection plot, just a murderer who tries to confess while the police refuse to see the truth.[89] Local gossip and legends in other stories do not provide much material for investigation, either. The countryside is more frequently just a stage for an urban detective to look for a criminal who is trying to benefit from rustic ignorance.[90] The few stories that involve true investigation work by small-town detectives share the same caustic image of national idiocy found in the city in the stories of Martínez de la Vega. Enrique Jiménez Jaime, in "Dosis mortal," uses a lazy and overweight local police chief as narrator. He complains about having to deal with "a pretty collection of morons called gendarmes" and with "stupid bosses" at the city council. He would rather continue drinking his soda, but, when forced to do it, he solves the mystery and surprises everyone, including the mayor.[91] The search for national identity central to "regionalist literature" was not on the agenda of crime fiction magazines.

Magazine editors also wanted to create good readers. The first step was to make them feel comfortable so they could enjoy a genre that had precise rules and a dense genealogy. The ideal reader would exercise taste and reason, possess sufficient literary culture, and know something about famous criminal cases. Introductions often placed the author in the context of past or present crime fiction with factoids or references to treatises about the genre. For example, they noted that in 1902 the Baroness de Orczy invented the "armchair detective," while Poe had created the closed-room problem.[92] Editors also taught readers that Cornell Woolrich was the same person as William Irish (whom "you, cultivated reader, must have already read"), a name invented by the "highly valued young man" to compete against himself, and that Erle Stanley Gardner was so prolific that he kept three secretaries constantly busy with his stories.[93] Editors helped readers situate stories in the coordinates of the multiple variations of the genre. They wrote that Hammett's "Una hora" combines "two styles of crime literature that prevail today in English-speaking countries: the tough, dynamic, sensational style in which the detective does not stop running back and forth, stopping once in a while to have a drink or have an encounter with a girl, and the purely intellectual one, where from his office's desk, or perfectly sprawled in his seat in a library, the detective is able to solve the most mysterious of all crimes based on reasoning and deductions."[94]

The "cultivated reader" could read with care and good sportsmanship. This reader would not, for example, jump to the end of a story, as the editors asked readers to avoid in the introduction to Miriam Allen Ford's "En relación con signos y figuras": "Afterwards you can tell us if once you read the last paragraph . . . you experienced the same surprise we did. Remember that your ingenuity and that of the author is at stake. Let's see if you can guess the denouement."[95] Editors dared readers to actively engage with the text; at the end of "El cartero que no llamaba," by José Dibildox, they asked: "Now reader, you are in possession of all the facts and, therefore, you will allow us, with all the irresponsibility of new authors, to throw down the gauntlet: Would you swear that the murderer is not Pedro Ramírez, the mailman?"[96] A knowledgeable reader was able to judge the quality of stories. Editors merely delivered authors to "the criticism of readers, because the opinion of the public is the one we judge to be really learned and capable."[97]

Mexican magazines proposed that the intellectual appreciation of murder and detection was akin to a sport. Since such a claim could further undermine the literary prestige of magazines, *Aventura y Misterio* announced itself as high literature at a low price and defined crime fiction as the loftiest mental adventure.[98] But references to sports were common. The detective-writer at the center of "Duelo a muerte," by Justo Rocha, proposes a bet to the police inspector in order to make deduction more interesting. Others investigate just to follow their "new hobby" without any concern for justice, like the students in "Los insectos del profesor," by Roberto Cruzpiñón.[99] Here and in other stories, students appeared as amateur detectives who solved cases because they were bored and liked to use their intelligence. One of the few policemen of true detective skill, Raymundo Quiroz Mendoza's Inspector Motolinía, interrupts a game of chess to work on a case, as if moving from one game to another.[100] In a comic aside in a Carlos Miranda story, Helú proposed that detection be declared an Olympic sport.[101] With an unreliable justice system, the thrill of victory seemed to be the only real incentive for characters and readers to solve crimes.

Competitive spirit and intellectual sportsmanship extended to narratives where readers adopted the perspective of the criminal. In those cases, the pleasure came from a just murder that could not be punished. In "No se olvide de darle cuerda," by Vicente Fe Álvarez, the murderer conceives his crime in a moment of creativity: "During the long and tedious hours of bureaucratic inaction, his thinking full of police fiction arguments, he planned the perfect crime, the impeccable solution that would allow him to get rid of the person he hated the most without losing, for that reason, his honorable place in society."[102] A crime is enjoyable when there is no moral guilt involved. This could be achieved through an unexpected event for which no one is criminally responsible, such as the intended victim's death of natural causes just before the planned murder is carried out; in other stories, told from the perspective of the criminal, murder is justifiable as a defense of male honor.[103]

The reader of crime magazines could identify with both the detective and the criminal because both had the same criminal literacy that readers themselves had to possess to enjoy the truth in fiction. Indeed, the paradox was that the very knowledge that helped the public understand crime could push someone to commit it. In Cruzpiñón's "El abanico de sándalo," a mother teaches her son how to kill by reading nota roja and crime fiction to him from an early age. The detective reflects on the connection: "Fondness for crimes and police novels increases acuity; it allows one to understand things that are not visible; but when the mind is weak and has not fully formed, it is damaging."[104] Such moral ambivalence was not a drawback of crime fiction but an additional reason to enjoy it. According to W. H. Auden, the detective genre was addictive because homicide gave pleasure and at the same time caused guilt in the reader. This guilt, according to Auden, was cleansed when knowledge restored the innocence of the reader by identifying the criminal. Assuming the impossibility of restoring the moral order upset by crime through punishment, Mexican authors and readers explored the possibilities of justice beyond the law. The results could be tragic, but readers could also find pleasure in the fantasy of impunity. In "Crimen legal," by Rogelio Gómez Díaz, a man who kills his victim cannot be punished because, due to a mistake, he had already served time in prison for the same crime. The law cannot touch him, and the newspapers give him $20,000 for the story.[105]

There was a problem, of course: the pleasure of crime could only be taken so far without openly challenging literary and moral norms. *Aventura y Misterio* recognized that it was hard to stick to the canon and continue to provide pleasure.[106] The detection plot was no longer so attractive, and the moral plot was unnecessary, in stories where the intellectual challenge gave way to other forms of satisfaction for the reader. This led to the decadence of the genre. In 1957, *Aventura y Misterio* declared victory in the enterprise of creating readers and by extension, writers: there were now multiple publications in the crime genre, and "the love in the public is now firmly rooted" since "everyday there is an increasing number of contributions by young authors, which demonstrates that there is also a reading public." [107] Yet it seemed that those new readers could easily direct their attention toward other genres. About a decade after the establishment of specialized magazines, crime fiction began to dissolve into other kinds of narratives. Mystery gave flexibility to the plot but lacked firm guidelines. Introducing a ghost story by Laurence Kirk, the editors of *Selecciones* confessed that "we do not know yet the full extent of the word 'mystery.' We think it has become a blanket term that now encompasses many genres: stories that are purely in the detective mold, sensational narratives, suspense . . . psychological, spy stories, etc." [108] The *Aventura y Misterio* story contest expanded after its second issue: at first, editors had considered only crime fiction and its variations, but later included "narratives from the different literary genres." [109] The editors of the magazine reflected on this change with a hint of regret: the best authors of detective fiction, like Borges and Bioy Casares, had used it to create a world of "imagination, but of imagination subject to logical and inevitable rules." The "intellectual" solidity of the crime story resided in its ability to challenge the reader "to solve an implacable syllogism whose propositions remain hidden." But the new popularity of mystery suggested that a transformation was under way: "Contemporary man does not want to renounce reason, nor does he want to renounce the basic component of mystery." The mystery novel was a product of the modern need "to escape from predictable, daily, uniform things." [110] The decay of the crime fiction into mystery expressed the inevitable uncertainty built into the former genre: when justice ceased to be necessary for the resolution of the detection plot, readers no longer concerned themselves with the moral plot. Ghost and other fantasy stories were less rigorous and satisfying from the intellectual perspective favored by editors and expected from readers and writers. However, in a perverse way, these stories were more realistic in that they no longer bothered with justice.

THE LITERARY MYSTERY OF LEO D'OLMO

From the mid-forties until the mid-fifties, every Sunday *La Prensa* published a story written by Leo D'Olmo featuring Chucho Cárdenas. I have counted 346 titles between 1945 and 1955. Most of these short novels had thirty-two folios made of eight folded newspaper pages, although some were printed in

FIGURE 16. Leo D'Olmo, *¿Quién mató a Rafael?* Mexico City: La Prensa, 1954.

the usual layout of the newspaper. Found next to the comics section, they included color drawings by Guillermo Nieto, with one image on the cover and another in the central pages typically depicting a colorful crime scene, a voluptuous woman, or a combination of the two (figure 16). A few had staged photographs of the main character in action. Chucho was a fictional reporter who worked in a newspaper also called *La Prensa,* and each installment usually solved a crime. The stories shared a specific outlook on the risks and rewards of urban life. Better than any other series in the genre, the adventures of Chucho Cárdenas expressed the views of the criminally literate reader about justice and social difference.

Authorship is intriguing but not very useful for understanding the Chucho Cárdenas series. It is not clear whether Leo D'Olmo actually existed. He was not invested, as most real writers are, in enhancing his literary reputation. Critics and scholars of crime fiction in Mexico barely mention him. Bermúdez excluded D'Olmo from the anthologies she edited. She proposes that the name was a pseudonym for an unknown author—a surprising contradiction in such an astute writer: how do we know it is a pseudonym if we do not know who was hiding behind it? I could find no traces of a person with that name. He may have been a writer or a journalist who wished to maintain his or her good name among the respectable public while earning some money on the side by selling stories for larger audiences. This would be consistent with the lack of stylistic pretensions in D'Olmo's novels. Other critics suggest that D'Olmo's name represented a group of authors, as in the cases of Nick Carter and Ellery Queen.[111] This is another speculation that is not supported by any evidence, although it involves several plausible conditions. As demonstrated by Carter's and Queen's followings, the loyalty of readers to a famous brand was easier to capitalize on without the uncertainties of authors' idiosyncratic work habits. This hypothesis would also account for the diversity of narrative approaches and themes in Chucho Cárdenas novels: rather than authors collaborating on each story, D'Olmo might have been several authors writing separately and consecutively, taking some liberties with readers' expectations. Given the straightforward presentation of crime, the lack of textual ornaments, and the simplicity of the characters involved, the authors could have been collaborators in the newspaper, perhaps reporters or editors. But this is also speculation.

However, there may have been an actual Leo D'Olmo. Someone using the same name wrote other books. This is the hypothesis of Vicente Francisco Torres, the most knowledgeable critic of crime fiction in Mexico during this period. He argues that D'Olmo was an exile from Spain, citing several Chucho Cárdenas stories that take place in the context of the Spanish Civil War expressing a sympathetic view of the republican side. The vocabulary in some novels supports the hypothesis: in a dialogue between Mexican domestic workers, for example, characters use verbal forms ("tenéis") that are common in Spain but not Latin America.[112] We may even guess at the identity of this Spanish author: Enrique Gual, a Catalonian better known as an art critic who came to Mexico during those years and published a few detective novels. One of them, *El crimen de la obsidiana,* was only tangentially connected to Mexico and resembled a Christie novel in cast and structure. Gual's books, however, were longer and more sophisticated than the Chucho Cárdenas adventures.[113] It would not be illogical to think that he or another Spanish exile, aware that article 33 of the Mexican constitution allowed the government to expel "undesirable" foreigners involved in national politics, would have preferred to remain anonymous while writing stories in which the Mexican police and justice system did not have a very glorious role. There is no evidence that a Leo D'Olmo was ever registered in the government's lists of foreigners entering Mexico, suggesting that Bermúdez's hypothesis might be valid. The possibility of a team of writers, perhaps one of them from Spain, seems likely but remains hypothetical. In any case, the absence of an author helps explain why those stories have remained in obscurity. A selection of Chucho Cárdenas stories published by Publilibros La Prensa in 1988 did nothing for the literary prestige of D'Olmo. This and earlier editions discouraged high-culture interest as they were printed in a cheap, massive run of poor quality, with few literary references, and were written in a simple, sometimes colloquial language. Particularly in the fifties, the novels tended to stress gore, their graphic design emphasizing the bloody corpses drawn by Nieto.[114]

A better way to approach these novels is to focus on their protagonist, Chucho Cárdenas, rather than on the evasive author. This angle is particularly useful for exploring how they articulated a specific understanding of gender, class, and ethnicity in Mexican society. As fiction, they could present opinions that were difficult to express in the newspaper. Readers and author shared a knowledge of nota roja references. Chucho's reporting is the starting point for most stories, and his boss at *La Prensa* supports him in his investigations, even when they get him in trouble with the law or distract him from "the routine work of the newsroom."[115] Sometimes the third-person narrator also works for *La Prensa,* calls Chucho "my friend," and claims to be "his biographer."[116] In a few stories, which otherwise do not depart much from the usual structure and themes, Chucho writes in the first person because D'Olmo is on vacation. Chucho is less prominent in a number of stories: he appears later in the plot, after the crime has been presented and witness statements have been transcribed. In one story, *Mortajas de cemento,* Chucho is even a potential victim: the narrator, a serial killer who reads his articles, is filled with hate for Chucho and decides to kill him.[117] The intricate slippage between fiction and reality extends to the question of his reputation. Journalism has already made him famous, and his popularity helps him get information. Career criminals read his articles and help him when they can, while newspaper vendors also give him a hand. Chucho's work of detection is integral to his job as a reporter, becoming almost an obligation as he solves more cases. The newspaper graphically frames the novel in the central pages of *Los cuatro últimos,* which contain a drawing of the front page of *La Prensa* with a large red headline linked to the plot, "Otro crimen del fantasma."[118] The framing was necessary so the novels could deepen some of the nota roja's fundamental ideas about justice in Mexico.

Chucho Cárdenas stories often referred to actual crime cases in the news. In *Robo en el Monte de Piedad,* the narrator indicates that "the episode we are recounting today is true. For reasons that will not escape the acuity of the reader, we have altered situations and changed names, while respecting the general lines that characterized the sensational development of the event." The last page, nevertheless, adds, "Author's note: This true to life novel . . . is based on the audacious robbery committed some years ago by Regato Ríos, famous in the world of crime."[119] Novels often alluded to knowledge about the underworld shared by newspaper readers. There were formal and thematic variations, including pre-Hispanic curses, murderers' monologues, and chronicles of social customs, but the dominant referents came from contemporary life, famous cases, and other anecdotal information that well-informed readers could easily understand. Details enhanced the sense of proximity, particularly those referring to the urban geography that *La Prensa* also used to contextualize famous cases: the cabaret Tenampa, the Lagunilla and San Juan markets, streets like Bucareli.[120] Referring to actual cases, D'Olmo suggested that fiction was more real than journalism, since Chucho could go beyond the bounds of nota roja without concern for the restrictions faced by real journalists.

This hyperrealism is further supported by Chucho's constant drive to challenge official explanations, even when doing so forces him to follow leads that put him at risk or take him as far as Madrid at his own expense. As with reporters in real life, Chucho closely follows the police investigation, and friendly officers encourage him to report the success of their work. The novels, however, dwell on the tension between the press and the police. When Chucho contradicts the official account, he does it as a detective in order to steer the case toward the correct resolution. In *El crimen del garage,* he publishes his own hypothesis and even argues his case before a judge. In the end, he tricks the real killer, the victim's Italian husband, who confesses and is captured by other reporters in the courtroom.[121] Referencing nota roja readers' involvement in famous cases, Chucho reminds the police that an inadequate official elucidation of the truth becomes a problem when a crime has "stirred popular imagination and was discussed with unusual passion" as a result of newspaper coverage.[122] Press conferences turn into tumultuous attacks on the police by journalists "instigated by the public's outrage." After all, Chucho reflects, "the police are there to put up with criticism as much as to capture criminals."[123] The journalist-police antagonism is personified with comic effect in the relationship between Chucho and Inspector Cifuentes, whom D'Olmo describes as "obese, apoplectic," and not very smart.[124] They exchange favors when necessary: Cifuentes gets Chucho out of jail after a night of drinking, and the reporter reciprocates by solving a case and saving the inspector's job. But sometimes Cifuentes is not happy when Chucho exposes his ineptitude, and Chucho in turn can grow angry with Cifuentes and refuse to help—until another victim is killed. Mindful of the inspector's dislike for bad publicity, Chucho forces his hand by publishing his own conclusions as if they had been obtained by Cifuentes. For all these disagreements, the stories make few references to police corruption or torture. Chucho is a better detective than Cifuentes, but he still needs to collaborate with the police, just like real nota roja reporters.[125]

Unlike Péter Pérez, Máximo Roldán, and Carlos Miranda, those morally ambiguous detectives of Mexican crime stories, Chucho Cárdenas has a strong ethical code. He is a modern man who relies both on his superior intelligence and his ability to adapt to a time and place when politics and class relations are rapidly changing. He can find the angles to prevail over criminals and the police, allying with both when necessary, but he never forgets the obligation to uphold the superiority of his masculinity, his class, and his nationality. Rather than defending privilege, which he lacks, his method is to embrace individualism: Chucho is a young man who lives an austere life in the company of his mother, sometimes visiting his girlfriend, but most of the time dedicated to his work. He does not like to carry a gun or use his connections for his benefit. He is not obsessed with money, but he is comfortable in a world of technology and consumption.[126] He moves through life with confidence, wit, and a modernized sense of honor. In most novels, Chucho's ethics are made explicit when he decides to take on a case. He does not do it because his work forces him, for pure intellectual curiosity, for money, or to avoid prison, yet he chooses to take on risks for reasons that would make sense to his contemporaries. Usually his "conscience" moves him to keep an innocent person from being punished, the honor of a family from being stained, or a killing spree from continuing. On the other hand, he will also enter the fray to enhance his reputation, to avenge the death of a good policeman, or because he hopes to boost the circulation of *La Prensa*.[127]

Chucho's modernized honor is not constrained by old gallantry. Women can be a good reason to take on a case, particularly when Chucho sees potential sexual rewards. He does have a "detail" in his life, a "prietita linda" (dark-skinned beauty) named María Luisa, whom he intends to marry but neglects when he is working.[128] More often, the stories include women who excite both Chucho's sense of honor and his libido. In *Robo en el Monte de Piedad*, he saves the reputation of the Escobar family by dispelling an accusation against the father for a theft he did not commit. The request to intervene comes from one of his daughters, a "pimpollo" (rosebud) so pretty that Chucho cannot refuse to help, moved simultaneously by "tenderness" and the temptation to "clutch that delicious little body in his hands."[129] Almost all women who appear in the novels are described in terms of their "mouth-watering forms." In *Herodes moderno,* a young widow comes crying to beg for Chucho's intercession and offers in exchange "my body, which is all I have." Without irony, Chucho praises her as a model of honesty "in these times of freedom, so often confused with libertinism."[130] Her opposite is the victim of *Tres gotas,* an aging widow with money who satisfies her "voluptuousness" with a retinue of lovers she can dismiss without a second thought. Female victims are also subject to these sexualized views: they can be passive and innocent, or overcome with lust, but in either case, sex is always part of the reason for their demise. Between the libidinous predator and the tearful widow, women respond to a logic that Chucho, a modern man, easily decodes since each one of them is no more than "a female, coquettish like all of them."[131] Men, by contrast, are inheritors of "the atavistic remainders of a remote past, those times when the strong sex fulfilled his mission of waging war all year round while his adored female waited for him with the most delicious reward."[132] In this evolutionist view of gender difference, sexual desire underlies a simple, natural order in which only men can face the modern equivalent of waging war: fighting for justice.

In D'Olmo's novels, women demonstrate the essential connection between sexual difference, crime, and justice. The capacity to understand reality and mete out justice is the key marker of gender exclusion in the few stories where women are more than sexual objects. A female police officer, Rafaela, collaborates with Chucho, proves her ability as an investigator, and participates in the arrest of the suspect. Yet he is sexually attracted to her, other characters harass her, and even suspects protest her intervention: "That's all we needed, that they give authority to women." [133] Another female detective is the opposite of Rafaela but prompts the same lesson when she becomes the lover of the cheating husband, kills his wife to keep $100,000, and provokes Chucho's scorn for "detectives with skirts." [134] If women's ability to find the truth is doubtful, their authority to impart justice is plainly transgressive. Several stories contain female murderers forced by circumstances to punish men who had offended their honor—as in *¿Quién mató a Rafael?*, where an upper-class mother kills the cynical Bolivian seducer of her daughter and is protected by Chucho (figure 16). These violent female characters do not upset gender hierarchies because they ultimately need a male detective to validate their actions. [135] The detective's combination of sexual appetite and sense of honor is mirrored by women's inherent sexuality and inability to decide about justice.

Men must have the monopoly of the truth about crime because, as Chucho's novels demonstrate, justice is best achieved by the detective through a privatized use of police violence. There are several cases in which Chucho sets things up for authorities to use the ley fuga against the criminal. In *¿Quién mató a Rafael?*, he not only helps the mother who killed a Bolivian seducer to escape prosecution, but also falsely accuses the Bolivian's Argentinian accomplice and arranges the scene so that he will fall victim to police bullets. [136] In other stories, murderers take revenge for an earlier transgression. Chucho's role then is to elucidate the moral plot, and let them escape. "Public opinion" prefers that kind of revenge to official justice, which is "slow and always benevolent with those who have money." The absence of the death penalty and the vindictive feelings of public opinion explain the need for that brand of punishment. [137] The police are better at supplying violence than at solving cases, yet a young police agent who killed a criminal in self-defense laments that "society . . . will not refrain from calling me a murderer through the newspapers. As if it was not itself so keen on having guys like that one disappeared!" In a moment of clarity, Cifuentes voices his loathing for defense lawyers who let criminals walk free and argues that they are the reason why the police allow lynchings. [138] The relationship linking crime, investigation, and punishment is constantly changing. In *Los cuatro últimos*, Chucho and the police show no consideration for the victims, drunk men killed by a middle-class woman whose family was ruined by drunk driving. Their lives are a minor aspect of the development of the moral plot: they can be sacrificed to a retaliatory notion of justice. [139]

Chucho's methods to obtain the truth are also heterogeneous and legally dubious. Rather than relying upon technical competence or genius-like omniscience, he uses a number of strategies that flaunt proper detection methods in favor of ingenuity, opportunism, and a shrewd knowledge of Mexican society. He can use disguises like Sherlock Holmes, set up fights like Hammett's Continental Op, poison a suspect's dog like Péter Pérez, or deploy a broad variety of other tricks: lying to witnesses, planting or stealing evidence, impersonating policemen, and breaking in. To execute this last strategy, he hires a friend from Tepito who has "retired from a none too honest trade." Prison is no threat: when Chucho lands in jail, he uses the opportunity to gain the confidence of prisoners, solve cases, or write, and when he is ready to leave he just calls in a favor from the police. Because he can move freely in such a broad gray zone, Chucho is more effective than the authorities: he finds crime scenes missed by police detectives, interrogates witnesses in indigenous languages, and sets up traps for suspects.[140] Violence is not part of his repertoire, though: Chucho does not carry a gun unless special caution is needed, and even then rarely fires at a criminal. Not that he cares much about collateral damage: besides poisoned dogs, the novels are full of victims caused by the detective's mistakes or neglect. In *El muerto se ríe,* he provokes a gunfight of epic proportions in order to lure the criminal into his hands.[141]

There was an overarching logic to D'Olmo's stories: class was the ultimate explanation for characters' actions, and the key to the narrative's moral plot. Psychology is of little value to him despite the authoritative voice of experts in contemporary cases. Only in a few stories does seeking to understand the suspect's mind actually lead to the solution. In *Se escapó el monstruo,* psychiatrists are recruited to help Chucho find a serial killer, but he soon discovers that one of them is a murderer with a Jekyll-Hyde personality.[142] Detection implied taking a critical view of strict social divides in the basic map of Mexican reality. Chucho is more intelligent and pragmatic than the police and everyone else because he belongs to a modest but ascending class of urban citizens. A humble hero, he is an expert who does not assume any status privilege, although, as noted above, he does seek sexual rewards for his work. Rigid class hierarchy, a basic fact of reality in the texts of authors from Martínez de la Vega to Agatha Christie, was a façade through which the hardworking, unassuming reporter could see with clarity. He explains the motives of criminals by situating them in a changing society. He, after all, has more "experience" because "the habit of dealing with all kinds of people has given him a unerring instinct to judge humans."[143] Chucho situates himself in a social middle ground defined by street savvy, ingenuity, aggressive masculinity, hard work, respectable ambitions, and constant comparisons with those above and below him—what in other contexts could be just called middle-class values. The poor and the rich are not always good or bad, but when they are, their behavior is determined by their origin and place in society. Virtue is codified as honor for the upper classes, and *humildad* (humility) or *honradez* (honesty) for those at the bottom, but only an intermediate perspective can see these traits with objectivity. For example, in *Robo en el Monte de Piedad,* Chucho explains to Cifuentes that the night watchman could not have been the author of the crime because "honesty, when it has been maintained through the years, is like a skin that covers the conscience of the citizen."[144] For the elite characters in *¿Dónde está el muerto?,* it is more important to protect the family's honor, endangered by women, than to uphold the law: "Killing a blackmailer might deserve forgiveness," reasons Chucho, "but giving him occasion for blackmail, that is really bad!"[145] There is no revolutionary egalitarianism here but rather a pragmatic recognition that members of different classes are fundamentally distinguished by the crimes they commit.

Chucho's map of crime and class in Mexican society cannot be rendered only within the coordinates of honor, however. The most dangerous spaces on this map are found in the rural world, always strange and brutal, never idyllic: "In Cuautla no sophisticated crimes are committed," notes the detective when called to solve a case outside the capital. Indians are "a primitive people" used to mistreatment.[146] Family vendettas cause violent crimes both in Tabasco and among migrants recently arrived in the city. *Las últimas horas del chacal* illustrates this savagery with its narrator, an illiterate peasant who killed his own mother. Ready for his execution, he only regrets being sentenced by a judge who did not understand the soul of country people, among whom rape is not a crime and a violent past is not a stigma: "We understand each other."[147] This view of a violent Mexican countryside essentially affirmed the picture proposed by criminologists like Julio Guerrero or writers like Juan Rulfo, yet D'Olmo used it not to define national identity but to contrast the deadly simplicity of rural violence against the intellectually engaging sophistication of urban crime.

When Chucho's adventures happen in the spaces of the urban poor, he evinces a detailed knowledge of customs based on personal familiarity, although his view of this space is no more positive than his opinion of the rural world. *Herodes moderno,* a story about a series of child kidnappings, offers the best example of the ambivalence that defines Chucho's combination of knowledge and disdain. The narrator describes a street world in which criminals and policemen are closely associated: "In Tepito there are people for all tastes. It is a gallery of soulless people where there is a neighborhood sample for each sinister activity. From the insignificant small-time thief to the bloodthirsty jackal. . . . Yet Chucho could never believe that, within that association of primitive depravities, there would be room for the refined cowardice of a kidnapper of babies." Knowing that immorality comes in different forms, Chucho seeks the help of an ex-convict, El Cacarizo. Even though El Cacarizo is a "monster," he is pleased to help locate the *robachicos* because, he notes, "even among criminals there are points of honor."[148] There is no idealization of the urban poor in other stories. In *Quemaron a Ricardo,* Chucho ventures into an unnamed suburban neighborhood to solve the murder of a newsboy, only to confront misery, dirt, and hostility from the boy's neighbors, among them a semi-naked woman who tries to seduce him. Chucho is almost killed by this mob, just before he uncharacteristically kills the murderer by smashing his head against the pavement, and is then rescued by soldiers.[149]

D'Olmo deepens these negative views of the Mexican lower classes in two novels where Chucho is absent and there is no detection plot, *Escuela de miserias* and *Lágrimas en la juerga.* The narrator listens in on the conversation of several female domestic workers in their room on the roof of a residential building—the *azotea,* an emblematic space of Mexico City working classes. The purpose is to present "fragments of real life" documenting "the animal slavery of the peasant woman" brought to work in the city. All the characters have been victims of rape, violence, and exploitation in the villages where they come from. Upon arriving in the city, they suffer new dangers: sexual harassment, prostitution, and vice. The "redemption of the victims" and the "sanitary prophylaxis of society" are potential benefits of the testimony. Unattended, the women's suffering can create a social threat that links biological decay with a revolutionary threat: "We are microbes!" one of them states. "We are the terrible vanguard of the worst ills, that Mexico still cannot defeat." They propose to form a union in order to improve their situation, and failing that, they plan "to contaminate the dominant classes" through their cleaning work and sexual contact with the masters.[150]

Biology and class are connected by race, another expression of social distance. Chucho does not use positivist criminology to explain crimes but often relies on phenotypic difference to describe class and moral difference.

Indigenous Mexicans combine ugliness with mental inferiority: one character is "uglier than a 'naco' Indian" while another is a "stubborn Chamula" who speaks "a guttural language of strange cadences."[151] The detective has read "the opinion of a great English criminologist who states that there are only three reasons for murder: insurmountable fear, greed, and love"; in Mexico, however, "several can be added: mental defects ... and, above all, revenge," with the latter also found in the rest of America, "at least in its semi tropical zones, among people of hot blood."[152] Despite subscribing to such determinism, Chucho does not apply racism to a single class or ethnicity. Criminals can be Chinese, Americans, Germans, Panamanians, Bolivians, all of them phenotypically repulsive. In *El avión de la muerte* the suspect is "a foreigner. You can see that from a mile away. With all the racial mixture in Mexico, here we do not see those bulky cheekbones nor that hay-colored hair, so straight and unappealing."[153] Chucho's visit to the archives of the Secretaría de Gobernación, in charge of immigration, prompts a sad revelation: "There are too many foreigners who pullulate in Mexico without paying the slightest attention to the laws of the country." They are a product of "the tide of refugees from Central Europe who were arriving in America."[154] Chucho's racism toward foreigners complicates the connection with class. Most of the criminals among them are closer to the upper classes, and they demonstrate a kind of sophistication that contrasts with lower-class Mexican criminals. Some are elegant men who seduce Mexican women or commit other kinds of professional crimes. Just as he can use indigenous languages, so Chucho is able to move comfortably among foreigners, speaking English and even flirting with an American suspect. Yet he keeps a nationalist distance. In *Arsenio Lupin en México,* he voices his rejection for the French elite residing in Mexico and of Mexicans who try to speak French.[155] D'Olmo, like many of his criminally literate readers, did not limit racial prejudice to the established positivistic correspondence of indigenous inferiority and crime. Racism articulated a new form of xenophobia in which crime was also an expression of national difference.

Chucho's xenophobia was not a nationalistic rejection of all outside influences. His adventures address world political events, alternatively invoking nationalism and cosmopolitanism. In several stories, the struggle against fascism during World War II serves as the context. In *Sangre y diamantes,* Chucho seeks the help of "his many good friends in the U.S. intelligence services" to solve the murder of Ruben Yaroslav, who is a "political refugee, Jewish, and diamond trader" and who becomes the victim of German spies who are looking for diamonds for the Luftwaffe.[156] Fascists pop up in the least expected places: the Italian wife-killer in *El crimen del garage* and the murderers of a famous artist in *El otro* are all fascists. *La ratonera del dentista: Dramas de espionaje* is set in civil-war era Barcelona days before the defeat of the Republicans. Chucho is not a character, and the narrative assumes a considerable knowledge of events in Spain from readers. Republicans lament their shortcomings in the defense of democracy: "The enemy gives no quarter and we . . . are not yet hard enough to deal with these beasts. It has been too much of a change from our peaceful lives of intellectuals, workers and students to these hateful depths in which we fight to death every instant."[157] The story reflects a retrospective self-criticism that Spanish exiles in Mexico (including perhaps D'Olmo himself) might have shared. Read next to other Chucho Cárdenas adventures involving fascists, the novel validates Mexico's alignment with the United States during WWII.[158]

Chucho's collaboration with the Allies does not translate into a straightforward acceptance of the United States. *Gringos* are the most frequent foreigners in D'Olmo's novels. They may be victims who deserved their fate, like the wealthy New Yorker suffering "neurasthenia with melancholy" who is the victim in *El inocente asesino;* or not, like Dan Blairs, a detective from San Francisco investigating a crime in a Mexican factory. U.S. nationals may be criminals involved in buying kidnapped children or in drug trafficking.[159] In *Cámara de la muerte,* Chucho goes to Texas to help a friend of his, Jorge Fernández, a bracero who has been falsely accused of a triple murder. Ethnicity defines character's morality in this case. In the ranch where the events took place, Chucho receives support from a Mexican American police agent and from a relative of the victims who does not hate Mexicans because he knows "the nobleness of that people whose blood runs in my veins." Chucho finally discovers that the murderer is an Anglo and saves Fernández from the gas chamber at the last minute with the help of a conscientious governor.[160]

The moral turpitude of upper-class life defines the last space of Chucho's moral map of Mexican society. Despite his middle-class skepticism toward luxury and idleness, Chucho moves easily in the world of Mexican elites, as his investigations take him from lowly cantinas to "sumptuous" cabarets where waiters sell stolen jewelry.[161] In several novels that closely follow the standard detective model, all characters are suspects and belong to wealthy families. As in the nota roja, murder opens the door into a world that the detective-journalist and the reader inspect with moral disapproval. In *La extraña casa de Tacubaya,* a family lives in isolation, behaving as if they were still living in the Porfiriato. In *¿Quién disparó?,* the members of another family are arrogant and a bit thick, perpetually fighting with each other over an inheritance. Revenge, greed, addiction, and the defense of honor find a pure criminal expression in these settings, although racism is not part of the explanation. Chucho summarizes the inferiority of such characters in his description of a woman who is beautiful "but as arrogant as other rich people, believing that she belongs to a superior caste only because her accounts have numbers with a lot of zeros." [162]

The adventures of Chucho Cárdenas document the moral outlook of urban middle-class readers in Mexico. The duration of the series, the sheer number of titles published, the newspaper's circulation, and the probability that more than one author was involved testify to its importance for the history of criminal literacy. D'Olmo's novels were part of a discussion of crime, justice, and society in which fiction allowed the detective to say and do things that nota roja reporters could not. The detection plot proved Chucho's superior intelligence and adaptability, while the moral plot of the stories sketched a comprehensive map of class and racial distinction in Mexico. Chucho was a character of middling social rank who moved ahead in life despite danger, corruption, and police ineptitude, all while brazenly expressing his own prejudices about women, foreigners, and almost everyone below or above him on the social ladder. As a journalist-detective, he could do something about Mexico's flawed justice institutions, employing unorthodox means to reach the truth or inciting the private use of violence. As a product of the imagination, Chucho fulfilled fantasies of justice that shaped people's understanding of reality. Yet, emerging from the pages of the newspaper, ultimately D'Olmo's novels did not transcend the medium through which they were disseminated, leaving few traces in the literary history of the country.

CONCLUSIONS

The early years of crime fiction in Mexico were not promising from a literary point of view. The situations and detectives favored by pioneers like Helú and Martínez de la Vega at first resembled parodies more than original attempts. What else could be expected from a country where justice and scientific policing were little more than a bad joke? Yet if we read these stories with some historical perspective, and without negative judgments about their aesthetic value, we can see that there was much more to them. This chapter looked at these texts through their authors, the conditions of their production and consumption, and their detectives. The results expand the insights of previous chapters.

Along with the nota roja, crime fiction explored the dangers of living in the city. Crime narratives focused on urban environments that had yet to be fully explored in national literature. These stories provided readers with vivid examples of the dangers associated with the big city but also showed the rewards of inhabiting this setting. Intelligence and daring allowed anyone to come out on the winning side of situations that endangered freedom and life. Going against the grain of essays and novels seeking the essence of Mexican identity, these stories painted an unflattering picture of Mexicans in the city and the countryside. Nationalism, after all, did not fit with fictions that centered on crime and state incompetence. Some of these writers had experienced the repression of the postrevolutionary regime on those very streets, and they now had dim hopes for democracy and the rule of law.

Narratives of crime allowed for a more truthful depiction of reality than newspapers because they did not need to mince words about the fact that in Mexico the norm was impunity, and the police could not be expected to provide closure for detection. This form of fiction, often referring to real cases, brought out the truth about crime in a way that was otherwise inconceivable in the public sphere. Its skeptical perspective found its ultimate validation in the detective's ability to dispense justice. The fundamental fantasy of these crime stories was not the idea that the state would take care of transgressors (as it was in the canonical narratives coming from the United States and Europe) but that the individualist hero could substitute for the state and provide justice through wit and daring. The cynicism in these stories was not paralyzing: it just required an ability to find solutions to transgression that would be as ingenious as the intelligence of the classic detectives and local criminals.

Mexican crime fiction provided an imaginary path to restore the causal links between crime, truth, and justice. In contrast with their police counterparts, fictional detectives were intelligent, adaptable, and cosmopolitan; they had a strong sense of honor and avoided unnecessary violence. They served as models for the modern Mexican man who wanted to advance in a dynamic and sometimes dangerous world of opportunity and risk. Their adventures communicated an intermediate perspective on Mexican society, critical of both the corruption of those at the top and the intellectual and cultural shortcomings of social inferiors. The main lesson fictional detectives offered was that intelligence could help citizens deal with crime, provided that they combined this intelligence with criminal literacy and a willingness to break the law and undermine or manipulate the representatives of the state. As a result, these detectives occupied a morally ambiguous gray zone: they could steal, abuse women, cause violence, protect criminals, and simultaneously conduct themselves as sleuths with great competence.

It is difficult to establish with certainty the extent to which these cynical models influenced the behavior of actual citizens. As explored in earlier chapters, we do know that the role of women was severely restricted when it came to demanding and enforcing the rule of law; that extrajudicial violence was acceptable for self-styled representatives of public opinion; and that police detectives were indeed more adept at torture and extortion than at the disinterested pursuit of the truth. And even with some of its repellent implications, crime fiction was a democratic form of literature. This chapter has shown how a genre whose rules were transparent and available through translations of the classics attracted many readers and inspired new writers. These texts did not require from readers a deep literary culture but rather familiarity with a few authors, the desire to read, and the cultural literacy necessary to catch the similarities and the ironies that linked fiction and reality. With such competent readers, Mexican crime fiction was able to adapt international models by balancing the fantasy of justice with the realism of familiar places and situations. To the standard plot of detection, it added a moral plot that pointed to a very accurate map of reality. Finally, there was another attribute of crime fiction that attracted readers and writers: the pleasure of looking closely at murder and of resolving the puzzle that it posed.

SEVEN

Our Models of Dread

CRIME AS REVENGE, JUSTICE, AND ART

The writers and editors considered in chapter 6 dealt with the gap between abstract and concrete justice through devices that revealed their ingenuity, daring, and disregard for the law. They allowed their readers to develop a critical perspective on justice and the police in Mexico. The four authors to be considered in this chapter probably had fewer readers, and they inhabited the margins of literary respectability. Their marginality was just as well, for it allowed them to play with the rules of the genre in a critical way. They grappled with the problem of truth and justice through various means, including psychoanalysis, art, and revenge. In doing so, they turned crime fiction into a reflective exercise about artistic creation: murder, whether their characters were aware of it, was their legacy for posterity. These authors inhabited the genre in a more deliberate way than their contemporaries examined in the previous chapter; they influenced the evolution of crime fiction after its early phase, adopting a darker tone that prefigured the tastes of later decades.

This chapter is not structured in a strict chronological order but is organized according to four authors' relationship with the rules of the genre. María Elvira Bermúdez was one of the few women to write detective stories in Mexico, and she was at the center of the effort to give the genre literary credentials. Thus, she articulated and enforced the rules of the genre with fervor. Her short stories and novels delved into the privacy of the upper-class world with microscopic detail, and her work proposed that the truth of crime resided in a mental realm that only intuition and arcane knowledge could reach. Her detection plots combined intuition and psychoanalytic determinism in a way that made her stories light on realism but heavy on literary references. Rodolfo Usigli published the first crime novel in Mexico but had little impact on the genre during his lifetime. Yet his *Ensayo de un crimen* was a critical exploration of murder as the artistic expression of a dark mind. It was also an ironic comment on the genre's superficial reliance on psychological mechanisms to explain acts of violence that in reality had no redeeming value or deep meaning. Juan Bustillo Oro was a movie director who published three short stories and directed four noir movies in the fifties. He used the craftsmanship and the themes deployed by Bermúdez and Usigli, but he put them at the service of revenge. In his stories, art promised a vicarious restoration of the relationship connecting crime, truth, and justice. That restoration proved to be an illusion for Rafael Bernal. He began writing crime fiction in the forties, but his last novel, *El complot mongol,* from 1969, marked the end of an era as the detective story gave way to a noir sensibility, and the pistolero took the quest for the truth and justice into his own hands. The result was that violence, not art or psychoanalysis, was all that was left, at least in his generation's effort to make sense of Mexican infamy through fiction.

THE LITERARY ANXIETY OF MARÍA ELVIRA BERMÚDEZ

María Elvira Bermúdez (1916 [or 1912]–1988) was not the only female author of crime fiction in Mexico, but she was the best known for the quantity of her production, her efforts to claim a literary status for the genre, and her proposal to use psychoanalysis as a validation of Mexican detectives' reliance on confessions to reach the truth.[1] She was atypical in a literary genre dominated by men, but she also had an unusual day job for women—she studied law and worked for many years in the Supreme Court. Recognition came slowly, and to a large extent it was determined by the fact that she was a woman writer, a curiosity rather than an influential figure in the field. Although she published more stories and novels than did most of her counterparts in the forties and fifties, her work was celebrated only in the eighties, when she was lauded as the elder female pioneer of a genre that was finally coming of age. The editors of *Selecciones Policiacas y de Misterio* introduced her in subtly gendered terms as "consistent," "enthusiastic," and "well trained," comparing her to other female writers.[2]

Bermúdez's double marginality (as a crime writer and a woman) might explain her sustained efforts to exalt the literary status of the genre. She was well aware of international debates about the literary merits of detective stories. On the one side, practitioners like S. S. Van Dine reckoned that detective stories should not be judged by standards by which they did not abide, saying that these stories were in reality a form of entertainment. More hostile critics, like Edmund Wilson, placed such stories "in a field which is mostly on a sub-literary level." G. K. Chesterton, by contrast, defended "the romance of police activity," and Mexican author and critic Alfonso Reyes claimed that "the police novel is the classic genre of our time."[3] Bermúdez reacted to this dilemma both as a writer and as a theorist of the genre. As a theorist, in interviews, essays, and anthologies, she often invoked the canon and its demanding rules. She was aware of the difficulties these rules posed for Mexican writers if they were to write stories with any references to social practices. In her introduction to *Los mejores cuentos policiacos mexicanos* (1955), she explained the literary establishment's disregard of crime fiction as an effect of the official dictates of social realism. Yet, she claimed, the "police genre" described "the social state" of the country, seeking to avoid its "shipwreck." The problem was that the genre came with a rigid view of justice, "extremely hard and inevitable strictures" which forced authors to make sure that criminals were always punished.[4] She was aware that such resolution flew in the face of Mexicans' view of reality and their "disdain" for "concrete justice." Rather than yielding to skepticism, however, she formulated a normative genealogy of the genre and a rigid classification of its variations that would guide legitimate Mexican stories.[5] Over the years, this orthodoxy took her from optimism to nostalgia. While in the fifties she could claim that Mexican authors were comparable to their foreign counterparts (Helú to Leblanc, Bernal to Chesterton), later in life she maintained that contemporary Mexican production was of low quality, resembled pornography, and included too much violence.[6]

As a writer, Bermúdez saw literature as a gentle form of redemption from the national "shipwreck." Her stories kept violence to a minimum, made almost all characters at the same time suspects and detectives, and solved the puzzle by penetrating into the mind of the criminal. She tried to challenge readers but also to reward them with explanations that assumed their sagacity and preserved the illusion of fair play.[7] These strategies, however, resulted in artificial settings, shallow characters, predictable structures, and overly elaborate resolutions. It is not surprising to see references to Christie in Bermúdez's narrative: in one story, the detective compares himself with Miss Marple, and in another, the victim identifies the killer by underlining a Christie book. Her plots and characters typically have literary qualities.

Armando H. Zozaya, the detective in most of her early stories, is a well-known journalist like Chucho Cárdenas, but more of an intellectual type. He lives comfortably, surrounded by servants at home, drives a nice coupe, and avidly reads and translates U.S. specialized books on crime ("they are very clever," he admits).[8] Solving a case is for him an extension of the act of reading: in "Crimen para inocentes," a body is a "document," the "epilogue to a terrible story" which he "wanted to read, page by page." In the same story, he introduces himself with modesty: "I am not a policeman. I am only an aficionado . . . interested in mysterious crimes."[9]

Another Bermúdez fictional detective is María Elena Morán, the wife of a federal deputy who solves cases to fight boredom and as an extension of her love for books. Her methods are even more literary than Zozaya's, using metaphors in lieu of logical explanations, or citing the books she reads as the key to interpret evidence.[10] Victims and suspects share that literary predilection. In *Diferentes razones tiene la muerte,* the murderer turns out to be a doctor who reads Nietzsche and kills for philosophical reasons. Victims leave literary clues. Literature empowers characters and author in their pursuit of the truth. The goal, beyond justice, is intellectual improvement: in "Ella fue testigo," an agent of the judicial police admits to Zozaya "that police literature might be helpful. The way you have disciplined your mind is proof of that."[11] Bermúdez saw *policial* literature as a way to redeem women, too. In her 1961 novel *Detente, sombra* all the characters, even taxi drivers, are female, and most are members of the cultural and political elite. The conceit is not meant to create a feminist utopia in which women can do everything that men now do. Characters embody the same jealousy, crime, and corruption usually dominated by men. The difference is that Morán solves the mystery because she has the intellectual discipline required by *policial* pursuits. In other words, Bermúdez placed more weight on the rules of the genre to engage the reader than on realism: those rules are so strong that the plot does not lose any value when set in an implausible social context.[12]

For Bermúdez, class and gender difference served as a plot device rather than as a reference to Mexican reality. In *Diferentes razones tiene la muerte,* for example, the setup is familiar to Christie's readers: a man gathers a group of upper-class characters in an elegant Mexico City mansion "to observe them . . . to perform an original experiment."[13] The murders allow Zozaya to enter a rarefied world of luxury that the police literally seal from the outside during the investigation. All the characters have reasons to commit the crimes, motivations that become increasingly complex as the murders add up, along with a nocturnal dance of people entering and leaving interconnected rooms. According to a dimwitted police detective, it all amounts to "a mess of divorces and crime among these rich and indolent people." The domestic workers at the mansion are not even interrogated: since there was no robbery, it is impossible to conceive of any reason for them to commit the crime. Only the sophistication of upper-class people could countenance such intricate crimes; the intellectual puzzle lies in their exceptionality. According to Zozaya, "In Mexico the majority of crimes, if not all of them, are crimes of passion, simple, evident, and not subtle and tortuous like these." [14]

Bermúdez dealt with these "tortuous" crimes with a synthesis of the detection and moral plots and an idiosyncratic appropriation of psychoanalysis. In *Diferentes razones,* Zozaya is not satisfied with material evidence, even though it is abundant, because it was probably planted by the culprit. The detective believes that an accusation "can only be supported by motives." [15] Thus, he looks for the psychological mechanisms behind the crime, reconstructing the "mental history" of the culprit, Dr. Requena. Earlier, in a chapter entitled "Psychoanalytical Summary," Requena cites psychiatric authorities to argue that anyone in the group could have committed the crime, and he classifies each character according to his or her kind of mental abnormality. [16] In the conclusion, Zozaya turns authority against the suspect and presents a didactic summary of psychoanalysis, citing loosely connected authors like Jung, Freud, Ferenczi, and "the criminal psychoanalysis of Jiménez de Azúa." [17] Family antecedents explain Requena's behavior: he had been abandoned and mistreated by his parents; guilt for his father's death lodged in his "subconscious" and remained "latent" until it emerged through his criminal actions, despite the "repression" exercised by his "conscience." [18]

This psychological determinism forced Bermúdez to violate the rules of crime fiction she defended in theory. Zozaya uses fairly conventional procedures to catch the culprit in *Diferentes razones:* unable to identify the killer, he sets up a scene in which all the characters are present. They discuss their motivations and alibis, and the scene ends with the criminal's emotional confession. The detective himself is part of this group self-examination, which helps characters dig into their "subconscious": he understood everything when he "heard a hidden voice." [19] This kind of group therapy undermined fair play since only in the final scene was the reader provided with the facts needed to solve the crime. Yet the scene did provide the swift and irrefutable resolution expected from the genre, particularly when the suspect attempted an escape after having described his murderous methods to the other characters. This way to validate the investigation fused the suspect's moral and material guilt. It also resonated with the reliance of Mexican police and judges on confessions. As we saw in chapters 2 and 4, murder as an act of self-expression was prominent in the public pursuit of the truth. Although confession had religious roots, psychoanalysis gave it a scientific imprimatur at a time when crime, rather than sin, required expiation. In *Diferentes razones,* as in other works by Bermúdez and her contemporaries, psychoanalysis seemed to make sense of the reasons why intelligent criminals would choose the self-defeating path of admitting their guilt: as in therapy, the relevant past could only emerge through the words of the subject.

Publicity, however, was necessary. Echoing nota roja settings for the narratives of famous murderers, fictional confessions had to happen in front of an audience. Only then could crime turn into a communicative act whose meaning was broadly shared. In *Diferentes razones,* Requena himself helps Zozaya gather the audience, and he confesses because he does not want to be accused for the wrong reasons: his "arrogance" would not countenance being considered "a simple and vulgar suspect." He admits that "everything he had done would be pointless if nobody learned about his accomplishment."[20] As we will see next, this notion of murder as a form of self-expression was developed in Usigli's *Ensayo de un crimen* and in stories by Bustillo Oro and Bernal.

RODOLFO USIGLI: THE CRIMINAL AND THE ARTIST

Rodolfo Usigli (1905–1979) wove the intricate connections between fiction and reality, both political and personal, into his 1944 crime novel *Ensayo de un crimen.* Murder was a vehicle for artistic creation in the novel, but it was also a window onto postrevolutionary corruption and impunity. As with other writers discussed in this book, Usigli felt lasting bitterness about Vasconcelos's 1929 electoral defeat.[21] Shortly after that experience, he reflected about crime in his diary in a way that seemed to both express this bitterness and anticipate the premise of the novel: "All crimes are simple, easy. Elementary gestures of suppression, violation, destruction"; they cause remorse in "the man of talent" because they return him to a "natural state" and plant doubts regarding "the divinity of the human spirit." He did not share this remorse, but he jotted down an idea that would be the seed for the novel: "Superiority of the aesthetic over the moral crime"; "nothing will bring me closer to people other than a great crime or a masterpiece."[22]

Despite his disappointment with the regime, Usigli went on to work for the Cárdenas government in the area of press relations. Under Ávila Camacho, he moved to the diplomatic service, perhaps a more pleasant job but one that also clearly indicated his growing distance from the centers of power. Readers of *Ensayo de un crimen* at the time of its publication could not have failed to notice Usigli's allusions to the rightward turn of the national government beginning in 1940 and the corruption associated with the new order. One character, the *gordo* Asuara, is the hedonistic organizer of illegal poker games for high-society players. He knows the police will not bother his operation because he has been familiar with them since the time "when policemen became thieves."[23] Asuara later becomes a member of the Supreme Court. The veiled criticism of the regime through fiction did not prevent Usigli from continuing his career as a diplomat while enjoying increasing success as a playwright, particularly after the 1947 opening of *El Gesticulador,* a critique of postrevolutionary politics set in a provincial town. It helped that *Ensayo de un crimen* had a small number of readers at first, and it was largely ignored by critics, too. In 1968, it was republished in Buenos Aires, and in the eighties Mexican presses made it widely available.[24]

Ensayo de un crimen would be Usigli's only published foray into crime fiction, although it revealed an unparalleled mastery of the rules of the genre and of the resources that Mexican crime fiction could use to critically represent Mexican reality. The book went beyond realism, exploiting the overlap between author, detective, and criminal. The resulting moral ambiguity was perhaps too much to take for the standard reader in the early times of the genre, thus explaining the book's long hibernation. The main character is Roberto de la Cruz, the scion of a decadent family, a dandy of perfect appearance but a stormy inner life. He wants to be a great artist of murder, committing crimes that would be beautiful and gratuitous (lacking a practical goal, like greed or passion) yet exhaustively planned and deliberately performed. The murders Roberto plans never pan out, however. His execution is clumsy, and he cannot control public perceptions of his creations. The first death is that of Patricia Terrazas, a wealthy, embarrassingly uninhibited socialite. When Roberto arrives at the planned location, he realizes that somebody has preempted him and she is already dead. In the second murder, whose intended victim is the aging homosexual art collector Count Schwartzemberg, a fire in the building where Roberto thought he had killed him prevents the press and the police from entering the crime scene, leaving responsibility uncertain. The third murder he does commit but not against the person he had in mind: instead of slitting the throat of a prostitute he had brought home for that purpose, he kills his wife, who has just returned from a trip.[25]

Ensayo de un crimen was longer than any piece of crime fiction produced in Mexico until then, giving Usigli ample room to develop several paradoxical contrapositions without turning to parody. The first concerns the criminal-detective. The narration is in the third person but closely follows Roberto's sensations, thoughts, and even dreams, highlighting the subjective perspective of the would-be murderer. The tune from a music box brings back traumatic childhood memories from the times of the revolution and triggers murderous desires. Usigli described Roberto's unconscious past, and the dreams that express them, in what seems to be an explanation of the crimes— a rather straightforward moral plot. Yet in key moments, such as those preceding a murder, the narrator's proximity to Roberto is interrupted, and the reader is kept ignorant of what happens inside and outside the protagonist's head. María Elvira Bermúdez expressed the perplexity of many readers when she mistakenly concluded that the novel "is not strictly *policial*" because the identity of the criminal is already known to the reader.[26] In fact, it is not. Usigli implicitly criticized the genre's reliance on moral or psychological reasoning by subtly interweaving a detection plot that ties the book together. The role of the detective here is played by a private investigator, former police inspector Valentín Herrera—his name and background clear references to Valente Quintana. He is a cunning sleuth and appears in the book at key moments, finally explaining to Roberto de la Cruz each one of the murders. The interaction between the two men allowed Usigli to fulfill the conventions of the genre by presenting a mystery and solving it with incontestable evidence. Herrera explains that a minor character in the story was actually the murderer of Terrazas and Schwartzemberg.[27] This provides the resolution for a detection plot that the reader could have easily neglected because of the narrative's focus on Roberto.

Usigli also ridiculed the notion that an artist could achieve superiority through crime, as he had believed when he was younger. Critics have long cited the novel's tacit parallelisms to Thomas de Quincey's "On Murder Considered as one of the Fine Arts." De Quincey's 1827 essay argued that murder could be an art if performed according to good taste and craftsmanship. A murder for lowly motives, therefore, could not be an act of aesthetic freedom and spiritual self-expression. Usigli avoided de Quincey's didactic irony, but he cited André Gide's narrative treatment of similar ideas.[28] Fundamentally, *Ensayo de un crimen* was a reflection on the uncertainty of truth and fame. The romantic idea of art for its own sake was no longer possible in modern Mexico, or at least it was no longer as important to the criminal-artist as the recognition of public opinion. But this recognition is evasive. Roberto wants his crimes to be admired as works of art. Yet the police accuse him of killing his wife because of her infidelities—which Roberto knows about but is not bothered by. Piqued in his artistic pride, he confesses to the other murders. Psychiatrists assess his mental condition and complete his humiliation by declaring him insane. He is frustrated by the misinterpretation of his artistic creations. "What he wanted was the truth, the reality of crime . . . as he had dreamt it: gratuitous, perfect; everything else was advertising." [29]

For Roberto, "the reality of crime" means the imprimatur of a judicial sentence but also the true publicity, as opposed to "advertising," of the nota roja. *Ensayo de un crimen* dissects the construction of Mexican reality at the roots of criminal literacy. Newspapers play a central role in the narrative: every morning, Roberto browses the police section of the newspapers before looking at the other sections. He looks for aesthetically satisfying murders, but he only finds an abundance of vulgar killings with base motivations. The novel cites headlines and texts, and describes caricatures and photographs from the nota roja. Although fictitious, these quotations are loaded with accurate satire: while *Excélsior* cruelly mocks victims, *La Prensa* demands harsh punishment in a bombastic tone. Journalists' characterizations of Roberto reveal the vagaries of publicity. When he finally appears in the newspapers, after confessing to Terrazas's murder, reporters describe Roberto as a coarse criminal. After he is exonerated and released from prison, they transform him into a gentleman, the victim of police ineptitude. When he kills his wife, he is again portrayed as a jealous brute, only to be later rehabilitated as a criminal of passion. All these erroneous depictions drive Roberto to tears because they miss the true meaning of his actions. The consequence is that his work is not "registered within the framework or reality by the police, the autopsy and the newspapers." [30]

This critical stance on reality does not mean that, for Usigli, the national infamy was an invention of journalists and creative murderers. Usigli provided references to contemporary life that any criminally literate reader of the mid-forties could easily have recognized. They would have found, for example, a clear connection between Terrazas and socialite Jacinta Aznar, murdered in 1932. The case, as we know, ended when the officially sentenced murderer, Alberto Gallegos (José Asturias, in the novel), suffered the ley fuga on the train to the Islas Marías. Both Terrazas and Aznar lived alone, and their bodies decayed for weeks before they were found. Both were aging women who did not hid their sexual appetites, had money, claimed to have friends in the European aristocracy, led an intense social life, and frequented the same upscale restaurants.[31] *Ensayo de un crimen* is closer than other contemporary Mexican productions to hard-boiled models in its detailed description of an urban life of danger, desire, mistrust, and corruption. Detection gave Usigli an opportunity to map out the moral geography of the city, with detailed descriptions of streets, restaurants, hotels, cabarets, mansions, prisons, and mental hospitals. Despite the dominance of upper-class characters, the novel presents an objective vision of the physical expanse and social diversity of Mexico City. Roberto and Schwartzemberg "went to the musical revues, the obscene burlesque, the neighborhood cabarets, living the night life of lowly Mexico.... Everywhere, without exception, the count would find acquaintances. Sometimes they were respectable people, sometimes drivers, wrestlers, professionals, sometimes writers or artists, sometimes elegant and [sexually] ambiguous young men like Luisito."[32] Usigli assumed that readers shared this negative view about the infamy of independent and dangerous women, homosexuals, policemen, and criminals. His own perspective on class difference was not as simple as those of D'Olmo or Bermúdez, and the result in *Ensayo de un crimen* presents a morally ambivalent, somber vision of Mexican society that noir novels and movies would echo in subsequent years.

Homosexuality occupied a particularly important place in Usigli's moral map, one that his fiction was better able to explore than nota roja or popular detective stories. The detection plot reveals this importance despite Roberto's reluctance to recognize it. The culprit in the murders of Terrazas and Schwartzemberg is Luisito, a character who appears sporadically in the first and second part of the novel. Both victims use Luisito to satisfy their sexual appetites, and he kills to steal from them—the most vulgar of motivations in Roberto's scale of values. Inspector Herrera recognizes this because he already knew about Luisito's connections with the victims, as he received daily "reports" on the habits of every person who was worth knowing in Mexico City.[33] Thus, he can explain why the crimes were inevitable: the murderer "is a devil, as a good representative of the society of faggots."[34] Although homophobia is not hidden in *Ensayo de un crimen,* a sense of risky ambivalence characterizes Roberto's ill-intentioned courtship of Schwartzemberg. Confronted by sexual insinuations from the count, Roberto "always kept his line, not allowing the slightest misunderstanding" while at the same time "penetrating the intimacy of the man."[35] While Schwartzemberg is ugly and embarrassing, his true killer, Luisito, is the portrait of the criminal consequences of any form of sexuality that did not match normative molds.[36]

These attitudes served Usigli well because they helped in the creation of plausible victims. In the novel, he disguised intolerance as procedural common sense. Usigli's depictions resonated with the rejection and even persecution of male homosexuals in Mexican public life that had occurred since the thirties. The association between criminality, mental illness, and homosexuality was a premise of studies of Goyo Cárdenas's personality. Crimes against homosexuals in general went unpunished because, police agents argued, they were particularly difficult to investigate due to the victims' discreet customs. As in other examples of crime fiction in Mexico, in *Ensayo de un crimen* victims were never blameless, and murderers were not necessarily despicable.[37] The victimization of wealthy and unmarried women like Terrazas had the same air of inevitable impunity as all violence against homosexuals. Even Carlota Cervantes, Roberto's wife and his unintended victim, occupies a morally dubious place. She belongs to a respectable family and would appear to be the moral opposite of Terrazas. Roberto is secretly in love with Carlota's mother, but she is married to a shy and educated man.[38] Suddenly, Roberto decides to marry her daughter, Carlota, whose first husband has just died. He was a closet homosexual and old friend of Roberto's who did not object to her keeping a lover. Roberto simply replaces him, perhaps because Carlota thinks Roberto is also gay, and she can continue to see her old lover. As a result, the police believe that Roberto was motivated by jealousy to kill Carlota, since he is most certainly not homosexual, as Usigli is keen to point out. In any case, the lives of an upper-class family are almost as morally decadent as the lives of Terrazas and Schwartzemberg. All deserved to die, reasons Herrera by the end of the novel.

Roberto's intended victims are easy to kill without regret. Thus, they facilitate murder as a freely creative act. Beauty, according to the young Usigli, is above the law.[39] A reading of the novel that considers Usigli's critique of de Quincey's idea of murder as a form of art would suggest, instead, that none of these murders, either executed or just planned, are true expressions of freedom. Roberto's intended victims are the object of his repulsion or desire: "I would love to kill her," he says about Terrazas the night they meet.[40] Murder as form of beauty no longer works because, by the early forties, Usigli had developed a deeper understanding of the communicative value of crime. He had seen criminals become authors whose work was discussed by large audiences. Like Roberto de la Cruz, Usigli wanted to produce a masterpiece that would be celebrated into posterity. But he also wrote Roberto as a sarcastic personification of his own younger self's romantic ideas about art. The decisive factor that made murder successful as a form of modern art was now public recognition, not disinterested beauty. Lowly criminals could achieve that fame, but it escapes Roberto because of the evasive quality of the truth in Mexico. In an ironic twist of Usigli's playing around with the roles of murderer, detective, and artist, his own recognition as a crime fiction author would have to wait four decades.

JUAN BUSTILLO ORO: THE DIRECTOR AND THE CRIMINAL

Juan Bustillo Oro (1904–1989) wrote only three crime short stories, a small body of work in comparison with his oeuvre as movie writer, director, and producer. He also directed four noir movies that were closely connected to those short stories in their ideas about murder and revenge. While he explored the same questions about art and crime formulated by Usigli in his novel, Bustillo Oro also exemplified the productive interactions between literature and cinema elicited by the pursuit of the truth. His noir movies were indebted to the narrative lessons of crime fiction, and, along with his short stories, they were among the most explicit reflections on the twisted ways of truth, justice, and crime to be found in Mexican fiction. The stories play with the identification between author and criminal and put that duality at the service of justice. During their youth, both Usigli and Bustillo Oro witnessed the kind of violence that defined the postrevolutionary regime for many members of their generation. In the fifties, Bustillo Oro was a victim of the pistolero-enforced domination of Mexican cinema by politically connected caciques. He used his art to take revenge.

In contrast with Usigli's critique of murder as an art form, Bustillo Oro told stories of murder as a way to obtain justice, in both judicial and artistic terms. The victims of his fictional violence correspond quite clearly with the sources of his own frustrations as a young defender of democracy and productive movie director. Compelled by his family to become a lawyer, he studied in the National University's Preparatoria and Jurisprudencia schools. But he wanted to be a writer, and he published several stories in *El Universal*

Ilustrado during the twenties. Politics, as much as vocation, determined his professional future. Supporting Vasconcelos's 1929 presidential campaign filled him with enthusiasm. With friends Antonio Helú and Germán de Campo, he participated in demonstrations in favor of their candidate and against official candidate Pascual Ortiz Rubio. Bustillo Oro remembers that Vasconcelos himself warned them to expect fraud and violence: "Those in government are not going to bother organizing voters but will be arming pistoleros." Bustillo Oro was traumatized by de Campo's death during a demonstration. In his memoirs, he describes the body of his friend, fallen near the Cine Monumental downtown, deploying a combination of gore and religious imagery that would reappear later in his fiction: "The wound, clearly and exactly calculated, is on the pure forehead of the Christian fighter. The bullet exited there after soaking in his encephalic mass, his noble brain thus escaping with his generous thoughts." The death of de Campo confirmed the "sacrifice of our generation, that henceforth would be forcefully and permanently expelled from public matters." [41] Like Helú, Bustillo Oro had to leave the country. After a trip to Europe, he began his long career in the movies, writing the script for the celebrated *El compadre Mendoza* (Fernando de Fuentes, 1933) and directing *Los dos monjes* the following year. Several of his movies were commercially profitable, yet he constantly shifted genres (from comedies to *rancheras,* suspense, and family dramas) despite the advice of his longtime producer Jesús Grovas.

Bustillo Oro's critical perspective on the postrevolutionary regime, already noticeable in the iconoclastic view of Pancho Villa in *El compadre Mendoza,* was clear throughout his oeuvre, particularly in his nostalgic period pieces about the Porfiriato. [42] In his memoirs, he explained several of his movies in terms of his political experience. *La honradez es un estorbo* (1937), for example, contains clear references to state corruption and a happy ending for the one honest character, who manages to earn a living from his writing. Bustillo Oro wrote that "today I realize that this happy ending, Yankee style, gave me the personal satisfaction of a biographical revenge." [43] An early and decisive success was *Ahí está el detalle* (1940), conceived as a vehicle for the popular theater comedian Mariano Moreno, known as "Cantinflas." Looking for a situation that would allow Cantinflas to use his vaudeville repertoire, Bustillo Oro recalled his experience as a lawyer arguing before a popular jury in the twenties. Cantinflas reminded him of those suspects who "dressed similarly, and answered questions with astutely confusing speech. Distrusting both the prosecutor and the defense attorneys, they slipped into funny jokes against themselves."[44] The trial scene in the movie satirized the dissonance of multiple voices and the ineptitude of the agents of the law that was examined in chapter 1. The defense attorney is unable to control Cantinflas, who is accused of killing someone named Bobby; he confesses, thinking that Bobby is a dog he had to put to sleep, but all is cleared up in the end.

Ahí está el detalle marked the beginning of a successful period for Bustillo Oro in which he earned a percentage of sales from his movies rather than a flat fee. The entire Mexican movie industry went through a phase of expansion. In the mid-forties, as Bustillo Oro remembered it, "great opaqueness" set in because of the "consolidation of the Ávila Camacho-Jenkins-Alarcón-Espinosa distribution monopoly." Thanks to its control over theaters, the group began to underpay distributors for the movies it projected, manipulate sales numbers, and force producers to take on expensive loans. Hoping to escape the monopoly's rule, Grovas and Bustillo Oro formed a partnership to build their own theater, the Cosmos, in the popular Tlaxpana neighborhood. Days before the opening, however, the building burned to the ground, and the partners had to sell the lot to the monopoly. After this defeat, Grovas chose to import movies from Europe while Bustillo Oro entered what he would later call a phase of "intellectual laziness" and minor movies.[45]

However, in the following years, Bustillo Oro would make four movies characterized by suspense, noir imagery, and a detection plot that reflected a productive dialogue between literary fiction and cinema. *El hombre sin rostro* (1950), *La huella de unos labios* (1952), *El asesino X* (1955), and *El medallón del crimen* (1956) showed Bustillo Oro's good instinct for the taste of audiences and his knowledge of the rules of detection and suspense. In *El hombre sin rostro,* a man kills women with a scalpel, causing wounds that, as in the case of Jack the Ripper, lead the police to think he is a physician or a scientist, like Goyo Cárdenas. The movie includes several dream sequences and scenes of lonely city streets, cabarets, the morgue, a scientific lab, and elegant but somber mansions.[46] Psychoanalytical therapy is key to the resolution of the mystery: during a long scene, Juan Carlos (Arturo de Córdova) lies on the couch while Dr. Britel (Miguel Ángel Ferriz), pipe in his mouth, invites him to free-associate, recount his dreams (where he finds "symbols of a sexual nature"), and look into his past for the origins of his anxiety. "We have to probe your soul, Juan," Britel says, "to its deepest levels." Britel discovers in Juan Carlos a fear of his dead mother and the consequent suppression of the libido. As in literary fiction, the movie drew references to reality from criminal literacy. In his memoirs, Bustillo Oro explains the eclectic genealogy of the movie's method of detection: the psychoanalysis classes he took at the preparatoria with Samuel Ramos, and his readings of Stevenson, Freud, Jung, Adler, and Kraft-Ebbing.[47] The movie included a psychiatric adviser in the credits, Dr. Gregorio Oneto Barenque, author of texts on the effects of marihuana and penal responsibility of the mentally ill. As mentioned in chapter 4, Oneto Barenque was also the director of the private clinic where Goyo Cárdenas was admitted in 1942 before he was arrested. Oneto Barenque's advice probably accounts for the precision of the psychological vocabulary in the movie's dialogue, but it also provides a suggestive connection with that famous case.

Going beyond Bermúdez's literary references to psychoanalysis, Bustillo Oro used the method, or at least his version of it, as a tool to explore the criminal mind and reflect on the problem of guilt. Juan Carlos, a former medical student, is frustrated by his failure to uncover the murderer. But he suffers from a split personality, and he has indeed committed the crimes, moved by his hatred of women. Britel shoots him near the end of the movie, when Juan Carlos is about to kill his own fiancée, Ana María (Carmen Molina). In his final moments, Juan Carlos believes he has killed the murderer. Ana María and Britel have compassion for him and do not tell him that he is in fact the murderer. Only at that point does the viewer realize that the confession with which Britel began the movie is that of killing Juan Carlos; by then, however, that murder is entirely justifiable. In a fitting example of the moral ambiguity of Mexican crime fiction, the two killers in the movie get to present their own narrative: Juan Carlos through therapy, and Britel through his confession. Both are also free of guilt and deserve the sympathy of the audience: Juan Carlos because of his illness, and Britel because of his heroic intervention to save Ana María.

La huella de unos labios was closer to Hollywood film noir conventions. The movie is set in dark, suffocating spaces and uses flashback and voice-over. Bustillo Oro adapted the script from "Collared," a 1949 short story by Cornell Woolrich whose rights he was able to acquire for a low price thanks to Antonio Helú's connection to Frederic Dannay (discussed in chapter 6). Bustillo Oro expanded the theme of revenge from the original story.[48] María (Rosario Granados) works in a cabaret but decides to leave her job in order to marry Felipe (Rubén Rojo). Her boss, Villa (Carlos López Moctezuma), covets María, and has Felipe hit by a car. Villa is a man of the underworld, surrounded by the prototypical pistoleros—smartly dressed thugs who speak with a lower-class accent, wield police badges, and are ready to follow orders even if they include beating, killing, or covering up. For María, by contrast, the story is that "of my dignity and my revenge," as she shifts from Felipe's innocent wife-to-be to Villa's domestic prisoner, and eventually becomes her own avenger.[49] The action takes place in city streets and cabarets, but mostly inside the apartment where María must suffer Villa's cruelty. Domestic violence, central to Woolrich's story, is depicted here in a straightforward manner that was not common in Mexican cinema. When Villa kills another woman and tries to pin it on her boyfriend, María manipulates the evidence so the police will get Villa. In order to do this, she paints her lips and presses them against the collar of one of Villa's shirts, the same kind as the one he had destroyed to avoid suspicion. In Woolrich's short story the villain is killed by the police when he is about to murder the protagonist. In the movie, revenge is consummated in a more perfect way, when one of Villa's own pistoleros accidentally runs him over. Once again, the death that ends the plot is morally legitimate.

For Bustillo Oro, the success of *La huella de unos labios* revealed a new taste for crime stories: "Even though the Mexican public came to the screenings of *La huella de unos labios* with obvious skepticism about the ability of Mexican cinema to tackle a story of suspense, our attempt worked." He believed that part of the success came from Woolrich's ability to break with "logic" in order to achieve effect: "He simply used surprise without bothering with improbability . . . [and had] the necessary artistry to hide the artificiality of the process behind emotions."[50]

Logic, or its absence, depended on the setting. *El asesino X* was an adaptation from a play by Alfredo Diestro that had unintended similarities to an O. Henry story, as Bustillo Oro recognized. It was shot in two weeks, with lots of voice-over and the feeling of a stage play. Manolo Fábregas played a Mexican migrant who is going to be executed in a U.S. court but refuses to identify himself in order to spare the shame to his family in Mexico.[51] A long trial scene shares some of the humor of *Ahí está el detalle,* but the U.S. setting allows Bustillo Oro to sustain the otherwise artificial premise that the police and justice system are effective and honest, and punishment is inevitable. The opposite was the case in the last of Bustillo Oro's noir films, where the setting was unmistakably Mexican. The plot of his 1956 *El medallón del crimen* revolves around two men: Ramón (Wolf Ruvinskis), a pistolero, and Raúl (Fábregas), a decent man married to devoted María (Granados). The two men become interested in each other because they can be blamed for the death of another María (Rita Macedo), who is Ramón's lover but flirts with Raúl.

Humor mixes uneasily with noir as Ramón's brutality contrasts with the domestic comedy between Fábregas and Granados. In the last scene, Raúl comically grimaces as María learns about his failed infidelity, even though they know the next-door neighbor has just been killed by Ramón.[52] The movie, which Bustillo Oro cowrote with Helú, paid homage to hard-boiled fiction by highlighting the importance of the urban setting. The initial scene at a police station shows the locations of Raúl and Ramón on a city map, the first one in the southern *colonia* Mixcoac, an area of new middle-class developments, and the other in the northern, seedy *barrio* Atlampa. A policeman traces a line between the two points on the map, and the rest of the movie follows the comings and goings of the two men across the city. The film opens with the usual panoramic images of a modern Mexico City and references to its four million inhabitants and their many stories, but this soon gives way to ground-level action in cabarets, bars, pharmacies, offices, highways, modern apartment buildings, and middle-class homes.

Bustillo Oro's crime fiction was closely connected to his movies. His early fiction had already explored the relation between art and crime. In *La penumbra inquieta: Cuentos cinematográficos,* published in 1925 in the weekly supplement "La novela semanal" of *El Universal Ilustrado,* Bustillo Oro narrated the fleeting relationships established between the main character, a young student, and women who went to the movies. In the intimacy of the darkness and the melody of the orchestra, cinema made possible anonymous sexual adventures: "Every man who goes to the movies is looking for something ... and usually ... finds it."[53] His crime stories were published in *Selecciones Policíacas y de Misterio* and in *Aventura y Misterio:* "Apuesta al crimen" (1951), "El asesino de los gatos" (1953), and "Cómo murió Charles Prague" (1960).[54] They adhere closely to the rules of crime fiction but still maintain explicit connections with cinema. Explaining *El medallón del crimen* in his memoirs, Bustillo Oro extended the literary rules of fair play and engagement with the audience to the movies. To achieve "suspense," according to Bustillo Oro, "sequences have to be combined as in a game of chess. Each move must lead to the expected results, leaving the enemy no possible escape. The enemy is the audience." Suspense resides in "carefully measuring the plot's tension" so that the audience can "forget criticism and be swept by anxiety." More than a competition, adds Bustillo Oro, this form of narrative resembles a premeditated crime in that the process "requires thought, treachery, and lots of deceit for the coincidences."[55] His three crime short stories develop the parallel between crime and art, but they are more provocative in defending revenge as a morally legitimate alternative to the weaknesses of justice and the police.

"Apuesta al crimen" deals with the pursuit of the artful crime, described and analyzed by the criminal himself. The theme cropped up frequently in Mexican crime fiction, from *Ensayo de un crimen* to Roberto Cruzpiñón's "El tercer paquete." Like Roberto de la Cruz, the narrator in Bustillo Oro's short story must recognize his own inability to control the ways in which the public interprets his actions. At the beginning of the story, he remembers the moment of "extraordinary lucidity" when he committed the crime, and he feels "again a pleasure that I could characterize as aesthetic." He had conceived the crime in a dream, "just as only in dreams I wrote a peerless novel or composed an immortal symphony." [56] His motivations, however, are a messy mix of greed and revenge. Fortune places in his hands the opportunity to take his uncle's money, which he needs to pay for his gambling debts. He is also seeking revenge: the uncle raised the narrator in a wealthy home but submitted him to extreme demands and humiliations. The resentment extends to the uncle's son, a fortunate young man of lesser intellectual abilities. One day, the narrator finds his uncle dead, shoots him in the head, and leaves everything ready for the police to accuse his cousin. When he is finished, feeling like a demiurge, the narrator states: "I completed my work and saw that it was good." So good, in fact, that there is no crime: the uncle had died of natural causes, and shooting a corpse is a physical action without moral value: "A corpse spits to our eyes its absolute and conclusive worthlessness. It is barely a thing." Yet soon the creation begins to unravel. It starts with self-doubt: he wonders whether putting the bullet in the man's head has "unleashed an inner demon." The police claim to have some evidence against him, and he confesses. He is not worried about "the long sentence with which murder is punished in Mexico . . . sometimes," but he regrets the failure of a creation that had required skill, opportunity, creativity, desire, and the intervention of the "subconscious." The failure extends to the story itself: the police do not believe him, the narrator tells the reader, "just as you do not believe me either." [57]

Justice is the goal of the murderer in "El asesino de los gatos," but the moral ambiguity is the same. The narrative is also a monologue with asides directed to the reader. The victim is another hated and dominant character, aptly named Güero Rico (literally, wealthy blond), who insults and beats the narrator, making him taste "the repulsion of my abject cowardice." The resentment reaches its climax when Rico kills, just for pleasure, the cats that the narrator fed and loved. The scene has the kind of graphic detail that was impossible to represent in film at the time, with the animals "almost beheaded, mixing blood and brains on the greasy floor." Revenge comes in a way that expresses its inherent justice: Rico dies when his head is crushed by an elevator, making "the noise of hundreds of walnuts breaking at the same time." As in the previous story, however, there is ambiguity as to the narrator's guilt: he is in control of the elevator, which accidentally starts when Rico is peaking through a gap. The narrator is not accused, and he does not feel guilty because "in the end, I had killed a wretched man." The crime is almost perfect not because of its premeditation but because of its indisputable moral legitimacy. "I was," he argues, an "instrument of that thing that one cannot see or touch, that can barely be guessed, that thing I would dare call Justice if I was not afraid of the pomposity of the term."[58]

"Cómo murió Charles Prague," published when Bustillo Oro had practically retired from the movies, took the relationship of crime, art, and justice to its ultimate consequences. The story takes place in 1920s Hollywood and is told by a gossip journalist who heard it from the secretary of a powerful producer, William Lane. The murderer is Lee Smith, a character actor. Prague is a handsome star, a favorite of the female audience of "typists." He dies, poisoned, while shooting a scene in a movie to be called *El triunfo de la justicia*. The agony is so impressive that the director lets the cameras roll even though the action departs from the script. Lane, who is in financial trouble, decides to use the footage in the movie but needs to change the script. Instead of the usual happy ending he allows for one of those rare "Europeanisms" in which the villain, in this case Smith, wins.[59] Now titled *La muerte encerrada*, the movie is a success, in good part because Lane pays newspapers to let the public know that Prague's actual death is shown in the movie.

The crime is so perfect that Smith feels compelled to confess. He tells Lane that he poisoned Prague, explaining that he was tired of portraying villains of superior "intelligence" who nevertheless end up defeated by the "stupid hero." As his career developed, Smith came to identify himself with his characters, "as a double exposure, to use the cinematographic term, or as a splitting of my personality, to use the language of psychology." He rebels against the "injustice" committed against him, both as a character and as an actor. His "self-respect" moves him "to seek the compensation of my own triumph, beautiful, just and categorical." After failing to sell scripts that reflect his hopes, he murders Prague, which yields the desired result. His confession to Lane responds to "the disinterested and pure pleasure of telling" details that nobody knows, and it is therefore intended to increase "the brightness of my victory." Lane nevertheless calls the police, knowing that the sensational trial will further benefit sales of the movie. Smith takes it in stride, and he promises to play the role of the villain one last time, now "in the magnificent scale of reality," even if it leads to his execution.[60] Unlike "Apuesta al crimen," "Cómo murió Charles Prague" contains the fulfillment of the plans of the criminal-artist, whose creation is properly appreciated by the public.

RAFAEL BERNAL: THE DETECTIVE
BECOMES THE PISTOLERO

The demise of the detective and the critique of the state is complete in the work of Rafael Bernal (1915–1972), an author whose crime fiction spans three decades and embodies the transformation of the genre during its golden years. Among its main authors, Bernal was perhaps the most distant, physically and symbolically, from the center of national literature. This allowed him to produce the most sarcastic critique of Mexican politics through crime fiction. He is now well known for the 1969 novel *El complot mongol,* a book that has been read as the first in a new era of noir and *neopoliciaco* that emerged in the seventies.[61] But a more expansive look at the continuities and transformations of Bernal's work after the forties can help us understand the dilemmas that defined the genre and reflected the time in which it was produced. This broader view also sheds light on the specifically Mexican contradiction regarding justice and truth that the genre could not transcend.

Like Helú, Usigli, and Bustillo Oro, Bernal came of age politically in the opposition to the postrevolutionary order. His sympathy for the Catholic resistance of Cristeros and Sinarquistas earned him a stint in prison. He was member of a family with deep intellectual prestige as the great-grandson of Joaquín García Icazbalceta and grandson of Luis García Pimentel, both historians, and brother of archeologist Ignacio Bernal, who excavated Monte Albán. Rafael worked in the family's haciendas, lived in the United States, and traveled widely, including a stint as a war correspondent. After 1960, he spent much of his time working for the Mexican foreign service until his death in Switzerland. He wrote in several genres and media (novels, short stories, scripts for radio, cinema, television) and on a range of themes (the history of travel to the Philippines, rural violence, fantasy), but initially

250 · CHAPTER SEVEN

literary scholars did not assign him a prominent place in Mexican letters, and some dismissed him later as xenophobic and reactionary.[62]

Bernal published two detective books with Catholic publisher Editorial Jus in 1946 (*Un muerto en la tumba* and *Tres novelas policiales*), and in 1949 he became the first Mexican writer to have a story in *Selecciones Policiacas y de Misterio,* for which he had already translated Dashiell Hammett.[63] These were standard detective narratives that maintained an illusion of fair play and interwove social satire and philosophical commentary. As in Helú and Martínez de la Vega, the humorous tone of Bernal's stories conveyed bitter views about Mexican customs and politics. In "La muerte poética," a bad poet reads a long composition invoking death in the theater of a provincial capital before a colorful gathering of corrupt bureaucrats, town literati, and inept policemen. When death does come, the intended victim is a deputy targeted by his own nephew, a blundering political protégé, but the bad poet is killed in an unintended act of literary justice. "El heróico don Serafín" is set in the political struggles of a state university. The president of the institution, an overrated philosopher, is murdered in the middle of a student protest. In "De muerte natural," all the greedy relatives of the millionaire victim are suspects.[64]

Teódulo Batanes, Bernal's detective in these stories, identifies meaningful clues that would seem irrelevant to less intuitive eyes: a pin that falls by coincidence in his hands, the last page in the prayer book that the victim was using.[65] He is a comically shy, absent-minded, short-sighted, thumb-sucking archeologist more interested in science than in the crimes that take place around him. Yet cases come to him: in "Muerte madrugadora," the suspect, an insomniac, sits next to Batanes on a park bench and presents the mystery, which the detective solves on the way to the police station. However, his relationship with the police is not very good; he annoys them with his distractedness and his habit of using multiple synonyms to say the same thing.[66] In *Un muerto en la tumba,* the death of a senator at the ruins of Monte Albán forces Batanes to team up with the local cacique, who wants to take revenge for his brother's death. The culprit is indeed killed trying to escape. Pistoleros hover around, but they are not suspects: they would not commit the kind of crimes that are interesting from a detective's point of view.[67]

The detection plot is of little importance in these stories because Batanes is not interested in the things of this world. In "De muerte natural," the detective acknowledges that God put the evidence in his hands.[68] In "La muerte madrugadora," he can use the clue from the prayer book because of his knowledge of the Christian calendar. The religious symbols in these early crime stories reflect Bernal's own Catholic beliefs but also include multiple references to G. K. Chesterton's Father Brown.[69] In the 1946 story "El extraño caso de Aloysius Hand," the detective is not Batanes but Rupert L. Brown. Instead of relying on physical evidence, Brown prefers to talk to suspects. Citing Chesterton, he reckons that "the most practical and important thing one can know about a man is his point of view about the Universe."[70] Thus, rather than advancing the cynical views of his contemporaries, Bernal's early stories present a benevolent skepticism toward secular institutions of justice. Discovering the culprit means revealing his moral inferiority and acknowledging the vanity of pursuing glory, material satisfaction, or even legal punishment.

"El extraño caso de Aloysius Hand" illustrates Bernal's peculiar views about justice and the communicative value of murder. The setting is a small town in the United States where several murders take place. The characters fit the familiar stereotypes of simple-minded Americans: they are not corrupt, but they lack imagination or any distinctive trait. Puzzled, Brown comments on the case with one of the locals, Hands, an avid reader of detective novels. Hands admires the "genius" of some criminals, and he enjoys "the problems that force one to think methodically." Brown, however, argues that sophisticated murders are not the product of a superior intelligence: "Those cases happen in novels, my dear Hands, but not in reality. You have to understand that between Edgar Poe, Conan Doyle, Agatha Christie and others, and a true murder there is a great difference, as much as between a movie star and his photograph." When Brown is about to abandon the case and leave town in frustration, Hands tells him his theory of murder as a form of art, including references to de Quincey. Hands then explains that he had considered being a detective, but his physique was not adequate; neither was he good enough to write murder novels. He had no choice, then, but to commit a murder with aesthetic value. To Brown's surprise, he confesses to the crimes and describes their execution. Hands knows that they are perfect crimes yet wishes to admit his guilt: to do otherwise would destroy the myth of the impossibility of the perfect crime, a myth necessary to prevent "common people" from attempting it. Above all, like Lee Smith and Roberto de la Cruz, Hands confesses so that his crimes can be admired by a learned public. But he also warns Brown that he will not be able to officially charge him because he has left no evidence. Brown, however, finds the way to get him: he accuses an innocent man and waits until Hands, desperate, writes his own confession, impelled by the "imbecility" of the police. Hands makes it clear that it is not guilt that moves him to confess "because I have used my art without benefit for me, moved by elevated sentiments." When the jury acquits him, considering him insane, he commits suicide and leaves a proud letter: "Like Cervantes, Shakespeare and Beethoven, I die misunderstood. Posterity will redeem my memory."[71]

El complot mongol was published twenty-three years later. Bernal finished it in Lima while he was on a diplomatic assignment. He had been diagnosed with cancer in 1967, which might explain the darker tone of the novel in comparison with his earlier crime fiction. But this is speculation, just like the claim that the novel caused Bernal problems in his diplomatic work because some characters could be read as references to actual politicians.[72] The novel does not cite famous cases, and it pays little mind to the rules of detection, but it closely follows the protagonist's use of violence in the pursuit of truth with a combination of third- and first-person narrative. Filiberto García is an aging pistolero whose inner feelings are as important as external events to move the story forward. He is commissioned by "El Coronel" to investigate and break a Chinese conspiracy to kill the U.S. president while he is visiting Mexico. Murders begin to happen, several of them at the hands of García, but there is "one too many": that of the woman García loves, Martita, a Chinese immigrant.

Some scholars have classified *El complot mongol* as a novel of espionage. Detection would be less important there than the uncovering of a conspiracy, and the interaction with the reader would rely more heavily on signposts from contemporary reality.[73] The novel does contain a motley international cast: Chinese immigrants engaged in all sorts of illegalities, Russian and American spies, Cuban infiltrators. Yet there is no ultimate rationality behind the international secrecy. The contrast with the adventures of Chucho Cárdenas is stark: for Chucho, there is no doubt that the Nazis and the *falangistas* are bad, while Mexicans are always on the right side of international conflict. García does not really care who wants to defeat whom on the international stage: he does as he is told and has no nationalist illusions. The Cold War is being fought in Mexico, but its heroism has dissipated, and even the binary of the superpowers is of little help in making sense of local violence and politics.[74] Trying to sort out real or imagined conspiracies only muddles a plot that, in the end, basically deals with Mexicans fighting each other.

The novel reflects the paranoia usually associated with the Cold War, with references to the eavesdropping prevalent at the time: spies who spy on other spies, men following each other in a secret caravan through the streets of the capital, responding to conspiracies that are impossible to prove.[75] Bernal's novel portrays the violence that such generalized suspicion engendered. Unlike most crime fiction in Mexico, violence is here in the hands of pistoleros who follow the orders of politicians and are by definition above the law. For García, that obedience is a virtue; he is not supposed to question his bosses much less seek publicity. García's job, killing, "is not for the newspapers."[76] His craft is to kill without ideology: "I do not care what party the deceased belongs to."[77] He is no spy, either. Comparing himself to the Russian or American agents, he recognizes their technical superiority but introduces a touch of grim Mexican pride: "We are amateurs" here, who only "know how to kill."[78] This meditation on historical change from the pistolero's perspective reflects the impact of the Mexican government's authoritarian tendencies in the sixties. The idea that crime fiction could help readers understand modernization, central to the magazines discussed in the previous chapter, or that murder could express the intelligence of an individual criminal, as proposed by Usigli and Bustillo Oro, and even the early Bernal, had turned into despair. Violence was losing meaning. García longed for the masculinity and popular values that prevailed in earlier times, and he laments the rise of a political class of *licenciados* who still need to use force but do not want to get their hands dirty. "Before one needed balls and now one needs a degree," he notes. It is as if now "there should be a professional school for pistoleros."[79] García had been part of a revolutionary tradition of unabashed political violence, but his bosses now are embarrassed by that raw use of power.

Reading Bernal either as a critic of the PRI or an apologist of authoritarianism misses the irony that the crime genre allowed him to share with readers. Bernal's early writings are useful for understanding this irony. In those stories, the detection plot was a thin layer that allowed detectives to find the truth through moral inquiries. The fair play, such as it was, lay in the assumption that the reader understood that the political context explained the murder. *El complot mongol* still included a detection plot, but now the state was represented not by blundering policemen but by powerful men who were smart enough to cover their tracks with conspiracies and violence. Even the reader could not be sure which was the crime that must be solved. The culprits no longer pull the trigger, and a wall of silence surrounds them.[80] In *El complot mongol*, García becomes a detective against his better judgment, and detection takes place through the brutal means that are available to him. He does not look at the crime scene but uses torture or espionage. The only verification of his findings is to extract confessions from those he is about to kill. The truth is validated by publicity in a negative way: the day after killing two men, García reads the newspaper just to make sure that the press is presenting it as "another mystery that the police cannot clarify."[81]

The old fictional detectives, even if they are also criminals, seem impossible in this new era of paranoia. García is a lonely man, insulated from feelings and people. He plays poker with Chinese immigrants whose language he does not understand, and he cites his international acquaintances as further evidence of his distance from reality: "What did they give me to drink that I only see foreigners now!"[82] The city around him is no longer populated by potential partners or allies, as with Máximo Roldán or Chucho Cárdenas; rather, the urban landscape is fragmented into dark spaces, like López Street, where the Chinese seclude themselves. Isolation also defines the relationship between García and Martita. She is an immigrant with forged papers who can only offer her loyalty in exchange for protection. Like other members of the Chinese community, she appreciates the little she is offered because back home her ancestors suffered much worse. China is a bit like Mexico in olden times, García admits with reluctant respect: "With the Chinese things are better. There they respect the elders and the elders rule. Lousy Chinese and lousy elders!" (¡Pinches chales y pinches viejos!)[83]

The last line of the novel summarizes the detective's predicament and setting: in the wake he improvises for Martita's body, he exclaims, "¡Pinche soledad!" The narrative hews close to the pistolero's subjectivity, haunted by his "lousy conscience." A school of pistoleros would indeed be useful, García admits, if it included "a year of study to learn how to forget all the death one has brought out."[84] He finds it increasingly difficult to deal with the victims from his past. "You have to respect the deceased. I make them and for that reason I respect them," he claims, but the bad memories still embitter his relationship with Martita.[85] Even his masculinity is degraded: he cannot have sexual relations with her because one memory returns to him, as he tells an alcoholic friend in a cantina: "In San Andrés Tuxtla I killed a man and then I raped his wife, in the same room."[86] There is no longer any artistic or moral redemption for the detective's crimes.

Scholars have claimed that *El complot mongol,* with all its evil sex and murder, renounces the Christian values of Bernal's early work.[87] But if we closely follow the thread of the pistolero's conscience and consider the novel's multiple references to Christian imagery, it is clear that repentance and expiation are central to its moral plot. García abandons the role of mindless pistolero and becomes a detective who eventually also dispenses justice, as do many of his Mexican fictional counterparts. As with Chandler's novels, there is not a sequence of methodical findings as much as a series of emotionally charged scenes that gradually reveal the truth. García realizes that the conspiracy he was sent to investigate was the scheme of an ambitious politician, Rosendo del Valle, in collaboration with one General Miraflores, to seize power in Mexico. García brings them together, forces them to confess, has del Valle kill Miraflores, and kills del Valle. He then finds Mr. Liu, Martita's boss and murderer, and kills him, too. By the end, justice has acquired the physical weight of guilt: "My hands are heavy. They hurt, like many deaths together." Back in his apartment, where Martita's body lies, he washes his blood-stained hands, and he asks his drunken cantina friend to pray for her.[88] While his friend intones the requiem in Latin, García feels the pain caused by the violence. "¡Pinche soledad!" can thus be a reference to Christ's dying words, "My God, my God, why have you forsaken me?"

CONCLUSIONS

During the middle decades of the twentieth century, fiction was the best way to imagine a country in which impunity would not mar the search for the truth. This did not produce utopian narratives or superheroes, but instead, it led to unconventional variations on the relationships between fiction and reality. This chapter has looked at four authors who explored that relationship by playing with the dualities of detective and criminal, art and murder, justice and revenge, and by mixing the moral and detection plots in peculiar ways. They exemplify the process through which the rules of the crime fiction genre changed from a hope of rational understanding through detection in a country of police ineptitude, in Bermúdez, to the impossibility of finding the truth in a world of conspiracy and violence, in Bernal.

Early Mexican crime fiction had already established multiple paths to uncover the truth, from the street smarts of Péter Pérez and Chucho Cárdenas through the psychological analysis of Bermúdez and Bustillo Oro's detectives, to the Catholic intuitions of Teódulo Batanes in the early Bernal. All of these writers were mindful of the rules of the genre, but all of them also tailored their work to Mexican circumstances. The notion that the genre was impossible in Mexico because of the absence of a proper justice system and an efficient police force is contradicted by this panorama. If anything, that absence created the one common feature of the works I have examined: the search for the resolution of a moral plot over the details of pure detection. The weakness of institutions made criminal literacy central to the reading of Mexican crime fiction.[89]

Imagining justice through fiction required a firm anchor in reality. This was clearly expressed in the role of detectives in Mexican crime fiction. None of the writers examined in this and the previous chapter created a police agent or other official figure as the central character in the detection plot. Even private professional sleuths were rare. The amateur detectives of Mexican stories present a broad range of attitudes and held a variety of day jobs, and they were generally unconcerned about the law. Máximo Roldán is a thief who solved cases in order to avoid being accused himself; Péter Pérez works for a few cents; Chucho Cárdenas and Armando Zozaya honor friendship and public opinion; former inspector Herrera and Filiberto García are cynical about institutions because they know the system from inside.[90] None of them affirms the classic premise that police or judges would tie up loose ends and assign blame according to the truth unearthed by detectives. Mexican fictional detectives must adapt their methods to local circumstances, whether through intuition, psychoanalysis, spying, Christian morality, or loose violence. They can be moved by their conscience, curiosity, or desire, but in any case, they know that the relationship between their findings and punishment is contingent and might require their own intervention to secure it.[91] Perhaps their ambiguous morality explains why they did not garner the popularity of their foreign counterparts and why they never jumped to the screen to be played by the stars that thrived in *ranchero* or melodrama movies.

The small part played by detectives in fiction was inversely proportional to the celebrity of murderers in the public sphere. The notion of the criminal as an author was a well-established pattern in the debates about famous cases, as discussed in chapter 4. In fiction, the creativity of killers meant that they could easily be protected from culpability. Victims in Usigli's and Bustillo Oro's fiction deserve their fate because of their flawed character (homosexuals or libertines for the former, dominant men for the latter). Along with Bermúdez and Bernal, these writers toyed with the parallels between artistic creation and murder. In Usigli and Bustillo Oro, murder could be a form of aesthetic transcendence equivalent to other arts. Bermúdez wrote bookish characters who used high culture as part of transgression and investigation. Bernal may have been more skeptical of the fantasies of Aloysius Hands, but he shared his contemporaries' use of fiction as a vehicle of revenge against an authoritarian and corrupt political system.

Considering murder as an aesthetic creation was not an expression of state ideology. On the contrary, it was a way to grapple with and draw some intellectual pleasure from the Mexican disconnection between justice and the truth.[92] The authors discussed in this chapter tackle the equivocal meanings of violence, and they recognize the impossibility of translating stories of crime or punishment into positive nationalist discourse. For all of them, postrevolutionary modernization meant corruption, impunity, and, for Bustillo Oro, business difficulties. Thus, even when they used their own version of psychoanalysis to probe the criminal's subjectivity, they did not use the method, like other contemporaneous intellectuals did, as an excuse to generalize about national identity. We should be cautious when placing these works of fiction in the context of state formation or political domination. Stressing their meaning in terms of political ideologies leads to missing their greater documentary value as critical treatments of the dilemmas of Mexican citizens in the face of violence and impunity.[93] The material for these stories, we should remember, consists of social relationships of a deeply personal nature, relationships that were also political insofar as they portrayed individual interactions with the state.

Fiction writers did not have the prestige of intellectuals who speculated about lo mexicano, but they might have played a greater role in giving narrative form to the national infamy. Crime fiction writers did not engage rural life because they shared with criminally literate readers the certainty that the big city was the scene where the cultural, psychological, and economic complications of modernization played out, offering both danger and promise. Writers like Usigli, Bustillo Oro, and Bernal mapped out the threatening and alluring areas of Mexico City and made space part of their plots. In Mexican crime stories (just as in actual police work), the density of social interactions in these spaces mattered more than material evidence. Thus, their dialogues and descriptions constituted a specific perspective on reality.[94] Writing about crime in these terms meant a choice that came at the expense of prestige for all of the writers discussed here. But they still wrote many pages. They probably did it for pleasure, but they also gained a measure of redemption, through their central yet overlooked role in shaping the ways in which stories of crime could be told and justice could be discussed in the public sphere.[95]

Key to this impact was the dialogue involved in reading crime fiction in Mexico. Fair play did not mean the rigorous administration of information so the reader could solve the mystery before the story's denouement—an ideal that was probably seldom fulfilled even among the classics.[96] It meant, instead, an ironic complicity with the reader. Rather than integrating clues into the detection plot, Mexican writers engaged criminally literate readers with whom they shared both the foundation of reality provided by the nota roja and public opinion's disdain for the police. The magazines discussed in the previous chapter took a didactic role in order to create an active public, and they often invoked sportsmanship as the way to draw intellectual pleasure from reading. They instructed readers on the proper ways to engage mysteries, and they encouraged some of them to become writers. The writers examined in this chapter went further, probing the moral limits of that pleasure. For them, the shortcomings of the police and judiciary were not just practical challenges in the detection process: they made it possible to justify murder as revenge or aesthetic realization. The national infamy was not a regrettable fact but a source of inspiration.

In the decades that followed, crime fiction in Mexico maintained some of the key features of its emergent period, such as its dialogical character and its underlying skepticism. Yet it underwent important stylistic and ideological changes. Bermúdez, Usigli, and Bernal were recognized as pioneers and their works were reedited in the eighties, but they still fell short of the political and social claims that narrative staked with the Latin American Boom. The emergence of the *neopoliciaco* was an expression of these shifting expectations. Paco Ignacio Taibo's successful novels revolved around a detective, Belascorán Shayne, who both endures and dispenses violence in his search for the truth. He faces the darkness of conspiracies of the powerful that prevent clear explanations. He knows that the truth will come from a historically correct set of beliefs rather than the minutia of detection. The enemy, and the culprit, is an abstract system that his heroism defeats through symbolic acts of violence.[97] As a member of a generation in which the repression of 1968 and possibility of revolutionary change inspired new thinking about the armed path to revolution, Taibo wrote novels that were a paean to honorable violence but lacked any of the moral and narrative nuance of *El complot mongol* and other works examined in this chapter.[98]

A bevy of true-crime books that emerged beginning in the 1970s represents a variation on the concerns about crime, corruption, and the absence of justice prefigured by early crime fiction and the nota roja. Some of these titles were fictionalized versions of cases well known to readers. In *Mitad oscura,* for example, Luis Spota presented a fictionalized version of the 1978 murder of the Flores Muñoz couple by their grandson Gilberto Flores Alavés. Spota described the corruption of power but also explained the crime as a product of the decadent moral influence of homosexuality. There were other books written on the case, the most notable being *Asesinato,* by Vicente Leñero, published in 1986. Leñero had written a novel about another true case, *Los albañiles* (1970), that also combined a critique of the justice system with a pursuit of the truth, and *El juicio,* on the Toral jury trial, mentioned in chapter 1. Leñero defined *Asesinato* as a "novel without fiction" and organized it as a critical examination of the newspaper coverage and the police investigation. The conclusion, predictably, is that the truth cannot be known in full, but its pursuit at least allows the author to take a peek into the lives of a wealthy family of the political elite. The debt to Mexican crime fiction is strong, from the role of the nota roja to the evidence of police brutality and ineptitude. Leñero justified the book as a "a literary adventure that, albeit focused on a single and precise event, exemplifies the stubborn, obsessive—often fruitless—pursuit to discover the truth."[99] Along with neopolicíaco, these books completed a shift from classic crime fiction and noir to a more brutal depiction of violence.[100] The plot seems indeed to have relinquished its centrality to realistic characterizations of criminals, policemen, and victims. The productive tension between fiction and reality had succumbed to political certainties that knowledgeable readers had to acquire outside narrative and nota roja.

CONCLUSION

Trying to Keep Our Eyes Open

IN HIS *HISTORIA UNIVERSAL DE LA INFAMIA,* Jorge Luis Borges conveyed the power of infamy as a "surface of images" with a dark underside. The narrator in "Hombre de la esquina rosada," the only story in the book set in Argentina, sees Francisco Real come into a neighborhood dance and establish his reputation by publicly offending a local strongman, Rosendo Juárez. Juárez chooses not to fight Real and leaves the dance in shame. The narrator is a minor figure in the crowd who witnesses the scene, but he feels insulted because Real has exposed the cowardice of one of his people; he feels that "in the barrio the more beaten down, the stronger the obligation to be tough."[1] He kills Real in the darkness of the night outside, where nobody can see him. As the story ends, without describing the murder itself, he tells Borges how he erased the single clue that could incriminate him. The narrator's understated confession thus entered the "meticulous glory" of the *Historia universal* as the punishment, and the mirror, of Real's flashy courage.

This book has told the stories of people who used violence and spoke about it and those who witnessed the dark side of crime and impunity. My goal has been to understand infamy as a "surface of images" while reconstructing the ways in which Mexican citizens critically engaged with this infamy. The first part of the book showed the transition from a system in which jury trials were the paradigmatic setting for the debates about crime and justice, to one in which the search for the truth, and the unofficial sentence, took place in the public sphere, mainly in the pages of the crime news. Nowhere else could readers find the material detail and the psychological characterizations that explained crimes such as those of Alberto Gallegos, Goyo Cárdenas, or the Tacubaya barbershop. The judiciary became increasingly remote and opaque for most people, while the images and words produced by crime had a stronger presence in everyday life. There were several consequences to this transition. One was that public opinion leaned toward acceptance of extrajudicial punishment against criminals who were particularly odious. Another was the creation of a criminally literate public that consumed narratives in the nota roja and crime fiction.

The second part of the book examined the reality behind debates about crime and justice through several figures that shaped perceptions of crime and the deterioration of justice. Official detectives were, with few exceptions, barely more than regular policemen, and like them, enjoyed very little respect. Their investigations were defined by the use of torture or, at best, technically flawed inquiries. Their private counterparts, usually former cops themselves, did not fare much better, but at least tried to keep their activities under a mantle of discretion. The reliance of investigators, judges, and journalists on suspects' confessions as the definitive proof of guilt had an unexpected consequence: the words of murderers acquired great authority when it came to the truth. This was especially the case regarding the events and the motivations behind the famous crimes that captured the public's interest. A number of those criminals used their authority to try to avoid punishment by weaving complex psychological explanations or dramatic narratives about honor. Although usually these devices did not work as intended, producing these narratives turned suspects into authors. Their first creation had been the crime, and the next one was the explanation. In contrast to these eloquent murderers stood the pistoleros, who were discreet when meting out violence on the orders of their bosses, yet flashy and entrepreneurial when it came to exploiting their impunity for profit. Pistoleros were emblematic of the close association between crime and politics that most citizens perceived as the defining feature of postrevolutionary life. Pistolerismo evolved from the thirties, when it still had strong connections to revolutionary and agrarian violence, to the fifties, when pistoleros' work became part of the country's modernization project.

The third part of the book examined a social field in which these situations and actors came together in the form of narratives. Short stories and novels from foreign and Mexican authors contributed to the creation of engaged and criminally literate readers. The rules of crime fiction facilitated reading as well as writing, and the middle decades of the century saw the emergence of the first generation of Mexican crime fiction authors. The stories, which readers avidly consumed, were not realistic or perfect in terms of the orthodox dictates of the genre, but they provided the best way to think about the Mexican disjuncture of truth and justice. Their detectives—Péter Pérez, Máximo Roldán, Chucho Cárdenas, and Teódulo Batanes—showed how the intelligence of amateurs was more effective than were institutions in reaching the truth and sometimes in dispensing punishment. These stories were also a guide to the dangers and rewards of modern urban life. Crime was redefined through fiction in a way that further removed the investigation from the state and breezily justified homicide in the name of justice. Fictional murderers like Roberto de la Cruz, Lee Smith, Aloysius Hand, and Filiberto García used violence to express their art or their bitterness toward modernization. They sought or evaded fame with the same cunning as the narrator in Borges's "Hombre de la esquina rosada."

From these findings, we can make a couple of observations of contemporary relevance and historiographical interest. First, impunity was not an obstacle to modernization but rather an integral component of it. The Mexican history of infamy cannot be reduced to the narrative of state formation that still guides much of the writing about the period.[2] The rapid economic, cultural, and demographic changes taking place during the middle decades of the twentieth century did not require a substantive improvement in law enforcement, from the perspective of the state or even of civil society. For the public, the outsized role of pistoleros in politics and business was not antithetical to progress but expressed, sometimes unpleasantly, the dynamism of postrevolutionary Mexico. The fact that pistoleros were not prosecuted was not an anecdotal aspect of state formation but a basic requirement for the consolidation of the political system. Judges and prosecutors had ample discretion to investigate or not, and police ineptitude was the perfect cover for the apparently unassailable "intellectual authors" behind many political and common crimes. Civil society was not ignorant or passive in the face of impunity, as we have seen, and periodically opposition movements made anticorruption a rallying cry that, if nothing else, managed to worry the government. But the strongest by-product of the integral role of crime in politics was a broadly shared disappointment with liberal institutions, particularly those involved with punishment and due process.

Second, the fundamental certainty of criminal literacy was that the state only punished those who did not have the means to circumvent justice, and it willingly left the most egregious criminals go free. As a result, the thirties to the fifties saw the normalization of extrajudicial violence, from ley fuga to lynching, and the devaluation of victims, attitudes that still inform the acceptance of violence in Mexico. If the state was not reliable and strict enough to deal with crime, the dehumanization of suspects and victims seemed a reasonable cost to pay to maintain the illusion of a causal connection between transgression and punishment. Another basic piece of criminal literacy was that justice was reserved for men. The visibility and agency of women in the judicial realm largely dissipated after the abolition of the criminal jury; before the jury system was abolished in 1929, a few women became criminal-authors despite the constraints of patriarchal expectations. Law enforcement and the use of violence remained two important realms of public life over which men had a monopoly. Especially after 1929, women were prominent mostly as victims and very occasionally as murderers who were merely reacting to male abuse.

Gender roles always have consequences beyond the relations between men and women. In twentieth-century Mexico, I would suggest, these consequences included the dehumanization of the casualties of crime and the legitimation of the state's discretional enforcement of the law. Voiceless, passive, and often identified with feminine subordination, victims became a minor consideration in debates about crime and justice. Somehow, they were always to blame for what they had suffered. A few of them, or their relatives, courageously disputed these attitudes, but nota roja accounts, murderers' explanations, and fiction narratives alike advanced a vision of victims that deprived them of dignity or any role in the process of uncovering the truth and achieving justice.[3] Extrajudicial violence was justified as their vindication.

These findings imply a specific way to interrogate the historical record. This book has emphasized the public sphere and everyday experience over high politics and the mechanics of the state. Doing so runs against the grain of the approaches embraced by historians of Latin American crime and punishment in the last two decades. They have largely embraced a state-centered perspective focused on sanctions and discipline while accepting criminological conceptions about the existence of "dangerous classes" as a legitimate object of study. I have given particular attention to the stories and voices of people who were directly interested in or affected by crime and impunity but less space to those who spoke in an official capacity. These official voices have received, and will continue to receive, plenty of attention from my colleagues. Official opinions were not as influential, though, as their authors liked to think. Instead, my assumptions are that laws and policies are only as effective as civil society can make them and that crime does not provide a useful criterion to classify people. In the realm of crime and punishment, support for or resistance to the law is largely determined by public discussions that necessarily involve a broad range of participants, as there is no single social group that is excluded from that realm.[4]

Those discussions involved the use of images and stories from the dark underside. I focused on these stories because they were a vehicle for different actors to convey their experience and understanding of violence. Murder, in particular, inspired narratives; the truth, when available, could be best presented in the form of a story; punishment, whether legal or extrajudicial, was justified as the moral consequence of a case. I used the category of criminal literacy to refer to the knowledge of reality into which those narratives had to fit in order to be effective. Any competent inhabitant of the modern city had to possess that knowledge, but criminal literacy also undergirded the attitudes toward violence and impunity mentioned above. There is much to be explored in the history of violence beyond the study of those attitudes.[5] My contribution has been to explore the communicative value of violence and its role as the focal point of exchanges in the public sphere. In contrast with the obscurity of institutions, stories about crime democratized knowledge, giving authority to a number of new voices. They represented actors who had been excluded from past discussions, when criminologists claimed that deviance was the object of science. These voices would continue to be excluded from discussions about other matters of common interest by an increasingly authoritarian government.

This book has explored the formative decades of national infamy. Today, Mexico is defined by violence to an extent that can only be compared to the first half-century after independence or the Mexican Revolution. But such comparison might easily reinforce the notion of the country as an essentially dangerous place where history does not matter. National identity was constructed as an unchanging essence that could only be known through a surface of violent images. The infamy that characterized mid-twentieth-century Mexico in the eyes of foreigners and many nationals was not so much the jovial familiarity with death observed by nationalist intellectuals of the time, but impunity. Its beneficiaries flaunted it because it was the result of political protection; victims and their relatives denounced impunity, invoking rage more often than the law; William Burroughs admired it as a "general atmosphere of freedom" which also happened to benefit him personally when he fled the country after killing his wife. Some particularly brazen manifestations of privilege exposed a fundamental contradiction of public life: that the truth was no longer connected to justice. It was difficult but not impossible to know what was behind a crime, but only the naïve thought this knowledge could be reached through institutions. In many cases, the truth came from the criminals themselves, and in other cases, it could be pieced together from the press. But either way, it could not be expected to lead to legally sanctioned punishment.

We can only understand Mexico's current reputation if we set aside cultural generalizations to consider historically its citizens' failed efforts to restore the broken nexus of crime, truth, and justice during the postrevolutionary period. This failure is apparent when we briefly review the decades following those covered by this book. Things have certainly changed, even if we agree that the repression of a student movement in 1968 was not the political turning point that many in that generation hoped it would be.[6] The most salient transformation has been the expansion and violence of the businesses associated with illegality. Throughout the late twentieth century, drug production and smuggling into the United States underwent several cycles of expansion around different kinds of commodities, from heroin, marihuana, and cocaine to methamphetamine. Each cycle fostered the evolution of increasingly sophisticated and well-funded criminal organizations. The insatiable demand for mind-altering substances across the border coincided with booming legal trade between the two countries even before the 1994 enactment of the North American Free Trade Agreement. Drug consumption in Mexico also expanded beginning in the sixties, particularly after oversupply and the entrance of new actors into the business facilitated low-price local retail. All along, Mexican drug traffickers partnered with transnational organizations from South America, China, Europe, and the United States. The collaboration between narcos and government agents was well established by the forties, in part because the business itself enjoyed considerable social tolerance until external and internal political factors increased the levels of violence associated with it. The most important among these was the U.S.-inspired "war on drugs," which began with interception and eradication operations in the seventies and justified an expansion of the security apparatus just as other parts of the state were being dismantled during the eighties. A remarkably long-lasting exercise in futility, the strategy absorbed growing state resources, caused human rights violations, and justified the militarization of drug enforcement.

The official anti-drug rhetoric and increased electoral competition in Mexico beginning in the nineties disrupted the gentlemen's agreements that had allowed the so-called cartels to prosper with the connivance of politicians. This opened the door for spurts of aggressive law enforcement. The militarization of operations against drug trafficking and closer collaboration with the United States in the capture of chieftains, particularly beginning with the presidency of Felipe Calderón (2006–2012), has increased the frequency and cruelty of drug-related violence committed by state and nonstate actors alike. The ensuing fragmentation of criminal organizations meant increasing competition among a diversified spectrum of actors and violence at an unprecedented scale. Groups that had been united by kinship broke apart, and experts in violence who had been subordinated to traffickers (like the Zetas to the Gulf Cartel) became independent and aggressively competed for business across the country. Local vigilantism (as in the state of Michoacán's autodefensas) complicated the uses of violence by claiming popular support for the informal detection and punishment of narcos. Finally, the business of crime itself changed: drug smuggling into the United States remained the most profitable pursuit, but a host of other activities became integral to the success of criminal organizations, notably retail drug sales, counterfeiting, extortion of businesses and local governments, human trafficking, and kidnapping.[7] The cost for the country is large but difficult to measure. The numbers of deaths and disappeared since 2006 are in the tens of thousands, with particular impact on poor young men, women, journalists, migrants, and other vulnerable sectors. Violence has reached an intensity that seems to have overwhelmed both the capacity of the state to contain it and the ability of citizens to make sense of it.

A common assumption among the crowd of security experts who have emerged in recent years is the idea that all the transformations sketched above were caused by drug trafficking, and that the current meanings and mechanisms of violence are entirely new. The vague notion of *narco-cultura* conveniently implies the novelty and all-encompassing influence of drug trafficking. The recent changes, however, would have not taken place, or they would have had very different scale and consequences, if they not had occurred in the context of weak police and judicial institutions. After the 1950s, the range of illegal activities undertaken by pistoleros continued to expand, and in recent decades these activities have received an injection of capital from drug trafficking-organizations. The broad range of crimes and illegal activities of today's criminal organizations carries the genetic code of the violent entrepreneurship of midcentury pistoleros. The difference is that now these practices involve bigger guns, more cars, plenty of accomplices, and a more plebeian style. But the basic structures exploited by today's counterparts of the pistoleros were already in place in the 1930s: police institutions selling badges and protection, a weak judiciary, and a political class tending to appropriate public resources for private gain. Although their budgets have increased, police agencies have continued to diversify, torture, partner in illicit activities, and generally lose what limited social legitimacy they might have had. The judiciary remains a black hole for the truth: trials are still long, insulated from public scrutiny, and vulnerable to bribes and pressures from the parties involved. The fundamental failure of both the police and the judiciary is encapsulated in the fact that very few homicides are investigated and punished, while charges against kingpins often involve offenses against public health rather than violent crimes.[8] A handful of particularly outrageous cases demonstrate that this failure is the basis for continuing impunity, ranging from the murder of women in Ciudad Juárez that began in the nineties to the disappearance of forty-three students from Iguala, Guerrero, on September 26, 2014. Although these and other cases have triggered protests at home and abroad, the large-scale violence underlying them has not been the object of mobilizations, nor has it become a point of reference in electoral politics. This book has tried to understand that indifference as much as the crimes and impunity behind it.

The transformations in recent decades would also have been very different had they not been facilitated by an authoritarian disposition among the public. The result of the discussions in the public sphere examined in this book was not a more democratic understanding of the rights of suspects and victims or more transparency when it came to the state's use of violence. These chapters reveal a consensus that limited citizenship rights, unfettered pistoleros, and extrajudicial violence are inevitable if not acceptable. From the disappointment of Vasconcelistas and Catholics expressed by fiction writers to the bitter requests for justice addressed to the president by common citizens, the evidence points to a growing disappointment with democracy and the legacy of the revolution. This authoritarian consensus has been best expressed and preserved in the realm of justice. The ambivalence toward the law documented by the nota roja and crime fiction contribute to an already heavy legacy for contemporary Mexico. The uncertainty of punishment during the years examined in this book created the conditions for today's implicit acceptance of ley fuga and torture as natural aspects of police and judicial processes. The levels of violence that afflict the country nowadays are acceptable to a large swath of the public because, as many have said, the victims of that violence deserve to be killed or tortured anyway.[9] Thus, the government's emphasis on security over justice is not simply a product of its authoritarianism or unawareness of the wishes of common people, as critics often argue. Rather, politicians know that most people will agree with the proposition that reforming the administration of justice is less important that enhancing the ability of the state to use force. Unlike the violence deployed by dictatorial regimes, state violence in Mexico is not a counterpart to the general absence of political representation. It is a product of a specific dysfunction of institutional representation. The discretional enforcement of penal law allows politicians to engage in practices of dubious legality while enjoying considerable safety and still claiming to represent society.

There is a feeling of nostalgia behind attitudes that accept the inevitability of state violence. Filiberto García, the veteran pistolero in *El complot mongol,* thought that in the old times pistoleros regulated themselves and upheld some sort of honor, or at least a cynical loyalty to the boss. A similar nostalgia is conveyed by the image of an aging pistolero on the cover of this book. The photograph shows Roberto "el Güero" Batillas half smiling, wearing an impeccable suit, and drawing his gun toward the camera, which is situated at a low angle. We, the readers, might momentarily identify with one of his victims and blink, but we will soon remember it is just an image enacted for a popular magazine.[10] We will also remember that Batillas launched his reputation when he appeared one night in the cabaret Waikiki and fought the strongest man in the place. Although the scene was similar, the outcome was different from that in the story "Hombre de la esquina rosada." Batillas was not murdered by an anonymous avenger but had a long career. He even managed to burnish the "meticulous glory" of his infamy when he posed for Rodrigo Moya's camera in 1966 after a stint in prison. With the privilege of fiction, Borges imagined a punishment for the arrogance of Francisco Real. Impunity, and the admiration of magazine readers, was Batillas's reward instead. The contemporary reader might even sympathize with the distant threat evoked by the image: Batillas was violent and immune to the law, but there were rules. As long as we think we understand those rules, we might say, the infamy that the image evokes can be forgotten, or even, ironically perhaps, embraced.

Resisting that sympathy with the devil, this book has tried to remind the reader that there is no justice without truth, and that truth has a history which is populated by other characters at the receiving end of the pistolero's gun. Victims were less stylish, perhaps, but they are still worth remembering because they tried not to close their eyes. We also have to keep our eyes open, like Bolaño's detectives, against a simplistic interpretation of reality that would relapse into the dream of nationalism. Today, it is very tempting to dismiss the postrevolutionary system on moral grounds: if only the national honor were restored and the corrupt politicians removed, the weight of national infamy would be lifted, and justice would reign. This neglects the intricate roots of the current situation, from the normalization of extrajudicial violence to the legacy of ideologically diverse movements and gestures of defiance against impunity, inside and outside the political spectrum.

There are strong dissenting voices against impunity today, and their influence may be growing. Such dissension does not occur in a historical vacuum; it is heir to the legacy of images, narratives, and debates from the middle decades of the century, which, as we have seen, were part of an effort to empower civil society in its pursuit of the truth. In response to the state's limited ability to determine the outcome of processes triggered by crime, citizens showed an unruly disposition to challenge authority and to deploy critical reason against the government's neglect. Skepticism did not result in passivity but in gestures of collective or individual defiance. Although the nota roja no longer has the influence it did in its early decades, there are plenty of courageous and professional crime news reporters and photographers who perform an invaluable service. The violence that some of them have suffered is a measure of their attempts to counter the use of violence as a means to impose propaganda, or silence, by state officials and organized crime.[11] A growing resistance to the dehumanization of criminals and victims is emerging as an expression of citizens' engagement with justice. This book surveyed the process through which the right to the truth was separated from the right to due process, yet managed to survive as a central topic of public life. Although justice has always been a central demand for Mexicans, the right to the truth, theoretically and legally formulated in other countries undergoing a transition from regimes responsible for massive human rights abuses, is only gradually becoming a political issue in Mexico. The immediate context for this is the intolerable number of disappearances and human rights abuses justified by drug enforcement, but the challenge to authority has long been there.[12] So, this is not only a history of infamy but also one about the persistent questions that Mexicans have been asking for more than a century.

Appendix

QUANTITATIVE EVIDENCE ABOUT CRIME IN
MEXICO IN THE LAST CENTURY

FIGURE 17 SHOWS THAT FROM 1926 (when the federal government began to systematically publish data from judicial sources) until the the 1980s, there was a steady decline in the rate of persons indicted for all crimes.[1] This trend suggests bookends: on one end, the violence of the revolution, when crime was probably very high, extending Porfirian tendencies in a context of lawlessness, and on the other end the cycle of economic crises of the latter twentieth century, when property crimes became more common than violent crimes and drugs came to dominate the interest of law enforcement. Figure 18 shows that an upward trend in federal prosecutions for crimes against public health (i.e., drug trafficking) began in the late 1960s, indicating new government priorities.[2] Table 1 shows the number of indictments per 100,000 inhabitants for different types of crimes, 1926–2005. While theft increased beginning in the 1980s, battery and homicide decreased until the end of the century. The overall trend between the late twenties and the eighties, then, is one of decreasing crime, and decreasing violence more specifically.

Although homicide rates were high on the eve of the disastrous war on drugs undertaken by President Felipe Calderón in 2006, particularly in certain cities and regions, they were still lower than in the years before and immediately after the revolution. In the Federal District, where that information is available for the prerevolutionary period, the rate of people indicted for homicide per 100,000 inhabitants was thirty-one in 1900 and thirty-seven in 1930, to diminish thereafter, hovering around six by the end of the century.[3] The decline, which is observable in most states, corresponds with that of criminality at the national level. Regional and temporal differences are noticeable but do not contradict the general trend: drug-related homicide

FIGURE 17. Total indicted per 100,000 inhabitants, Mexico, 1926–2005. Source: Pablo Piccato, "Estadísticas del Crimen en México: Series históricas, 1901–2001," 2003. http://www.columbia.edu/~pp143/estadisticascrimen/EstadisticasSigloXX.htm.

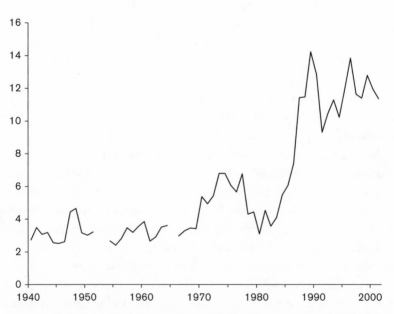

FIGURE 18. Indicted for crimes against public health per 100,000 inhabitants, Mexico, 1940–2001. Source: Pablo Piccato, "Estadísticas del crimen en México: Series históricas, 1901–2001," 2003. http://www.columbia.edu/~pp143/estadisticascrimen /EstadisticasSigloXX.htm.

TABLE 1 Indicted per 100,000 inhabitants, selected offenses, Mexico, 1926–2005

	Total	Homicide	Battery	Theft	Rape
1926–1930	263	25	84	36	3
1931–1935	218	35	76	53	4
1936–1940	203	38	66	47	4
1941–1945	208	31	56	58	4
1946–1950	210	29	60	53	4
1951–1955	166	22	46	45	3
1956–1960	145	18	42	33	3
1961–1965	131	15	38	29	3
1966–1970	128	14	37	25	4
1971–1975	122	12	35	25	3
1976–1980	119	11	34	24	3
1981–1985	134	9	35	31	3
1986–1990	176	9	38	44	4
1991–1995	185	9	37	42	4
1996–2000	191	7	34	59	4
2001–2005	203	7	36	63	5

SOURCE: Pablo Piccato, "Estadísticas del crimen en México: Series históricas, 1901–2001," 2003, http://www.columbia.edu/~pp143/estadisticascrimen/EstadisticasSigloXX.htm.

rates in Sinaloa and Baja California increased beginning in the 1980s, but remained very low in Yucatán.

Crime was experienced very differently across states. Table 2 provides nuance to the national picture, showing crime rates for selected crimes, by state, from 1926 to 2005. Some states had high rates for all crimes throughout the period, like Baja California and Tamaulipas, while others were consistently on the low side, like Guerrero, Hidalgo, Oaxaca, and Tlaxcala. States like Chihuahua and Baja California Sur saw an increase in crime rates starting in the 1970s, in the latter case specifically murder. Theft rates varied broadly, with the Federal District having some of the highest rates. Paradoxically, the battery rate in the capital was more than twice the national average, while its murder rate was below the national average. Breaking up these rates at the municipal levels, only possible for recent years, suggests that the differences are starker the closer we look.[4] State priorities also influenced the distribution of offenses across the national territory during the period in question. Drug-related indictments in the early twenty-first century, for example, were concentrated in the Federal District, Chihuahua, Sinaloa, Tamaulipas, Baja California, and Chihuahua, together comprising 51 percent

TABLE 2 Average crime rates per 100,000 inhabitants by state, selected
offenses, Mexico, 1926–2005

	Total	Homicide	Battery	Theft
Estados Unidos Mexicanos	174.88	18.23	47.41	38.49
Aguascalientes	172.46	11.19	45.00	53.23
Baja California Norte	388.90	18.00	97.10	122.72
Baja California Sur	266.35	13.61	64.82	82.51
Campeche	161.84	12.64	39.01	56.16
Chiapas	163.89	17.71	58.30	28.83
Chihuahua	152.76	17.90	41.95	42.02
Coahuila	141.61	14.73	32.58	46.73
Colima	231.15	30.51	47.86	68.77
Durango	158.50	26.91	36.55	42.85
Federal District	285.95	12.52	108.69	74.65
Guanajuato	154.42	16.32	37.46	40.37
Guerrero	109.00	18.00	20.38	25.72
Hidalgo	112.63	21.64	31.75	21.97
Jalisco	129.58	13.92	30.92	36.50
México (state)	140.70	19.03	37.10	26.33
Michoacán	123.88	21.00	27.78	31.76
Morelos	182.62	21.44	44.29	44.37
Nayarit	185.94	24.08	48.78	46.61
Nuevo León	135.34	12.43	33.07	39.21
Oaxaca	111.44	16.29	36.26	19.75
Puebla	111.93	16.58	29.88	21.66
Querétaro	154.41	19.02	46.63	34.57
Quintana Roo	177.93	15.71	33.16	51.93
San Luis Potosí	165.49	19.29	46.69	34.99
Sinaloa	123.78	16.30	27.03	41.92
Sonora	233.80	14.67	65.26	94.48
Tabasco	220.35	19.22	62.44	45.95
Tamaulipas	276.75	21.08	81.40	75.68
Tlaxcala	111.21	11.70	38.42	18.67
Veracruz	131.03	18.20	44.11	29.04
Yucatán	183.39	6.68	50.38	65.54
Zacatecas	146.13	16.64	42.85	33.98

SOURCE: Pablo Piccato, "Estadísticas del crimen en México: Series históricas, 1901–2001," 2003,
http://www.columbia.edu/~pp143/estadisticascrimen/EstadisticasSigloXX.htm.

of prosecutions even though they represent only 37 percent of total crimes.[5] In order to understand the period from the 1920s to the 1960s, however, we must move away from the focus on drug trafficking, not only because it was not a significant factor until the 1970s but, more importantly, because it reflects a state policy rather than an actual transformation in practices and perceptions of crime among the population.

Scholars usually assume that statistics on murder are more reliable than those for other types of crime, as officials are obligated by law to investigate it. But in Mexico the number of cases that escape prosecution is large. Figure 19 compares the evidence from judicial sources with that from health authorities counting homicide as a cause of death. The number of deaths reported as homicide by forensic sources is consistently higher than that of judicial statistics. Part of this might be the result of cases in which a corpse leads to an investigation but not to an indictment. The difference—a national average of 65 percent more between 1926 and 2005, and a Federal District average of 91 percent more—demonstrates that justice only reached a limited number of cases. This is still a problem in certain places, such as the northern border: in Nuevo Laredo during 2004 there were 130 reported cases of homicide but only 11 indicted for the crime.[6] Federal prosecutors usually give priority to their investigations of organized crime over individual homicides, but this does not explain the spike in recent years: if we consider the evidence in figure 19 it becomes apparent that the problem of impunity has been a constant. The lack of investigation and punishment explains why the decline in murder rates noted above did not lead to a decrease in public concern about the problem. Falling indictment rates did not necessarily mean falling crime rates. This disparity is reflected in the ways in which homicide has been depicted, explained, and discussed, where suspicion of the police and judicial corruption are repeating themes. Another factor influencing public perception of crime rates might be the increasing use of guns as murder weapons after the revolution, rather than the more traditional knives.[7] Death by firearms was often associated with an unfair disparity of power between victim and attacker, unlike the "clean duels" fought with knives.

While institutional factors are important, a close look at the data on offenders suggests that one variable explaining the overall trend might be demographic. As in other modern societies, most offenders in Mexico are young men; crime rates are positively correlated with the percentage of men between twenty and forty years of age. Growing crime rates in the last decades of the twentieth century correspond with a demographic structure that

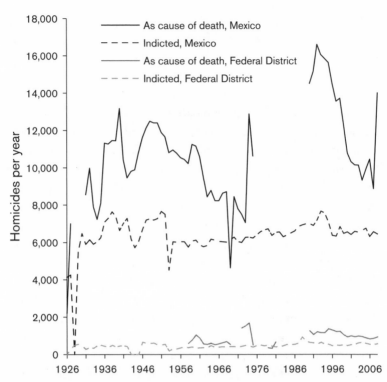

FIGURE 19. Homicide, indicted and as a cause of death, Mexico, 1926–2005. Source: Pablo Piccato, "Estadísticas del crimen en México: Series históricas, 1901–2001," 2003. http://www.columbia.edu/~pp143/estadisticascrimen/EstadisticasSigloXX. htm; Departamento de la Estadística Nacional, *Anuario de 1930;* Secretaría de Economía-Dirección General de Estadística, *Anuario estadístico de los Estados Unidos Mexicanos,* various years; Secretaría de Industria y Comercio-Dirección General de Estadística, *Anuario estadístico de los Estados Unidos Mexicanos,* various years; Secretaría de Programación y Presupuesto-Coordinación General de los Servicios Nacionales de Estadística, Geografía e Informática, *Anuario estadístico de los Estados Unidos Mexicanos,* various years; Instituto Nacional de Estadística, Geografía e Informática, *Anuario estadístico de los Estados Unidos Mexicanos,* various years.

had the highest percentage of young people in the country's history. Natality was still high in 1970 (the birth rate at 44.6 per 1,000 inhabitants was more than twice the contemporary level), but infant mortality decreased sharply during that decade, with birth rates declining only by the mid-1990s. In 1970, the percentage of the population between twenty and thirty-nine years was the highest ever (38.89 percent, against 35.34 in 1950).[8]

The availability of socioeconomic statistical series for the entire period makes it difficult to argue that a specific factor can explain change over time or regional differences. It is not easy, for example, to establish long-term correlations between poverty and crime. A negative hypothesis in this regard seems safer: poverty does not explain crime because the poorest areas of the country in recent decades are not the ones with the highest rates. But it would be risky to project that finding all the way back to the 1920s. We can say with some certainty, however, that schooling has a negative correlation with crime. If we pair judicial series for the twentieth century with the changes in the percentage of the population attending school, we obtain a negative Pearson number for total rates ($r = -.78$), and an even stronger one for homicide ($r = -.98$). Literacy rates increased throughout the century and across the country, and indictment rates decreased. This confluence might not reflect a causal connection but at least points to the complexity of causal factors.[9] One might argue, for example, that educated young men will be less prone to break the law, or, alternatively, that greater access to schools in certain places and periods expresses a stronger presence of the state, which in turns reflects greater capacity of institutions to punish or prevent transgressions. Thus, while quantitative evidence is useful to support the thesis that the mid-twentieth century should be considered as a distinct chapter in the history of Mexican crime, the same evidence achieves little in terms of understanding transgression, punishment, and their social impact. Further, given the apparent disparity between indictment rates and crime rates, it is not surprising that criminal statistics were of little interest to non-experts during most of the twentieth century. Narratives spoke louder than numbers.

ABBREVIATIONS FOR ARCHIVAL SOURCES

ABR:	Archivo Bernardo Reyes, Centro de Estudios Históricos Condumex
AGN, ALM:	Archivo General de la Nación, Fondo Presidentes, Adolfo López Mateos
AGN, ARC:	Archivo General de la Nación, Fondo Presidentes, Adolfo Ruiz Cortines
AGN, ATSJDF:	Archivo General de la Nación, Archivo del Tribunal Superior de Justicia del Distrito Federal
AGN, DFS:	Archivo General de la Nación, Fondo Secretaría de Gobernación, Dirección Federal de Seguridad
AGN, DGG:	Archivo General de la Nación, Fondo Secretaría de Gobernación, Dirección General de Gobierno
AGN, DGIPS:	Archivo General de la Nación, Fondo Secretaría de Gobernación, Dirección General de Investigaciones Políticas y Sociales
AGN, FB:	Archivo General de la Nación, Fondo Francisco Bulnes
AGN, LC:	Archivo General de la Nación, Fondo Presidentes, Lázaro Cárdenas
AGN, MAC:	Archivo General de la Nación, Fondo Presidentes, Miguel Ávila Camacho
AGN, MAV:	Archivo General de la Nación, Fondo Presidentes, Miguel Alemán Valdés

AGN, SCEP:	Archivo General de la Nación, Sociedad Cooperativa Editora de Periódicos
AHDF, GDF:	Archivo Histórico del Distrito Federal, Gobierno del Distrito Federal
AHDF, JJC:	Archivo Histórico del Distrito Federal, Justicia, Jurados Criminales
AHDF, JJI:	Archivo Histórico del Distrito Federal, Justicia Jurados de Imprenta
AHDF, JP, ISSS:	Archivo Histórico del Distrito Federal, Sección Jefatura de Policía, Serie Investigación y Seguridad, Servicio Secreto
DDCD:	Diario de los Debates de la Cámara de Diputados
FAECFT:	Fideicomiso Archivo Elías Calles y Fernando Torreblanca
RCH:	Fondo Rafael Chousal, Centro de Estudios sobre la Universidad, Universidad Nacional Autónoma de México

NOTES

INTRODUCTION

1. Historical scholarship has moved beyond the official narratives of crime control. Elisa Speckman, *Crimen y castigo: Legislación penal, interpretaciones de la criminalidad y administración de justicia (Ciudad de México, 1872–1910)* (Mexico City: El Colegio de México, 2002); Robert Buffington, *Criminal and Citizen in Modern Mexico* (Lincoln: University of Nebraska Press, 2000); Mayra Lizzete Vidales Quintero, *Legalidad, género y violencia contra las mujeres en Sinaloa durante el porfiriato* (Mexico City: Plaza y Valdés, 2009); Pablo Piccato, *City of Suspects: Crime in Mexico City, 1900–1931* (Durham: Duke University Press, 2001).

2. On continuities, see, for example, Martha Santillán Esqueda, "Delincuencia femenina: Representación, prácticas y negociación judicial, Distrito Federal (1940–1954)" (PhD diss., Universidad Nacional Autónoma de México, 2013); Saydi Núñez Cetina, "El homicidio en el Distrito Federal: Un estudio sobre la violencia y la justicia entre 1920 y 1940" (PhD diss., CIESAS, 2012); Ricardo Pérez Montfort, *Cotidianidades, imaginarios y contextos: Ensayos de historia y cultura en México, 1850–1950* (Mexico City: CIESAS, 2008); on legal reform, Elisa Speckman Guerra, *Del Tigre de Santa Julia, la princesa italiana y otras historias: Sistema judicial, criminalidad y justicia en la Ciudad de México (siglos XIX y XX)* (Mexico City: UNAM-INACIPE, 2014); on modernity, Jesse Lerner, *El impacto de la modernidad: Fotografía criminalística en la Ciudad de México* (Mexico City: Turner; Consejo Nacional para la Cultura y las Artes; Instituto Nacional de Antropología e Historia; Editorial Océano, 2007); Everard Kidder Meade, "Anatomies of Justice and Chaos: Capital Punishment and the Public in Mexico, 1917–1945" (PhD diss., University of Chicago, 2005); Fernando Fabio Sánchez, *Artful Assassins: Murder as Art in Modern Mexico* (Nashville: Vanderbilt University Press, 2010); Eric Zolov, *Refried Elvis: The Rise of the Mexican Counterculture* (Berkeley: University of California Press, 1999); James Alex Garza, *The Imagined Underworld: Sex, Crime, and Vice in Porfirian Mexico City* (Lincoln: University of Nebraska Press, 2007); on drug trafficking, Luis Astorga, *El siglo de las drogas* (Mexico City: Espasa-Calpe Mexicana, 1996); Elaine

Carey, *Women Drug Traffickers: Mules, Bosses, and Organized Crime* (Albuquerque: University of New Mexico Press, 2014); Diego Enrique Osorno and Froylán Enciso, *El Cártel de Sinaloa: Una historia del uso político del narco* (Mexico City: Grijalbo, 2009). On foreign paradigms, David E. Ruth, *Inventing the Public Enemy: The Gangster in American Culture, 1918–1934* (Chicago: University of Chicago Press, 1996), 2, 3, 25, 40–45, 64–73, 119; John Carter Wood and Paul Knepper, "Crime Stories: Criminality, Policing and the Press in Inter-War European and Transatlantic Perspectives," *Media History* 20:4 (2 October 2014): 345–51.

3. Wil Pansters, ed., *Violence, Coercion, and State-Making in Twentieth-Century Mexico: The Other Half of the Centaur* (Stanford: Stanford University Press, 2012); Stephen R. Niblo, *Mexico in the 1940s: Modernity, Politics, and Corruption* (Wilimington, Del.: Scholarly Resources, 1999); Alan Knight, "Cardenismo: Juggernaut or Jalopy?," *Journal of Latin American Studies* 26:1 (1994): 73–107; Paul Gillingham and Benjamin T. Smith, eds., *Dictablanda: Politics, Work, and Culture in Mexico, 1938–1968* (Durham: Duke University Press, 2014). On the dirty war, Sergio Aguayo Quezada, *La charola: Una historia de los servicios de inteligencia en México* (Mexico City: Grijalbo, 2001); Alexander Aviña, *Specters of Revolution: Peasant Guerrillas in the Cold War Mexican Countryside* (New York: Oxford University Press, 2014); Tanalís Padilla, *Rural Resistance in the Land of Zapata: The Jaramillista Movement and the Myth of the Pax Priísta, 1940–1962* (Durham: Duke University Press, 2008). On new crime, Myriam Laurini and Rolo Díez, *Nota roja 70's: Lla crónica policiaca en la ciudad de México* (Mexico City: Diana, 1993).

4. On the riddle, and the role of detectives to explain modern life, Todd Herzog, *Crime Stories: Criminalistic Fantasy and the Culture of Crisis in Weimar Germany* (New York: Berghahn Books, 2009), 17; Raymond Chandler, *The Notebooks of Raymond Chandler and English Summer: A Gothic Romance* (New York: Harper, 2006). Michel Foucault defines problematization as the moments when people realize that certain things that were already there, as practices, social relations, or ideas, need to be dealt with, and proposes "an analysis of a specific problematization as the history of an answer—the original, specific, and singular answer of thought—to a certain situation." Michel Foucault, *Fearless Speech* (Los Angeles: MIT Press, 2001), 173.

5. Pablo Piccato, "Estadísticas del crimen en México: Series históricas, 1901–2001," 2003, http://www.columbia.edu/~ppi43/estadisticascrimen/Estadisticas-SigloXX.htm.

6. Manuel Múzquiz Blanco, "El horripilante asesinato: El relato de una anciana de claro perfil indígena que uniera su via a la del rico pulquero muerto," *Detective* 1:5 (9 Nov. 1931): 7. For a history of the truth that implies the production of "the subject of knowledge" see Michel Foucault, "Truth and Juridical Forms," *Social Identities: Journal for the Study of Race, Nation and Culture* 2:3 (1996): 327–42; Nildo Avelino, "Sujeito a política: Tecnologia confessional e controle da subjetividade," in Nildo Avelino and Salvo Vaccaro, *Governamentalidade: Segurança* (Sao Paulo: Editora Intermeios, 2014), 309–42.

7. On crime in the era of science, and the lasting influence of romanticism, Lawrence Frank, *Victorian Detective Fiction and the Nature of Evidence: The Scien-*

tific Investigations of Poe, Dickens and Doyle (New York: Palgrave, 2003). Truth is verified by juridical institutions, according to Boltanski, solving a mystery that threatens state power. He recognizes, however, the tensions between official truth and the truth which cannot be said publicly. Luc Boltanski, *Enigmes et Complots: Une Enquête à Propos D'enquêtes* (Paris: Gallimard, 2012).

8. Although the study of the public sphere in Latin America is expanding, the historiography has focused on the nineteenth century, ignoring less prestigious and more recent publics and struggling to consider gender and class. See Jürgen Habermas, *The Structural Transformation of the Public Sphere: An Inquiry into a Category of Bourgeois Society* (Cambridge: MIT Press, 1991); Craig J. Calhoun, *Habermas and the Public Sphere* (Cambridge: MIT Press, 1992). On Latin America see Pablo Piccato, "Public Sphere in Latin America: A Map of the Historiography," *Social History* 35:2 (2010): 165–92; Elías José Palti, "Guerra y Habermas: Ilusiones y realidad de la esfera pública latinoamericana," in *Conceptualizar lo que se ve: François-Xavier Guerra, historiador: Homenaje,* ed. Erika Pani and Alicia Salmerón (Mexico City: Instituto Mora, 2004), 461–83. The role of violence has not been incorporated into our historical understanding of the public sphere—even though violence was a central reference point for Habermas and other authors in the tradition of critical theory, as they attempted to make sense of the role of fascism and other forms of oppression in the transformation of modern liberal politics. Hannah Arendt, *On Violence* (New York: Harcourt, Brace, 1969); Enzo Traverso, *L'histoire comme champ de bataille: Interpréter les violences du XXe siècle* (Paris: La Découverte, 2010). Particularly useful from a criminological perspective is Stanley Cohen, "Crime and Politics: Spot the Difference," *British Journal of Sociology* 47:1 (1996): 1–21.

9. On the creation of reality through crime narratives, Boltanski, *Enigmes et Complots;* Jerome Bruner, "The Narrative Construction of Reality," *Critical Inquiry* 18:1 (1991): 1–21. See also Pierre Bourdieu, *Outline of a Theory of Practice* (New York: Cambridge University Press, 1977); Jürgen Habermas, *The Theory of Communicative Action,* vol. 1, *Reason and the Rationalization of Society* (Boston: Beacon Press, 1984). On places, Dominique Kalifa, "Crime Scenes: Criminal Topography and Social Imaginary in Nineteenth-Century Paris," *French Historical Studies* 27:1 (December 21, 2004): 175–94.

10. Jorge García-Robles, *Stray Bullet: William S. Burroughs in Mexico,* trans. Daniel J. Schechter (Minneapolis: University of Minnesota Press, 2013), 38. For a similarly cynical view of Mexican police see Patricia Highsmith, *A Game for the Living* (New York: Harper, 1958). On drug fiends, Isaac Campos, *Home Grown: Marijuana and the Origins of Mexico's War on Drugs* (Chapel Hill: University of North Carolina Press, 2012).

11. From the 1954 prologue: "La palabra infamia aturde en el título, pero bajo los tumultos no hay nada. No es otra cosa que apariencia, que una superficie de imágenes." Jorge Luis Borges, *Obras completas* (Barcelona: Emecé Editores, 1996), 1:307.

12. Ibid., 338, 322. Mexicans are only mentioned in the book as victims of Billy the Kid, who does not bother to count them among the deaths he owes justice. On Borges and his embrace of literary, and criminal, tradition, see Alejandra Laera, *El*

tiempo vacío de la ficción: Las novelas argentinas de Eduardo Gutiérrez y Eugenio Cambaceres (Buenos Aires: Fondo de Cultura Económica de Argentina, 2004); Beatriz Sarlo, *Borges, un escritor en las orillas* (Buenos Aires: Ariel, 1995).

13. Quote from *Excélsior*, 21 Jun. 1936, sec. 3a, p. 3; Carlos Monsiváis, *Los mil y un velorios: Crónica de la nota roja* (Mexico City: Consejo Nacional para la Cultura y las Artes; Alianza Editorial, 1994). Earlier criminological works had already dwelled on the violence of popular language and interactions, describing underclass intemperance and peasants' melancholic brutality and indifference to death. Octavio Paz, *El laberinto de la soledad* (Mexico City: Fondo de Cultura Económica, 1963); Samuel Ramos, *El perfil del hombre y la cultura en México* (Mexico City: P. Robredo, 1938). Critical views of this literature in Roger Bartra, *La jaula de la melancolía: Identidad y metamorfosis del mexicano* (Mexico City: Grijalbo, 1987), 49, 52, 86–87, 130, 160; Claudio Lomnitz, *Exits from the Labyrinth: Culture and Ideology in the Mexican National Space* (Berkeley: University of California Press, 1992); Julio Guerrero, *La génesis del crimen en México: Estudio de psiquiatría social* (Paris: Vda. de Ch. Bouret, 1901). Imagining the underworld "had both intensely local and broadly transnational aspects." Wood and Knepper, "Crime Stories," 347.

14. The reader will notice some slippage between "crime" and "murder" in these pages. This is inevitable because murder provided the emblematic narratives of crime. For studies centered on a case, the classic is Michel Foucault, *I, Pierre Riviere, Having Slaughtered My Mother, My Sister, and My Brother . . . : A Case of Parricide in the 19th Century* (New York: Pantheon Books, 1975); a model, Sarah C. Maza, *Violette Nozière: A Story of Murder in 1930s Paris* (Berkeley: University of California Press, 2011). On a case recovered to combat collective amnesia, Gayle K. Brunelle, *Murder in the Métro: Laetitia Toureaux and the Cagoule in 1930s France* (Baton Rouge: Louisiana State University Press, 2010). A discussion of the format in Robert Buffington and Pablo Piccato, eds., *True Stories of Crime in Modern Mexico* (Albuquerque: University of New Mexico Press, 2009). A reminder of the different roles in Carlo Ginzburg, "The Inquisitor as Anthropologist," in *Clues, Myths, and the Historical Method*, trans. John Tedeschi (Baltimore: John Hopkins University Press, 1992), 156–64.

15. Josefina Ludmer, *El cuerpo del delito: Un manual* (Buenos Aires: Perfil Libros, 1999), 12, 217. Karl Marx wrote in the *Economic Manuscripts*: "A criminal produces crimes," he wrote. "The criminal produces not only crimes but also criminal law, and with this also the professor who gives lectures on criminal law and in addition to this the inevitable compendium in which this same professor throws his lectures onto the general market as 'commodities.' . . . This brings with it augmentation of national wealth." Karl Marx, "Digression: (On Productive Labour)," in *The Production Process of Capital: A Contribution to the Critique of Political Economy, Third Chapter, Capital in General*, in *Marx's Economic Manuscripts of 1861–63*, http://www.marxists.org/archive/marx/works/1861/economic/ch33.htm. On other cases see Dominique Kalifa, *L'encre et le sang: Récits de crimes et société à la belle epoque* (Paris: Fayard, 1995); Herzog, *Crime Stories*; Lila Caimari, *Mientras la ciudad duerme: Pistoleros, policías y periodistas en Buenos Aires, 1920–1945* (Buenos

Aires: Siglo Veintiuno Editores, 2012), forthcoming as *While the City Sleeps: A History of Pistoleros, Policemen, and the Crime Beat in Buenos Aires before Perón* (Berkeley: University of California Press).

16. Concepción Dueñas to Adolfo Ruiz Cortines, 28 Jan. 1954, AGN ARC 541/272.

17. Eric Monkkonen, "Homicide: Explaining America's Exceptionalism," *American Historical Review* 111:1 (2006): 76–94. The role of civil society in crime control is also central in those societies. David Garland, *The Culture of Control: Crime and Social Order in Contemporary Society* (Oxford: Oxford University Press, 2001), 33.

CHAPTER 1. FROM TRANSPARENCY TO DARKNESS

1. Elisa Speckman Guerra, *Del Tigre de Santa Julia, la princesa italiana y otras historias: Sistema judicial, criminalidad y justicia en la Ciudad de México (siglos XIX y XX)* (Mexico City: UNAM-INACIPE, 2014), 109–10, 113. Speckman sees the diversity of the audiences and the lack of interest for public affairs as further symptoms of the jury's decadence. The cases examined here reveal a great deal of public interest.

2. For a productive dialogical approach to judicial sources David Carey, *I Ask for Justice: Maya Women, Dictators, and Crime in Guatemala, 1898–1944* (Austin: University of Texas Press, 2013); Carlo Ginzburg, *History, Rhetoric, and Proof* (Hanover, N.H.: University Press of New England, 1999). Famous cases "offer vivid illustrations of the ways in which the public discussion of private life helped to shape the culture of the new public sphere." Sarah C. Maza, *Private Lives and Public Affairs: The Causes Célèbres of Prerevolutionary France* (Berkeley: University of California Press, 1993), 264; see also 3, 24, 68, 320. See also Richard Sennett, *The Fall of Public Man* (New York: Knopf, 1977); Katherine Fischer Taylor, *In the Theater of Criminal Justice: The Palais de Justice in Second Empire Paris* (Princeton: Princeton University Press, 1993), xix; Eugenia Lean, *Public Passions: The Trial of Shi Jianqiao and the Rise of Popular Sympathy in Republican China* (Berkeley: University of California Press, 2007); Joan B. Landes, "The Public and the Private Sphere: A Feminist Reconsideration," in *Feminism, the Public and the Private* (Oxford: Oxford University Press, 1998), 135–63.

3. Editorial, "Jurados" por Francisco de P. Segura, *El Foro* 5:13 (19 Jul. 1877): 50, 57; Emilio Islas, "Disertación sobre la institución de jurados en materia criminal," *El Foro* 6:40 (2 Mar. 1876). Taylor, *In the Theater,* xix, 6, 8, 38, 127. On the history of the jury and its opposition in France, see James M. Donovan, "Magistrates and Juries in France, 1791–1952," *French Historical Studies* 22:3 (1999): 379, 420; Bernard Schnapper, "Le jury français aux XIX et XXème siècles," in *The Trial Jury in England, France, Germany: 1700–1900* (Berlin: Duncker u. Humbolt, 1987), 165–239.

4. Paradoxically, the scholarship on the jury in Mexico looks at the institution as one of the last holdovers against the increasing unification of codes and

monopolization of justice by the legal profession. Representing public opinion in a collective body, the jury was a legacy of colonial notions of justice as a negotiation in which the public persona of vecinos played a key role. The best overview of legislation in Speckman Guerra, *Del Tigre de Santa Julia,* 93–128. For colonial antecedents see Tamar Herzog, *Upholding Justice: Society, State, and the Penal System in Quito (1650–1750)* (Ann Arbor: University of Michigan Press, 2004), 258. See also Manuel González Oropeza, "El juicio por jurado en las constituciones de México," *Cuestiones Constitucionales: Revista Mexicana de Derecho Constitucional* 2 (July 2000): 78; Guillermo Colín Sánchez, *Derecho mexicano de procedimientos penales* (Mexico City: Porrúa, 1980), 47–49, 103, 617; *Ley de jurados en materia criminal para el Distrito Federal* (Mexico City: Boletin Judicial, 1892), 28; Antonio Padilla Arroyo, "Los jurados populares en la administración de justicia en México en el siglo XIX," *Secuencia: Revista de Historia y Ciencias Sociales* 47 (2000): 137–70.

5. *Ley de jurados en materia criminal para el Distrito Federal* (Mexico City, 1869), 24. President Juárez decreed a press law in 1861 whereby offenses committed through the press (including defamatory, immoral, and subversive writings) would be tried in front of a jury of citizens summoned by the city council. Pablo Piccato, *The Tyranny of Opinion: Honor in the Construction of the Mexican Public Sphere* (Durham: Duke University Press, 2010), chap. 1.

6. *Principes de politique* [1815], in Benjamin Constant, *Œuvres* (Paris: Gallimard, 1979), 1208. On judicial public opinion Elías José Palti, *La invención de una legitimidad: Razón y retórica en el pensamiento mexicano del siglo XIX: Un estudio sobre las formas del discurso político* (Mexico City: Fondo de Cultura Económica, 2005), 256–57. On early Mexican liberalism Charles A. Hale, *Mexican Liberalism in the Age of Mora* (New Haven: Yale University Press, 1968).

7. Guillermo Prieto, *Obras completas,* ed. Boris Rosen Jélomer (Mexico City: Consejo Nacional para la Cultura y las Artes, 1994), 9:65–67. Several *cartillas,* or jury handbooks, guided jurors in their deliberations. In 1892 the Federal District government paid jurist José María Gamboa to write a cartilla that was printed in a run of a thousand copies. AHDF, JJI, 2743, 152. Cartillas continued to be updated with selections from new legislation as late as 1929. *Cartilla de instrucción para jurados del fuero común en el Distrito Federal: Edición oficial* (Mexico City, 1929); *Cartilla a que se refiere el Art. 97 del reglamento de la ley de organización de tribunales del Distrito Federal y del territorio de La Baja-California* (Mexico City: Imprenta del Gobierno Federal, 1885); *Cartilla de instrucción para jurados del fuero común en el Distrito Federal* (Mexico City: Imprenta del Gobierno, 1895); *El Monitor Republicano,* 16 Apr. 1869, p. 3. The initial law assumed jurors lacked "conocimiento de la ley." *Ley de jurados* (1869), 29; *Gaceta de Policía* 1:11 (7 Jan. 1906): 2–3; for Rabasa, "Si el jurado da en absolver a los acusados por cierta clase de delitos, es porque la pena es excesiva en el común sentir." Emilio Rabasa, "Deberes de los jurados," *Revista de Legislación y Jurisprudencia* (July 1889): 196; Juvenal, "Un paso atrás," *El Monitor Republicano,* 27 Apr. 1880, p. 1; Elisa Speckman Guerra, "El Congreso Constituyente de 1916–1917 y la justicia penal," *eScholarship* (23 Nov. 2011): 5, http://escholarship.org/uc/item/5jj6r82h. This was clearly the case in press juries and, as we will see.

8. *Monitor Republicano,* 15 Apr. 1869, p. 3. Testimonies of corruption abound. See for example *Monitor Republicano,* 2 May 1880, p. 1. On *"consignas"* from above to be followed by judges, Francisco Bulnes, *El verdadero Díaz y la revolución* (Mexico City: Editora Nacional, 1960 [1920]), 88–89; Rodolfo Reyes to Antonio Sarabia, ABR, copiadores, 34, 16886, 347–50. A judge asking Díaz for a job for his son in Mariano Botello to Rafael Chousal, Mexico City, RCH, 29, 251, f. 19. Ignorant judges according to Jesús Urueta, cited by Demetrio Sodi, *El jurado en México: Estudios sobre el jurado popular* (Mexico City: Imp. de la Secretaría de Fomento, 1909), 70–71; Padilla Arroyo, "Los jurados populares," 138, 44. Similar situations and uses in Osvaldo Barreneche, *Dentro de la ley, todo: La justicia criminal de Buenos Aires en la etapa formativa del sistema penal moderno de la Argentina* (Buenos Aires: Ediciones al Margen, 2001); Taylor, *In the Theater,* 8.

9. Juvenal, "Un paso atrás," *Monitor Republicano,* 27 Apr. 1880, p. 1. For the characterization as a democratic institution, and the unanimous vote in Congress, see *Monitor Republicano,* 16 Apr. 1869, p. 3; *Monitor Republicano,* 28 Apr. 1869, pp. 3–4. As a new guarantee, "Crónica parlamentaria," *Monitor Republicano,* 24 Apr. 1869, p. 3. Even Porfirio Díaz supported it in his 1871 Plan de la Noria against Juárez. The Plan de la Noria in Ramon Prida, *¡De la dictadura a la anarquía! Apuntes para la historia política de México durante los últimos cuarenta y tres años (1871–1913)* (Mexico City: Botas, 1958), 29. For defense of the jury since independence as a guarantee of democracy and justice, Speckman Guerra, *Del Tigre de Santa Julia,* 98–99.

10. Ignacio Ramírez, *México en pos de la libertad* (Mexico City: Partido Revolucionario Institucional, 1986), 181. See also Segura, "Jurados," 58.

11. "Crónica parlamentaria," *Monitor Republicano,* 17 Apr. 1869, p. 3. Despite their struggles with the Catholic Church, few Mexican liberals of this time were atheistic. Early formulations of this individual autonomy in Constant, *Œuvres,* 1208; José María Luis Mora, *Mora legislador* (Mexico City: Cámara de Diputados, 1994), 182. See also Speckman Guerra, *Del Tigre de Santa Julia,* 114; Santiago Sierra, "Suspension de garantias: La ley de jurados," *La Libertad,* 26 Feb. 1880, p. 1; *Cartilla* (1895), 38; *Ley de jurados en materia criminal para el Distrito Federal* (Mexico City: Impr. del Gobierno Federal, 1891), 112.

12. Islas, "Disertación sobre la institución de jurados en materia criminal," 157; Emilio Monroy, "Jurados: Resultados prácticos de la institución en el Distrito Federal," *El Foro* 8:24 (3 Aug. 1880): 88.

13. *Ley de jurados* (1891) xxi. The questions in Homicide, 1926, AGN, ATSJDF, 18516.

14. *Cartilla* (1895), 23.

15. Intelligence cited by city council commission considering excuses of prospective jurors, 21 Feb. 1870, AHDF, JJC, 2731, exp. 2. Excluding the "moral component" from the questionnaire was equivalent to destroying the jury itself. "Los jurados," *Monitor Republicano,* 3 Aug. 1880, p. 2; *Cartilla* (1885), 26.

16. *Monitor Republicano,* 15 Apr. 1849, p. 3; *Monitor Republicano,* 1 Jun. 1969, p. 3; *Ley de jurados* (1869), 25, 29.

17. Sodi, *El jurado en México*, 41–44, 49, 52. Eliminated in Jalisco, see *El Siglo Diez y Nueve*, 12 Apr. 1880, p. 3. On the 1907 reform, *Diario del Hogar*, 26 Nov. 1907, p. 1.

18. Speckman Guerra, "El Congreso Constituyente," 18; Sodi, *El jurado en México*, 58.

19. For example, Santiago Sierra, "Suspension de garantias: La ley de jurados," *La Libertad*, 26 Feb. 1880, p. 1.

20. Bulnes, *El verdadero Díaz*, 96–97.

21. Ibid., 82.

22. Sodi, *El jurado en México*, 58. An accusation of corruption against him in J. M. Benítez, *El lisiado trágico: Apuntes sobre la interesante e íntima vida de Salvador Díaz Mirón* (Mexico City, 1932), 93.

23. Sodi, *El jurado en México*, 91–95, 70–71, 219–21, 257–58, 364, 372.

24. J. D. Fernández, "Editorial: El Jurado," *El Foro* (14 Apr. 1880). In a press jury "se habló de la santidad del hogar doméstico, del honor de la familia, del amor puro y de los sentimientos de honradez; todo esto no está (preciso es confesarlo) al alcance de nuestro pueblo," "Crónica: El jurado del 'Federalista,'" *El Foro* 2:28 (19 Aug. 1877): 123. On selfishness and acquittals, Emilio Monroy, "Jurados: Resultados prácticos de la institución en el Distrito Federal," *El Foro* 8:19 (27 Jul. 27, 1880): 69–70. Guerrero's case in *El Imparcial*, 14 Jan. 1897, p. 2. An acquittal despite a confession in Homicide, 1922, against Florencio Sánchez, AGN, ATSJDF, 1051492; and Homicide, 1926, AGN, ATSJDF, 18516. The play is Juan A. Mateos, *Los dioses se van* (Mexico City, 1877). Porfirio Díaz requesting suspension of guarantees after the suspects in a train robbery in San Ángel, outside the capital, were acquitted, in *El Siglo Diez y Nueve*, 2 Apr. 1880, p. 1. Hurried jurors in *Monitor Republicano*, 3 Aug. 1880, p. 2. On Bribes, *Monitor Republicano*, 3 Aug. 1880, pp. 20–22; Amado Manuel Lay, "Visión del Porfiriato en cuatro narradores mexicanos: Rafael Delgado, Federico Gamboa, José López Portillo y Rojas y Emilio Rabasa" (PhD diss., University of Arizona, 1981), 130. On lawyers, J. Alberto Salinas y Rivera, "Editorial: Colaboración; La defensa de los reos," *El Foro* 5:32 (24 Aug. 1877): 127; "Defensores de pobres," *Monitor Republicano*, 22 Jul. 1880, p. 3. Routine reports in, for example, *El Monitor Republicano*, 7 Jan. 1869, p. 3. The propensity to acquit discussed in Sodi, *El jurado en México*, 49–50.

25. *La Voz de México*, 12 Jan. 1906, p. 1. For examples of famous cases ending in conviction see, against El Chalequero, Alonso Rodríguez Miramón, *Requisitoria pronunciada por el agente del ministerio público . . . en la vista en jurado de la causa instruida contra Francisco Guerrero (a) Antonio El Chalequero y contra José Montoya, por robos, violaciones, heridas y homicidios perpetrados del año de 1881 a julio de 1888* (Mexico City: Antigua Imprenta; Librería de Murguía, 1891); against La Chiquita, *El Imparcial*, 19 Sept. 1897, pp. 1–2, 4; against Timoteo Andrade, Francisco Serralde, *Escrito presentado a la suprema corte de justicia de la Nación por el Lic . . . fundando los recursos de revisión, en el amparo promovido por Timoteo Andrade* (Mexico City: Talleres de "La Ciencia Jurídica," 1899); against Arnulfo Villegas, *El País*, 13 Feb. 1908, p. 1. For guilty verdicts that vindicated the jury, Editorial, "La reivindicación del jurado popular," *El Universal*, 12 Oct. 1923, p. 3.

26. *El Universal,* 13 Aug. 1929, p. 1.

27. Emilio Monroy, "Jurados. Resultados prácticos de la institución en el Distrito Federal," *El Foro* 8:23, July 31, 1880, p. 86.

28. For the selection of juries, *Excélsior,* 27 Apr. 1924, sec. 2, p. 1. The names and portraits in *Excélsior,* 29 Apr. 1924, p. 1.

29. See requests for such exceptions in AHDF, JJC, 2731, exp. 1. They were often rejected when the prospective juror had a stable livelihood. Jurors had to answer questions of fact about the crime and the mitigating or aggravating circumstances, as posed by the judge, but did not vote on the penalty itself. *Ley de jurados* (1869).

30. "Crónica parlamentaria," *Monitor Republicano,* 21 Apr. 1869, p. 3.

31. AHDF, JJC, 2731, exp. 1. Filomeno Villarreal stated that he could not read or write and had poor sight.

32. Petition by Felipe Rodríguez, 3 Sept. 1869, AHDF, JJC, 2731, exp. 1; Santiago Sierra, "Suspensión de garantias: La ley de jurados," *La Libertad,* 26 Feb. 1880, p. 1. For another opinion in favor of a "jurado de clases," see Bulnes, *El verdadero Díaz,* 96–97.

33. *Ley de jurados* (1891).

34. AHDF, JJC, v. 2744, exp. 1. See also *Diario Oficial* 130:1–27 (Jan. 1914).

35. Juez presidente de jurados Alberto Martinez to Ayuntamiento, AHDF, JJC, 2731, exp. 2; Minister of Justice to City Council, 22 Nov. 1869, AHDF, JJC, 2731, exp. 7. The civil registry did not have complete lists of citizens. AHDF, JJC, 2731, exp. 8. Various letters requesting exemption from 1869 in AHDF, JJC, 2731, exp. 1. Similar requests since 1918 in AHDF, JJC, 2744. On process of selection see Speckman Guerra, *Del Tigre de Santa Julia,* 101–3. In 1891 the governor of the Federal District, who was appointed by the president, took charge of the process from the city council. Juvenal, Editorial, "Reformas necesarias," *El Monitor Republicano,* 29 Apr. 1880, p. 1; *El Monitor Republicano,* 1 May 1880, p. 3; *Cartilla* (1895), 9–10; Sodi, *El jurado en México,* 81, 120–21. Problems in 1920 in AHDF, JJC, 2744, 73.

36. Federico Sodi, *El jurado resuelve: Memorias* (Mexico City: F. Trillas, 1961), 160–62. On milperos, by Federico's half-brother, Sodi, *El jurado en México,* 111–12; *El Universal,* 7 Aug. 1929, p. 3. "Jurados profesionales" in Querido Moheno, *Sobre la brecha* (Mexico City: Botas, 1925), 119. "Coyotes" in *El Universal,* 12 Oct. 1923, p. 3. Drunks and immigrants in *La Voz de México,* 14 Jan. 1906, p. 1; Sodi, *El jurado en México,* 75–76, 115; Juvenal, "Reformas necesarias," *Monitor Republicano,* 29 Apr. 1880, p. 3.

37. *El Universal,* 7 Aug. 1929, p. 3.

38. They were all imprisoned by agents of the judicial police. *El Universal,* 11 Aug. 1929, sec. 2, p. 1; *El Universal,* 11 Aug. 1929, sec. 3, p. 1.

39. *Cartilla* (1895), 27 citing the Code of Penal Procedures, art. 448, and the Juries Law, art. 63. See also *Cartilla* (1885), 474.

40. Carlos Roumagnac, "Mis recuerdos de Belem," *El Nacional,* 24 Sept. 1933, p. 2. Roumagnac was a Spanish-born journalist and criminologist. See for example the September 1897 trial of María Villa, "La Chiquita," in *El Foro* 50:66 (13 Apr. 1898): 263. After 1903 a different judge, called *presidente de debates,* conducted the

public phase of the trial, replacing the judge who had been in charge of the investigatory phase of the process. Speckman Guerra, "El Congreso Constituyente," 3.

41. Carlos Roumagnac, "Recuerdos de Belem," *El Nacional,* 5 Jul. 1933, p. 2; some judges even dismissed defense lawyers who challenged them. Sodi, *El jurado en México,* 210.

42. *Cartilla* (1895), 27, 33.

43. Lawyers cited Castelar, Victor Hugo, Shakespeare, and others. *La Voz de México,* 14 Jan. 1906, p. 1. This did not work when "talento" was absent, *Gaceta de Policía* 1:32 (17 Jun. 1906): 10; Sodi, *El jurado en México,* 214–17; Sodi, *El jurado resuelve,* 243.

44. Moheno was born in Pichucalco, Chiapas, in 1873, and died in Mexico City in 1933. He graduated from the Escuela Nacional de Jurisprudencia in 1896. François-Xavier Guerra, *México: Del antiguo régimen a la revolución* (Mexico City: Fondo de Cultura Económica, 1988), 1:437, 2:13. On his ideas and political activities under Madero see Pablo Piccato, *Congreso y revolución: El parlamentarismo en la XXVI Legislatura* (Mexico City: Instituto Nacional de Estudios Históricos de la Revolución Mexicana, 1992). Moheno's main works on politics include Querido Moheno, *¿Hacia dónde vamos? Bosquejo de un cuadro de instituciones políticas adecuadas al pueblo mexicano* (Mexico City: I. Lara, 1908); Moheno, *Mi actuación política después de la decena trágica* (Mexico City: Botas, 1939); Moheno, *Problemas contemporáneos* (Mexico City, 1903). As a speaker, Moheno was described as an "artist" because of his shrewd use of emotion. Moheno, *Procesos célebres: Rubin; Discurso en defensa de la acusada* (Mexico City: Botas, 1925), 7–8; Moheno, *Mis últimos discursos: La caravana pasa . . . (Preliminar), discursos ante el congreso jurídico, defensa de la Sra. Jurado, defensa de la Sra. Alicia Olvera* (Mexico City: Botas, 1923), 78.

45. Speech by Antonio Díaz Soto y Gama, DDCD, year 2, Thirty-First Legislature, no. 33, 23 Oct. 1925, p. 25; Moheno, *Mis últimos discursos,* 10–12, 118, 20.

46. Gustave Le Bon, *Psychologie des foules* (Paris: Alcan, 1921), 51, 142–47. Sodi, who was Moheno's law teacher, also cited Le Bon when analyzing speeches. Sodi, *El jurado en México,* 238–56.

47. *El Universal,* 4 Oct. 1923, sec. 2, p. 1.

48. Moheno, *Mis últimos discursos,* 20; Antonio Ramos Pedrueza, *Conferencias* (Mexico City: Eusebio Gómez de la Puente, 1922), 99, 116.

49. Le Bon, *Psychologie,* 55. On Le Bon's influence on Mexican rhetoricians see Jorge Aguilar Mora, *Una muerte sencilla, justa, eterna: Cultura y guerra durante la revolución mexicana* (Mexico City: ERA, 1990), 254. On oratory, see Piccato, *The Tyranny of Opinion,* chap. 3. Le Bon studied and cited in Francisco Bulnes, AGN FB, 21, exps. 25, 27; Salvador Díaz Mirón and Antonio Castro Leal, *Díaz Mirón: Su vida y su obra* (Mexico City: Porrúa, 1970); Salvador Alvarado, *El Universal,* 6 Oct. 1916, p. 6.

50. Moheno, *Mis últimos discursos,* 15. Similar opinions cited in Speckman Guerra, *Del Tigre de Santa Julia,* 121.

51. Moheno, *Mis últimos discursos,* 7, 26, 30, 103–6; Moheno, *Sobre la brecha,* 186, 89, 202, 203; *Excélsior,* 30 Apr. 1924, sec. 2, p. 6.

52. The Mexican present was one characterized by anomie and the masses' "excessive claims." Moheno, *Mis últimos discursos*, 18, 26, 30, 88, 105, 58; Moheno, *Rubin*, 25, 32.

53. Moheno, *Mis últimos discursos*, 14–15, 17. Through income requirements, the law sought to "excluir cierto grupo de notoria ineptitud" (to exclude a certain group of notorious ineptitude). *Ley de jurados* (1891), 82, 96. Antonio Ramos Pedrueza also saw these requirements as a way to improve an institution that was more reliable than, if just as emotional as, judges. Ramos Pedrueza, *Conferencias*, 107, 17. This was a response to a period when these requirements were not established yet and "men of certain social position stubbornly refuse to be jurors." *El Siglo Diez y Nueve*, 26 Apr. 1880, p. 1. On the "professional juries" favorable to judges see Sodi, *El jurado en México*.

54. Moheno, *Mis últimos discursos*, 55.

55. *El Universal*, 20 Jul. 1922, p. 1, 6. Against indigenism and federalism, another *bête noire* of conservatives, see *El Universal*, 20 Jul. 1922, pp. 34, 44. For similar views expressed in another jury, this time against lower-class Mexicans, see Victor Manuel Macías González, "El caso de una beldad asesina: La construcción narrativa, los concursos de belleza y el mito nacional posrevolucionario (1921–1931)," *Historia y Grafía* 13 (1999): 146.

56. A black witness was the object of mockery in one of his cases. *Excélsior*, 29 Apr. 1924, p. 6; Moheno, *Mis últimos discursos*, 83; Moheno, *Sobre la brecha*, 191, 203.

57. See Francisco Bulnes, *Los grandes problemas de México* (Mexico City: El Universal, 1927).

58. For an expression of concern about the ability of lawyers to influence jurors, speech by Deputy Jara, *Diario de los debates del Congreso Constituyente, 1916–1917* (Mexico City: Comisión Nacional para la Celebración de Sesquicentenario de la Independencia Nacional, 1960), 1:825. On abolition and scandalous acquittals, Speckman Guerra, *Del Tigre de Santa Julia*, 127.

59. *Cartilla* (1895), 30–31, 33; Sodi, *El jurado en México*, 91–95, 130; José María Lozano and Manuel Dublán, *Legislación mexicana; ó, colección completa de las disposiciones legislativas expedidas desde la independencia de la república . . . ordenada por los Lics. Manuel Dublan y Jose María Lozano . . . [1687–1904]* (Mexico City: Impr. de E. Dublán, 1876), 14: 527–52; Rabasa, "Deberes de los jurados," 196; *Requisitoria del ministerio público y alegatos de los defensores en el jurado de José de León Toral y Concepción Acevedo y de la Llata: Reos del delito de homicidio proditorio del General Álvaro Obregón, 8 de noviembre de 1928* (Mexico City: Talleres Gráficos de la Nación, 1928), 22.

60. Through stories and anecdotes, Federico's book fondly remembers his stint as prosecutor and defense attorney in the 1920s. Sodi, *El jurado resuelve*, 24, 27, 221.

61. *Excélsior*, 27 Apr. 1924, p. 1; Sodi, *El jurado resuelve*, 68, 104.

62. Sodi, *El jurado resuelve*, 102.

63. Ibid., 111, 260.

64. Ibid., 26–27, 56–58, 186. The two men in *Gran jurado nacional: A consecuencia de la muerte del Sr. D. José C. Verástegui, y en virtud de los rumores que aseguraban*

que esa lamentable desgracia había acaecido en un duelo . . . en el cual sucumbió el Sr. Verástegui, y en cuyo suceso habían figurado como autores el occiso, y el Sr. D. Francisco Romero: Como testigos del Sr. Verástegui, los sres. Apolinar Castillo y Ramón Prida . . . (Mexico City: Cámara de Diputados, 1895), 292.

65. *El Siglo Diez y Nueve*, 17 Dec. 1890, p. 2; *El Universal*, 7 Aug. 1929, sec. 2, p. 1.

66. María Teresa Morfín was sixteen when she killed her husband. After her acquittal she danced naked in cabarets and ended up murdered. Sodi, *El jurado resuelve*, 71; *Excélsior* 30 Apr. 1928, sec. 2, p. 1.

67. Luz González was the suspect. *El Universal*, 7 Oct. 1923, sec. 2, p. 1; *Nueva Era*, 26 Aug. 1911, p. 3.

68. Sodi, *El jurado en México*, 139–38, 215–16.

69. Sodi, *El jurado resuelve*, 147; see also 96–100. Rebeca Monroy Nasr and Enrique Díaz Reyna, *Historias para ver: Enrique Díaz, fotorreportero* (Mexico City: UNAM; Instituto de Investigaciones Estéticas, 2003), 127; Federico Gamboa, *Santa* (Mexico City: Eusebio Gómez de la Puente, 1927), 243–60. Anyone older than fourteen could attend as long as they behaved properly. *Cartilla* (1895), 71–72.

70. *El Universal*, 2 Oct. 1923, sec. 2, 1; Federico Gamboa, *La llaga* (Mexico City: Eusebio Gómez de la Puente, 1922), 17; Federico Gamboa, *Mi diario IV (1905–1908): Mucho de mi vida y algo de la de otros* (Mexico City: Consejo Nacional para la Cultura y las Artes, 1995), 136–37. *El Universal*, 7 Aug. 1929, sec. 2, p. 1; *El Siglo Diez y Nueve*, 15 Dec. 1890, p. 2. For trials that in the U.S. "hypnotized the nation," see William Marling, *The American Roman Noir: Hammett, Cain, and Chandler* (Athens: University of Georgia Press, 1995), 5.

71. *Excélsior*, 8 Oct. 1929, sec. 2, p. 1; *El Universal*, 6 Aug. 1929, sec. 2, p. 1; Monroy Nasr and Díaz Reyna, *Historias para ver*, 115–38. The legal journal *El Foro* published in 1895 a detailed chronicle of the murder trial of Luz Gómez, including transcriptions of the exchanges between lawyers and the suspect. *El Foro* 44:3 (4 Jan. 1895): 11.

72. *Excélsior*, 29 Apr. 1928, sec. 2, p. 1.

73. Federico Gamboa, *Mi diario I (1892–1896): Mucho de mi vida y algo de la de otros* (Mexico City: Consejo Nacional para la Cultura y las Artes, 1995), 36. The students in *El Diario del Hogar*, 26 Sept. 1906, p. 1.

74. Carlos Roumagnac, *Elementos de policía científica: Obra de texto para la escuela científica de policía de México* (Mexico City: Botas, 1923), 148–49.

75. Carlos Roumagnac, *Matadores de mujeres: Segunda parte de "Crímenes sexuales y pasionales"* (Mexico City: Ch. Bouret, 1910), 96. For jury trials as learning experiences for all kinds of people, Carlos Roumagnac, *Los criminales en México: Ensayo de psicología criminal: Seguido de dos casos de hermafrodismo observado por los Señores Doctores Ricardo Egea . . . Ignacio Ocampo* (Mexico City: 1904), 266. Debates in front of the jury included criticisms of the government that were difficult to find elsewhere. Carlos Roumagnac, "Mis recuerdos de Belem," *El Nacional*, 7 May 1933, p. 5.

76. Novelist Federico Gamboa noted his disapproval of the murder in his diary. Federico Gamboa, *Mi diario VII (1920–1939): Mucho de mi vida y algo de la de otros* (Mexico City: CNCA, 1995), 78–79. A Supreme Court justice's "deep reflections" in *El Heraldo,* 13 Jul. 1922, p. 1. See also *El Heraldo,* 11 Jul. 1922, p. 1, 3; *El Heraldo,* 14 Jul. 1922, p. 5. The case would be remembered as one of the most famous tried in front of a popular jury. *Excélsior,* 8 Oct. 1929, sec. 2, p. 1. I discussed this case in Pablo Piccato, "The Girl Who Killed a Senator: Femininity and the Public Sphere in Post-Revolutionary Mexico," in *True Stories of Crime in Modern Mexico,* ed. Robert Buffington and Pablo Piccato (Albuquerque: University of New Mexico Press, 2009), 128–53.

77. *El Universal,* 25 May 1922, p. 1; *El Heraldo,* 25 May 1922, p. 1; *El Heraldo,* 28 May 1922, p. 1; *El Heraldo,* 31 May. 1922, p. 8; *El Heraldo,* 14 Jul. 1922, p. 5. Jesús Moreno had suffered prison before the revolution, fought for Madero, and more recently supported Obregón and Calles in their rebellion against Carranza, although some in Veracruz saw him as an outsider. María del Pilar Moreno, *La tragedia de mi vida: Memorias escritas por la niña* (Mexico City: Phoenix, 1922), 74, 6–7, 28; DDCD, Twenty-Ninth Legislature, 11 Oct. 1920, pp. 30–31. Calles considered Moreno "a person of my complete confidence and well-known probity." Plutarco Elías Calles to Adolfo de la Huerta, 29 Apr. 1921, FAECFT, 4755, gaveta 54, exp. 73, inv. 3855, 1920–21. See also Jesús Moreno to Plutarco Elías Calles, 18 Dec. 1920, FAECFT, ser. 12010400, exp. 25, leg. 2/3, inv. 70, f. 131. Tejeda Llorca had links with the Porfirian elite, too. *El Universal,* 25 May 1922, p. 1; *El Heraldo de México,* 25 May 1922, p. 1; *El Heraldo de México,* 14 Jul. 1922, p. 5; *Excélsior,* 27 Apr. 1924, sec. 2, p. 8; *Excélsior,* 29 Apr. 1924, p. 6; Francisco Tejeda Llorca to Alvaro Obregón, FAECFT, exp. D; *El Universal,* 13 Jul. 1922, sec. 2, p. 3; Plutarco Elías Calles to Adalberto Tejeda, 24 May 1922, FAECFT, gaveta 54, exp. 96, inv. 3878; Adalberto Tejeda to Plutarco Elías Calles, 10 Jul. 1922, FAECFT, gaveta 72, exp. 26, inv. 5558, leg 4/15, PEC, fs. 160–210. On the debates about fuero and congressmen's honor, see Glenn James Avent, "Representing Revolution: The Mexican Congress and the Origins of Single-Party Rule, 1916–1934" (PhD diss., University of Arizona, 2004), chap. 5. See also Pablo Piccato, ed., *El poder legislativo en las décadas revolucionarias, 1908–1934* (Mexico City: Instituto de Investigaciones Legislativas-Cámara de Diputados, 1997).

78. *Excélsior,* 24 Apr. 1924, sec. 2, p. 6; *Excélsior,* 29 Apr. 1924, p. 1; Enrique Plasencia de la Parra, *Personajes y escenarios de la rebelión delahuertista, 1923–1924* (Mexico City: Instituto de Investigaciones Históricas UNAM; M.A. Porrúa, 1998).

79. *El Universal,* 26 May 1922, p. 6.

80. "En medio de una ovación cerrada y pisando flores, la niña Ana María del Pilar Moreno quedó libre," *Excélsior,* 30 Apr. 1924, p. 6.

81. Moreno, *La tragedia,* 18, 21, 23, 57; *Excélsior,* 17 Apr. 1924, p. 1. For a similarly successful narrative presented in front of the jury trial, in the case of Magdalena Jurado, see Aurelio de los Reyes, *Cine y sociedad en México, 1896–1930: Bajo el cielo de México (1920–1924)* (Mexico City: Universidad Nacional Autónoma de México, 1993), 2:85; Moheno, *Mis últimos discursos,* 88–140. Other women accused of murder

wrote memoirs. Mary S. Hartman, *Victorian Murderesses: A True History of Thirteen Respectable French and English Women Accused of Unspeakable Crimes* (New York: Schocken Books, 1975), 20.

82. Moreno, *La tragedia,* 54–57; *El Universal,* 11 Jul. 1922, p. 1; *El Universal,* 13 Jul. 1922, sec. 2, p. 1, 11; *El Universal,* 14 Jul. 1922, sec. 2, p. 10; *El Universal,* 15 Jul. 1922, p. 1; *El Universal,* 18 Jul. 1922, sec. 2, p. 1, 8; *El Heraldo,* 11 Jul. 1922, p. 3; *El Heraldo,* 12 Jul. 1922, p. 1; *El Heraldo,* 14 Jul. 1922, pp. 1, 5.

83. She and her attorneys (Abel C. Salazar, later joined by "prominent lawyers" Telésforo Ocampo, Manuel Zamora, Juan B. Cervantes, José Moreno Salido, and Querido Moheno) denounced the "hatred" of the judge in charge of the investigation. *El Universal,* 23 Jul. 1922, sec. 2, p. 1; *Excélsior,* 29 Apr. 1924, sec. 2, p. 8; *El Universal,* 16 Jul. 1922, p. 9; *El Universal,* 19 Jul. 1922, p. 1, 8; *El Universal,* 22 Jul. 1922, sec. 2, p. 1; *El Universal,* 4 Aug. 1922, sec. 2, p. 1; *El Universal,* 25 Aug. 1922, p. 5. On her defense team and the delay, *El Universal,* 25 Jul. 1922, sec. 2, p. 1; *El Universal,* 26 Jul. 1922, sec. 2, p. 7.

84. The Morenos had one car and Jesús had just bought a second when he was murdered. Moheno, *Sobre la brecha,* 178, 84; Moreno, *La tragedia,* 17, 24, 28, 31–35, 43. Not a great departure here from Porfirian models. Carmen Ramos et al., *Presencia y transparencia: La mujer en la historia de México* (Mexico City: El Colegio de México, 1987).

85. *Excélsior,* 27 Apr. 1924, sec. 2, p. 1; Moreno, *La tragedia,* 4, 7, 11, 14, 17, 21, 41–42, 44. In his 1923 defense of another female charged with killing a man, Moheno argued that women feared guns, contrasting their ignorance with the skill of revolutionary gunmen. Moheno, *Mis últimos discursos.* For women's relatively limited involvement in cases of serious violence, see Elisa Speckman, "Las flores del mal: Mujeres criminales en el porfiriato," *Historia Mexicana* 47:1 (1997): 189. But see, for lower-class women's participation in the revolution, Gabriela Cano, "Soldaderas and Coronelas," in *Encyclopedia of Mexico: History, Society and Culture* (Chicago: Fitzroy Dearborn Publishers, 1997), 2:1357–60; Ana Lau and Carmen Ramos, *Mujeres y revolución, 1900–1917* (Mexico City: Instituto Nacional de Estudios Históricos de la Revolución Mexicana, 1993). Mexican cases of women using guns in Macías González, "El caso de una beldad." On narratives of self-representations and notions of honor by women accused of crimes, Ruth Harris, "Melodrama, Hysteria and Feminine Crimes of Passion in the Fin-de-Siècle," *History Workshop* 25 (1988): 32, 34, 38; Hartman, *Victorian Murderesses,* esp. 1, 5, 8. See also Kristin Ruggiero, "Honor, Maternity, and the Disciplining of Women: Infanticide in Late Nineteenth-Century Buenos Aires," *Hispanic American Historical Review* 72:3 (1992): 353–73. On violence in the chambers see *El Universal,* 3 Oct. 1923, p. 1; Pablo Piccato, "El parlamentarismo y la construcción de una esfera pública posrevolucionaria," *Historias* 39 (1998): 65–85.

86. Moreno, *La tragedia,* 1, 2; *Excélsior,* 27 Apr. 1924, sec. 2, p. 1; *El Heraldo,* 11 Jul. 1922, p. 1.

87. *Excélsior,* 30 Apr. 1924, p. 1; *Excélsior,* 29 Apr. 1924, p. 6. When she was told that Tejeda Llorca had been elected senator, she asked Calles: "Won't the people of

Veracruz be ashamed of having a murderer as their representative?" *Excélsior,* 29 Apr. 1924, p. 6. Photographs included reconstructions of María del Pilar's shooting of Tejeda Llorca, images of her talking to the court, and the crowd outside the courthouse. *Excélsior,* 29 Apr. 1924, p. 1; but see Avent, "Representing Revolution," 236. On other female suspects dressed in black see de los Reyes, *Cine y sociedad,* 2:18, 80.

88. Moheno, *Mis últimos discursos,* 13; *El Universal,* 4 Oct. 1923, sec. 2, p. 1. Government officials, all the way up to cabinet level, were indeed "obsessed" to defeat Moheno. Sodi, *El jurado resuelve,* 119.

89. *Excélsior,* 29 Apr. 1924, p. 1; *Excélsior,* 30 Apr. 1924, sec. 2, p. 6; Moheno, *Sobre la brecha,* 175, 78, 84; Moreno, *La tragedia,* 28, 32, 33, 34; *Excélsior,* 29 Apr. 1924, p. 6.

90. Moheno, *Sobre la brecha,* 180.

91. *Excélsior,* 27 Apr. 1924, sec. 2, p. 1; *Excélsior,* 30 Apr. 1924, p. 1; Moheno, *Sobre la brecha,* 177, 181–83, 191; "¡María del Pilar Moreno fue absuelta!" *El Heraldo de México* (Los Angeles), 1 May 1924, p. 1. Moheno reminded jurors that they had to decide within the sovereignty of their "conscience" and "intimate belief." Moheno, *Mis últimos discursos,* 18–19, 22, 23; Querido Moheno, *Procesos célebres: Honorio Rodríguez, discurso de defensa* (Mexico City: Botas, 1928). Critics of the jury, and of Moheno, mention press campaigns on behalf of defendants as part of defense strategy. Speckman Guerra, *Del Tigre de Santa Julia,* 120.

92. *Excélsior,* 29 Apr. 1924, p. 1; *Excélsior,* 30 Apr. 1929, p. 1.

93. *El Heraldo,* 12 Jul. 1922, p. 5; *Excélsior,* 13 Jul. 1922, p. 5; Moreno, *La tragedia,* 59, 68; *El Universal,* 13 Jul. 1922, sec. 2, p. 1.

94. *El Heraldo,* 13 Jul. 1922, p. 5. For similar responses, among women and lawyers, de los Reyes, *Cine y sociedad,* 2:87.

95. *El Universal,* 7 Aug. 1929, sec. 2, 1.

96. He was acquitted. Sodi, *El jurado resuelve,* 86, 91.

97. Speech by public defender Rafael Rodríguez Talavera, *El Imparcial,* 19 Sept. 1897. See also on this case Robert Buffington and Pablo Piccato, "Tales of Two Women: The Narrative Construal of Porfirian Reality," *Americas* 55:3 (1999): 391–424. The "harapos" in *El Foro* 44:6 (8 Jan. 1895): 24. On female offenders through criminology's eyes see Lisette Rivera Reynaldos, "Crímenes pasionales y relaciones de género en México, 1880–1910," *Nuevo Mundo/Mundos Nuevos,* 2006, http://nuevomundo.revues.org/2835.

98. For example, Luz González, *El Universal,* 4 Oct. 1923, sec. 2, p. 1; *El Universal,* 17 Aug. 1922, sec. 2, p. 1. The fearful witnesses were Manuel Zapata and Rafael Rebollar. *El Universal,* 20 Jul. 1922, sec. 2, p. 1; *Excélsior,* 30 Apr. 1924, p. 1. De Landa's case in Víctor Macías González, "The Case of the Murdering Beauty: Narrative Construction, Beauty Pageants, and the Postrevolutionary Mexican National Myth (1921–1931)," in *True Stories of Crime in Modern Mexico,* ed. Robert Buffington and Pablo Piccato (Albuquerque: University of New Mexico Pres, 2009), 215–47. On Morfín, Sodi, *El jurado resuelve,* 42, 71. As suspects or witnesses, women proved to have, as predicted by Le Bon, greater influence over jurors than men. Sodi, *El jurado en México,* 240.

99. Moheno, *Mis últimos discursos,* 81; Moheno, *Rubin,* 61; Moheno, *Sobre la brecha,* 194, 200, 193.

100. Moheno, *Sobre la brecha,* 185, 188–89. The argument of Mexican women's oppression was central in the defense of Nydia Camargo, who had killed a Chilean man. Moheno, *Rubin,* 23, 71. He concluded this defense with a strong call intended to move jurors: "Kill him!!" Moheno, *Rubin,* 61. See also Moheno, *Mis últimos discursos,* 147–48, 53.

101. *El Heraldo,* 12 Jul. 1922, p. 1. Letters came from the interns of General Hospital, from a mechanics union, from a violinist, from railroad workers, from Guanajuato, Hidalgo, Jalisco, and Veracruz. *El Heraldo,* 12 Jul. 1922, p. 1; *El Heraldo,* 14 Jul. 1922, p. 1; *El Heraldo,* 19 Jul. 1922, p. 1, 8. Even the Salvation Army offered money to pay for the defense of María del Pilar. Moheno, *Sobre la brecha,* 93, 173, 178, 187; Cesare Lombroso, *Crime: Its Causes and Remedies,* trans. Henry P. Horton (Boston: Little, Brown, 1918), 256. See also Cesare Lombroso, *L'uomo delinquente in rapporto all'antropologia, alla giurisprudenza ed alle discipline carcerarie,* vol. 2, *Delinquente epilettico, d'impeto, pazzo e criminaloide* (Torino: Fratelli Bocca, 1889), 238.

102. *El Heraldo,* 15 Jul. 1922, p. 5; *Excélsior,* 29 May 1924, sec. 2, p. 1; *El Heraldo,* 11 Jul. 1922, p. 1; *El Heraldo,* 14 Jul. 1922, p. 1; *El Universal,* 14 Jul. 1922, sec. 2, p. 10; *El Heraldo,* 13 Jul. 1922, p. 5.

103. Moheno, *Sobre la brecha,* 179, 93.

104. Moheno, *Rubin,* 13, 19, 21; Maza, *Private Lives and Public Affairs,* 66; Moheno, *Sobre la brecha,* 188.

105. DDCD, year 2, Thirty-First Legislature, no. 33, 23 Oct. 1925, p. 23.

106. Ibid., p. 24.

107. Moheno, *Honorio Rodríguez,* 78. He argued elsewhere that women were simpler than men, and as such could be more criminal than them, their natural differences paralleling those between whites and blacks. Moheno, *Mis últimos discursos,* 80–82. *Excélsior,* 11 May 1924, p. 7; *Excélsior,* 12 May 1924, p. 3; *Excélsior,* 21 May 1924, sec. 2, p. 8. On dueling, Pablo Piccato, "Politics and the Technology of Honor: Dueling in Turn-of-the-Century Mexico," *Journal of Social History* 33:2 (1999): 331–54. On the memorandum, and the release of a man who killed his wife and her lover avenging "his insulted honor," *Excélsior,* 31 May 1924, p. 3. See also *Excélsior,* 1 Apr. 1924, p. 6; *Excélsior,* 29 Apr. 1924, p. 1; *Excélsior,* 31 May 1924, p. 3; de los Reyes, *Cine y sociedad,* 2:64. The autopsy in *El Heraldo,* 30 May 1922, sec. 2, p. 1; *El Anti-Reeleccionista* 1:13 (24 Aug. 1909): 4; *El Heraldo,* 11 Jul. 1922, p. 3.

108. Session of January 26, 1917, *Diario de los debates del Congreso Constituyente,* 982, 986–88. In postrevolutionary France, courts were part of a public sphere that changed from an iconic, oral, symbolically feminine language to one that was more male in its preference for textuality and rationality. Maza, *Private Lives,* 110, 314. On the new regulations, see Armando Z. Ostos, *Breves comentarios sobre el nuevo código de procedimientos penales para el Distrito y Territorios Federales* (Mexico City: 1921), 27, 31, 40; on the last cases, against women, *Excélsior,* 8 Oct. 1929, sec. 2, 1. Not that courtrooms had been welcoming places for women. Attorneys had no compunction about praising the bodies of good-looking female witnesses. Sodi, *El jurado resuelve,* 99.

109. Jean Franco, *Plotting Women: Gender and Representation in Mexico* (New York: Columbia University Press, 1988); Enriqueta Tuñón Pablos, "El otorgamiento del sufragio femenino en México" (PhD diss., Universidad Nacional Autónoma de México, 1997), 3–4, 62; Gabriela Cano, "Revolución, feminismo y ciudadanía en México (1915–1940)," in *Historia de las mujeres en occidente* (Madrid: Taurus, 1993), 303; Alexandra Minna Stern, "Responsible Mothers and Normal Children: Eugenics, Nationalism, and Welfare in Post-Revolutionary Mexico, 1920–1940," *Journal of Historical Sociology* 12:4 (Nov. 1999): 370, 377; Mary Kay Vaughan, "Modernizing Patriarchy: State Policies, Rural Households, and Women in Mexico, 1930–1940," in *Hidden Histories of Gender and the State in Latin America* (Durham: Duke University Press, 2000), 194–215.

110. Emilio Portes Gil, *Autobiografía de la revolución* (Mexico City: IMC, 1964), 411–12.

111. Renato González Mello, Irma Hernández, et al., *Los pinceles de la historia: La arqueología del régimen 1910–1955* (Mexico City: Museo Nacional de Arte, 2003). The cult of Pro became popular and he was beatified in 1988.

112. Jaymie Heilman, "The Demon Inside: Madre Conchita, Gender, and the Assassination of Obregón," *Mexican Studies/Estudios Mexicanos* 18:1 (1 Feb. 2002): 31. This is the best historical treatment of the case. See also Robert Weis, "The Revolution on Trial: Assassination, Christianity, and the Rule of Law in 1920s Mexico," *Hispanic American Historical Review* 96:2 (May 2016): 319–353. Quotation from *Requisitoria del ministerio público*, 59; see also 7, 23, 31; Orlando Balderas Martínez, "José de León Toral: Proceso histórico-jurídico (1928–1929)" (BA thesis, Universidad Nacional Autónoma de México, n.d.), 114, 128 132, 135. The proceedings in *El jurado de Toral y La Madre Conchita: Lo que se dijo y lo que no se dijo en el sensacional juicio: Versión taquigráfica textual*, vol. 1 (Mexico City, 1928); *New York Times*, 21 Jul. 1928, p. 1; *Washington Post*, 10 Nov. 1928, p. 6; *Chicago Daily Tribune*, 31 Oct. 1928, p. 38; *New York Times*, 7 Nov. 1928, p. 26. The 1857 and 1917 constitutions mentioned "delitos políticos," but the 1871 penal code did not include any reference to them. Felipe Tena Ramírez, *Leyes fundamentales de México* (Mexico City: Porrúa, 1989), 610, 825.

113. Monroy Nasr and Díaz Reyna, *Historias para ver*, 127–29; *Chicago Daily Tribune*, 2 Nov. 1928, p. 20; *Excélsior*, 2 Nov. 1928, p. 1; *New York Times*, 1 Aug. 1928, p. 5; Raúl Carrancá y Rivas, *Derecho penitenciario: Cárcel y penas en México* (Mexico City: Editorial Porrúa, 1986), 222.

114. *Excélsior*, 4 Nov. 1928, p. 5.

115. *Excélsior*, 2 Nov. 1928, p. 1; *Excélsior*, 4 Nov. 1928, sec. 2, p. 1.

116. *Excélsior*, 4 Nov. 1928, pp. 1, 4, 8; *Excélsior*, 2 Nov. 1928, p. 3.

117. *Excélsior*, 3 Nov. 1928, p. 3.

118. Ibid.

119. *Excélsior*, 4 Nov. 1928, p. 1.

120. Quotation from *Excélsior*, 3 Nov. 1928, p. 6; see also *Excélsior*, 3 Nov. 1928, p. 1, and sec. 2, p. 1; *Excélsior*, 1 Nov. 1928, sec. 2, p. 1. For Toral's "gendered weakness" see Heilman, "The Demon Inside," 35–36.

121. *Excélsior,* 4 Nov. 1928, English section, p. 1.

122. *Excélsior,* 1 Nov. 1928, p. 11; *Excélsior,* 4 Nov. 1928, p. 3; *El jurado de Toral y la Madre Conchita,* 1:149; *Washington Post,* 4 Aug. 1928, p.1; *New York Times,* 23 Oct. 1928, p. 60.

123. *Excélsior,* 4 Nov. 1928, p. 1. The construction of a martyr narrative that places the life of the martyr at the center analyzed for the case of Agustín Pro in Marisol López-Menéndez, "The Holy Jester: A Story of Martyrdom in Revolutionary Mexico," *The New School Psychology Bulletin* 6:2 (2009): 59–66; *El jurado de Toral y la Madre Conchita,* 1:90.

124. *El jurado de Toral y la Madre Conchita,* 1:53–62.

125. Ibid., 56, 93.

126. In the King James version of John 18:36, "Jesus answered, 'My kingdom is not of this world: if my kingdom were of this world, then would my servants fight, that I should not be delivered to the Jews: but now is my kingdom not from hence.' Pilate therefore said unto him, 'Art thou a king then?' Jesus answered, 'Thou sayest that I am a king. To this end was I born, and for this cause came I into the world, that I should bear witness unto the truth. Every one that is of the truth heareth my voice.'" *King James Bible* (Project Gutenberg, n.d.).

127. María Elena Sodi de Pallares, *Los cristeros y José de León Toral* (Mexico City: Editorial "Cvltvra," 1936), 100–101.

128. Ibid., 96; Renato González Mello, "Of Intersections and Parallel Lives: José de León Toral and David Alfaro Siqueiros," in *True Stories of Crime in Modern Mexico,* ed. Robert Buffington and Pablo Piccato (Albuquerque: University of New Mexico Press, 2009), 179–214.

129. She claimed to act with the consent of Archbishop Mora y del Río. Concepción Acevedo y de la Llata, *Obregón: Memorias inéditas de la Madre Conchita,* ed. Armando de María y Campos (Mexico City: Libro-Mex, 1957), 79, 89, 92, 119. Acevedo complained during the trial that Correa Nieto had promised her not to divulge the information about the brands. *El jurado de Toral y la Madre Conchita,* 1:235.

130. Gonzalo N. Santos, *Memorias* (Mexico City: Grijalbo, 1984), 329; *El jurado de Toral y la Madre Conchita,* 1:185, 204, 213. In her memoirs she suggests that she did not welcome Toral's decision. Before his execution she told him, through another person, that he was a "shameless abuser, who was only good to take her to prison," yet she forgave him. Acevedo y de la Llata, *Obregón,* 42, 52, 58, 82.

131. Acevedo y de la Llata, *Obregón,* 79. On the use of gender arguments against and in defense of Acevedo, see Heilman, "The Demon Inside."

132. Yet, according to Armando de María y Campos, she did not mind being compared with Saint Teresa. Concepción Acevedo y de la Llata, *Memorias de la madre Conchita,* ed. Armando de María y Campos (Mexico City: Libro-Mex, 1962), 71; *El jurado de Toral y la Madre Conchita,* 1:168, 229, 235; quote from Rogelio Jiménez Marce, "Una monja descarriada: La Madre Conchita y su imaginario de la vida religiosa," *Repositorio Institucional Zaloamati,* December 2012, http://zaloamati.azc.uam.mx/handle/11191/2096.

133. Heilman, "The Demon Inside," 46.

134. Múgica was a governor of Michoacán, minister under Cárdenas, and prominent socialist. Acevedo y de la Llata, *Obregón*, 230; Jiménez Marce, "Una monja descarriada," 80. On other publications by Acevedo after her release from the Islas Marías in 1942 see Heilman, "The Demon Inside," 46, 48–59. She was released in 1942 and went on to do charity work outside the Catholic Church (which had excommunicated her after her indictment), and to write and give lectures and interviews about her experience. Jiménez Marce, "Una monja descarriada," 81, 84; *El jurado de Toral y la Madre Conchita*, 1:235.

135. *El jurado de Toral y la Madre Conchita*, 1:120–21, 164; *Excélsior*, 6 Nov. 1928, pp. 3, 4; *Requisitoria del Ministerio Público y alegatos; Excélsior*, 4 Nov. 1928, pp. 1, 11; Heilman, "The Demon Inside," 39.

136. *Requisitoria del ministerio público y alegatos*, 48–49, 54, 55.

137. Querido Moheno, "Mis impresiones del jurado: El regicida," *Excélsior*, 3 Nov. 1928, pp. 1, 11.

138. Querido Moheno, "Interrogatorio que el procurador de justicia hizo ayer a José de León Toral," *Excélsior*, 4 Nov. 1928, p. 1. "Mystics do not hope to get elected to Congress," reasoned Moheno. Moheno, "Mis impresiones del jurado," p. 11.

139. Moheno, "Interrogatorio," pp. 1, 11.

140. *El jurado de Toral y la Madre Conchita*, 1:101, 103, 107; *Requisitoria del ministerio público y alegatos*, 27, 32. A fictional extrapolation of the conspiracy theory in Francisco Martín Moreno, *México acribillado: Una novela histórica en cuatro actos* (Mexico City: Alfaguara, 2008).

141. *Requisitoria del ministerio público y alegatos*, 32, 84.

142. Ibid., 29, 30, 60, 62, 80, 88.

143. Ibid., 35.

144. *Excélsior*, 6 Nov. 1928, p. 4; Sodi de Pallares, *Los Cristeros*, 116.

145. *Requisitoria del ministerio público y alegatos*, 23.

146. Ibid., 22; Sodi de Pallares, *Los Cristeros*, 111; Sodi, *El jurado resuelve*, 112.

147. Sodi de Pallares, *Los Cristeros*, 115; *Requisitoria del ministerio público y alegatos*, 115.

148. Sodi de Pallares, *Los Cristeros*, 13, 20, 39–40. *Excélsior* portrayed María Elena arriving at the San Ángel courtroom with her father. *Excélsior*, 4 Nov. 1928, sec. 3, p. 1.

149. Acevedo y de la Llata, *Obregón*, 83.

150. *Excélsior*, 1 Nov. 1928, p. 1.

151. *Excélsior*, 5 Nov. 1928, p. 1; *Requisitoria del ministerio público y alegatos*, 11, 14; *Excélsior*, 6 Nov. 1928, pp. 1, 3 and 4.

152. *Excélsior*, 6 Nov. 1928, pp. 1, 10; Monroy Nasr and Díaz Reyna, *Historias para ver*, 40, 113; *New York Times*, 6 Nov. 1928, p. 30.

153. *Excélsior*, 6 Nov. 1928, p. 10.

154. Ibid., p. 4; *New York Times*, 7 Nov. 1928, p. 26; *Atlanta Constitution*, 9 Nov. 1928, p. 1; Balderas Martínez, "Toral: Proceso histórico-jurídico," 142–44; David C. Bailey, *!Viva Cristo Rey! The Cristero Rebellion and the Church-State Conflict in*

Mexico (Austin: University of Texas Press, 1974), 228–29; *New York Times*, 6 Nov. 1928, p. 30; *Excélsior*, 7 Nov. 1928, p. 1, 4; *Excélsior*, 8 Nov. 1928, p. 1; *Excélsior*, 9 Nov. 1928, pp. 1, 4; *New York Herald Tribune*, Nov. 9, 1928, p. 1.

155. *El jurado de Toral y la Madre Conchita*, 204.

156. DDCD, Legislatura XXXIII, no. 25, 5 Nov. 1928. *Excélsior* printed blank boxes with the national shield on top, indicating the ads that had been withdrawn. According to Acevedo, after breaking into the courtroom the group of deputies went to the *Excélsior* building to set it on fire. Acevedo y de la Llata, *Obregón*, 81.

157. *Excélsior*, 6 Nov. 1928, p. 5.

158. Balderas Martínez, "Toral: Proceso histórico-jurídico," 150; Arno Burkholder de la Rosa, "El periódico que llegó a la vida nacional: Los primeros años del diario 'Excélsior' (1916–1932)," *Historia Mexicana* 58:4 (1 Apr. 2009): 1407–13; Miguel Velasco Valdes, *Historia del periodismo mexicano: Apuntes* (Mexico City: Librería de Manuel Porrúa, 1955), 199.

159. Bailey, *¡Viva Cristo Rey!*, 239; Monroy Nasr and Díaz Reyna, *Historias para ver*, 138; *Los Angeles Times*, 11 Feb. 1929, p. 1. For the influence of the case on a police journalist, Eduardo Téllez Vargas and José Ramón Garmabella, *¡Reportero de Policía! El Güero Téllez* (Mexico City: Ediciones Océano, 1982), 17–19.

160. Jorge Ibargüengoitia, *El atentado*, in *Teatro mexicano contemporáneo: Antología* (Madrid: Sociedad General de Escritores de México, 1991).

161. Vicente Leñero, *El juicio: El jurado de León Toral y la Madre Conchita* (Mexico City: J. Mortiz, 1972).

162. Gamboa, *Mi diario I*, 184–85.

163. *El Universal*, 17 Sept. 1929, p. 3; Moheno, *Honorio Rodríguez*, 29.

164. *El Universal*, 7 Aug. 1929, p. 3. A similar formulation in *El Universal*, 12 Oct. 1923, p. 3. For the use of melodrama as the dramatization of social forces Angus McLaren, *The Trials of Masculinity: Policing Sexual Boundaries, 1870–1930* (Chicago: University of Chicago Press, 1997); Sarah C. Maza, *Violette Nozière: A Story of Murder in 1930s Paris* (Berkeley: University of California Press, 2011).

165. Luis Cabrera to Rafael Nieto, 13 Jun. 1922, FAECFT, Fondo Fernando Torreblanca, ser. 010203, exp. 1/2: Cabrera, Luis, inv. 142; Saydi Núñez Cetina, "¿Pena de muerte o indulto? La justicia penal en el Distrito Federal durante la institucionalización del estado revolucionario," *Revista Historia y Justicia* 2 (April 2014): 21.

166. *El Universal*, 2 Aug. 1929, p 1. See a fuller discussion in Speckman Guerra, *Del Tigre de Santa Julia*, 127; Núñez Cetina, "¿Pena de muerte o indulto?"

167. *Excélsior* journalist Víctor Alba recognized that he had to adapt his writing to the new setting: "If the reports about crimes I had to write in the form of novels now, for judicial news, I have to use the dramatic form, with dialogues and comments as if it was theater, and it often was." Víctor Alba, *Sísifo y Su Tiempo: Memorias de un cabreado, 1916–1996* (Barcelona: Laertes, 1996), 300. The activities in courtrooms were rarely described. An unflattering description of the Texcoco penal courts in *La Prensa*, 1 Jul. 1936, pp. 1–2. On science, Luis Garrido, *Ensayos penales* (Mexico City: Botas, 1952), 78; R. Zubarán Capmany, "El nuevo código penal mexicano," *El Universal*, 23 Aug. 1929, p. 3. On this process see Ariel Rodríguez Kuri, *La*

experiencia olvidada: El ayuntamiento de México: Política y administración, 1876–1912 (Mexico City: El Colegio de México, 1996). Although a new penal code for the Federal District was passed in 1931, reestablishing the authority of judges, the jury no longer decided over most criminal causes. The code maintained extensive prescriptions for the jury, but the institution was only to be used for crimes committed by the press and federal officials. See Codigo de Procedimientos Penales para el Distrito Federal, accessed 29 Dec. 2014, http://www.metro.df.gob .mx/transparencia/imagenes/fr1/normaplicable/2014/2/cppdf14042014.pdf.

168. Francisco Valencia Rangel, *El crimen, el hombre y el medio: Principios de geografía criminal para la República mexicana* (Mexico City: Cicerón, 1938), 207; Carlos Franco Sodi, *Don Juan Delincuente y otros ensayos* (Mexico City: Botas, 1951); J. Alberto Salinas y Rivera, "Jurados de la capital: Un jurado notable," *El Foro* 5:31 (23 Aug. 1877); *El Heraldo de Mexico,* 19 Jul. 1925, p. 5; Juan Bustillo Oro, *Ahí está el detalle* (Grovas-Oro Films, 1940). Commemorations in *Excélsior,* 8 Oct. 1929, sec. 2, p. 1; Victoriano Salado Álvarez, *Memorias: Tiempo viejo, tiempo nuevo* (Mexico City: Porrúa, 1985), 219.

CHAPTER 2. A LOOK AT THE CRIME SCENE

1. *El Universal Gráfico,* 1 Jan. 1947, p. 5; *La Prensa,* 1 Jan. 1947, p. 1.

2. *La Prensa,* 29 Apr. 1934, p. 6.

3. No discussion of nota roja, for example, in Humberto Musacchio, *Historia gráfica del periodismo mexicano* (Mexico City: Gráfica, Creatividad y Diseño, 2003); or in María del Carmen Ruiz Castañeda et al., *El periodismo en México: 450 años de historia* (Mexico City: Editorial Tradición, 1974).

4. J.M. Servín, *D.F. Confidencial: Crónicas de delincuentes, vagos y demás gente sin futuro* (Oaxaca: Editorial Almadia, 2010), 31. I agree on this with Benjamin T. Smith and Paul Gillingham, "Introduction," in their forthcoming volume on the history of the press in Mexico. On the press in general, Ruiz Castañeda et al., *El periodismo en México.*

5. Carlos Monsiváis, *Los mil y un velorios: Crónica de la nota roja* (Mexico City: Consejo Nacional para la Cultura y las Artes: Alianza Editorial, 1994), 5, 7, 10, 13. Monsiváis's work is invaluable. Other useful studies include Víctor Ronquillo, *Nota roja 50's: La crónica policiaca en la ciudad de México* (Mexico City: Editorial Diana, 1993); Ana Luisa Luna, *La crónica policiaca en México: Nota roja 40s* (Mexico City: Diana, 1993); Victoria Brocca, *Nota roja 60's: La crónica policiaca en la ciudad de México* (Mexico City: Diana, 1993).

6. Robert Buffington, *A Sentimental Education for the Working Man: The Mexico City Penny Press, 1900–1910* (Durham: Duke Uiversity Press, 2015); Rafael (el Fisgón) Barajas Durán, *El país de "El Llorón de Icamole": Caricatura mexicana de combate y libertad de imprenta durante los gobiernos de Porfirio Díaz y Manuel González (1877–1884)* (Mexico City: Fondo de Cultura Económica, 2007).

7. Eduardo Téllez Vargas and José Ramón Garmabella, *¡Reportero de policía! El Güero Téllez* (Mexico City: Ediciones Océano, 1982), 33; Francesc Barata and Marco Lara Klahr, *Nota(n) roja: La vibrante historia de un género y una nueva manera de informar* (Mexico City: Random House Mondadori, 2009), 55–62.

8. Monsiváis, *Los mil y un velorios,* 29, 31; Julio Scherer García and Carlos Monsiváis, *Tiempo de saber: Prensa y poder en México* (Mexico City: Aguilar, 2003).

9. Ricardo Pérez Montfort, *Cotidianidades, imaginarios y contextos: Ensayos de historia y cultura en México, 1850–1950* (Mexico City: CIESAS, 2008), 388. The best example for this in Mexico, and a reference throughout this chapter, is Jesse Lerner, *El impacto de la modernidad: Fotografía criminalística en la Ciudad de México* (Mexico City: Turner; Consejo Nacional para la Cultura y las Artes; Instituto Nacional de Antropología e Historia; Editorial Océano, 2007). See also Guy Reel, *The National Police Gazette and the Making of the Modern American Man, 1879–1906* (New York: Palgrave Macmillan, 2006); Paulina Brunetti, *Relatos de prensa: La crónica policial en los diarios cordobeses de comienzos del siglo XX (1900–1914)* (Córdoba, Argentina: Jorge Sarmiento Editor-Universitaslibros, 2006), 21; Dominique Kalifa, *L'encre et le sang: Récits de crimes et société à la belle epoque* (Paris: Fayard, 1995); Sylvia Saítta, *Regueros de tinta: El diario "Crítica" en la década de 1920* (Buenos Aires: Editorial Sudamericana, 1998); John R. Brazil, "Murder Trials, Murder, and Twenties America," *American Quarterly* 33:2 (1 Jul. 1981): 163–84.

10. Servín, *D.F. confidencial,* 37, 51; and, paradoxically, Monsiváis, *Los mil y un velorios,* 87–88.

11. Monsiváis, *Los mil y un velorios,* 31; Cuauhtémoc Medina, "*¡Alarma!* Crimen y circulación," *Poliester* 2:6 (1993): 18–27, for the link between nota roja and judicial narratives; Miguel Donoso Pareja, *Picaresca de la nota roja* (Mexico City: Editorial Samo, 1973).

12. Max Aub, *Crímenes ejemplares* (Madrid: Calambur, 1996), 27; Sonia Adriana Peña, "José Revueltas y la crónica policial," *Literatura Mexicana* 20:1 (2009): 79–88; *El Universal Gráfico,* 3 Jan. 1955, p. 5; Wilberto L. Cantón, *Nota roja: Reportaje en dos actos* (Mexico City: Ecuador, 1965). For Roland Barthes the arbitrary relationship established between two events, a caricature of causality, defined the French *fait divers.* "Structure de fait divers" in Roland Barthes, *Essais critiques* (Paris: Éditions du Seuil, 1964), 188–97. The possibilities of this compressed language were explored also in Félix Fénéon et al., *Nouvelles en trois lignes* (Paris: Éd. Macula, 1990).

13. Examples of the latter in Gerardo Villadelángel Viñas and Edgardo Ganado Kim, *El libro rojo, continuación: I, 1868–1928* (Mexico City: Fondo de Cultura Económica, 2008); Enrique Metinides and Photographers' Gallery, *Enrique Metinides* (London: Ridinghouse, 2003). But see Enrique Metinides, *101 Tragedies of Enrique Metinides,* ed. Trisha Ziff (New York: Aperture, 2012). See Cuauhtémoc Medina, "SEMEFO, The Morgue," in *The Mexico City Reader,* ed. Rubén Gallo and Lorna Scott Fox (Madison: University of Wisconsin Press, 2004); Pablo Piccato, "Art, Homicide, and the Anonymous Dead in Latin America," *Public Seminar,* 30 Nov. 2015, http://www.publicseminar.org/2015/11/art-homicide-and-the-anonymous-dead-in-latin-america/.

14. Colin Sparks, "Introduction: The Panic over Tabloid News," in *Tabloid Tales: Global Debates over Media Standards,* ed. Colin Sparks and John Tulloch (Oxford: Rowman and Littlefield, 2000), 11.

15. See Pablo Piccato, "Altibajos de la esfera pública en México, de la dictadura republicana a la democracia corporativa: La era de la prensa," in *Independencia y revolución: Pasado, presente y futuro,* ed. Gustavo Leyva (Mexico City: Fondo de Cultura Económica-Universidad Autónoma Metropolitana, 2010), 240–91; Ruiz Castañeda et al., *El periodismo en México; Silvia González Marín, Prensa y poder político: La elección presidencial de 1940 en la prensa mexicana* (Mexico City: XXI Siglo Veintiuno, 2006), 17–18, 27, 35.

16. Diego Arenas Guzmán, *El Periodismo en la Revolución Mexicana* (Mexico City: Patronato del Instituto Nacional de Estudios Históricos de le Revolución Mexicana, 1966); F. Ibarra de Anda, *El periodismo en México, lo que es y lo que debe ser: Un estudio del periódico y del periodista mexicanos y de las posibilidades de ambos para el futuro* (Mexico: Imprenta Mundial, 1934); González Marín, *Prensa y poder político.* A scarcity of sources is in part to be blamed for the lack of a proper business history of Mexican newspapers.

17. Jacinto Rodríguez Munguía, *La otra guerra secreta: Los archivos prohibidos de la prensa y el poder* (Mexico City: Random House Mondadori, 2007), 90, 94, 149.

18. U.S. Consulate Mexico City, National Archives, Department of State, M274, roll 240, 812.91/18; Scherer García and Monsiváis, *Tiempo de saber,* 165; Rodríguez Munguía, *La otra guerra secreta,* 242; Gabriela Aguilar and Ana Cecilia Terrazas, *La prensa, en la calle: Los voceadores y la distribución de periódicos y revistas en México* (Mexico City: Grijalbo, 1996), 119.

19. Luis Novaro to Consejo de Administración, 2 Feb. 1939, AGN, SCEP, leg. 1, f. 1340. The Sunday edition went from forty-five thousand to forty thousand.

20. *Detectives* 1:1 (15 Aug. 1932); *Detectives* 1:2 (22 Aug. 1932): 8–9.

21. Brocca, *Nota roja 60's,* 111.

22. Cited in Angel Miquel, *Disolvencias: Literatura, cine y radio en México (1900–1950)* (Mexico City: Fondo de Cultura Económica, 2005), 156–57. Sensationalized crime coverage helped William Randolph Hearst's *New York Journal* sell 1.5 million copies in 1900. Roy Lotz, *Crime and the American Press* (New York: Praeger, 1991), 11.

23. Miguel Velasco Valdes, *Historia del periodismo mexicano: Apuntes* (Mexico City: Librería de Manuel Porrúa, 1955), 199.

24. In 1939 the DAPP's functions in relation to the media were absorbed by the Secretaría de Gobernación. Joy Elizabeth Hayes, *Radio Nation: Communication, Popular Culture, and Nationalism in Mexico, 1920–1950* (Tucson: University of Arizona Press, 2000), 66–67, 83–85; Fernando Mejía Barquera, *La industria de la radio y la televisión y la política del estado mexicano* (Mexico City: Fundación Manuel Buendía, 1989), 64; González Marín, *Prensa y poder político,* 106–7, 121–22, 130–36.

25. Scherer García and Monsiváis, *Tiempo de saber,* 31, 145, 149; Arellano Martínez, "El mirador de los días," *Revista de Policía* 23:281 (Jul. 1964): 1–3, 43; Aguilar

and Terrazas, *La prensa, en la calle;* Rodríguez Munguía, *La otra guerra secreta,* 243; Annick Lempérière, *Intellectuels, etat et société au Mexique: Les clercs de la nation (1910–1968)* (Paris: L'Harmattan, 1992).

26. Ibarra de Anda, *El periodismo en México,* 51. For the state-centered view, Roberto Blanco Moheno, *Memorias de un reportero* (Mexico City: Editorial V Siglos, 1975), 225; Vanessa Freije, "Journalists, Scandal, and the Unraveling of One-Party Rule in Mexico, 1960–1988" (PhD diss., Duke University, 2015).

27. Paul Gillingham, "Maximino's Bulls: Popular Protest after the Mexican Revolution, 1940–1952," *Past and Present,* no. 206 (2010): 175–211. On consumption, Velasco Valdes, *Historia del periodismo mexicano;* Víctor Macías González, "The Case of the Murdering Beauty: Narrative Construction, Beauty Pageants, and the Postrevolutionary Mexican National Myth (1921–1931)," in *True Stories of Crime in Modern Mexico,* ed. Robert Buffington and Pablo Piccato (Albuquerque: University of New Mexico Pres, 2009), 215–47.

28. Contrast with U.S. tabloids, whose ideal reader was a "secretary and stenographer" only attracted by melodrama. V. Penelope Pelizzon and Nancy Martha West, *Tabloid, Inc.: Crimes, Newspapers, Narratives* (Columbus: Ohio State University Press, 2010), 34.

29. González Marín, *Prensa y poder político,* 24, 29; *El Universal Gráfico,* 1 Jan. 1929, p. 1; *El Universal Gráfico,* 2 Jan. 1929; *El Universal Gráfico,* 2 Jan. 1929, pp. 25–28.

30. *La Prensa,* 24 Jan. 1957, p. 9. Compare *La Prensa,* 3 May 1951, p. 16, and *Alarma!* 2:27 (12 May 1951): 6. In 1972, *La Prensa* was the first to use color on its cover.

31. Velasco Valdes, *Historia del periodismo mexicano,* 217.

32. Enrique E. Sánchez Ruiz, "Apuntes para una historia de la prensa en Guadalajara," *Comunicación y Sociedad* 22 (December 2014): 19–20; González Marín, *Prensa y poder político,* 32–33; Ruiz Castañeda et al., *El periodismo en México,* 280–82. I thank Benjamin T. Smith for his notes on Ordorica.

33. AGN, LC, 704.1/18, 1.22.35; Velasco Valdes, *Historia del periodismo mexicano,* 218.

34. An attempt to acquire the newspaper by Callista banker Luis Montes de Oca fell through, AGN, LC, 704.1/71, 3.28.35; one of the employees was the Güero Téllez, Téllez Vargas and Garmabella, *¡Reportero de policía!,* 40; Geo W. Glass to President Cárdenas, 4 Feb. 1936, AGN, LC, 704.1/72.

35. AGN, LC, 704.1/72, 3.30.35, 9 Nov. 1937; Ignacio Muñoz and others to Luis Rodríguez, secretary to President Cárdenas, 4 Jul. 1935, AGN, LC, 704.1/18.

36. See complaints against George W. Glass, manager, in José García Plaza et al. to Lázaro Cárdenas, 24 Nov. 1936, AGN, LC, 704.1–72; Abacuc P. Cuevas to Cárdenas, 18 Dec. 1936, AGN, LC, 704.1/71. See *La Prensa,* 12 Jul. 1936, p. 8; Fco. Cardona y Rosell, "Sobre la política racial alemana," *La Prensa,* 4 Jul. 1936, p. 11. Later on, editors expressed their sympathy toward Franquismo. *La Prensa,* 9 May 1934, p. 10; *La Prensa,* 26 Feb. 1948, pp. 3, 13.

37. Report on general assembly of 14 Aug. 1937, AGN, SCEP, leg. 1, f. 1151.

38. González Marín, *Prensa y poder político*, 31.

39. AGN, LC, Luis Novaro, director of *La Prensa*, to Cárdenas, 27 Sept. 1938, 704.1/72; AGN, LC, 704.1/18, 1.22.35.

40. Minutes of assembly, 11 Nov. 1942, AGN, SCEP, leg. 2.

41. "Versión taquigráfica de las declaraciones rendidas por los CC. Luis Novaro y Miguel Gil en la sesión efectuada por el consejo de administración el día 3 de noviembre de 1942," AGN, SCEP, leg. 2; Reporte de pérdidas y ganancias, 1–30 Sept. 1938, AGN, SCEP, leg. 3, f. 1310; Editora de Periódicos, SCL, Estado de rendimientos por el periodo de 10 de enero al 31 de diciembre de 1943, AGN, SCEP, leg. 3 bis.

42. AGN, SCEP, leg. 1, f. 1164; Relación de saldos acreedores de los agentes de circulación, correspondiente al 31 de Dic. de 1943, AGN, SCEP, leg. 3 bis. An estimate of circulation based on data from the Unión de Voceadores, in "Cuánto imprimen y cuánto venden los diarios capitalinos," *etcetera*, 1 Aug. 2003, http://www.etcetera.com.mx/articulo.php?articulo = 325. *Esto* is also owned by OEM. An extensive treatment of the press in the period in Benjamin T. Smith, *Stories from the Newsroom, Stories from the Street: A History of the Press in Modern Mexico* (unpublished manuscript).

43. Minutes of assembly, 11 Nov. 1942, AGN, SCEP, leg. 2.

44. Velasco Valdes, *Historia del periodismo mexicano*, 233.

45. *La Prensa*, 1 Jan. 1947, pp. 8, 9, 16; *La Prensa*, 2 Jan. 1947, pp. 3, 15; *La Prensa*, 4 Jan. 1947, p. 8; *La Prensa*, 11 Jan. 1947, p. 9; *La Prensa*, 2 May 1951, pp. 1, 6, 8; *La Prensa*, 13 Sept. 1954, pp. 6, 33; *La Prensa*, 4 Mar. 1957, pp. 27, 34; "Vox Populi," *La Prensa*, 16 Mar. 1959, p. 9.

46. *La Prensa*, 1 Jan. 1929, p. 6; Velasco Valdes, *Historia del periodismo mexicano*, 236; Reglamento de labores del departamento de redacción, 28 Apr. 1939, AGN, SCEP, leg. 3 bis.

47. Servín, *D.F. Confidencial*, 40, 57; *La Prensa*, 1 May 1934, pp. 4, 18.

48. Medina, "*Alarma!*"; Brocca, *Nota roja 60's*; Lerner, *El impacto de la modernidad*, 77; Servín, *D.F. confidencial*, 40, 57. *Detectives* claimed to print 42,720 copies in 1932. It sold for ten cents. *Detectives* 1:1 (15 Aug. 1932); *Detectives* 1:2 (22 Aug. 1932): 8–9. See for example of narratives *Detectives*, 5:266 (20 Sept. 1937): 14–15.

49. *Alarma* 2:27 (12 May 1951).

50. On the death of Arnulfo R. Gómez, for example, see *Detectives* 1:12 (31 Oct. 1932): 3. Comics also included drawings of female murder victims. Lerner, *El impacto de la modernidad*, 80, 88.

51. *Alarma* 2:28 (19 May 1951): 4; *Alarma* 2:27 (12 May 1951): 4.

52. "Suplemento especial sobre campaña de Luis Echeverría," *Alarma!* 352 (28 Jan. 1970): 5.

53. Rodríguez Munguía, *La otra guerra secreta*, 208, 217–18. I thank Benjamin T. Smith for his notes on *Por Qué?*

54. *Argos* 1:5–6 (1 Jan. 1945); Lerner, *El impacto de la modernidad*, 36–37. Praise for brave policemen and official speeches by police inspector in *Policía Internacional: Magazine Mensual de Criterio Independiente al Servicio de la Policía Nacional y del Extranjero* 1:1 (Feb. 1948); see also *Detectives* 1:1 (9 Jun. 1959): 2; Vicente

Lombardo Toledano, "Acelerar la revolución," *Revista de Policía* 23:281 (Jul. 1964): 40–42, 65. *Revista de Policía* defined itself not as "official publication of the Police Department but the voice of its staff." "Veinticuatro años de '*Revista de Policía*,'" *Revista de Policía* 24:288 (Feb. 1965): 6–8.

55. Arellano Martínez, "Mirador de los días," *Revista de Policía,* 23:280 (Jun. 1964): 4, 35, 37.

56. *Detectives* 1:1 (9 Jun. 1959): 2, 23, 25.

57. *Revista de Policía* 24:280 (Jun. 1964): 1.

58. *Argos, Órgano de la Unión Nacional de Detectives y Técnicos Policiales* 1:5–6 (Jan. 1945): 11.

59. *El Sol de Culiacán,* 6 Mar. 1975, p. 2; *Don Paco* 1:3 (10 Aug. 1947): 1; *Don Paco* 1:22 (28 Dec. 1947): 1 and ff. According to Benjamin T. Smith, "By the 1950s, most provincial capitals had their own versions of the afternoon press," often linking common crime with state politics. As in Mexico City, crime news was key to building sales. Smith, *Stories from the Newsroom.*

60. Alvaro A. Fernández Reyes, *Crimen y suspenso en el cine mexicano 1946–1955* (Zamora, Michoacán: El Colegio de Michoacán, 2007), 52, 102, 98. Monsiváis, *Los mil y un velorios;* Rafael Aviña, "De la nota roja a la pantalla," *Reforma,* 7 Jul. 1996; "Cuidado con el hampa," magnetic audio tape, Colección Televisa Radio, Fonoteca Nacional; Ismael Rodríguez, *Nosotros los pobres,* 1948, starring Pedro Infante as a falsely accused man. A studio of radio audiences in Aguascalientes in 1958 found that the most popular program was *La policía vigila.* National Archives and Records Administration, Record Group 306, Box 16, IRI Mex 17, International Research Associates, A Study of Newspaper Readership in Aguascalientes and Reader Attitudes toward "Suplemento Semanal." Thanks to Benjamin T. Smith for the reference.

61. *Exélsior,* 3 Jul. 1936, 1. See also Vicente Lombardo Toledano, *El Universal,* 18 Oct. 1923, p. 1.

62. *Exélsior,* 3 Jul. 1936, p. 1. See also *Novedades,* 8 Oct. 1942, p. 7. Another proposal in DDCD, XXXVII Legislature, 20 Oct. 1938, vol. 3, year 2, no. 9.

63. Ibid.

64. *Novedades,* 8 Oct. 1942, p. 7.

65. Velasco Valdes, *Historia del periodismo mexicano,* 209. A Supreme Court judge praised *Excélsior* for toning down on its reporting of suicide and similar events. Kathryn A. Sloan, *Death in the City: Suicide and the Social Imaginary in Modern Mexico* (Berkeley: University of California Press, 2017). For law that would have limited display of crimes in comics and other publications in 1944 but failed to have much effect, Anne Rubenstein, *Bad Language, Naked Ladies, and Other Threats to the Nation: A Political History of Comic Books in Mexico* (Durham: Duke University Press, 1998): 95.

66. Vicente Lombardo Toledano to criminological congress, *El Universal,* 18 Oct. 1923, p. 1. See also *Exélsior,* 3 Jul. 1936, p. 1. A similar argument made against fait divers in France in Kalifa, *L'encre et Le Sang,* 199. In the U.S., against yellow journalism, David R. Spencer, *The Yellow Journalism: The Press and America's Emergence as a World Power* (Evanston: Northwestern University Press, 2007), 100.

67. Rodríguez Munguía, *La otra guerra secreta*, 122.

68. *La Prensa*, 4 Jul. 1936, p. 10.

69. *Alarma* 2:28 (19 May 1951): 4; Will Straw, "Nota Roja and Journaux Jaunes: Popular Crime Periodicals in Quebec and Mexico," in *Aprehendiendo al delincuente: Crimen y medios en América del Norte*, ed. Graciela Martínez-Zalce, Will Straw, and Susana Vargas (Mexico City: CISAN-UNAM, 2011), 53–70.

70. Rubenstein, *Bad Language*; José Herrera H., "Las películas cinematográficas mexicanas," *Revista de Policía* 23:280 (1 Jun. 1964):1; Blanco Moheno, *Memorias de un reportero*, 275; Brocca, *Nota roja 60's*, 97. On the moral project of the revolution see Katherine Elaine Bliss, *Compromised Positions: Prostitution, Public Health, and Gender Politics in Revolutionary Mexico City* (University Park: Pennsylvania State University Press, 2001). On violence against the press see Gillingham, "Maximino's Bulls"; Benjamin T. Smith, *Pistoleros and Popular Movements: The Politics of State Formation in Postrevolutionary Oaxaca* (Lincoln: University of Nebraska Press, 2009). Journalists suffering violence in *Don Roque* (Apizaco, Tlaxcala) (10 Mar. 1946): 1; *Policía Internacional* 12:2 (Feb. 1949): 12, 16; *Alarma!* 350 (14 Jan. 1970): 39.

71. Servín, *D.F. Confidencial*, 211.

72. AGN, DFS, exp. 48-2-959, H-97- L-12, 13 Jun. 1959; AGN, DFS, 13 Feb. 1968, exp. 11–142–68, H-72 L-7; AGN, DFS, exp. 11–206–73, H-5, L-7. Clippings in AGN, DGIPS, 7:1, 223fs, Jan. 1924–Jun. 1925; AGN, DGIPS, 34:29, 6fs, Sept. 1935. See also AGN, DGG, 2/014. (29) 4, c. 0, exp. 0, 1929.

73. AGN, DFS, report by agents dated 23 Jan. 1975, exp. 100–13–1-75, H-14, L-13; AGN, DFS, 29 Dec. 1967, exp. 34–15–67, H-23 L-1; AGN, DFS, 9 Aug. 1971, exp. 35–17–71, H-323 L-2. Reporters profited, in other cases, by publishing false information. AGN, DFS, 23 Aug. 1976, exp. 9–76–76, H-151, L-2. A visit by victims to the newspaper could indeed result in additional pressure against authorities to solve a case. *La Prensa*, 11 Sept. 1954, pp. 23, 35.

74. Sergio Aguayo Quezada, *La charola: Una historia de los servicios de inteligencia en México* (Mexico City: Grijalbo, 2001), 92, 134; Rodríguez Munguía, *La otra guerra secreta*, 149–50, 160–61, 348.

75. Téllez Vargas and Garmabella, *¡Reportero de policía!*, 38, 74–75, 64–65; Roberson, "Diario de una instructora de baile," *Revista de Policía* 24:286 (Dec. 1964): 24–27, 57; Leo D'Olmo, *¿Quién disparó? Novela original de Leo D'Olmo* (Mexico City: La Prensa, 1954), 10; *La Prensa*, 17 Mar. 1959, p. 40.

76. Cantón, *Nota roja;* Vicente Leñero, "Prólogo: La belleza del crimen," in Villadelángel Viñas and Ganado Kim, *El libro rojo*, xxvi; Ronquillo, *Nota roja 50's*, 8; Everard Kidder Meade, "Anatomies of Justice and Chaos: Capital Punishment and the Public in Mexico, 1917–1945" (PhD diss, University of Chicago, 2005), 581; Scherer García and Monsiváis, *Tiempo de saber*, 152.

77. Interview with Carlos Peláez Fuentes, Mexico City, 31 Jul. 2013; Metinides, *101 Tragedies*; Reglamento de labores del Departamento de Redacción, 28 Apr. 1939, AGN, SCEP, leg. 3 bis.

78. Rebeca Monroy Nasr and Enrique Díaz Reyna, *Historias para ver: Enrique Díaz, fotorreportero* (Mexico City: UNAM; Instituto de Investigaciones Estéticas,

2003), 111; John Mraz, *Nacho López, Mexican Photographer,* vol. 14 (Minneapolis: University of Minnesota Press, 2003); Lerner, *El impacto de la modernidad,* 101.

79. Lerner, *El impacto de la modernidad,* 101. But see Metinides, *101 Tragedies.*

80. Reglamento de labores del Departamento de Redacción, 28 Apr. 1939, AGN, SCEP, leg. 3 bis. The director made 810 pesos a month. AGN, SCEP, leg. 1, f. 1294–95.

81. Ibarra de Anda, *El periodismo en México,* 95, 102–10. Similarly in the U.S., Spencer, *The Yellow Journalism,* 12, 98. See also Blanco Moheno, *Memorias de un reportero,* 88, 119, 120, 132, 191; Roberto Blanco Moheno, *La noticia detrás de la noticia* (Mexico City: Litográfica Zacatecana, 1966), 140–41; Piccato, "Altibajos de la esfera pública"; Julio Scherer García, *La terca memoria* (Mexico City: Grijalbo, 2007), 92–93.

82. Rigoberto, "Tribunal de la opinión pública en la jefatura de policía," *Revista de Policía* (Jul. 1964) 23:281, 16–18, 80; Rodríguez Munguía, *La otra guerra secreta,* 158; Scherer García and Monsiváis, *Tiempo de saber,* 240; *Detectives* 1:11 (27 Oct. 1929): 3; *Alarma!* 349 (7 Jan. 1970): 2; José Marín Castillo, "Una antigua teoría," *Revista de Policía* 23:283 (Sept. 1964): 28; Téllez Vargas and Garmabella, *¡Reportero de policía!,* 100; Cantón, *Nota roja;* Roberson, "Diario de una instructora de baile," *Revista de Policía* 24:286 (Dec. 1964): 24; J. García-Robles, *La bala perdida: William S. Burroughs en México, 1949–1952* (Mexico City: Ediciones del Milenio, 1995), 79.

83. Editorial, *Detectives* 1:2 (23 Jun. 1959): 10.

84. Aguayo Quezada, *La charola,* 79, 239; Rodríguez Munguía, *La otra guerra secreta,* 158; Scherer García and Monsiváis, *Tiempo de saber,* 240; Julio Scherer García, *Historias de muerte y corrupción: Calderón, Mouriño, Zambada, El Chapo, la Reina del Pacífico* (Mexico City: Grijalbo, 2011), 90–97; Freije, "Journalists, Scandal."

85. José Marín Castillo, "El cumplimiento del deber," *Revista de Policía* 23:280 (Jun. 1964): 26–27, 51; see also *Detectives* 1:1 (15 Aug. 1932): 2; Diane Davis, *Policing and Mexican Regime·Change: From Post-Authoritarianism to Populism to Neo-Liberalism* (London: London School of Economics, 2007); Diane E. Davis, "The Political and Economic Origins of Violence and Insecurity in Contemporary Latin America: Past Trajectories and Future Prospects," in *Violent Democracies in Latin America,* ed. Enrique Desmond Arias and Daniel M. Goldstein (Durham: Duke University Press, 2010), 35–62.

86. Lerner, *El impacto de la modernidad,* 124; Federico Navarrete, "Foto-Violencia en México," *Poliester* 4:13 (1995): 16–25; Medina, *"Alarma!"*

87. *La Prensa,* 22 Jan. 1957, pp. 18, 35; *La Prensa,* 16 Mar. 1932, p. 5; *La Voz de Sinaloa,* 3 Jul. 1963, 1; *La Prensa,* 15 Mar. 1955, pp. 20, 38; *La Prensa,* 12 Mar. 1957, p. 9.

88. *Detectives* 1:2 (22 Aug. 1932): 11; *Detectives* 1:9 (10 Oct. 1932): 4.

89. "Son los verdugos de la frontera! Odiosos patrulleros," *Alarma!* 350 (4 Jan. 1970): 14; "Justicia: ¿Cuánto vales?," *Don Roque* (Apizaco, Tlaxcala) 1:1 (17 Feb. 1946): 4; "Atropellos a granel de la POLICIA LOCAL," *Don Roque* (Apizaco, Tlaxcala) 1:7 (31 Mar. 1946): 4; *La Voz de Sinaloa,* 1 Jul. 1963, pp. 1, 3.

90. Téllez Vargas and Garmabella, *¡Reportero de policía!*, 165. Contradicting the police also raised sales. "Versión taquigráfica de las declaraciones rendidas por los CC. Luis Novaro y Miguel Gil en la sesión efectuada por el consejo de administración el día 3 de noviembre de 1942," AGN, SCEP, leg. 2. Similar competition with the police in Spencer, *The Yellow Journalism*, 1, 39.

91. Servín, *D.F. Confidencial*, 57.

92. Ibid., 48–49; Michel de Certeau, *The Practice of Everyday Life*, trans. Steven Rendall (Berkeley: University of California Press, 1984).

93. AGN ARC, 541/676. Another example in AGN MAC, 541/57. These letters, almost two thousand per presidential period between Cárdenas and López Mateos, are catalogued under "Homicidio" in presidential archives at the AGN. Police investigators also included clippings among their notes, or sent hundreds of copies of Mexico City newspapers to other cities in order to help find and capture suspects still at large. AHDF, JP, ISSS, c. 12, exp. 80, 1957; AHDF, JP, ISSS, c. 10, exp. 65, 1948; AHDF, JP, ISSS, c. 12, exp. 80, 1957; *Alarma!* 371 (10 Jun. 1970): 8. The police using the press in Amy Chazkel, *Laws of Chance: Brazil's Clandestine Lottery and the Making of Urban Public Life* (Durham: Duke University Press, 2011), chap. 6.

94. *La Prensa,* 2 Mar. 1932, p. 3. On the way simultaneity of different events created a narrative; Pelizzon and West, *Tabloid, Inc.,* 58–60. On traffic accidents, *El Universal Gráfico,* 3 Jan. 1955, p. 5; *El Universal Gráfico,* 1 Jan. 1955, p. 1; *La Prensa,* 9 Mar. 1932, p. 2; *El Universal Gráfico,* 1 Jan. 1937, p. 1; *El Sol del Pacífico* (Mazatlán), 4 Nov. 1963, p. 1; *La Prensa,* 11 Mar. 1957, p. 20. On suicides caused by "penosa enfermedad," *La Prensa,* 13 Mar. 1932, p. 1.

95. Jerome Bruner, "The Narrative Construction of Reality," *Critical Inquiry* 18:1 (1991): 1–21. The truth, therefore, is not a transparent relationship between language and events. Damián Fernández Pedemonte, *La violencia del relato: Discurso periodístico y casos policiales* (Buenos Aires: La Crujía Ediciones, 2001), 23. On reality as a way to organize life I follow, in general lines, Jürgen Habermas, *Moral Consciousness and Communicative Action* (Cambridge: MIT Press, 1990); Habermas, *The Theory of Communicative Action,* vol. 1, *Reason and the Rationalization of Society* (Boston: Beacon Press, 1984).

96. "Encuesta relámpago: ¿Es posible la regeneración del delincuente? ¿Cómo puede lograrse?" Miguel Roa, *La Prensa,* 24 Apr. 1934, p. 8; Gabriela Torres-Mazuera, "La delincuencia como conflicto político en la prensa de la ciudad de México 1994–1996," *Estudios Políticos, Medellín* 30 (June 2007): 16, 18. Opinions in favor of death penalty in Prof. Juan B. Sepúlveda Lozano, "Escuela de padres de familia," *Revista de Policía* 23:281 (Jul. 1964): 30–31.

97. *Alarma!* 361 (1 Apr. 1970): 23, 28, 31; *Alarma!* 352 (28 Jan. 1970): 8; *La Prensa,* 3 Sept. 1932, pp. 2, 15; *El Universal Gráfico,* 7 Jan. 1937, p. 1; *Alarma!* 350 (14 Jan. 1970): 6, 9; *Amanecer* (Querétaro), 4 Mar. 1959, p. 6; *Alarma!* 353 (4 Feb. 1970): 39–40; *Alarma!* 371 (10 Jun. 1970): 8.

98. *Alarma!* 350 (14 Jan. 1970): 19. For portraits see also *Argos* 1:7 (Feb. 1945): 1.

99. *Cuidado con el hampa,* Colección Televisa Radio, Fonoteca Nacional. Other radio shows included *La policía siempre vigila* and *El que la hace la paga.*

100. *Alarma!* 351 (28 Jan. 1970): 2. On the uses of information Oscar Lewis, *Five Families: Mexican Case Studies in the Culture of Poverty* (New York: New American Library, 1959), 179–81.

101. Ricardo Ojeda to Manuel Mendoza, 17 Feb. 1957, AHDF, JP, ISSS, c. 12, exp. 80, 1957. Rewards were also offered. *La Prensa,* 28 Apr. 1934, p. 6. The number of traffic accidents grew very fast between the 1940s and 1970s. Pablo Piccato, "Estadísticas del crimen en México: Series históricas, 1901–2001," 2003, http://www.columbia.edu/~pp143/estadisticascrimen/EstadisticasSigloXX.htm. Examples of images in *La Prensa,* 6 Mar. 1959, p. 1. On fear, Rossana Reguillo, "The Oracle in the City: Beliefs, Practices, and Symbolic Geographies," *Social Text* 81:4 (2004): 35–46.

102. *La Prensa,* 25 Mar. 1959, p. 9; *La Prensa,* 8 May 1934, p. 11; *La Prensa,* 13 Mar. 1959, p. 25. On anonymous mail, *La Prensa,* 8 May 1934, p. 11. Some published letters were about officials. *La Prensa,* 25 Mar. 1959, p. 9.

103. *Detectives* 1:8 (8 Sept. 1959): 12–13. Examples in *La Prensa,* 2 Mar. 1957, pp. 20–21; *La Prensa,* 5 Mar. 1957, p. 9; *La Prensa,* 7 Mar. 1957, p. 9; *La Prensa,* 8 Mar. 1957, p. 9; *La Prensa,* 10 Mar. 1957, pp. 9, 41; *La Prensa,* 11 Mar. 1957, p. 9; *La Prensa,* 25 Jan. 1957, p. 10; *Revista de Policía* 24:285 (Nov. 1964): 20; *Detectives* (1:3) 7 Jul. 1959: 4–5; *La Prensa,* 7 Sept. 1954, pp. 23, 24; *La Prensa,* 19 Sept. 1954, p. 40; AGN, ARC, 542.1/74; *La Prensa,* 11 Mar. 1957, p. 9; *Alarma!* 872 (16 Jan. 1980): 16–17; Téllez Vargas and Garmabella, *¡Reportero de policía!,* 261–62; *La Prensa,* 22 Jan. 1957, pp. 12, 18; *La Prensa,* 20 Aug. 1954, pp. 2, 10; *La Prensa,* 25 Jan. 1957, p. 10. Others dealt with urban problems such as neglected potholes, dumpsters, or lost children. *Alarma!* 353 (4 Feb. 1970): 39–40; *Alarma!* 371 (10 Jun. 1970): 8; *La Prensa,* 25 Mar. 1959, p. 9. Similar role in U.S. newspapers in Torres-Mazuera, "La delincuencia como conflicto," 113.

104. *La Prensa,* 28 Apr. 1934, p. 6.

105. *La Prensa,* 27 Apr. 1934, p. 3; *La Prensa,* 23 Jan. 1957, p. 3; *La Prensa,* 24 Jan. 1957, p. 9.

106. *Detective* 1:29 (18 Apr. 1932): 2.

107. *Alarma!* 349 (7 Jan. 1970): 1, 3; *Alarma!* 1 (17 Apr. 1963): 1.

108. Queja de Severo Fragoso, AHDF, GDF, Oficina Central de Quejas, f. 1, p. 2.

109. See for example the case of Olympic medalist, murderer, and drug trafficker Humberto Mariles. Brocca, *Nota roja 60's,* 120; Monsiváis, *Los mil y un velorios,* 38–39. Novels that used the same resource were popular. See for example Luis Spota, *La mitad oscura* (Mexico City: Grijalbo, 1982); Vicente Leñero, *Asesinato: El doble crimen de los Flores Muñoz* (Mexico: Plaza y Janés, 1988); Paco Ignacio Taibo and Víctor Ronquillo, *El caso Molinet* (Mexico City: Difusión Editorial, 1992).

110. Donoso Pareja, *Picaresca de la nota roja,* 77–89, 37–44, 10, 19. In the 1950s U.S. tabloids began to include stories about UFOs and other paranormal phenomena, with retouched or staged images. Pelizzon and West, *Tabloid, Inc.,* 60.

111. *Alarma!* 361 (1 Apr. 1970): 36; *Alarma!* 367 (13 May 1960): 8; *Alarma!* 354 (11 Feb. 1970): 33–35; *Alarma!* 355 (18 Feb. 1970): 1, 4–6.

112. *La Prensa,* 2 Mar. 1932, pp. 4, 13; *La Prensa,* 3 Mar. 1932, pp. 2, 12; *La Prensa,* 4 Mar. 1932, pp. 2, 13; *La Prensa,* 20 Mar. 1932, pp. 3, 14.

113. *La Prensa,* 29 Apr. 1934, pp. 1, 15.

114. Minutes of assembly, 11 Nov. 1942, AGN, SCEP, leg. 2.

115. Gosserez was sentenced to eight years of confinement in Islas Marías. *La Prensa,* 2 Mar. 1932, pp. 4, 13; *La Prensa,* 3 Mar. 1932,p p. 2, 12; *La Prensa,* 4 Mar. 1932, pp. 2, 13; *La Prensa,* 20 Mar. 1932, pp. 3, 14.

116. On new notions of love Ana Lidia García Peña, "Amor y pasión sexual en el México posrevolucionario: El caso de Eduardo Pallares," in *Amor e historia: La expresión de los afectos en el mundo de ayer* (Mexico City: El Colegio de Mexico, 2013), 245–72; Martha Santillán Esqueda, "Delincuencia femenina: Representación, Prácticas y negociación judicial, Distrito Federal (1940–1954)" (PhD diss., Universidad Nacional Autónoma de México, 2013), 79–80, 306–7, 381. See also Pablo Piccato, *City of Suspects: Crime in Mexico City, 1900–1931* (Durham: Duke University Press, 2001), chap. 5.

117. "Mató a tiros a su esposa un comerciante: Tragedia por celos en Santa María la Ribera," *La Prensa,* 5 Mar. 1957, pp. 20–21, 39; "El pollero autovioudo habla mal de su mujer," *La Prensa,* 7 Mar. 1957, pp. 22, 32.

118. *La Prensa,* 11 Mar. 1957, pp. 21, 36.

119. *Alarma!* 1 (17 Apr. 1963): 27.

120. *El Universal Gráfico,* 31 Dec. 1928, pp. 8–9.

121. Clemente Cámara Ochoa, *Redactor de guardia: Cuentos* (Mexico City, 1955), 140–52.

122. Téllez Vargas and Garmabella, *¡Reportero de policía!,* 22.

123. *La Prensa,* 18 Mar. 1932, p. 1; *La Prensa,* 20 Mar. 1932, p. 3; *La Prensa,* 23 Mar. 1932, p. 3.

124. A similar case in *La Prensa,* 7 Mar. 1959, p. 2. On Cárdenas, Blanco Moheno, *Memorias de un reportero,* 211.

125. *Alarma!* 373 (24 Jun. 1970): 6–7; Servín, *D.F. Confidencial,* 57; Téllez Vargas and Garmabella, *¡Reportero de policía!,* 165. Celebrity reporter Carlos Denegri benefited from such transactions. Scherer García and Monsiváis, *Tiempo de saber,* 24, 165. In France, interviews themselves could become events in press coverage. Kalifa, *L'encre et le sang,* 64.

126. *La Prensa,* 24 Apr. 1934, p. 3; *La Prensa,* 28 Apr. 1934, p. 6; Francisco Martinez Baca and Vergara Manuel, *Estudios de antropología criminal: Memoria que por disposición del superior gobierno del estado de Puebla presentan* (Puebla: Benjamín Lara, 1892).

127. *La Prensa,* 4 Mar. 1932, p. 5. See also *Detective* 1:21 (29 Feb. 1932): 9.

128. Téllez Vargas and Garmabella, *¡Reportero de policía!,* 109, 112, 113, 114; Carlos Roumagnac, *Los criminales en México: Ensayo de psicología criminal* (Mexico City, 1904).

129. *La Prensa,* 1 May 1934, p. 9.

130. Karen Halttunen, *Murder Most Foul: The Killer and the American Gothic Imagination* (Cambridge: Harvard University Press, 1998), 93, 100, 116. See also

Barthes, *Essais critiques*, 188. Even when U.S. reporters abandoned that structure, the presentation of "tantalizing facts" followed a logical order. Spencer, *The Yellow Journalism*, 42–43, 104.

131. Kalifa, *L'encre et le sang*, 290.

132. Cited in Spencer, *The Yellow Journalism*, 105; *La Prensa*, 28 Apr. 1934, p. 18. Criminals' life stories did not necessarily mean, as in *Crítica*, in Buenos Aires, the use of psychological explanations. Sylvia Saítta, *Regueros de tinta: El diario "Crítica" en la década de 1920* (Buenos Aires: Editorial Sudamericana, 1998), 205–6.

133. Monsiváis, *Los mil y un velorios*, 5, 7, 10, 13; Roberson, "Diario de una instructora de baile," *Revista de Policía* 24:286 (Dec. 1964): 24–27, 57–58; *El Universal Gráfico*, 31 Dec. 1928, pp. 8–9.

134. *La Prensa*, 24 Apr. 1934, p. 3. In Mexican narratives, unlike crime stories in France, police detectives did not occupy a prominent place. Kalifa, *L'encre et le sang*, 75.

135. *La Prensa*, 25 Apr. 1932, p. 18.

136. Kalifa, *L'encre et le sang*, 287; Jorge Luis Borges and Adolfo Bioy Casares, *Seis problemas para Don Isidro Parodi* (Buenos Aires: Sur, 1942); "The Mystery of Marie Roget," in Edgar Allan Poe, *The Works of Edgar Allan Poe*, vol. 1, 2000, http://www.gutenberg.org/ebooks/2147.

137. Robert Buffington and Pablo Piccato, "Tales of Two Women: The Narrative Construal of Porfirian Reality," *The Americas* 55:3 (1999): 391–424; Lerner, *El impacto de la modernidad*; Servín, *D.F. Confidencial*, 39, 211.

138. Monsiváis, *Los mil y un velorios*, 29; Rodríguez Munguía, *La otra guerra secreta*, 218.

139. Servín, *D.F. Confidencial*, 207. Examples in *La Prensa*, 1 Mar. 1957, p. 39. On presentation of suspects, Navarrete, "Foto-violencia en México"; Lerner, *El impacto de la modernidad*; interview with Carlos Peláez Fuentes, Mexico City, 31 Jul. 2013.

140. *Alarma!* 353 (14 Feb. 1970): 2.

141. *Alarma!* 353 (4 Feb. 1970): 2–3, 4; *Alarma!* 354 (18 Feb. 1970): 29.

142. Lerner, *El impacto de la modernidad*, 62–67. See "The Photographic Message," in Roland Barthes, *Image, Music, Text: Essays Selected and Translated by Stephen Heath* (London: Fontana Press, 1977); *Revista de Policía* 280 (1 Jun. 1964): 1. On pornography and American gothic, Halttunen, *Murder Most Foul*, 66–67. In Europe, Iain McCalman, *Radical Underworld: Prophets, Revolutionaries and Pornographers in London, 1795–1840* (London: Clarendon, 1992); Lisa Z. Sigel, "Filth in the Wrong People's Hands: Postcards and the Expansion of Pornography in Britain and the Atlantic World, 1880–1914," *Journal of Social History* 33:4 (2000): 859–85; Lynn Hunt, introduction, in Lynn Hunt, ed., *The Invention of Pornography: Obscenity and the Origins of Modernity, 1500–1800* (New York: Zone Books, 1993).

143. Large portrait of suspect in *La Prensa*, 1 Mar. 1934, p. 2. A drawing in *La Prensa*, 6 Mar. 1932, p. 3. A composition with several subjects in *La Prensa*, 3 Mar. 1932, p. 1; *Argos* 3:6 (Jun. 1946): 1, 4; *Detective* 1:1 (10 Oct. 1931): 6–7. Porfirian mug shots in *Gaceta de Policía* 1:9 (17 Dec. 1905): 9. See Lerner, *El impacto de la modernidad*, 44. Collective portrait of drug addicts in *La Prensa*, 19 Feb. 1932, p. 9.

144. *La Prensa,* 28 Apr. 1934, p. 6.

145. Ibid., and back cover.

146. *La Prensa,* 25 Apr. 1934, pp. 3, 18; *La Prensa,* 26 Apr. 1934, pp. 3, 6, 18, 21; *La Prensa,* 29 Apr. 1934, p. 30.

147. *La Prensa,* 28 Apr. 1934, p. 3.

148. Statement by Rosendo Islas Mendoza, 1 Mar. 1932, AHDF, JP, ISSS, c. 2, exp. 9, 1932; *La Prensa,* 1 May 1934, pp. 3, 15.

149. *La Prensa,* 28 Apr. 1938, p. 8; Everard Meade, "La ley fuga y la tribuna improvisada: Extrajudicial Execution and Public Opinion in Mexico City, 1929–1940," paper presented at the colloquium "Crime and Punishment in Latin America: Practices and Representations," University of Colorado, Boulder, October 7 and 8, 2011. A poll of readers in favor of the death penalty in *Detective* 1:23 (21 Mar. 1932): 2.

150. On historical approaches to reason see Jürgen Habermas, "The Public Sphere: An Encyclopedia Article," *New German Critique,* no. 3 (1974): 53; Habermas, *Moral Consciousness; Elías José Palti, La invención de una legitimidad: Razón y retórica en el pensamiento mexicano del siglo XIX (Un estudio sobre las formas del discurso político)* (Mexico City: Fondo de Cultura Económica, 2005), 89, 194–95; François-Xavier Guerra, *Modernidad e independencias: Ensayos sobre las revoluciones hispánicas* (Mexico City: Editorial MAPFRE; Fondo de Cultura Económica, 2000), 23; Rafael Rojas, *La escritura de la independencia: El surgimiento de la opinión pública en México* (Mexico City: Taurus—Centro de Investigación y Docencia Económicas, 2003), 124–25, 84–85; Daniel Gordon, "Philosophy, Sociology, and Gender in the Enlightenment Conception of Public Opinion," *French Historical Studies* 17:4 (1992): 882–911.

151. Trinidad Manuel Chávez to Miguel Ávila Camacho, 28 Apr. 1945, AGN, MAC, -549.44/963. Criticism against another agent who did not file charges against men who defended their honor in *Detective* 1:5 (9 Nov. 1931): 2, 11.

152. *Detectives* 1:20 (27 Dec. 1932): 2. An editorial against impunity on behalf of readers and the people, in *La Prensa,* 7 Jan. 1947, p. 8. Denunciations of false journalists and their powerful patrons in *Alarma* 2:27 (12 May 1951): 4.

153. *La Prensa,* 25 Apr. 1934, p. 3.

154. *La Prensa,* 29 Apr. 1934, p. 6; *La Prensa,* 3 May 1934, pp. 10, 12; *La Prensa,* 4 May 1934, p. 10; *La Prensa,* 5 May 1934, pp. 3, 26. The police report in AHDF, JP, ISSS, c. 3, exp. 20, N/522/1204.

155. Barata and Lara Klahr, *Nota(n) roja,* 42–43. On the loss of quality, Leñero, *Asesinato,* 27, 75, 311; Taibo and Ronquillo, *El caso Molinet,* 49, 97; Vicente Leñero, "Prólogo: La belleza del crimen," in Villadelángel Viñas and Ganado Kim, *El libro rojo,* xxvi; Téllez Vargas and Garmabella, *¡Reportero de policía!,* 34. In the United States something similar happened with tabloids. Pelizzon and West, *Tabloid, Inc.,* 15, 183. *Ovaciones* began publication in 1947; *Esto,* from the García Valseca network, in 1941. Smaller crime sections in industrial newspapers exemplified in *Novedades,* 1 Oct. 1942; *Exélsior,* 15 Mar. 1970, p. 25; *El Universal,* 5 Mar. 1970. See also González Marín, *Prensa y poder político,* 28; Miquel, *Disolvencias,* 171.

156. *La policía siempre vigila* and *Cuidado con el hampa* recordings held at the Fonoteca Nacional, Colección Televisa Radio; Brocca, *Nota roja 60's,* 27. For example of the new style, "Nacho López Tarso maniático sexual: El notable actor desconcierta a todo el mundo," in *De la verdad,* quoted in Donoso Pareja, *Picaresca de la nota roja,* 27–32. Téllez Vargas and Garmabella, *¡Reportero de policía!,* 10. On the contrast between the tone of headlines and the text itself see, for example, *Alarma!* 354 (11 Feb. 1970): 28.

157. Carlos Monsiváis, *A ustedes les consta: Antología de la crónica en México* (Mexico City: ERA, 1980), 334. The TV show in TV Azteca was *Ciudad desnuda.* Televisa competed with it. Daniel C. Hallin, "*La nota roja*: Popular Journalism and the Transition to Democracy in Mexico," in *Tabloid Tales: Global Debates over Media Standards,* ed. Colin Sparks and John Tulloch (Oxford: Rowman and Littlefield, 2000), 268–70.

158. Sparks, "Introduction"; Kalifa, *L'encre et le sang,* 246; Pelizzon and West, *Tabloid, Inc.,* 3, 5, 10, 46; James T. Siegel, *A New Criminal Type in Jakarta: Counter-Revolution Today* (Durham: Duke University Press, 1998); Lila Caimari, *Mientras la ciudad duerme: Pistoleros, policías y periodistas en Buenos Aires, 1920–1945* (Buenos Aires: Siglo Veintiuno Editores, 2012).

159. This relationship is still contingent in contemporary society. John Braithwaite, *Crime, Shame and Reintegration* (New York: Cambridge University Press, 1989).

160. AHDF, JP, ISSS, c. 10, exp. 65, 1948. Editorials on ley fuga in *La Prensa,* 28 Apr. 1934, p. 10, and "El que a hierro mata . . . [a hierro muere]," *La Prensa,* 28 Apr. 1934, pp. 18–20; Téllez Vargas and Garmabella, *¡Reportero de policía!,* 25; Meade, "La ley fuga y la tribuna improvisada."

161. Stanley Cohen, "Crime and Politics: Spot the Difference," *British Journal of Sociology* 47:1 (1996): 1–21; Siegel, *A New Criminal Type.* On the efforts of the emerging national state to impose "monismo jurídico" in Mexico see Elisa Speckman, "Los jueces, el honor y la muerte: Un análisis de la justicia (Ciudad de México, 1871–1931)," *Historia Mexicana* 55:4 (2006): 1435. Engagement with justice has not been part of studies of citizenship in Mexico. Contrast with the literature on transitional justice in Argentina and Chile, for example, where the crimes committed by military regimes offered a more identifiable target and the opportunity to tailor institutions to the search for the truth. Hugo Vezzetti, *Pasado y presente: Guerra, dictadura y sociedad en la Argentina* (Buenos Aires: Siglo XXI, 2002), 21–22; Carlos Santiago Nino, *Radical Evil on Trial* (New Haven: Yale University Press, 1996).

CHAPTER 3. LOST DETECTIVES

1. Dominique Kalifa, *Histoire des détectives privés en France, 1832–1942* (Paris: Nouveau Monde, 2007), 9, 11–17, 104–6, 161, 201; Robert P. Weiss, "The Emergence and Transformation of Private Detective Industrial Policing in the United States,

1850–1940," *Crime and Social Justice* 9–10 (1978): 35–48; Luc Boltanski, *Enigmes et complots: Une enquête à propos d'enquêtes* (Paris: Gallimard, 2012), 100, 113.

2. Jacinto Barrera Bassols, *El caso Villavicencio: Violencia y poder en el porfiriato* (Mexico City: Alfaguara, 1997).

3. Eduardo Téllez Vargas and José Ramón Garmabella, *¡Reportero de policía! El Güero Téllez* (Mexico City: Ediciones Océano, 1982), 263; Ilan Stavans, *Antihéroes: México y su novela policial* (Mexico City: Joaquín Mortiz, 1993), 79–83; "Veinticuatro años de '*Revista de Policía*,'" *Revista de Policía* 24:288 (Feb. 1963): 6–8.

4. *Detectives* 1:4 (5 Sept. 1932): 12–14; José Marín Castillo, "Una antigua teoría," *Revista de Policía* 23:283 (Sept. 1964): 27.

5. Letters from Juan González Alejo, Omealco Ver., 30 Jun. 1962, and Antonio Robles Oropeza, Paredones, BC, May 1964, to Federal District police, AHDF, JP ISSS, c. 13, exp. 99, 1962.

6. Carlos Isla, *El mejor caso de Valente Quintana: Los "corta mechas"* (Mexico City: Fontamara, 2004), 16. For the growing international production of handbooks, Kalifa, *Histoire des détectives privés*, 167; Carlos Monsiváis, "Prólogo," in *La obligación de asesinar: Novelas y cuentos policiacos* (Mexico City: M. A. Porrúa, 1998), 13; *Argos, órgano de la Unión Nacional de Detectives y Técnicos Policiales* 3:1 (Jan. 1946): 5–6; *Selecciones Policiacas y de Misterio* 4:82 (Oct. 1950): 5.

7. *La Prensa,* 13 Mar. 1957, p. 23. For a school in Culiacán, *Argos* 3:1 (Jan. 1946): 14; courses offered by the Unión Nacional de Detectives y Técnicos Policiales, at the "Maestro Roumagnac" school, advertised in *Argos* 4:12 (Dec. 1947): 3. Roumagnac, a well-known Porfirian criminologist, created his own technical school and published a textbook in 1923. Stavans, *Antihéroes*, 73; Carlos Roumagnac, *Elementos de policía científica: Obra de texto para la Escuela Científica de Policía de México* (Mexico City: Botas, 1923). On textbooks, Kalifa, *Histoire des détectives privés*, 176–80.

8. AGN, DGG, 2.014(29)22, c. 2, exp. 15, f. 28.

9. For an agency that provided "investigaciones privadas, solvencias, localizaciones, vigilancias, conducta y antecedentes personales" associated with the "International Directory of Detective Agencies Association de New York City USA," see *Argos* 3:1 (Jan. 1946): 16.

10. Rodolfo Sweegers to Secretario de Gobernación, 1 Feb. 1934, AGN, DGG, 2.014(29)748, c. 2, exp. 6. For the authorization granted to the American Secret Service, see R. Zaleta Cuevas to Secretario de Gobernación, 12 Apr. 1934, AGN, DGG, 2.014(29)28, c. 2, exp. 9. For a request denied see Sobre solicitud para establecer el Servicio de Investigación Comercial Lic. José Benitez, Oficina Jurídica del Gobierno DF, 21 Jan. 1932, AGN, DGG, 2.014(29)22, c. 2, exp. 15. Other requests in AGN, DGG, 2.014(29)23, c. 2. exp. 14. On the bad reputation of private investigators Octavio B. Barona to Secretario de Gobernación, 10 Feb. 1934, AGN, DGG, 2.014(29)22, c. 2, exp. 15. Another request in AGN, DGG, 2.014(29)22, c. 2, exp. 15; AGN, DGG,2.014(29)20, c. 2, exp. 17.

11. Letters of merchants and musicians' organizations attached to Juan Cachú Ramírez, Juan J. Gómez, Benjamin Vélez, José Pedroza al Secr. de Gobernación, 14 Mar. 1933, AGN, DGG, 2.014(29)22, c. 2, exp. 15, f. 16.

12. Cristóbal Trápaga, Mexico City, to Secretaría de Gobernación, 24 Oct. 1933. Agencia Polmex's request in AGN, DGG, 2.014(29)22, c. 2, exp. 15.

13. Enrique Jiménez D. to Secretario de Gobernación, 28 Jul. 1934, AGN, DGG, 2.014(29)27, c. 2, exp. 10.

14. Reglamento para los investigadores, detectives y policías privados o pertenecientes a organismos de servicio público descentralizado o concesionado, *Diario Oficial de la Federación* 170:35 (13 Oct. 1948): 1–4; AGN, DGG, 2.014(29)28, c. 2, exp. 9; Alfonso Quiroz Cuarón, *Asaltos a bancos en Venezuela y América* (Mexico City: Morales Hermanos, 1964), 175; Diane Davis, "Policing and Regime Transition: From Postauthoritarianism to Populism to Neoliberalism," in *Violence, Coercion, and State-Making in Twentieth-Century Mexico: The Other Half of the Centaur,* ed. Wil Pansters (Stanford: Stanford University Press, 2012).

15. *Argos* 1:5–6 (Jan. 1945): 6, 8–13.

16. *Argos* 3:3 (Mar. 1946): 9; *Argos* 3:2 (Feb. 1946): 12–13; *Argos* 3:1 (Jan. 1946): 4.

17. *Argos* 3:2 (Feb. 1946): 12–18. On the complaints for the theft by police agents, Téllez Vargas and Garmabella, *¡Reportero de policía!,* 115–20.

18. Isla, *El mejor caso,* 11–13. Valente Quintana, *Memorias de Valente Quintana* (Mexico City: Ediciones Populares, 1961), 6, 126–27, 134, 168; *Detectives* 1:6 (19 Sept. 1932): 15.

19. *Lebanon Daily News* (Lebanon, Pa.), 11 Nov. 1929, p. 8; *San Antonio Express,* 28 Jan. 1930, p. 3.

20. Carlos Monsiváis, *Los mil y un velorios: Crónica de la nota roja* (Mexico City: Consejo Nacional para la Cultura y las Artes; Alianza Editorial, 1994), 21; Juan Manuel Aurrecoechea, *Puros cuentos: La historia de la historieta en México* (Mexico City: Consejo Nacional para la Cultura y las Artes, Dirección General de Publicaciones, 1988), 3:292, 210, 295. As a boxing promoter in Texas see *Chicago Daily Tribune,* 14 Feb. 1929, p. 13; *Los Angeles Times,* 11 Feb. 1932, p. A11.

21. Quintana, *Memorias de Valente Quintana,* 10–11, 18, 25, 39, 176, quotation on 145. Other police detectives liked to use disguises. *Novedades,* 11 Oct. 1942, p. 10, for example.

22. *Kerrville Times,* 29 Dec. 1929, p. 4.

23. Gonzalo N. Santos, *Memorias* (Mexico City: Grijalbo, 1984), 323.

24. Quintana, *Memorias de Valente Quintana,* 72; María Toral de De León, *Memorias de María Toral de De León, madre de José de León Toral* (Mexico City: Editorial Tradición, 1972), 134; Alfonso Quiroz Cuarón and Samuel Máynez Puente, *Psicoanálisis del magnicidio* (Mexico City: Editorial Jurídica Mexicana, 1965), 110.

25. *Excélsior,* 17 Mar. 1951, p. 1, 9.

26. Quintana, *Memorias de Valente Quintana,* 202; Isla, *El mejor caso de Valente Quintana,* 149.

27. Jose Marín Castillo, "Otro triunfo resonante del servicio secreto," *Revista de Policía* 25:291 (May 1965): 33. On the lack of regulation, Enrique Jiménez D. to Secretario de Gobernación, 28 Jul. 1934, AGN, DGG, 2.014(29)27, c. 2, exp. 10. Its agents "were not exactly saints but at least kept criminals at bay." Its name was

changed in 1972 and it was dissolved in 1983. "El Servicio Secreto mexicano," *Foro extraoficial de la fuerza aérea mexicana,* no. 13, Sept. 2007, accessed 26 Jan. 2015, http://extrafam.mforos.com/365894/6254085-servicio-secreto-mexicano/; "Veinticuatro años de *'Revista de Policía,'" Revista de Policía* 24:288 (Feb. 1963): 6–8; editorial, *Detectives* 1:2 (23 Jun. 1959): 16–17. As a intelligence agency, Sergio Aguayo Quezada, *La charola: Una historia de los servicios de inteligencia en México* (Mexico City: Grijalbo, 2001), 74. Its members could easily be fired. *Argos* 1:7 (Feb. 1945): 3, 16. An example of brutal methods in *Detectives* 1:3 (7 Jul. 1959): 9.

28. *Alarma* (4 Jun. 1953): 28–29. The break on the Cárdenas case came thanks to agent Ana María Dorantes, *Últimas Noticias,* 11 Sept. 1942, p. 1. On training, *Policía Internacional* 1:3 (Apr. 1948): 8–9; Téllez Vargas and Garmabella, *¡Reportero de policía!,* 257. A school in Culiacán from 1934 in *Argos* 3:1 (Jan. 1946): 14. On the need to have experience and know the criminals, Jesús Mata Montemayor, "Temas policíacos," *Argos* 3:13 (Jan. 1947): 7.

29. "Nuevas quejas del personal de policía metropolitana," *La Prensa,* 13 Feb. 1932, p. 4; *El universal,* 3 Aug. 1929, sec. 2, p. 1.

30. AHDF, JP ISSS, c. 13, exp. 99, 1962. Two policemen killed in a traffic stop in *Policía Internacional* 1 (1 Sept. 1948): 1, 4; *Policía Internacional* 14 (1 Apr. 1948): 6–7.

31. The brother of a murder victim who was asked by police for money to arrest the killer pleaded with President López Mateos, "Mr President: is it true that in Mexico justice is only for the rich and the poor have to get with their own hands?" José Antonio Boneta and Fernández Guerra to Adolfo López Mateos, 20 Jul. 1960, AGN, ALM, 541/290; Téllez Vargas and Garmabella, *¡Reportero de policía!,* 117.

32. *Detectives* 1:1 (9 Jun. 1959): 24. For the perks of a police job in recent times see Aguayo Quezada, *La charola,* 78–79, 88.

33. *Argos* 3:6 (Jun. 1946): 3.

34. *Policía Internacional* 2:18 (Feb. 1949): 5.

35. José Marín Castillo, "Una antigua teoría," *Revista de Policía* 23:283 (Sept. 1964): 27, 30.

36. *Policía Internacional* 5:4 (May 1948): 9.

37. Resourcefulness in Agente Joaquín Soto Villegas to Director Servicio Secreto, 9 Jul. 1962, AHDF, JP ISSS, c. 13, exp. 99, 1962. On technical issues Téllez Vargas and Garmabella, *¡Reportero de policía!,* 168, 38, 236, 286. Few cases saw the use of fingerprints collected at the crime scene. *El Universal,* 5 Aug. 1929, sec. 3, p. 1.

38. "Veinticuatro años de *'Revista de Policía,'" Revista de Policía* 24:288 (Feb. 1963): 6–8, 57; *Argos* 4:3 (Mar. 1947): 3; *Policía Internacional* 5:53 (15 Nov. 1963): 38. A literary reference in José Martínez de la Vega, *Péter Pérez, detective de Peralvillo y anexas* (Mexico City: Joaquín Mortiz, 1994), 83. Competition in Jose Marín Castillo, "Otro triunfo resonante del Servicio Secreto," *Revista de Policía* 25:291 (May 1965): 59; AHDF, JP, ISSS, c. 12, exp. 88, 1959. Secret Service stepping aside to let police examine the crime scene, but continuing with their investigation, in Col. Manuel Mendoza Domínguez to Gral de Div. Jefe de la Policía del DF, 18 Jan. 1957, p. 62, and s. AHDF, JP, ISSS, c. 12, exp. 80, 1957.

39. Téllez Vargas and Garmabella, *¡Reportero de policía!,* 168.

40. *Alarma!* 2:32 (12 Jun. 1959): 1–2.

41. Manuel Rojas to Vicente Gonzalez, Jefe Policía, 18 Jul. 1936, AHDF, JP ISSS, c. 4, exp. 30, legs. 1 and 2, 1936; *La Prensa,* 19 Aug. 1954, p. 25. Agents fired for using it in *Alarma* (4 Jun. 1953): 26–27. As feature of judicial investigations, Gabriel Trujillo Muñoz, *Testigos de cargo* (Mexico City: CONACULTA-CECUT, 2000), 41. Denounced in *Argos* 3:9 (Sept. 1946): 3. See also Monsiváis, *Los mil y un velorios,* 17. Torture was also applied against Cristero rebels. María Elena Sodi de Pallares, *Demetrio Sodi y su tiempo* (Mexico City, 1947), 206. On the use of torture among judiciary police today see Elena Azaola Garrido and Miguel Angel Ruiz Torres, *Investigadores de papel: Poder y derechos humanos entre la policía judicial de la Ciudad de México* (Mexico City: Distribuciones Fontamara, 2009), 61.

42. Manuel Rojas to Vicente Gonzalez, 18 Jul. 1936, AHDF, JP ISSS, c. 4, exp. 30, legs. 1 and 2, 1936; anonymous letter to Inspector General de Policía, undated, AHDF, JP, ISSS, c. 2, exp. 9, 1932, 194, p. 54. Recent use of torture for same purposes in Guillermo Zepeda Lecuona, *Crimen sin castigo: Procuración de justicia penal y ministerio público en México* (Mexico City: Fondo de Cultura Económica-Cidac, 2004), 330–34; Paul Chevigny, *Edge of the Knife: Police Violence in the Americas* (New York: New Press, 1995), 240–42; *La Prensa,* 5 Sept. 1954, pp. 23–24.

43. *Alarma!* (4 Jun. 1953): 26–27; *El jurado de Toral y la Madre Conchita: Lo que se dijo y lo que no se dijo en el sensacional juicio; Versión taquigráfica textual* (Mexico City, 1928), 1:53–59, 62, 100; Toral de De León, *Memorias de María Toral,* 60, 71; *Detectives* 1:13 (26 Jan. 1960): 3; Téllez Vargas and Garmabella, *¡Reportero de policía!,* 156; Víctor Velásquez, *El caso Alarcón* (Mexico City, 1955), 46.

44. Federico Finchelstein, *The Ideological Origins of the Dirty War: Fascism, Populism, and Dictatorship in Twentieth Century Argentina* (New York: Oxford University Press, 2014).

45. *Detectives* 1:8 (31 Jul. 1959): 19.

46. *Alerta: Revista de Detectives* (Guadalajara) 3:33 (Feb. 1951): 15; a 1930 murder case in AGN, ATSJDF, 23196, 17. The Code of Penal Procedures required confessions to be supported by other evidence, made by adults in full knowledge of their own deeds, in front of an officer of the judicial police, and ratified in front of a judge. For a sentence that rejects accounts changed by suspects, AGN, ATSJDF, 23196, 237v–38. *La Prensa,* 18 Sept. 1954, pp. 2, 30. The wife of a suspect who went to the police in Apizaco, Tlaxcala, to find him was raped, beaten, and tortured, according to her account. Manuela López to Miguel Aleman Valdés, AGN, MAV, 541/347. A late use of the simulated torture of relatives in Vicente Leñero, *Asesinato: El doble crimen de los Flores Muñoz* (Mexico City: Plaza y Janés, 1988), 316–17. AHDF, JP, ISSS, c. 11, exp. 75, 1954; Velásquez, *El caso Alarcón.* Despite penal code reforms, confessions obtained under torture continue to be accepted in penal courts. "En México, confesiones bajo tortura: Amnistía Internacional," *Proceso,* 16 Dec. 2011, http://www.proceso.com.mx/?p = 291699.

47. Torture and death threats in AGN, ATSJDF, 23196, 155v. See also Orlando Balderas Martínez, "José de León Toral: Proceso histórico-jurídico (1928–1929)"

(BA thesis, Universidad Nacional Autónoma de México, n.d.), 114; *La Prensa*, 14 Jul. 1936, p. 3.

48. He obtained the injunction. AHDF, JP, ISSS, c. 11, exp. 75, 1954.

49. Rafael Cornejo Armenta to Procurador de la República, 1936, AHDF, JP ISSS, c. 4, exp. 30, legs. 1 and 2, 1936; Ezequiel Padill Rechy to Vicente González, 5 Jul. 1936, AHDF, JP ISSS, c. 4, exp. 30, legs. 1 and 2, 1936.

50. Monsiváis, *Los mil y un velorios*, 29.

51. *La Prensa*, 11 Jul. 1936, p. 10.

52. "Sogas siniestras en la penitenciaría," *Alarma* (13 May 1953): 21–22, 24.

53. Gral. José Juan Méndez, AHDF, JP, ISSS, c. 3, exp. 20, N/522/1204.

54. *La Prensa*, 25 Apr. 1934, p. 3, 18; *La Prensa*, 26 Apr. 1934, pp. 3, 6, 18, 21; *La Prensa*, 29 Apr. 1934, p. 30.

55. Téllez Vargas and Garmabella, *¡Reportero de policía!*, 25; Vito Alessio Robles, "La ley fuga," *La Prensa* (San Antonio), 1 Sept. 1933, p. 3.

56. Téllez Vargas and Garmabella, *¡Reportero de policía!*, 27; Jesse Lerner, *El impacto de la modernidad: Fotografía criminalística en la Ciudad de México* (Mexico City: Turner; Consejo Nacional para la Cultura y las Artes; Instituto Nacional de Antropología e Historia; Editorial Océano, 2007), 76–77. Prisoners could also suffer a similar fate on the islands. Elena Azaola Garrido and Cristina José Yacamán, *Las mujeres olvidadas: Un estudio sobre la situación actual de las cárceles de mujeres en la República Mexicana* (Mexico City: El Colegio de México, 1996), 76, 91.

57. *La Prensa*, 19 Mar. 1932, p. 3; Téllez Vargas and Garmabella, *¡Reportero de policía!*, 27.

58. Everard Meade, "La ley fuga y la tribuna improvisada: Extrajudicial Execution and Public Opinion in Mexico City, 1929–1940," paper presented at the colloquium "Crime and Punishment in Latin America: Practices and Representations," University of Colorado, Boulder, October 7 and 8, 2011. A broader treatment of the ideas below in Pablo Piccato, "Ley Fuga as Justice: The Consensus around Extrajudicial Violence in Twentieth-Century Mexico," in *Violence and Crime in Latin America*, ed. Gema Santamaría and David Carey (Norman: University of Oklahoma Press, 2017)..

59. *La Prensa*, 28 Apr. 1934, p. 10; *Excélsior*, 11 Oct. 1929, p. 5; *La Prensa*, 7 Mar. 1932, p. 5; *La Prensa*, 16 Mar. 1932, p. 5.

60. Querido Moheno, *Procesos célebres: Rubin: Discurso en defensa de la acusada* (Mexico City: Botas, 1925), 177, 187, 168; similar arguments used in another case, in Pablo Piccato, "The Girl Who Killed a Senator: Femininity and the Public Sphere in Post-Revolutionary Mexico," in *True Stories of Crime in Modern Mexico* (Albuquerque: University of New Mexico Press, 2009), 128–53. On the political and communicative uses of lynching see Daniel M. Goldstein, *The Spectacular City Violence and Performance in Urban Bolivia* (Durham: Duke University Press, 2004); Christopher Krupa, "Histories in Red: Ways of Seeing Lynching in Ecuador," *American Ethnologist* 36:1 (1 Feb. 2009): 20–39. Isaac Mendicoa Juárez was an emblematic case: a bandit from the southern suburbs of the capital whose death by ley fuga in 1933 illustrated the influence of the press, public frustration with light sentences, and

the inability of prisons to rehabilitate criminals. Saydi Núñez Cetina, "El caso de el 'Tigre del Pedregal,'" in *Crimen y justicia en la historia de México: Nuevas miradas,* ed. Elisa Speckman and Salvador Cárdenas (Mexico City: Suprema Corte de Justicia de la Nación, 2011), 315–53.

61. *La Prensa,* 16 Mar. 1932, p. 5.

62. Clippings, n.d., AHDF, JP, ISSS, c. 10, exp. 65, 1948.

63. Clippings from *Últimas Noticias* de *Excélsior,* 27 Feb. 1948, AHDF, JP, ISSS, c. 10, exp. 65, 1948.

64. Fernando Novoa to Alemán, Federal District, 21 Feb. 1948, AGN, MAV, 541/347.

65. AHDF, JP ISSS, c. 4, exp. 30, legs. 1 and 2, 1936.

66. *La Prensa,* 28 Feb. 1948, p. 1.

67. *La Prensa,* 27 Feb. 1948, p. 1; *La Prensa,* 28 Feb. 1948, p. 3. A judicial official declared that, even if the police explanation was true, nobody would believe it. The same was believed by readers surveyed by the newspaper. *La Prensa,* 3 May 1934, pp. 2, 3.

68. Paulino Nava Olivarria, Acaponeta Nay, 3 Aug. 1962, to Police Chief, AHDF, JP ISSS, c. 13, exp. 99, 1962.

69. Arturo Villarreal Palo, "Ministerio público y policía de investigación en México: Una reforma incompleta," *Letras jurídicas* 5 (fall 2007); Diane E. Davis, "The Political and Economic Origins of Violence and Insecurity in Contemporary Latin America: Past Trajectories and Future Prospects," in *Violent Democracies in Latin America,* ed. Enrique Desmond Arias and Daniel M. Goldstein (Durham: Duke University Press, 2010), 35–62.

70. Nick Carter, "Cazando a Teodoro Villanueva," *Detectives* 1:3 (29 Aug. 1932): 15. A similar argument, by police chief José Mijares Palencia, in *El Universal,* 5 Jul. 1930, sec. 2, p. 1.

71. AHDF, JP ISSS, c. 4, exp. 30, legs. 1 and 2, 1936.

72. Azaola Garrido and Ruiz Torres, *Investigadores de papel,* 20, 24, 47, 56, 67. A first-person account of torture techniques in J. L. Trueba Lara, *Los primeros en morir: Biografía de un policía mexicano* (Mexico City: Nueva Imagen, 1996), 43; Gustavo Fondevilla, "Controlling the Madrinas: The Police Informer Management and Control System in Mexico," *Police Journal* 86 (2014): 116–42.

CHAPTER 4. HORRIBLE CRIMES

1. *El Universal,* 15 Jun. 1930, p. 1. On the museum, Director de la Escuela de Policía to Prof. Benjamín A. Martínez, 16 Jun. 1932, AHDF, JP, ISSS, c. 2, exp. 9, 1932. On police museums see Amy Chazkel, "Police Museums in Latin America: Preface," *Radical History Review,* no. 113 (20 Mar. 2012): 127–33.

2. Ana Luisa Luna, *La crónica policíaca en México: Nota roja 40s* (Mexico City: Diana, 1993), 92; *Últimas Noticias,* 30 Sept. 1942, p. 1.

3. *Detectives* 1:10 (17 Oct. 1932): 4; Eduardo Téllez Vargas and José Ramón Garmabella, *¡Reportero de policía! El Güero Téllez* (Mexico City: Ediciones Océano,

1982), 105–8; Myriam Laurini and Rolo Díez, *Nota roja 70's: La crónica policiaca en la Ciudad de México* (Mexico City: Diana, 1993), 67.

4. The recent historiography on Mexican criminals is expanding and has generated remarkable products; to cite a few: Lisette Rivera Reynaldos, Elisa Speckman, Saydi Núñez Cetina, Everard Meade. On murder as a source for diverse cultural products, a sample is *Novedades*, 10 Jan. 1942, p. 9; Victoria Brocca, *Nota roja 60's: La crónica policiaca en la Ciudad de México* (Mexico City: Diana, 1993), 85, 94, 95; Vicente Leñero, "Prólogo, La belleza del crimen," in Gerardo Villadelángel Viñas and Edgardo Ganado Kim, *El libro rojo, continuación. I, 1868–1928* (Mexico City: Fondo de Cultura Económica, 2008), xxvi, xxvii; J.M. Servín, *D.F. confidencial: Crónicas de delincuentes, vagos y demás gente sin futuro* (Oaxaca: Editorial Almadia, 2010), 37, 51.

5. An example in *La Prensa*, 9 Mar. 1932, pp. 2, 15. On crimes of passion Pablo Piccato, *City of Suspects: Crime in Mexico City, 1900–1931* (Durham: Duke University Press, 2001), 106; *Gaceta de Policía* 1:14 (11 Mar. 1906): 2–3. These crimes attracted more attention before the revolution. Carlos Roumagnac, *Crímenes sexuales y pasionales: Estudios de psicología morbosa*, vol. 1, *Crímenes sexuales* (Mexico City: Librería de Ch. Bouret, 1906).

6. Querido Moheno, *Procesos célebres: Honorio Rodríguez, discurso de defensa* (Mexico City: Botas, 1928), 193, 196, 200; *La Prensa*, 2 Mar. 1932, pp. 4, 13; *La Prensa*, 3 Mar. 1932, pp. 2, 12, 20; *La Prensa*, 4 Mar. 1932, pp. 2, 13.

7. *La Prensa*, 17 May 1941, pp. 2, 8.

8. *Alarma!* 356 (25 Feb. 1970): 29.

9. Robert Buffington, *Criminal and Citizen in Modern Mexico* (Lincoln: University of Nebraska Press, 2000); Pablo Piccato, "La construcción de una perspectiva científica: Miradas porfirianas a la criminalidad," *Historia Mexicana* 187:1 (1997): 133–81; Elisa Speckman, *Crimen y castigo: Legislación penal, interpretaciones de la criminalidad y administración de justicia (Ciudad de México, 1872–1910)* (Mexico City: El Colegio de México, 2002).

10. Both were sentenced to death and executed during the last years of the Porfiriato. Elisa Speckman Guerra, *Del Tigre de Santa Julia, la princesa italiana y otras historias: Sistema judicial, criminalidad y justicia en la Ciudad de México (siglos XIX y XX)* (Mexico City: UNAM-INACIPE, 2014); Pablo Piccato, "El Chalequero, or 'the Mexican Jack the Ripper': The Meanings of Sexual Violence in Turn-of-the-Century Mexico City," *Hispanic American Historical Review* 81:3–4 (2001): 623–51.

11. Speckman Guerra, *Del Tigre de Santa Julia*, chap. 2.

12. Matt Houlbrook, "Commodifying the Self Within: Ghosts, Libels, and the Crook Life Story in Interwar Britain," *Journal of Modern History* 85:2 (June 2013): 321–63. See also Dominique Kalifa, *L'encre et le sang: Récits de crimes et société à la belle epoque* (Paris: Fayard, 1995), 123, 188; Roland Barthes, *Ensayos críticos* (Buenos Aires: Seix y Barral, 2003), 271. On murder as education and edification, Eugenia Lean, *Public Passions: The Trial of Shi Jianqiao and the Rise of Popular Sympathy in Republican China* (Berkeley: University of California Press, 2007), 17, 27.

13. See for example Leo D'Olmo, *El crimen del garage* (Mexico City: La Prensa, n.d.), 28–29; María Elvira Bermúdez, *Muerte a la zaga* (Tlahuapan, Puebla: Premià, 1985), 28, 29; María Elvira Bermúdez, *Cuento policiaco mexicano: Breve antología* (Mexico City: UNAM, 1987), 230–31; Antonio Helú, *La obligación de asesinar: Novelas y cuentos policiacos* (Mexico City: M.A. Porrúa, 1998), 213. For the "mercy ... engendered ... with the humble confession of guilt in full display of regret" in front of a jury, see *El Universal,* 4 Oct. 1923, sec. 2, p. 1. See also Paul J. Vanderwood, *Juan Soldado: Rapist, Murderer, Martyr, Saint* (Durham: Duke University Press, 2004), 14. For the central juridical role of confession, both intimate and public, during the colonial period see Andrés Lira, "Dimensión jurídica de la conciencia: Pecadores y pecados en tres confesionarios de la Nueva España, 1545–1732," *Historia Mexicana* 55:4 (2006): 1141, 1147. Barthes contrasts the unity of the *fait divers* with the need to complete the story of political crimes with external information. As we will see, the distinction was not as clear in the Mexican case. "Structure de fait divers," in Roland Barthes, *Essais critiques* (Paris: Éditions du Seuil, 1964), 188–91.

14. *"Sádico"* used in Carlos Roumagnac, *Elementos de policía científica: Obra de texto para la Escuela Científica de Policía de México* (Mexico City: Botas, 1923), 150–51; "Líder obrero convertido en asesino," *Detectives* 2:266 (20 Sept. 1937): 11, 31. *"Sadismo"* in Mariano Ruiz Funes, "Prólogo," in Alfonso Quiroz Cuarón, *Un estrangulador de mujeres* (Mexico City, 1952); *Últimas Noticias,* 10 Sept. 1942, p. 1. See Thomas De Quincey, *On Murder* (New York: Oxford University Press, 2006). For reference to Krafft-Ebing, see Comisión Revisora del Código Penal, *Trabajos de revisión del Código Penal: Proyecto de reformas y exposición de motivos* (Mexico City: Tip. de la Oficina Impresora de Estampillas, 1912).

15. Marquis de Sade, *The Marquis de Sade: The 120 Days of Sodom, and Other Writings,* trans. Austryn Wainhouse and Richard Seaver (New York: Grove Press, 1966), 183; Marquis de Sade, *Juliette* (New York: Grove, 1988); Simone de Beauvoir, "Must We Burn Sade?" [1955] in Sade, *The Marquis de Sade,* 31, 38–39. "The lives of all the women who dwell on the face of the earth, are as insignificant as the crushing of a fly." Sade, *The 120 Days,* 231.

16. Octavio Paz, *Un más allá erótico: Sade* (Mexico City: Editorial Vuelta, 1995), 11–13. The poem first published in Octavio Paz, *Libertad bajo palabra* (Mexico City: Tezontle, 1949). See also Carlos Monsiváis, *Los mil y un velorios: Crónica de la nota roja* (Mexico City: Consejo Nacional para la Cultura y las Artes; Alianza Editorial, 1994), 11; Karen Halttunen, *Murder Most Foul: The Killer and the American Gothic Imagination* (Cambridge: Harvard University Press, 1998), 61; Lynn Hunt, ed., *The Invention of Pornography: Obscenity and the Origins of Modernity, 1500–1800* (Zone Books, 1993), 35.

17. Nick Carter, "Chucho el Roto, personaje tangible," *Detectives* 1:1 (9 Jun. 1959): 8–9, 13. Piccato, *City of Suspects,* chap. 5; Elisa Speckman, "I Was a Man of Pleasure, I Can't Deny it: Histories of José de Jesús Negrete, a.k.a. 'The tiger of Santa Julia,'" in Robert Buffington and Pablo Piccato, eds., *True Stories of Crime in Modern Mexico* (Albuquerque: University of New Mexico Press, 2009); Monsiváis, *Los mil y un velorios,* 13. There is a broad literature on bandits. One can start with Rich-

ard W. Slatta, *Bandidos: The Varieties of Latin American Banditry* (New York: Greenwood, 1987); Juan Pablo Dabove, *Nightmares of the Lettered City: Banditry and Literature in Latin America, 1816–1929* (Pittsburgh: University of Pittsburgh Press, 2007); E.J. Hobsbawm, *Bandits* (London: Weidenfeld and Nicolson, 1969); Gilbert M. Joseph, "On the Trail of Latin American Bandits: A Reexamination of Peasant Resistance," in *Patterns of Contention in Mexican History* (Irvine: University of California Press, 1992), 293–336; Paul J. Vanderwood, *Disorder and Progress: Bandits, Police and Mexican Development* (Wilmington, Del.: Scholarly Resources, 1992).

18. On reporters' anonymity, Téllez Vargas and Garmabella, *¡Reportero de policía!*, 76. On common criminals' use of violence to communicate with their peers and the public, Diego Gambetta, *Codes of the Underworld: How Criminals Communicate* (Princeton: Princeton University Press, 2009). "Autor del crimen" used, for example, in *El Universal*, 1 Feb. 1917, p. 3.

19. Michel Foucault, *I, Pierre Rivière, Having Slaughtered My Mother, My Sister, and My Brother . . . : A Case of Parricide in the 19th Century* (New York: Pantheon Books, 1975), 200; Michel Foucault, *Language, Counter-Memory, Practice: Selected Essays and Interviews* (Ithaca: Cornell University Press, 1977). For Roland Barthes, the author is the past of the text, the necessary antecedent to it. This, as we will see, applied to criminals as authors: their past was essential to their explanations of their felonies. Roland Barthes, *Image, Music, Text: Essays Selected and Translated by Stephen Heath* (London: Fontana Press, 1977), 145.

20. Roberson, "Diario de una instructora de baile," *Revista de Policía* 24:286 (Dec. 1964): 26.

21. *Memoria del Primer Congreso nacional penitenciario celebrado en la Ciudad de México del 24 de noviembre al 3 de diciembre de 1932, convocado por la Dirección Antialcohólica* (Mexico City: Talleres Gráficos de la Nación, 1935), p. 83; Antonio Saborit, *Los doblados de Tomóchic* (Mexico City: Cal y Arena, 1994), 174; Heriberto Frías, "Crónicas desde la cárcel," *Historias* 11 (Oct.–Dec. 1985): 47–71. The compilation and publication of such texts had been a project for French criminologist Gabriel Tarde, as well as American tabloids. Philippe Artières, *Le livre des vies coupables: Autobiographies de criminels (1896–1909)* (Paris: Albin Michel, 2000); V. Penelope Pelizzon and Nancy Martha West, *Tabloid, Inc.: Crimes, Newspapers, Narratives* (Columbus: Ohio State University Press, 2010), 129.

22. *La Prensa*, 21 Mar. 1932, p. 1.

23. *La Prensa*, 1 May 1934, p. 1.

24. *Detective* 1:21 (29 Feb. 1932): 2. The case was remembered as one of the most shocking of its time. Téllez Vargas and Garmabella, *¡Reportero de policía!*, 25. Laboratorio de Criminalística e Identificación to Juez 20 de la Primera Corte Penal, 3 Jun. 1932, AHDF, JP, ISSS, c. 2, exp. 9, 1932, pp. 166–69.

25. Unsigned memorandum to Jefe de la Oficina de Investigación y Seguridad Pública, 26 Feb. 1932, AHDF, JP, ISSS, c. 2, exp. 9, 1932, p. 20.

26. *La Prensa*, 3 Mar. 1932, p. 18.

27. *Detective* 1:21 (29 Feb. 1932): 2.

28. Francisco [unintelligible] to Jefe de la Policía, Mexico, 2 Mar. 1932; unintelligible signature to Inspección de Policía, 23 Feb. 1923, both in AHDF, JP, ISSS, c. 2, exp. 9, 1932, pp. 3, 54, 156.

29. Undated letter, AHDF, JP, ISSS, c. 2, exp. 9, 1932, p. 56. The author cites the press as his or her source to suggest potential avenues of investigation.

30. *La Prensa,* 1 Mar. 1932, pp. 3, 18.

31. Ibid., p. 18.

32. *Detective* 1:23 (21 Mar. 1932): 5. On the length of the interrogation *La Prensa* (San Antonio), 5 Mar. 1932, p. 4. To a question from the police chief, however, Gallegos answered that he had not been coerced. This, and quote by the man leaving the house in Declaración rendida por el detenido Alberto Gallegos Sánchez, 27 Feb. 1932, AHDF, JP, ISSS, c. 2, exp. 9, 1932, pp. 26–38, 75.

33. *La Prensa* (San Antonio), 8 Mar. 1932, p. 9.

34. Declaración rendida por el detenido Alberto Gallegos Sánchez, 27 Feb. 1932, AHDF, JP, ISSS, c. 2, exp. 9, 1932, p. 33.

35. *La Prensa,* 20 Mar. 1932, pp. 1, 3; *La Prensa,* 1 Mar. 1932, p. 3; *La Prensa,* 4 Mar. 1932, pp. 3, 5; *La Prensa* (San Antonio), 19 Mar. 1932, p. 1. Declaración rendida por Alberto Gallegos ante el C. jefe de la Policía del D.F., 1 Mar. 1932, AHDF, JP, ISSS, c. 2, exp. 9, 1932, p. 67.

36. *La Prensa* (San Antonio), 24 Mar. 1932, p. 1; *La Prensa,* 22 Mar. 1932, p. 3; *La Prensa* (San Antonio), 3 May 1933, p. 2.

37. *La Prensa,* 1 Mar. 1932, p. 3; *La Prensa,* 4 Mar. 1932, p. 5. See also *Detective* 1:21 (29 Feb. 1932): 9; Jesse Lerner, *The Shock of Modernity: Crime Photography in Mexico City* (Mexico City: Turner, 2007), 76–77.

38. Statement by Alberto Gallegos, 1 Mar. 1932, AHDF, JP, ISSS, c. 2, exp. 9, 1932, p. 75; *La Prensa* (San Antonio), 7 Mar. 1932, p. 1.

39. *Detective* 1:23 (14 Mar. 1932): 4–5; *La Prensa,* 3 Mar. 1932, p. 1.

40. *La Prensa,* 21 Mar. 1932, pp. 3, 13.

41. *La Prensa* (San Antonio), 20 Mar. 1932, p. 1; *La Prensa* (San Antonio), 25 Aug. 1933, p. 4.

42. *Novedades,* 4 Oct. 1942, p. 11. The best treatments, from different perspectives, are Monsiváis, *Los mil y un velorios,* and Everard Kidder Meade, "Anatomies of Justice and Chaos: Capital Punishment and the Public in Mexico, 1917–1945" (PhD diss., University of Chicago, 2005).

43. *El Universal Gráfico,* 11 Sept. 1942, p. 3.

44. The investigation is documented extensively in AHDF, JP, ISSS, c. 7, exp. 53, p. 5.

45. Undated clippings in AHDF, JP, ISSS, c. 7, exp. 53; *El Universal Gráfico,* 9 Sept. 1942, p. 22.

46. Anonymous to general Leopoldo Treviño Garza, 10 Sept. 1942, in AHDF, JP, ISSS, c. 7, exp. 53; Reinalda Salgado, Cuernavaca, to Miguel Ávila Camacho, 8 Sept. 1942, AGN MAC, -541/630; *Últimas Noticias,* 11 Sept. 1942, p. 1. "Hundreds of letters" were sent to the judge according to *El Universal Gráfico,* 29 Sept. 1942, p. 3.

47. Ríos Molina argues that Cárdenas did not commit the crime but covered up for others. He offers no evidence other than a statement Cárdenas made under the influence of Pentothal. Andrés Ríos Molina, *Memorias de un loco anormal: El caso de Goyo Cárdenas* (Mexico City: Editorial Debate, 2010), 82.

48. Monsiváis, *Los mil y un velorios*, 26; Meade, "Anatomies of Justice."

49. Dr. A. Martín Lucenay, "Apuntes para una breve biografía sexual de Gregorio Cárdenas" and Lucenay to Fernando Mora, director of *La Prensa*, Mexico City, 11 Sept. 1942, in AGN, DGIPS, gaveta 743, exp. 1. Lucenay, also a former communist, had been a prolific author of popular texts about sexology. Richard Cleminson, "El libro Homosexualidad del Dr. Martín de Lucenay: Entre el conocimiento científico y la recepción pública de la ciencia sexológica en España a principios del siglo XX," *Hispania* 54:218 (2004): 961–86.

50. *Últimas Noticias*, 17 Sept. 1942, p. 1.

51. *El Universal Gráfico*, 10 Sept. 1942, p. 5.

52. Declaración del detenido ingeniero químico Gregorio Cárdenas Hernández, 9 Sept. 1942, AHDF, JP, ISSS, c. 7, exp. 53. folios 94–97.

53. *Últimas Noticias*, 17 Sept. 1942, p. 1; *El Universal Gráfico*, 17 Sept. 1942, pp. 3, 21; *Últimas Noticias*, 1 Sept. 1942, p. 2; *El Universal Gráfico*, 18 Sept. 1942, p. 23; José Ramón Garmabella, *El criminólogo: Los casos más importantes del Dr. Quiroz Cuarón* (Mexico City: Debolsillo, 2007). Article 68 of the penal code was broad in defining the exception, and the authority of experts. *Código penal para el Distrito y Territorios Federales y para toda la República en materia de fuero federal [1931]* (Mexico City: Botas, 1938).

54. AHDF, JP, ISSS, c. 7, exp. 53. f. 64. He asked his lawyer for paper because "he plan[ned] to start a narrative about his life." *Novedades*, 3 Oct. 1942, p. 9; *El Universal Gráfico*, 12 Sept. 1942, p. 3. He also asked readers to send him books by Plato, Papini, and Lafragua. *El Universal Gráfico*, 14 Sept. 1942, p. 3.

55. *Últimas Noticias*, 17 Sept. 1942, p. 1.

56. Alicia Arias Ávalos to President Alemán, Mexico City, 15 Jan. 1948, AGN, MAV, 444.1/146.A.

57. Quiroz Cuarón, *Un estrangulador de mujeres*, 118–21. On La Castañeda, see Cristina Rivera Garza, *La Castañeda: Narrativas dolientes desde el Manicomio General, México, 1910–1930* (Mexico City: Tusquets, 2010).

58. Carlota, Guadalupe, Hermelina, and Rosa Cárdenas Hernández to President Alemán, 22 Mar. 1951; Gregorio Cárdenas to President Alemán, 9 Sept. 1948; Gregorio Cárdenas to President Alemán, 30 Sept. 1948. All at AGN, MAV, 444.1/146.A. His memoir of the harsher times of incarceration is compelling. Gregorio Cárdenas Hernández, *Celda 16* (Mexico City: Editorial Diana, 1970). He argued that Quiroz Cuarón was not a true scientist and only produced a report intended to punish him. Luna, *Nota roja 40s*, 91. Meade, "Anatomies of Justice," 481; Monsiváis, *Los mil y un velorios*, 92; Ríos Molina, *Memorias de un loco anormal*.

59. Meade, "Anatomies of Justice," 607, 687, 703, 705; Cárdenas Hernández, *Celda 16*, 91, 98; Luna, *Nota roja 40s*, 92; *La Prensa*, 5 Feb. 1970, p. 1; *El Universal Gráfico*, 9 Sept. 1942, pp. 3, 22.

60. Quiroz Cuarón, *Un estrangulador de mujeres*, 126–27.

61. Cárdenas Hernández, *Celda 16*, 192; *Últimas Noticias* 10 Sept. 1942, p. 1; *Últimas Noticias*, 19 Sept. 1942, p. 1; Oficial Mayor Procuraduría General de Justicia Distrito Federal to Jorge Casasus, 21 Jul. 1943, AGN MAC, -541/630; *Novedades*, 4 Oct. 1942, p. 11. Lafora was the object of nationalist attacks by Mexican experts for his intervention in this case. Sonia Adriana Peña, "José Revueltas y la crónica policial," *Literatura mexicana* 20:1 (2009): 83.

62. *Últimas Noticias*, 30 Sept. 1942, p. 1. On the effects of the deregulation of prostitution see Katherine Elaine Bliss, *Compromised Positions: Prostitution, Public Health, and Gender Politics in Revolutionary Mexico City* (University Park: Pennsylvania State University Press, 2001). On Cárdenas's accusation against Quiroz Cuarón, Meade, "Anatomies of Justice," 705–6; Luna, *Nota roja 40s*, 92.

63. Garmabella, *El criminólogo*, 34, 40.

64. Ibid., 78, 167, 187, 190.

65. *Detectives* 1:1 (9 Jun. 1959): 6–9. A multinational gang portrayed in *Argos* 1:7 (Feb. 1945): 1; *Argos* 1:7 (Feb. 1945): 7; Alfonso Quiroz Cuarón, *Asaltos a bancos en Venezuela y América* (México City: Morales Hermanos, 1964), 10–41; Garmabella, *El criminólogo*, 97.

66. *Detectives* 1:5 (5 Sept. 1932): 8–9, 15; *Argos* 4:12 (Mar. 1948): 3. See also *Policía Internacional* 18:3 (Feb. 1941); *Policía Internacional* 1:3 (Apr. 1948): 8–9. It can be argued that "international crime" was a product of police collaborations. Paul Knepper and Jacqueline Azzopardi, "International Crime in the Interwar Period: A View from the Edge," *Crime, Law and Social Change* 56:4 (1 Nov. 2011): 407–19.

67. Mariano Ruiz Funes, "Prólogo," in Quiroz Cuarón, *Un estrangulador de mujeres*, 8. Among other publications in the field, see Alfonso Quiroz Cuarón, José Gómez Robleda, and Benjamín Argüelles, *Tendencia y ritmo de la criminalidad en México, D.F.* (Mexico City: Instituto de Investigaciones Estadísticas, 1939); Alfonso Quiroz Cuarón and Raúl Quiroz Cuarón, *El costo social del delito en México: Symposium sobre el costo social del crimen y la defensa social contra el mismo* (Mexico City: Botas, 1970); Alfonso Quiroz Cuarón, *La criminalidad en la República Mexicana* (Mexico City: UNAM, 1958).

68. Alfonso Quiroz Cuarón and Liborio Martínez, "El Tigre de Santa Julia: J. Jesús Negrete, delincuente constitucional, por tendencia o por diatesis criminal," *Criminalia*, cited in Alfonso Quiroz Cuarón, *Estudios criminológicos* (Mexico City, 1954), 260–61; Quiroz Cuarón, *Asaltos a bancos*, 89.

69. For lobotomy see Alfonso Quiroz Cuarón, Alfonso Millán, and José Sol Casao, "Higinio sobera de la flor: Dictamen técnico sobre la personalidad del delincuente," *Criminalia* 20:4 (Apr. 1954): 175–224, cited in Quiroz Cuarón, *Estudios criminológicos*. See also Garmabella, *El criminólogo*, 36–37, 40, 43, 46, 45, 68; Quiroz Cuarón, *Asaltos a bancos*, 206, 13, quotation on 89; Rubén Gallo, *Freud's Mexico: Into the Wilds of Psychoanalysis* (Cambridge: MIT Press, 2010), 221. An anonymous letter from 1959 proposes that the authors of a crime should read Freud and use it to distract investigators. AHDF, JP, ISSS, c. 12, exp. 88, 1959.

70. Quiroz Cuarón, *Un estrangulador de mujeres;* Quiroz Cuarón, *Estudios criminológicos.* Ruiz Funes agreed that such strange phenomena were better kept "confined to the study of science." Mariano Ruiz Funes, "Prólogo," in Quiroz Cuarón, *Un estrangulador de mujeres,* 10–11.

71. "Un caso de miedo grave," in *Criminalia* 20:6 (Jun. 1954), cited in Quiroz Cuarón, *Estudios criminológicos,* 316.

72. Quiroz Cuarón and Martínez, "El Tigre de Santa Julia," 257.

73. Alfonso Quiroz Cuarón and Samuel Máynez Puente, *Psicoanálisis del magnicidio* (Mexico City: Editorial Jurídica Mexicana, 1965), 120, 129, quote from 130.

74. Ibid., 131–32, 135.

75. Garmabella, *El criminólogo,* 167; Quiroz Cuarón and Máynez Puente, *Psicoanálisis del magnicidio,* 139.

76. Natalia Sedova Trotsky to President Avila Camacho, Mexico City, 26 Nov. 1941, AGN, MAC, 541/115.

77. He produced a newspaper in Lecumberri, according to Roberto Blanco Moheno, who tried to interview him there. Roberto Blanco Moheno, *Memorias de un reportero* (Mexico City: Editorial V Siglos, 1975), 214; Quiroz Cuarón and Máynez Puente, *Psicoanálisis del magnicidio,* 149, 139. A novel with documentary support that reconstructs Mercader's story is Leonardo Padura, *El hombre que amaba a los perros* (Barcelona: Tusquets Editores, 2011).

78. Anonymous to Demetrio Medina, 18 Feb. 1957, in AHDF, JP, ISSS, c. 12, exp. 80, 1957. A subsequent letter from the same person requested a reward for helping the capture of the fugitives. Jesús Gálvez Pérez, "Un grito de alarma," *La Prensa,* 24 Jan. 1957, p. 13; *La Prensa,* 12 Jan. 1957, p. 29; "'Que lo maten,' clamaron en la reconstrucción," read the front-page headline of *La Prensa,* 17 Jan. 1957, p. 1. For a letter to the president requesting justice in the case see extract from Luis Mejía and others to the president, Tehuacán, 15 Jan. 1957, AGN, ARC, 541/828.

79. *La Prensa,* 11 Jan. 1957, p. 14. Most of the information below comes from AHDF, JP, ISSS, c. 12, exp. 80, 1957.

80. *La Prensa,* 15 Jan. 1957, p. 43.

81. Téllez Vargas and Garmabella, *¡Reportero de policía!,* 176.

82. Manuel Mendoza Domínguez to Police Chief, 18 Jan. 1957, p. 62, AHDF, JP, ISSS, c. 12, exp. 80, 1957. The information about the armlock that killed the priest and the failed robberies come from El Chundo's testimony.

83. AHDF, JP, ISSS, c. 12, exp. 80, 1957, p. 25.

84. *La Prensa,* 11 Jan. 1957, p. 14; *La Prensa,* 14 Jan. 1957, pp. 1, 31; *La Prensa,* 15 Jan. 1957, pp. 1, 32.

85. Téllez Vargas and Garmabella, *¡Reportero de policía!,* 173.

86. *La Prensa,* 21 Jan. 1957, p. 31. Panchito's mother, who lived in Ciudad Juárez, Chihuahua, disputed his custody. *La Prensa,* 25 Jan. 1957, pp. 1, 20–21.

87. *La Prensa,* 27 Jan. 1957, p. 38; Téllez Vargas and Garmabella, *¡Reportero de policía!,* 175.

88. Víctor Ronquillo, *Nota roja 50's: La crónica policiaca en la Ciudad de México* (Mexico City: Editorial Diana, 1993), 68–69; Téllez Vargas and Garmabella, *¡Reportero de policía!,* 169, 178.

89. The original in Spanish has its own color: "-Pa qué, ay na más se sueltan ustedes de argüenderos y laberintosos. . . . pa qué hablo, mejor me asilencio." *El Universal,* 5 Aug. 1929, sec. 3, p. 1; quote from *El Universal,* 7 Aug. 1929, sec. 2, p. 1; Manuel Múzquiz Blanco, "Un viaje circular por el alma obscura de Romero Carrasco," *Detective* 1:7 (23 Nov. 1931): 3; *La Prensa,* 19 Mar. 1932, pp. 1, 3; *Detective* 1:23 (21 Mar. 1932): 13; Téllez Vargas and Garmabella, *¡Reportero de policía!,* 26.

90. *Detectives* 1:1 (9 Jun. 1959): 4–5; *El Universal,* 14 May 2007, accessed 6 Apr. 2015, http://www.eluniversal.com.mx/espectaculos/76419.html. The governor of Coahuila pardoned Fernández, who had continued to direct the movie while formally in prison. Paco Ignacio Taibo, *"Indio" Fernández: El cine por mis pistolas* (Mexico City: J. Mortiz/Planeta, 1986), 189, 192.

91. Brocca, *Nota roja 60's,* 33, 38. On the privileges of famous people accused of murder, see *Alarma!* 355 (18 Feb. 1970): 14–15.

92. *Novedades,* 4 Oct. 1942, p. 7; *Novedades,* 6 Oct. 1942, p. 13; *Novedades,* 7 Oct. 1942, p. 5. José Revueltas, then a nota roja reporter in *El Popular,* described Ricarda López as intelligent and clear in her explanations. Peña, "José Revueltas," 84.

93. Monsiváis, *Los mil y un velorios,* 64–65.

94. *La Prensa,* 17 Mar. 1959, p. 20; *La Prensa,* 19 Mar. 1959, pp. 20–21; *La Prensa,* 20 Mar. 1959, p. 22.

95. Manuel Buendía, "Red privada," *La Prensa,* 19 Mar. 1959, p. 9.

96. *Detectives* 1:9 (29 Sept. 1959): 13. A long prison sentence in 1964 in Brocca, *Nota roja 60's,* 39, 47. For a case of an early autoviuda who left prison after a couple of months, perhaps because of her friendship with politicians like Emilio Portes Gil, see Luna, *Nota roja 40s,* 113–16.

97. *Alarma!* 349 (7 Jan. 1970): 10. For neighbors in favor of an autoviuda see *Alarma!* 367 (13 May 1970): 14.

98. For a woman who killed a man "atenazada por el histerismo," *La Prensa,* 4 Feb. 1932, p. 1; *Alarma!* (13 May 1953): 12–13, 27; a "brava hembra que en un momento de coraje" killed a man who tried to abuse her, *La Prensa,* 13 Mar. 1959, p. 9.

99. *La Prensa,* 19 Mar. 1959, p. 9.

100. *Amanecer* (Querétaro), 7 Mar. 1959, pp. 1, 3–4.

101. *La Prensa,* 7 Mar. 1959, p. 2; *La Prensa,* 8 Mar. 1959, p. 44; *Novedades* 7 Mar. 1959, pp. 1, 8.

102. *El Universal Gráfico,* 16 Mar. 1959, pp. 1, 3.

103. Ema Martinez to Adolfo Lopez Mateos, Mexico City, 31 Jan. 1959, AGN, ALM, 703.2/25.

104. *La Prensa,* 14 Mar. 1959, pp. 20–21, 34.

105. *El Universal Gráfico,* 11 Mar. 1959, p. 5; *Novedades,* 11 Mar. 1959, sec. 2, p. 1; *El Universal Gráfico,* 9 Mar. 1959, p. 14. An initial psychological assessment had established that she was was aware of her actions. *La Prensa,* 13 Mar. 1959, pp. 2, 39.

106. *Novedades,* 7 Mar. 1959, p. 8.

107. *Amanecer* (Querétaro), 6, 7, and 8 Mar. 1959; *El Universal Gráfico,* 7 Mar. 1959, pp. 1, 3–4.

108. Lisette Rivera and other researchers on the Porfirian period show how generally the press did not accept the "violent emotions" rationale when it came to women killing men. Lisette Rivera Reynaldos, "Crímenes pasionales y relaciones de género en México, 1880–1910," *Nuevo Mundo/Mundos Nuevos,* 2006, http://nuevomundo.revues.org/2835.

109. Paz, *Un más allá erótico,* 30, 42, 53.

110. In France, they entered a discursive field whose logic they had to understand if they wanted to survive. Artières, *Le livre des vies coupables,* 25, 13.

CHAPTER 5. CAREFUL GUYS

1. AHDF, JP, ISSS, c. 10, exp. 65, 1948, p. 125.

2. Roberto Blanco Moheno, *Memorias de un reportero* (Mexico City: Editorial V Siglos, 1975), 96.

3. AHDF, JP ISSS, c. 4, exp. 30, legs. 1 and 2, 1936. Another description in David García Salinas, *Gendarmes y guaruras (50 años del servicio secreto): 1a. parte* (Mexico City: Populibros La Prensa, 1985), 15–16.

4. Luquín, *Análisis espectral del mexicano: El lambiscón, el madrugador, el picapedrero, el pistolero* (Mexico City: Costa-Amic, 1961), 79.

5. *Don Roque* 1:8 (7 Apr. 1946): 3.

6. *Detectives* 1:8 (8 Sept. 1959): 12–13; *La Prensa,* 1. Jan. 1953, p. 2.

7. Blanco Moheno, *Memorias de un reportero,* 147; Carlos Ferreira, "El Regis," *Milenio* 26 Sept. 2009, accessed 5 Nov. 2010, http://impreso.milenio.com/node/8647226. Another prominent tough guy was future police chief Arturo Durazo. Jorge González González, *Lo negro del negro Durazo* (Mexico City: Editorial Posada, 1983), 39.

8. Adriana Gómez, "El trenecito de Rodrigo Moya," *Ciudad Viva,* Sept. 2007, http://www.ciudadviva.gov.co/septiembre07/magazine/2/index.php; Alberto del-Castillo Troncoso, *Rodrigo Moya: Una visión crítica de la modernidad* (Mexico City: Consejo Nacional para la Cultura y las Artes, 2006), 24–25.

9. Luquín, *Análisis espectral del mexicano;* Rodolfo Usigli, *Ensayo de un crimen* (Mexico City: Secretaría de Educación Pública, 1986), 78.

10. *Excélsior,* 26 Jun. 1936, p. 5. On the daily carrying of guns for non-pistoleros, *La Prensa,* 12 Aug. 1954, p. 35.

11. AGN, MAC, 705.2/276, 14 Apr. 1948. On the use of charolas until the seventies, Sergio Aguayo Quezada, *La charola: Una historia de los servicios de inteligencia en México* (Mexico City: Grijalbo, 2001), 76; Luis Ramírez de Arellano to Miguel Alemán, 10 Mar. 1948, AGN MAV 541/353. The practice was widespread and well established. In 1930 the Mexico City police chief promised to ban it. *El Universal,* 7 Jun. 1930, p. 1.

12. Cabarets were the setting for melodrama, dance, and music, and a platform for the careers of such important artists as exotic dancer Tongolele and songwriter Agustín Lara. Susanne Eineigel, "Culture and the Public Sphere in 1920s Mexico City," presented at the the the annual meeting of the Latin American Studies Association, Montreal, 2007; Alvaro A. Fernández Reyes, *Crimen y suspenso en el cine mexicano 1946–1955* (Zamora, Michoacán: El Colegio de Michoacán, 2007), 52–53.

13. Juan Orol, *Gángsters contra charros* (España Sono Films, 1947).

14. *La Prensa*, 18 Aug. 1954, p. 8. Comic strips depicted them with broad hats and smoking guns in their hands, a mix of detective and gunman. *Novedades*, 2 Oct. 1942, p. 4.

15. Matías was a suspect in "El espantoso asesinato de Mensolete." José Martínez de la Vega, *Péter Pérez, detective de Peralvillo y anexas* (Mexico City: Joaquín Mortiz, 1994), 45.

16. *La Prensa*, 14 Mar. 1957, pp. 9, 34; *Alarma!* 1:1 (17 Apr. 1963): 11; *Alarma!* 1:2 (11 May 1963): 9; *Detectives* 1:11 (27 Oct. 1959): 23. On the underworld, see James Alex Garza, *The Imagined Underworld: Sex, Crime, and Vice in Porfirian Mexico City* (Lincoln: University of Nebraska Press, 2007); Dominique Kalifa, *Les bas-fonds: Histoire d'un imaginaire* (Paris: Seuil, 2013); Richard J. Evans, *Tales from the German Underworld: Crime and Punishment in the Nineteenth Century* (New Haven: Yale University Press, 1998). These studies see the underworld as a self-contained realm with only negative links to the world "above ground."

17. *El Universal*, 5 Jul. 1930, sec. 2, p. 1.

18. El Caballero de Moriscount, "La aristocracia del hampa," *Revista de Policía* 23:282 (Aug. 1964): 26–28. Infamous police chief Arturo Durazo Moreno started his career as tough guy in a small cabarets. González González, *Lo negro del negro*, 39.

19. *El Universal Gráfico*, 31 Dec. 1928, pp. 8–9. A witness told *La Prensa* about "the adventurous life of Guadalupe," whose body showed "up to twenty scars, unequivocal signals of the consequences of a busy life." *La Prensa*, 1 Jan. 1929, sec. 2, p. 5. Similar places in smaller localities, see *Don Roque* (Apizaco, Tlaxcala) 1:8 (7 Apr. 1946): 3.

20. Jose Raul Aguilar, *Los métodos criminales en Mexico, cómo defendernos* (Mexico City: Ediciones Lux, 1941), 15, 16, 17, 163, 167–68. International criminals in *La Prensa*, 10 Mar. 1932, p. 19; *Detectives* 1:2 (23 Jun. 1959): 8–9; Eduardo Téllez Vargas and José Ramón Garmabella, *¡Reportero de policía!: El Güero Téllez* (Mexico City: Ediciones Océano, 1982), 112, 113, 114. For American gangsters dressing and behaving like businessmen see David E. Ruth, *Inventing the Public Enemy: The Gangster in American Culture, 1918–1934* (Chicago: University of Chicago Press, 1996), 2, 40–43. On kickbacks see letters to Ávila Camacho in AGN MAC, -703.4/88; *La Prensa*, 22 Jan. 1957, pp. 1–2; *La Prensa*, 25 Jan. 1957, p. 10; *La Prensa*, 7 Sept. 1954, pp. 23–24; *Alarma!* 1135 (30 Jan. 1985): 1–5.

21. *Detective* 1:11 (21 Dec. 1931): 4. Boxing was an increasingly popular form of exercise and entertainment. *La Prensa*, 2 Mar. 1959, p. 18; *Excélsior*, 28 Jun. 1936, p. 1. In his explorations of the city with Count Schwartzemberg, Roberto de la Cruz also goes to the boxing and wrestling arenas. Usigli, *Ensayo*, 164. See also Stephen

R. Niblo, *Mexico in the 1940s: Modernity, Politics, and Corruption* (Wilimington, Del.: Scholarly Resources, 1999), 64. For an officer at the Servicio Secreto accused of torturing a suspect, who had been a boxer, Víctor Velásquez, *El caso Alarcón* (Mexico City, 1955), 54.

22. AHDF, JP ISSS, c. 4, exp. 30, legs. 1 and 2, 1936.

23. Alejo Llamas Suárez, "Gangsterismo autóctono," *La Prensa,* 7 Jul. 1936, p. 9. Similar words were used by Octavio Paz years later in his description of "modern criminals" and their "disdain for life." Octavio Paz, *El laberinto de la soledad* (Mexico City: Fondo de Cultura Económica, 1963), 54.

The word "raquetero" was, according to experts, a "pochismo" used to refer to criminals acting in concert, with certain methods, and using violence. Aguilar, *Los métodos,* 15.

24. Jorge García-Robles, *Stray Bullet: William S. Burroughs in Mexico* (Minneapolis: University of Minnesota Press, 2013), 38.

25. Mark Overmyer-Velázquez, "Portraits of a Lady: Visions of Modernity in Porfirian Oaxaca City," *Mexican Studies/Estudios Mexicanos* 23:1 (1 Feb. 2007): 63–100.

26. "La ola de sangre," editorial, *Excélsior,* 2 Aug. 1939, p. 8; *Alarma!* 361 (1 Apr. 1970): 15; *Detectives* 1:9 (Sept. 29, 1959): 31. Pistoleros who abused women in the state of Hidalgo with the protection of politicians in *La Prensa,* 2 Jul. 1936, p. 10. Murderers protected by official positions and guns denounced by Rafael Mendiola to Adolfo López Mateos, 26 Feb. 1963, AGN, ALM, 541/449. "Despistolización" campaigns against the use of guns were recurrent. *Excélsior,* 26 Jun. 1936, p. 5.

27. *Novedades,* 5 Nov. 1947, sec. 2, p. 1.

28. AHDF, JP ISSS, c. 4, exp. 30, legs. 1 and 2, 1936; AGN MAV 541/50; Luis Ramírez de Arellano to Miguel Alemán, 10 Mar. 1948, AGN MAV 541/353.

29. Javier Torres Pérez to Adolfo Ruiz Cortines, 28 Aug. 1958, AGN ARC, 541/1003.

30. AHDF, JP, ISSS, c. 10, exp. 65, 1948.

31. *La Prensa,* 1 Feb. 1932, p. 15. For a correspondent murdered in Morelos by a "well-known pistolero" see *Alarma!* 362 (8 Apr. 1970): 34. A drunk Sinaloa major running wild in a cantina in *La Voz de Sinaloa,* 23 Jul. 1963, p. 4. For attacks against journalists see Blanco Moheno, *Memorias de un reportero,* 149; Carlos Moncada, *Oficio de muerte: Periodistas asesinados en el país de la impunidad* (Mexico City: Penguin; Random House; Grupo Editorial México, 2012); Víctor Alba, *Sísifo y su tiempo: Memorias de un cabreado, 1916–1996* (Barcelona: Laertes, 1996), 300.

32. It was applied to supporters of opposition candidate Andrew Almazán. The Twenty-Eighth Legislature (1940–1942) had the greatest number of uses of the word in any two-year period: six. The database starts in 1917. Cámara de Diputados, Mexico, "Diario de los Debates dela Cámara de Diputados del Congreso de los Estados Unidos Mexicanos," http://cronica.diputados.gob.mx/. The use of "pistolero" and "pistolerismo" saw a sharp increase in usage in the early 1930s, reaching a first peak in the early 1940s, according to Google Books Ngram Viewer, accessed May 5, 2016, https://books.google.com/ngrams/graph?content = pistolero%2Cpistolerismo&year_start =

1800&year_end = 2000&corpus = 21&smoothing = 3&share = &direct_url = t1%3B%2Cpistolero%3B%2Cco%3B.t1%3B%2Cpistolerismo%3B%2Cco. The database does not separate by country.

33. On guns among deputies, Antonio Helú, *La obligación de asesinar: Novelas y cuentos policiacos* (Mexico City: M.A. Porrúa, 1998). On the murder of deputies and senators, AHDF, JP, ISSS, c. 10, exp. 65, 1948. The word could also be applied to political crimes in other countries. Orantes Arnoldo, Telegramas, 15 Nov. 1954, AGN ARC 541/458.

34. The murder of the deputy is discussed below. AHDF, JP ISSS, c. 4, exp. 30, legs. 1 and 2, 1936.

35. "La ola de sangre," editorial, *Excélsior*, 2 Aug. 1939, p. 8.

36. *La Prensa*, 12 Aug. 1954, p. 1. See also Luquín, *Análisis espectral del mexicano*, 79; *La Prensa*, 23 Feb. 1948, p. 8.

37. Mateo Podan "¡Pistoleros del país: Uníos!," *La Prensa*, 3 Jul. 1936, p. 11; Mateo Podan, "Humo y ecos de los disparos," *La Prensa*, 4 Jul. 1936, p. 11. For examples of uses of pistoleros in elections and other political situations see Paul Gillingham, "'We Don't Have Arms, but We Do Have Balls': Fraud, Violence, and Popular Agency in Elections," in *Dictablanda: Politics, Work, and Culture in Mexico, 1938–1968,* ed. Paul Gillingham and Benjamin T. Smith (Durham: Duke University Press, 2014), 149–72. For Gillingham, "most violence–whether committed by state or non-state actors–was profoundly political." Paul Gillingham, "Who Killed Crispín Aguilar? Violence and Order in the Post-Revolutionary Countryside," in *Violence, Insecurity and the State in Mexico,* ed. Wil Pansters (Stanford: Stanford University Press, 2012), 100. For a "despistolización" campaign, *Excélsior*, 26 Jun. 1936, pp. 5, 8. The futility of such campaigns in Alan Knight, "Caciquismo in Twentieth-Century Mexico," in *Caciquismo in Twenieth-Century Mexico,* ed. W.G. Pansters and Alan Knight (London: Institute for the Study of the Americas, 2005), 16.

38. *La Prensa*, 20 Feb. 1948, p. 24.

39. Gonzalo N. Santos, *Memorias* (Mexico City: Grijalbo, 1984), 397, 399. His favorite estate was "El Gargaleote." On the political and economic bases of Santos's power in San Luis Potosí, see Wil G. Pansters, "Tropical Passion in the Desert: Gonzalo N. Santos and Local Elections in Northern San Luis Potosí, 1943–1958," in *Dictablanda: Politics, Work, and Culture in Mexico, 1938–1968,* ed. Paul Gillingham and Benjamin T. Smith (Durham: Duke University Press, 2014), 126–49.

40. *Policía Internacional* 1:2 (Mar. 1948): 1.

41. *La Prensa*, 13 Aug. 1954, p. 8. A similar concern, *Don Paco* (Apizaco, Tlaxcala): 1:19 (7 Dec. 1947): 2.

42. Blanco Moheno, *Memorias de un reportero*, 97.

43. Oscar Lewis, *Five Families: Mexican Case Studies in the Culture of Poverty* (New York: New American Library, 1959), 286. See also *La Prensa*, 2 Jan. 1953, p. 2; *La Prensa*, 2 Feb. 1932, pp. 3, 7; Alfredo López Cisneros, "Rey Lopitos ... sanguinario cacique," *Alarma!* 356 (25 Feb. 1970): 2.

44. Paul Friedrich, "A Mexican Cacicazgo," *Ethnology* 4:2 (April 1, 1965): 190–209. A Chiapas case study in Stephen E. Lewis, "Dead-End Caudillismo and

Entrepreneurial Caciquismo in Chiapas, 1910–1955," in *Caciquismo in Twentieth-Century Mexico,* ed. W. G. Pansters and Alan Knight (London: Institute for the Study of the Americas, 2005), 151–68.

45. Salvador Maldonado Aranda, "Between Law and Arbitrariness: Labour Union Caciques in Mexico," in *Caciquismo in Twenieth-Century Mexico,* ed. W. G. Pansters and Alan Knight (London: Institute for the Study of the Americas, 2005), 230; Veronique Flanet, *Viviré, si dios quiere: Un estudio de la violencia en la mixteca de La Costa,* trans. Tununa Mercado (Mexico City: Instituto Nacional Indigenista, 1977), 66–67, 127; Wil Pansters, "Goodbye to Caciques? Definition, the State and the Dynamics of Caciquismo in Twentieth-Century Mexico," in *Caciquismo in Twentieth-Century Mexico,* ed. W. G. Pansters and Alan Knight (London: Institute for the Study of the Americas, 2005), 324–25; Iñigo Laviada, *Los caciques de La Sierra* (Mexico City: Jus, 1977), 22–23. I owe this reference to Benjamin T. Smith. Knight, "Caciquismo in Twentieth-Century Mexico," 16; Alan Knight, "Habitus and Homicide: Political Culture in Revolutionary Mexico," in *Citizens of the Pyramid: Essays on Mexican Political Culture,* ed. Wil G. Pansters (Amsterdam: Thela, 1997), 109.

46. Gillingham, "Who Killed Crispín Aguilar?"

47. Benjamin T. Smith, *Pistoleros and Popular Movements: The Politics of State Formation in Postrevolutionary Oaxaca* (Lincoln: University of Nebraska Press, 2009), 42–43, 133. See also Maldonado Aranda, "Between Law and Arbitrariness," 227.

48. The parallels, noted by Smith and others, with the disciplining of the political class since the 1930s are very suggestive. Smith, *Pistoleros and Popular Movements;* Gillingham, "Who Killed Crispín Aguilar?"

49. The organization of violence embodied by pistoleros was ironically depicted in fiction: Filiberto García, the pistolero of *El complot mongol,* by Rafael Bernal, spoke with bitterness about the need for a "faculty for pistoleros" that would teach one how to forget death. Rafael Bernal, *El complot mongol* (Mexico City: Joaquín Mortiz, 1969), 187; *El Momento,* 23 May 1943, quoted in Smith, *Pistoleros,* 217; AHDF, JP, ISSS, c. 10, exp. 65, 1948; *Alarma!* 361 (1 Apr. 1970): 15.

50. Santos, *Memorias,* 27.

51. The reform focused on limiting the use of certain weapons. *El Universal Gráfico,* 19 Sept. 1942, p. 3. Machine guns, rifles, automatic weapons, handguns with calibers greater than 6.5 mm, and other weapons were reserved for the use of the armed forces. The government could make exceptions for individuals, however. See "Ley que declara las armas que la nación reserva para uso del ejército, armada e institutos armados para la defensa nacional," *Diario Oficial* 80:8 (9 Sept. 1933): 118–19.

52. González González, *Lo negro del negro.* He married a sister of Hugo Izquierdo Ebrard. Alfonso Diez García, "Hugo Izquierdo Ebrard desde el manicomio," *Codigo Diez,* 10 Mar. 2014, accessed 20 May 2016, http://www.codigodiez .mx/cronicaspdf/36cronica10mar14.pdf. Thanks to Benjamin T. Smith for this reference.

53. AHDF, JP ISSS, c. 4, exp. 30, legs. 1 and 2, 1936. This ethos examined in depth in Bernal, *El complot mongol,* 11. For Oaxacan caciques using trusted Afro-Mexican pistoleros, Flanet, *Viviré, si dios quiere,* 37.

54. Santos, *Memorias,* 25, 223.

55. AHDF, JP, ISSS c. 8, exp. 54, leg. 3.

56. The request was forwarded to the governor of Puebla. Gaspar Cruz to Adolfo López Mateos, 8 Sept. 1961, AGN, ALM, 541/520.

57. *Detectives* 1:8 (8 Sept. 1959): 12–13. The leader was Norberto Treviño Zapata. *Alarma* 21 May 1953): 24–25.

58. Juana Jara, Margarita Jara, and Ventura Jara to Adolfo López Mateos, 9 Nov. 1959, AGN, ALM, 541/187. Caciques who used pistoleros and concocted judicial cases against adversaries in Laviada, *Los caciques de La Sierra,* 30, 41.

59. *Detectives* 1:8 (8 Sept. 1959): 12–13. Cattle rustler with police badges in AHDF, JP, ISSS, c. 12, exp. 84, 1958. Criminals using police identifications denounced in *La Prensa,* 15 Mar. 1932, pp. 2, 13.

60. *Detectives* 1:1(27 Oct. 1959): 24. The best contemporary studies of this phenomenon are Aguayo Quezada, *La charola,* and Gustavo Fondevilla, "Controlling the Madrinas: The Police Informer Management and Control System in Mexico," *Police Journal* 86 (2014): 116–42.

61. Thomas G. Rath, *Myths of Demilitarization in Postrevolutionary Mexico, 1920–1960* (Chapel Hill: University of North Carolina Press, 2013); Aguayo Quezada, *La charola.*

62. *La Prensa,* 2 Feb. 1932, pp. 3, 15; Diane E. Davis, "Policing and Regime Transition: From Postauthoritarianism to Populism to Neoliberalism," in *Violence, Coercion, and State-Making in Twentieth-Century Mexico: The Other Half of the Centaur,* ed. Wil Pansters (Stanford: Stanford University Press, 2012), 68–90.

63. Téllez Vargas and Garmabella, *¡Reportero de policía!,* 182, 186; Víctor Ronquillo, *Nota roja 50's: La crónica policiaca en la Ciudad de México* (Mexico City: Editorial Diana, 1993), 71–81; *La Prensa,* 26 Aug. 1954, p. 7; *La Prensa,* 1 Mar. 1957. On the Burroughs case García-Robles, *Stray Bullet.* For a fictionalized biography see Eugenio Aguirre, *El abogánster* (Mexico City: Planeta, 2014).

64. Luquín, *Análisis espectral del mexicano,* 78.

65. Téllez Vargas and Garmabella, *¡Reportero de policía!,* 195–96.

66. Santos, *Memorias,* 224.

67. *La Prensa,* 23 Apr. 1934, p. 20; "Editorial: Los cabaret y dancing tan abundantes en nuestra multicolor metrópoli, siempre han servido de refugio para aquellos que en una forma o en otra rinden culto al crimen," *Argos* 3:1 (Jan. 1946): 1; Carlos Monsiváis, *A ustedes les consta: Antología de la crónica en México* (Mexico City: ERA, 1980), 327.

68. "El enigma de la muerte de Miravete," *Detectives* 5:266 (20 Sept. 1937): 32–33.

69. Niblo, *Mexico in the 1940s,* 178, 227, 260, citing the 1948 memo.

70. *Alarma* (21 May 1953): 24–25. See also, for Acapulco in 1963, AGN, ALM, 541/520. Violence in the creation of urban settlements became a permanent fixture of political control by the PRI. Markus-Michael Müller, *Policing the Fragments: Public Security and the State in Mexico City* (Berlin, 2009), 56, 58–59.

71. AGN, ALM, 541/520; AHDF, JP, ISSS, c. 10, exp. 65, 1948.

72. AHDF, JP, ISSS, c. 10, exp. 65, 1948.

73. "Triste e implacable epílogo de tres siniestros y sombríos superpistoleros," *Policía Internacional* 1:2 (Mar. 1948): 12.

74. AHDF, JP, ISSS, c. 11, exp. 75, 1954; *La Prensa,* 10 Aug. 1956, pp. 1, 2.

75. "El asesinato de Eduardo Franzoni," *Detectives* 5:266 (20 Sept. 1937): 14–15.

76. *Alarma!* 513 (28 Feb. 1973), cited by Miguel Donoso Pareja, *Picaresca de la nota roja* (Mexico City: Editorial Samo, 1973), 71–76. On the rates, higher in cities, for murder, Flanet, *Viviré, si dios quiere,* 135–36.

77. Manuel Muzquiz Blanco, "La libertad de Eva de la O," *Detective* 1:4 (2 Nov. 1931). On the ideas about marihuana, see Isaac Campos, *Home Grown: Marijuana and the Origins of Mexico's War on Drugs* (Chapel Hill: University of North Carolina Press, 2012). For a broader reference, Luis Astorga, *El siglo de las drogas* (Mexico City: Espasa-Calpe Mexicana, 1996).

78. See for example *La Palabra* (Culiacán), 3 Nov. 1955, p. 7; *La Palabra* (Culiacán) 10 Nov. 1955, p. 1. For two agents killed next to four hundred kilos of marihuana, AHDF, JP ISSS, c. 13, exp. 99, 1962. On La Bandida, Carlos Ferreyra, "El Regis," *Milenio,* 26 Sept. 2009, http://impreso.milenio.com/node/8647226. The best social history of trafficking at this time in Elaine Carey, *Women Drug Traffickers: Mules, Bosses, and Organized Crime* (Albuquerque: University of New Mexico Press, 2014). On Corvera, Téllez Vargas and Garmabella, *¡Reportero de policía!,* 197.

79. Bernal, *El complot mongol,* 184; *La Prensa,* 3 May 1951, p. 42. On pimps, *Detective* 1:12 (28 Dec. 1931): 8–9. The best treatment of the evolution of prostitution after the revolution is Katherine Elaine Bliss, *Compromised Positions: Prostitution, Public Health, and Gender Politics in Revolutionary Mexico City* (University Park: Pennsylvania State University Press, 2001), 196–97. The police tended to collect the tax from prostitutes directly. González González, *Lo negro del negro,* 110.

80. *La Prensa,* 6 May 1951, pp. 38, 40. *Alarma!* 356 (25 Feb. 1970): 30–31; AHDF, JP, ISSS, c. 12, exp. 84, 1958. Ronquillo, *Nota roja 50's,* 71–81. Corvera's gang included Hugo Izquierdo Ebrard, one of the men convicted for the murder of Angulo. Ibid., 87–88; Téllez Vargas and Garmabella, *¡Reportero de policía!,* 190–91.

81. AHDF, JP ISSS, c. 4, exp. 30, legs. 1 and 2, 1936. Unless otherwise noted, statements from witnesses, suspects, and detectives were extracted from this file, which lacks pagination.

82. *Excélsior,* 16 Jul. 1936, sec. 2, p. 1.

83. *Excélsior,* 13 Nov. 1924, p. 1.

84. Antonio Santoyo, *La mano negra: Poder regional y estado en México: Veracruz, 1928–1943* (Mexico City: Consejo Nacional para la Cultura y las Artes, 1995), 135.

85. Clipping from *Crítica,* 29 Jul. 1936: "Por fin, ¿quién asesinó a Altamirano?" in AHDF, JP ISSS, c. 4, exp. 30. On venadear, see "Cobardemente fue 'venadeada' toda una familia en el Río Tamesí," *Policía Internacional* 9:1 (Nov. 1948); Flanet, *Viviré, si dios quiere,* 137.

86. *Excélsior,* 27 Jun. 1936, sec. 2, p. 8.

87. *Excélsior,* 26 Jun. 1936, pp. 1, 4; *Excélsior,* 27 Jun. 1936, pp. 1, 3; *Excélsior,* 29 Jun. 1936, sec. 2.

88. *Excélsior,* 27 Jun. 1936, p. 3.

89. *La Prensa,* 1 Jul. 1936, p. 10.

90. Undated clipping, AHDF, JP ISSS, c. 4, exp. 30, legs. 1 and 2, 1936.

91. Vicente González Fernández to Heriberto Jara, AHDF, JP ISSS, c. 4, exp. 30.

92. AHDF, JP ISSS, c. 4, exp. 30, legs. 1 and 2, 1936.

93. Salvador Altamirano to president Alemán, 26 Jun. 1949, AGN MAV 541/71.

94. Anonymous report, 16 Nov. 1936, in AHDF, JP ISSS, c. 4, exp. 30, legs. 1 and 2, 1936.

95. Gillingham, "Who Killed Crispín Aguilar?," 94; Knight, "Habitus and Homicide"; Santoyo, *La mano negra,* 150.

96. *Excélsior,* 27 Jun. 1936, p. 1.

97. Friedrich, "A Mexican Cacicazgo," 198–99.

98. Statement by Gildardo Lovillo Martínez, 6 Jul. 1936, AHDF, JP ISSS, c. 4, exp. 30, legs. 1 and 2, 1936. Lovillo's statement (spelling his last name as Lobillo) also reproduced in *La Prensa,* 6 Jul. 1936, pp. 3, 5; *La Prensa,* 8 Jul. 1936, pp. 2, 5.

99. Santoyo, *La mano negra,* 150–51.

100. Blanco Moheno, *Memorias de un reportero,* 83–86; Santoyo, *La mano negra,* 156.

101. Gillingham, "Who Killed Crispín Aguilar?," 92.

102. *Don Roque* 1:31 (29 Feb. 1948): 2; *Don Roque* 1:37 (11 Apr. 1948): 1. *Don Roque* reported earlier that Armenta Castillo was preparing a rebellion against the government. *Don Roque,* 1:19 (7 Dec. 1947): 2. See also undated clipping, "Por el ojo de la llave: Política versus policía," AHDF, JP ISSS, c. 4, exp. 30.

103. *La Prensa,* 19 Feb. 1948, pp. 3, 18. The concern about Mexican "political gangsterism" was also mentioned in a report from the U.S. embassy to the Department of State. Niblo, *Mexico in the 1940s,* 227, 261; León, Aurelio, AGN MAV, 541/300, 541/308, 541/347. The Federal District's governor, Fernando Casas Alemán, was a former Veracruz governor and close collaborator of his cousin, President Alemán.

104. Unless otherwise noted, references to statements in this case were extracted from AHDF, JP, ISSS, c. 10, exp. 65, 1948.

105. Statement by Rafael Barradas Osorio, 23 Feb. 1948, AHDF, JP, ISSS, c. 10, exp. 65, 1948.

106. AHDF, JP, ISSS, c. 10, exp. 65, 1948. Thanks to Paul Gillingham for the reference to the Armentas. Other Armentas involved in a political assassination, this one of deputy Manlio Fabio Altamirano in 1936, were Rafael Armenta Cornejo and Armando Armenta. Salvador Altamirano to Presidente Alemán, 26 Jun. 1949, AGN MAV, 541/71; AHDF, JP, ISSS, c. 4, exp. 30, 1936.

107. Agents Pedro C. Balderas Salinas and Gonzalo Balderas Castelazo to Jefe Servicio Secreto, 26 Feb. 1948, AHDF, JP, ISSS, c. 10, exp. 65, 1948; *La Prensa,* 26 Feb. 1948, p. 3. In the 1940 presidential election Andrew Almazán mounted a strong challenge against Ávila Camacho.

108. For Armenta Barradas's involvement in a case connected to the inheritance of Maximino Ávila Camacho see *La Prensa,* 28 Jan. 1947, pp. 3, 30. For his involve-

ment in the murder of leader Eduardo Guichard, and probably Altamirano, too, see *Excélsior,* 1 Aug. 1939, p. 1.

109. AGN, MAC, 705.2/276, 14 Apr. 1948. The hotel was indeed severely damaged during the 1985 earthquake.

110. *Policía Internacional* 1:2 (Mar. 1948): 1.

111. *La Prensa,* 27 Feb. 1948, pp. 3, 13, 27, 28.

112. *La Prensa,* 28 Feb. 1948, p. 10.

113. Report dated 29 Feb. 1948, in AHDF, JP, ISSS, c. 10, exp. 65, 1948. An army officer based in Veracruz wrote to his superiors reporting that, after reading about the death of Armenta Castillo and the other two, he ordered the arrest of the Izquierdo Ebrard brothers, "finishing that way the useless life of those pistoleros who had established a school of crime and terror." Alfonso Chanona López to Alejandro Mange, 2 Mar. 1948, in AHDF, JP, ISSS, c. 10, exp. 65, 1948.

114. Clippings, n.d., AHDF, JP, ISSS, c. 10, exp. 65, 1948.

115. *La Prensa,* 28 Feb. 1948, pp. 1, 8, 10; clipping from *Últimas Noticias,* 27 Feb. 1948, AHDF, JP, ISSS, c. 10, exp. 65, 1948.

116. "Do not neglect to answer me because I am humble and poor," she concluded defiantly. Gloria Flores to Miguel Alemán, Apizaco, 10 Mar. 1948, AGN, MAV, 541/347.

117. Gillingham, "Who Killed Crispín Aguilar?," 104–5.

118. Alba, *Sísifo y su tiempo,* 302; *Alarma* (7 Jul. 1951); Alfonso Chanona López to Alejandro Mange, 2 Mar. 1948, in AHDF, JP, ISSS, c. 10, exp. 65, 1948.

119. *Alarma!* (7 Jul. 1951); Téllez Vargas and Garmabella, *¡Reportero de policía!,* 195.

120. Blanco Moheno, *Memorias de un reportero,* 224, 266; Aguayo Quezada, *La charola,* 66.

121. Davis, "Policing and Regime Transition"; Diane E. Davis, "The Political and Economic Origins of Violence and Insecurity in Contemporary Latin America: Past Trajectories and Future Prospects," in *Violent Democracies in Latin America,* ed. Enrique Desmond Arias and Daniel M. Goldstein (Durham: Duke University Press, 2010), 35–62.

122. *Detectives* 1:1 (9 Jun. 1959): 24.

123. *La Prensa,* 19 Feb. 1948, pp. 3, 18.

124. Aguayo Quezada, *La charola.* On the absence of regulations for the Secret Service, see Enrique Jiménez D. to Secretario de Gobernación, 28 Jul. 1934, AGN, DGG, 2.014(29)27, c. 2, exp. 10.

125. *La Prensa,* 12 Sept. 1954, pp. 1, 28. A suspect in the Angulo case was a member of the secret police; statement by Rafael Barradas Osorio, 23 Feb. 1948, AHDF, JP, ISSS, c. 10, exp. 65, 1948.

126. *La Prensa,* 12 Aug. 1954, p. 35.

127. *La Prensa,* 11 Aug. 1954, pp. 1, 6, 36. The case was the most prominent in the newspaper's crime coverage for a week and continued to be reported well into October.

128. *La Prensa,* 11 Aug. 1954, p. 6; Velásquez, *El caso Alarcón,* 55. On the ascent of union charrismo since Alemán's presidency see Michael Snodgrass, "The Golden

Age of Charrismo: Workers, Braceros, and the Political Machinery of Postrevolutionary Mexico," in *Dictablanda: Politics, Work, and Culture in Mexico, 1938–1968,* ed. Paul Gillingham and Benjamin T. Smith (Durham: Duke University Press, 2014), 175–95; Marcos Aguila and Jeffrey Bortz, "The Rise of Gangsterism and Charrismo: Labor Violence and the Postrevolutionary Mexican State," in *Violence, Coercion and State-Making in Twentieth Century Mexico,* ed. Wil G. Pansters (Stanford: Stanford University Press, 2012), 185–211.

129. The history of sugar mills is long. See Tanalís Padilla, *Rural Resistance in the Land of Zapata: The Jaramillista Movement and the Myth of the Pax Priísta, 1940–1962* (Durham: Duke University Press, 2008); *El Sol de Culiacán,* 1 Mar. 1975, p. 1. On the movie industry, see *La Prensa,* 18 Feb. 1948, p. 9; Liberato Carrasco to Miguel Molinar, Sept. 22, 1954, AHDF, JP, ISSS, c. 11, exp. 75, 1954. See for example "Líder obrero convertido en asesino," *Detectives* 5:266 (20 Sept. 1937): 11, 31. For violence and unionism, see Maldonado Aranda, "Between Law and Arbitrariness," 245.

130. *La Prensa,* 13 Aug. 1954, pp. 2, 5; See Andrew Paxman, "William Jenkins, Business Elites, and the Evolution of the Mexican State 1910–1960" (PhD diss., University of Texas, 2008).

131. *La Prensa,* 14 Aug. 1954, pp. 2, 26; *La Prensa,* 15 Aug. 1954, pp. 2, 7.

132. *La Prensa,* 12 Sept. 1954, pp. 1, 28; Velásquez, *El caso Alarcón,* 22.

133. The Servicio Secreto file in AHDF, JP, ISSS, c. 11, exp. 75, 1954. Quote from pp. 14–15.

134. *La Prensa,* 22 Sept. 1954, p. 2.

135. *La Prensa,* 17 Sept. 1945, pp. 14, 16; *La Prensa,* 7 Oct. 1954, pp. 2, 13.

136. *La Prensa,* 12 Sept. 1954, pp. 1, 28; Beatriz Cubillas de Ponce de León requesting amparo on behalf of her husband Alejandro Ponce de León, AHDF, JP, ISSS, c. 11, exp. 75, p. 28.

137. *La Prensa,* 20 Sept. 1954, pp. 1, 2.

138. AHDF, JP, ISSS, c. 11, exp. 75, pp. 189, 83.

139. *La Prensa,* 3 Oct. 1954, pp. 2, 11, 13.

140. Even the chief of police of the Federal District avoided reporters' questions about progress on the case. *La Prensa,* 14 Sept. 1954, pp. 1, 6; *La Prensa,* 14 Sept. 1954, p. 6; *La Prensa,* 15 Sept. 1954, p. 6.

141. *La Prensa,* 3 Oct. 1954, pp. 1, 2.

142. *La Prensa,* 3 Oct. 1954, pp. 1, 2; Juan Bustillo Oro, *Vida cinematográfica* (Mexico City: Cineteca Nacional, 1984), 247; AHDF, JP, ISSS, c. 11, exp. 75.

143. *La Prensa,* 18 Sept. 1954, pp. 2, 30; *La Prensa,* 22 Sept. 1954, pp. 1, 2; Paxman, "William Jenkins," 384. For Alarcón's defense (basically, that he did not know Mascarúa and had nothing to gain from his death), see Velásquez, *El caso Alarcón,* iii, 50. I owe this reference to Benjamin T. Smith.

144. *La Prensa,* 12 Sept. 1954, pp. 1, 28. The signatories of several letters published in support of Alarcón included the names of Luis Spota, Antonio Badú, Jesús Galindo, Raúl de Anda, and Luis Azcárraga. *La Prensa,* 19 Sept. 1954, pp. 23, 32; Niblo, *Mexico in the 1940s,* 52.

145. Carlo Ginzburg, *The Judge and the Historian: Marginal Notes on a Late-Twentieth-Century Miscarriage of Justice* (London: Verso, 1999).

146. For Batillas interview from prison, see *Alarma* (13 May 1953): 4–5. On Ríos Galeana see "Carlos Monsiváis habla de la experiencia y contactos de Ríos Galeana," *El Universal,* 14 Jul. 2005, online edition, accessed 11 Jul. 2016, http://archivo.eluniversal.com.mx/primera/23004.html.

147. In Mexico, however, the cost of murder as a communicative action was relatively low, and it was impossible to distinguish criminals from policemen. Diego Gambetta, *Codes of the Underworld: How Criminals Communicate* (Princeton: Princeton University Press, 2009), 7, 24.

148. Paul Gillingham and Benjamin T. Smith, eds., *Dictablanda: Politics, Work, and Culture in Mexico, 1938–1968* (Durham: Duke University Press, 2014), xi, 22.

149. On the consensual violence of pistoleros, as opposed to authoritarianism, see Knight, "Caciquismo in Twentieth-Century Mexico," 17. On the the mistake of trying to distinguish modern and traditional cacique rule, Smith, *Pistoleros and Popular Movements,* 42–43.

150. Luquín, *Aguila de oro: Espejo del pistolero* (Mexico City: Costa-Amic, 1950), 123.

151. García-Robles, *Stray Bullet,* 38.

152. Just to mention two authors cited above: Knight, "Habitus and Homicide," 108; Paxman, "William Jenkins," 208.

CHAPTER 6. OUR TIMES, OUR PERSPECTIVES

1. The integral relation with urban life was formulated in 1902 by G. K. Chesterton in "A Defence of Detective Stories": "A city is, properly speaking, more poetic even than a countryside, for while Nature is a chaos of unconscious forces, a city is a chaos of conscious ones." Chesterton, *The Defendant,* 120, reproduced in Howard Haycraft, *The Art of the Mystery Story: A Collection of Critical Essays, Edited, and with a Commentary* (New York: Simon and Schuster, 1946), 4–5. Scholars highlight the ability of crime fiction to provide readers with a map of the complex reality of Latin American cities in the mid–twentieth century. Glen S. Close, *Contemporary Hispanic Crime Fiction: A Ttransatlantic Discourse on Urban Violence* (New York: Palgrave Macmillan, 2008), 28–29; Miguel G. Rodríguez Lozano, *Pistas del relato policial en México: Somera expedición* (Mexico City: Universidad Nacional Autónoma de México, 2008), 6; Persephone Braham, *Crimes against the State, Crimes against Persons: Detective Fiction in Cuba and Mexico* (Minneapolis: University of Minnesota Press, 2004), 18; Anis Bawarshi, "The Genre Function," *College English* 62:3 (January 1, 2000): 336–38. A useful conceptualization of "reality" as a predictable set of events regulated by the state in Western societies in Luc Boltanski, *Énigmes et complots: Une enquête à propos d'enquêtes* (Paris: Gallimard, 2012), 31, 38; Close, *Contemporary Hispanic Crime Fiction,* 19, 28.

2. The decades of the popularity of crime fiction coincided with the publication of prestigious texts on lo mexicano. Georg Leidenberger, "Samuel Ramos: La historia de la filosofía en México (1943)," in *México como problema: Esbozo de una historia intelectual,* ed. Carlos Illades, Rodolfo Suarez, and Brian Francis Connaughton Hanley (Mexico City: Universidad Autónoma Metropolitana, 2012), 228–29; Braham, *Crimes against the State,* 67. Recent studies of crime fiction propose that homicide was a tool to build the nation as a "grand narrative" and to enhance the role of the state by tracing "national boundaries" which excluded people judged inimical to modernity. Fernando Fabio Sánchez, *Artful Assassins: Murder as Art in Modern Mexico* (Nashville: Vanderbilt University Press, 2010), 13.

3. Ilan Stavans, *Antihéroes: México y su novela policial* (Mexico City: Joaquín Mortiz, 1993), 22; Julio Guerrero, *La génesis del crimen en México: Estudio de psiquiatría social* (Paris: Vda. de Ch. Bouret, 1901); Pablo Piccato, "Julio Guerrero, la génesis del crimen en México: Estudio de psiquiatría social (1901)," in *México como problema: Esbozo de una historia intelectual,* ed. Carlos Illades, Brian Connaughton Hanley, and Rodolfo Suárez (Mexico City: Universidad Autónoma Metropolitana, 2012).

4. See for example Silvia González Marín, *Prensa y poder político: La elección presidencial de 1940 en la prensa mexicana* (Mexico: Siglo Veintiuno, 2006); Jeffrey M. Pilcher, "Mexico's Pepsi Challenge: Traditional Cooking, Mass Consumption, and National Identity," in *Fragments of a Golden Age: The Politics of Culture in Mexico since 1940,* ed. Gilbert M. Joseph, Anne Rubestein, and Eric Zolov (Durham: Duke University Press, 2001), 71–90; Stephen R. Niblo, *Mexico in the 1940s: Modernity, Politics, and Corruption* (Wilmington, Del.: Scholarly Resources, 1999).

5. Carlos Monsiváis, *Los mil y un velorios: Crónica de la nota roja* (Mexico City: Consejo Nacional para la Cultura y las Artes; Alianza Editorial, 1994), 223; Monsiváis, "Prólogo," in Antonio Helú, *La obligación de asesinar: Novelas y cuentos policiacos* (Mexico City: M. A. Porrúa, 1998), 13.

6. The novel takes place in 1912 but the date of printing is not available. The book was edited in San Antonio, Texas. Quiroga, *Vida y milagros de Pancho Reyes.*

7. This was a basic function of the genre elsewhere. Ernest Mandel, *Delightful Murder: A Social History of the Crime Story* (Minneapolis: University of Minnesota Press, 1984), 31.

8. W. H. Auden, "The Guilty Vicarage," *Harper's Magazine,* May 1948, 407.

9. Ernest Mandel explains the popularity of the genre as a result of death becoming an obsession of bourgeois society. Mandel, *Delightful Murder,* 42; Karen Halttunen, *Murder Most Foul: The Killer and the American Gothic Imagination* (Cambridge: Harvard University Press, 1998). Since murder is by definition a failure of social order, any mystery narrative has a strong "sociological implication." The investigation has to keep a distance from those implications and mind "its own business," namely, solving the case. Raymond Chandler, *The Simple Art of Murder* (New York: Vintage Books, 1988), 2.

10. María Elvira Bermúdez, *Cuento policiaco mexicano, breve antología* (Mexico City: UNAM, 1987), 9; María Elvira Bermúdez, "Qué es lo policiaco en la narra-

tiva," *Estudios Filosofía-Historia-Letras* (Fall 1987), http://biblioteca.itam.mx/estudios/estudio/estudio10/sec_30.html. A contemporaneous omnibus of the prescriptive in Haycraft, *The Art of the Mystery Story*. Mexican authors borrowed a few tricks from serials like those about Holmes and Nick Carter, such as the focus on a single detective and the reappearance of secondary figures that established a past for him. "The Five Orange Pips," in Arthur Conan Doyle, *The Adventures and Memoirs of Sherlock Holmes* (New York: Modern Library, 2001); Raymond Chandler, *The Notebooks of Raymond Chandler and English Summer: A Gothic Romance* (New York: Harper, 2006); Boltanski, *Énigmes et complots,* 72.

11. Stavans, *Antihéroes,* 41–48; Agatha Christie, *Murder Is Easy* (New York: St. Martin's Paperback, 2001), 214, 262, 14, 57, 6; Dominique Kalifa, *L'encre et le sang: Récits de crimes et société à la belle epoque* (Paris: Fayard, 1995), 29, 30, 73, 77. Kalifa draws from the works of Tzvetan Todorov. For the distinction between the story itself, the course of events, and the plot, the discourse presenting them, as a basic divide made productively transparent by the detective novel, see Peter Brooks, *Reading for the Plot: Design and Intention in Narrative* (New York: Vintage Books, 1985), 13, 18, 24, 29. "The Mystery of Marie Roget" in Poe, *Works of Edgar Allan Poe,* vol. 1; Peter Thoms, "Poe's Dupin and the Power of Detection," in *Cambridge Companion to Edgar Allan Poe,* ed. Kevin J. Hayes (West Nyack, N.Y.: Cambridge University Press, 2002), 133–46. Newspapers were also important in the first detective books in Argentina; Sonia Mattalía, *La ley y el crimen: Usos del relato policial en la narrativa argentina* (Frankfurt: Ediciones de Iberoamericana, 2008), 28–29.

12. Chandler, *Notebooks of Raymond Chandler.* The writer must work hard to produce a true story, regardless of the scorn of critics who take more seriously the realism of "any fourth-rate, ill-constructed, mock-serious account of the life of a bunch of cotton pickers in the deep south." Doroty Gardiner and Kathrine Sorley Walker, *Raymond Chandler Speaking* (London: Penguin, 1988), 48. Manuel Valle, *El signo de los cuatro: II, Agatha Christie: Historias sin historia de la naturaleza humana* (Albolote, Spain: Editorial Comares, 2006), 103, 15, 39, 42, 168; Christie, *Murder Is Easy,* 80, 67–68, 84. Agatha Christie, *And Then There Were None* (New York: St. Martin's Press, 2001).

13. Chandler, *The Simple Art of Murder,* 17; Dashiell Hammett, *Red Harvest* (New York: Pockett Books, 1929); Joseph C. Porter, "The End of the Trail: The American West of Dashiell Hammett and Raymond Chandler," *Western Historical Quarterly* 6:no. 4 (October 1975): 411–24.

14. Chandler, *The Simple Art of Murder,* 274, 368. The criminal should always be punished "in one way or another, not necessarily by operation of the law" so as not to irritate the reader. Chandler, *Notebooks of Raymond Chandler,* 37.

15. Sean McCann, "The Hard-Boiled Novel," in *The Cambridge Companion to American Crime Fiction,* ed. Catherine Ross Nickerson (New York: Cambridge University Press, 2010), 50; Mandel, *Delightful Murder,* 25, 31, 33–39, 43, 47. Luc Boltanski sees that connection with social life a condition for what he proposes is the genre's common denominator: explaining the causes of a riddle that seems to contradict the order of reality. Boltanski, *Énigmes et complots.*

16. Catherine Nickerson, "Murder as Social Criticism," *American Literary History* 9:4 (Winter 1997): 744–57; citing Klein, *Easterns, Westerns, and Private Eyes,* 179. On the "outer structure" and the "inner, personalized plot" of Chandler's novels see Stephen Knight, "'A Hard Cheerfulness': An Introduction to Raymond Chandler," in *American Crime Fiction: Studies in the Genre,* ed. Brian Docherty (New York: St. Martin's Press, 1988), 82–83; Stephen Knight, *Form and Ideology in Crime Fiction* (London: Macmillan, 1980), 153. A similar distinction between an "apparent plot" and a "revealed plot" that contains the moral key of the story in William Marling, *The American Roman Noir: Hammett, Cain, and Chandler* (Athens: University of Georgia Press, 1995), xiii, 40. For a broad perspective on plotting, see Brooks, *Reading for the Plot,* 13, 18, 29.

17. On the moral lessons of winning and losing, Clifford Geertz, "Deep Play: Notes on the Balinese Cockfight," in *The Interpretation of Cultures: Selected Essays* (New York: Basic Books, 1973); Hammett, *Red Harvest;* Boltanski, *Énigmes et complots,* 87.

18. They corrected themselves and provided the author's address. *Aventura y Misterio* 3 (Jan. 1957): 3.

19. Monsiváis, "Prólogo," in Helú, *La obligación de asesinar,* 13–15; José Luis de la Fuente, "Rodolfo Usigli busca la verdad: Ensayo de un crimen, antecedente policiaco mexicano," *Alter Texto* 1:1 (2003): 93; M.M. Bakhtin, *The Dialogic Imagination: Four Essays* (Austin: University of Texas Press, 1981); M.M. Bakhtin, *Problems of Dostoevsky's Poetics* (Minneapolis: University of Minnesota Press, 1984).

20. John D. Dorst, "Neck-Riddle as a Dialogue of Genres: Applying Bakhtin's Genre Theory," *Journal of American Folklore* 96:382 (1 Oct. 1983): 413–15; Bawarshi, "The Genre Function," 336–38.

21. Bakhtin, *Problems of Dostoevsky's Poetics;* Pierre Bourdieu, *Outline of a Theory of Practice* (New York: Cambridge University Press, 1977); Rebecca Martin, ed., *Crime and Detective Fiction* (Ipswich, Mass.: Salem Press, 2013).

22. Braham, *Crimes against the State,* x, ix, xii, xiii; Alfonso Reyes, "Sobre la novela policial" (1946), in Alfonso Reyes, *Obras completas,* vol. 9, *Norte y Sur; Los trabajos y los días; História Natural Das Laranjeiras* (Mexico City: Fondo de Cultura Económica, 1959), 457–61; Sánchez, *Artful Assassins,* 3, 62; Stavans, *Antihéroes,* xx, 11, 38–39. On the early exclusion of policial from high literature see Gerardo García Muñoz, *El enigma y la conspiración: Del cuarto cerrado al laberinto neopoliciaco* (Saltillo: Universidad Autómoma de Coahuila, 2010), 34–35, 37, 38. Flat characters also defined the classics of the genre. Heather Worthington, *Key Concepts in Crime Fiction* (New York: Palgrave Macmillan, 2011), 118.

23. María Elvira Bermúdez, *Los mejores cuentos policíacos mexicanos* (Mexico City: Libro-Mex, 1955), 15. A similar opinion expressed by Xavier Villaurrutia in 1946, cited in García Muñoz, *El enigma y la conspiración,* 41. For the golden period see Gabriel Trujillo Muñoz, *Testigos de cargo* (Mexico City: CONACULTA-CECUT, 2000), 19. A model to read crime stories at the intersection of fiction and reality, and the gaps of literary history, in Josefina Ludmer, *El cuerpo del delito: Un manual* (Buenos Aires: Perfil Libros, 1999), 158.

24. Vicente Francisco Torres, *El cuento policial mexicano* (Mexico City: Editorial Diógenes, 1982), 12; Monsiváis, "Prólogo," in Helú, *La obligación de asesinar,* 18–19.

25. Haycraft, *The Art of the Mystery Story,* 198.

26. Helú to Frederic Dannay, México, D.F, 11 Oct. 1946, in Frederic Dannay Papers, Columbia University Libraries, New York (hereafter Dannay Papers).

27. Besides publishing Helú and Gual and translating Conan Doyle, Albatros published such books as *Pensamientos para tarjetas y postales,* from 1951, and *Declamador nacional, antología poética,* in 1950. Monsiváis, "Prólogo," in Helú, *La obligación de asesinar,* 13; Trujillo Muñoz, *Testigos de cargo,* 32; Vicente Francisco Torres, *Muertos de papel: Un paseo por la narrativa policial mexicana* (Mexico City: CNCA; Sello Bermejo, 2003), 44–47. Ilan Lytle Stavans, *Antiheroes: Mexico and Its Detective Novel* (Madison, N.J.: Fairleigh Dickinson University Press, 1997), 75–79.

28. Helú to Dannay, Mexico City, 22 Feb. 1944, Dannay Papers.

29. Helú, *La obligación de asesinar,* 79–97. Critics have nevertheless accused him of being derivative. Monsiváis, "Prólogo," in ibid, 18–19; Torres, *Muertos de papel,* 45; Helú, *La obligación de asesinar,* 11–21.

30. Helú to Dannay, Mexico City, 8 Nov. 1944, Dannay Papers. He wrote Máximo Roldán's adventures for the radio, too. A similar criticism is found in "Los predestinados," where dueling and slander are vehicles for professional advancement for journalists. Most of Helú's scripts were directed by Juan Bustillo Oro (discussed in chapter 7), a friend from the times of the Vasconcelos campaign. On the Vasconcelos campaign and some of its literary consequences Christopher Domínguez Michael, *Tiros en el concierto: Literatura mexicana del siglo V* (Mexico City: ERA, 1997), 128–47.

31. Helú, *La obligación de asesinar,* 165, 160; Helú to Dannay, Mexico City, 12 Jan. 1944, Dannay Papers.

32. Antonio Helú and Adolfo Fernández Bustamante, *El crimen de insurgentes: Comedia policíaca en tres actos* (Mexico City: Sociedad General de Autores de México, 1940), 39, 74. The 1935 staging included Andrea Palma, of cinematographic fame from *La mujer del puerto* (1934).

33. Antonio Helú to Frederick Dannay, Mexico City, 4 Dec. 1943, Dannay Papers. In another letter, Helú asked that the title of a story be corrected because Roldán "is not a detective." Antonio Helú to Frederick Dannay, Mexico City, 31 Mar. 1944, Dannay Papers.

34. Helú, *La obligación de asesinar,* 177. See also Monsiváis, "Prólogo," in ibid, 18–19, 171–91. Roldán inhabited "una zona nebulosa donde la ley y el crimen no llegan a distinguirse," Trujillo Muñoz, *Testigos de cargo,* 33.

35. This is probably a reference to S. S. Van Dine's idea of the detective story as a sporting event. Helú, *La obligación de asesinar,* 49, 62, 69, 73, 74. A movie with the same title, now apparently lost, had been directed by Helú in 1937.

36. Ibid, 197–203.

37. Ibid, 214–17.

38. Ibid., 151.

39. Bermúdez, *Los mejores cuentos,* 17. See also José Martínez de la Vega, *Péter Pérez, detective de Peralvillo y anexas* (Mexico City: Joaquín Mortiz, 1994); Torres, *El cuento policial mexicano,* 12, 17; Monsiváis, "Prólogo," in Helú, *La obligación de asesinar,* 17; Torres, *Muertos de papel,* 40–41; Stavans, *Antiheroes,* 108.

40. For Close, in Martínez de la Vega this means the early recognition that foreign examples had limits when it came to writing about modern Latin American cities. Close, *Contemporary Hispanic Crime Fiction,* 28.

41. Martínez de la Vega, *Peter Pérez, detective,* 81. In another story he is given tacos made with human flesh.

42. José Martínez de la Vega, *Humorismo en camiseta: Aventuras de Peter Pérez* (Mexico City: Talleres Gráficos de la Nación; Excélsior, 1946), 48; Martínez de la Vega, *Peter Pérez, detective,* 63, 17–18.

43. Martínez de la Vega, *Peter Pérez, detective,* 28; Trujillo Muñoz, *Testigos de cargo,* 41.

44. Martínez de la Vega, *Peter Pérez, detective,* 95; Martínez de la Vega, *Humorismo en camiseta,* 12, 20, 44.

45. Martínez de la Vega, *Humorismo en camiseta,* 57.

46. Ibid, 81, 35–36, 125; Martínez de la Vega, *Peter Pérez, detective,* 54, 96–97.

47. Torres, *Muertos de papel,* 41; Martínez de la Vega, *Humorismo en camiseta,* 142, 89.

48. Martínez de la Vega, *Peter Pérez, detective,* 101 and ff.; Torres, *Muertos de papel,* 43. Radio shows with police content were broadcast since at least 1942. AGN, MAC, 541/630.

49. Martínez de la Vega, *Humorismo en camiseta,* 87, 25, 111.

50. Ibid, 84, 24; Martínez de la Vega, *Peter Pérez, detective,* 49, 40, 83, 53.

51. Martínez de la Vega, *Humorismo en camiseta,* 92.

52. Ibid, 137–39, 170–73; Martínez de la Vega, *Peter Pérez, detective,* 19.

53. Martínez de la Vega, *Peter Pérez, detective,* 22, 39; Martínez de la Vega, *Humorismo en camiseta,* 75, 87, 112.

54. Martínez de la Vega, *Peter Pérez, detective,* 13, 16, 36.

55. Ibid, 178.

56. The same problem mentioned by Torres, *Muertos de papel,* 23. On the category of the author, see "Death of the Author," in Roland Barthes, *Image, Music, Text: Essays Selected and Translated by Stephen Heath* (London: Fontana Press, 1977); and "What Is an Author?," in Michel Foucault, *Language, Counter-Memory, Practice: Selected Essays and Interviews* (Ithaca: Cornell University Press, 1977).

57. *Selecciones Policiacas y de Misterio* 5:70 (Jan. 1950); Bermúdez, *Los mejores cuentos.* Bermúdez's "Muerte a la zaga" was later published in book form: María Elvira Bermúdez, *Muerte a la zaga* (Tlahuapan, Puebla: Premià, 1985). The book was published by the Fondo Cultura Económica a year after the Premià edition.

58. In *Argos,* which also published poetry and criminological studies. Jesse Lerner, *El impacto de la modernidad: Fotografía criminalística en la Ciudad de México* (Mexico City: Turner; Consejo Nacional para la Cultura y las Artes, 2007), 36–37.

59. Monsiváis, "Prólogo," in Helú, *La obligación de asesinar,* 13.

60. *Aventura y Misterio* 1 (1 Nov. 1956): 2.

61. Stories under the Ellery Queen pseudonym had been published by *Últimas Noticias* since 1942. *Últimas Noticias,* 1 Sept. 1942, p. 2.

62. Helú to Ellery Queen, 4 Dec. 1943; Helú to Dannay, 6 Jan. 1944. All in Dannay Papers. Only the letters from Helú are preserved in the collection.

63. Helú to Dannay, Mexico City, 30 May 1944, Dannay Papers. The concern about money was as old as the genre, and even established authors in the U.S. had to write scripts to make a living. Chandler, *Notebooks of Raymond Chandler.*

64. Juan Bustillo Oro, *Vida cinematográfica* (Mexico City: Cineteca Nacional, 1984), 281–83.

65. *Selecciones Policiacas y de Misterio* 5:84 (Dec. 1950); *Selecciones Policiacas y de Misterio* 9:127 (1 Jan. 1955). The debt discussed in Helú to Dannay, 20 May 1947; Helú to Dannay, 12 Apr. 1949. Both in Dannay Papers.

66. *Aventura y Misterio* 1 (Nov. 1956); *Novelas y Cuentos Mercury* 11 (14 Sept. 1957): 1. According to its editors, by 1956 *Selecciones* had published 795 stories in 14,800 pages. *Selecciones Policiacas y de Misterio* 11:149 (1 Dec. 1956): 5–6.

67. Torres, *Muertos de papel,* 23, 16; Torres, *El cuento policial mexicano,* 14. For contemporary scholars, magazine authors are not easy to group by nationality, gender, or any of the standard categories used to divide up research. Stavans, *Antihéroes,* 93; Monsiváis, "Prólogo," in Helú, *La obligación de asesinar,* 13; Trujillo Muñoz, *Testigos de cargo,* 32.

68. *Aventura y Misterio* 2 (Dec. 1956), back cover; *Aventura y Misterio* 1 (Nov. 1956): 1: the genre is indeed "frequently mistreated."

69. Helú to Dannay, Mexico City, 30 May 1944, Dannay Papers.

70. *Selecciones Policiacas y de Misterio* 4:69 (15 Dec. 1949): 22. Rodolfo Walsh was one of them. Rudolf J. Walsh, "Suerte en el juego," *Aventura y Misterio* 4 (Feb. 1957). Another, from Cuba, was Marcos Alexander. *Aventura y Misterio* 1 (Nov. 1956): 24.

71. Roberto Cruzpiñón, "La vivienda del 18," *Selecciones Policiacas y de Misterio* 95 (1952); Roberto Cruzpiñón, "En un automóvil," *Selecciones Policiacas y de Misterio* 105 (1952); Roberto Cruzpiñón, "El abanico de sándalo," *Selecciones Policiacas y de Misterio* 125 (1954); Roberto Cruzpiñón, "Los insectos del profesor," *Selecciones Policiacas y de Misterio* 135 (1956); Roberto Cruzpiñón, "Mauricio," *Selecciones Policiacas y de Misterio* 169 (1959); Roberto Cruzpiñón, "El tercer paquete," *Selecciones Policiacas y de Misterio* 175 (1960). He was later a professor and wrote a science textbook. The neglect toward authors published in *Aventura y Misterio* noted by Torres, *El cuento policial mexicano,* 14.

72. *Aventura y Misterio* 3 (Jan 1957): 72.

73. *Aventura y Misterio* 1 (1 Nov. 1956): 81.

74. *Selecciones Policiacas y de Misterio* 4:69 (25 Dec. 1949): 5. When the magazine celebrated its eleven-year anniversary, its editors claimed to have read more than ten thousand stories in English, French, and Spanish. *Selecciones Policiacas y de Misterio* 11:149 (1 Dec. 1956): 4–6.

75. *Aventura y Misterio* 1 (Nov. 1956): 3.

76. Trujillo Muñoz, *Testigos de cargo,* 32. Ernesto Monato translated many stories and wrote a few of his own, was an editor of *Selecciones,* and also a minor movie actor in films by Bustillo Oro, as well as films produced in Cuba. His name could have been another alias: "Monato" means "month" in Esperanto; volume 125 of *Selecciones Policiacas y de Misterio* included a story by one Ornato Tomasen, anagram of Ernesto Monato. *Selecciones Policiacas y de Misterio* 9:125 (1 Dec. 1954): 25.

77. *Selecciones Policiacas y de Misterio* 2:4 (1 Jan. 1947): 9. Hammett "revolutionized the style of police novel" with *The Maltese Falcon* and created "a new style . . . a hundred percent North American." *Selecciones Policiacas y de Misterio* 1:3 (1 Dec. 1946): 23, 63.

78. Luis Garrido, "El arcano del No. 12," *Aventura y Misterio* 1 (1956): 30.

79. The stories are quite different except for a few details and the detective-thief. Helú, *La obligación de asesinar,* 370, 45; Torres, *Muertos de papel,* 25, 45; Antonio Helú to Frederick Dannay, Mexico City, 4 Dec. 1943, Dannay Papers.

80. Torres, *Muertos de papel,* 25.

81. José Manuel Enríquez, "Un corazón amante," *Selecciones Policiacas y de Misterio* 42 (1954). *Ellery Queen's Mystery Magazine* also used introductory texts to engage readers, comment on the authors, and describe editorial input. A selection in Haycraft, *The Art of the Mystery Story,* 409.

82. Ernesto Alonso, "La cabeza de Adán," *Selecciones Policiacas y de Misterio* 171 (1959); Carlos Pérez Ruíz, "A treinta pasos," *Aventura y Misterio* 3 (January 1957); Ernesto Monato, "El diamante del rajá," *Selecciones Policiacas y de Misterio* (149) 1956.

83. Habacuc Pérez Castillo, "Los dos dedos del muerto," *Aventura y Misterio* 2 (Dec. 1956); Vicente Fe Álvarez, "Se le helaban los huesos," *Selecciones Policiacas y de Misterio* 153 (1957); Henry García-Herreros, "Circunstancia imprevista," *Aventura y Misterio* 3 (Jan. 1957).

84. Raymundo Quiroz Mendoza, "Sin novedad en Berlín," *Selecciones Policiacas y de Misterio* 116 (1954). Quiroz Mendoza also wrote for the theater.

85. Juan Miguel de Mora, "Estar de suerte," *Aventura y Misterio* 4 (Feb. 1957).

86. García-Herreros, "Circunstancia imprevista." Other stories focused on Mexican students who played football, then still an American novelty, or included Mexican detectives solving Cold War intrigues in the U.S. Cruzpiñón, "La vivienda del 18"; Guillermo R. Galindo, "El asesino juega futbol," *Aventura y Misterio* 4 (Feb. 1957); Carlos Z. Hernández, "Engranaje de muerte," *Aventura y Misterio* 5 (Mar. 1957).

87. Pérez Castillo, "Los dos dedos," 70. A similar comment in *Aventura y Misterio* 3 (Jan. 1957): 83.

88. Arturo Perucho, "La muerte aprende a cantar," *Selecciones Policiacas y de Misterio* 107 (1952); see also Carlos Méndez Ochoa, "Carta de un suicida," *Selecciones Policiacas y de Misterio* 73 (1950).

89. Luis Gutiérrez y González, "Junto al zapote licenciado," *Aventura y Misterio* 14 (Dec. 1957).

90. Hernán Hoyos, "Intruso del más allá," *Aventura y Misterio* 10 (Sept. 1957). Ernesto Monato, "El papelerillo de Uruapan," *Selecciones Policiacas y de Misterio* 167

(1959). Gossip and legends in Xavier Fierro, "Amelia Otero," *Aventura y Misterio* 12 (Oct. 1957); Raúl Pérez Arce, "Las cruces en la arena," *Aventura y Misterio* 12 (Oct. 1957).

91. Enrique Jiménez Jaime, "Dosis mortal," *Aventura y Misterio* 1 (Nov. 1956). Rafael Bernal, discussed in chapter 7, explored the funny possibilities of provincial criminal comedy. Rafael Bernal, "De muerte natural," in Bermúdez, *Los mejores cuentos*, 41–61; Rafael Bernal, *Un muerto en la tumba* (Mexico City: Jus, 1946).

92. *Selecciones Policiacas y de Misterio* 1:3 (1 Dec. 1946): 23, 63; *Selecciones Policiacas y de Misterio* 1:1 (1 Nov. 1946): 67. On the creation of readers through crime fiction see Umberto Eco, "El bautizo de la rosa," *Nexos*, 1 Oct. 1984, http://www .nexos.com.mx/?p = 4399; Knight, *Form and Ideology*, 71.

93. Also a reference to treatises by Douglas Thomson and Dorothy Sayers, *Selecciones Policiacas y de Misterio* 1:1 (1 Nov. 1946): 42; *Selecciones Policiacas y de Misterio* 2:4 (1. Jan. 1947): 47.

94. *Selecciones Policiacas y de Misterio* 1:1 (1 Nov. 1946): 24.

95. *Selecciones Policiacas y de Misterio* 1:2 (15 Nov. 1946): 65. A similar challenge in Frank Gruber, "La copa de oro," *Selecciones Policiacas y de Misterio* 133 (1955): 13.

96. José Dibildox, "El cartero que no llamaba," *Aventura y Misterio* 3 (1957): 57.

97. *Selecciones Policiacas y de Misterio* 9:119 (1 Aug. 1954): 56; Alonso Tégula, "La muerte piadosa," *Aventura y Misterio* 1 (1956): 24.

98. For example, Reyes, "Sobre la novela policial"; Garrido, "El arcano del No. 12," 38, 56; Rebecca Martin, "On Crime and Detective Fiction," in *Crime and Detective Fiction*, ed. Rebecca Martin (Ipswich, Mass.: Salem Press, 2013), xv, xxi.

99. Justo Rocha, "Duelo a muerte," *Aventura y Misterio* 5 (1957); Cruzpiñón, "Los insectos del profesor," 42.

100. Galindo, "El asesino juega futbol"; Mario Aguirre, "Hay huellas en el jardín," *Aventura y Misterio* 2 (1956); Guido J. Guerra Faife, "El asesinato del colono," *Aventura y Misterio* 5 (1957); Raymundo Quiroz Mendoza, "Motolinía habla de toros," *Selecciones Policiacas y de Misterio* 74 (Apr. 1950); Gabriel Doria, "El espectro de Medea," *Aventura y Misterio* 2 (Dec. 1956); Quiroz Mendoza, "Sin novedad." The main character in *El caso de la fórmula española* is a reporter as well as an expert on bullfighting. Enrique Gual, *El caso de la fórmula española* (Mexico City: Editorial Albatros-Libros y Revistas, 1947). Modernizing students in Cruzpiñón, "La vivienda del 18"; Cruzpiñón, "Los insectos del profesor."

101. This is probably a reference to S. S. Van Dine's idea of the detective story as a sporting event. Helú, *La obligación de asesinar*, 49, 62, 69, 73, 74. In the late 1920s Willard Huntington Wright wrote a formulation of the rules of detective stories and the sportsmanship required, comparing the form with the crossword puzzle or "a sporting event." Willard Huntington Wright, "The Detective Novel," *Scribner's* (Nov. 1926); S. S. Van Dine, "Twenty Rules for Writing Detective Stories," in *The Winter Murder Case: A Philo Vance Story,* by S. S. Van Dine (London: Cassell, 1939), 149–58; S. S. Van Dine, "The Art of the Mystery Story," in Haycraft, *The Art of the Mystery Story;* on the combination of intellectual and moral enjoyment of the genre, Martin, "On Crime."

102. Vicente Fe Álvarez, "No se olvide de darle cuerda," *Selecciones Policiacas y de Misterio* 119 (1953): 55. See also Juan Bustillo Oro, "Apuesta al crimen," *Selecciones Policiacas y de Misterio* 92 (1951): 44; Rogelio Gómez Díaz, "Crimen legal," *Aventura y Misterio* 6 (1957).

103. Marcos Alexanders, "El teléfono está sonando," *Aventura y Misterio* 5 (1957); Blanca Edwiges de Ramos, "Aprendiz de asesino," *Aventura y Misterio* 3 (1957); Agusto Bondani, "Cuestión de suerte," *Aventura y Misterio* 3 (1957); Enrique Jiménez Jaime, "¿Servicio completo, señor?," *Aventura y Misterio* 3 (1957); Antonio Helú, "Un día antes de morir," *Aventura y Misterio* 3 (1957). First-person narrators in Bustillo Oro, "Apuesta al crimen"; Gómez Díaz, "Crimen legal." On thefts Eduardo Zanonni, "Un olor peculiar," *Aventura y Misterio* 1 (1956); Paulino Masip, "Un ladrón," *Selecciones Policiacas y de Misterio* 106 (1952).

104. Cruzpiñón, "El abanico de sándalo," 62. Another killer who reads the nota roja in Roberto Cruzpiñón, "El tercer paquete," *Selecciones Policiacas y de Misterio* 175 (1960). For the "literatura podrida" linked to drug consumption and murder, Tégula, "La muerte piadosa." Novels condemned but secretly read by the police in Guerra Faife, "El asesinato del colono." On similarities between criminals and police, José Rosa, "La dama blanca," *Aventura y Misterio* 6 (1957).

105. Gómez Díaz, "Crimen legal." The innocent killed by pursuers in Ernesto Monato, "Libertad prematura," *Selecciones Policiacas y de Misterio* 124 (1954). In other stories, as mentioned above, the criminal was making justice while committing murder. Such is the case of "El asesino de los gatos," by Bustillo Oro (to be discussed in chapter 7). In "Estar de suerte," by Juan Miguel de Mora, the Mexican petty thieves who kill the U.S. pedophile unwittingly preempt another crime. de Mora, "Estar de suerte"; Auden, "The Guilty Vicarage," 407.

106. *Aventura y Misterio* 1 (Nov. 1956): 2. Magazines began to publish spy stories, adventure, *costumbrista* narratives, ghost, and fantasy stories. See *Aventura y Misterio* 2 (Dec. 1956); *Aventura y Misterio* 4 (Mar. 1957); *Aventura y Misterio* 10 (Oct. 1957); *Aventura y Misterio* 11 (Sept. 1957); *Aventura y Misterio* 12 (Oct. 1957); *Aventura y Misterio* 14 (Dic. 1957). The dream in Sergio Fernández, "La llamada," *Aventura y Misterio* 13 (1957). The parody of literary life in Ulalume, "Un poema y un cuento," *Aventura y Misterio* 11 (1957). The monologue in Carlos Mendez Ochoa, "Carta de un suicida," *Selecciones Policiacas y de Misterio* 73 (1950); Raúl Pérez Arce, "La venganza," *Aventura y Misterio* 10 (Sept. 1957). See also José C. Baeza Campos, "Historia de sobremesa," *Aventura y Misterio* 12 (Oct. 1957); Alfredo Cardona Peña, "Más allá, también más allá," *Aventura y Misterio* 10 (Sept. 1957).

107. *Aventura y Misterio* 3 (Jan. 1957): 2.

108. *Selecciones Policiacas y de Misterio* 133 (1955): 80.

109. *Aventura y Misterio* 2 (Dec. 1956): 2.

110. *Aventura y Misterio* 5 (Apr. 1957): 2.

111. Torres, *Muertos de papel,* 74; Stavans, *Antihéroes,* 104; Larry N. Landrum, *American Mystery and Detective Novels: A Reference Guide* (Westport, Conn.: Greenwood, 1999), 7.

112. Leo D'Olmo, *Escuela de miserias: Un drama que se desarrolla todos los días y a todas las horas, delante de tus ojos, lector: ¿Por qué no lo ves? ¿Por qué no se busca un remedio salvador para tanta mujer desgraciada?* (Mexico City: La Prensa, 1947); Leo D'Olmo, *Herodes modernos* (Mexico City: La Prensa, n.d.), 5; see also Leo D'Olmo, *El papelerillo ahorcado* (Mexico City: La Prensa, 1951); Torres, *Muertos de papel*, 75. According to Alfredo Pavón, D'Olmo also published eleven stories, five of them by *La Prensa*. Alfredo Pavón, *Cuento y figura: La ficción en México* (Tlaxcala: UA Tlaxcala, 1999), xvi, 71n30, 72. A Worldcat search yields the following book titles, too, both published by La Prensa, but without a date: *Ha muerto un patriota: Estampa dramática de la guerra* and *El vengador (novela de guerra)*.

113. Enrique F. Gual, *El crimen de la obsidiana*, translated from Catalan by Ma. Luisa Algarra (Mexico City: Minerva, 1942). Another novel set in Mexico is Gual, *El caso*. Bermúdez notes that Gual was also a journalist; he arrived in Mexico in 1937. Bermúdez, *Cuento policiaco mexicano*. Gual was a member of the Club de la Calle Morgue. He published in *Selecciones Policiacas y de Misterio* and *Aventura y Misterio* and wrote several books on art criticism up to the 1960s. See *Selecciones Policiacas y de Misterio* 4:78 (Jul. 1950).

114. Leo D'Olmo, *El muerto que se ríe* (Mexico City: La Prensa, 1954); Leo D'Olmo, *Tres gotas de sangre* (Mexico City: La Prensa, 1954); Leo D'Olmo, *¿Quién disparó?* (Mexico City: La Prensa, 1954); Leo D'Olmo, *Juego con sangre* (Mexico City: La Prensa, 1954). On the registry of foreigners, personal communication from Pablo Yankelevich.

115. D'Olmo, *Herodes modernos,* 15, 16; Leo D'Olmo, *Lucha a muerte: Aventura de Chucho Cárdenas, el popular detective-reportero mexicano; Segunda y última parte de "Herodes modernos"* (Mexico City: La Prensa, n.d.). 14. As a reporter who takes on the role of detective, Chucho was not an exception within crime fiction. See Sylvia Saítta, *Regueros de tinta: El diario "Crítica" en la década de 1920* (Buenos Aires: Editorial Sudamericana, 1998), 199. Understanding author and detective in parallel is a useful devise in other cases as well; see Knight, *Form and Ideology,* 159, 165.

116. Leo D'Olmo, *Rafaela* (Mexico City: La Prensa, 1951); the same expression used in Leo D'Olmo, *Dinamiteros* (Mexico City: La Prensa, 1953); Leo D'Olmo, *Se escapó el monstruo* (Mexico City: La Prensa, 1953); Leo D'Olmo, *La cabeza diabólica* (Mexico City: La Prensa, 1952).

117. Leo D'Olmo, *Muñeco de seda* (Mexico City: La Prensa, 1951); Leo D'Olmo, *El misterio de la fundición* (Mexico City: La Prensa, n.d.), 8–9. In another novel the gangsters from a dangerous neighborhood admire his weekly adventures, but when he uncovers their schemes they try to kill him. Leo D'Olmo, *Mortajas de cemento* (Mexico City: La Prensa, 1953); Leo D'Olmo, *Quemaron a Ricardo* (Mexico City: La Prensa, 1953). In the first person, Leo D'Olmo, *El fantasma de Cuautla* (Mexico City: La Prensa, 1952); Leo D'Olmo, *La muerte del ruletero* (Mexico City: La Prensa, 1955); also in first person, Leo D'Olmo, *Panteón en el 22* (Mexico City: La Prensa, 1953).

118. Leo D'Olmo, *Los cuatro últimos: La captura del fantasma* (Mexico City: La Prensa, 1951), 4–5. On his reputation, D'Olmo, *La cabeza diabólica;* D'Olmo,

Herodes modernos, 23, 24. For the participation of reporters in investigations as a way to increase their status see Kalifa, *L'encre et le sang,* 97.

119. Leo D'Olmo, *Robo en el Monte de Piedad* (Mexico City: La Prensa, n.d.), 1, 31.

120. Leo D'Olmo, *El caíd de Tenampa* (Mexico City: La Prensa, 1954); Leo D'Olmo, *El vengador de la Lagunilla* (Mexico City: La Prensa, 1954); Leo D'Olmo, *Muerte en el mercado de San Juan* (Mexico City: La Prensa, 1955); Leo D'Olmo, *La despedazada de Bucareli* (Mexico City: La Prensa, 1955). Contemporary references in D'Olmo, *Escuela de miserias,* 3; D'Olmo, *¿Quién disparó?;* D'Olmo, *Herodes modernos;* Leo D'Olmo, *El rubí de Tonantzin* (Mexico City: La Prensa, n.d.); Leo D'Olmo, *Las últimas horas del chacal: Drama de la vida, ¡de la mala vida!* (Mexico City: La Prensa, n.d.); D'Olmo, *El misterio de la fundición.* Similar references in Kalifa, *L'encre et le sang,* 107.

121. Leo D'Olmo, *El crimen del garage* (Mexico City: La Prensa, n.d.), 28–29. Articles can also influence criminals. When he believes that the police are not trying hard enough to catch a serial child killer, Chucho exaggerates the danger and manipulates the murderer, through his articles, into believing that he is about to catch him, thus forcing him to try to kill him. D'Olmo, *Herodes modernos,* 22. He deceives the police when necessary, too. Leo D'Olmo, *La cámara de la muerte* (Mexico City: La Prensa, n.d.); D'Olmo, *Quemaron a Ricardo;* Leo D'Olmo, *Vuela la muerte: Aventuras de Chucho Cárdenas: Toda semejanza entre los protagonistas de esta novela y personajes de la realidad, será puramente casual* (Mexico City: La Prensa, n.d.); D'Olmo, *Tres gotas;* Leo D'Olmo, *El inocente asesino* (Mexico City: La Prensa, n.d.). In Madrid, Leo D'Olmo, *El secreto del cantinero* (Mexico City: La Prensa, 1954), 27–28.

122. D'Olmo, *El crimen del garage,* 14–15; D'Olmo, *El misterio de la fundición,* 22–23; Leo D'Olmo, *La extraña casa de Tacubaya* (Mexico City: La Prensa, n.d.), 22. The reporter's activism is an example of "the evolution of journalism." D'Olmo, *El misterio de la fundición,* 3. See also Leo D'Olmo, *Sangre y diamantes* (Mexico City: La Prensa, n.d.), 3.

123. Leo D'Olmo, *¡Era justo!* (Mexico City: La Prensa, 1951). Press conference in Leo D'Olmo, *Madruga la muerte: ¡La serie más espantosa de crímenes!* (Mexico City: La Prensa, 1951), 1.

124. D'Olmo, *¿Quién disparó?,* 6.

125. D'Olmo, *El rubí;* D'Olmo, *Vuela la muerte.* On pistoleros D'Olmo, *Últimas horas del chacal,* 23–24; D'Olmo, *La extraña casa de Tacubaya,* 13–15; D'Olmo, *El inocente asesino,* 26, 30. For other reporters who think Chucho is receiving exclusive information, although he acts as intermediary between them and the police, see D'Olmo, *¿Quién disparó?,* 10; D'Olmo, *Juego con sangre,* 5; D'Olmo, *Los cuatro últimos.* A similar situation in Leo D'Olmo, *Cuatro días* (Mexico City: La Prensa, 1951).

126. D'Olmo, *El misterio de la fundición,* 2, 4. Leo D'Olmo, *Otros cinco hermanos* (Mexico City: La Prensa, 1947), 16, 30. This is different from American roman noir as a "master narrative about consumerism." Marling, *The American Roman Noir,* ix.

127. He will not keep a 20,000-peso reward, instead giving it to a colleague who needs the money. D'Olmo, *La extraña casa de Tacubaya*, 19, 20; D'Olmo, *El crimen del garage*, 16, 31; D'Olmo, *Robo en el Monte de Piedad*, 30; D'Olmo, *Vuela la muerte*, 29, 32; D'Olmo, *Sangre y diamantes*, 6.

128. D'Olmo, *El misterio de la fundición*, 2, 4. This vision of women is not surprising in crime fiction. Knight, *Form and Ideology*, 23, 157; Joseph Paul Moser, "From 'Hard-Boiled' Detective to 'Fallen Man': The Literary Lineage and Postwar Emergence of Film Noir," in *Crime and Detective Fiction*, ed. Rebecca Martin (Ipswich, Mass.: Salem Press, 2013), 161–62; McCann, "The Hard-Boiled Novel," 54.

129. D'Olmo, *El misterio de la fundición*, 14–15.

130. D'Olmo, *Herodes modernos*, 3, 7, 9. Female forms described in D'Olmo, *Vuela la muerte*, 11–12; Leo D'Olmo, *Barba azul con faldas: El misterio del degollado* (Mexico City: La Prensa, 1951).

131. D'Olmo, *El crimen del garage*, 15; Leo D'Olmo, *La llorona* (Mexico City: La Prensa, 1951); D'Olmo, *Secreto del cantinero*, 15; D'Olmo, *La cabeza diabólica*. The widow in D'Olmo, *Tres gotas*, 6, 18, 23, 29. A similar case, covered by the press in similarly lurid detail, was the murder of Mercedes Cassola Meller, in 1959, in Lucerna Street. AHDF, JP, ISSS, c. 12, exp. 88, 1959.

132. D'Olmo, *El misterio de la fundición*, 5–6.

133. D'Olmo, *Rafaela*.

134. D'Olmo, *Fantasma de Cuautla*.

135. D'Olmo, *Rafaela*; Leo D'Olmo, *¿Inocente?* (Mexico City: La Prensa, 1951); Leo D'Olmo, *¿Dónde está el muerto? Suceso extraño: Un cadáver extraviado* (Mexico City: La Prensa, 1949); Leo D'Olmo, *¿Quién mató a Rafael?* (Mexico City: La Prensa, 1954); Leo D'Olmo, *Fueron seis amigos* (Mexico City: La Prensa, n.d.); Leo D'Olmo, *Un muerto en la cajuela* (Mexico City: La Prensa, 1953); D'Olmo, *Panteón 22*; D'Olmo, *Quemaron a Ricardo*. This is also the case in U.S. noir. Cornell Woolrich, *The Bride Wore Black* (New York: Ace Books, 1940); David Schmid, "Cornell Woolrich (4 December 1903–25 September 1968)," in *American Hard-Boiled Crime Writers*, ed. George Parker Anderson and Julie B. Anderson (Detroit: Gale Group, 2000), 349–63.

136. D'Olmo, *¿Quién mató a Rafael?*, 31. Chucho prepares the ground for the suspect to attempt an escape and be killed by the police, a result he deems honorable, in D'Olmo, *¿Dónde está el muerto?*, 31. For other authors using the press as an instrument of informal justice see Rafael Solana, *El crimen de las tres bandas* (Mexico City: Colección Lunes, 1945), 176, 174; Monato, "El papelerillo de Uruapan."

137. D'Olmo, *El crimen del garage*; Leo D'Olmo, *El misterio de los suicidas* (Mexico City: La Prensa, 1988); Leo D'Olmo, *Cárcel a domicilio* (Mexico City: La Prensa, n.d.); D'Olmo, *Herodes modernos*, 14; D'Olmo, *Últimas horas del chacal*, 7–9; Leo D'Olmo, *El crimen de insurgentes* (Mexico City: La Prensa, 1955).

138. D'Olmo, *Lucha a muerte*, 4. Further reflections on the irrelevance of legal punishment, its short penalties, and the new crimes it breeds in prison in Leo D'Olmo, *Se fraguó en La Peni: El doble crimen del callejón del Otero* (Mexico City:

La Prensa, 1951), 3, 4. Lynchings, ley fuga, and "people's law" are equivalent to official laws. D'Olmo, *Últimas horas del chacal*, 24. This also applies outside Mexico. D'Olmo, *Secreto del cantinero*, 3, 27–28, 32. See chapter 2 for newspapers editorializing in favor of the death penalty and the ley fuga.

139. D'Olmo, *Los cuatro últimos*.

140. Leo D'Olmo, *El otro* (Mexico City: La Prensa, 1947), 19; D'Olmo, *El caíd de Tenampa;* Leo D'Olmo, *Panteón en el rancho: Segunda parte de "Vuela la muerte"* (Mexico City: La Prensa, n.d.); the Tepito friend in D'Olmo, *El inocente asesino,* 12. D'Olmo, *Sangre y diamantes,* 28; D'Olmo, *Tres gotas,* 4, 30; D'Olmo, *Herodes modernos,* 22; D'Olmo, *La cámara de la muerte,* 32; D'Olmo, *El rubí,* 14, 21, 29; D'Olmo, *Juego con sangre,* 14.

141. D'Olmo, *Otros cinco hermanos,* 16; D'Olmo, *Muerto se ríe,* 30; D'Olmo, *Fueron seis amigos,* 30; Leo D'Olmo, *Cuatro muertos y medio* (Mexico City: La Prensa, 1988); D'Olmo, *Cárcel a domicilio;* D'Olmo, *Papelerillo ahorcado;* D'Olmo, *¿Inocente?;* D'Olmo, *Fantasma de Cuautla.* Chucho allows a killing spree to go on so Cifuentes can take credit for solving more cases. D'Olmo, *Los cuatro últimos*.

142. D'Olmo, *Se escapó el monstruo.* A similar situation in Bustillo Oro's movie *El hombre sin rostro,* examined in the following chapter, and premiered three years before the story. He discards a suspect because he is a "poor retard" who cannot tell good from evil. D'Olmo, *La extraña casa de Tacubaya,* 21. Insanity is faked in D'Olmo, *La cabeza diabólica;* D'Olmo, *Panteón en el rancho,* 21. A killer is offended for being called "loco" in D'Olmo, *Mortajas de cemento*.

143. D'Olmo, *Otros cinco hermanos,* 12. This view of social classes resonates with that of the hard-boiled novel detective who, according to McCann, occupied a middle ground between flawed members of the elite and dangerous members of the underclass. In the U.S. this perspective would "lay the outlines of an emergent white, working-class populism. McCann, "The Hard-Boiled Novel," 47. See also Worthington, *Key Concepts,* 122–27. For a good example of historical readings of noir, Dennis Broe, *Film Noir, American Workers, and Postwar Hollywood* (Gainesville: University Press of Florida, 2009).

144. D'Olmo, *Robo en el Monte de Piedad,* 11, 17. See Louise E. Walker, *Waking from the Dream: Mexico's Middle Classes after 1968* (Stanford: Stanford University Press, 2013).

145. D'Olmo, *Dónde está el muerto?,* 31.

146. D'Olmo, *El rubí,* 12, 18; D'Olmo, *Fantasma de Cuautla*.

147. D'Olmo, *Últimas horas del chacal,* 8. Vendettas in Leo D'Olmo, *¿Corsos o tabasqueños?* (Mexico City: La Prensa, 1954); D'Olmo, *Escuela de miserias,* 3.

148. D'Olmo, *Herodes modernos,* 25, 24. The despicable nature of the crimes prompts a paradoxical call for unity from Cifuentes: "To lay hands on the neck of a robachicos is a mission for all of us" that makes lynching acceptable. Ibid, 4, 11. Child-stealing is particularly heinous, evoking the famous 1932 case of the kidnapping of Charles Lindbergh's son. Leo D'Olmo, *Cara de palo: El crimen más odioso*

(Mexico City: La Prensa, 1951). On the Lindbergh case, closely followed in Mexico, see *La Prensa*, 2 Mar. 1932, pp. 9, 31, and following days.

149. D'Olmo, *Quemaron a Ricardo*.

150. D'Olmo, *Escuela de miserias*, 3, 17–19, 24, 29; Leo D'Olmo, *Lágrimas en la juerga: Segunda parte de "Escuela de miserias"* (Mexico City: La Prensa, n.d.), 3, 4, 14, 21, 22, 24. The Porfirian concern about contamination by domestic workers in Luis Lara y Pardo, *La prostitución en México: Estudios de higiene social* (Mexico City: Bouret, 1908), 22–26.

151. D'Olmo, *El rubí*, 8, 11, 12, 18; D'Olmo, *Cárcel a domicilio*.

152. D'Olmo, *Fueron seis amigos*, 8, 14–16. On Chandler's novels as expression of the anxieties of privatized individuals see Knight, "A Hard Cheerfulness," 84–85.

153. Leo D'Olmo, *El avión de la muerte* (Mexico City: La Prensa, n.d.), 4. Ugly foreigners in Leo D'Olmo, *Trampa mortal* (Mexico City: La Prensa, 1952); D'Olmo, *El avión de la muerte*, 3.

154. D'Olmo, *Lucha a muerte*, 23, 31. He laments the lack "of control" or the "excess of freedom" that allows so many foreigners to enter Mexico. D'Olmo, *Sangre y diamantes*, 13–14, 17, 23, 31.

155. D'Olmo, *Robo en el Monte de Piedad*, 8; D'Olmo, *¿Quién mató a Rafael?*; D'Olmo, *Panteón en el 22;* Leo D'Olmo, *La equivocación fatal* (Mexico City: La Prensa, n.d.), 21, 32.

156. D'Olmo, *Sangre y diamantes*, 13–14, 15.

157. Leo D'Olmo, *La ratonera del dentista: Dramas del espionaje por Leo D'Olmo* (Mexico City: La Prensa, n.d.), 5, 6, 10, 32. Fascists in D'Olmo, *El crimen del garage*, 30; D'Olmo, *El otro*, 13. Chucho against foreign criminals waging war over control of radio signals in D'Olmo, *El avión de la muerte*, 30.

158. For U.S. theorists of the mystery novel there was no contradiction between ideology and fair play in the writing of crime fiction. The genre was only possible in democratic regimes, and could be effectively used to indoctrinate against fascism. Anthony Boucher, "The Ethics of the Mystery Novel" (first published in Oct. 1944, in *Tricolor*), in Haycraft, *The Art of the Mystery Story*, 385, 389.

159. D'Olmo, *El inocente asesino*, 4. Blairs in D'Olmo, *El misterio de la fundición*, 15. Other victims in D'Olmo, *El otro;* D'Olmo, *La extraña casa de Tacubaya*. Bad Americans in D'Olmo, *Lucha a muerte;* D'Olmo, *Misterio de los suicidas*.

160. D'Olmo, *La cámara de la muerte*, 5–6; Leo D'Olmo, *Horas de agonía: Final de "La cámara de la muerte"* (Mexico City: La Prensa, n.d.), 10, 13, 27–29.

161. D'Olmo, *Sangre y diamantes*, 19.

162. D'Olmo, *¿Quién disparó?*, 2. Revenge in D'Olmo, *Mortajas de cemento*. Greed in D'Olmo, *Secreto del cantinero;* D'Olmo, *Crimen de Insurgentes*. Cocaine in D'Olmo, *Misterio de los suicidas*. Morphine in D'Olmo, *La llorona*. For the details on upper-class sociability as providing examples of immoral behavior see, e.g., Quiroz Mendoza, "Motolinía habla," 5–53. Strange families in D'Olmo, *La extraña casa de Tacubaya;* D'Olmo, *Otros cinco hermanos;* D'Olmo, *¿Quién disparó?*, 2–4, 13, 15; D'Olmo, *Tres gotas*, 8; D'Olmo, *Cara de palo*.

CHAPTER 7. OUR MODELS OF DREAD

1. Besides her work on crime, she did several translations and wrote an essay about the customs of Mexicans. María Elvira Bermúdez, *La vida familiar del mexicano* (Mexico City: Antigua Librería Robredo, 1955). See Juan José Reyes, "Vidas Paralelas," *Siempre!*, Dec. 2012, http://www.siempre.com.mx/2012/12/vidas-paralelas/.

2. *Selecciones Policiacas y de Misterio* 5:70 (1 Jan. 1950): 6. See Vicente Francisco Torres, *Muertos de papel: Un paseo por la narrativa policial mexicana* (Mexico City: CNCA; Sello Bermejo, 2003), 102; J. Patrick Duffey, "María Elvira Bermúdez (1916–1988)," in *Latin American Mystery Writers: An A-to-Z Guide*, ed. Darrell B. Lockhart (Westport, Conn.: Greenwood, 2004), 24.

3. Gilbert Keith Chesterton, *The Defendant* (Londont: Dent, 1902), 122. See Willard Huntington Wright, "The Great Detective Stories," and Edmund Wilson, "Who Cares Who Killed Roger Ackroyd?," both in Howard Haycraft, *The Art of the Mystery Story: A Collection of Critical Essays, Edited, and with a Commentary* (New York: Simon and Schuster, 1946), quotation on 392; Alfonso Reyes, "Sobre la novela policial," cited in *Aventura y Misterio* 1 (Nov. 1956): 2.

4. María Elvira Bermúdez, *Los mejores cuentos policiacos mexicanos* (Mexico City: Libro-Mex, 1955), 7, 8, 13–14.

5. María Elvira Bermúdez, *Cuento policiaco mexicano, breve antología* (Mexico City: UNAM, Coordinación de Difusión Cultura, Dirección de Literatura, 1987), 15–17.

6. Bermúdez, *Los mejores cuentos*, 16; Bermúdez, *Cuento policaco mexicano*, 11, 12. *El complot mongol*, she added, had forced critics to accept "that a police novel can be a great novel." Torres, *Muertos de papel*, 104–5.

7. Torres, *Muertos de papel*, 104–6.

8. María Elvira Bermúdez, *Muerte a la zaga* (Tlahuapan, Puebla: Premià, 1985), 7, 36, 62; María Elvira Bermúdez, *Detente, sombra* (Mexico City: Universidad Autónoma Metropolitana, 1984), 240.

9. María Elvira Bermúdez, "Crimen para inocentes," *Selecciones Policiacas y de Misterio* 9:126 (Jan. 1955): 64, 76. He pretends to be a writer in one case, and in another he reaches the solution by reading a Russian author. On his disinterest see also Bermúdez, *Muerte a la zaga*, 9, 24, 29; Bermúdez, *Detente, sombra*, 100.

10. Bermúdez, *Detente, sombra*, 180; Bermúdez, *Muerte a la zaga*; Duffey, "María Elvira Bermúdez," 26.

11. Bermúdez, *Detente, sombra*, 168. Clues in Bermúdez, *Detente, sombra*; María Elvira Bermúdez, "Un indicio tangible," *Selecciones Policiacas y de Misterio* 9:121 (Sept. 1954) 58. A judicial investigator likes to collect rare books and brags to Zozaya about his recent acquisition, "a very rare copy of *Pathology* from the eighteenth century." Bermúdez, "Crimen para inocentes," 63; María Elvira Bermúdez, *Diferentes razones tiene la muerte* (Mexico City: Plaza y Valdés, 1987), 212. The book opens

with an epigraph from *Thus spoke Zarathustra*. Christie's works also had abundant references to their own literary character. Agatha Christie, *Murder Is Easy* (New York: St. Martin's, 2001), 65, 73.

12. Bermúdez, *Detente, sombra*, 185, 189, 191, 196, 203. On the author's feminism, Duffey, "María Elvira Bermúdez," 25. According to her grandson, Bermúdez struggled within the PRI for feminine suffrage. Reyes, "Vidas paralelas." Stories in which Zozaya is the main character do not critique Mexican machismo; on the contrary, they show him dispensing sexual innuendo to female characters or treating them as passive elements of the story. Bermúdez, "Crimen para inocentes," 81.

13. Bermúdez, *Diferentes razones tiene la muerte*, 90. First published in the late forties in an edition sponsored by fellow admirer of the genre and future president Adolfo López Mateos.

14. Ibid., 109, 213, 101. According to Van Dine, "servants" could not be suspects in a proper mystery. S. S. Van Dine, "Twenty Rules for Writing Detective Stories," in *The Winter Murder Case: A Philo Vance Story*, by S. S. Van Dine (London: Cassell, 1939), 149–58.

15. Bermúdez, *Diferentes razones tiene la muerte*, 34.

16. Ibid., 181, 136.

17. The method, another character admits, "is useful and necessary for all criminal investigations." Ibid., 224, 222.

18. Ibid., 223. A combination of hatred, trauma, and desire to punish also lead Requena to commit mistakes that lead to his capture. Ibid., 212, 223, 225, 228, 227, 230. See chapter 4 for the use of psychoanalysis in criminal cases. The discipline had considerable prestige at the time but lacked academic or institutional cohesion. Other crime fiction writers invoked psychoanalysis and alluded to these studies. Gabriel Doria, "El espectro de Medea," *Aventura y Misterio* 2 (Dec. 1956); María Elvira Bermúdez, "Un segundo después de la muerte," in *Muerte a la zaga* (Mexico City: FCE, 1986). Anonymous letters to the police cited Freud in order to elucidate sexual crimes. Alfonso Quiroz Cuarón, José Gómez Robleda, and Benjamín Argüelles, *Tendencia y ritmo de la criminalidad en México, D.F.* (Mexico City: Instituto de Investigaciones Estadísticas, 1939); Rubén Gallo, *Freud's Mexico: Into the Wilds of Psychoanalysis* (Cambridge: MIT Press, 2010); José Ramón Garmabella, *El criminólogo: Los casos más importantes del Dr. Quiroz Cuarón* (Mexico City: Debolsillo, 2007).

19. Bermúdez, *Diferentes razones tiene la muerte*, 158. Bermúdez, "Crimen para inocentes," 86. This device, common in classical detective stories, also in Antonio Helú, *La obligación de asesinar* (Mexico City: Editorial Albatros, 1946).

20. A public confession in María Elvira Bermúdez, "Dando en el clavo," *Aventura y Misterio* 1 (Nov. 1956); Bermúdez, *Diferentes razones tiene la muerte*, 231. See also Agatha Christie, *And Then There Were None* (New York: St. Martin's Press, 2001). Chandler criticized the weakness of the motivations in this novel. Dorothy Gardiner and Kathrine Sorley Walker, *Raymond Chandler Speaking* (London: Penguin, 1988), 47.

21. Usigli was the son of an immigrant family, like Helú; his father died when he was a child, and the household had little money left to support Rodolfo's refined sartorial tastes.

22. Rodolfo Usigli, *Voces: Diario de trabajo, 1932–1933* (Mexico City: Seminario de Cultura Mexicana, 1967), 276, 225–26, 29. Cited by Torres, *Muertos de papel*, 30.

23. Rodolfo Usigli, *Ensayo de un crimen* (Mexico City: Secretaría de Educación Pública, 1986), 18, 219; Carlos Isla, *El mejor caso de Valente Quintana: Los "corta mechas"* (Mexico City: Fontamara, 2004); Monsiváis, "Prólogo," in Helú, *La obligación de asesinar*, 13. Carlos Monsiváis, *Los mil y un velorios: Crónica de la nota roja* (Mexico City: Consejo Nacional para la Cultura y las Artes; Alianza Editorial, 1994), 20.

24. Guillermo Schmidhuber de la Mora, "Rodolfo Usigli, a cien años de su nacimiento," in *Tiempo, texto y contexto teatrales* (Buenos Aires: Galerna, 2006), 142. Bermúdez fails to mention him in her 1955 anthology but devotes a paragraph to the novel in the 1987 essay preceding her second compilation of the genre. Bermúdez, *Los mejores cuentos policiacos mexicanos;* Bermúdez, *Cuento policiaco mexicano,* 10. There is a mention in *Aventura y Misterio* 3 (Jan. 1957): 2. Critics have characterized the novel as either a literary exercise totally disconnected from Mexican reality or, more recently, an echo of the official postrevolutionary discourse of social and cultural homogenization. For the first position, see Ilan Stavans, *Antihéroes: México y su novela policial* (Mexico City: Joaquín Mortiz, 1993), 98. For the second, also discussed below, see Fernando Fabio Sánchez, *Artful Assassins: Murder as Art in Modern Mexico* (Nashville: Vanderbilt University Press, 2010), 45, 49. A more balanced view in Torres, *Muertos de papel*, 28–33; Schmidhuber de la Mora, "Rodolfo Usigli."

25. Usigli, *Ensayo de un crimen*, 211.

26. Torres, *Muertos de papel*, 105.

27. Raymond Chandler, *The Notebooks of Raymond Chandler and English Summer: A Gothic Romance* (New York: HarperCollins, 2006), 35–39. The comparison with "The Simple Art of Murder" in José Luis de la Fuente, "Rodolfo Usigli busca la verdad: *Ensayo de un crimen,* antecedente policiaco mexicano," *Alter Texto* 1:1 (2003): 106. See also Torres, *Muertos de papel*, 2–32. A 1955 movie by Spanish director Luis Buñuel based on the book departed from Usigli's basic detection narrative and made substantive changes to its plot. Buñuel gave greater weight to hidden drives than rational design, but Usigli disapproved. The movie was released with the same title as the novel, but Usigli came close to removing his name from the credits and forced the producers to change the name of the protagonist to Archibaldo de la Cruz. Schmidhuber de la Mora, "Rodolfo Usigli," 142; Carolyn Wolfenzon, "Los dos ensayo(s) de un crimen: Buñuel y Usigli," *Chasqui* 35:1 (2006): 36.

28. Torres, *Muertos de papel*, 29–31; Thomas De Quincey, *On Murder* (New York: Oxford University Press, 2006); Usigli, *Ensayo de un crimen*, 163; André Gide, *Judge Not,* trans. Benjamin Ivry (Urbana: University of Illinois Press, 2003). A 1943 translation of "Murder" was published in Buenos Aires. Although Usigli had collaborated with Diego Rivera in 1938 to present the surrealists in Mexico, the evi-

dence is not clear in the novel that automatism was part of Roberto's method. Sánchez, *Artful Assassins,* 48; "Rodolfo Usigli, Apostle of Mexican Drama: The Walter Havighurst Special Collections Library," Walter Havighurst Special Collections Library, Miami University Libraries, 2007, http://spec.lib.miamioh.edu /home/usigli/.

29. I translate "publicidad" as "advertising," although it could also more broadly mean "publicity." Usigli, *Ensayo de un crimen,* 116.

30. Ibid., 185, 79, 13. For an analysis that highlights the search for the truth and the role of newspapers see De la Fuente, "Rodolfo Usigli," 27; Torres, *Muertos de papel.*

31. The connection was noted by Jesse Lerner, *El impacto de la modernidad: Fotografía criminalística en la Ciudad de México* (Mexico City: Turner; Consejo Nacional para la Cultura y las Artes; Editorial Océano, 2007), 76–77. See also Eduardo Téllez Vargas and José Ramón Garmabella, *¡Reportero de policía! El Güero Téllez* (Mexico City: Ediciones Océano, 1982), 22, 25; *La Prensa,* 1 Mar. 1932; *Detective* 1:21 (29 Feb. 1932): 2. On the restaurants, Unsigned memorandum to Jefe de la Oficina de Investigación y Seguridad Pública, 26 Feb. 1932, AHDF, JP, ISSS, c. 2, exp. 9, 1932, p. 22. Usigli refers to other cases and people widely known by the criminally literate: the murder of an entire family by Luis Romero Carrasco, in 1929, and the imprisonment of painter Manuel Rodríguez Lozano.

32. For De la Fuente the problem of truth is at the center of Usigli's novel, making him a "provocateur" and an "iconoclast." De la Fuente, "Rodolfo Usigli," 94, 93, 97, 109, 110, 99. See also Schmidhuber de la Mora, "Rodolfo Usigli," 140–41. See also Wolfenzon, "Los dos ensayo(s)," 35–36; Torres, *Muertos de papel,* 31. It is not simple to define the noir sensibility, in part because the label is mostly retrospective and applies to a set of values expressed through multiple media. Andrew Pepper, "The American Roman Noir," in *The Cambridge Companion to American Crime Fiction,* ed. Catherine Ross Nickerson (New York: Cambridge University Press, 2010), 60; William Marling, *The American Roman Noir: Hammett, Cain, and Chandler* (Athens: University of Georgia Press, 1995), ix. "Noir" is sometimes taken as synonymous with "hard-boiled." Ernest Mandel, *Delightful Murder: A Social History of the Crime Story* (Minneapolis: University of Minnesota Press, 1984), 34–35.

33. Usigli, *Ensayo de un crimen,* 38. See chapter 3 of *Ensayo* for the "complete history, past and present, of every resident of Mexico City" that Quintana claimed to possess. *Kerrville Times,* 29 Dec. 1929, p. 4.

34. Usigli, *Ensayo de un crimen* 273.

35. Ibid., 184.

36. According to Stavans, the crime of Schwartzemberg alluded to a similar case that had taken place in Yucatán years earlier. Stavans, *Antihéroes,* 99. Critics have interpreted these characterizations as an expression of Usigli's rivalry with another playwright of the time, Salvador Novo. Novo's fondness for young men and drivers was an open secret in literary circles. Carlos Monsiváis, "El mundo soslayado (donde se mezclan la confesión y la proclama)," in Salvador Novo, *La estatua de sal* (Mexico

City: Consejo Nacional para la Cultura y las Artes, 1998), 19, 24. There are plenty of examples. On a murder between "afeminados": "Horrenda tragedia pasional entre dos homosexuales!" *Alarma* 2:36 (14 Jul. 1951): 3. Also *Alarma!* 355 (Feb. 1970).

37. My interpretation differs from that of Sánchez, who sees the homophobic violence of *Ensayo de un crimen* as an expression of a state project of national modernization. It is, I would argue, an expression of broadly shared views about reality. Sánchez, *Artful Assassins,* 9; *Alarma!* 356 (25 Feb. 1970): 6–7. See also Téllez Vargas and Garmabella, *¡Reportero de policía!,* 22. On Goyo Cárdenas, *Últimas Noticias,* 19 Sep. 1942, p. 1. For a crime involving interrogations of many suspects defined as homosexuals see AHDF, JP, ISSS, c. 12, exp. 88, 1959. A particularly homophobic novel inspired by a later case is Luis Spota, *La mitad oscura* (Mexico City: Grijalbo, 1982).

38. Critics have identified him as archeologist Alfonso Caso. Wolfenzon, "Los dos ensayo(s)," 36; Usigli, *Ensayo de un crimen,* 142.

39. He writes that much in his 1932 diaries. Usigli, *Voces,* 15.

40. Usigli, *Ensayo de un crimen,* 24, 34. Fernando Fabio Sánchez sees the novel as an example of the postrevolutionary regime's project of social hygiene and modernization. His is a productive reading of the novel yet loses sight of its detection plot. Roberto does not actually kill any of the victims he chooses—he is far, in other words, from the alleged efficiency of state modernization. Luisito, instead, kills for self-interest. Sánchez, *Artful Assassins,* 46, 54–55.

41. Juan Bustillo Oro, *Vientos de los veintes: Cronicón testimonial* (Mexico City: Secretaría de Educación Pública, 1973), 134, 95, 174.

42. Juan Bustillo Oro, *La penumbra inquieta y otros relatos* (Mexico City: Universidad Nacional Autónoma de México, 2009); Juan Bustillo Oro, *Vida cinematográfica* (Mexico City: Cineteca Nacional, 1984); Bustillo Oro, *Vientos de los veintes.*

43. Bustillo Oro, *Vida cinematográfica,* 158.

44. Ibid., 187.

45. Ibid., 249, 313–14. Jenkins and Alarcón would be implicated in the murder of Alonso Mascarúa in 1954, discussed in chapter 5.

46. Juan Bustillo Oro, *El hombre sin rostro* (Mexico City: Mexcinema Video de Mexico, 1950). See a suggestive treatment in Sánchez, *Artful Assassins,* 64.

47. Bustillo Oro, *Vida cinematográfica,* 268; Sánchez, *Artful Assassins,* 66.

48. Cornell Woolrich, "Collared," *Ellery Queen's Mystery Magazine* 14:68 (Jul. 1949): 125–44; Bustillo Oro, *Vida cinematográfica,* 281; Juan Bustillo Oro, *La huella de unos labios* (1952).

49. David Schmid, "Cornell Woolrich (4 December 1903–25 September 1968)," in *American Hard-Boiled Crime Writers,* ed. George Parker Anderson and Julie B. Anderson (Detroit: Gale Group, 2000), 349–46. She resembles other resourceful women who seek justice in Woolrich's stories. See for example Cornell Woolrich, *The Bride Wore Black* (New York: Ace Books, 1940).

50. Bustillo Oro, *Vida cinematográfica,* 282–83.

51. Ibid., 298–313; Juan Bustillo Oro, *El asesino X* (1955).

52. Emilio García Riera, *Historia documental del cine mexicano* (Guadalajara: Universidad de Guadalajara, 1992), 8:50–53.

53. Bustillo Oro, *La penumbra inquieta*, 59. Also Armando C. Amador, ed., *Dieciocho novelas de "El Universal Ilustrado" (1922–1925)* (Mexico City: Instituto Nacional de Bellas Artes, Departamento de Literatura, 1969). For the new sociability of movie theaters see Ann Blum and Katherine Bliss, "Dangerous Driving: Adolescence, Sex, and the Gendered Experience of Public Space in Early 20th-Century Mexico City," in *Gender, Sexuality and Power in Modern Latin America,* ed. Katherine Bliss and William E. French (Lanham, Md.: Rowman and Littlefield, 2007), 163–86.

54. Juan Bustillo Oro, "El asesino de los gatos," *Selecciones Policiacas y de Misterio* 123 (1954); Juan Bustillo Oro, "Apuesta al crimen," *Selecciones Policiacas y de Misterio* 92 (1951); Juan Bustillo Oro, "Cómo murió Charles Prague," *Selecciones Policiacas y de Misterio* 175 (1960). There is a clear attempt, in the words of Jael Tercero Andrade, to "blend cinema and literature." Bustillo Oro also wrote science fiction and fantasy stories. Tercero Andrade, introduction to Bustillo Oro, *La penumbra inquieta,* 23. See for example a mix that includes detection and ghosts in Juan Bustillo Oro, *Lucinda del polvo lunar* (Mexico City: Domés, 1985).

55. Bustillo Oro, *Vida cinematográfica,* 315.

56. Bustillo Oro, "Apuesta al crimen," 44. See Roberto Cruzpiñón, "El tercer paquete," *Selecciones Policiacas y de Misterio* 91 (1960).

57. Bustillo Oro, "Apuesta al crimen," 52, 57, 58, 60, 56, 68.

58. Bustillo Oro, "El asesino de los gatos," 48, 47, 51, 43.

59. Bustillo Oro, "Cómo murió Charles," 37, 43.

60. Ibid., 41–45.

61. Miguel G. Rodríguez Lozano, *Pistas del relato policial en México: Somera expedición,* Colección de bolsillo (Mexico City: Universidad Nacional Autónoma de México, 2008), 10–11. A recent, valuable literary discussion of Bernal in *El complot anticanónico: Ensayos sobre Rafael Bernal,* ed. Joserra Ortiz (Mexico City: CONACULTA, 2015).

62. The novel was republished in the eighties and appreciated for its affinities with *neopoliciaco*. Stavans, *Antihéroes,* 119–20; Torres, *Muertos de papel,* 34–37; Mauricio Bravo Correa, "Pesquisa biobibliográfica de Rafael Bernal: Resultados preliminares de un rescate literario" (BA thesis, Universidad Nacional Autónoma de México, 2006), 13–24; Persephone Braham, *Crimes against the State, Crimes against Persons: Detective Fiction in Cuba and Mexico* (Minneapolis: University of Minnesota Press, 2004), 70.

63. Rafael Bernal, *Tres novelas policiacas* (Mexico City: Jus, 1946); Rafael Bernal, *Un muerto en la tumba* (Mexico City: Jus, 1946). "La muerte poética" was published in *Selecciones Policiacas y de Misterio* 5 (1947), "La muerte madrugadora" in *Selecciones Policiacas y de Misterio* 15 (1948), and "De muerte natural" in *Selecciones Policiacas y de Misterio* 41 (1950). The translation is Dashiel Hammett, "Demasiado han vivido," *Selecciones Policiacas y de Misterio* 1:3 (Dec. 1946).

64. Rafael Bernal, "La muerte poética," in Bermúdez, *Cuento policiaco mexicano,* 56, 61, 63; Rafael Bernal, "El heróico Don Serafín," in *Tres novelas policiacas* (Mexico City: Jus, 1946), 129; Rafael Bernal, "De muerte natural," in Bermúdez, *Los mejores cuentos,* 41–61.

65. Bernal, "De muerte natural," 42; Bernal, "La muerte madrugadora."

66. Bernal, "La muerte madrugadora"; Rafael Bernal, "El extraño caso de Aloysius Hands," in *Tres novelas policiacas* (Mexico City: Jus, 1946), 6.

67. Bernal, *Un muerto en la tumba.*

68. Bernal, "De muerte natural," 60.

69. Torres, *Muertos de papel,* 33.

70. Bernal, "El extraño caso de Aloysius Hands," 82.

71. Ibid., 41, 18, 55, 51, 60, 72, 74, 95–97.

72. The influence of Chandler and Hammett has also been pointed out as a key difference from his earlier works. Torres, *Muertos de papel,* 35; Bravo Correa, "Pesquisa biobibliográfica," 24. The novel was not widely read after its publication, and Bernal continued in the employment of the Foreign Ministry until his death in 1972. Torres, *Muertos de papel,* 34–35; Sánchez, *Artful Assassins,* 91. For the possibility that the novel, not widely distributed until the eighties, may have been the object of censorship, see Braham, *Crimes against the State,* 69.

73. See, e.g., Stavans, *Antihéroes,* 116–20. See Luc Boltanski, *Énigmes et complots: une enquête à propos d'enquêtes* (Paris: Gallimard, 2012).

74. See Patrick Iber, "Managing Mexico's Cold War: Vicente Lombardo Toledano and the Uses of Political Intelligence," *Journal of Iberian and Latin American Research* 19:1 (2013): 11–19.

75. The Mexican's state compulsion to eavesdrop on its own agents is documented in Tanalís Padilla and Louise E. Walker, "In the Archives: History and Politics," *Journal of Iberian and Latin American Research* 19:1 (2013): 1–10; Aaron W. Navarro, *Political Intelligence and the Creation of Modern Mexico, 1938–1954* (University Park: Pennsylvania State University Press, 2010).

76. Rafael Bernal, *El complot mongol* (Mexico City: Joaquín Mortiz, 1969), 21.

77. Ibid., 75.

78. Ibid., 174.

79. Ibid., 187, 11.

80. This pessimistic epistemology is taken to its extreme by Paco Ignacio Taibo: the truth is impossible to reach in the end because power itself is a vast conspiracy. Paco Ignacio Taibo, *Cosa fácil* (Barcelona: Editorial Grijalbo, 1977). For other readings see Sánchez, *Artful Assassins,* 110; Stavans, *Antihéroes,* 119.

81. Bernal, *El complot mongol,* 89. Compare with Marcus Klein, *Easterns, Westerns, and Private Eyes* (Madison: University of Wisconsin Press, 1994), 170; Dashiell Hammett, *Red Harvest* (New York: Pocket Books, 1929).

82. Bernal, *El complot mongol,* 40. García likes his Chinese friends: they focus on gambling and drug trafficking; they know much, but "are very discreet." Ibid., 10. On Chinese opium dens in Mexico City see Ricardo Pérez Montfort, "De vicios

populares, corruptelas, y toxicomanías," in *Juntos y medio revueltos* (Mexico City: Sones-Unios, 2000), 113–34. Policemen believed that crimes committed among Chinese immigrants were impossible to solve. *Detectives* 1:9 (10 Oct. 1932): 12.

83. Bernal, *El complot mongol,* 12.

84. Ibid., 243, 187.

85. Ibid., 57–58.

86. Ibid., 188. He treats women like he treats his victims: "you have to go straight to what you want." Ibid., 98.

87. Torres, *Muertos de papel,* 34.

88. Bernal, *El complot mongol,* 239–40, 229, 232. On the sequence of scenes in Chandler see Stephen Knight, *Form and Ideology in Crime Fiction* (London: Macmillan, 1980), 150.

89. As mentioned above, this was not an exception but the norm in crime fiction. See Sonia Mattalía, *La ley y el crimen: Usos del relato policial en la narrativa argentina* (Frankfurt: Ediciones de Iberoamericana, 2008), 14. The importance of criminal literacy explains the close association between these stories and other narrative media: theater in Helú, comics and nota roja in D'Olmo, movies in Bustillo Oro.

90. One exception can be found in "Dosis mortal," by Enrique Jiménez Jaime, centered on an obese small-town police chief who solved crimes from his chair despite the "pretty collection of idiots called gendarmes" under his orders and the "dumb bosses" above him. Enrique Jiménez Jaime, "Dosis mortal," *Aventura y Misterio* 1 (1 Nov.1956): 108. The procedural narrative, as in Georges Simenon's inspector Maigret novels, was never explored by Mexican authors. In the U.S. the procedural could bring a sense of order during depression. Heather Worthington, *Key Concepts in Crime Fiction* (New York: Palgrave Macmillan, 2011), 145.

91. Joseph Paul Moser, "From 'Hard-Boiled' Detective to 'Fallen Man': The Literary Lineage and Postwar Emergence of Film Noir," in *Crime and Detective Fiction,* ed. Rebecca Martin (Ipswich, Mass.: Salem Press, 2013), 161. This is not an exclusively Mexican phenomenon. As one police officer exclaimed in a Chandler short story: "Hell with the loose ends." Raymond Chandler, *The Simple Art of Murder* (New York: Vintage Books, 1988), 274.

92. Sánchez interprets *Ensayo de un crimen* and *El hombre sin rostro* from the premise that "murder is a metaphor of aesthetic creation," yet he deems both works a reflection of the regime's modernizing effort to impose homogeneity on society. As he admits, his analysis is not concerned with "the relationship between crime and notions of justice and truth." Sánchez, *Artful Assassins,* 6, 13.

93. Here I am inverting the analysis proposed in Marling, *The American Roman Noir.*

94. Compare with Boltanski, *Énigmes et complots,* 38, 40. Crime was, for Paz or Ramos, a permanent symptom of Mexicans' psychological tendencies, but not the product of social conditions, much less a matter of justice. See introduction, above.

95. María Pía Lara, *Narrating Evil: A Postmetaphysical Theory of Reflective Judgment* (New York: Columbia University Press, 2007), 12, 16–17.

96. Haycraft, *The Art of the Mystery Story*, 396.

97. Braham, *Crimes against the State*, 66, chap. 6; Taibo, *Cosa fácil*. For a similar process elsewhere see Natalia Jacovkis, "Latin American Crime Fiction," in *Crime and Detective Fiction*, ed. Rebecca Martin (Ipswich, Mass.: Salem Press, 2013), 116–18.

98. See also Glen S. Close, *Contemporary Hispanic Crime Fiction: A Ttransatlantic Discourse on Urban Violence* (New York: Palgrave Macmillan, 2008), 31, 38. Torres, *Muertos de papel*, 80–81. For an analysis in terms of middle-class anxieties see Louise E. Walker, *Waking from the Dream: Mexico's Middle Classes after 1968* (Stanford: Stanford University Press, 2013), chap. 3. Taibo is at least mindful of the conventions of the genre. Resolution of a mystery is also a pretext in Carlos Fuentes's *La cabeza de la hidra*, where crime and espionage are assembled, again, without much concern for coherence. Carlos Fuentes, *La cabeza de la hidra* (Mexico City: J. Mortiz, 1978). On other authors in the genre see Gabriel Trujillo Muñoz, *Testigos de cargo* (México: CONACULTA, 2000), 19.

99. Vicente Leñero, *Asesinato: El doble crimen de los Flores Muñoz* (Mexico City: Plaza y Janés, 1988), 6, 548. On the same case, see Luis Guillermo Piazza, *Los cómplices* (Mexico City: Diana, 1983). For a novel inspired by and critical of the nota roja see Jorge Ibargüengoitia, *Las muertas* (Mexico City: J. Mortiz, 1977).

100. Close, "The Detective Is Dead: Long Live the Novela Negra!," in *Hispanic and Luso-Brazilian Detective Fiction: Essays on the Género Negro Tradition*, ed. Renée W. Craig-Odders, Jacky Collins, and Glen S. Close (Jefferson, N.C.: McFarland, 2006), 143–61.

CONCLUSION

1. Jorge Luis Borges, *Obras completas* (Barcelona: Emecé Editores, 1996), 1:352.

2. For example Gilbert M. Joseph and Daniel Nugent, *Everyday Forms of State Formation: Revolution and the Negotiation of Rule in Modern Mexico* (Durham: Duke University Press, 1994). But see Jeffrey Rubin, *Decentering the Regime: Ethnicity, Radicalism, and Democracy in Juchitán, Mexico* (Durham: Duke University Press, 1997); Paul Gillingham and Benjamin T. Smith, eds., *Dictablanda: Politics, Work, and Culture in Mexico, 1938–1968* (Durham: Duke University Press, 2014). Most of studies of security and drug trafficking in Mexico are centered on the state, probing its capacity to reverse the trend and the willingness of its leaders to do it.

3. But see, on mourning, Kathryn A. Sloan, *Death in the City: Suicide and the Social Imaginary in Modern Mexico* (Berkeley: University of California Press, 2017), chap. 6.

4. Norbert Lechner, *Los patios interiores de la democracia* (Santiago: FLASCO, 1988); David Carey, *I Ask for Justice: Maya Women, Dictators, and Crime in Guatemala, 1898–1944* (Austin: University of Texas Press, 2013).

5. Enzo Traverso, *L'histoire comme champ de bataille: Interpréter les violences du XXe siècle* (Paris: La Découverte, 2010).

6. Pablo Piccato, "Comments: How to Build a Perspective on the Recent Past," *Journal of Iberian and Latin American Research* 19:1 (1 Jul. 2013): 91–102.

7. The bibliography on the recent period is vast. The remaining footnotes should be read as suggestions for further reading. See on the points above Paul Gootenberg, *Andean Cocaine: The Making of a Global Drug* (Chapel Hill: University of North Carolina Press, 2008), chaps. 6 and 7; Luis Alejandro Astorga Almanza, *El siglo de las drogas: El narcotráfico, del porfiriato al nuevo milenio* (Mexico City: Plaza y Janés, 2005); Ioan Grillo, *El Narco: Inside Mexico's Criminal Insurgency* (New York: Bloomsbury Press, 2012); Elaine Carey, *Women Drug Traffickers: Mules, Bosses, and Organized Crime* (Albuquerque: University of New Mexico Press, 2014).

8. The best overview is Guillermo Zepeda Lecuona, *Crimen sin castigo: Procuración de justicia penal y ministerio público en México* (Mexico City: Fondo de Cultura Económica-Cidac, 2004). See also Wayne A. Cornelius and David A. Shirk, *Reforming the Administration of Justice in Mexico* (Notre Dame: University of Notre Dame Press 2007). Current data provided by the Justice in Mexico Project, at the University of San Diego, justiceinmexico.org.

9. Alan Knight, "Habitus and Homicide: Political Culture in Revolutionary Mexico," in *Citizens of the Pyramid: Essays on Mexican Political Culture,* ed. Wil G. Pansters (Amsterdam: Thela, 1997), 110. On contemporary violence, Alvaro Delgado, "Asoman los paramilitares," *Proceso,* 26 Sept. 2011, http://www.proceso.com .mx/?p = 282499.

10. The perspective described by Alberto del Castillo Troncoso, *Rodrigo Moya: Una visión crítica de la modernidad* (Mexico City: CONACULTA, 2006), 24–25.

11. Pablo Piccato, "'Ya Saben Quién': Journalism, Crime and Impunity in Mexico Today," in *Mexico's Struggle for Public Security: Organized Crime and State Responses,* ed. Susana Berruecos and George Philip (London: Palgrave Macmillan, 2012), 47–70.

12. On the effects of fear, Rossana Reguillo, "The Oracle in the City: Beliefs, Practices, and Symbolic Geographies," *Social Text* 22:481 (2004): 35–46. On the links between social and civil rights and the risks of the denial of justice, Guillermo O'Donnell, "Reflections on Contemporary South American Democracies," *Journal of Latin American Studies* 33:3 (2001): 599–609. For the juridical formulation of the right to truth by the Interamerican Court of Human Rights see Laurence Burgorgue-Larsen, "La lutte contre l'impunité dans le système interaméricain des droits de l'homme," in *Cursos de derechos humanos de Donostia-San Sebastián* (Bilbao: Universidad del País Vasco, 2009), 10:89–110; Carlos Santiago Nino, *Radical Evil on Trial* (New Haven: Yale University Press, 1996). The UN International Convention for the Protection of All Persons from Enforced Disappearance (signed in New York, 20 Dec. 2006) states in article 24 that "each victim has the right to know the truth regarding the circumstances of the enforced disappearance, the progress and results of the investigation and the fate of the disappeared person. Each State Party shall take appropriate measures in this regard." Office of the United Nations High Commissioner for Human Rights, "International Convention for the Protection of

All Persons from Enforced Disappearance," http://www2.ohchr.org/english/law/disappearance-convention.htm.

APPENDIX. QUANTITATIVE EVIDENCE ABOUT CRIME IN MEXICO IN THE LAST CENTURY

1. Indicted, or *presunto,* means those suspects charged and imprisoned but not sentenced. Their cases constitute the most reliable figure available to compile long-term series. Even though they may not represent the entire number of homicides, as we will see below, indicted suspects are more important in public perceptions of crime than those found guilty, and certainly more visible than those not arrested. Figures based on my compilation of judicial figures. The dataset and some analysis at Pablo Piccato, "Estadísticas del crimen en México: Series Históricas, 1901–2001," 2003, http://www.columbia.edu/~pp143/estadisticascrimen/EstadisticasSigloXX.htm.

2. See Pablo Piccato, "A Historical Perspective on Crime in Twentieth-Century Mexico City," in *The Administration of Justice in Mexico* (Notre Dame, Ind.: University of Notre Dame Press, 2006).

3. *Anuario estadístico de la República Mexicana* (Mexico City: Secretaría de Fomento, 1896); Dirección General de Estadística, *Estadística del ramo criminal en la República Mexicana que comprende un periodo de quince años, de 1871 a 1885* (Mexico City: Secretaría de Fomento, 1890); Pablo Piccato, *City of Suspects: Crime in Mexico City, 1900–1931* (Durham, N.C.: Duke University Press, 2001).

4. Instituto Nacional de Estadística y Geografía (INEGI), Sistema para la Consulta del Cuaderno Estadístico Municipal de Nuevo Laredo, Tamaulipas, Edición 2005, accessed 29 Apr. 2008, http://www.inegi.gob.mx; INEGI, Sistema para la Consulta del Cuaderno Estadístico Municipal Juárez, Chihuahua, Edición 2006, accessed 29 Apr. 2008, http://www.inegi.gob.mx; INEGI, Sistema para la Consulta del Anuario Estadístico del Distrito Federal, Edición 2006, accessed 29 Apr. 2008, http://www.inegi.gob.mx.

5. Instituto Nacional de Estadística y Geografía, *Estadísticas judiciales en materia penal de los Estados Unidos Mexicanos* 2006, accessed 29 Apr. 2008, http://www.inegi.gob.mx.

6. Piccato, *City of Suspects;* James Greenberg, *Blood Ties: Life and Violence in Rural Mexico* (Tucson: University of Arizona Press, 1989); Pablo Piccato, "Murder as Politics in Modern Mexico," in *Murder and Violence in Modern Latin America,* ed. Eric A. Johnson, Ricardo Donato Salvatore, and Petrus Cornelis Spierenburg (Bulletin of Latin American Research book series, 2013), 104–25. See data in INEGI, Sistema para la Consulta del Cuaderno Estadístico Municipal de Nuevo Laredo, Tamaulipas, Edición 2005, accessed 29 Apr. 2008, http://www.inegi.gob.mx; INEGI, Sistema para la Consulta del Cuaderno Estadístico Municipal Juárez, Chihuahua, Edición 2006, accessed 29 Apr. 2008, http://www.inegi.gob.mx; INEGI, Sistema para la Consulta del Anuario Estadístico del Distrito Federal, Edición 2006, accessed 29 Apr. 2008, http://www.inegi.gob.mx.

7. Alfonso Quiroz Cuarón, José Gómez Robleda, and Benjamín Argüelles, *Tendencia y ritmo de la criminalidad en México, D.F.* (Mexico City: Instituto de Investigaciones Estadísticas, 1939).

8. INEGI, *Estadísticas históricas de México* (Aguascalientes, Ags.: INEGI, 1999), 4; INEGI, Pirámide de población—grupos de edad, accessed 8 May 2008, http://www.inegi.gob.mx; Instituto Nacional de Estadística y Geografía (México), *Estadísticas históricas de México 2009,* México 2010, Colección memoria(Aguascalientes: INEGI, 2009), table 1.7.

9. See analysis in Ira Beltrán and Pablo Piccato, "Crimen en el siglo XX: Fragmentos de análisis sobre la evidencia cuantitativa," in *Los últimos cien años, los próximos cien años* (Mexico City: Universidad Autónoma Metropolitana, 2004), 13–44.

INDEX

abogángster, 172
Acevedo de la Llata, Concepción (madre
    Conchita), 45–48, 60, 113, 126; trial of,
    51–59
Acosta Juárez, José, 116
Aguilar Crispín, 180, 183
Ahí está el detalle (Bustillo Oro), 243–244,
    246
Alarcón, Gabriel, 119, 187
Alarma!, 67, 73, 74, 76, 83, 84, 85, 87, 95,
    101, 127, 171, 174
Alducín, Rafael, 58, 69
Alemán, Miguel, 70, 76, 77, 141, 168, 173,
    179, 180, 181, 183, 184, 189
Alessio Robles, Vito, 72
Almazán, Juan Andreu, 181
Altamirano, Rafael. *See* murder, of Rafael
    Altamirano
Altamirano, Manlio Fabio, 124, 156, 157,
    158, 166, 180. *See also* murder; of Manlio
    Fabio Altamirano.
Álvarez Bravo, Manuel, 96
Amanecer, 158
amparo (writ of protection), 45, 119, 122,
    172, 178, 182, 187
Anda, Agustín de, 153
Angulo, Mauro, 122, 173, 174, 178. *See also*
    murder; of Mauro Angulo.
anticommunism, 68
anti-Semitism, 71
Aréchiga, Rafael, 157
Argos, 74, 75, 109, 111, 144
Arias Ávalos, Graciela, 137, 140, 141

Arias Córdova, Manuel, 137
Arredondo, José Antonio, 185, 186
Asesino X, El (Bustillo Oro), 244, 246
assassination: of Álvaro Obregón, *see under*
    Obregón, Álvaro; regicide, 52–53; as
    religious resistance, 52; as solution to
    disputes, 183; in Mexican history, 53;
    attempt against Emilio Portes Gil, 58;
    See also murder
Armenta Barradas, Armando, 167, 178, 181,
    188
Armenta Castillo, Marciano, 122, 123, 163,
    174, 181, 182, 188
Aub, Max, 66
Auden, W.H., 195
authoritarianism: of crowd behavior, 26; in
    everyday life, 189–190
autoviudas, 154, 158
Aventura y Misterio, 198, 207, 208–15,
    247
Ávila Bretón, Rafael, 180, 181
Ávila Camacho, Manuel, 70, 72, 99, 168,
    183, 236, 244
Ávila Camacho, Maximino, 72, 168, 187
Ávila Camacho, Rafael, 187
Aznar, Jacinta, 99, 121, 131, 132, 133, 136

Barrio Atlampa, 113, 247
Barba González, Silvano, 75, 76
Barbosa, Ricardo, 149, 150
Batanes, Teódulo, 251, 256, 263
Batillas, Roberto ("El Güero"), 162, 163,
    167, 174, 188, 269

Belem (prison/courthouse), 31, 35, 40, 82, 131, 134
Bermúdez, María Elvira, 199, 203, 206, 209, 210, 217, 218, 231, 232, 238, 240, 245, 256, 257, 259; on crime fiction as genre, 233–34; use of psychoanalysis, 235, 236
Bernal, Rafael, 200, 206, 210, 236, 251–52, 257, 258, 259; *El complot mongol*, 232–233, 250, 253–55, 259, 269
Bioy Casares, Adolfo, 208, 215
Blanco Moheno, 179, 180
Bojórquez, Dolores, 5
Borges, Jorge Luis, 7, 8, 164, 208, 215, 261, 263, 269
Botellita de Jerez (band), 66
Buendía, Manuel, 77, 154; ties to DFS, 80
Bulnes, Francisco, 22
Burroughs, William, 6, 80, 166, 172, 190, 265
Bustillo Oro, Juan, 75, 209, 210, 232, 236, 242, 250, 254, 256, 257, 258; *Ahí está el detalle*, 243–44, 246; *El asesino X*, 244, 246; *El cuello de la camisa*, 207; *El hombre sin rostro*, 244–45; *El medallón del crimen*, 244, 246–48; *La huella de unos labios*, 244–246; and psychoanalysis, 244–45

Cabrera, Luis, 60
Cadena García Valseca, 70
Calles, Plutarco Elías, 34, 38, 44, 45, 49, 50, 54, 55, 58, 68, 71, 200
Canchola, José, 170, 171
Cantinflas (Mario Moreno), 243
Cárdenas, Gregorio ("Goyo"), 86, 91, 115, 126, 129, 130, 137, 145, 146, 157, 158, 159, 163, 244, 261; capture, 116; criminal profile, 138–141; in popular culture, 143; release, 142
Cárdenas, Chucho, 199, 215, 216, 217, 218, 219, 220, 227, 228, 234, 255, 256, 257, 263
Cárdenas, Lázaro, 43, 68, 70, 71, 75, 168, 177, 204, 237
Cárdenas de la Cruz, Patricio, 87
Cardona, Rafael, 48, 49
Carranza, Venustiano, 21, 53
Casasola, Miguel V., 71
Casasola family, 78, 79

Castro Leal, Antonio, 206
Castro, Pedro J., 122, 167, 182
Cervantes, César, 134, 136
Chandler, Raymond, 195, 196, 210
Chesterton, G.K., 200, 233, 252
Christie, Agatha, 132, 196, 223, 233
Chucho El Roto, 130
Ciudad Juárez, 41
Ciudad Nezahualcóyotl, 95
civilization, 3, 57, 71, 84
Club de la Calle Morgue, 200, 201
Colonia Asturias, 184
Colonia Mixcoac, 247
Colonia Peralvillo, 204
Colonia Portales, 37, 38
Colonia Vallejo, 170
Complot mongol, El (Bernal), 232, 250, 253–254, 269
confession, 91, 96, 117, 118–19, 124, 135, 152, 186, 236; as truth, 129, 130, 133, 138
Constant, Benjamin, 19
Cornejo Armenta, Rafael, 178, 179, 180, 183
Correa Nieto, Juan, 46, 47, 51, 52, 53, 56
Corvera Ríos, Fidel, 172, 174, 175, 183
Coyoacán, 78
crime: as authorship, 130–31, 158–59, 188; and class hierarchies, 223, 226; indictment rates, 273–74; and modernization, 2–3, 263; of passion, 23, 37, 42–43, 86–89, 127, 158, 235; political, 46, 52, 53, 54; and punishment, 4; and race/ethnicity, 226–227; reconstruction of, 116–17; as sadism, 129–130, 159; and sexuality, 129, 138–39, 145, 221, 240–1
crime fiction: and class/gender, 199, 221–28, 234–35; and criminal literacy, 10, 193, 201, 205, 212–14, 216, 219, 228–30, 234, 239, 252, 254, 257–59; in England, 200, 207; and film, 200–1, 204–5, 210, 242, 244, 247; as genre, 193, 195, 197–98, 206–7, 211–15, 230–31, 254, 256–59, 262; international circulation of, 206–208; and moral ambiguity, 202–3, 214, 230, 237, 248, 257; and nationalism, 194, 206, 226, 229; neopoliciaco, 250, 259–260; and nota roja, 214, 218–220, 228, 239; narrative elements, 196–197, 213–14; and originality, 210–11; as outward

looking, 194, 199–200, 211–212, 226–27, 230, 253–255; parody in, 204–205; as political and cultural critique, 194, 199, 201, 203–5, 251–52, 254, 258; readership, 193, 195, 207–208, 217; role of editors, 208–12; scholarly disdain of, 198–99; in the United States, 197, 207, 229

criminal literacy, 6, 8, 9, 60, 110, 124, 126, 137, 143, 153, 159, 163, 169, 175, 188, 190, 193, 261–262, 265; as critical instrument, 11, 261, 263; and gender/class, 12–13, 38, 75, 264; in jury trials, 33, 40; in film, 244–45; through nota roja, 64, 66, 75–76, 82–83, 89, 91, 94, 96, 99, 102–3, 205, 218; through radio, 75; and private detectives, 109, 111

criminology, 5, 25, 41, 127, 142, 144; and crime fiction, 209; and nota roja, 145; and truth, 147

Cristeros, 45, 52, 53, 54, 58, 73, 250

Cruzpiñón, Roberto, 209, 213, 214, 248

Cuautla, 224

Cuello de la camisa, El (Bustillo Oro), 207

Cuidado con el hampa (radio show), 75, 83, 92, 101, 165

Dannay, Frederic, 200, 202, 207, 208, 210, 245

death penalty, 23, 46, 53, 83, 121, 203, 222

De la Cruz, Roberto, 10, 237, 238–241, 248, 263

Delgado, Agustín, 205

Departamento Autónomo de Prensa y Publicidad (DAPP), 68

detectives: private, 108–9; knowledge/expertise, 109–10, 114, 234; as business/enterprise, 110; regulation of, 110–11; role in crime fiction, 196, 197, 201–206, 219, 220, 223, 228, 230, 238, 257; ethics/honor, 196, 220–2

Detective, 5, 74, 84, 174

Detectives, 67, 74, 84, 100, 118, 154, 171, 173, 184

Detectives School of America, 112

Díaz, Enrique, 78–79

Díaz Mirón, Salvador, 152

Díaz Ordaz, Gustavo, 74, 76

Díaz, Porfirio, 25, 108

Díaz Soto y Gama, Antonio, 42, 43, 56

Dirección Federal de Seguridad, 76, 80, 180, 182, 183, 184

D'Olmo, Leo, 216, 217, 218, 219, 220, 221, 240

drug trafficking, 174–75, 266–267

due process, 11, 45, 263, 270

Durazo Moreno, Arturo, 170

Echenique Sagarramundi, Andrés, 154

Echeverría, Luis, 64, 74, 76

Ellery Queen's Mystery Magazine, 200, 202, 207, 208, 210

El que la hace la paga (radio show), 101

Ensayo de un crimen (Usigli), 112, 232, 248; criminal literacy in, 239–240; homosexuality in, 240–41

Escuela Correccional (juvenile detention center), 42

Escuela Normal para Profesoras, 37

Espinosa Tagle, Manuel, 46, 47

Excélsior, 7, 38, 40, 46, 47, 49, 50, 55, 57, 58, 64, 67, 68, 69, 78, 80, 131, 153, 162, 177, 180, 203, 239

fiction, 8, 12

Federal Bureau of Investigation, 77

Fellig, Arthur (Wegee), 96

Fernández Bustamente, Adolfo, 201

Fernández, Donato, 170

Fernández, Emilio (El Indio), 152, 172; *Salón México*, 164; *Herencia macabra*, 153

Fernández, Silvestre, 111, 112

fiction, 7–8, 190, 193, 195, 218, 219, 256, 258, 263. See also reality

fotorreportajes (graphic stories), 79

Foucault, Michel, 130

Franco, Francisco, 71

Franco Sodi, Carlos, 122

French Revolution, 19

Freud, Sigmund, 129, 235

fuero (parliamentary immunity), 34

Fullana Taberner, Juan, 148, 149, 150

Gaceta de Policía, 74

Gallegos, Alberto, 89, 91, 96, 97*fig.*, 99, 126, 131, 132, 137, 138, 158, 160, 163, 261, 324n32; killing of, 121, 123, 239–240; murder confession, 132–136

Gamboa, Federico, 30, 33, 59
Gángsters contra charros (Orol), 164–166
García Filiberto, 253, 257, 263, 269, 333n49
García Cabral, Ernesto, 46, 47
García Castillo, Fernando, 127
García, Filiberto, 253–255
García Salinas, David, 78
Garrido, Luis, 209, 210
Genial detective Péter Pérez, El (Delgado), 205
Gil, Miguel, 86, 134
Glass, George W., 71, 72, 72
Gómez Mont, Felipe, 154, 156
Gómez Robleda, José, 147
Gosserez, Guillermo, 85, 127. *See also* murder; Restaurant Broadway case.
Gual, Enrique F., 200, 209, 217
guardias blancas, 178. *See also* Mano Negra
guaruras (bodyguards), 170, 172, 174, 184
Guerra al Crimen, 74
Guerrero, Felipe, 23
Guichard, Eduardo, 167
guitarreros (money counterfeiters), 92
Guzmán, Martín Luis, 68, 119

Halttunen, Karen, 93
Hammett, Dashiell, 197, 210, 212, 223, 251
Healy, John, 80
Helú, Antonio, 75, 199, 243; international connections, 200–2, 210, 233, 245; as crime fiction author, 206–8, 213, 228, 250–51
Heraldo de México, El, 33, 35, 40, 187
Herencia macabra (Fernández), 153
Hernández, Magdalena, 154, 155*fig.*, 156*fig.*
Herrera Pérez, Arturo, 171, 173
Hitler, Adolf, 71
Hockney, David, 82
Holmes, Sherlock, 195, 204, 223
Holofernes (biblical character), 49
Hombre sin rostro, El (Bustillo Oro), 244–245
Homicide. *See* murder. *See also* assassination
honor: in crime fiction, 201, 224–25, 228; and gender, 12, 42, 87; in jury trials, 23–24, 54; as justification for crime, 41–43, 87, 127, 153, 201, 214

Huella de unos labios, La (Bustillo Oro), 244–246
Huerta, Gral. Victoriano, 25, 70

Ibargüengoitia, Jorge, 58
Imparcial, El, 66, 67, 70
impunity, 4, 102, 116, 122, 124, 141, 166, 171–73, 188, 214, 256, 258, 263, 265; and authoritarian regime, 189–190, 193–94, 254, 268–269
infamy: as reputation and morality, 7–8; and gender, 12, 87; and violence, 163, 190, 265
Infante, Pedro, 75
Infante, Manuel, 83
Instituto Mexicano de Policía, 115
Islas Marías (penal colony), 42, 51, 121, 136, 152, 239
Issasi, Adolfo, 42
Ixtapalapa, 24
Ixtapan de la Sal, 77
Izquierdo Ebrard, Hugo, 172, 181, 182, 188

Jamaica (neighborhood), 148
Jaramillo, Rubén, 185
Jenkins, William, 185, 187, 244
Jordán, Gonzalo, 89
Jornada, La, 101
Juárez, Benito, 19
judicial system, 27; corruption in, 59, 84; weakness, 267–268
Judith (biblical character), 49
Jurado, Bernabé, 172, 175
jury trials: abolition of, 60–61, 102; as citizen education, 19–20; crowd behavior in, 47, 61; criticism of, 21–24, 26, 40–41, 54; deliberation in, 28; emotion and sentiment in, 19, 25–30, 38, 39, 40, 42–43, 59, 291n53; in film, 243; as expression of popular sovereignty, 20; and patriarchy, 40, 43; and politics, 34–35, 38–40, 42, 49, 55; in popular culture, 61–62; power of judges in, 24–25; as public opinion, 26–27, 59, 160, 296n108; in radio broadcasts, 57; as spectacle, 30–33, 38, 40, 47, 60; use of rhetoric, 25, 28, 39; women in, 47, 59–60, 295n98

Kerouac, Jack, 166
Krafft-Ebing, Richard von, 129

La Castañeda, 140, 141, 157
Landa, Maria Teresa de, 41, 126
La policía siempre vigila (radio show), 101
Leblanc, Maurice, 210, 233
Le Bon, Gustave, 26, 39, 53
Lecumberri (prison), 141, 142, 147, 152f
Leñero, Vicente, 58, 260
León, Aurelio, 181, 183
Lepe, Ana Berta, 153
Lepe, Guillermo, 153
Lewis, Oscar, 169
ley fuga, 9, 61, 99, 108, 114, 136, 142, 148, 151, 152; as extralegal punishment, 121–23; as justice, 182, 222, 268
Liga de la decencia, 154
Lindbergh, Charles, 82
Lobillo, Gildardo, 177, 179, 188
Lombardo Toledano, Vicente, 71, 177
Lombroso, Cesare, 53, 128, 144
López, Ignacio ("Nacho"), 79
López Mateos, Adolfo, 157, 171
López Portillo, José, 170
López Rosales, Ricarda, 153
Lucenay, Martín de, 138, 139
lynching, 103, 121, 122, 148, 153, 204

Maas Patiño, Joaquín, 161, 163
Madero, Francisco I., 25, 27, 53, 70
Mano Negra, 178–80, 181, 183
Margolles, Teresa, 66
María Félix, 74
Mariscal, Ignacio, 19, 20
Martínez, Ema, 131, 154, 155, 156*fig.*, 157, 158
Martínez de la Vega, José, 164, 199, 200, 203, 204, 205, 206, 210, 211, 212, 223, 228, 251
Marx, Karl, 11
Mascarúa, Alonso. *See* murder; of Alonso Mascarúa
Mayo brothers, 78
Meade, Everard, 121, 142
Medallón del crimen, El (Bustillo Oro), 244, 246–248
Mellado, Guillermo ("Nick Carter"), 81, 108
Mendoza, Manuel, 152

Mercader, Ramón ("Jacques Mornard"), 78, 144, 145, 147, 160
mestizaje, 27; and honorability, 55
Metinides, Enrique, 79, 95, 96
Ministerio Público, 110, 116,
Miranda, Carlos, 201, 202, 203, 213, 220
Moheno, Querido, 25, 26, 29, 34, 37, 38, 39, 40, 43, 46, 55, 58, 59, 61; on crimes of passion, 127; on ley fuga, 122; views on race, 27; on politics and religion, 53, 54; press: and state, 67–68, 70–71, 101; as business, 66–70. *See also* nota roja
Moll, José, 149, 150
Monsiváis, Carlos, 7, 138; views on nota roja, 65
Moreno, Jesús, 34, 35
Moreno, María del Pilar, 29, 32*fig.*, 40, 41, 43, 91, 130, 153; trial of, 33–39
Morfín, Maria Teresa: trial of, 41
Morones, Luis N., 44, 56
Moya, Rodrigo, 162, 269
Múgica, Gral. Francisco J., 52
murder: of Alonso Mascarúa, 184–87; as art, 232, 236–9, 248–50, 252–3, 257–259; as communicative act, 10, 235, 252, 339n147; in crime narratives, 10, 194–5, 198, 203, 214, 265; of Father Juan Fullana Taberner, 149–50; and femininity, 35, 37–43, 86–87, 158; of Manlio Fabio Altamirano, 176–79; of Mauro Angulo, 180–184; as political, 195; of Rafael Altamirano, 156–8; Restaurant Broadway case, 86–87; as revenge, 36, 38–39, 222, 245, 259; as story, 128–129; Tacubaya barbershop case, 85, 90*fig.*, 99–100, 103, 117, 119, 131, 261; of Villar Lledías brothers, 111, 113; of women, 42–43, 87; by women, 33–38, 52, 153–55, 222
Mussolini, Benito, 71
Múzquiz Blanco, Manuel, 5

Nacional, El, 71, 76
Nagore, Alfonso Francisco, 40
Nava, Pepe, 7
Negrete, Jesús ("El Tigre de Santa Julia"), 128, 146
neopoliciaco. *See* crime fiction; nepoliciaco

INDEX · 371

nota roja (crime news), 9, 131, 193, 195, 196; as aesthetic of the ordinary, 65; and critiques of government, 64, 72, 73, 74, 81, 83, 84, 103; notions of justice in, 12, 64, 81–82, 92; glorification of crime, 74; as journalistic genre, 63, 64, 66, 76, 77, 96, 102, 300n167; government censorship of, 75–77, 270; legacies, 101–102; photography, 79, 94–96, 103; reporters, 78–81; relationship to police, 80–82, 101, 220; and truth/reality, 82–85, 92–93, 99, 102, 129, 263; and gender/sexual norms, 86–89, 92, 95–96, 103; and pistolero violence, 168–169; and reader's emotions, 96, 99; role of interviews, 91–92, 96; as narrative, 85–93, 96, 235; on radio, 75, 83, 92, 101

Nota Roja, 76, 84

Novaro, Luis, 71

Novedades, 78, 153, 158

Novelas y Cuentos Mercury, 208

Obregón, Álvaro, 34, 49, 52, 53, 54, 58, 69, 200; assassination of, 44–46, 51, 53, 143, 179

Oneto Barenque, Gregorio, 137, 138, 140, 157, 245

Ordorica, Miguel, 70

Organización Editorial Mexicana (OEM), 72

Orol, Juan: *Gángsters contra charros*, 164–166

Ortiz Rubio, Pascual, 112, 243

Padilla, Ezequiel, 56

Palavicini, Félix, 65, 69

Parra, Manuel, 170, 175, 177, 178, 179, 180, 183, 188

Partido Acción Nacional, 77, 154

Partido Nacional Cooperatista, 34

Partido Nacional Revolucionario, 177

Paz, Octavio, 7, 130, 159

Peláez Fuentes, Carlos, 78

Pérez Moreno, José, 40

Pérez, Péter, 204, 205, 207, 220, 223, 256, 257, 263

Pinkerton Agency, 108

pistolerismo, 175, 186, 261, 263, 267; as business, 173–74, 179, 184; and caciq-

uismo, 168–69, 180; in crime fiction, 205, 251, 253–56; as political violence, 177–78, 180; public imagery, *162fig.*, *165fig.*, 188, 190; relation to public sphere, 163, 175; and the state, 166–71, 173, 175, 182, 188–89; as "violent entrepreneurship," 169, 175. *See also* nota roja; on pistolero violence

Poe, Edgar Allan, 195, 196, 200, 212

Policía Internacional, 74

Policía Judicial, 111, 113, 114, 116

Ponce de León, Alejandro, 118, 173, 185, 188; arrest, 186–87

Popular, El (newspaper), 66

Porfiriato, 2, 6, 25, 41, 92, 108, 122, 128, 131, 145, 228, 243

Portes Gil, Emilio, 44, 112, 176, 328n96

Por Que?, 73, 74

Posada, José Guadalupe, 7, 65, 66

Prensa, La: depiction of ley fuga, 119–122; on female murderers, 154–156, 158; and nota roja, 63, 66–70, 75, 84–85, 87, 89, 91, 99–102, 184, 185; on pistoleros, 164, 166, 168, 182–3; portrayal of famous murder cases, 131–132, 134, 138–139, 151, 154–6, 158, 187; reporters and photographers, 78–82, 95–96; as publisher of crime fiction, 199, 215; readership and sales, 71–72, 86; surveillance on, 76–77

Prieto, Guillermo, 19

Pro, Miguel Agustín, 45, 49, 51, 52, 58, 113

prostitution, 26, 80, 95, 125, 144–45, 164, 175, 225; and victims of crime, 137, 143

public sphere, 4, 5, 9, 13, 55, 59, 64, 85, 195, 264–265, 268, 283n8; criminals in, 146, 159, 257; fiction in, 229; justice in, 12, 17, 18, 60, 258, 261; press and, 102. See also pistolerismo

punishment, 89, 262; detached from justice, 102, 214, 222, 265

Querétaro, 76, 151, 158

Quiroga, Pablo, 176, 177, 178

Quiroz Cuarón, Alfonso, 130, 141, 142, 143; as criminological expert, 144–147

Quiroz Mendoza, Raymundo, 211, 213

Quincey, Thomas de, 129, 238, 241, 252

Quintana, Valente, 44, 45, 93, 108, 110, 114, 124, 144, 166, 238; detection methods, 111–113

Ramírez, Ignacio, 20, 27
Ramírez Romero, María de Jesús, 82
Ramos, Samuel, 7, 245
reality, 6–7, 64, 66, 77, 82. 85, 159, 239, 250, 259, 265, 283n9; and fiction 7, 8, 197, 218, 228, 229–230, 236–237, 256, 260. See also *nota roja*
Revista de Policía, 74, 130
revolution: French, 19; Mexican, 2, 3, 4, 6, 21, 25, 27
Revueltas, José, 66
robbery, 173, 175, 182; Tren de Laredo case, 112
Rodríguez Lafora, Santiago, 142, 143
Rodríguez Silva, Santiago, 84, 86, 91, 92, 93, 94, 96, 98*fig.*, 99, 100, 103, 117, 131; killing of, 119–21, 123, 131
Roldán, Máximo, 201, 202, 203, 210, 220, 255, 257, 263
Romero Carrasco, Luis, 40, 121, 126, 136, 152
Roumagnac, Carlos, 25, 33, 91, 130
Ruiz Cortines, Adolfo, 11, 76, 82, 157, 167, 182,
Rulfo, Juan, 212, 224
Rush, Bernice, 28, 30

Sade, Marquis de, 129, 130
Salazar Mallén, Rubén, 206
Salón México (Fernández), 164
San Ángel, 44, 45, 46, 47, 48, 49, 52, 57
San Luis Potosí, 56
Santa María la Ribera, 87
Santos, Gonzalo N., 56, 57, 168, 170
Secretaría de la Defensa Nacional, 172
Secretaría de Educación Pública, 46, 200
Secretaría de Gobernación, 67, 77, 170
Selecciones policíacas y de misterio, 200, 206, 207, 208, 209, 210, 215, 232, 247, 251
SEMEFO (art collective), 66
Servicio Secreto, 114, 116, 124, 148, 150, 151, 152, 176, 180, 181, 182, 184, 185, 186, 188
Sierra, Santiago, 21, 23
Sobera de la Flor, Higinio, 145

Sodi, Demetrio, 22, 24, 45, 46, 47, 49, 53, 54, 55, 57, 60, 61
Sodi de Pallares, María Elena, 55
Sodi, Federico, 28, 29, 30, 41, 55, 60
Sol de Guadalajara, El, 70
Spanish Civil War, 69, 194, 227
Spota, Luis, 259–260
Steffens, Lincoln, 93
Suárez, Teresa, 87, 88*fig.*, 92

Tabasco, 224
Tacubaya, 121, 148. *See also* murder; Tacubaya barbershop case
Taibo, Paco Ignacio, 259
Tejeda Llorca, Francisco, 42: assassination of, 33–39
Téllez Vargas, Eduardo, 65, 74, 78, 79, 81, 82
Téllez Vargas, Pedro, 185, 187
Tenampa cabaret, 219
Tepito, 148, 149, 150, 223
Texas, 71, 112, 113, 132, 133, 227
Tlatelolco massacre, 3, 74
Thomalen, Consuelo, 58, 68
Topete, Ricardo, 44, 45
Toral, José de León, 44, 45, 60, 61, 68, 113, 126, 131, 143, 179; trial, 46–59, 260; personality, 48–49; as martyr, 49–50, 53, 55, 56; as regicide, 53; execution, 58
Trápaga, Cristóbal, 110
Trotsky, Leon, 78, 79, 144, 147
Trujeque, Antonio, 186, 188
truth: and public opinion, 5–6; 82–83, 102, 159; in crime fiction, 193–7, 199, 204, 206–14, 222–3, 229–34, 241–42, 236, 250, 253–6, 260
torture, 4, 9, 45, 50, 58, 107, 113, 122, 123, 124, 129, 133, 149; techniques of, 118; as tool of investigation, 117–118, 119, 254–255, 268

Últimas Noticias, 69, 70, 122, 203
Unión de Voceadores, 67, 68, 74
United States, 7, 19, 20, 57, 108
Universal, El, 24, 26, 40, 41, 59, 65, 67, 69
Universal Gráfico, El, 67, 69, 87
unomásuno, 101
Uruchurtu, Ernesto P., 74

Usigli, Rodolfo, 10, 112, 231–232, 250, 254, 258, 259; on murder as artistic creation, 236, 257. See also *Ensayo de un crimen*

Valencia Rangel, Francisco, 61
Valentín Vázquez, José ("Pancho Valentino"), 131, 149, 150, 151*fig.*, 158
Valle, Rafael Heliodoro, 46
Vallejo Becerra, Pedro ("El México"), 149, 150
Varela, Demetrio, 82
Vasconcelos, José, 200, 236, 242
Vázquez Raña, Mario, 71
Velázquez, Fidel, 185
Veracruz, 34, 85, 109, 114, 122, 138; pistoleros in, 176–183, 188

violence: in detective work, 113, 117–119; extrajudicial, 9, 45, 61, 102, 121–122, 261, 263; and the everyday, 102–103, 166, 168; and honor, 27, 36, 39, 42, 43, 59–60, 87, 92, 122–123, 127, 157; naturalization of, 190, 254, 268; as resistance to tyranny, 27, 58; urban vs. rural, 224–225
Villa, María, 41, 129

Waikiki cabaret, 162, 166, 269
Woolrich, Cornell, 207, 212, 245, 246

xenophobia, 226–27

Zapata, Emiliano, 27
Zozaya, Armando H., 234, 235, 236, 257, 354n11, 355n12